"A MASTERPIECE OF THE ART OF CONVERSATION . . . A BOOK YOU MUST READ."
The Los Angeles Times

"*WORKING* is good reading in the sense that the people we meet are not digits in a poll but real people with real names who share their anecdotes, adventures, and aspirations with us. . . . a splendid book—important in what it has to say and impressive in the manner in which it is said."

Business Week

"NO JOURNALIST ALIVE WIELDS A TAPE RECORDER AS EFFECTIVELY AS STUDS TERKEL, or is as adroit at eliciting . . . private fears and dreams."

Newsweek

"A NO-NONSENSE BOOK . . . The characters in it make a great river of people. . . . This is uninhibited stuff. . . . Somebody should have added an interview with Studs Terkel, who performed a heroic job of work in his own grinding routine of interviewing. . . . A beautfully balanced look at ourselves from the inside, a fascinating Big Parade."
The San Francisco Chronicle

WORKING

People Talk About What They Do All Day and How They Feel About What They Do

Studs Terkel

BALLANTINE BOOKS • NEW YORK

Library of Congress Catalog Card Number: 73-18037

ISBN 0-345-32569-9

This edition published by arrangement with Pantheon Books

Manufactured in the United States of America

First Ballantine Books Edition: November 1985
Sixth Printing: June 1988

For Jude Fawley; for Ida, who
shares his vision; for Annie, who didn't.

Acknowledgments

As in two previous works, *Division Street: America* and *Hard Times,* my benefactors were friends, acquaintances, and wayfaring strangers. A suggestion, a casual comment, a tip, a hunch: a collective thoughtfulness led to the making of this book.

Among these singularly unselfish scouts were: Marge Abraham, Joe Agrella, Marvin David, Lucy Fairbank, Lou Gilbert, De Witt Gilpin, Bill Gleason, Jake Green, Lois Greenberg, Pete Hamill, Denis Hamill, Noel Meriam, Sam Moore, Bill Moyers, John Mulhall, Bryce Nelson, Patricia O'Brien, Jessie Prosten, Al Raby, Kelly Sanders, Florence Scala, Ida Terkel, Anne Thurson, Warren Weaver, Steven Yahn, Beverly Younger, Connie Zonka, and Henry de Zutter.

For the third time, Cathy Zmuda transcribed hundreds of thousands of spoken words—perhaps millions in this instance—onto pages that sprang to life. Her constant good humor and perceptiveness were as rewarding to me as her astonishing technique. Nellie Gifford's acute observations as a volunteer editor, at a time the manuscript was *really* gargantuan, helped immeasurably in cutting the lean from the fat. A perspective was offered by both that might otherwise have been missing.

My gratitude, too, to Nan Hardin, for her generosity of time and spirit, as a knowing guide during a memorable trip through Indiana and eastern Kentucky. My colleagues at radio station WFMT, notably Ray Nordstrand, Norman Pellegrini, and Lois Baum, were once again remarkably understanding and ingenious during my prolonged leaves of absence. I know I gave them a hard time, but theirs was truly grace under pressure.

Especially am I grateful to my editor, André Schiffrin, whose idea this was, as twice before. His insistence and quiet encouragement, especially during recurring moments of self-doubt, are evident in all these pages. And to his nimble associates, Myriam Portnoy and Dian Smith, for their bright-eyed look at what was becoming burdensome matter—a salute.

Every man's work shall be made manifest: for the day shall declare it, because it shall be revealed by fire; and the fire shall try every man's work of what sort it is.
—I Corinthians 3:13

You can't eat for eight hours a day nor drink for eight hours a day nor make love for eight hours a day—all you can do for eight hours is work. Which is the reason why man makes himself and everybody else so miserable and unhappy.

—William Faulkner

The "work ethic" holds that labor is good in itself; that a man or woman becomes a better person by virtue of the act of working. America's competitive spirit, the "work ethic" of this people, is alive and well on Labor Day, 1971.

—Richard M. Nixon

I like my job and am good at it, but it sure grinds me down sometimes, and the last thing I need to take home is a headache.

—TV commercial for Anacin

WORKING

INTRODUCTION

This book, being about work, is, by its very nature, about violence—to the spirit as well as to the body. It is about ulcers as well as accidents, about shouting matches as well as fistfights, about nervous breakdowns as well as kicking the dog around. It is, above all (or beneath all), about daily humiliations. To survive the day is triumph enough for the walking wounded among the great many of us.

The scars, psychic as well as physical, brought home to the supper table and the TV set, may have touched, malignantly, the soul of our society. More or less. ("More or less," that most ambiguous of phrases, pervades many of the conversations that comprise this book, reflecting, perhaps, an ambiguity of attitude toward The Job. Something more than Orwellian acceptance, something less than Luddite sabotage. Often the two impulses are fused in the same person.)

It is about a search, too, for daily meaning as well as daily bread, for recognition as well as cash, for astonishment rather than torpor; in short, for a sort of life rather than a Monday through Friday sort of dying. Perhaps immortality, too, is part of the quest. To be remembered was the wish, spoken and unspoken, of the heroes and heroines of this book.

There are, of course, the happy few who find a savor in their daily job: the Indiana stonemason, who looks upon his work and sees that it is good; the Chicago piano tuner, who seeks and finds the sound that delights; the bookbinder, who saves a piece of history; the Brooklyn fireman, who saves a piece of life ... But don't these satisfactions, like Jude's hunger for knowledge, tell us more about the person than about his task? Perhaps. Nonetheless, there is a common attribute here: a meaning to their work well over and beyond the reward of the paycheck.

For the many, there is a hardly concealed discontent. The blue-collar blues is no more bitterly sung than the white-collar moan. "I'm a machine," says the spot-welder. "I'm caged," says the bank teller, and echoes the hotel clerk. "I'm a mule," says the steelworker. "A monkey can do what I do," says the receptionist. "I'm less than a farm implement," says the migrant worker. "I'm an object," says the high-fashion model. Blue collar and white call upon the identical phrase: "I'm a robot." *"There is nothing to talk about,"* the young accountant despairingly enunciates. It was some time ago that John Henry sang, "A man ain't nothin' but a man." The hard, unromantic fact is: he died with his hammer in his hand, while the machine pumped on. Nonetheless, he found immortality. He is remembered.

As the automated pace of our daily jobs wipes out name and face—and, in many instances, feeling—there is a sacrilegeous question being asked these days. To earn one's bread by the sweat of one's brow has always been the lot of mankind. At least, ever since Eden's slothful couple was served with an eviction notice. The scriptural precept was never doubted, not out loud. No matter how demeaning the task, no matter how it dulls the senses and breaks the spirit, one *must* work. Or else.

Lately there has been a questioning of this "work ethic," especially by the young. Strangely enough, it has touched off profound grievances in others, hitherto devout, silent, and anonymous. Unexpected precincts are being heard from in a show of discontent. Communiqués from the assembly line are frequent and alarming: absenteeism. On the evening bus, the tense, pinched faces of young file clerks and elderly secretaries tell us more than we care to know. On the expressways, middle management men pose without grace behind their wheels as they flee city and job.

There are other means of showing it, too. Inchoately, sullenly, it appears in slovenly work, in the put-down of craftsmanship. A farm equipment worker in Moline complains that the careless worker who turns out more that is bad is better regarded than the careful craftsman who turns out less that is good. The first is an ally of the Gross National Product. The other is a threat to it, a kook—and the sooner he is penalized the better. Why, in these circumstances, should a man work with care? Pride does indeed precede the fall.

Others, more articulate—at times, visionary—murmur of a hunger for "beauty," "a meaning," "a sense of pride." A veteran car hiker sings out, "I could drive any car like a baby, like a woman changes her baby's diaper. Lots of customers say, 'How you do this?' I'd say, 'Just the way you bake a cake, miss.' When I was younger, I could swing with that car. They called me Lovin' Al the Wizard."

Dolores Dante graphically describes the trials of a waitress in a fashionable restaurant. They are compounded by her refusal to be demeaned. Yet pride in her skills helps her make it through the night. "When I put the plate down, you don't hear a sound. When I pick up a glass, I want it to be just right. When someone says, 'How come you're just a waitress?' I say, 'Don't you think you deserve being served by me?' "

Peggy Terry has her own sense of grace and beauty. Her jobs have varied with geography, climate, and the ever-felt pinch of circumstance. "What I hated worst was being a waitress. The way you're treated. One guy said, 'You don't have to smile; I'm gonna give you a tip anyway.' I said, 'Keep it. I wasn't smiling for a tip.' Tipping should be done away with. It's like throwing a dog a bone. It makes you feel small."

In all instances, there is felt more than a slight ache. In all instances, there dangles the impertinent question: Ought not there be an increment, earned though not yet received, from one's daily work—an acknowledgement of man's *being?*

An American President is fortunate—or, perhaps, unfortunate—that, offering his Labor Day homily, he didn't encounter Maggie Holmes, the domestic, or Phil Stallings, the spot-welder, or Louis Hayward, the washroom attendant. Or especially, Grace Clements, the felter at the luggage factory, whose daily chore reveals to us in a terrible light that Charles Dickens's London is not so far away nor long ago.

Obtuseness in "respectable" quarters is not a new phenomenon. In 1850 Henry Mayhew, digging deep into

London's laboring lives and evoking from the invisible people themselves the wretched truth of their lot, astonished and horrified readers of the *Morning Chronicle*. His letters ran six full columns and averaged 10,500 words. It is inconceivable that Thomas Carlyle was unaware of Mayhew's findings. Yet, in his usual acerbic—and, in this instance, unusually mindless—manner, he blimped, "No needlewoman, distressed or other, can be procured in London by any housewife to give, for fair wages, fair help in sewing. Ask any thrifty housemother. No *real* needlewoman, 'distressed' or other, has been found attainable in any of the houses I frequent. Imaginary needlewomen, who demand considerable wages, and have a deepish appetite for beer and viands, I hear of everywhere. . . ."* A familiar ring?

Smug respectability, like the poor, we've had with us always. Today, however, and what few decades remain of the twentieth century, such obtuseness is an indulgence we can no longer afford. The computer, nuclear energy for better or worse, and sudden, simultaneous influences flashed upon everybody's TV screen have raised the ante and the risk considerably. Possibilities of another way, discerned by only a few before, are thought of—if only for a brief moment, in the haze of idle conjecture—by many today.

The drones are no longer invisible nor mute. Nor are they exclusively of one class. Markham's Man with the Hoe may be Ma Bell's girl with the headset. (And can it be safely said, she is "dead to rapture and despair"? Is she really "a thing that grieves not and that never hopes"?) They're in the office as well as the warehouse; at the manager's desk as well as the assembly line; at some estranged company's computer as well as some estranged woman's kitchen floor.

Bob Cratchit may still be hanging on (though his time is fast running out, as did his feather pen long ago), but Scrooge has been replaced by the conglomerate. Hardly a chance for Christmas spirit here. Who knows Bob's name in this outfit—let alone his lame child's? ("The last place I worked for, I was let go," recalls the bank teller. "One of my friends stopped by and asked where I was at. They

---

* E. P. Thompson and Eileen Yeo, *The Unknown Mayhew* (New York: Pantheon Books, 1971).

said, 'She's no longer with us.' That's all. I vanished.") It's nothing personal, really. Dicken's people have been replaced by Beckett's.

"Many old working class women have an habitual gesture which illuminates the years of their life behind. D. H. Lawrence remarked it in his mother: my grandmother's was a repeated tapping which accompanied an endless working out of something in her head; she had years of making out for a large number on very little. In others, you see a rhythmic smoothing out of the hand down the chair arm, as though to smooth everything out and make it workable; in others, there is a working of the lips or a steady rocking. None of these could be called neurotic gestures, nor are they symptoms of acute fear; they help the constant calculation."*

In my mother's case, I remember the illuminating gesture associated with work or enterprise. She was a small entrepreneur, a Mother Courage fighting her Thirty Years' War, daily. I remember her constant feeling of the tablecloth, as though assessing its quality, and her squinting of the eye, as though calculating its worth.

Perhaps it was myopia, but I rarely saw such signs among the people I visited during this adventure. True, in that dark hollow in Eastern Kentucky I did see Susie Haynes, the black lung miner's wife, posed in the doorway of the shack, constantly touching the woodwork, "as though to smooth everything out and make it workable." It was a rare gesture, what once had been commonplace. Those who did signify—Ned Williams, the old stock chaser, Hobart Foote, the utility man—did so in the manner of the machines to which they were bound. Among the many, though the words and phrases came, some heatedly, others coolly, the hands were at rest, motionless. Their eyes were something else again. As they talked of their jobs, it was as though it had little to do with their felt lives. It was an alien matter. At times I imagined I was on the estate of Dr. Caligari and the guests poured out fantasies.

* Richard Hoggart, *The Uses of Literacy* (New York: Oxford University Press, 1957).

To maintain a sense of self, these heroes and heroines play occasional games. The middle-aged switchboard operator, when things are dead at night, cheerily responds to the caller, "Marriott Inn," instead of identifying the motel chain she works for. "Just for a lark," she explains bewilderedly. "I really don't know what made me do it." The young gas meter reader startles the young suburban housewife sunning out on the patio in her bikini, loose-bra'd, and sees more things than he would otherwise see. "Just to make the day go faster." The auto worker from the Deep South will "tease one guy 'cause he's real short and his old lady left him." Why? "Oh, just to break the monotony. You want quittin' time so bad."

The waitress, who moves by the tables with the grace of a ballerina, pretends she's forever on stage. "I feel like Carmen. It's like a gypsy holding out a tambourine and they throw the coin." It helps her fight humiliation as well as arthritis. The interstate truckdriver, bearing down the expressway with a load of seventy-three thousand pounds, battling pollution, noise, an ulcer, and kidneys that act up, "fantasizes something tremendous." They all, in some manner, perform astonishingly to survive the day. These are not yet automata.

The time study men of the General Motors Assembly Division made this discomfiting discovery in Lordstown. Gary Bryner, the young union leader, explains it. "Occasionally one of the guys will let a car go by. At that point, he's made a decision: 'Aw, fuck it. It's only a car.' It's more important to just stand there and rap. With us, it becomes a human thing. It's the most enjoyable part of my job, that moment. I love it!" John Henry hardly envisioned that way of fighting the machine—which may explain why he died in his prime.

There are cases where the job possesses the man even after quitting time. Aside from occupational ticks of hourly workers and the fitful sleep of salaried ones, there are instances of a man's singular preoccupation with work. It may affect his attitude toward all of life. And art.

Geraldine Page, the actress, recalls the critique of a backstage visitor during her run in *Sweet Bird Of Youth*. He was a dentist. "I was sitting in the front row and looking up. Most of the time I was studying the fillings in your mouth. I'm curious to know who's been doing your dental work." It was not that he loved theater less, but that he loved dentistry more.

At the public unveiling of a celebrated statue in Chicago, a lawyer, after deep study, mused, "I accept Mr. Picasso in good faith. But if you look at the height of the slope on top and the propensity of children who will play on it, I have a feeling that some child may fall and be hurt and the county may be sued. . . ."

In my own case, while putting together this book, I found myself possessed by the mystique of work. During a time out, I saw the film *Last Tango in Paris*. Though Freud said *lieben und arbeiten* are the two moving impulses of man, it was the latter that, at the moment, consumed me. Thus, I saw on the screen a study not of redemption nor of self-discovery nor whatever perceptive critics may have seen. During that preoccupied moment I saw a study of an actor *at work*. He was performing brilliantly in a darkened theater (apartment), as his audience (the young actress) responded with enthusiasm. I interpreted her moans, cries, and whimpers as bravos, huzzahs, and olés. In short, I saw the film as a source of a possible profile for this book. Such is the impact of work on some people.

A further personal note. I find some delight in my job as a radio broadcaster. I'm able to set my own pace, my own standards, and determine for myself the substance of each program. Some days are more sunny than others, some hours less astonishing than I'd hoped for; my occasional slovenliness infuriates me . . . but it is, for better or worse, in my hands. I'd like to believe I'm the old-time cobbler, making the whole shoe. Though my weekends go by soon enough, I look toward Monday without a sigh.

The danger of complacency is somewhat tempered by my awareness of what might have been. Chance encounters with old schoolmates are sobering experiences. Memories are dredged up of three traumatic years at law school. They were vaguely, though profoundly, unhappy times for me. I felt more than a slight ache. Were it not for a fortuitous set of circumstances, I might have become a lawyer—a determinedly failed one, I suspect. (I flunked my first bar examination. Ninety percent passed, I was told.)

During the Depression I was a sometime member of the Federal Writers' Project, as well as a sometime actor in radio soap operas. I was usually cast as a gangster and just as usually came to a violent and well-deserved end. It was always sudden. My tenure was as uncertain as that of a radical college professor. It was during these moments—though I was unaware of it at the time—that the surreal nature of my work made itself felt. With script in hand, I read lines of stunning banality. The more such scripts an actor read, the more he was considered a success. Thus the phrase "Show Business" took on an added significance. It was, indeed, a business, a busyness. But what was its meaning?

If Freud is right—"his work at least gives him a secure place in a portion of reality, in the human community"*—was what I did in those studios really work? It certainly wasn't play. The sales charts of Proctor & Gamble and General Mills made that quite clear. It was considered *work*. All my colleagues were serious about it, deadly so. Perhaps my experiences in making life difficult for Ma Perkins and Mary Marlin may have provided me with a metaphor for the experiences of the great many, who fail to find in their work their "portion of reality." Let alone, a secure place "in the human community."

Is it any wonder that in such surreal circumstances, status rather than the work itself becomes important? Thus the prevalance of euphemisms in work as well as in war. The janitor is a building engineer; the garbage man, a sanitary engineer; the man at the rendering plant, a factory mechanic; the gravedigger, a caretaker. They are not themselves ashamed of their work, but society, they feel, looks upon them as a lesser species. So they call upon promiscuously used language to match the "respectability" of others, whose jobs may have less social worth than their own.

(The airline stewardess understands this hierarchy of values. "When you first start flying . . . the men you meet are airport employees: ramp rats, cleaning airplanes and things like that, mechanics. . . . After a year we get tired of that, so we move into the city to get involved with men that are usually young executives. . . . They wear their hats and their suits and in the winter their black gloves.")

* Sigmund Freud, *Civilization and Its Discontents* (New York: W. W. Norton and Co., 1962).

Not that these young men in white shirts and black gloves are so secure, either. The salesman at the advertising agency is an account executive. "I feel a little downgraded if people think I'm a salesman. Account executive—that describes my job. It has more prestige than just saying, 'I'm a salesman.' " A title, like clothes, may not make the man or woman, but it helps in the world of peers—and certainly impresses strangers. "We're all vice presidents," laughs the copy chief. "Clients like to deal with vice presidents. Also, it's a cheap thing to give somebody. Vice presidents get fired with great energy and alacrity."

At hospitals, the charming bill collector is called the patients' representative! It's a wonderland that Alice never envisioned. Consider the company spy. With understandable modesty, he refers to himself as an industrial investigator. This last—under the generic name, Security—is among the most promising occupations in our society today. No matter how tight the job market, here is a burgeoning field for young men and women. Watergate, its magic spell is everywhere.

In a further bizarre turn of events (the science of medicine has increased our life expectancy; the science of business frowns upon the elderly), the matter of age is felt in almost all quarters. "Thirty and out" is the escape hatch for the elderly auto worker to the woods of retirement, some hunting, some fishing. ... But thirty has an altogether different connotation at the ad agency, at the bank, at the auditing house, at the gas company. Unless he/she is "with it" by then, it's out to the woods of the city, some hunting, some fishing of another sort. As the work force becomes increasingly younger, so does Willy Loman.

Dr. John R. Coleman, president of Haverford College, took an unusual sabbatical during the early months of 1973. He worked at menial jobs. In one instance, he was fired as a porter-dishwasher. "I'd never been fired and I'd never been unemployed. For three days I walked the streets. Though I had a bank account, though my children's tuition was paid, though I had a salary and a job waiting for me back in Haverford, I was demoralized. I had an inkling of how professionals my age feel when they lose *their job and their confidence begins to sink."* Dr. Coleman is 51.*

Perhaps it is this specter that most haunts working men and women: the planned obsolescence of people that is of a piece with the planned obsolescence of the things they make. Or sell. It is perhaps this fear of no longer being needed in a world of needless things that most clearly spells out the unnaturalness, the surreality of much that is called work today.

"Since Dr. Coleman happens to be chairman of the Federal Reserve Bank of Philadelphia, he quit his ditchdigging job to preside over the bank's monthly meeting. When he looked at the other members of the board, he could not keep from feeling that there was something unreal about them all."†

Something unreal. For me, it was a feeling that persisted throughout this adventure. (How else can I describe this undertaking? It was the daily experience of *others*, their private hurts, real and fancied, that I was probing. In lancing an especially obstinate boil, it is not the doctor who experiences the pain.)

I was no more than a wayfaring stranger, taking much and giving little. True, there were dinners, lunches, drinks, some breakfasts, in posh as well as short order places. There were earnest considerations, varying with what I felt was my companion's economic condition. But they were at best token payments. I was the beneficiary of others' generosity. My tape recorder, as ubiquitous as the carpenter's tool chest or the doctor's black satchel, carried away valuables beyond price.

On occasions, overly committed, pressed by circumstance of my own thoughtless making, I found myself neglecting the amenities and graces that offer mutual pleasure to visitor and host. It was the Brooklyn fireman who astonished me into shame. After what I had felt was an overwhelming experience—meeting him—he invited me to stay "for supper. We'll pick something up at the Italian joint on the corner." I had already unplugged my tape rec-

* *New York Times*, June 10, 1973.
† Ibid.

order. (We had had a few beers.) "Oh, Jesus," I remember the manner in which I mumbled. "I'm supposed to see this hotel clerk on the other side of town." He said, "You runnin' off like that? Here we been talkin' all afternoon. It won't sound nice. This guy, Studs, comes to the house, gets my life on tape, and says, 'I gotta go' . . ." It was a memorable supper. And yet, looking back, how could I have been so insensitive?

In a previous work, a middle-aged black hospital aide observed, "You see, there's such a thing as a feeling tone. And if you don't have this, baby, you've had it." It is a question I ask myself just often enough to keep me uncomfortable. Especially since my host's gentle reprimand. Not that it was a revelatory experience for me. Though I had up to that moment succeeded in burying it, this thief-in-the-night feeling, I knew it was there. The fireman stunned me into facing up to it.

(Is it any wonder that in some societies, which we in our arrogance call "primitive," offense is taken at being photographed? It is the stealing of the spirit. In remembering such obscenities, a South African "adventure" comes to mind. In 1962, on the road to Pretoria, a busload of us, five Americans and thirty Germans, stopped off at a Zulu village.

As the bare-breasted women ran toward the tourists, the cameras clicked busily. "Tiki! Tiki!" cried the women. A tiki is worth about three cents. The visitors, Reetmeister cigars poised on their pouting lips, muttered, "Beggars." They were indignant. A simple quid pro quo—and a dirt cheap one, at that—was all their subjects had in mind. Their spirit for a tiki . . .)

The camera, the tape recorder . . . misused, well-used. There are the *paparazzi;* and there is Walker Evans. The portable tape recorder, too, is for better or for worse. It can be, tiny and well-concealed, a means of blackmail, an instrument of the police state or, as is most often the case, a transmitter of the banal. Yet, a tape recorder, with microphone in hand, on the table or the arm of the chair or on the grass, can transform both the visitor and the host. On one occasion, during the play-back, my companion murmured in wonder, "I never realized I felt that way." And I was filled with wonder, too.

It can be used to capture the voice of a celebrity, whose answers are ever ready and flow through all the expected straits. I have yet to be astonished by one. It can be used to capture the thoughts of the non-celebrated—on the steps of a public housing project, in a frame bungalow, in a furnished apartment, in a parked car—and these "statistics" become persons, each one unique. I am constantly astonished.

As with my two previous books, I was aware of paradox in the making of this one. The privacy of strangers is indeed trespassed upon. Yet my experiences tell me that people with buried grievances and dreams unexpressed do want to let go. Let things out. Lance the boil, they say; there is too much pus. The hurts, though private, are, I trust, felt by others too.

When André Schiffrin, my editor, who persuaded me to undertake the other assignments (*Division Street: America* and *Hard Times*), suggested this one, I was, as before, hesitant. I am neither an economist nor a sociologist nor The Inquiring Reporter. How am I to go about it?

Seven years ago, seeking out the feelings of "ordinary" people living out their anonymous lives in a large industrial city, "I was on the prowl for a cross-section of urban thought, using no one method or technique." Three years later, I was on the prowl for the memories of those who survived the Great Depression. In each case, my vantage was that of a guerrilla. I was somewhat familiar with the terrain. In the first instance, it was the city in which I had lived most of my life. It concerned an actual present. In the second, it was an experience I had shared, if only peripherally. It concerned an actual past. But this one—in which the hard substance of the daily job fuses to the haze of the daydream—was alien territory. It concerned not only "what is" but "what I imagine" and "what might be."

Though this was, for me, a more difficult assignment, my approach was pretty much what it had been before. I had a general idea of the kind of people I wanted to see; who, in reflecting on their personal condition, would touch on the circumstances of their fellows. Yet, as I suspected, improvisation and chance played their roles. "A tip from an acquaintance. A friend of a friend telling me of a friend or non-friend. A face, vaguely familiar, on the morning bus. An indignant phone call from a listener or a friendly one. . . ."*

Cases come to mind.

While riding the el, I was approached by a singularly tall stranger. Hearing me talking to myself (as I have a habit of doing), he recognized my voice as "the man he listens to on the radio." He told me of his work and of his father's work. His reflections appear in the sequence "Fathers and Sons." He told me of two of his students: a young hospital aide and a young black man who works in a bank. They, too, are in this book.

There was a trip to eastern Kentucky to see the remarkable Joe Begley, who is worth a book by himself, though none of his reflections are found in this one. It was his suggestion that I visit Joe and Susie Haynes, who live in the hollow behind the hills. They, in turn, guided me to Aunt Katherine. One life was threaded to another, and so tenuously . . .

It was a young housewife in a small Indiana town who led me to the strip miner, with whom she had some words, though recognizing his inner conflicts. She told me, too, of the stonemason, who, at the moment, was nursing a beer at the tavern near the river. And of the farmer having his trials in the era of agribusiness. And of the three newsboys, who might have a postscript or two to offer readers of Horatio Alger.

"I realized quite early in this adventure that interviews, conventionally conducted, were meaningless. Conditioned clichés were certain to come. The question-and-answer technique may be of some value in determining favored detergents, toothpaste and deordorants, but not in the discovery of men and women."† There were questions, of course. But they were casual in nature—at the beginning: the kind you would ask while having a drink with someone; the kind he would ask you. The talk was idiomatic rather than academic. In short, it was conversation. In time, the sluice gates of dammed up hurts and dreams were opened.

As with the other books, there are deliberate ommisions in this one: notably, clergymen (though a young priest is

* From the preface to *Division Street: America* (New York: Pantheon Books, 1967).

† From the preface to *Division Street: America*.

here), doctors (there is a dentist), politicians, journalists and writers of any kind (the exception is a film critic; her subject, work as reflected or non-reflected in movies). I felt that their articulateness and expertise offered them other forums. My transcribing their attitudes would be nothing more than self-indulgence. I was interested in other counties not often heard from.

Choices were in many instances arbitrary. People are engaged in thousands of jobs. Whom to visit? Whom to pass by? In talking to the washroom attendant, would I be remiss in neglecting the elevator operator? One felt his job "obsolete." Wouldn't the other, too? In visiting the Chicago bookbinder, I missed the old Massachusetts basket weaver. I had been told about the New Englander, who found delight in his work. So did my Chicago acquaintance. Need I have investigated the lot of an assembler at the electronics plant, having spent time with spot-welders at Ford? An assembly line is a line is a line.

An unusually long sequence of this book is devoted to the automobile—its making, its driving, its parking, its selling. Also its servicing. There is its residue, too: traffic, noise, accident, crime, pollution, TV commercials, and human orneriness at its worst.

"The evil genius of our time is the car," Barry Byrne, an elderly architect, observed several years ago. "We must conquer the automobile or become enslaved by it." (He was a disciple of Frank Lloyd Wright, who spoke of the *organic* nature of things. "It was his favorite word. When you look at a tree, it is a magnificent example of an organic whole. All parts belong together, as fingers belong to one's hands. The car today is a horrible example of something not belonging to man.") Less than a year after our conversation, Mr. Byrne, on his way to Sunday mass, was run down by a car and killed.

As for the men and women involved in its manufacture, a UAW local officer has his say: "Every time I see an automobile going down the street, I wonder whether the person driving it realizes the kind of human sacrifice that has to go in the building of that car. There's no question there's a better way. And they can build fewer cars and resolve many of the human problems . . ." Though the sequence is headed "The Demon Lover," the title of another Child ballad might have just as appropriately been used: "The False Knight upon the Road."

But it provides millions with jobs. So does ordnance work (another euphemism called upon; "war" has only one syllable).

As some occupations become obsolete, others come into being. More people are being paid to watch other people than ever before. A cargo inspector says, "I watch the watchman." He neglected to tell who watches *him*. A young department head in a bank finds it amusing. "Just like Big Brother's watching you. Everybody's watching somebody. It's quite funny when you turn and start watching them. I do that quite a bit. They know I'm watching them. They become uneasy."

Here, too, grievances come into play. The most profound complaint, aside from non-recognition and the nature of the job, is "being spied on." There's the foreman at the plant, the supervisor listening in at Ma Bell's, the checker who gives the bus driver a hard time, the "passenger" who gives the airline stewardess a gimlet eye . . . The indignation of those being watched is no longer offered in muted tones. Despite the occasional laugh, voices rise. Such humiliations, like fools, are suffered less gladly than before.

In the thirties (as rememberers of "Hard Times" remembered), not very many questioned their lot. Those rebels who found flaws in our society were few in number. This time around, "the system stinks" was a phrase almost as recurrent as "more or less."

Even the "company girl" had a few unexpected things to say. I was looking for an airline stewardess, who might tell me what it was really like. Pressed for time, I did what would ordinarily horrify me. I called a major airline's public relations department. They were most cooperative. They suggested Terry Mason (that's not her name). I assumed it would be a difficult experience for me—to find out what it was really like, under these circumstances. I underestimated Miss Mason's spunkiness. And her sense of self. So, apparently, did the PR department. She concluded, "The younger girls don't take that guff any more. When the passenger is giving you a bad time, you talk back to him." Her name may be Terry, but obviously nobody can "fly her."

Not that being young makes one rebellious. Another well-nurtured myth we live by. This may be "The Age of Charlie Blossom," but Ralph Werner, twenty, is far more amenable to the status quo and certainly more job-conscious than Bud Freeman, sixty-seven. And Ken Brown, a tycoon at twenty-six, respects the "work ethic" far, far more than Walter Lundquist, forty-eight. It isn't the calendar age that determines a man's restlessness. It is daily circumstance, an *awareness* of being hurt, and an inordinate hunger for "another way." As Lundquist, who gave up a "safe" job for "sanity" puts it: "Once you wake up the human animal you can't put it back to sleep again."

Perhaps it is time the "work ethic" was redefined and its idea reclaimed from the banal men who invoke it. In a world of cybernetics, of an almost runaway technology, things are increasingly making things. It is for our species, it would seem, to go on to other matters. Human matters. Freud put it one way. Ralph Helstein puts it another. He is president emeritus of the United Packinghouse Workers of America. "Learning is work. Caring for children is work. Community action is work. Once we accept the concept of work as something meaningful—not just as the source of a buck—you don't have to worry about finding enough jobs. There's no excuse for mules any more. Society does not need them. There's no question about our ability to feed and clothe and house everybody. The problem is going to come in finding enough ways for man to keep occupied, so he's in touch with reality." Our imaginations have obviously not yet been challenged.

"It isn't that the average working guy is dumb. He's tired, that's all." Mike LeFevre, the steelworker, asks rhetorically, "Who you gonna sock? You can't sock General Motors . . . you can't sock a system." So, at the neighborhood tavern, he socks the patron sitting next to him, the average working guy. And look out below! It's predetermined, his work being what it is.

"Even a writer as astringent and seemingly unromantic as Orwell never quite lost the habit of seeing working classes through the cozy fug of an Edwardian music hall. There is a wide range of similar attitudes running down through the folksy ballyhoo of the Sunday columnists, the journalists who always remember with admiration the latest bon mot of their pub pal, 'Alf.'" *

* Richard Hoggart, *The Uses of Literacy*.

Similarly, on our shores, the myth dies hard. The most perdurable and certainly the most dreary is that of the cabdriver-philosopher. Our columnists still insist on citing him as the perceptive "diamond in the rough" social observer. Lucky Miller, a young cabdriver, has his say in this matter. "A lot of drivers, they'll agree to almost anything the passenger will say, no matter how absurd. They're angling for that tip." Barbers and bartenders are probably not far behind as being eminently quotable. They are also tippable. This in no way reflects on the nature of their work so much as on the slothfulness of journalists, and the phenomenon of tipping. "Usually I do not disagree with a customer," says a barber. "That's gonna hurt business." It's predetermined, his business—or work—being what it is.

Simultaneously, as our "Alf," called "Archie" or "Joe," is romanticized, he is caricatured. He is the clod, put down by others. The others, who call themselves middle-class, are in turn put down by still others, impersonal in nature—The Organization, The Institution, The Bureaucracy. "Who you gonna sock? You can't sock General Motors . . ." Thus the dumbness (or numbness or tiredness) of both classes is encouraged and exploited in a society more conspicuously manipulative than Orwell's. A perverse alchemy is at work: the gold that may be found in their unexamined lives is transmuted into the dross of banal being. This put-down and its acceptance have been made possible by a perverted "work ethic."

But there are stirrings, a nascent flailing about. Though "Smile" buttons appear, the bearers are deadpan because nobody smiles back. What with the computer and all manner of automation, new heroes and anti-heroes have been added to Walt Whitman's old work anthem. The sound is no longer melodious. The desperation is unquiet.

Nora Watson may have said it most succinctly. "I think most of us are looking for a calling, not a job. Most of us, like the assembly line worker, have jobs that are too small for our spirit. Jobs are not big enough for people."

During my three years of prospecting, I may have, on more occasions than I had imagined, struck gold. I was constantly astonished by the extraordinary dreams of ordinary people. No matter how bewildering the times, no matter how dissembling the official language, those we call ordinary are aware of a sense of personal worth—or more often a lack of it—in the work they do. Tom Patrick, the Brooklyn fireman whose reflections end the book, similarly brings this essay to a close:

"The fuckin' world's so fucked up, the country's fucked up. But the firemen, you actually see them produce. You see them put out a fire. You see them come out with babies in their hands. You see them give mouth-to-mouth when a guy's dying. You can't get around that shit. That's real. To me, that's what I want to be.

"I worked in a bank. You know, it's just paper. It's not real. Nine to five and it's shit. You're lookin' at numbers. But I can look back and say, 'I helped put out a fire. I helped save somebody.' It shows something I did on this earth."

CONTENTS

BOOK TWO

COMMUNICATIONS

A PECKING ORDER

DID YOU EVER HEAR THE ONE ABOUT THE FARMER'S DAUGHTER?

THE COMMERCIAL

BOOK THREE

CLEANING UP

WATCHING

BOOK FOUR

THE DEMON LOVER

THE MAKING

THE DRIVING

THE PARKING

THE SELLING

BOOK FIVE

APPEARANCE

BOOK SIX

THE QUIET LIFE

BROKERS

BUREAUCRACY

ORGANIZER

BOOK SEVEN

THE SPORTING LIFE

IN CHARGE

MA AND PA COURAGE

REFLECTIONS ON IDLENESS
AND RETIREMENT

BOOK EIGHT

THE AGE OF
CHARLIE BLOSSOM

BOOK NINE

THE QUIZ KID
AND THE CARPENTER

IN SEARCH OF A CALLING

SECOND CHANCE

FATHERS AND SONS

Preface I

WHO BUILT THE PYRAMIDS?

Who built the seven towers of Thebes?
The books are filled with the names of kings.
Was it kings who hauled the craggy blocks of stone? . . .
In the evening when the Chinese wall was finished
Where did the masons go? . . .

—Bertolt Brecht

MIKE LEFEVRE

It is a two-flat dwelling, somewhere in Cicero, on the out-skirts of Chicago. He is thirty-seven. He works in a steel mill. On occasion, his wife Carol works as a waitress in a neighborhood restaurant; otherwise, she is at home, caring for their two small children, a girl and a boy.

At the time of my first visit, a sculpted statuette of Mother and Child was on the floor, head severed from body. He laughed softly as he indicated his three-year-old daughter: "She Doctor Spock'd it."

I'm a dying breed. A laborer. Strictly muscle work . . . pick it up, put it down, pick it up, put it down. We handle between forty and fifty thousand pounds of steel a day. (Laughs) I know this is hard to believe—from four hundred pounds to three- and four-pound pieces. It's dying.

You can't take pride any more. You remember when a guy could point to a house he built, how many logs he stacked. He built it and he was proud of it. I don't really think I could be proud if a contractor built a home for me. I would be tempted to get in there and kick the carpenter in the ass (laughs), and take the saw away from him. 'Cause I would have to be part of it, you know.

It's hard to take pride in a bridge you're never gonna

1

cross, in a door you're never gonna open. You're mass-producing things and you never see the end result of it. (Muses) I worked for a trucker one time. And I got this tiny satisfaction when I loaded a truck. At least I could see the truck depart loaded. In a steel mill, forget it. You don't see where nothing goes.

I got chewed out by my foreman once. He said, "Mike, you're a good worker but you have a bad attitude." My attitude is that I don't get excited about my job. I do my work but I don't say whoopee-doo. The day I get excited about my job is the day I go to a head shrinker. How are you gonna get excited about pullin' steel? How are you gonna get excited when you're tired and want to sit down?

It's not just the work. Somebody built the pyramids. Somebody's going to build something. Pyramids, Empire State Building—these things just don't happen. There's hard work behind it. I would like to see a building, say, the Empire State, I would like to see on one side of it a foot-wide strip from top to bottom with the name of every bricklayer, the name of every electrician, with all the names. So when a guy walked by, he could take his son and say, "See, that's me over there on the forty-fifth floor. I put the steel beam in." Picasso can point to a painting. What can I point to? A writer can point to a book. Everybody should have something to point to.

It's the not-recognition by other people. To say a woman is *just* a housewife is degrading, right? Okay. *Just* a housewife. It's also degrading to say *just* a laborer. The difference is that a man goes out and maybe gets smashed.

When I was single, I could quit, just split. I wandered all over the country. You worked just enough to get a poke, money in your pocket. Now I'm married and I got two kids ... (trails off). I worked on a truck dock one time and I was single. The foreman came over and he grabbed my shoulder, kind of gave me a shove. I punched him and knocked him off the dock. I said, "Leave me alone. I'm doing my work, just stay away from me, just don't give me the with-the-hands business."

Hell, if you whip a damn mule he might kick you. Stay out of my way, that's all. Working is bad enough, don't bug me. I would rather work my ass off for eight hours a day with nobody watching me than five minutes with a guy watching me. Who you gonna sock? You can't sock

General Motors, you can't sock anybody in Washington, you can't sock a system.

A mule, an old mule, that's the way I feel. Oh yeah. See. (Shows black and blue marks on arms and legs, burns.) You know what I heard from more than one guy at work? "If my kid wants to work in a factory, I am going to kick the hell out of him." I want my kid to be an effete snob. Yeah, mm-hmm. (Laughs.) I want him to be able to quote Walt Whitman, to be proud of it.

If you can't improve yourself, you improve your posterity. Otherwise life isn't worth nothing. You might as well go back to the cave and stay there. I'm sure the first caveman who went over the hill to see what was on the other side—I don't think he went there wholly out of curiosity. He went there because he wanted to get his son out of the cave. Just the same way I want to send my kid to college.

I work so damn hard and want to come home and sit down and lay around. *But I gotta get it out.* I want to be able to turn around to somebody and say, "Hey, fuck you." You know? Laughs.) The guy sitting next to me on the bus too. 'Cause all day I wanted to tell my foreman to go fuck himself, but I can't.

So I find a guy in a tavern. To tell him that. And he tells me too. I've been in brawls. He's punching me and I'm punching him, because we actually want to punch somebody else. The most that'll happen is the bartender will bar us from the tavern. But at work, you lose your job.

This one foreman I've got, he's a kid. He's a college graduate. He thinks he's better than everybody else. He was chewing me out and I was saying, "Yeah, yeah, yeah." He said, "What do you mean, yeah, yeah, yeah. Yes, *sir*." I told him, "Who the hell are you, Hitler? What is this *"Yes, sir"* bullshit? I came here to work, I didn't come here to crawl. There's a fuckin' difference." One word led to another and I lost.

I got broke down to a lower grade and lost twenty-five cents an hour, which is a hell of a lot. It amounts to about ten dollars a week. He came over—after breaking me down. The guy comes over and smiles at me. I blew up. He didn't know it, but he was about two seconds and two feet away from a hospital. I said, "Stay the fuck away from me." He was just about to say something and was pointing his finger. I just reached my hand up and just grabbed his finger and I just put it back in his pocket. He walked away. I grabbed his finger because I'm married. If I'd a been single, I'd a grabbed his head. That's the difference.

You're doing this manual labor and you know that technology can do it. (Laughs.) Let's face it, a machine can do the work of a man; otherwise they wouldn't have space probes. Why can we send a rocket ship that's unmanned and yet send a man in a steel mill to do a mule's work?

Automation? Depends how it's applied. It frightens me if it puts me out on the street. It doesn't frighten me if it shortens my work week. You read that little thing: what are you going to do when this computer replaces you? Blow up computers. (Laughs.) Really. Blow up computers. I'll be goddamned if a computer is gonna eat before I do! I want milk for my kids and beer for me. Machines can either liberate man or enslave 'im, because they're pretty neutral. It's man who has the bias to put the thing one place or another.

If I had a twenty-hour workweek, I'd get to know my kids better, my wife better. Some kid invited me to go on a college campus. On a Saturday. It was summertime. Hell, if I had a choice of taking my wife and kids to a picnic or going to a college campus, it's gonna be the picnic. But if I worked a twenty-hour week, I could go do both. Don't you think with that extra twenty hours people could really expand? Who's to say? There are some people in factories just by force of circumstance. I'm just like the colored people. Potential Einsteins don't have to be white. They could be in cotton fields, they could be in factories.

The twenty-hour week is a possibility today. The intellectuals, they always say there are potential Lord Byrons, Walt Whitmans, Roosevelts, Picassos working in construction or steel mills or factories. But I don't think they believe it. I think what they're afraid of is the potential Hitlers and Stalins that are there too. The people in power fear the leisure man. Not just the United States. Russia's the same way.

What do you think would happen in this country if, for one year, they experimented and gave everybody a twenty-hour week? How do they know that the guy who digs Wallace today doesn't try to resurrect Hitler tomorrow? Or the guy who is mildly disturbed at pollution doesn't decide to go to General Motors and shit on the

guy's desk? You can become a fanatic if you had the time.
The whole thing is time. That is, I think, one reason rich
kids tend to be fanatic about politics: they have time.
Time, that's the important thing.

It isn't that the average working guy is dumb. He's
tired, that's all. I picked up a book on chess one time.
That thing laid in the drawer for two or three weeks,
you're too tired. During the weekends you want to take
your kids out. You don't want to sit there and the kid
comes up: "Daddy, can I go to the park?" You got your
nose in a book? Forget it.

I know a guy fifty-seven years old. Know what he tells
me? "Mike, I'm old and tired *all* the time." The first thing
happens at work: When the arms start moving, the brain
stops. I punch in about ten minutes to seven in the morning. I say hello to a couple of guys I like, I kid around
with them. One guy says good morning to you and you
say good morning. To another guy you say fuck you. The
guy you say fuck you to is your friend.

I put on my hard hat, change into my safety shoes, put
on my safety glasses, go to the bonderizer. It's the thing I
work on. They rake the metal, they wash it, they dip it in
a paint solution, and we take it off. Put it on, take it off,
put it on, take it off, put it on, take it off . . .

I say hello to everybody but my boss. At seven it starts.
My arms get tired about the first half-hour. After that, they
don't get tired any more until maybe the last half-hour at
the end of the day. I work from seven to three thirty. My
arms are tired at seven thirty and they're tired at three
o'clock. I hope to God I never get broke in, because I
always want my arms to be tired at seven thirty and three
o'clock. (Laughs.) 'Cause that's when I know that there's
a beginning and there's an end. That I'm not brainwashed.
In between, I don't even try to think.

If I were to put you in front of a dock and I pulled up a
skid in front of you with fifty hundred-pound sacks of
potatoes and there are fifty more skids just like it, and
this is what you're gonna do all day, what would you
think about—potatoes? Unless a guy's a nut, he never
thinks about work or talks about it. Maybe about baseball
or about getting drunk the other night or he got laid or he
didn't get laid. I'd say one out of a hundred will actually
get excited about work.

Why is it that the communists always say they're for the

workingman, and as soon as they set up a country, you
got guys singing to tractors? They're singing about how
they love the factory. That's where I couldn't buy communism. It's the intellectuals' utopia, not mine. I cannot
picture myself singing to a tractor, I just can't. (Laughs.)
Or singing to steel. (Singsongs.) Oh whoop-dee-doo, I'm
at the bonderizer, oh how I love this heavy steel. No
thanks. Never hoppen.

Oh yeah, I daydream. I fantasize about a sexy blonde
in Miami who's got my union dues. (Laughs.) I think of
the head of the union the way I think of the head of my
company. Living it up. I think of February in Miami.
Warm weather, a place to lay in. When I hear a college
kid say, "I'm oppressed," I don't believe him. You know
what I'd like to do for one year? Live like a college kid.
Just for one year. I'd love to. Wow! (Whispers) Wow!
Sports car! Marijuana! (Laughs.) Wild, sexy broads. I'd
love that, hell yes, I would.

Somebody has to do this work. If my kid ever goes to
college, I just want him to have a little respect, to realize
that his dad is one of those somebodies. This is why even
on—(muses) yeah, I guess, sure—on the black thing . . .
(Sighs heavily.) I can't really hate the colored fella that's
working with me all day. The black intellectual I got no
respect for. The white intellectual I got no use for. I got
no use for the black militant who's gonna scream three
hundred years of slavery to me while I'm busting my ass.
You know what I mean? (Laughs.) I have one answer for
that guy: go see Rockefeller. See Harriman. Don't bother
me. We're in the same cotton field. So just don't bug me.
(Laughs).

After work I usually stop off at a tavern. Cold beer.
Cold beer right away. When I was single, I used to go into
hillbilly bars, get in a lot of brawls. Just to explode. I got
a thing on my arm here (indicates scar). I got slapped
with a bicycle chain. Oh, wow! (Softly) Mmm. I'm getting older. (Laughs.) I don't explode as much. You might
say I'm broken in. (Quickly) No, I'll never be broken in.
(Sighs.) When you get a little older, you exchange the
words. When you're younger, you exchange the blows.

When I get home, I argue with my wife a little bit.
Turn on TV, get mad at the news. (Laughs.) I don't even
watch the news that much. I watch Jackie Gleason. I look
for any alternative to the ten o'clock news. I don't want to

go to bed angry. Don't hit a man with anything heavy at
five o'clock. He just can't be bothered. This is his time to
relax. The heaviest thing he wants is what his wife has to
tell him.

When I come home, know what I do for the first
twenty minutes? Fake it. I put on a smile. I got a kid
three years old. Sometimes she says, "Daddy, where've
you been?" I say, "Work." I could have told her I'd been
in Disneyland. What's work to a three-year-old kid? If I
feel bad, I can't take it out on the kids. Kids are born innocent of everything but birth. You can't take it out on
your wife either. This is why you go to a tavern. You
want to release it there rather than do it at home. What
does an actor do when he's got a bad movie? I got a bad
movie every day.

I don't even need the alarm clock to get up in the
morning. I can go out drinking all night, fall asleep at
four, and bam! I'm up at six—no matter what I do.
(Laughs.) It's a pseudo-death, more or less. Your whole
system is paralyzed and you give all the appearance of
death. It's an ingrown clock. It's a thing you just get used
to. The hours differ. It depends. Sometimes my wife wants
to do something crazy like play five hundred rummy or
put a puzzle together. It could be midnight, could be ten
o'clock, could be nine thirty.

What do you do weekends?

Drink beer, read a book. See that one? *Violence in
America.* It's one of them studies from Washington. One
of them committees they're always appointing. A thing
like that I read on a weekend. But during the weekdays,
gee ... I just thought about it. I don't do that much reading from Monday through Friday. Unless it's a horny
book. I'll read it at work and go home and do my homework. (Laughs.) That's what the guys at the plant call
it—homework. (Laughs.) Sometimes my wife works on
Saturday and I drink beer at the tavern.

I went out drinking with one guy, oh, a long time ago.
A college boy. He was working where I work now. Always preaching to me about how you need violence to
change the system and all that garbage. We went into a
hillbilly joint. Some guy there, I didn't know him from
Adam, he said, "You think you're smart." I said, "What's

your pleasure?" (Laughs.) He said, "My pleasure's to kick your ass." I told him I really can't be bothered. He said, "What're you, chicken?" I said, "No, I just don't want to be bothered." He came over and said something to me again. I said, "I don't beat women, drunks, or fools. Now leave me alone."

The guy called his brother over. This college boy that was with me, he came nudging my arm, "Mike, let's get out of here." I said, "What are you worried about?" (Laughs.) This isn't unusual. People will bug you. You fend it off as much as you can with your mouth and when you can't, you punch the guy out.

It was close to closing time and we stayed. We could have left, but when you go into a place to have a beer and a guy challenges you—if you expect to go in that place again, you don't leave. If you have to fight the guy, you fight.

I got just outside the door and one of these guys jumped on me and grabbed me around the neck. I grabbed his arm and flung him against the wall. I grabbed him here (indicates throat), and jiggled his head against the wall quite a few times. He kind of slid down a little bit. This guy who said he was his brother took a swing at me with a garrison belt. He just missed and hit the wall. I'm looking around for my junior Stalin (laughs), who loves violence and everything. He's gone. Split. (Laughs.) Next day I see him at work. I couldn't get mad at him, he's a baby.

He saw a book in my back pocket one time and he was amazed. He walked up to me and he said, "You read?" I said, "What do you mean, I read?" He said, "All these dummies read the sports pages around here. What are you doing with a book?" I got pissed off at the kid right away. I said, "What do you mean, all these dummies? Don't knock a man who's paying somebody else's way through college." He was a nineteen-year-old effete snob.

Yet you want your kid to be an effete snob?

Yes. I want my kid to look at me and say, "Dad, you're a nice guy, but you're a fuckin' dummy." Hell yes, I want my kid to tell me that he's not gonna be like me . . .

If I were hiring people to work, I'd try naturally to pay them a decent wage. I'd try to find out their first names, their last names, keep the company as small as possible, so I could personalize the whole thing. All I would ask a man is a handshake, see you in the morning. No applications, nothing. I wouldn't be interested in the guy's past. Nobody ever checks the pedigree on a mule, do they? But they do on a man. Can you picture walking up to a mule and saying, "I'd like to know who his granddaddy was?"

I'd like to run a combination bookstore and tavern. (Laughs.) I would like to have a place where college kids came and a steelworker could sit down and talk. Where a workingman could not be ashamed of Walt Whitman and where a college professor could not be ashamed that he painted his house over the weekend.

If a carpenter built a cabin for poets, I think the least the poets owe the carpenter is just three or four one-liners on the wall. A little plaque: Though we labor with our minds, this place we can relax in was built by someone who can work with his hands. And his work is as noble as ours. I think the poet owes something to the guy who builds the cabin for him.

I don't think of Monday. You know what I'm thinking about on Sunday night? Next Sunday. If you work real hard, you think of a perpetual vacation. Not perpetual sleep ... What do I think of on a Sunday night? Lord, I wish the fuck I could do something else for a living.

I don't know who the guy is who said there is nothing sweeter than an unfinished symphony. Like an unfinished painting and an unfinished poem. If he creates this thing one day—let's say, Michelangelo's Sistine Chapel. It took him a long time to do this, this beautiful work of art. But what if he had to create this Sistine Chapel a thousand times a year? Don't you think that would even dull Michelangelo's mind? Or if da Vinci had to draw his anatomical charts thirty, forty, fifty, sixty, eighty, ninety, a hundred times a day? Don't you think that would even bore da Vinci?

Way back, you spoke of the guys who built the pyramids, not the pharaohs, the unknowns. You put yourself in their category?

Yes. I want my signature on 'em, too. Sometimes, out of pure meanness, when I make something, I put a little dent in it. I like to do something to make it really unique.

Hit it with a hammer. I deliberately fuck it up to see if it'll get by, just so I can say I did it. It could be anything. Let me put it this way: I think God invented the dodo bird so when we get up there we could tell Him, "Don't you ever make mistakes?" and He'd say, "Sure, look." (Laughs.) I'd like to make my imprint. My dodo bird. A mistake, *mine*. Let's say the whole building is nothing but red bricks. I'd like to have just the black one or the white one or the purple one. Deliberately fuck up.

This is gonna sound square, but my kid is my imprint. He's my freedom. There's a line in one of Hemingway's books. I think it's from *For Whom the Bell Tolls*. They're behind the enemy lines, somewhere in Spain, and she's pregnant. She wants to stay with him. He tells her no. He says, "if you die, I die," knowing he's gonna die. But if you go, I go. Know what I mean? The mystics call it the brass bowl. Continuum. You know what I mean? This is why I work. Every time I see a young guy walk by with a shirt and tie and dressed up real sharp, I'm lookin' at my kid, you know? That's it.

Preface II

WHO SPREAD THE NEWS?

BILLY CARPENTER

Newburgh, Indiana is Lincoln boyhood country. It borders Kentucky to the northwest. The Ohio River sluggishly flows alongside the town; industrial sludge in its waters.

He is twelve. He has been a newsboy, off and on, for seven years. He delivers by bicycle. After school each day he works his paper route for about an hour. On Sunday, he's up at four in the morning. "It's dark and it's spooky. You gotta cut through these woods. It's scary." He has sixty-nine customers.

I like my work. You know a lot of guys on your route. If you're nice, they tell everybody about how nice you are and they would pass it on. But now I'm kind of in a hurry and I do it just any old way to get it done. 'Cause it's wintertime. It gets dark earlier. And if I don't get home in time, the stuff's cold and it ain't any good.

Before, I'd put it anywhere they'd want me to. I still do for this old man, he's a cripple. I put it on the table. But for the guys who can walk, if I have to put it on the porch for everybody, it'd take me about two hours. This one lady, she lives about thirty yards from the street. I just throw the paper. She came one day and started to bawl me out 'cause she got a box. You gotta go up this alley, turn around, and go to the box on the side of the house. It takes about a minute. If I had to do it for everybody, I'd never get done. Then she says. "Put it in the door." I'll put it in the door. Now she keeps the door locked, so I just throw it on the porch.

11

They used to bawl us out more. They don't do it so much now. They hold back payin' you. I collect at the beginning of the month. About three of my people, it's hard to collect. This one is always gone. He comes home around twelve o'clock and he leaves about six in the morning. I'd usually be able to catch him. I can't now.

Will your experience as a newsboy help you get along in the world?

Oh yeah. You can get a good job as a salesman, like selling encyclopedias and stuff in your later life. I would. Because you would get a lot of money.

CLIFF PICKENS

A colleague of Billy Carpenter, he too is twelve. He has fifty-four customers.

It's fun throwing papers. Sometimes you get it on the roof. But I never did that. You throw the paper off your bicycle and it lands some place in the bushes. It'll hit part of the wall and it'll bounce down into the bushes and the bushes are so thick that it'll go—boongg! That's pretty fun, because I like to see it go boongg! (Laughs.) It bounces about a foot high. You never expect bushes to bounce. I always get it out of the bushes and throw it back on their porch.

The people down at the pool hall, they reach back in my basket while I'm not lookin' and steal my papers. But they always give 'em back. They just tease me. I don't know their names. They're all kinds of guys, young guys, older guys. I usually go up there and say, "Okay, hand it over. I know you guys stuff it up your shirt." If they don't give it to me, I raise up their shirt and grab it. It's good to be a newsboy. You get to really like people.

TERRY PICKENS

Cliff's brother. He is fourteen. He has a Prince Valiant haircut. He is Newburgh's leading collector of rock recordings as well as its most avid reader of science fiction. There are fifty-seven customers on his paper route, yet it takes him considerably longer to get his work done than Cliff or Billy. "I ride the bike all over the place. I go both sides of the street. Cliff hasn't got any hills. Mine's all hills."

I've been having trouble collecting. I had one woman hid from me once. I had another woman tell her kids to tell me she wasn't home. He says, "Mom, newsboy." She says (whispers), "Tell him I'm not home." I could hear it from the door. I came back in half an hour and she paid me. She's not a deadbeat. They'll pay you if you get 'em. Sometimes you have to wait . . .

If I don't catch 'em at home, I get pretty mad. That means I gotta come back and come back and come back and come back until I catch 'em. Go around about nine o'clock at night and seven o'clock in the morning. This one guy owed me four dollars. He got real mad at me for comin' around at ten o'clock. Why'd I come around so late? He probably was mad 'cause I caught him home. But he paid me. I don't care whether he gets mad at me, just so I get paid.

I like to have money. It's nice to have money once in a while instead of being flat broke all the time. Most of my friends are usually flat broke. I spent $150 this summer. On nothing—candy, cokes, games of pool, games of pinball. We went to McDonald's a couple of times. I just bought anything I wanted. I wonder where the money went. I have nothing to show for it. I'm like a gambler, the more I have, the more I want to spend. That's just the way I am.

It's supposed to be such a great deal. The guy, when he came over and asked me if I wanted a route, he made it sound so great. Seven dollars a week for hardly any work at all. And then you find out the guy told you a bunch of bull. You mistrust the people. You mistrust your customers because they don't pay you sometimes.

Then you get mad at the people at the printing corporation. You're supposed to get fifty-seven papers. They'll send me forty-seven or else they'll send me sixty-seven. Sunday mornings they get mixed up. Cliff'll have ten or eleven extras and I'll be ten or eleven short. That happens all the time. The printers, I don't think they care. They make all these stupid mistakes at least once a week. I think they're half-asleep or something. I do my job, I don't see why they can't do theirs. I don't like my job any more than they do.

Sunday morning at three—that's when I get up. I stay up later so I'm tired. But the dark doesn't bother me. I run into things sometimes, though. Somebody's dog'll come out and about give you a heart attack. There's this one woman, she had two big German shepherds, great big old things, like three or four feet tall. One of 'em won't bite you. He'll just run up, charging, bark at you, and then he'll go away. The other one, I didn't know she had another one—when it bit me. This dog came around the bush. (Imitates barking.) When I turned around, he was at me. He bit me right there (indicates scar on leg). It was bleeding a little. I gave him a real dirty look.

He ran over to the other neighbor's lawn and tried to keep me from gettin' in there. I walked up and delivered the paper. I was about ready to beat the thing's head in or kill it. Or something with it. I was so mad. I called up that woman and she said the dog had all its shots and "I don't believe he bit you." I said, "Lady, he bit me." Her daughter started giving me the third degree. "What color was the dog?" "How big was it?" "Are you sure it was our yard and our dog?" Then they saw the dogs weren't in the pen.

First they told me they didn't think I needed any shots. Then they said they'd pay for the doctor. I never went to the doctor. It wasn't bleeding a whole lot. But I told her if I ever see that dog again, she's gonna have to get her papers from somebody else. Now they keep the dog penned up and it barks at me and everything. And I give it a dirty look.

There's a lot of dogs around here. I got this other dog, a little black one, it tried to bite me too. It lunged at me, ripped my pants, and missed me. (With the glee of W. C.

Fields) I kicked it *good*. It still chases me. There are two
black dogs. The other one I've kicked so many times that
it just doesn't bother me any more. I've kicked his face in
once when he was biting my leg. Now he just stays under
the bushes and growls at me. I don't bother to give him a
dirty look.

There were these two other dogs. They'd always run out
in the street and chase me. I kicked them. They'd come
back and I'd kick 'em again. I don't have any problems
with 'em any more, because they got hit chasin' cars.
They're both dead.

I don't like many of my customers, 'cause they'll cuss
me if they don't get their papers just exactly in the right
place. This one guy cussed me up and down for about fifteen minutes. I don't want to repeat what he called me.
All the words, just up and down. He told me he drives
past all those blank drugstores on his blank way home and
he would stop off at one of 'em and get a blank newspaper. And I'm just a blank convenience.

I was so mad at him. I hated his guts. I felt like taking
a lead pipe to him or something. But I kept my mouth
shut, 'cause I didn't know if the press guy'd get mad at me
and I'd lose my route. You see, this guy could help me or
he could hurt me. So I kept my mouth shut.

A lot of customers are considerate but a lot of 'em
aren't. Lot of 'em act like they're doing you such a favor
taking the paper from you. It costs the same dime at a
drugstore. Every time they want you to do something they
threaten you: (imitates nasty, nasal voice) "Or I'll quit."

What I really can't stand: you'll be collecting and somebody'll come out and start telling you all their problems.
"I'm going to visit my daughter today, yes, I am. She's
twenty-two, you know." "Look here, I got all my sons
home, see the army uniforms?" They'll stand for like half
an hour. I got two or three like that, and they always got
something to say to me. I'll have like two hours wasted listening to these people blabbin' before they pay me. Mmm,
I don't know. Maybe they're lonely. But they've got a
daughter and a son, why do they have to blab in my ear?

A lot of the younger customers have had routes and
they know how hard it is, how mean people are. They'll
be nicer to you. They tend to tip you more. And they
don't blab all day long. They'll just pay you and smile at

you. The younger people frequently offer me a coke or something.

Older people are afraid of me, a lot of them. The first three, four weeks—(muses) they seemed so afraid of me. They think I'm gonna rob 'em or something. It's funny. You wouldn't think it'd be like this in a small town, would you? They're afraid I'm gonna beat 'em up, take their money. They'd just reach through the door and give me the money. Now they know you so well, they invite you in and blab in your ear for half an hour. It's one or the other. I really don't know why they're afraid. I'm not old, so I wouldn't know how old people feel.

Once in a while I come home angry, most of the time just crabby. Sometimes kids steal the paper out of people's boxes. I lose my profits. It costs me a dime. The company isn't responsible, I am. The company wouldn't believe you probably that somebody stole the paper.

I don't see where being a newsboy and learning that people are pretty mean or that people don't have enough money to buy things with is gonna make you a better person or anything. If anything, it's gonna make a worse person out of you, 'cause you're not gonna like people that don't pay you. And you're not gonna like people who act like they're doing you a big favor paying you. Yeah, it sort of molds your character, but I don't think for the better. If anybody told me being a newsboy builds character, I'd know he was a liar.

I don't see where people get all this bull about the kid who's gonna be President and being a newsboy made a President out of him. It taught him how to handle his money and this bull. You know what it did? It taught him how to hate the people in his route. And the printers. And dogs.

THE MASON

CARL MURRAY BATES

We're in a tavern no more than thirty yards from the banks of the Ohio. Toward the far side of the river, Alcoa smokestacks belch forth: an uneasy coupling of a bucolic past and an industrial present. The waters are polluted, yet the jobs out there offer the townspeople their daily bread.

He is fifty-seven years old. He's a stonemason who has pursued his craft since he was seventeen. None of his three sons is in his trade.

As far as I know, masonry is older than carpentry, which goes clear back to Bible times. Stone mason goes back way *before* Bible time: the pyramids of Egypt, things of that sort. Anybody that starts to build anything, stone, rock, or brick, start on the northeast corner. Because when they built King Solomon's Temple, they started on the northeast corner. To this day, you look at your courthouses, your big public buildings, you look at the cornerstone, when it was created, what year, it will be on the northeast corner. If I was gonna build a septic tank, I would start on the northeast corner. (Laughs.) Superstition, I suppose.

With stone we build just about anything. Stone is the oldest and best building material that ever was. Stone was being used even by the cavemen that put it together with mud. They built out of stone before they even used logs. He got him a cave, he built stone across the front. And he learned to use dirt, mud, to make the stones lay there without sliding around—which was the beginnings of mortar, which we still call mud. The Romans used mortar that's almost as good as we have today.

Everyone hears these things, they just don't remember 'em. But me being in the profession, when I hear something in that line, I remember it. Stone's my business. I, oh, sometimes talk to architects and engineers that have made a study and I pick up the stuff here and there.

Every piece of stone you pick up is different, the grain's a little different and this and that. It'll split one way and break the other. You pick up your stone and look at it and make an educated guess. It's a pretty good day layin' stone or brick. Not tiring. Anything you like to do isn't tiresome. It's hard work; stone is heavy. At the same time, you get interested in what you're doing and you usually fight the clock the other way. You're not lookin' for quittin'. You're wondering you haven't got enough done and it's almost quittin' time. (Laughs.) I ask the hod carrier what time it is and he says two thirty. I say, "Oh, my Lord, I was gonna get a whole lot more than this."

I pretty well work by myself. On houses, usually just one works. I've got the hod carrier there, but most of the time I talk to myself, "I'll get my hammer and I'll knock the chip off there." (Laughs.) A good hod carrier is half your day. He won't work as hard as a poor one. He knows what to do and make every move count makin' the mortar. It has to be so much water, so much sand. His skill is to see that you don't run out of anything. The hod carrier, he's above the laborer. He has a certain amount of prestige.

I think a laborer feels that he's the low man. Not so much that he works with his hands, it's that he's at the bottom of the scale. He always wants to get up to a skilled trade. Of course he'd make more money. The main thing is the common laborer—even the word *common* laborer—just sounds so common, he's at the bottom. Many that works with his hands takes pride in his work.

I get a lot of phone calls when I get home: how about showin' me how and I'll do it myself? I always wind up doin' it for 'em. (Laughs.) So I take a lot of pride in it and I do get, oh, I'd say, a lot of praise or whatever you want to call it. I don't suppose anybody, however much he's recognized, wouldn't like to be recognized a little more. I think I'm pretty well recognized.

One of my sons is an accountant and the other two are

bankers. They're mathematicians, I suppose you'd call 'em that. Air-conditioned offices and all that. They always look at the house I build. They stop by and see me when I'm aworkin'. Always want me to come down and fix somethin' on their house, too. (Laughs.) They don't buy a house that I don't have to look at it first. Oh sure, I've got to crawl under it and look on the roof, you know . . .

I can't seem to think of any young masons. So many of 'em before, the man lays stone and his son follows his footsteps. Right now the only one of these sons I can think of is about forty, fifty years old.

I started back in the Depression times when there wasn't any apprenticeships. You just go out and if you could hold your job, that's it. I was just a kid then. Now I worked real hard and carried all the blocks I could. Then I'd get my trowel and I'd lay one or two. The second day the boss told me: I think you could lay enough blocks to earn your wages. So I guess I had only one day of apprenticeship. Usually it takes about three years of being a hod carrier to start. And it takes another ten or fifteen years to learn the skill.

I admired the men that we had at that time that were stonemasons. They knew their trade. So naturally I tried to pattern after them. There's been very little change in the work. Stone is still stone, mortar is still the same as it was fifty years ago. The style of stone has changed a little. We use a lot more, we call it golf. A stone as big as a baseball up to as big as a basketball. Just round balls and whatnot. We just fit 'em in the wall that way.

Automation has tried to get in the bricklayer. Set 'em with a crane. I've seen several put up that way. But you've always got in-between the windows and this and that. It just doesn't seem to pan out. We do have a power saw. We do have an electric power mix to mix the mortar, but the rest of it it's done by hand as it always was.

In the old days they all seemed to want it cut out and smoothed. It's harder now because you have no way to use your tools. You have no way to use a string, you have no way to use a level or a plumb. You just have to look at it because it's so rough and many irregularities. You have to just back up and look at it.

All construction, there's always a certain amount of injuries. A scaffold will break and so on. But practically no real danger. All I ever did do was work on houses, so we

don't get up very high—maybe two stories. Very seldom
that any more. Most of 'em are one story. And so many
of 'em use stone for a trim. They may go up four, five
feet and then paneling or something. There's a lot of
skinned fingers or you hit your finger with a hammer.
Practically all stone is worked with hammers and chisels.
I wouldn't call it dangerous at all.

Stone's my life. I daydream all the time, most times it's
on stone. Oh, I'm gonna build me a stone cabin down on
the Green River. I'm gonna build stone cabinets in the
kitchen. That stone door's gonna be awful heavy and I
don't know how to attach the hinges. I've got to figure out
how to make a stone roof. That's the kind of thing. All
my dreams, it seems like it's got to have a piece of rock
mixed in it.

If I got some problem that's bothering me, I'll actually
wake up in the night and think of it. I'll sit at the table
and get a pencil and paper and go over it, makin' marks
on paper or drawin' or however . . . this way or that way.
Now I've got to work this and I've only got so much. Or
they decided they want it that way when you already got
it fixed this way. Anyone hates tearing his work down. It's
all the same price but you still don't like to do it.

These fireplaces, you've got to figure how they'll throw
out heat, the way you curve the fireboxes inside. You have
to draw a line so they reflect heat. But if you throw too
much of a curve, you'll have them smoke. People in these
fine houses don't want a puff of smoke coming out of the
house.

The architect draws the picture and the plans, and the
draftsman and the engineer, they help him. They figure
the strength and so on. But when it comes to actually
makin' the curves and doin' the work, you've got to do it
with your hands. It comes right back to your hands.

When you get into stone, you're gettin' away from the
prefabs, you're gettin' into the better homes. Usually at
this day and age they'll start into sixty to seventy thousand
and run up to about half a million. We've got one goin'
now that's mighty close, three or four hundred thousand.
That type of house is what we build.

The lumber is not near as good as it used to be. We
have better fabricating material, such as plywood and
sheet rock and things of that sort, but the lumber itself is
definitely inferior. Thirty, forty years ago a house was al-

most entirely made of lumber, wood floors ... Now they have vinyl, they have carpet, everything, and so on. The framework wood is getting to be of very poor quality.

But stone is still stone and the bricks are actually more uniform than they used to be. Orignally they took a clay bank ... I know a church been built that way. Went right on location, dug a hole in the ground and formed bricks with their hands. They made the bricks that built the building on the spot.

Now we've got modern kilns, modern heat, the temperature don't vary. They got better bricks now than they used to have. We've got machines that make brick, so they're made true. Where they used to, they were pretty rough. I'm buildin' a big fireplace now out of old brick. They run wide, long, and it's a headache. I've been two weeks on that one fireplace.

The toughest job I ever done was this house, a hundred years old plus. The lady wanted one room left just that way. And this doorway had to be closed. It had deteriorated and weathered for over a hundred years. The bricks was made out of broken pieces, none of 'em were straight. If you lay 'em crooked, it gets awful hard right there. You spend a lifetime trying to learn to lay bricks straight. And it took a half-day to measure with a spoon, to try to get the mortar to match. I'd have so much dirt, so much soot, so much lime, so when I got the recipe right I could make it in bigger quantity. Then I made it with a coffee cup. Half a cup of this, half a cup of that ... I even used soot out of a chimney and sweepin's off the floor. I was two days layin' up a little doorway, mixin' the mortar and all. The boss told the lady it couldn't be done. I said, "Give me the time, I believe I can do it." I defy you to find where that door is right now. That's the best job I ever done.

There's not a house in this country that I haven't built that I don't look at every time I go by. (Laughs.) I can set here now and actually in my mind see so many that you wouldn't believe. If there's one stone in there crooked, I know where it's at and I'll never forget it. Maybe thirty years, I'll know a place where I should have took that stone out and redone it but I didn't. I still notice it. The people who live there might not notice it, but I notice it. I never pass that house that I don't think of it. I've got one house in mind right now. (Laughs.) That's the work of my hands. 'Cause you see, stone, you don't prepaint it, you don't camouflage it. It's there, just like I left it forty years ago.

I can't imagine a job where you go home and maybe go by a year later and you don't know what you've done. My work, I can see what I did the first day I started. All my work is set right out there in the open and I can look at it as I go by. It's something I can see the rest of my life. Forty years ago, the first blocks I ever laid in my life, when I was seventeen years old. I never go through Eureka—a little town down there on the river—that I don't look thataway. It's always there.

Immortality as far as we're concerned. Nothin' in this world lasts forever, but did you know that stone—Bedford limestone, they claim—deteriorates one-sixteenth of an inch every hundred years? And it's around four or five inches for a house. So that's gettin' awful close. (Laughs.)

BOOK ONE

WORKING THE LAND

PIERCE WALKER

An autumn evening in a southern Indiana farmhouse. The city, Evansville, industrial and distending, is hardly fifteen miles away—and coming on fast.

It's a modern, well-appointed house. A grandfather's clock, tick-tocking, is the one memento of a "country" past. His father and his grandfather worked this land. "My father was born on the same spot this house is sittin'. And I was born here. We tore the old house down."

His wife, who has a job in the city, and their fourteen-year-old daughter live with him. His older child, a son, is elsewhere. Though he has a few head of beef cattle, soy beans and corn are his source of income. He describes himself as "a poor farmer."

I farm about five-hundred acres. I own in the neighborhood of two-hundred. The rest of it I sharecrop. I give the owners two-fifths and I keep three-fifths. They're absentee. One would be a doctor. And a bricklayer. One would be a contractor widow. (Glances toward his wife) What would you call Roger? An aeronautical engineer. I guess all of 'em have inherited from their parents. They hold it for an investment. If I owned a lot of farm land myself, if I had that much money, I don't think I'd be farming it. I'd let somebody else worry with it.

For a farmer, the return on your investment is so small now that it isn't really worthwhile. A younger person cannot start farming unless they have help from the father or somebody. 'Cause you have to be almost able to retire a

25

rich man to start out. The only way the farmers are making it today is the ones in business keep getting bigger, to kinda offset the acreage, the margin income. I don't know what's gonna happen in the future. I'm afraid it's gonna get rough in time to come.

Your cities are moving out, taking the farm land. If you want to stay in the farming business, it's best not to be too close to the city. But if you're thinking of disposing of your farm in a few years, why then it's an advantage, 'cause it'll be worth a lot more.

I don't see how I'll keep the thing goin'. As I get older and want to slow down ... Well, that's one way of looking at it, retirement. It's either gritting it out or selling. It seems nowadays a lot of 'em do retire and rent it out to a neighbor or somebody. The end of the day, the older you get, the tireder you get.

City people, they think you're well off. When they drive by, I hear a lot of comments, 'cause most of my friends are city people. They drive by and see a big tractor and things settin' down. They envy me, but they don't know what's behind all that.

Farming, it's such a gamble. The weather and the prices, and everything that goes with it. You don't have too many good days. It scares when you see how many working days you actually have. You have so many days to get the crop planted and the same in the fall to harvest it. They have this all figured down to the weather and it's just a few days. You try to beat the weather. It tenses you up. Whether we needed rain or we didn't need rain, it affects you in different ways. I have seen a time when you're glad to hear the thunder and lightning. Then again, I've wished I didn't hear it. (Laughs.)

Mrs. Walker interjects: In his busy season, every morning when we get up the radio goes on right away so we can get the weather report. About ten to six every morning. We just eagerly listen to this report. In the summer when he isn't too busy or like in the winter, we never pay too much attention to it. Otherwise, we watch it close."

Weather will make ya or break ya. The crops have to have enough moisture. If they don't have enough, they hurt. If you have too much, it hurts. You take it like you git. There's nothing you can do about it. You just don't think too much about it. My wife says it doesn't bother me too much. Of course, you still worry . . .

I don't believe farmers have as much ulcers as business people 'cause their life isn't quite as fast. But I'll say there will be more as times goes on. 'Cause farming is changing more. It's more a business now. It's getting to be a big business. It's not the labor any more, it's the management end of it.

Your day doesn't end. A farmer can't do like, say, a doctor—go out of town for the weekend. He has to stay with it. That's just one of the things you have to learn to live with. I'd say a majority of the time a farmer, when he comes in at night and goes to bed, he's tired enough he's not gonna have trouble sleepin'. Of course, he'll get wore down.

He touches a weary cadence as he recounts a twelve-plus-hour workday in the fall: up at six (an earlier rising in the spring, four thirty-five) . . . "haul my grain to the elevator in town, which takes about an hour and a half . . . combine about three or four loads a day . . . there's headlights on the combine, so if I start a load, I'll finish it even though it's after dark . . . that'll run from fifteen hundred to two thousand bushel . . . five hundred bushels a truckload . . . first thing next morning, I'll take the load to town . . ."

In the winter he "loafs," helping his wife with her housework, preparing the machinery for spring, planning the fertilizer program, and "a lot of book work," getting all the records up to date for "tax time."

We'll soon be storing the fall harvest. Machinery and a lot of equipment and everything ready to go when the crops mature. That's the big problem: machinery. Combine, you're speaking of twenty thousand dollars. And the eight-row planter for the spring, that's expensive. It's such a large investment for what small return you really get out of it. You won't use it but a month or two out of the year.

My father-in-law helps me an awful lot in the spring and a little in the fall. He drives the tractor for me. My daughter, she drives a tractor when school is out. When I was home there on the farm, there was five children, three boys, and we were on an eighty-acre farm. It took all of us, my father and three boys. You can see the difference machinery plays in it.

The number of farmers are getting less every day and just seems like it's getting worse every year. The younger ones aren't taking over. The majority of the people originated from the farm years ago. But it's been so long ago that the young ones now don't realize anything about the farm. What goes with it or anything like that. The gamble that the farmer takes.

The city people, when they go to the grocery store and the price of meat is raised, they jump up and down. They don't realize what all is behind that. They're thinking of their own self. They don't want to put up that extra money—which I don't blame them either. The same way when I go to buy a piece of equipment. I go jump up and down.

Break the dollar down for food and the farmer's down at the bottom of the list. He's got the most invested of all but he's the smallest percentage-wise out of the food dollar. The processors, it seems like that's the big end of it. The ladies like to buy this ready-prepared and frozen and all that, and that costs 'em.

And chemicals in farming, it's getting to be quite expensive. It seems as though we can't farm without it. They're tryin' to outlaw a lot of 'em, but I don't know. From my end of it, I'd hate to be without 'em. Seems as though if we didn't have chemicals, we wouldn't have crops. It seems like the bugs and the weeds would just about take care of 'em if we didn't have the chemicals. But I don't know ... on the other end, either ... whether it's good for our country or not.

What do you call these—organic farming? They have a lot of good points, but I never did see a large organic farm. They're just more or less small operators. I don't think you can do it on a large scale enough to be feeding a nation. You can see many small organic farms. They used to call 'em truck farmers. They had routes to town and deliver produce and like that. He more or less retailed his product to individual homes. He just couldn't get big enough, just like everybody else.

They're using airplanes more all the time. We had our corn sprayed this year by a plane—for blight. You hire a plane, he furnishes the material, and he does it for so much an acre. We had it sprayed twice—with fungicide.

When you get a good crop, that's more or less your reward. If you weren't proud of your work, you wouldn't have no place on the farm. 'Cause you don't work by the hour. And you put in a lot of hours, I tell ya. You wouldn't stay out here till dark and after if you were punchin' a clock. If you didn't like your work and have pride in it, you wouldn't do that.

You're driving a tractor all day long, you don't talk to anyone. You think over a lot of things in your mind, good and bad. You're thinking of a new piece of equipment or renting more land or buying or how you gonna get through the day. I can spend all day in the field by myself and I've never been lonesome. Sometimes I think it's nice to get out by yourself.

The grass is greener on the other side of the fence, they say. When I got out of high school I worked one summer in a factory in Evansville. I didn't like it. I've always been glad I worked that one summer. I know what it is to work in a factory for a little while. The money part of it's good, but the atmosphere, confined. The air and everything like that. I wasn't used to a smelly factory. They have a certain odor, you don't have it out in the field.

I might say I've been real lucky in farming. My wife has helped me an awful lot. She's worked ever since we've been married. My girl, she likes it and loves to get out on the tractor. Our boy really worked. He liked the farm and worked from the time he was old enough until he left. He graduated from Purdue last spring. From observing him from the time he grew up, I would say he'd make a good farmer. He's in Georgia now. He's in management training. He realized he could make more money in some other position than he can farming. I hope he isn't putting money ahead of what he really wants to do. He says he likes what he's doin', so . . .

It seems like if they once get out and go to college, there's very few of 'em do come back. They realize that as far as the future and the money could be made from farming, it just wasn't there. So that was one thing that turned his mind away from it. Of course, he can always change. I'm hoping . . .

I do believe farmers are going to have to band together a little bit more than they have in the past. Whether it'll be through a cooperative or a union, I can't say. The trouble is they're too much individual for the rest of the country nowadays. You're bucking against the organized country, it seems like. And the farmers aren't organized, it seems like.

The big complaint you hear is that when you take your product to the market, you take what they give you. And when you go buy on the other end, you pay what they say. So you're at their mercy on both ends, more or less.

I don't like to—farmers really don't want to, deep in their hearts—but when it gets to a certain point, there's no alternative. 'Cause when a person gets desperate or is about to lose his farm, he'll do about anything he wouldn't do otherwise.

I hate to look at it that way, if the farmer is part of an organization, that would take all the—I wouldn't say enjoyment, no—but it'd be just like any other business. When you all had to sell at a certain time and all that went with it. But I believe it is going to come to that.

POSTSCRIPT: *"The family farm has never been stronger than it is now, and it has never been better serviced by the Department of Agriculture."—Earl L. Butz, Secretary of Agriculture, in the keynote speech at the 51st National 4-H Congress* (Chicago Sun-Times, *November 27, 1972*).

ROBERTO ACUNA

I walked out of the fields two years ago. I saw the need to change the California feudal system, to change the lives of farm workers, to make these huge corporations feel they're not above anybody. I am thirty-four years old and I try to organize for the United Farm Workers of America.

His hands are calloused and each of his thumbnails is singularly cut. "If you're picking lettuce, the thumbnails fall off 'cause they're banged on the box. Your hands get swollen. You can't slow down because the foreman sees you're so many boxes behind and you'd better get on. But people would help each other. If you're feeling bad that day, somebody who's feeling pretty good would help. Any people that are suffering have to stick together, whether

*they like it or not, whether they are black, brown, or
pink."*

According to Mom, I was born on a cotton sack out in
the fields, 'cause she had no money to go to the hospital.
When I was a child, we used to migrate from California
to Arizona and back and forth. The things I saw shaped
my life. I remember when we used to go out and pick carrots and onions, the whole family. We tried to scratch a
livin' out of the ground. I saw my parents cry out in
despair, even though we had the whole family working. At
the time, they were paying sixty-two and a half cents an
hour. The average income must have been fifteen hundred
dollars, maybe two thousand.*

This was supplemented by child labor. During those
years, the growers used to have a Pick-Your-Harvest
Week. They would get all the migrant kids out of school
and have 'em out there pickin' the crops at peak harvest
time. A child was off that week and when he went back to
school, he got a little gold star. They would make it seem
like something civic to do.

We'd pick everything: lettuce, carrots, onions, cucum-
bers, cauliflower, broccoli, tomatoes—all the salads you
could make out of vegetables, we picked 'em. Citrus fruits,
watermelons—you name it. We'd be in Salinas about four
months. From there we'd go down into the Imperial Valley. From there we'd go to picking citrus. It was like a cycle. We'd follow the seasons.

After my dad died, my mom would come home and
she'd go into her tent and I would go into ours. We'd
roughhouse and everything and then we'd go into the tent
where Mom was sleeping and I'd see her crying. When I
asked her why she was crying she never gave me an answer. All she said was things would get better. She retired
a beaten old lady with a lot of dignity. That day she
thought would be better never came for her.

*"One time, my mom was in bad need of money, so she got
a part-time evening job in a restaurant. I'd be helping her.
All the growers would come in and they'd be laughing,*

* "Today, because of our struggles, the pay is up to two
dollars an hour. Yet we know that is not enough."

*making nasty remarks, and make passes at her. I used to
go out there and kick 'em and my mom told me to leave
'em alone, she could handle 'em. But they would embarrass her and she would cry.*

*"My mom was a very proud woman. She brought us up
without any help from nobody. She kept the family strong.
They say that a family that prays together stays together.
I say that a family that works together stays together—because of the suffering. My mom couldn't speak English too
good. Or much Spanish, for that matter. She wasn't educated. But she knew some prayers and she used to make
us say them. That's another thing; when I see the many
things in this world and this country, I could tear the
churches apart. I never saw a priest out in the fields trying
to help people. Maybe in these later years they're doing it.
But it's always the church taking from the people.*

*"We were once asked by the church to bring vegetables
to make it a successful bazaar. After we got the stuff
there, the only people havin' a good time were the rich
people because they were the only ones that were buyin'
the stuff . . ."*

I'd go barefoot to school. The bad thing was they used
to laugh at us, the Anglo kids. They would laugh because
we'd bring tortillas and frijoles to lunch. They would have
their nice little compact lunch boxes with cold milk in
their thermos and they'd laugh at us because all we had
was dried tortillas. Not only would they laugh at us, but
the kids would pick fights. My older brother used to do
most of the fighting for us and he'd come home with black
eyes all the time.

What really hurt is when we had to go on welfare. Nobody knows the erosion of man's dignity. They used to
have a label of canned goods that said, "U. S. Commodities. Not to be sold or exchanged." Nobody knows how
proud it is to feel when you bought canned goods with
your own money.

*"I wanted to be accepted. It must have been in sixth
grade. It was just before the Fourth of July. They were
trying out students for this patriotic play. I wanted to do
Abe Lincoln, so I learned the Gettysburg Address inside
and out. I'd be out in the fields pickin' the crops and I'd
be memorizin'. I was the only one who didn't have to read*

the part, 'cause I learned it. The part was given to a girl who was a grower's daughter. She had to read it out of a book, but they said she had better diction. I was very disappointed. I quit about eighth grade.

"Any time anybody'd talk to me about politics, about civil rights, I would ignore it. It's a very degrading thing because you can't express yourself. They wanted us to speak English in the school classes. We'd put out a real effort. I would get into a lot of fights because I spoke Spanish and they couldn't understand it. I was punished. I was kept after school for not speaking English."

We used to have our own tents on the truck. Most migrants would live in the tents that were already there in the fields, put up by the company. We got one for ourselves, secondhand, but it was ours. Anglos used to laugh at us. "Here comes the carnival," they'd say. We couldn't keep our clothes clean, we couldn't keep nothing clean, because we'd go by the dirt roads and the dust. We'd stay outside the town.

I never did want to go to town because it was a very bad thing for me. We used to go to the small stores, even though we got clipped more. If we went to the other stores, they would laugh at us. They would always point at us with a finger. We'd go to town maybe every two weeks to get what we needed. Everybody would walk in a bunch. We were afraid. (Laughs.) We sang to keep our spirits up. We joked about our poverty. This one guy would say, "When I get to be rich, I'm gonna marry an Anglo woman, so I can be accepted into society." The other guys would say, "When I get rich I'm gonna marry a Mexican woman, so I can go to that Anglo society of yours and see them hang you for marrying an Anglo." Our world was around the fields.

I started picking crops when I was eight. I couldn't do much, but every little bit counts. Every time I would get behind on my chores, I would get a carrot thrown at me by my parents. I would daydream: If I were a millionaire, I would buy all these ranches and give them back to the people. I would picture my mom living in one area all the time and being admired by all the people in the community. All of a sudden I'd be rudely awaken by a broken carrot in my back. That would bust your whole dream apart and you'd work for a while and come back to day-dreaming.

We used to work early, about four o'clock in the morning. We'd pick the harvest until about six. Then we'd run home and get into our supposedly clean clothes and run all the way to school because we'd be late. By the time we got to school, we'd be all tuckered out. Around maybe eleven o'clock, we'd be dozing off. Our teachers would send notes to the house telling Mom that we were inattentive. The only thing I'd make fairly good grades on was spelling. I couldn't do anything else. Many times we never did our homework, because we were out in the fields. The teachers couldn't understand that. I would get whacked there also.

School would end maybe four o'clock. We'd rush home again, change clothes, go back to work until seven, seven thirty at night. That's not counting the weekends. On Saturday and Sunday, we'd be there from four thirty in the morning until about seven thirty in the evening. This is where we made the money, those two days. We all worked.

I would carry boxes for my mom to pack the carrots in. I would pull the carrots out and she would sort them into different sizes. I would get water for her to drink. When you're picking tomatoes, the boxes are heavy. They weigh about thirty pounds. They're dropped very hard on the trucks so they have to be sturdy.

The hardest work would be thinning and hoeing with a short-handled hoe. The fields would be about a half a mile long. You would be bending and stooping all day. Sometimes you would have hard ground and by the time you got home, your hands would be full of calluses. And you'd have a backache. Sometimes I wouldn't have dinner or anything. I'd just go home and fall asleep and wake up just in time to go out to the fields again.

I remember when we just got into California from Arizona to pick up the carrot harvest. It was very cold and very windy out in the fields. We just had a little old blanket for the four of us kids in the tent. We were freezin' our tail off. So I stole two brand-new blankets that belonged to a grower. When we got under those blankets it was nice and comfortable. Somebody saw me. The next morning the grower told my mom he'd turn us in unless we gave him back his blankets—sterilized. So my mom and I and my kid brother went to the river and cut some wood and made a fire and boiled the water and she scrubbed the blankets. She hung them out to dry, ironed them, and sent them back to the grower. We got a spanking for that.

I remember this labor camp that was run by the city. It was a POW camp for German soldiers. They put families in there and it would have barbed wire all around it. If you were out after ten o'clock at night, you couldn't get back in until the next day at four in the morning. We didn't know the rules. Nobody told us. We went to visit some relatives. We got back at about ten thirty and they wouldn't let us in. So we slept in the pickup outside the gate. In the morning, they let us in, we had a fast breakfast and went back to work in the fields.*

The grower would keep the families apart, hoping they'd fight against each other. He'd have three or four camps and he'd have the people over here pitted against the people over there. For jobs. He'd give the best crops to the people he thought were the fastest workers. This way he kept us going harder and harder, competing.

When I was sixteen, I had my first taste as a foreman. Handling braceros, aliens, that came from Mexico to work. They'd bring these people to work over here and then send them back to Mexico after the season was over. My job was to make sure they did a good job and pushin' 'em ever harder. I was a company man, yes. My parents needed money and I wanted to make sure they were proud of me. A foreman is recognized. I was very naïve. Even though I was pushing the workers, I knew their problems. They didn't know how to write, so I would write letters home for them. I would take 'em to town, buy their clothes, outside of the company stores. They had paid me $1.10 an hour. The farm workers' wage was raised to eighty-two and a half cents. But even the braceros were making more money than me, because they were working piecework. I asked for more money. The manager said, "If you don't like it you can quit." I quit and joined the Marine Corps.

"I joined the Marine Corps at seventeen. I was very mixed up. I wanted to become a first-class citizen. I wanted to be accepted and I was very proud of my uniform. My mom

* "Since we started organizing, this camp has been destroyed. They started building housing on it."

didn't want to sign the papers, but she knew I had to better myself and maybe I'd get an education in the services.

"I did many jobs. I took a civil service exam and was very proud when I passed. Most of the others were college kids. There were only three Chicanos in the group of sixty. I got a job as a correctional officer in a state prison. I quit after eight months because I couldn't take the misery I saw. They wanted me to use a rubber hose on some of the prisoners—mostly Chicanos and blacks. I couldn't do it. They called me chicken-livered because I didn't want to hit nobody. They constantly harassed me after that. I didn't quit because I was afraid of them but because they were trying to make me into a mean man. I couldn't see it. This was Soledad State Prison."

I began to see how everything was so wrong. When growers can have an intricate watering system to irrigate their crops but they can't have running water inside the houses of workers. Veterinarians tend to the needs of domestic animals but they can't have medical care for the workers. They can have land subsidies for the growers but they can't have adequate unemployment compensation for the workers. They treat him like a farm implement. In fact, they treat their implements better and their domestic animals better. They have heat and insulated barns for the animals but the workers live in beat-up shacks with no heat at all.

Illness in the fields is 120 percent higher than the average rate for industry. It's mostly back trouble, rheumatism and arthritis, because of the damp weather and the cold. Stoop labor is very hard on a person. Tuberculosis is high. And now because of the pesticides, we have many respiratory diseases.

The University of California at Davis has government experiments with pesticides and chemicals. To get a bigger crop each year. They haven't any regard as to what safety precautions are needed. In 1964 or '65, an airplane was spraying these chemicals on the fields. Spraying rigs they're called. Flying low, the wheels got tangled on the fence wire. The pilot got up, dusted himself off, and got a drink of water. He died of convulsions. The ambulance attendants got violently sick because of the pesticides he had on his person. A little girl was playing around a sprayer. She stuck her tongue on it. She died instantly.

These pesticides affect the farm worker through the lungs. He breathes it in. He gets no compensation. All they do is say he's sick. They don't investigate the cause.

There were times when I felt I couldn't take it any more. It was 105 in the shade and I'd see endless rows of lettuce and I felt my back hurting ... I felt the frustration of not being able to get out of the fields. I was getting ready to jump any foreman who looked at me cross-eyed. But until two years ago, my world was still very small.

I would read all these things in the papers about Cesar Chavez and I would denounce him because I still had that thing about becoming a first-class patriotic citizen. In Mexicali they would pass out leaflets and I would throw 'em away. I never participated. The grape boycott didn't affect me much because I was in lettuce. It wasn't until Chavez came to Salinas, where I was working in the fields, that I saw what a beautiful man he was. I went to this rally, I still intended to stay with the company. But something—I don't know—I was close to the workers. They couldn't speak English and wanted me to be their spokesman in favor of going on strike. I don't know—I just got caught up with it all, the beautiful feeling of solidarity.

You'd see the people on the picket lines at four in the morning, at the camp fires, heating up beans and coffee and tortillas. It gave me a sense of belonging. These were my own people and they wanted change. I knew this is what I was looking for. I just didn't know it before.

My mom had always wanted me to better myself. I wanted to better myself because of her. Now when the strikes started, I told her I was going to join the union and the whole movement. I told her I was going to work without pay. She said she was proud of me. (His eyes glisten. A long, long pause.) See, I told her I wanted to be with my people. If I were a company man, nobody would like me any more. I had to belong to somebody and this was it right here. She said, "I pushed you in your early years to try to better yourself and get a social position. But I see that's not the answer. I know I'll be proud of you."

All kinds of people are farm workers, not just Chicanos. Filipinos started the strike. We have Puerto Ricans and Appalachians too, Arabs, some Japanese, some Chinese. At one time they used us against each other. But now they can't and they're scared, the growers. They can organize conglomerates. Yet when we try organization to better our lives, they are afraid. Suffering people never dream it could be different. Ceasar Chavez tells them this and they grasp the idea—and this is what scares the growers.

Now the machines are coming in. It takes skill to operate them. But anybody can be taught. We feel migrant workers should be given the chance. They got one for grapes. They got one for lettuce. They have cotton machines that took jobs away from thousands of farm workers. The people wind up in the ghettos of the city, their culture, their families, their unity destroyed.

We're trying to stipulate it in our contract that the company will not use any machinery without the consent of the farm workers. So we can make sure the people being replaced by the machines will know how to operate the machines.

Working in the fields is not in itself a degrading job. It's hard, but if you're given regular hours, better pay, decent housing, unemployment and medical compensation, pension plans—we have a very relaxed way of living. But the growers don't recognize us as persons. That's the worst thing, the way they treat you. Like we have no brains. Now we see they have no brains. They have only a wallet in their head. The more you squeeze it, the more they cry out.

If we had proper compensation we wouldn't have to be working seventeen hours a day and following the crops. We could stay in one area and it would give us roots. Being a migrant, it tears the family apart. You get in debt. You leave the area penniless. The children are the ones hurt the most. They go to school three months in one place and then on to another. No sooner do they make friends, they are uprooted again. Right here, your childhood is taken away. So when they grow up, they're looking for this childhood they have lost.

If people could see—in the winter, ice on the fields. We'd be on our knees all day long. We'd build fires and warm up real fast and go back onto the ice. We'd be picking watermelons in 105 degrees all day long. When people have melons or cucumber or carrots or lettuce, they don't know how they got on their table and the consequences to the people who picked it. If I had enough money, I would take busloads of people out to the fields and into the labor camps. Then they'd know how that fine salad got on their table.

AUNT KATHERINE HAYNES

A worked-out mining town in eastern Kentucky, Blackey. It is near the Virginia border. The Cumberlands are in view; is it fog, smoke, or a heavy dust that causes them to appear more distant than they really are? The people of the town, population 350—the young have gone—are, many of them, of Revolutionary War stock. Most are on welfare.

Along the superhighway, cutting through the mountains, gangs of men are casually engaged in road repair. All day trucks and half-trucks rumble by, kicking up clouds of coughing dust. During the trip to Blackey, there were glimpses of deep "hollers" and shacks; and an occasional person. Half-hidden by the mountain greenery were the ubiquitous small mountains of slag.

We're behind the mountains, deep in the hollow, Bull Creek. It's a long, winding, tortuous dirt road, some seven miles from Blackey.

Aunt Katherine Haynes is seventy-seven. She lives by herself in a cottage, on the rocks, at the foot of the mountains. It is surrounded by caterpillar tractors and bulldozers. On the wall, among olden photographs, is the legend: God Bless Our Home. It is a spare place, singularly neat: a folded umbrella in one corner, a homemade broom in another; an ancient brass bedstead is the one conspicuous piece of furniture.

She recalls the hollow of her small girlhood: "The road, a horse could travel it, but that was all. No cars, no wagons, or no nothin' back then. Then they went to have wagons and kinda widened the road up. Each man used to work six days a year, free labor. On the roads. If he wasn't out on the days the others was, why they laid him off a bigger piece to finish and he had to do that. That was the law. They always done it in the fall of the year.

"In the fall of the year, it's the prettiest place you've ever seen. When the leaves is colored . . . it's beautiful to see the hills when it's colored like that, brown and red and green and yeller. The pines always looks green and if the rest is all colored, the pines shows up.

*"There was more big trees then, but the fields were
cleaned up and tended. You can see there's nothin' cleaned
up any more, 'cause I ain't able to do it . . ."*

Housework and farmin' is all I done, never worked at
nothin' else. Eighteen hours out of every twenty-four.
Out-of-doors and then in the house at night. I have
worked out in the fodder field and carry it in some time
after dark. We'd stack it by moonlight. Never got much
rest on what little time I was in bed. (Laughs.)

You usually didn't get much rest on Sunday, had to
cook for ten children on Sunday. I've raised ten and I had
eleven. Three meals a day I cooked on Sunday. I got so I
couldn't cook like I used to. I used to be out here just
runnin' and cookin' those meals in a few minutes and fillin'
the table full. But my mind just jumps from here to there
and I can't do that no more. Just hard work, that's all I
ever knowed.

I can run circles around every girl I've got in the house
today. I'm awful thankful for it, but I won't hold up much
longer. I'm a gittin' down. Used to be I could stand and
split wood all day long, but now I go out there and split a
little while and it hurts the back of my legs to stoop over.
But I done awful well I think.

I just don't know. I was just raised an old hillbilly and
I'll die one. Radio, it's sittin' up there, but I can't hear too
good. Don't have a television. I say there's too much foolishness on for me to watch. I hear a little about Vietnam.
And I study a lot about it. But I have enough to worry on
my mind without listenin' to that to worry more about.
What was to be would be. No, I don't guess I have a
grandson in Vietnam now. Terry's boy, I actually don't
know if he's out of Vietnam or not.

They wasn't much to think on when you didn't have an
education. I didn't get half through the third reader, so
I've got no education at all. Only five months of school. I
just quit out until we got the fodder saved. Then it got so
cold, I couldn't go back. I'm just a flat old hillbilly. That's
the only way I know to talk and the only way I'll ever try
to talk.

There was fifteen in the family and we were raised in a
log house. There wasn't a window in the house. If we seen
how to do anything in the winter, we done it by firelight.
There wasn't even a kerosene lamp. We had to keep the

door open regardless of how cold it was. If you needed to work at somethin' we either done it by the light of the fire in the grate or opened the door. We always kept a good fire.

That was the way I learnt to write. I'd get me a piece of clay dirt out of the cracks and write on the side of the log house. I couldn't write a line when I was goin' to school. Now that's the truth.

JOE AND SUSIE HAYNES

Aunt Katherine's newphew and his wife. On this morning, a piece of sun peers over the Cumberlands. "That's young white oaks up there a growin'," he says. "They'll be there till the strip and auger* people pushes 'em down and they get diggin' for lumber."

His speech comes with difficulty, due to partial paralysis of his face and shortage of breath. Frequently during the conversation we take time out. He wears a hearing aid. She is hanging out the wash. A small dog runs about; a few chickens peck away.

"Minin's about all the work here, outside highway work or farmin' a little. My father started workin' in the mines when he was eleven years old. I guess he was fifty-seven when he quit, he had to. He had to walk across the big mountain and it'd be late into the night when he'd come back. So we never got to see daddy but on Sunday."

JOE: I graduated from high school in 1930, November. I went to work in the mines. We worked for fifteen cents a ton. If we made a dollar and a half a day, we made pretty good money. You got up between three thirty and four in the morning. You'd start work about six. We usually got out around maybe dark or seven or eight, nine o'clock. I come back as late as ten o'clock at night. Sometimes I just laid down to sleep, not even sleep—then wash up.

I just got short-winded and just couldn't walk across the street. I'm better now than I used to be. The doctor advised me to quit work. My heart got bad to where I

* A variation of strip mining.

couldn't get enough oxygen. March of '68 I quit. They turned me down for black lung. I'm paid through Social Security. My old uncle, he retired forty-nine years old. He's been dead a long time now. Guess he had too much sand.

My hearin' . . . It coulda been affected with so much noise. I was tampin' up, shootin' the coal down, just behind the machine. I worked that continuous miner. That made lotsa noise. This hearin' aid cost me $395.

I think the United Mine Workers has let us down a little bit. I think they sold us out is what I do. They teamed up with the operators, I think.

SUSIE: I went to school with a young boy and he got mashed up in the mines. He was about eighteen years old when he got killed.

JOE: Oh, I remember lots of accidents. I guess there was eight or nine men killed while I worked at one. These truck mines I worked in was all. They wasn't union mines. The strip and the auger about got 'em all shut down right now. I have a nephew of mine run a mine. He worked about seventeen men. They all gone to unemployment now.

Yeah, I was born in an old log cabin here. I had a great-great-great-grandfather or somethin' fought that Revolution. Grandfather Fields and his brothers was in the Civil War. One on each side of it. My grandfather owned 982 acres in here. He sold his minerals* for twenty-seven and a half cents an acre.

You're in one of the richest areas in the world and some of the poorest people in the world. They's about twenty-eight gas and oil wells. They have one here they claim at least a three-million-dollar-a-year gas well. One of the men that works for the gas company said they valued it at twenty-five million dollars, that one well. They offered a woman seventy-five dollars on the farm that the gas well's just laid on, for destroyin' half an acre of her place to set that well up.

They can do that legally because they have the mineral rights—broad from deed. Eighteen eighty-nine, my grandfather sold this, everything known and all that might be

* Mineral rights.

found later—gas, oil, coal, clay, stone ... My grandfather and grandmother signed in with two X's. They accepted the farmin' rights. Company can dig all your timber, all your soil off, uncover everything, just to get their coal. Go anywhere they want to, drill right in your garden if they want to.

They took bulldozers and they tore the top off the ground. I couldn't plow it or nothin' where they left it. Come through right by that walnut tree. I've got corn this year, first year I raised it. About four years since they left. Nice corn over there. I had to move a lot of rock where they took the bulldozers.

They threatened my wife with trespassin' here because she called up the water pollution man, the gas and oil company did. (Laughs.) If the oil runs down this creek, it'd kill the fish and everything in it. And I had a lot of chickens to die, too, from drinkin' that oil.

SUSIE: When they come through with them bulldozers and tear it up like that, the dirt from it runs down to our bottom land and it ruins the water. Our drinkin' water gets muddy. So we don't have much of a chance, don't look like.

Our boy in the Navy when he comes back, he says all he can see is the mountain tore up with bulldozers. Even the new roads they built, they's debris on it and you can't hardly get through it sometimes. I guess that's what they send our boys off to fight for, to keep 'em a free country and then they do to us like that. Nothin' we can do about it. He said it was worse here than it was over in Vietnam. Four times he's been in Vietnam. He said this was a worse toreup place than Vietnam. He said, "What's the use of goin' over there an' fightin' and then havin' to come back over here an' pay taxes on somethin' that's torn up like that?"

JOE: If we don't organize together, why these big companies is just gonna take anything they want. That's the only chance on earth we got. It's all gone over to the rich man. Even the President. And we don't have a governor.

SUSIE: Everybody talk about it all the time. Especially Aunt Katherine up here, that's all me an' her talk about—what they done to us. My mother and father sold all their land out, where my mother's buried. Company said they sold the mineral to some other company and they was goin' to auger it. They won't have to dig the holes for the ones if they're goin' into my mother's grave. 'Cause there won't be enough left of 'em to dig a hole for. We're not gonna let it happen to my mother's grave because there's seven of us children and I know that five of us will stay right there and see that they don't do that.

They said, men from the company, we'd get a road up to the cemetery that's on top of the hill. I said, "Well, it won't be any use goin' up there, because there won't be any dead up there. There'll just be tombstones settin' there. Because the coal is under the graves." An old preacher down there, they augered under the grave where his wife was buried. And he's nearly blind and he prayed an' everything.

It's something to think about, that a man to make a few dollars would go through and under a cemetery like that. Not even respecting the dead. You can't talk to 'em. They won't talk to you about it. They walk off and leave you. They know they're doin' wrong.

Our son just come back from Vietnam, he went to work for a strip mine. We told him we wouldn't allow him to work for them and stay home. So he quit. He was tellin' me yesterday, looks like he's gonna have to go back to work. I said, "Well, do you want me to pack your clothes tonight or do you want to wait until morning to get 'em? 'Cause," I said, "when you start workin' for the strip mines, you're not comin' back here. I'm not responsible for anything that happens to ya." Don't want none of ours in that, no way.

You and Joe have very little money. Life is rough and life is hard ... Your son could pick up about fifty dollars a day ...

SUSIE: From forty-five to eighty a day.

JOE: He's an equipment operator.

SUSIE: Yeah, he worked and he made good. But we didn't want him in that. He was gonna get killed over there and we wouldn't be responsible for no doctor bills and no funeral bills for him—if he was gonna do that kind of work.

Then he said he had to make a livin' some way. Well, he's gonna have to go back to the army, look like. I said, "Go to the army and come back. Maybe you can get a job then." He said he didn't want to go to the army. And he went to work for one of his cousins, night watchin'. He makes $150 a week. But he told me yesterday that they were gonna close down over there and he was gonna have to go back and work for the strip mines. I said, "When you start work, I'll pack your clothes. You're not gonna stay here."

We sent him to school for him to take his heavy equipment. I worked and cooked over at the school, helped send him there. I said, "I'm not sendin' you to school to come out here and go to work for these strip mines." I'd rather see him in Vietnam than see him doin' strip jobs.

I just think if it's not stopped by officials and governor and all, we're just gonna have to take guns and stop it. When they come to your land ... We got tax receipts here dated back to 1848 that the Haynes and Fields paid tax on this place. Do you think we should let some money grabber come here and destroy it? For nothin'? And have to move out?

JOE: They sweated my grandfathers out of it. Millions of dollars ...

BOB SANDERS

His home is Boonville, Indiana. It is an area of newly built one-family dwellings: pleasantly arbored, front lawns uniformly well-trimmed, two-car garages to the rear. It was somewhat difficult to distinguish this house from the others, though a good distance separated them.

It is said young Lincoln studied law in this town, along the Indiana-Kentucky border. Today the natural landscape of this region is overwhelmed by slag heaps, huge banks of shale. It is strip mine country; one of the earliest.

He's been a strip miner for more than twenty years; his father was one too. He earns about twenty thousand dollars a year. Casually he voices his one regret: he might have been a major league baseball player. He had a tryout with the New York Giants some twenty-five years ago; it looked promising. Marriage plus his father's illness cut short the promise. He lost the chance of proving himself a major-leaguer.

At first he spoke with a great deal of reluctance; his comments short, cryptic. Gradually, he let go ...

I don't dig coal. I take the dirt off coal. You have to know how to handle dirt, to get the best advantage of your machinery. You just can't take a piece of equipment that's developed to take eighty foot of dirt and go on and get ninety, ninety-five. That's *management*, you follow me? All you get over the maximum, that's gravy. You have to uncover it as cheap as possible.

From the time you go to work, like eight o'clock in the morning, when you step up on that piece of equipment and get the seat, why there's not a piece of equipment that's not movin' all day. We run around the clock. We're on a continuous operation, three shifts a day, seven days a week. I work at least forty-eight hours every week.

You don't ever stop it. Eighty dollars a minute down time is what they figure. You have an oiler that you break him in to operate. When I'm eatin' lunch, thirty minutes lunch time, that machine's still runin'. The only time the machine stops is when you change shifts. Most machines have even got a time clock on how long it takes you to swing, how long it takes you to grease, how long it takes you to load your bucket and go to the bank, how long it takes you to dump it, how long this and that. I drink coffee and smoke and never miss a lay. There is no break. They don't pay you for that.

I know what this piece of equipment's raised to do. I always try to get that and to better it. Any company, if they're worth 150 million dollars you don't need to think for a minute they're not gonna know what you're doin'. They didn't get there that way ... and if I want to go any place ... If I'm supposed to move five thousand cubic feet of dirt an hour, if that's what the machine's rated at, you know damn well they know it. Sure, you're gonna get a certain amount of fatigue.

"There's some dangers to it, yeah. There's danger if you go out on the highway. If you get 125 feet in the air, you

might fall and slip. You're dealing with 4,160 volts of elec-
tricity all the time. If you don't have a good ground
system, you can step right off this floor and you'd be dead.
Same way shootin' explosives. Say, they put two thousand
pounds of dynamite in a hole, maybe eight, nine inches in
diameter, maybe it's seventy feet deep. If you don't get
this hole tamped right and this kicks out, instead of goin'
vertical it goes horizontal—well hell, I've seen it go sev-
enty-five foot high and the house covered up . . . people. It
still isn't as dangerous as underground. But around the tip-
ples, even in strip mining, the dust is tremendous. These
people have to wear inhalators to stay on the job. I do.
They can be subjected to black lung."

We go as deep as ninety-five feet. From the operator's
standpoint it's more profitable. From the consumer's
standpoint, they stand to benefit by the profit the company
gets. The cheaper they produce the coal, the cheaper the
electricity gets.

The company I work for produces five, six thousand ton
of coal a day. A million ton a year. Our coal runs from
four to seven foot thick. Four-foot coal runs six thousand
tons to the acre. We'll mine an acre a day. You have
bastard veins, where the coal runs fifteen foot thick.
They're gettin' ready to put in three and a half million ton
a year mines.

People's misinformed about this environmental thing.
About your soil being dug up and not put back. Ninety
percent of this ground, even twenty-five years ago, was
rundown. Ninety percent of the ground I've seen tore up,
you'd starve to death tryin' to raise a roastin' ear on it.
But in the next ten years you're gonna see good farm land
that'll be bought up by the coal companies. You're gonna
see some good topsoil move because the companies are
gonna pay prices. They're gonna get this coal.

There's ground that doesn't look too good now, but
that's all gonna be changed. The companies are makin' the
money to go and do this. They're gonna level it. I can take
you to a place right now where they're throwin' banks up
eighty feet high. They have tractors up there running
twenty-four hours a day and it's leveler than my yard.
That ground is in much better shape than it was before it
was turned over.

Don't misunderstand me. For years these things went on

and the companies have been at fault. Hell, they're just like you and me. They done got the gravy, and when they have to go puttin' it back, it's just a dead cost to them. But hell, they can afford to do it, so there's no problem. They're gonna do this. I'm no operator, I'm a working-man, but I don't think it's fair to the industry for this kind of talk to go on.

There's a lot of things I don't like about my work. I've never really appreciated seeing ground tore up. Especially if that ground could be made into something. I think about it all the time. You tear somethin' up that you know has taken years and years and years ... and you dig into rock. You get to talkin' about the glacier went through there and what caused this particular rock to come out of the bank like it does. You see things come out of that bank that haven't been moved for years. When you see 'em, you have to think about 'em.

"Only about fifteen percent of strip miners are veterans. See, in 1954 mining industry was dead. Hell, everybody quit burnin' coal. Everybody went off to gas and oil. Coal mines were dead. Then in 1954 we had a few power plants that started bringin' it back. Up till the last three years, your natural gas people consumed that tremendous rate. They don't have natural gas hardly to last a century. All right, look at your oil. The cheapest thing in this world right now is coal. This is for heat, light, anything. So now coal minin's boomin'. From the time we got our last con-tract three years ago, companies were gettin' three dollars a ton for coal power plants. Now they're gettin' six, six and a half a ton. And they're not even diggin' their coal out."

You go on a piece of equipment and say it's worth ten million, fifteen million dollars. You don't expect people to go out there and take care of that for thirty or forty dol-lars a day. If you got that kind of money to spend for equipment ... it just doesn't add up. I make more money than anybody at the mine. Still and all, they don't have the responsibility I have. The difference is maybe eight, ten dollars a day between what I do and the men down there. All he has to do is get his bucket and go to work and come home. But if I don't uncover the coal, nobody's gonna work.

Aw no, I don't feel tense. I've been around this stuff ever since I was a kid. I started working a coal mine when I was in high school back during the war. I started in the laboratory and then went to survey. These are company jobs. A miner is a UMW man. I don't think there's a union man that wants to see the ground torn up.

I don't think anybody's gonna say their work's satisfyin', gratifyin', unless you're in business for yourself. I don't think you're satisfied workin' for the other person. But I make a good livin' at it. I've been offered better jobs. But I've got a year and a half to go, I'll have my pension time in. Then I'll go company-wise. I entertain the idea of being an operator, put it that way.

HUB DILLARD

A lower middle class suburb south of Chicago. It is a one-family brick dwelling with a two-car garage in the rear. "This one next door is a contractor. The fella across the street, he's an electrician. We have one that's an engineer for Allis-Chalmers. We have two policemen that live here. Everybody kind of minds their own business."

He is a forty-eight-year-old construction worker who has been at it for twenty-two years. His wife works; his two married children live elsewhere. He is considerably overweight and his breathing is labored. "I'm a heavy equipment operator. I run a crane."

There is a pecking order: apprentices; "dirt work"—sewers, water mains, tunnels, roads; buildings; "soft jobs" for the older or disabled. "They're supposed to be in the union at least ten years and fifty-five years old."

There's no job in construction which you could call an easy job. I mean, if you're out there eating dust and dirt for eight, ten hours a day, even if you're not doing anything, it's work. Just *being* there is . . .

The difficulty is not in running a crane. Anyone can run it. But making it do what it is supposed to do, that's the big thing. It only comes with experience. Some people learn it quicker and there's some people can never learn it. (Laughs.) What we do you can never learn out of a book.

You could never learn to run a hoist or a tower crane by reading. It's experience and common sense.

There's a bit more skill to building work. This is a boom crane. It goes anywhere from 80 feet to 240 feet. You're setting iron. Maybe you're picking fifty, sixty ton and maybe you have ironworkers up there 100, 110 feet. You have to be real careful that you don't bump one of these persons, where they would be apt to fall off.

At the same time, they're putting bolts in holes. If they wanted a half-inch, you have to be able to give them a half-inch. I mean, not an inch, not two inches. Those holes must line up exactly or they won't make their iron. And when you swing, you have to swing real smooth. You can't have your iron swinging back and forth, oscillating. If you do this, they'll refuse to work with you, because their life is at stake.

They're working on beams, anywhere from maybe a foot wide to maybe five or six inches. These fellas walk across there. They have to trust you. If there's no trust there, they will not work with you. It has to be precision. There has been fellows that have been knocked off and hurt very seriously. If there's someone careless or drinking ... I had a serious accident myself. My one leg is where I don't trust to run a crane any more with 239, 240 feet of stake.

These cranes are getting bigger and bigger, so there's more tension. Now they're coming out with a hydraulic crane. Cherry pickers they're called. They're so very easy to upset if you don't know exactly what you supposed to do. And it happens so quick.

They're more dangerous if you don't respect 'em. Everything inside your cab has got a capacity, tells you what it can lift, at what degree your boom is. But there's some of these foremen that are trying to make a name for themselves. They say, We're only gonna pick this much and that much and there's no use we should put this down. A lot of times they want you to carry things that weighs three or four ton. On level ground this can be done, but if you're going down a slope, you're asking for trouble.

It's not so much the physical, it's the mental. When you're working on a tunnel and you're down in a hole two hundred feet, you use hand signals. You can't see there. You have to have something else that's your eyes. There has been men dropped and such because some fellow gave the wrong signal.

Then there's sometimes these tunnels, they cave in. There's been just recently over here in Midlothian, it was four fellas killed. They encountered some gas in there. Sometimes you get a breakthrough in water. There was one of 'em in Calumet City about a year ago. It was muck. This thing caved in their mushing machine. A big percentage of 'em, the accidents, come from a habit. You're just not thinkin' about your work, becomes second nature. Maybe you're thinkin' about somethin' else, and right there in that instant something happens.

The average age of the workingman, regular, is seventy-two. The average crane operator lives to be fifty-five years old. They don't live the best sort of life. There's a lot of tension. We've had an awful lot of people have had heart attacks. Yeah, my buddy.

There was eleven of them in an elevator downtown. They built Marina Towers. The company that built that elevator, it was supposed to be fool-proof. If it got going so fast, it would automatically stop—which it didn't. It fell twelve floors and they were all hurt bad. Two of them had heart attacks when this was falling. There was one fella there that was completely paralyzed. He had eleven children. The only thing he could move is his eyes, that's all. It's because somebody made a mistake. A lot of stuff that comes out of the factory isn't exactly right. It's faulty. They don't know until it's used on a job. It's not just one person that's hurt. It's usually four or five.

Before I had this heart attack, I sure wanted a drink. (Laughs.) Sure, it relaxes. You're tense and most everybody'd stop and have a beer or a shot. They'd have a few drinks and then they'd go home. They have a clique, like everybody has. Your ironworkers, they go to one tavern. Maybe the operators go to another one. The carpenters go to another place. They build buildings and tear 'em down in the tavern. (Laughs.)

There's a lot of times you have to take another man's word for something and a lot of people get hurt. I was hurt because I took another man's word. I was putting the crane on a lowboy—the tractor that hauls it. This foreman told me to swing this stub section of the boom from the front of the lowboy to the back. I said it couldn't be done. He said it's been done a number of times. The lowboy wasn't big enough for the crane and the crane went over backward. They had some extra weight on the back of the crane, which is an unsafe practice. When the crane went over backwards and threw me out, a five-hundred-pound weight went across my leg and crushed my ankle and hip. I was in the hospital, had three operations on my leg and was out of work eighteen months.

With an air of fatalism, he relives the moment: "It threw me out and it was a real hot day. I said, 'My leg is broke.' He said, 'No, it can't be broke.' They seen me lyin' there, these women came over and started throwin' blankets on me. I said, 'Jesus, as hot as it is now, you're gonna smother me.' The ambulance came. They started takin' the shoe off. They ended cuttin' it off. And the bone came out."

"This doctor showed me everything he did. It was crushed. It wouldn't heal. He told me to go home, walk on it. I'd get outside and I'd scream. So finally they took me back in the hospital and operated again. There was a piece of four-inch bone never mended. He said it didn't show on the x-ray.

"Comin' downstairs or goin' down a ramp, it bothers me. We have a boat, it's an awful nice boat and it's awful hard for me to get in and out of it. I used to do an awful lot of huntin'. I'm a farm boy. Boy! I can't do any huntin' now. It was three years ago, August twenty-second."

What were you thinking of during those eighteen months?

Trying to feed my family and make my house payments—which was very hard. My wife worked a little bit and we managed. The union gave us thirty-one dollars a week, Workmen's Compensation gave us sixty-nine dollars a week. And after I was off for six months, I received $180 in Social Security.

The work I'm doin' now, sewers, water mains, and such as that—dirt work—there's no chance of hurting anybody. If I was doing the same work as before, set irons, such as that, there's a chance somebody could be killed. Your hands and feet, the pairs of them, have to work together.

You take other crafts, like an ironworker, he needs a belt, two spud wrenches, a knife which costs him fifteen dollars, and he makes more than a crane operator. The crane operator, he's responsible for a machine that cost over a quarter of a million dollars. Regardless of what kind of machine it is, they all cost anywhere from thirty-five, forty thousand dollars and up. So why isn't he worth as much money?

In the wintertime, sometimes you're off several months. People will say, look at the money this man's making. But when other people are working, he's getting nothing. In the steel mill, when they get laid off, they get so much money per week for so many weeks. When I get laid off, there's nothing more than to get another job. We have no paid holidays, no paid vacations.

We can't go out and get our own jobs. When we get laid off we have to call the union hall and they send you to a job whenever it's your turn. But there's so many people work for a contractor, say, for twelve, fifteen years, these people will do anything to keep their job. They don't think of the safety of another operator, of his equipment or anything. They're doing things to please the contractor. You have some contractors that'll try to get an operator to work below scale. But not like you used to. The majority of contractors are pretty good.

Instead of asking for more money, the union should ask for better conditions. Conditions are being improved, though. Our union has hired a man, he can call a man out on a job if he thinks it was unsafe. Years ago, if you said it was unsafe, they fired you.

Oh yeah, every union has a clique. I don't care what union it is, their own people are going to work more. I mean their brothers and their son and such like that. And as the machinery gets more complicated, you have to learn how to read them. Somebody has to teach you. But if you're just another person and have no pull, why then you're not gonna have an opportunity to learn it.

Sure, there's a lot of colored boys do real good work. You set down with 'em and you have your lunch and there's no hard feelings. But there again, they hate you because you are something. You didn't get this just through a friend. You got it through hard work and that's the only way you're gonna get it. I was an apprentice and I worked my way up.

My father was a crane operator since 1923. We lived on a farm and he was away from home a lot. So I said I'd never do this. When I got out of the service, I went to school and was a watchmaker. I couldn't stay in the pack. It was the same thing, every day and every day. It was inside. And being a farm boy ... So I went to work with my father, construction work, and stayed with it ever since.

I have one son doin' this work. But his youngest one, he's pretty intelligent, I'd like to see him be a professional man if he will. Of course, I wanted the other one too. But ... there's so many changes now. When I started, to build a road a mile it took you two or three months. Now they can build a mile a day. The work is so much more seasonal because they can do it so much quicker. Your chances of being off work in the wintertime is a lot greater now than it was years ago.

When they put up this new strip on the Dan Ryan,* they had one machine there that did the work of five machines fifteen years ago. It did it faster and so much better. It would take one man to do that. Fifteen years ago, it took five men and it took all summer. They did it now in three months. I just don't know ...

There's a certain amount of pride—I don't care how little you did. You drive down the road and you say, "I worked on this road." If there's a bridge, you say, "I worked on this bridge." Or you drive by a building and you say, "I worked on this building." Maybe it don't mean anything to anybody else, but there's a certain pride knowing you did your bit.

That building we put up, a medical building. Well, that granite was imported from Canada. It was really expensive. Well, I set all this granite around there. So you do this and you don't make a scratch on it. It's food for your soul that you know you did it good. Where somebody walks by this building you can say, "Well, I did that."

---

* A major multilane expressway running through Chicago.

BOOK TWO

COMMUNICATIONS

In coming of age, communications has
become an end in itself. . . . We are
all wired for sound. . . .
                                    —Wright Morris

SHARON ATKINS

A receptionist at a large business establishment in the
Midwest. She is twenty-four. Her husband is a student. "I
was out of college, an English Lit. major. I looked around
for copywriting jobs. The people they wanted had majored
in journalism. Okay, the first myth that blew up in my
face is that a college education will get you a job."

I changed my opinion of receptionists because now I'm
one. It wasn't the dumb broad at the front desk who took
telephone messages. She had to be something else because
I thought I was something else. I was fine until there was
a press party. We were having a fairly intelligent conversation. Then they asked me what I did. When I told them,
they turned around to find other people with name tags. I
wasn't worth bothering with. I wasn't being rejected because of what I had said or the way I talked, but simply
because of my function. After that, I tried to make up
other names for what I did—communications control, ser-
vomechanism. (Laughs.)

I don't think they'd ever hire a male receptionist.
They'd have to pay him more, for one thing. You can't
pay someone who does what I do very much. It isn't
economically feasible. (Laughs.) You're there just to filter
people and filter telephone calls. You're there just to handle the equipment. You're treated like a piece of equipment, like the telephone.

You come in at nine, you open the door, you look at
the piece of machinery, you plug in the headpiece. That's

how my day begins. You tremble when you hear the first ring. After that, it's sort of downhill—unless there's somebody on the phone who is either kind or nasty. The rest of the people are just non, they don't exist. They're just voices. You answer calls, you connect them to others, and that's it.

I don't have much contact with people. You can't see them. You don't know if they're laughing, if they're being satirical or being kind. So your conversations become very abrupt. I notice that in talking to people. My conversations would be very short and clipped, in short sentences, the way I talk to people all day on the telephone.

I never answer the phone at home. It carries over. The way I talk to people on the phone has changed. Even when my mother calls, I don't talk to her very long. I want to *see* people to talk to them. But now, when I see them, I talk to them like I was talking on the telephone. It isn't a conscious process. I don't know what's happened. When I'm talking to someone at work, the telephone rings, and the conversation is interrupted. So I never bother finishing sentences or finishing thoughts. I always have this feeling of interruption.

You can think about this thing and all of a sudden the telephone rings and you've got to jump right back. There isn't a ten-minute break in the whole day that's quiet. I once worked at a punch press, when I was in high school. A part-time job. You sat there and watched it for four, five hours. You could make up stories about people and finish them. But you can't do that when you've got only a few minutes. You can't pick it up after the telephone call. You can't think, you can't even finish a letter. So you do quickie things, like read a chapter in a short story. It has to be short-term stuff.

I notice people have asked me to slow down when I'm talking. What I do all day is to say what I have to say as quickly as possible and switch the call to whoever it's going to. If I'm talking to a friend, I have to make it quick before I get interrupted.

You try to fill up your time with trying to think about other things: what you're going to do on the weekend or about your family. You have to use your imagination. If you don't have a very good one and you bore easily, you're in trouble. Just to fill in time, I write real bad poetry or letters to myself and to other people and never mail them. The letters are fantasies, sort of rambling, how I feel, how depressed I am.

I do some drawings—Mondrian, sort of. Peaceful colors of red and blue. Very ordered life. I'd like to think of rainbows and mountains. I never draw humans. Things of nature, never people. I always dream I'm alone and things are quiet. I call it the land of no-phone, where there isn't any machine telling me where I have to be every minute.

The machine dictates. This crummy little machine with buttons on it—you've got to be there to answer it. You can walk away from it and pretend you don't hear it, but it pulls you. You know you're not doing anything, not doing a hell of a lot for anyone. Your job doesn't mean anything. Because *you're* just a little machine. A monkey could do what I do. It's really unfair to ask someone to do that.

Do you have to lie sometimes?

Oh sure, you have to lie for other people. That's another thing: having to make up stories for them if they don't want to talk to someone on the telephone. At first I'd feel embarrassed and I'd feel they knew I was lying. There was a sense of emptiness. There'd be a silence, and I'd feel guilty. At first I tried to think of a euphemism for "He's not here." It really bothered me. Then I got tired of doing it, so I just say, "He's not here." You're not looking at the person, you're talking to him over the instrument. (Laughs.) So after a while it doesn't really matter. The first time it was live. The person was there. I'm sure I blushed. He probably knew I was lying. And I think he understood I was just the instrument, not the source.

Until recently I'd cry in the morning. I didn't want to get up. I'd dread Fridays because Monday was always looming over me. Another five days ahead of me. There never seemed to be any end to it. Why am I doing this? Yet I dread looking for other jobs. I don't like filling out forms and taking typing tests. I remember on applications I'd put down, "I'd like to deal with the public." (Laughs.) Well, I don't want to deal with the public any more.

I take the bus to work. That was my big decision. I had to go to work and do what everyone else told me to do, but I could decide whether to take the bus or the el. To me, that was a big choice. Those are the only kinds of decisions you make and they become very important to you.

Very few people talk on the bus going home. Sort of sit there and look dejected. Stare out the window, pull out their newspaper, or push other people. You feel tense until the bus empties out or you get home. Because things happen to you all day long, things you couldn't get rid of. So they build up and everybody is feeding them into each other on the bus. There didn't seem to be any kind of relief about going home. It was: Boy! Did I have a lot of garbage to put up with!

One minute to five is the moment of triumph. You physically turn off the machine that has dictated to you all day long. You put it in a drawer and that's it. You're your own man for a few hours. Then it calls to you every morning that you have to come back.

I don't know what I'd like to do. That's what hurts the most. That's why I can't quit the job. I really don't know what talents I may have. And I don't know where to go to find out. I've been fostered so long by school and didn't have time to think about it.

My father's in watch repair. That's always interested me, working with my hands, and independent. I don't think I'd mind going back and learning something, taking a piece of furniture and refinishing it. The type of thing where you know what you're doing and you can create and you can fix something to make it function. At the switchboard you don't do much of anything.

I think the whole idea of receptionists is going to change. We're going to have to find machines which can do that sort of thing. You're wasting an awful lot of human power.

I'll be home and the telephone will ring and I get nervous. It reminds me of the telephone at work. It becomes like Pavlov's bell. (Laughs.) It made the dogs salivate. It makes me nervous. The machine invades me all day. I'd go home and it's still there. It's a very bad way to talk to people, to communicate. It may have been a boon to business but it did a lot to wreck conversation. (Laughs.)

FRANCES SWENSON

A bungalow in a lower-middle-class neighborhood in the city. A widow, she lives with her grown son. "How would I describe myself? A happy-go-lucky middle-aged woman." (Laughs.)

The walls are decorated with paper tole. It is her handi-work. "It actually looks like real flowers. I enjoy keeping my hands busy. It keeps me out of trouble. I also sew, but I wouldn't want to make my living doing that. The eyes kinda get faded after you get older. You have to have extra strong glasses to see to sew."

She is a switchboard operator at a large motel frequented by conventioneers. She has had this job for three years, though she has been a telephone operator for at least fifteen.

"There are always five girls at the board. They can only take lunch one at a time. I'm fifty. The little one next to me is twenty. The one next to her is twenty. The other one's about forty. And the other one's about thirty-five. Oh, I love 'em and they love me. They think I'm a great old lady." (Laughs.)

You have to have a nice smiling voice. You can't be angry or come in like you've been out the night before. (Laughs.) You always have to be pleasant—no matter how bad you feel.

I had one gentleman the other day and he wanted an outside call. I asked his name and room number, which we have to charge to his room. And he says, "What's it to you?" I said, "I'm sorry, sir, this is our policy." And he gets a little hostile. But you just take it with a grain of salt and you just keep on working. Inside you and in your head you get mad. But you still have to be nice when the next call comes in. There's no way to let it out. I'm pretty easy to get along with. I'm not the type to get angry on the phone.

You try to imagine what they look like, which is very hard. Even age is hard to tell on the phone. My phone voice is a lot different than my home voice. I can call the switchboard right now and they wouldn't know it was me.

First thing I do is get my headset on, and I sit down at the board to relieve the girl that's been working all night. This is a board that's twenty-four hours. It's the type of chair that a stenographer would sit on. Believe me, after eight hours, it's not a comfortable chair. (Laughs.) We are constantly kept busy. There isn't an idle moment. There's not much time to converse. I have worked in different offices and you can even take the chance to pick up a crochet hook, to keep your fingers busy. Not here.

I worked 125 hours last two weeks. We asked the boss why we didn't get time and a half overtime. He says, "Well, the girls at the front desk are getting it, I don't see why you don't. You'll get it starting the first of the month." We were informed today we were not going to get it. The one that told us okayed it, but there are two higher in the hotel than he.

At one time, they tried to bring the union in, but two girls voted it down and then they decided to quit. But it has to be. Because I lost my weekend. I was invited to a cookout and I didn't go. They needed me, so I figured okay, I'll go, they need me. But I lost out on a little fun.

It's the tension you're under while you're sitting there working. At one time Illinois Bell had a rest home. Years ago, when the switchboard operators became tense, overwrought, they sent them there. They had nervous breakdowns. They don't have it now because I think things have gotten easier.

I'm tired at the end of the day. Say you pick up a thousand calls a day, and these cords are on heavy weights, and they get pretty heavy at the end of eight hours. You go to pick 'em up and they'll slide right out of your hand, and you drop it. I worked with an operator who said she had more strength in her hand than a man because of using her hand all day.

This board where I'm at now, you have to reach. The jacks are up pretty high. It's not easy on the arms. Sometimes the cords are so close together as your fingers and you've got to reach in-between if they want that number in-between, so you break your fingernails.

When you get up like in my age and go to work, it's a grind. We can't take even one break because you're constantly needed.

If you got to go, you've got to come right back. 'Cause

you don't get a fifteen-minute break. This last week, when we were so busy, I said it would be nice if we had a place to stretch out. Sometimes you get so wound up you don't want to eat. I didn't want to eat for a couple of days, not because I wasn't hungry, but I didn't want to eat downstairs and there was nowhere else to go to get food. I went and sat in a different department just to get away from the switchboard. Because it's the yackety-yak and constant conversation, and it's really noisy.

You're never without your headset. Your cords are retractable and you're talking as you get a drink of water. It's a pitcher we have about fifteen feet away. We're still plugged in and we're saying, "Can I help you, sir?"

When you see one girl kinda slow down and relax, it puts the burden on the other girls. The main thing is to get the cord out of your hand and get rid of the call. If a customer wants to know how much the meals are, you don't sit and tell them, you give the call to the restaurant. Some of these people I work with will sit and they will explain everything. You've got to get rid of the call. The telephone company trains you to pick up more than one call at a time.

A lot of men don't realize what a switchboard is and how complicated they are. We had one of the young men—an assistant manager trainee—he worked just the lunch hour, and he had it. You got to memorize all the departments. You can't keep looking at your sheets, you gotta remember these things.

I think switchboard operators are the most underpaid, 'cause we are the hub of everything. When you call somebody, you want immediate service. Of course, I chose the job. If you choose the job, it's your responsibility. Just because I feel I'm not paid enough doesn't mean I'm not gonna give 'em good work.

The kids today don't work like the older women. They take a job as it comes. If they want to work, they work. If they don't, they fool around. We have a couple that sit on the phone half of the day, take time out. That puts the burden on the rest of the girls. The older women are more loyal, they're more conscientious, they don't take time off.

I had to have plumbing done in the back yard here. I asked a girl to switch shifts with me so I wouldn't keep them hanging that they couldn't get a girl to come in. I said if you can work my trick, I'll work yours. Where the other girls, they'd say, "I'm staying home tomorrow."

Anybody that has done switchboard likes switchboard. It's not lonesome. You're talking to people. You ask another switchboard operator, they like it.

Want to hear a good one? (Laughs.) It was one o'clock in the morning. A phone call came in. I worked the night shift. And I said, "Holiday Inn." I said it because we're not Holiday Inn, I was just fooling around. The little girl I worked with turned me in. So the boss called me in. She said, "Why did you do it?" I said, "Just for a lark. It was quiet, nothing to do." She said, "Fran, you're a good operator and we all love you, but I don't know why you did it." I said, "I wanted to have a little fun."

The little girl, after she did it, she said she was sorry. About a week later, I said to her, "Young lady, I was gonna quit, but I wouldn't do it for the likes of you." And she says, "Fran, I admire you because you didn't say anything to me in front of the boss." And I said, "Well, you're pretty low because you have done things I would never have told on."

The operators' code is: You don't hear what the one next to you is saying. This is the way I was taught. Whether she's flirtin' with somebody is none of my business. What I done I did for fun. I didn't think it was very bad. (Laughs.)

I never listen in on a phone conversation, but I'll tell you what. I worked for Illinois Bell and I don't care who the operator is, the greatest thing is listening on phone calls. (Laughs.) When you're not busy. At the motel, no. At Bell, I did. If you work nights and it's real quiet, I don't think there's an operator who hasn't listened in on calls. The night goes faster.

At the phone company, during the war, there were times when we had to listen in on a call that would be—I'll say a Spanish-speaking person. They were being monitored. We'd have to say, "This is the Spanish-speaking call." You can monitor any switchboard.

I always had my fingers in the switchboard. We get real friendly. We're supposed to wear our names. Mine's just Frances. It's not even Frances, I'm Fran. The assistant manager, we refer to him as mister. I've always respected a name. These young kids today don't. They call people by their first names. The last place I worked, we called him mister. He was a buyer and I figured he should have respect. I'm only a switchboard operator. I'm Fran. It wouldn't be miss.

But I feel they need us badly. They need us to be polite and they need us to be nice. You cannot have a business and have a bad switchboard operator. We are the hub of that hotel.

And we don't get respect. We don't get it from the bosses or the guests. Although they are nice to us. But if they knew how hard we worked. Today communications is the big thing. So much business is over the phone. I really think we demand a little more respect.

We sit there and we joke, "Wouldn't it be great if we could just take this handful of plugs and just *yank* 'em?" (Laughs.) We think of it, we think of it. Like I said, you get so tense ... If we could just *pull* 'em. (Laughs.) Disconnect them and see what happens. You accidentally disconnect somebody, which happens quite often. You don't do it on purpose, although there are times when you feel you'd like to do it.

HEATHER LAMB

For almost two years she has been working as a long distance telephone operator at Illinois Bell. A naval base is nearby. She works three nights a week, split shift, during the high-school season and a full forty hours in the summertime. She is turning eighteen.

I'ts a strange atmosphere. You're in a room about the size of a gymnasium, talking to people thousands of miles away. You come in contact with at least thirty-five an hour. You can't exchange any ideas with them. They don't know you, they never will. You feel like you might be missing people. You feel like they put a coin in the machine and they've got you. You're there to perform your service and go. You're kind of detached.

A lot of the girls are painfully shy in real life. You get some girls who are outgoing in their work, but when they have to talk to someone and look them in the face, they can't think of what to say. They feel self-conscious when they know someone can see them. At the switchboard, it's a feeling of anonymousness.

There are about seven or eight phrases that you use and that's it: "Good morning, may I help you?" "Operator, may I help you?" "Good afternoon." "Good evening." "What number did you want?" "Would you repeat that again?" "I have a collect call for you from so-and-so, will you accept the charge?" "It'll be a dollar twenty cents." That's all you can say.

A big thing is not to talk with a customer. If he's upset, you can't say more than "I'm sorry you've been having trouble." If you get caught talking with a customer, that's one mark against you. You can't help but want to talk to them if they're in trouble or if they're just feeling bad or something. For me it's a great temptation to say, "Gee, what's the matter?" You don't feel like you're really that much helping people.

Say you've got a guy on the line calling from Vietnam, his line is busy and you can't interrupt. God knows when he'll be able to get on his line again. You know he's lonesome and he wants to talk to somebody, and there you are and you can't talk to him. There's one person who feels badly and you can't do anything. When I first started, I asked the operator and she says, "No, he can always call another time."

One man said, "I'm lonesome, will you talk to me?" I said, "Gee I'm sorry, I just can't." But you *can't*. (Laughs.) I'm a communications person but I can't communicate.

I've worked here almost two years and how many girls' first names do I know? Just their last name is on their headset. You might see them every day and you won't know their names. At Ma Bell they speak of teamwork, but you don't even know the names of the people who are on your team.

It's kind of awkward if you meet someone from the company and say, "Hi there, Jones," or whatever. (Laughs.) It's very embarrassing. You sit in the cafeteria and you talk to people and you don't even know their names. (Laughs.) I've gone to a lot of people I've been talking to for a week and I've said, "Tell me your name." (Laughs.)

You have a number—mine's 407. They put your number on your tickets, so if you made a mistake they'll know who did it. You're just an instrument. You're there to dial a number. It would be just as good for them to punch out the number.

The girls sit very close. She would be not even five or six inches away from me. The big thing is elbows, especially if she's left-handed. That's why we have so many colds in the winter, you're so close. If one person has a cold, the whole office has a cold. It's very catchy.

You try to keep your fingernails short because they break. If you go to plug in, your fingernail goes. You try to wear your hair simple. It's not good to have your hair on top of your head. The women don't really come to work if they've just had their hair done. The headset flattens it.

Your arms don't really get tired, your mouth gets tired. It's strange, but you get tired of talking, 'cause you talk constantly for six hours without a break.

Half the phones have a new system where the quarter is three beeps, a dime is two beeps, and a nickel is one beep. If the guy's in a hurry and he keeps throwing in money, all the beeps get all mixed up together (laughs), and you don't know how much money is in the phone. So it's kinda hard.

When you have a call, you fill it out on this IBM card. Those go with a special machine. You use a special pencil so it'll go through this computer and pick up the numbers. It's real soft lead, it just goes all over the desk and you're all dirty by the time you get off. (Laughs.) And sometimes your back hurts if your chair isn't up at the right height and you have to bend over and write. And keeping track. You don't get just one call at a time.

There is also the clock. You've got a clock next to you that times every second. When the light goes off, you see the party has answered, you have to write down the hour, the minute, and the second. Okay, you put that in a special slot right next to the cord light. You're ready for another one. Still you've got to watch the first one. When the light goes on, they disconnect and you've got to take that card out again and time down the hour, the minute, and the second—plus keeping on taking other calls. It's hectic.

If you work the day shift, conversations are short, so they come down in time amount to trying to take down a man's credit card number and collecting another man's money. One man waiting for his overtime, another man

waiting for you to put his call through. Sometimes your
tickets get all messed up—and that makes people even
madder. And it doesn't help when people are crabby and
they don't talk loud enough.

Businessmen get very upset if they have to repeat their
credit card number. Sometimes they're talking to you and
they're talking to their partner and you're trying to listen
for the number. They'll say something to their partner and
you think it's for you and they get irritated. You get very
sensitive to people's voices. Sometimes you get mad. Why
should this man be yelling at me? I do feel put-down a lot.

But other times there's a real sense of power. I can tell
you when you have to stop talking. You have to pay me
the money. If you don't pay me the money, I can do this
and this to you. You feel that more when you're talking to
people who have to pay for their calls, like sailors at the
base. But with the businessmen, you get a feeling of help-
lessness. He can ruin you. You've got real power over the
poorer people. They don't even have a phone, so they
can't complain. This businessman can write a letter to Ma
Bell. I'm more tolerant of the people who are calling from
a pay phone and haven't got much money. But businessmen, I make him pay for every second of this call.
(Laughs.) I'm more powerful than him at the moment.
(Laughs.)

I think telephone prices are really too high. Dialing direct is cheap, but the poorer people who don't have private phones and have to use pay phones, the costs are exhorbitant. It's preying on poor people.

You can always get a date over the phone if you want.
I've gotten asked so many times. (Laughs.) You always
make some little comment, especially when you're bored
late at night. I talk with a Southern accent or a Puerto Rican accent. Or try to make your voice real sexy, just to
see what kind of reaction ... No, no, I never accepted
dates. (Laughs.) Nobody ever sounded . . .

A lot of times, they leave the phone and bill it to others. You call the number they gave and they say, "I don't
know him." The operator isn't charged for any of this, but
they do keep track. How many calls you take, how well
you mark your tickets, how many errors you make.
You're constantly being pushed.

If you're depressed 'cause the day hasn't gone right, it
shows in how you talk to people. But again, some days are

hysterically funny. I don't keep with all the regulations. I always try to make a couple of jokes. Especially if you're working late at night. Sometimes people on the lines are so funny, you'll just sit there and laugh and laugh until tears roll down your face. (Laughs.)

Do I listen in on conversations? (Lowers voice) Some girls really do. I've never had the temptation to flip the switch. I don't know why. This company is the kind who watches you all the time. The supervisor does listen to you a lot. She can push a button on this special console. Just to see if I'm pleasant enough, if I talk too much to the customers, if I'm charging the right amount, if I make a personal call. Ma Bell is listening. And you don't know. That's why it's smart to do the right thing most of the time. Keep your nose clean.

They never asked me to listen in. 'Cause they'd be reversing all the things they ever said: secrecy of communications, privacy for the customers. I don't think I would anyway. They can have the job.

Most people who have stayed as telephone operators are older women. Not too many young girls are there forever. Girls are more patient than older women. I was sitting next to one today. This man evidently left the phone and she was trying to get money from him. She yells, "Look at that bastard!" She started ringing real hard, "You come back here, you owe me money!" Really crabbily. If I did that, the supervisor would yell at me. But this lady's been there for twenty years. They're very permissive with their older ladies. A lot of them have ugly voices. But again, you've been working there twenty years and saying the same things for twenty years, my God, can you blame them? After twenty years you get real hard.

It's a hard feeling when everyone's in a hurry to talk to somebody else, but not to talk to you. Sometimes *you* get a feeling of need to talk to somebody. Somebody who wants to listen to you other than "Why didn't you get me the right number?"

It's something to run into somebody who says, "It's a nice day out, operator. How's your day, busy? Has it been a rough day?" You're so thankful for these people. You say, "Oh yes, it's been an awful day. Thank you for asking."

JACK HUNTER

It was an accidental encounter, while he was in the city during a convention of the American Communications Association. It was at the time of the Christmas season bombings of North Vietnam. En route to a restaurant, the subject came up: "What else could President Nixon do? He had no alternative."

I'm a college professor. As a communications specialist, I train students to become more sensitive and aware of interpersonal communication—symbolic behavior, use of words, as well as nonverbal behavior. I try to ignite symbols in your mind, so we can come to a point of agreement on language. This is an invisible industry. Since the Second World War we've had phenomenal growth. There are seven-thousand-plus strong teachers in this discipline.

I'm high on the work because this is the way life is going to be—persuading people. We're communicating animals. We're persuadeable animals. It's not an unethical thing. It's not the black mustache and the black greasy hair bit. There is an unethical way—we're cognizant of the ways of demagogic persuasion—but we train students in the ethical way. Business communication is a very important field in our industry. We train people so they can humanize the spirit of both parties, the interviewer and the interviewee. In the first ten minutes of an interview, the interviewer has usually made up his mind. We find out the reasons. Through our kind of research we tell business: what you're doing is productive or counterproductive.

I'm talking about specialists, that we're accustomed to in the movie world. One guy blew up bridges, that's all he could do. Here's a guy who's an oral specialist or writing or print or electronics. We're all part of the family. Nobody has a corner on communication.

Many Ph.D.s in the field of speech are now in business as personnel directors. I have good friends who are religious communicators. I had the opportunity to go with a bank in a Southern state as director of information. I would have overseen all the interoffice and intraoffice communication behavior—all the written behavior—to get the whole system smoother. And what happens? Profit. Happiness in job behavior. Getting what's deep down from them, getting their trust.

B.F. Skinner reaches over into our field. Good friends of mine study this kind of behavior so they can make better comments about interpersonal relationships. Communication figures in our lives whether it's John Smith at the plant or President Kennedy during the Cuban missile crisis. Friends of mine are studying conflict communication: how people communicate when they're under fire.

Take Jerry Friedheim.* He appears to me to be a machine—dash—human voice of the Nixon administration on this very touchy issue. He is, in my perception, mechanical. His voice has the lack of emotion. It is like a voice typewriter. He produces. It's good. Heads have to keep cool. Nixon uses his people wisely and gets the information he needs to help him: what kinds of behavior can be attracted to what kinds of messages. In the past four years, he has so carefully softened the power of the press that it's being taken more lightly than ever before. That's why the Watergate affair was so delicately brushed aside by the American people.

Communications specialists do have a sense of power. People will argue it's a misuse of power. When a person has so much control over behavior, we're distrustful. We must learn how to become humane at the same time.

* During the Christmas bombing of North Vietnam, Friedheim, a public relations officer of the Defense Department, was the Administration's spokesman in dealing with the press.

A PECKING ORDER

TERRY MASON

She has been an airline stewardess for six years. She is twenty-six-years old, recently married. "The majority of airline stewardesses are from small towns. I myself am from Nebraska. It's supposed to be one of the nicest professions for a woman—if she can't be a model or in the movies. All the great benefits: flying around the world, meeting all those people. It is a nice status symbol.

"I have five older sisters and they were all married before they were twenty. The minute they got out of high school, they would end up getting married. That was the thing everybody did, was get married. When I told my parents I was going to the airlines, they got excited. They were so happy that one of the girls could go out and see the world and spend some time being single. I didn't get married until I was almost twenty-five. My mother especially thought it would be great that I could have the ambition, the nerve to go to the big city on my own and try to accomplish being a stewardess."

When people ask you what you're doing and you say stewardess, you're really proud, you think it's great. It's like a stepping stone. The first two months I started flying I had already been to London, Paris, and Rome. And me from Broken Bow, Nebraska. But after you start working, it's not as glamorous as you thought it was going to be.

They like girls that have a nice personality and that are pleasant to look at. If a woman has a problem with blemishes, they take her off. Until the appearance counselor thinks she's ready to go back on. One day this girl showed up, she had a very slight black eye. They took her off. Little things like that.

We had to go to stew school for five weeks. We'd go through a whole week of make-up and poise. I didn't like this. They make you feel like you've never been out in public. They showed you how to smoke a cigarette, when to smoke a cigarette, how to look at a man's eyes. Our teacher, she had this idea we had to be sexy. One day in class she was showing us how to accept a light for a cigarette from a man and never blow it out. When he lights it, just look in his eyes. It was really funny, all the girls laughed.

It's never proper for a woman to light her own cigarette. You hold it up and of course you're out with a guy who knows the right way to light the cigarette. You look into their eyes as they're lighting your cigarette and you're cupping his hand, but holding it just very light, so that he can feel your touch and your warmth. (Laughs.) You do not blow the match out. It used to be really great for a woman to blow the match out when she looked in his eyes, but she said now the man blows the match out.

The idea is not to be too obvious about it. They don't want you to look too forward. That's the whole thing, being a lady but still giving out that womanly appeal, like the body movement and the lips and the eyes. The guy's supposed to look in your eyes. You could be a real mean woman. You're a lady and doing all these evil things with your eyes.

She did try to promote people smoking. She said smoking can be part of your conversation. If you don't know what to say, you can always pull out a cigarette. She says it makes you more comfortable. I started smoking when I was on the airlines.

Our airline picks the girl-next-door type. At one time they wouldn't let us wear false eyelashes and false fingernails. Now it's required that you wear false eyelashes, and if you do not have the right length nails, you wear false nails. Everything is supposed to be becoming to the passenger.

That's the whole thing: meeting all these great men that either have great business backgrounds or good looking or different. You do meet a lot of movie stars and a lot of political people, but you don't get to really visit with them that much. You never really get to go out with these men. Stewardesses are impressed only by name people. But a normal millionaire that you don't know you're not impressed about. The only thing that really thrills a stewardess is a passenger like Kennedy or movie stars or somebody political. Celebrities.

I think our average age is twenty-six. But our supervisors tell us what kind of make-up to wear, what kind of lipstick to wear, if our hair is not the right style for us, if we're not smiling enough. They even tell us how to act when you're on a pass. Like last night I met my husband. I was in plain clothes. I wanted to kiss him. But I'm not supposed to kiss anybody at the terminal. You're not supposed to walk off with a passenger, hand in hand. After you get out of the terminal, that's all yours.

The majority of passengers do make passes. The ones that do make passes are married and are business people. When I tell them I'm married, they say, "I'm married and you're married and you're away from home and so am I and nobody's gonna find out." The majority of those who make passes at you, you wouldn't accept a date if they were friends of yours at home.

After I was a stewardess for a year, and I was single, I came down to the near North Side of Chicago, which is the swinging place for singles. Stewardess, that was a dirty name. In a big city, it's an easy woman. I didn't like this at all. All these books—*Coffee, Tea and Me.*

I lived in an apartment complex where the majority there were stewardesses.* The other women were secretaries and teachers. They would go to our parties and they would end up being among the worst. They never had stories about these secretaries and nurses, but they sure had good ones about stewardesses.

I meet a lot of other wives or single women. The first minute they start talking to me, they're really cold. They think the majority of stewardesses are snobs or they may be jealous. These women think we have a great time, that we are playgirls, that we have the advantage to go out

* "In New York, stewardesses live five or six girls to one apartment. They think they can get by because they're in and out so much. But there's gonna be a few nights they're all gonna be home at once and a couple of 'em will have to sleep on the floor."

with every type of man we want. So when they first meet us, they really turn off on us.

When you first start flying, the majority of girls do live in apartment complexes by the airport. The men they meet are airport employees: ramp rats, cleaning airplanes and things like that, mechanics, and young pilots, not married, ones just coming in fresh.

After a year we get tired of that, so we move into the city to get involved with men that are usually young executives, like at Xerox or something. Young businessmen in the early thirties and late twenties, they really think stewardesses are the gals to go out with if they want to get so far. They wear their hats and their suits and in the winter their black gloves. The women are getting older, they're getting twenty-four, twenty-five. They get involved with bartenders too. Stewardesses and bartenders are a pair. (Laughs.)

One time I went down into the area of swinging bars with two other girls. We just didn't want anybody to know that we were stewardesses, so we had this story made up that we were going to a women's college in Colorado. That went over. We had people that were talking to us, being nice to us, being polite. Down there, they wouldn't even be polite. They'd buy you drinks but then they'd steal your stool if you got up to go to the restroom. But when they knew you weren't stewardesses, just young ladies that were going to a women's college, they were really nice to us.

They say you can spot a stewardess by the way she wears her make-up. At that time we all had short hair and everybody had it cut in stew school exactly alike. If there's two blondes that have their hair cut very short, wearing the same shade of make-up, and they get into uniform, people say, "Oh, you look like sisters." Wonder why? (Laughs.)

The majority of us were against it because they wouldn't let you say how *you'd* like your hair cut, they wouldn't let you have your own personality, *your* makeup, *your* clothes. They'd tell you what length skirts to wear. At one time they told us we couldn't wear anything one inch above the knees. And no pants at that time. It's different now.

Wigs used to be forbidden. Now it's the style. Now it's permissible for nice women to wear wigs, eyelashes, and false fingernails. Before it was the harder looking women that wore them. Women showing up in pants, it wasn't ladylike. Hot pants are in now. Most airlines change style every year.

She describes stewardess schools in the past as being like college dorms: it was forbidden to go out during the week; signing in and out on Friday and Saturday nights. "They've cut down stewardess school quite a bit. Cut down on how to serve meal classes and paperwork. A lot of girls get on aircraft these days and don't know where a magazine is, where the tray tables are for passengers ... Every day we used to have an examination. If you missed over two questions, that was a failure. They'd ask us ten questions. If you failed two tests out of the whole five weeks, you would have to leave. Now they don't have any exams at all. Usually we get a raise every year. We haven't been getting that lately."

We have long duty hours. We can be on duty for thirteen hours. But we're not supposed to fly over eight hours. This is in a twenty-four-hour period. During the eight hours, you could be flying from Chicago to Flint, to Moline, short runs. You stop twenty minutes. So you get to New York finally, after five stops, let's say. You have an hour on your own. But you have to be on the plane thirty minutes before departure time. How many restaurants can serve you food in thirty minutes? So you've gone thirteen hours, off and on duty, having half-hours and no time to eat. This is the normal thing. If we have only thirty minutes and we don't have time to eat, it's our hard luck.

Pilots have the same thing too. They end up grabbing a sandwich and eating in the cockpit. When I first started flying we were not supposed to eat at all on the aircraft, even though there was an extra meal left over. Now we can eat in the buffet. We have to stand there with all those dirty dishes and eat our meals—if there's one left over. We cannot eat in the public eye. We cannot bring it out if there's an extra seat. You can smoke in the cockpit, in the restrooms, but not in the public's eye.

"We have a union. It's a division of the pilots union. It helps us out on duty time and working privileges. It makes sure that if we're in Cleveland and stuck because of

weather and thirteen hours have gone by, we can go to bed. Before we had a union the stew office would call and say, 'You're working another seven.' I worked one time thirty-six hours straight."

The other day I had fifty-five minutes to serve 101 coach passengers, a cocktail and full-meal service. You do it fast and terrible. You're very rude. You don't mean to be rude, you just don't have time to answer questions. You smile and you just ignore it. You get three drink orders in a hurry. There's been many times when you miss the glass, pouring, and you pour it in the man's lap. You just don't say I'm sorry. You give him a cloth and you keep going. That's the bad part of the job.

Sometimes I get tired of working first class. These people think they're great, paying for more, and want more. Also I get tired of coach passengers asking for something that he thinks he's a first-class passenger. We get this attitude of difference from our airlines. They're just dividing the class of people. If we're on a first-class pass, the women are to wear a dress or a nice pants suit that has a matching jacket, and the men are to dress with suit jacket and tie and white shirt. And yet so many types of first-class passengers: some have grubby clothes, jeans and moccasins and everything. They can afford to dress the way they feel . . .

If I want to fly first class, I pay the five dollars difference. I like the idea of getting free drinks, free champagne, free wine. In a coach, you don't. A coach passenger might say, "Could I have a pillow?" So you give him a pillow. Then he'll say, "Could you bring me a glass of water?" A step behind him there's the water fountain. In first class, if the guy says, "I want a glass of water," even if the water fountain is right by his arm, you'd bring it for him. We give him all this extra because he's first class. Which isn't fair . . .

When you're in a coach, you feel like there's just head and head and head of people. That's all you can see. In first class, being less people, you're more relaxed, you have more time. When you get on a 727, we have one coatroom. Our airline tells us you hang up first-class coats only. When a coach passenger says, "Could you hang up my coat?" most of the time I'll hang it up. Why should I hang up first class and not coach?

One girl is for first class only and there's two girls for coach. The senior girl will be first class. That first-class girl gets used to working first class. If she happens to walk through the coach, if someone asks her for something, she'll make the other girls do it. The first stew always stays at the door and welcomes everybody aboard and says good-by to everybody when they leave. That's why a lot of girls don't like to be first class.

There's an old story on the airline. The stewardess asks if he'd like something to drink, him and his wife. He says, "I'd like a martini." The stewardess asks the wife, "Would you like a drink?" She doesn't say anything, and the husband says, "I'm sorry, she's not used to talking to the help." (Laughs.) When I started flying, that was the first story I heard.

I've never had the nerve to speak up to anybody that's pinched me or said something dirty. Because I've always been afraid of these onion letters. These are bad letters. If you get a certain amount of bad letters, you're fired. When you get a bad letter you have to go in and talk to the supervisor. Other girls now, there are many of 'em that are coming around and telling them what they feel. The passenger reacts: She's telling me off! He doesn't believe it. Sometimes the passenger needs it.

One guy got his steak and he said, "This is too medium, I want mine rarer." The girl said, "I'm sorry, I don't cook the food, it's precooked." He picked up the meal and threw it on the floor. She says, "If you don't pick the meal up right now, I'll make sure the crew members come back here and make you pick it up." (With awe) She's talking right back at him and loud, right in front of everybody. He really didn't think she would yell at him. Man, he picked up the meal ... The younger girls don't take that guff any more, like we used to. When the passenger is giving you a bad time, you talk back to him.

It's always: the passenger is right. When a passenger says something mean, we're supposed to smile and say, "I understand." We're supposed to *really* smile because stewardesses' supervisors have been getting reports that the girls have been back-talking passengers. Even when they pinch us or say dirty things, we're supposed to smile at them. That's one thing they taught us at stew school. Like he's rubbing your body somewhere, you're supposed to just put his hand down and not say anything and smile at him. That's the main thing, smile.

When I first went to class, they told me I had a crooked smile. She showed me how to smile. She said, "Kinda press a little smile on"—which I did. "Oh, that's great," she said, "that's a *good* smile." But I couldn't do it. I didn't feel like I was doing it on my own. Even if we're sad, we're supposed to have a smile on our face.

I came in after a flight one day, my grandfather had died. Usually they call you up or meet you at the flight and say, "We have some bad news for you." I picked up this piece of paper in my mailbox and it says, "Mother called in. Your grandfather died today." It was written like, say, two cups of sugar. Was I mad! They wouldn't give me time off for the funeral. You can only have time off for your parents or somebody you have lived with. I had never lived with my grandparents. I went anyway.

A lot of our girls are teachers, nurses, everything. They do this part-time, 'cause you have enough time off for another kind of job. I personally work for conventions. I work electronic and auto shows. Companies hire me to stay in their booth and talk about products. I have this speech to tell. At others, all I do is pass out matches or candy. Nowadays every booth has a young girl in it.

People just love to drink on airplanes. They feel adventurous. So you're serving drinks and meals and there's very few times that you can sit down. If she does sit down, she's forgotten how to sit down and talk to passengers. I used to play bridge with passengers. But that doesn't happen any more. We're not supposed to be sitting down, or have a magazine or read a newspaper. If it's a flight from Boston to Los Angeles, you're supposed to have a half an hour talking to passengers. But the only time we can sit down is when we go to the cockpit. You're not supposed to spend any more than five minutes up there for a cigarette.

We could be sitting down on our jump seat and if you had a supervisor on board, she would write you up—for not mixing with the crowd. We're supposed to be told when she walks on board. Many times you don't know. They do have personnel that ride the flights that don't give their names—checking, and they don't tell you about it. Sometimes a girl gets caught smoking in the cabin. Say it's a long flight, maybe a night flight. You're playing cards with a passenger and you say, "Would it bother you if I smoke?" And he says no. She would write you up and get you fired for smoking in the airplane.

They have a limit on how far you can mix. They want you to be sociable, but if he offers you a cigarette, not to take it. When you're outside, they encourage you to take cigarettes.

You give your time to everybody, you share it, not too much with one passenger. Everybody else may be snoring away and there's three guys, maybe military, and they're awake 'cause they're going home and excited. So you're playing cards with 'em. If you have a supervisor on, that would be a no-no. They call a lot of things no-no's.

They call us professional people but they talk to us as very young, childishly. They check us all the time on appearance. They check our weight every month. Even though you've been flying twenty years, they check you and say that's a no-no. If you're not spreading yourself around passengers enough, that's a no-no. Not hanging up first-class passengers' coats, that's a no-no, even though there's no room in the coatroom. You're supposed to somehow make room. If you're a pound over, they can take you off flight until you get under.

Accidents? I've never yet been so scared that I didn't want to get in the airplane. But there've been times at take-offs, there's been something funny. Here I am thinking, What if I die today? I've got too much to do. I can't die today. I use it as a joke.

I've had emergencies where I've had to evacuate the aircraft. I was coming back from Las Vegas and being a lively stewardess I stayed up all night, gambled. We had a load full of passengers. The captain tells me we're going to have an emergency landing in Chicago because we lost a pin out of the nose gear. When we land, the nose gear is gonna collapse. He wants me to prepare the whole cabin for the landing, but not for two more hours. And not to tell the other stewardesses, because they were new girls and would get all excited. So I had to keep this in me for two more hours, wondering, Am I gonna die today? And this is Easter Sunday. And I was serving the passengers drinks and food and this guy got mad at me because his omelet was too cold. And I was gonna say, "You just wait, buddy, you're not gonna worry about that omelet." But I was nice about it, because I didn't want to have trouble with a passenger, especially when I have to prepare him for an emergency.

I told the passengers over the intercom: "The captain says it's just a precaution, there's nothing to worry about." I'm just gonna explain how to get out of the airplane fast, how to be in a braced position. They can't wear glasses or high heels, purses, things out of aisles, under the seats. And make sure everybody's pretty quiet. We had a blind woman on with a dog. We had to get people to help her off and all this stuff.

They were fantastic. Nobody screamed, cried, or hollered. When we got on the ground, everything was fine. The captain landed perfect. But there was a little jolt, and the passengers started screaming and hollering. They held it all back and all of a sudden we got on the ground, blah.

I was great. (Laughs.) That's what was funny. I thought, I have a husband now. I don't know how he would take it, my dying on an airplane. So I thought, I can't die. When I got on the intercom, I was so calm. Also we're supposed to keep a smile on our face. Even during an emergency, you're supposed to walk through the cabin and make everybody feel comfortable with a smile. When you're on the jump seat everybody's looking at you. You're supposed to sit there, holding your ankles, in a position to get out of that airplane fast with a big fat smile on your face.

Doctors tell stewardesses two bad things about them. They're gonna get wrinkles all over their face because they smile with their mouth and their eyes. And also with the pressurization on the airplane, we're not supposed to get up while we're climbing because it causes varicose veins in our legs. So they say being a stewardess ruins your looks.

A lot of stewardesses wanted to be models. The Tanya girl used to be a stewardess on our airline. A stewardess is what they could get and a model is what they couldn't get. They weren't the type of person, they weren't that beautiful, they weren't that thin. So their second choice would be stewardess.

What did you want to be?

I wanted to get out of Broken Bow, Nebraska. (Laughs.)

POSTSCRIPT: *"Every time I go home, they all meet me at the airplane. Not one of my sisters has been on an airplane. All their children think that Terry is just fantastic, because their mom and dad—my sisters and their husbands—feel so stupid, 'Look at us. I wish I could have done that.' I know they feel bad, that they never had the chance. But they're happy I can come home and tell them about things. I send them things from Europe. They get to tell all their friends that their sister's a stewardess. They get real excited about that. The first thing they come out and say, 'One of my sisters is a stewardess.'*

"My father got a promotion with his company and they wrote in their business news that he had a family of seven, six girls and a boy, and one girl is a stewardess in Chicago. And went on to say what I did, and didn't say a word about anything else."

BERYL SIMPSON

Prior to her present job as an employment counselor, she had been an airline reservationist for twelve years.

My job as a reservationist was very routine, computerized. I hated it with a passion. Getting sick in the morning, going to work feeling, Oh, my God! I've got to go to work.

I was on the astrojet desk. It has an unlisted number for people who travel all the time. This is a special desk for people who spend umpteen millions of dollars traveling with the airlines. They may spend ten thousand dollars a month, a hundred thousand a month, depending on the company. I was dealing with the same people every day. This is so-and-so from such-and-such a company and I want a reservation to New York and return, first class. That was the end of the conversation. They brought in a computer called Sabre. It's like an electric typewriter. It has a memory drum and you can retrieve that information forever. Sabre was so expensive, everything was geared to it. Sabre's down, Sabre's up, Sabre's this and that. Everything was Sabre.

With Sabre being so valuable, you were allowed no more than three minutes on the telephone. You had twenty seconds, busy-out time it was called, to put the information into Sabre. Then you had to be available for another phone call. It was almost like a production line. We adjusted to the machine. The casualness, the informality that had been there previously was no longer there. The last three or four years on the job were horrible. The computer had arrived.

They monitored you and listened to your conversations. If you were a minute late for work, it went into your file. I had a horrible attendance record—ten letters in my file for lateness, a total of ten minutes. You took thirty minutes for your lunch, not thirty-one. If you got a break, you took ten minutes, not eleven.

When I was with the airlines, I was taking eight tranquilizers a day. I came into this business, which is supposed to be one of the most hectic, and I'm down to three a day. Even my doctor remarked, "Your ulcer is healed, it's going away." With the airline I had no free will. I was just part of that stupid computer.

I remember when I went to work for the airlines, they said, "You will eat, sleep, and drink airlines. There's no time in your life for ballet, theater, music, anything." My first supervisor told me that. Another agent and I were talking about going to the ballet or something. He overheard us and said we should be talking about work. When you get airline people together, they'll talk about planes. That is all they talk about. That and Johnny Carson. They are TV-oriented people.

I had much more status when I was working for the airlines than I have now. I was always introduced as Beryl Simpson, who works for the airlines. Now I'm reduced to plain old Beryl Simpson. I found this with boyfriends. I knew one who never dates a girl with a name. He never dates Judy, he never dates Joan. He dates a stewardess or a model. He picks girls for the glamor of their jobs. He never tells you their names. When I was with the airlines, I was introduced by my company's name. Now I'm just plain old everyday me, thank God.

I have no status in this man's eyes, even though I probably make twice as much as the ones he's proud of. If I'd start to talk about some of the stocks I hold, he'd be impressed. This is true of every guy I ever dated when I was working on the airlines. I knew I had a dumb, stupid, ridiculous, boring job, and these people were glamorizing it. "Oh, she works for the airlines." Big deal. When I used to go back home, the local paper would run my picture and say that I work for the airlines and that I had recently returned from some exotic trip or something. Romance.

A lot of times we get airline stewardesses into our office who are so disillusioned. We'd like to frame their applications when we get a bright-eyed, starry-eyed kid of eighteen who wants a career in the airlines. Big as life disillusionment. We want to say, "It's not what it's cracked up to be, girlie." If a girl's a stewardess, she might as well forget it after twenty-six. They no longer have compulsory retirement, but the girls get into a rut at that age. A lot of them start showing the rough life they've lived.

JILL TORRANCE

She is a photographer's model, high fashion. Her face is a familiar one in magazine ads as well as on television commercials. She has been engaged in this work for eight years. She earns the city's top rate: fifty dollars an hour.

I do whatever kind of products anyone wants. This week I had a job for some South American product. They said, "We want you to be sexy, coy, pert, but not too effervescent." It always means the same smile and open eyes. For forty-five minutes they tell you what they want. They explain and explain and you sort of tune out and do the same thing.

There are a lot of people there: the person who has the product, the man from the ad agency, a couple of people from the photography studio, the stylist, who poses your dress to make sure it hangs right ... suddenly there are a dozen people standing around. Each is telling you to do something else. You know they are even more insecure than you. You pretend you're listening and you do what you'd planned to do in the first place. When you've worked before a camera long enough, you know what they want even though they don't.

At first you work very hard to try to discover different

looks and hairdos. After a while, you know them all. Someone once asked me, "Why do high-fashion models pose with their mouths open? They look like they're catching flies." (Laughs.) This look has been accepted for a long time. They want everything to be sexy, subtle or overt. After a while, it's automatic.

Now the natural look is in. Jumping up and down or staring out there ... What's natural about looking into space? They want you natural but posed. (Laughs.) How can you feel natural with three pounds of make-up, in some ridiculous costume, standing there and looking pretty? What they think of as being natural is very phony.

You never know from day to day. I did a job for a snow blower in Michigan. It's a little machine that ladies are able to push to get snow out of the way. It was ten below. We flew over at five thirty in the morning. I had my long underwear on, but I forgot to wear my heavy shoes and I froze my feet. You're either doing fur coats in 110 degrees in the summer or bathing suits in the winter. I do whatever they ask me. I take the money and run.

Someone will call you at seven in the morning and say be ready at eight thirty. Can you be there in forty minutes? You're a basket case trying to get your wardrobe together and be there on time. You're having a cup of coffee, suddenly the phone rings and you have to run. It's terrible. Somehow you manage to make it on time. I'm very seldom late. I'm amazed at myself.

I'd like to say I'm sick and can't make it, but I seldom turn something down unless I think it's really awful. Usually I'm just rushing and do the job. I feel guilty if I say no. When you're working for one agency, they expect you to be on call. Otherwise the client may think you're too pampered.

You go out of your house with your closetful on your arm. Different colors and shoes to match and purses and wigs. Every time I get a taxi, they think I'm going to the airport. They're upset when I'm going ten blocks away. I've never found one to help me in or out of a cab. And I'm a good tipper. So I've developed these very strong muscles with one shoulder lower than the other from carrying all the wardrobe about. (Laughs.)

In the middle of the winter it's really horrendous, because you're fighting all the people to get a taxi. I have three or four pieces of luggage. It's pretty heavy. Then I

struggle out of the cab and upstairs to the studio. You're
supposed to look fresh and your hair is supposed to be
sparkling. By the time you get there, you're perspiring like
crazy, and it's difficult to feel fresh under all those hot
lights when you've had such a struggle to get there.

*What's your first reaction when the phone rings in the
morning and it's a job call?*

Oh, crap.

"*I hadn't set out to be a model. I worked as a receptionist
in a beauty shop during high school. This was in South
Dakota. A woman who had worked for Eileen Ford and
had been in* Vogue *and* Harper's Bazaar *said to me, 'Why
don't you go to New York and be a model?' I didn't know
what a model was. I thought they were dummies in cata-
logues. I thought the people in the photographs were just
cutouts. I didn't think they were really people. I paid no
attention to advertising.*

"*I wanted to go to college, but I had saved only three
hundred dollars. So I went to New York at eighteen. I
had never put anything on but lipstick and had never worn
high-heeled shoes. I walked up and down Lexington Avenue for three hours 'cause my room at the Y wasn't ready.
I didn't dare turn left or right. I just kept walking. A hamburger in South Dakota was twenty-five cents and in this
drugstore suddenly it was a dollar and a quarter.*"

At Eileen Ford, they told me I was too long-waisted
and that maybe I should think about something else, and
it was too bad since I had come all the way from South
Dakota. I was so green.

I looked in the telephone book. Huntington Hartford
had just bought this agency. So I went there. I was so
bashful I couldn't even give my name to the receptionist.
About a half an hour later, this guy who had just taken
over the agency—he'd been a male model—came in. He
was the first man I'd seen in New York, close up. I was
just staring at him. He said, "You! Come into my office!"
I thought I had really been discovered. He probably called
me because I was staring at him and he liked himself a
lot. (Laughs.)

A week or two later there was a cocktail party. I'd

never had a drink in my life. They said you should be there at five o'clock. At five I was the only person there. They asked me what I wanted to drink. I didn't know. I said, "Bourbon and water is really nice." It was awful. The party was for Sammy Kaye. I'd never heard of Sammy Kaye.

The guy just wanted us to be there. He was having fifteen of his favorite models over. You just go. No pay. If there's an opening at a photography studio or whatever you go, because advertising people are there and you should be seen and you should make sure they remember your face. All the ridiculous things ... That's what happens to a lot of girls who go into modeling. They're very vulnerable. They don't know what they're doing. Usually they come from very poor families. This seems glamorous. Most of the girls I met were from Ohio or Indiana or some place like that.

I had fifty cents left in my pocket when I got my first job. I worked two hours and made sixty dollars. It was absolutely incredible to me. I pinned a corsage on a guy. It was some hotel ad in a trade magazine. It was a very silly shot that was terribly simple. It was getting all this money for smiling and pinning a flower on a guy. It didn't turn out to be that simple.

Most people have strange feelings about standing before a camera. You have to learn to move and make different designs with your body. Some girls know how to puff their nose in and out to make it change or their lips or cheekbones. They practice in front of a mirror.

Usually you're competing with anywhere from thirty to sixty girls. They're cattle calls. Sometimes they take you in ten at a time. You wait from forty-five minutes to an hour before you're called. They narrow it down and ask for three or four to come back. It's like going out on a job interview every day. Everybody is very insecure. You walk into a room and see thirty beautiful girls and say, "What am I doing here?" Immediately you feel you should leave. But you think you might get three out of fifteen jobs, so ...

There's no training needed, no kind of background. People spend thousands of dollars going to charm schools to learn make-up. It's ridiculous. They just take money from young girls. You learn while you're working. I didn't think it was funny the first few years because I was so nervous. After you relax, you see how absurd it all is.

I've always had a problem gaining weight. I told a photographer I had gained two pounds. I was happy about it. The agency said, "She's too fat, tell her to lose weight." They wouldn't have known if I hadn't told them.

I think the shyest people get into show business or modeling. They were wallflowers in their classes. You never really feel at ease and you force yourself to do things not natural to you. It's always something that you really aren't, that someone else wants you to be.

You feel like you're someone's clothes hanger. One day someone will say you're great. In the next studio, they'll say you're terrible. It changes from minute to minute: acceptance, rejection. Suddenly it doesn't mean anything. Why should you base your whole day on how you look in the morning?

My feelings are ambivalent. I like my life because it does give me freedom. I can have half a day off to do things I like. I couldn't do that if I had a normal job. I could never be a secretary. I make as much money working three hours as a secretary makes in a week. If I had to sit in an office for eight hours a day filing, I would find that more degrading than modeling. I don't look down at secretaries. Most are talented women who could do better jobs than their bosses probably, but will never get the chance—because they're women.

I'd probably join women's lib, but they don't believe in make-up and advertising, so I couldn't very well go to their meetings as I am. At school, where I'm studying photography, they said if I had any interest in women's lib I wouldn't be modeling. I was trying to tell them women are so underpaid that I couldn't earn a comparable wage at any other job. They disagreed, but in the next breath they were talking about something they'd seen advertised and wanted to buy the next day.

I feel guilty because I think people should do something they really like to do in life. I should do something else, but there is nothing I can do really well. I'm established and make a steady living, so it becomes pretty easy. It's not very fulfilling ... but I'm lazy, I admit it. It's an easier thing to do.

You stop thinking when you're working. But it does take a lot of nervous energy because the camera goes one, two, three very fast, and you have to move very fast. There's a *kind* of thinking about what you're doing. If your left knee is at the right angle . . .

I usually don't tell people that I model. I say I'm an actuary or something. You're a celebrity because your picture is in a magazine or there's the negative connotation. If strippers or whores are arrested, they usually say, "I'm a model." There's also the thing about models being free and easy. I've never had the problem of men making passes at me. I've always managed to maintain a distance. I would never have become a model had I known . . .

Mrs. Paley—what's her name? Babs Paley—said the greatest thing is being very thin and very rich. I'm afraid that turns me off. I don't like to look at my pictures. I don't like to ride by and see some advertisement and tell everyone that's me.

Most models, after one or two years, can't be very interested in it. But they get involved with money, so it's difficult for them to quit. And there's always the possibility of the commercial that's going to make you twenty thousand dollars at one crack. You can work very hard all year on photos and not make as much as you can on two television commercials.

Male models are even worse. They're always talking about that lucky streak. They're usually ex-beach boys or ex-policemen or ex-waiters. They think they're going to get rich fast. Money and sex are the big things in their life. They talk about these two things constantly. Money more than sex, but sex a lot. Dirty jokes and the fast buck. You see this handsome frame and you find it empty.

I go off into my own world most of the time. It's difficult for me to talk with the others, because most people I work with are very conservative and play it safe. I usually get emotional, so since I'm not going to change them and they're not going to change me, we sort of talk about everyday gossip. You end up smiling and being nice to everyone. You can't afford not to be.

POSTSCRIPT: *"When I visit that Baptist family back home, they ask if I drink and what do I drink. When I say, 'Seven-Up,' they don't believe me. When I come home once a year, I try to make my people happy or bring them gifts. Probably like the guilty father who brings gifts for his children . . ."*

ANNE BOGAN

We're on the thirty-second floor of a skyscraper, the office of a corporation president. She is his private secretary. The view of the river, railroad yards, bridges, and the city's skyline is astonishing.

"I've been an executive secretary for eight years. However, this is the first time I've been on the corporate end of things, working for the president. I found it a new experience. I love it and I feel I'm leaning a lot."

I become very impatient with dreamers. I respect the doers more than the dreamers. So many people, it seems to me, talk about all the things they want to do. They only talk without accomplishing anything. The drifters are worse than the dreamers. Ones who really have no goals, no aspirations at all, just live from day to day . . .

I enjoy one thing more than anything else on this job. That's the association I have with the other executives, not only my boss. There's a tremendous difference in the way they treat me than what I've known before. They treat me more as . . . on the executive level. They consult me on things, and I enjoy this. It stimulates me.

I know myself well enough to know that I've always enjoyed men more than women. Usually I can judge them very quickly when I meet a woman. I can't judge men that quickly. I seek out the few women I think I will enjoy. The others, I get along with all right, but I feel no basic interest. I don't really enjoy having lunch with them and so on.

You can tell just from conversation what they talk about. It's quite easy. It's also very easy to tell which girls are going to last around the office and which ones aren't. Interest in their work. Many of them aren't, they just don't dig in. They're more interested in chatting in the washroom. I don't know if that's a change from other years. There's always been some who are really not especially career-minded, but they have to give a little bit and try a little harder. The others get by on as little as possible.

I feel like I'm sharing somewhat of the business life of the men. So I think I'm much happier as the secretary to an executive than I would be in some woman's field, where I could perhaps make more money. But it wouldn't be an extension of a successful executive. I'm perfectly happy in my status.

She came from a small town in Indiana and married at eighteen. She had graduated from high school and began working immediately for the town's large company. "My husband was a construction worker. We lived in a trailer, we moved around a lot. There's a lot of community living in that situation and I grew pretty tired of it. You can get involved, you can become too friendly with people when you live too close. A lot of time can be wasted. It was years before I started doing this."

I have dinner with businessmen and enjoy this very much. I like the background music in some of these restaurants. It's soothing and it also adds a little warmth and doesn't disturb the conversation. I like the atmosphere and the caliber of people that usually you see and run into. People who have made it.

I think if I've been at all successful with men, it's because I'm a good listener and interested in their world. I enjoy it, I don't become bored with it. They tell me about their personal life too. Family problems, financial, and the problems of raising children. Most of the ones I'm referring to are divorced. In looking through the years they were married, I can see this is what probably happened. I know if I were the wife, I would be interested in their work. I feel the wife of an executive would be a better wife had she been a secretary first. As a secretary, you learn to adjust to the boss's moods. Many marriages would be happier if the wife would do that.

ROBERTA VICTOR

She had been a prostitute, starting at the age of fifteen. During the first five or six years, she worked as a high-

priced call girl in Manhattan. Later she was a street-
walker . . .

You never used your own name in hustling. I used a
different name practically every week. If you got busted, it
was more difficult for them to find out who you really
were. The role one plays when hustling has nothing to do
with who you are. It's only fitting and proper you take another name.

There were certain names that were in great demand.
Every second hustler had the name Kim or Tracy or Stacy
and a couple others that were in vogue. These were all
young women from seventeen to twenty-five, and we
picked these very non-ethnic-oriented WASP names, rich
names.

A hustler is any woman in American society. I was the
kind of hustler who received money for favors granted
rather than the type of hustler who signs a lifetime contract for her trick. Or the kind of hustler who carefully
reads women's magazines and learns what it is proper to
give for each date, depending on how much money her
date or trick spends on her.

The favors I granted were not always sexual. When I
was a call girl, men were not paying for sex. They were
paying for something else. They were either paying to act
out a fantasy or they were paying for companionship or
they were paying to be seen with a well-dressed young woman. Or they were paying for somebody to listen to them.
They were paying for a *lot* of things. Some men were
paying for sex that *they* felt was deviant. They were
paying so that nobody would accuse them of being perverted or dirty or nasty. A large proportion of these guys
asked things that were not at all deviant. Many of them
wanted oral sex. They felt they couldn't ask their wives or
girl friends because they'd be repulsed. Many of them
wanted somebody to talk dirty to them. Every good call
girl in New York used to share her book and we all knew
the same tricks.

We know a guy who used to lie in a coffin in the middle
of his bedroom and he would see the girl only once. He
got his kicks when the door would be open, the lights
would be out, and there would be candles in the living
room, and all you could see was his coffin on wheels. As

you walked into the living room, he'd suddenly sit up. Of course, you screamed. He got his kicks when you screamed. Or the guy who set a table like the Last Supper and sat in a robe and sandals and wanted you to play Mary Magdalene. (Laughs.)

I was about fifteen, going on sixteen. I was sitting in a coffee shop in the Village, and a friend of mine came by. She said; "I've got a cab waiting. Hurry up. You can make fifty dollars in twenty minutes." Looking back, I wonder why I was so willing to run out of the coffee shop, get in a cab, and turn a trick. It wasn't traumatic because my training had been in how to be a hustler anyway.

I learned it from the society around me, just as a woman. We're taught how to hustle, how to attract, hold a man, and give sexual favors in return. The language that you hear all the time, "Don't sell yourself cheap." "Hold out for the highest bidder." "Is it proper to kiss a man good night on the first date?" The implication is it may not be proper on the first date, but if he takes you out to dinner on the second date, it's proper. If he bring you a bottle of perfume on the third date, you should let him touch you above the waist. And go on from there. It's a market place transaction.

Somehow I managed to absorb that when I was quite young. So it wasn't even a moment of truth when this woman came into the coffee shop and said; "Come on." I was back in twenty-five minutes and I felt no guilt.

She was a virgin until she was fourteen. A jazz musician, with whom she had fallen in love, avoided her. "So I went out to have sex with somebody to present him with an accomplished fact. I found it nonpleasurable. I did a lot of sleeping around before I ever took money."

A precocious child, she was already attending a high school of demanding academic standards. "I was very lonely. I didn't experience myself as being attractive. I had always felt I was too big, too fat, too awkward, didn't look like a Pepsi-Cola ad, was not anywhere near the American Dream. Guys were mostly scared of me. I was athletic, I was bright, and I didn't know how to keep my mouth shut. I didn't know how to play the games right.

"I understood very clearly they were not attracted to me for what I was, but as a sexual object. I was attractive. The year before I started hustling there were a lot of

*guys that wanted to go to bed with me. They didn't want
to get involved emotionally, but they did want to ball. For
a while I was willing to accept that. It was feeling intimacy, feeling close, feeling warm.*

*"The time spent in bed wasn't unpleasant. It just wasn't
terribly pleasant. It was a way of feeling somebody cared
about me, at least for a moment. And it mattered that I
was there, that I was important. I discovered that in bed it
was possible. It was one skill that I had and I was proud
of my reputation as an amateur.*

*"I viewed all girls as being threats. That's what we were
all taught. You can't be friends with another woman, she
might take your man. If you tell her anything about how
you really feel, she'll use it against you. You smile at other
girls and you spend time with them when there's nothing
better to do, but you'd leave any girl sitting anywhere if
you had an opportunity to go somewhere with a man. Because the most important thing in life is the way men feel
about you."*

How could you forget your first trick? (Laughs.) We
took a cab to midtown Manhattan, we went to a pent-
house. The guy up there was quite well known. What he
really wanted to do was watch two women make love, and
then he wanted to have sex with me. It was barely sex. He
was almost finished by the time we started. He barely
touched me and we were finished.

Of course, we faked it, the woman and me. The ethic
was: You don't participate in a sexual act with another
woman if a trick is watching. You always fake it. You're
putting something over on him and he's paying for something he didn't really get. That's the only way you can
keep any sense of self-respect.

The call girl ethic is very strong. You were the lowest
of the low if you allowed yourself to feel anything with a
trick. The bed puts you on their level. The way you
maintain your integrity is by acting all the way through.
It's not too far removed from what most American women do—which is to put on a big smile and act.

It was a tremendous kick. Here I was doing absolutely
nothing, *feeling* nothing, and in twenty minutes I was
going to walk out with fifty dollars in my pocket. That just
made me feel absolutely marvelous. I came downtown. I
can't believe this! I'm not changed, I'm the same as I was

twenty minutes ago, except that now I have fifty dollars in my pocket. It really was tremendous status. How many people could make fifty dollars for twenty minutes' work? Folks work for eighty dollars take-home pay. I worked twenty minutes for fifty dollars clear, no taxes, nothing! I was still in school, I was smoking grass. I was shooting heroin, I wasn't hooked yet, and I had money. It was terrific.

After that, I made it my business to let my friend know that I was available for more of these situations. (Laughs.) She had good connections. Very shortly I linked up with a couple of others who had a good call book.

Books of phone numbers are passed around from call girl to call girl. They're numbers of folks who are quite respectable and with whom there is little risk. They're not liable to pull a knife on you, they're not going to cheat you out of money. Businessmen and society figures. There's three or four groups. The wealthy executive, who makes periodic trips into the city and is known to several girls. There's the social figure, whose name appears quite regularly in the society pages and who's a regular once-a-week John. Or there's the quiet, independently wealthy type. Nobody knows how they got their money. I know one of them made his money off munitions in World War II. Then there's the entertainer. There's another crowd that runs around the night spots, the 21 Club . . .

These were the people whose names you saw in the paper almost every day. But I knew what they were really like. Any John who was obnoxious or aggressive was just crossed out of your book. You passed the word around that this person was not somebody other people should call.

We used to share numbers—standard procedure. The book I had I got from a guy who got it from a very good call girl. We kept a copy of that book in a safe deposit box. The standard procedure was that somebody new gave half of what they got the first time for each number. You'd tell them: "Call so-and-so, that's a fifty-dollar trick." They would give you twenty-five dollars. Then the number was theirs. My first book, I paid half of each trick to the person who gave it to me. After that, it was my book.

The book had the name and phone number coded, the

price, what the person wants, and the contact name. For four years I didn't turn a trick for less than fifty dollars. They were all fifty to one hundred dollars and up for twenty minutes, an hour. The understanding is: it doesn't get conducted as a business transaction. The myth is that it's a social occasion.

You're expected to be well dressed, well made up, appear glad to see the man. I would get a book from somebody and I would call and say, "I'm a friend of so-and-so's, and she thought it would be nice if we got together." The next move was his. Invariably he'd say, "Why don't we do that? Tonight or tomorrow night. Why don't you come over for a drink?" I would get very carefully dressed and made up . . .

There's a given way of dressing in that league—that's to dress well but not ostentatiously. You have to pass doormen, cabdrivers. You have to look as if you belong in those buildings on Park Avenue or Central Park West. You're expected not to look cheap, not to look hard. Youth is the premium. I was quite young, but I looked older, so I had to work very hard at looking my age. Most men want girls who are eighteen. They really want girls who are younger, but they're afraid of trouble.

Preparations are very elaborate. It has to do with beauty parlors and shopping for clothes and taking long baths and spending money on preserving the kind of front that gives you a respectable address and telephone and being seen at the right clubs and drinking at the right bars. And being able to read the newspapers faithfully, so that not only can you talk about current events, you can talk about the society columns as well.

It's a social ritual. Being able to talk about what is happening and learn from this great master, and be properly respectful and know the names that he mentions. They always drop names of their friends, their contacts, and their clients. You should recognize these. Playing a role . . .

At the beginning I was very excited. But in order to continue I had to turn myself off. I had to disassociate who I was from what I was doing.

It's a process of numbing yourself. I couldn't associate with people who were not in the life—either the drug life or the hustling life. I found I couldn't turn myself back on when I finished working. When I turned myself off, I was numb—emotionally, sexually numb.

At first I felt like I was putting one over on all the other poor slobs that would go to work at eight-thirty in the morning and come home at five. I was coming home at four in the morning and I could sleep all day. I really thought a lot of people would change places with me because of the romantic image: being able to spend two hours out, riding cabs, and coming home with a hundred dollars. I could spend my mornings doing my nails, going to the beauty parlor, taking long baths, going shopping . . .

It was usually two tricks a night. That was easily a hundred, a hundred and a quarter. I always had money in my pocket. I didn't know what the inside of a subway smelled like. Nobody traveled any other way except by cab. I ate in all the best restaurants and I drank in all the best clubs. A lot of people wanted you to go out to dinner with them. All you had to do was be an ornament.

Almost all the call girls I knew were involved in drugs. The fast life, the night hours. At after-hours clubs, if you're not a big drinker, you usually find somebody who has cocaine, 'cause that's the big drug in those places. You wake up at noon, there's not very much to do till nine or ten that night. Everybody else is at work, so you shoot heroin. After a while the work became a means of supplying drugs, rather than drugs being something we took when we were bored.

The work becomes boring because you're not part of the life. You're the part that's always hidden. The doormen smirk when you come in, 'cause they know what's going on. The cabdriver, when you give him a certain address—he knows exactly where you're going when you're riding up Park Avenue at ten o'clock at night, for Christ sake. You leave there and go back—to what? Really, to what? To an emptiness. You've got all this money in your pocket and nobody you care about.

When I was a call girl I looked down on streetwalkers. I couldn't understand why anybody would put themselves in that position. It seemed to me to be hard work and very dangerous. What I was doing was basically riskless. You never had to worry about disease. These were folks who you know took care of themselves and saw the doctor regularly. Their apartments were always immaculate and the liquor was always good. They were always polite. You didn't have to ask them for money first. It was always implicit: when you were ready to leave, there would be an envelope under the lamp or there'd be something in your pocketbook. It never had to be discussed.

I had to work an awful lot harder for the same money when I was a streetwalker. I remember having knives pulled on me, broken bottles held over my head, being raped, having my money stolen back from me, having to jump out of a second-story window, having a gun pointed at me.

As a call girl, I had lunch at the same places society women had lunch. There was no way of telling me apart from anybody else in the upper tax bracket. I made my own hours, no more than three or so hours of work an evening. I didn't have to accept calls. All I had to do was play a role.

As a streetwalker, I didn't have to act. I let myself show the contempt I felt for the tricks. They weren't paying enough to make it worth performing for them. As a call girl, I pretended I enjoyed it sexually. You have to act as if you had an orgasm. As a streetwalker, I didn't. I used to lie there with my hands behind my head and do mathematics equations in my head or memorize the keyboard typewriter.

It was strictly a transaction. No conversation, no acting, no myth around it, no romanticism. It was purely a business transaction. You always asked for your money in front. If you could get away without undressing totally, you did that.

It's not too different than the distinction between an executive secretary and somebody in the typing pool. As an executive secretary you really identify with your boss. When you're part of the typing pool, you're a body, you're hired labor, a set of hands on the typewriter. You have nothing to do with whoever is passing the work down to you. You do it as quickly as you can.

What led you to the streets?

My drug habit. It got a lot larger. I started looking bad. All my money was going for drugs. I didn't have any money to spend on keeping myself up and going to beauty parlors and having a decent address and telephone.

If you can't keep yourself up, you can't call on your old tricks. You drop out of circulation. As a call girl, you have to maintain a whole image. The trick wants to know he can call you at a certain number and you have to have a stable address. You must look presentable, not like death on a soda cracker.

I looked terrible. When I hit the streets, I tried to stick to at least twenty dollars and folks would laugh. I needed a hundred dollars a night to maintain a drug habit and keep a room somewhere. It meant turning seven or eight tricks a night. I was out on the street from nine o'clock at night till four in the morning. I was taking subways and eating in hamburger stands.

For the first time I ran the risk of being busted. I was never arrested as a call girl. Every once in a while a cop would get hold of somebody's book. They would call one of the girls and say, "I'm a friend of so-and-so's." They would try to trap them. I never took calls from people I didn't know. But on the streets, how do you know who you're gonna pick up?

As a call girl, some of my tricks were upper echelon cops, not patrolmen. Priests, financiers, garment industry folks, bigtimers. On the street, they ranged from *junior* executive types, blue-collar workers, upwardly striving postal workers, college kids, suburban white collars who were in the city for the big night, restaurant workers . . .

You walk a certain area, usually five or six blocks. It has a couple of restaurants, a couple of bars. There's the step in-between: hanging out in a given bar, where people come to you. I did that briefly.

You'd walk very slowly, you'd stop and look in the window. Somebody would come up to you. There was a ritual here too. The law says in order to arrest a woman for prostitution, she has to mention money and she has to tell you what she'll do for the money. We would keep within the letter of the law, even though the cops never did.

Somebody would come up and say, "It's a nice night, isn't it?" "Yes." They'd say, "Are you busy?" I'd say, "Not particularly." "Would you like to come with me and have a drink?" You start walking and they say, "I have fifteen dollars or twelve dollars and I'm very lonely." Something to preserve the myth. Then they want you to spell out exactly what you're willing to do for the money.

I never approached anybody on the street. That was the ultimate risk. Even if he weren't a cop, he could be some kind of supersquare, who would call a cop. I was trapped by cops several times.

The first one didn't even trap me as a trick. It was three in the morning. I was in Chinatown. I ran into a trick I knew. We made contact in a restaurant. He went home and I followed him a few minutes later. I knew the address. I remember passing a banana truck. It didn't dawn on me that it was strange for somebody to be selling bananas at three in the morning. I spent about twenty minutes with my friend. He paid me. I put the money in my shoe. I opened the door and got thrown back against the wall. The banana salesman was a vice squad cop. He'd stood on the garbage can to peer in the window. I got three years for that one.

I was under age. I was four months short of twenty-one. They sent me to what was then called Girls' Term Court. They wouldn't allow me a lawyer because I wasn't an adult, so it wasn't really a criminal charge. The judge said I was rehabilitable. Instead of giving me thirty days, he gave me three years in the reformatory. It was very friendly of him. I was out on parole a couple of times before I'd get caught and sent back.

I once really got trapped. It was about midnight and a guy came down the street. He said he was a postal worker who just got off the shift. He told me how much money he had and what he wanted. I took him to my room. The cop isn't supposed to undress. If you can describe the color of his shorts, it's an invalid arrest. Not only did he show me the color of his shorts, he went to bed with me. Then he pulled a badge and a gun and busted me.

He lied to me. He told me he was a narc and he didn't want to bust me for hustling. If I would tell him who was dealing in the neighborhood, he'd cut me loose. I lied to him, but he won. He got me to walk out of the building past all my friends and when we got to the car, he threw me in. (Laughs.) It was great fun. I did time for that—close to four years.

What's the status of the streetwalker in prison?

It's fine. Everybody there has been hustling. It's status in reverse. Anybody who comes in saying things like they could never hustle is looked down on as being somewhat crazy.

She speaks of a profound love she had for a woman who

she'd met in prison; of her nursing her lover after the wo-man had become blind.

"I was out of the country for a couple of years. I worked a house in Mexico. It had heavy velour cur-tains—a Mexican version of a French whorehouse. There was a reception area, where the men would come and we'd parade in front of them.

"The Mexicans wanted American girls. The Americans wanted Mexican girls. So I didn't get any American tricks. I had to give a certain amount to the house for each trick I turned and anything I negotiated over that amount was mine. It was far less than anything I had taken in the States.

"I was in great demand even though I wasn't a blonde. A girl friend of mine worked there two nights. She was Norwegian and very blonde. Every trick who came in wanted her. Her head couldn't handle it all. She quit after two nights. So I was the only American.

"That was really hard work. The Mexicans would play macho. American tricks will come as quickly as they can. Mexicans will hold back and make me work for my money. I swear to God they were doing multiplication tables in their heads to keep from having an orgasm. I would use every trick I knew to get them to finish. It was crazy!

I was teaching school at the same time. I used Alice in Wonderland *as the text in my English class. During the day I tutored English for fifth- and sixth-grade kids. In the evening, I worked in the call house.*

"The junk down there was quite cheap and quite good. My habit was quite large. I loved dope more than any-thing else around. After a while I couldn't differentiate be-tween working and not working. All men were tricks, all relationships were acting. I was completely turned off."

She quit shooting dope the moment she was slugged, brutally beaten by a dealer who wanted her. This was her revelatory experience. "It was the final indignity. I'd had tricks pulling broken bottles on me, I'd been in razor fights, but nobody had ever hit me." *It was a threat to her status.* "I was strong. I could handle myself. A tough broad. This was threatened, so . . ."

I can't talk for women who were involved with pimp's. That was where I always drew the line. I always thought pimps were lower than pregnant cockroaches. I didn't want anything to do with them. I was involved from time to time with some men. They were either selling dope or stealing, but they were not depending on my income. Nor were they telling me to get my ass out on the street. I never supported a man.

As a call girl I got satisfaction, an unbelievable joy— perhaps perverted—in knowing what these reputable folks were really like. Being able to open a newspaper every morning, read about this pillar of society, and know what a pig he really was. The tremendous kick in knowing that I didn't feel anything, that I was acting and they weren't. It's sick, but no sicker than what every woman is taught, all right?

I was in *control* with every one of those relationships. You're vulnerable if you allow yourself to be involved sexually. I wasn't. They were. I called it. Being able to manipulate somebody sexually, I could determine when I wanted that particular transaction to end. 'Cause I could make the guy come. I could play all kinds of games. See? It was a tremendous sense of power.

What I did was no different from what ninety-nine percent of American women are taught to do. I took the money from under the lamp instead of in Arpege. What would I do with 150 bottles of Arpege a week?

You become your job. I became what I did. I became a hustler. I became cold, I became hard, I became turned off, I became numb. Even when I wasn't hustling, I was a hustler. I don't think it's terribly different from somebody who works on the assembly line forty hours a week and comes home cut off, numb, dehumanized. People aren't built to switch on and off like water faucets.

What was really horrifying about jail is that it really isn't horrifying. You adjust very easily. The same thing with hustling. It became my life. It was too much of an effort to try to make contact with another human being, to force myself to care, to feel.

I didn't care about me. It didn't matter whether I got up or didn't get up. I got high as soon as I awoke. The first thing I'd reach for, with my eyes half-closed, was my dope. I didn't like my work. It was messy. That was the biggest feeling about it. Here's all these guys slobbering over you all night long. I'm lying there, doing math or conjugations or Spanish poetry in my head. (Laughs.)

And they're slobbering. God! God! What enabled me to do it was being high—high and numb.

The overt hustling society is the microcosm of the rest of the society. The power relationships are the same and the games are the same. Only this one I was in control of. The greater one I wasn't. In the outside society, if I tried to be me, I wasn't in control of anything. As a bright, assertive woman, I had no power. As a cold, manipulative hustler, I had a lot. I knew I was playing a role. Most women are taught to *become* what they act. All I did was act out the reality of American womanhood.

DID YOU EVER HEAR THE ONE ABOUT THE FARMER'S DAUGHTER?

BARBARA HERRICK

She is thirty; single. Her title is script supervisor/producer at a large advertising agency; working out of its Los Angeles office. She is also a vice president. Her accounts are primarily in food and cosmetics. "There's a myth: a woman is expected to be a food writer because she is assumed to know those things and a man doesn't. However, some of the best copy on razors and Volkswagens has been written by women."

She has won several awards and considerable recognition for her commercials. "You have to be absolutely on target, dramatic and fast. You have to be aware of legal restrictions. The FTC gets tougher and tougher. You must understand budgetary matters: will it cost a million or can it be shot in a studio in one day?"

She came off a Kansas farm, one of four daughters. "During high school, I worked as a typist and was an extremely good one. I was compulsive about doing every tiny job very well." She graduated from the University of Missouri. According to Department of Labor statistics, she is in the upper one percent bracket of working women.

In her Beverly Hills apartment are paintings, sculpted works, recordings (classic, folk, jazz, and rock), and many books, most of them obviously well thumbed.

Men in my office doing similar work were being promoted, given raises and titles. Since I had done the bulk of the work, I made a stand and was promoted too. I needed the title, because clients figured that I'm just a face-man.

A face-man is a person who looks good, speaks well, and presents the work. I look well, I speak well, and I'm pleasant to have around after the business is over with—if they acknowledge me in business. We go to the lounge and have drinks. I can drink with the men but remain a lady. (Laughs.)

That's sort of my tacit business responsibility, although this has never been said to me directly. I know this is why I travel alone for the company a great deal. They don't anticipate any problems with my behavior. I equate it with being the good nigger.

On first meeting, I'm frequently taken for the secretary, you know, traveling with the boss. I'm here to keep somebody happy. Then I'm introduced as the writer. One said to me after the meeting was over and the drinking had started, "When I first saw you, I figured you were a—you know. I never knew you were the person *writing* this all the time." (Laughs.) Is it a married woman working for extra money? Is it a lesbian? Is it some higher-up's mistress?

I'm probably one of the ten highest paid people in the agency. It would cause tremendous hard feelings if, say, I work with a man who's paid less. If a remark is made at a bar—"You make so much money, you could buy and sell me"—I toss it off, right? He's trying to find out. He can't equate me as a rival. They wonder where to put me, they wonder what my salary is.

Buy and sell me—yeah, there are a lot of phrases that show the reversal of roles. What comes to mind is swearing at a meeting. New clients are often very uptight. They feel they can't make any innuendoes that might be suggestive. They don't know how to treat me. They don't know whether to acknowledge me as a woman or as another neuter person who's doing a job for them.

The first time, they don't look at me. At the first three meetings of this one client, if I would ask a direction question, they would answer and look at my boss or another man in the room. Even around the conference table. I don't attempt to be—the glasses, the bun, and totally asexual. That isn't the way I am. It's obvious that I'm a woman and enjoy being a woman. I'm not overly provocative either. It's the thin, good nigger line that I have to toe.

. I've developed a sixth sense about this. If a client will say, "Are you married?" I will often say yes, because

that's the easiest way to deal with him if he needs that
category for me. If it's more acceptable to him to have a
young, attractive married woman in a business position
comparable to his, terrific. It doesn't bother me. It makes
me safer. He'll never be challenged. He can say, "She'd be
sensational. I'd love to get her. I could show her what a
real man is, but she's married." It's a way out for him.

Or there's the mistress thing: well, she's sleeping with
the boss. That's acceptable to them. Or she's a frustrated,
compulsive castrator. That's a category. Or lesbian. If I
had short hair, wore suits, and talked in a gruff voice, that
would be more acceptable than I am. It's when I tran-
scend their labels, they don't quite know what to do. If
someone wants a quick label and says, "I'll bet you're a
big women's libber, aren't you?" I say, "Yeah, yeah." They
have to place me.

I travel a lot. That's what gets very funny. We had a
meeting in Montreal. It was one of those bride's magazines, honeymoon-type resorts, with heart-shaped beds and
the heated pool. I was there for three days with nine men.
All day long we were enclosed in this conference room.
The agency account man went with me. I was to talk
about the new products, using slides and movies. There
were about sixty men in the conference room. I had to
leave in such a hurry, I still had my gaucho pants and
boots on.

The presentation went on for an hour and a half. There
was tittering and giggling for about forty minutes. Then
you'd hear the shift in the audience. They got interested in
what I was saying. Afterwards they had lunch sent up.
Some of them never did talk to me. Others were interested
in my life. They would say things like, "Have you read
The Sensuous Woman?" (Laughs.) They didn't really want
to know. If they were even more obvious, they probably
would have said, "Say, did you hear the one about the
farmer's daughter?" I'd have replied, "Of course, I'm one
myself."

The night before, there was a rehearsal. Afterwards the
account man suggested we go back to the hotel, have a
nightcap, and get to bed early. It was a 9:00 A.M. meeting. We were sitting at the bar and he said, "Of course,
you'll be staying in my room." I said, "What? I have a
room." He said, "I just assumed. You're here and I'm here
and we're both grown up." I said, "You assumed? You

never even asked me whether I wanted to." My feelings obviously meant nothing to him. Apparently it was what you *did* if you're out of town and the woman is anything but a harelip and you're ready to go. His assumption was incredible.

We used to joke about him in the office. We'd call him Mr. Straight, because he was Mr. Straight. Very short hair, never grew sideburns, never wore wide ties, never, never swore, never would pick up an innuendo, super-super-conservative. No one would know, you see?

Mr. Straight is a man who'd never invite me to have a drink after work. He would never invite me to lunch alone. Would never, never make an overture to me. It was simply the fact that we were out of town and who would know? That poor son of a bitch had no notion what he was doing to my ego. I didn't want to destroy his. We had to work together the next day and continue to work together.

The excuse I gave is one I use many times. "Once when I was much younger and innocent, I slept with an account man. The guy turned out to be a bastard. I got a big reputation and he made my life miserable because he had a loose mouth. And even though you're a terrifically nice guy and I'd like to sleep with you, I feel I can't. It's my policy. I'm older and wiser now. I don't do it. You have to understand that." It worked. I could never say to him, "You don't even understand how you insulted me."

It's the always-having-to-please conditioning. I don't want to make any enemies. Only of late, because I'm getting more secure and I'm valued by the agency, am I able to get mad at men and say, "Fuck off!" But still I have to keep egos unruffled, smooth things over . . . I still work with him and he never mentioned it again.

He'll occasionally touch my arm or catch my eye: We're really sympatico, aren't we baby? There may be twelve men and me sitting at the meeting and they can't call on one of the girls or the receptionist, he'd say, "Let's have some coffee, Barbara. Make mine black." I'm the waitress. I go do it because it's easier than to protest. If he'd known my salary is more than his I doubt that he'd have acted that way in Denver—or here.

Part of the resentment toward me and my salary is that I don't have a mortgage on a home in the Valley and three kids who have to go to private schools and a wife who spends at Saks, and you never know when you're going to lose your job in this business. Say, we're having a convivial drink among peers and we start grousing. I'm not allowed to grouse with the best of them. They say, "Oh, you? What do you need money for? You're a single woman. You've got the world by the balls." I hear that all the time.

If I'm being paid a lot of attention to, say by someone to whom I'm attracted, and we've done a job and we're in New York together for a week's stretch, we're in the same hotel, suppose I want to sleep with him? Why not? Here's my great double standard. You never hear it said about a man in my capacity—"He sleeps around." It would only be to his glory. It's expected, if he's there with a model, starlet, or secretary. In my case, I constantly worry about that. If I want to, I must be very careful. That's what I'm railing against.

This last shoot, it was an exasperating shot. It took hours. We were there all day. It was exhausting, frustrating. Between takes, the camera man, a darling man, would come back to where I was standing and put his arms around me. I didn't think anything of it. We're hardly fucking on the set. It was his way of relaxing. I heard a comment later that night from the director: "You ought to watch your behavior on the set with the camera man." I said, *"Me* watch it? Fuck that! Let *him* watch it." He was hired by me. I could fire him if I didn't like him. Why *me,* you see? *I* have to watch.

Clients. I get calls in my hotel room: "I want to discuss something about production today that didn't go right." I know what that means. I try to fend it off. I'm on this tightrope. I don't want to get into a drunken scene ever with a client and to literally shove him away. That's not going to do me any good. The only smart thing I can do is avoid that sort of scene. The way I avoid it is by suggesting an early morning breakfast meeting. I always have to make excuses: "I drank too much and my stomach is really upset, so I couldn't do it right now. We'll do it in the morning." Sometimes I'd like to say, "Fuck off, I know what you want."

"I've had a secretary for the last three years. I hesitate to use her ... I won't ask her to do typing. It's hard for me to use her as I was used. She's bright and could be much

more than a secretary. So I give her research assignments, things to look up, which might be fun for her. Rather than just say, 'Here, type this.'

"*I'm an interesting figure to her. She says, 'When I think of Women's Lib I don't think of Germaine Greer or Kate Millett. I think of you.' She sees my life as a lot more glamorous than it really is. She admires the externals. She admires the apartment, the traveling. We shot two commercials just recently, one in Mexico, one in Nassau. Then I was in New York to edit them. That's three weeks. She takes care of all my travel details. She knows the company gave me an advance of well over a thousand dollars. I'm put up in the fine hotels, travel first class. I can spend ninety dollars at a dinner for two or three. I suppose it is something—little Barbara from a Kansas farm and Christ! look where I am. But I don't think of it, which is a funny thing.*"

It used to be the token black at a big agency was very safe because he always had to be there. Now I'm definitely the token woman. In the current economic climate, I'm one of the few writers at my salary level getting job offers. Unemployment is high right now among people who do what I do. Yet I get calls: "Will you come and write on feminine hygiene products?" Another, involving a food account: "We need you, we'll pay you thirty grand and a contract. Be the answer for Such-an'-such Foods." I'm ideal because I'm young enough to have four or five solid years of experience behind me. I know how to handle myself or I wouldn't be where I am.

I'm very secure right now. But when someone says to me, "You don't have to worry," he's wrong. In a profession where I absolutely cannot age, I cannot be doing this at thirty-eight. For the next years, until I get too old, my future's secure in a very insecure business. It's like a race horse or a show horse. Although I'm holding the job on talent and responsibility, I got here partly because I'm attractive and it's a big kick for a client to know that for three days in Montreal there's going to be this young brunette, who's very good, mind you. I don't know how they talk about me, but I'd guess: "She's very good, but to look at her you'd never know it. She's a knockout."

I have a fear of hanging on past my usefulness. I've seen desperate women out of jobs, who come around with their samples, which is the way all of us get jobs. A lot of women have been cut. Women who had soft jobs in an agency for years and are making maybe fifteen thousand. In the current slump, this person is cut and some bright young kid from a college, who'll work for seven grand a year, comes in and works late every night.

Talk about gaps. In a room with a twenty-two-year-old, there are areas in which I'm altogether lost. But not being a status-quo-type person, I've always thought ahead enough to keep pace with what's new. I certainly don't feel my usefulness as a writer is coming to an end. I'm talking strictly in terms of physical aging. (Laughs.) It's such a young business, not just the consumer part. It's young in terms of appearances. The client expects agency people, especially on the creative end, to dress a certain way, to be very fashionable. I haven't seen many women in any executive capacity age gracefully.

The bellbottoms, the beads, beards, and sideburns, that's the easy, superficial way to feel part of the takeover culture. It's true also in terms of writing. What kind of music do you put behind the commercial? It's ridiculous to expect a sheltered forty-two-year-old to anticipate progressive rock. The danger of aging, beyond touch, out of reach with the younger market . . .

The part I hate—it's funny. (Pause.) Most people in the business are delighted to present their work and get praise for it—and the credit and the laughter and everything in the commercial. I always hate that part. Deep down, I feel demeaned. Don't question the adjectives, don't argue, if it's a cologne or a shampoo. I know, 'cause I buy 'em myself. I'm the biggest sucker for buying an expensively packaged hoax thing. Face cream at eight dollars. And I sell and convince.

I used Erik Satie music for a cologne thing. The clients didn't know Satie from Roger Williams. I'm very good at what I do, dilettantism. I go into my act: we call it dog and pony time, show time, tap dance. We laugh about it. He says, "Oh, that's beautiful, exactly right. How much will it cost us?" I say, "The music will cost you three grand. Those two commercials you want to do in Mexico and Nassau, that's forty grand. There's no way I can bring it in for less." I'm this young woman, saying, "Give me forty thousand dollars of your money and I will go away to Mexico and Nassau and bring you back a commercial and you'll love it." It's blind faith.

Do I ever question what I'm selling? (A soft laugh.) All the time. I know a writer who quit a job equivalent to mine. She was making a lot of money, well thought of. She was working on a consumer finance account. It's blue collar and black. She made this big stand. I said to her, in private, "I agree with you, but why is this your test case? You've been selling a cosmetic for years that is nothing but mineral oil and women are paying eight dollars for it. You've been selling a cake mix that you know is so full of preservatives that it would kill every rat in the lab. Why all of a sudden . . . ?"

If you're in the business, you're in the business, the fucking business! You're a hustler. But because you're witty and glib . . . I've never pretended this is the best writing I can do. Every advertising writer has a novel in his drawer. Few of them ever do it.

I don't think what I do is necessary or that it performs a service. If it's a very fine product—and I've worked on some of those—I love it. It's when you get into that awful area of hope, cosmetics—you're just selling image and a hope. It's like the arthritis cure or cancer—quackery. You're saying to a lady, "Because this oil comes from the algae at the bottom of the sea, you're going to have a timeless face." It's a crock of shit! I know it's part of my job, I do it. If I made the big stand my friend made, I'd lose my job. Can't do it. I'm expected to write whatever assignment I'm given. It's whorish. I haven't written enough to know what kind of writer I am. I suspect, rather than a writer, I'm a good reader. I think I'd make a good editor. I have read so many short stories that I bet you I could turn out a better anthology than anybody's done yet, in certain categories. I remember, I appreciate, I have a feeling I could . . .

POSTSCRIPT: *Shortly afterward she was battling an ulcer.*

THE COMMERCIAL

JOHN FORTUNE

*He is thirty-six. He has been with an advertising agency
for eight years. "I started out in philosophy at Prince-
ton ..."*

I am what is called a creative supervisor. Creative is a
pretentious word. I have a group of about six people who
work for me. They create radio commercials, print ads,
billboards that go up on highways, television commercials
too. Your purpose is to move goods off the shelf (laughs):
your detergents, your soaps, your foods, your beers, cigarettes ...

It's like the fashion business. There's a look to advertising. Many techniques are chosen because they're in vogue
at the time. Then a new look will emerge. Right now, a
kind of angry stand-up is popular. A guy who's all pissed
off up there and he says, "Look, other products are rotten
and ours is good—buy it or I'll kill you." The hortatory
kind is in fashion now.

It's an odd business. It's serious but it isn't. (Laughs.)
Life in an advertising agency is like being at a dull party,
interrupted by more serious moments. There's generally a
kind of convivial attitude. Nobody's particularly uptight.
Creativity of this kind flourishes better.

They're aware that they're talking about little bears
capering around a cereal box and they're arguing which
way the bears should go. It's a silly thing for adults to be
doing. At the same time, they're aware the client's going
to spend a million dollars on television time to run this

commercial. Millions of dollars went into these little bears, so that gave them an importance of their own. That commercial, if successful, can double salaries. It's serious, yet it isn't. This kind of split is in everybody's mind. Especially the older generation in advertising, people like me.

I was a writer *manqué*, who came into advertising because I was looking for a way to make money. My generation is more casual about it. Many will be writers who have a novel in the desk drawer, artists who are going to quit someday and paint. Whereas the kids coming up consider advertising itself to be the art form. They've gone to school and studied advertising. There's an intensity about what they do. They don't laugh at those little bears capering around the cereal. Those little bears are it for them. They consider themselves fine artists and the advertising business owes them the right to create, to express themselves.

And there's a countertendency among young people. The other day I was challenged by someone: "I find this commercial offensive. It's as if you're trying to manipulate people." This kind of honesty is part of it. But he's in the business himself. His bread is in the same gravy. Though the older ones start out casual, they become quite serious as they go along. You become what you behold. You turn into an advertising man.

My day is so amorphous. Part of it is guiding other people. I throw ideas out and let them throw ideas back, shoot down ideas immediately. In some ways it's like teaching. You're trying to guide them and they're also guiding you. I may sit with a writer and an art director who are going to create a commercial—to sell garbage bags, okay? A number of ideas are thrown out. What do you think of this? What do you think of that? Last year we tried this. Don't make it that wild. We stick, say, to a family situation.

Let's have a big family reunion, right? We'll use fast motion and slow motion as our visual technique. A reunion right after dinner. They're outside, they're at a picnic, right? Grampa's in the hammock and so forth. Everything's in slow motion. But when it comes time to clean up things go pretty fast if you use these garbage bags. Everything begins to move in fast motion, which is a funny technique. Fast motion tends to distance people from what they're watching. I didn't like it. I thought it lacked focus.

You have to set things up. You have to characterize everybody, grampa, uncle ... You don't have the effective relationships clearly marked in the beginning. You have to do this in a commercial that may be only thirty seconds. Sometimes you're writing a play, creating a vehicle. You begin with a human problem and then you see how it's satisfied by the product.

The way you sell things is to make some kind of connection between the attributes of the product and what people want, human needs. Some years ago, there was a product called Right Guard, an underarm deodorant. It was positioned at that time for men. It was not going anywhere. A copy-writer noticed that it was a spray, so the whole family could use it. He said, "Let's call it the all-family spray." There was no change in the product, merely in the way it was sold. What any product is selling is a package of consumer satisfactions. A dream in the flesh or something.

A Mustang is a machine that was designed with human fantasies in mind. It's not just a piece of machinery. Somebody did a lot of research into what people wanted. That research went into the design, very subtly into the shape. Then the advertising came along and added another layer. So when a person drives a Mustang, he's living in a whole cocoon of satisfaction. He's not just getting transportation. With detergents people are buying advertising. With cigarettes they're buying an image, not just little things in a box.

They're all very similar. That raises the question: How important is advertising? Is there a justification for it? It's a question people are asking all over the country. I myself am puzzled by it. There's big change going on right now. The rules are becoming more stringent. In another five years you'll just have a lawyer up there. He'll say, "This is our product. It's not much different from any other product. It comes in a nice box, no nicer than anybody else's. It'll get your clothes pretty clean, but so will the others. Try it because we're nice people, not that the other company isn't nice."

I enjoy it actually. I think any kind of work, after a while, gets a kind of functional autonomy. It has an intensity of its own. You start out doing something for a reason and if you do it long enough, even though the reason may have altered, you continue to do it, because it gives you its own satisfaction.

It's very hard to know if you know something in this business. There are very few genuine experts. It's a very fragile thing. To tell somebody they should spend ten million dollars on this tiger that's gonna represent their gasoline, that's quite a thing to sell somebody on doing. Gee, why should it be a tiger? Why shouldn't it be a llama?

The way, you see, is by being very confident. Advertising is full of very confident people. (Laughs.) Whether it's also full of competent people is another question. Coming into a meeting is a little like swimming in a river full of piranha fish. If you start to bleed, they're gonna catch you. You have to build yourself up before you're gonna sell something. You have to have an attitude that it's terrific.

I say to myself, Isn't it terrific? It could be worse—that's another thing I say. And I whistle and skip around and generally try to get my juices moving. Have a cup of coffee. I have great faith in coffee. (Laughs.) There's an element of theater in advertising. When I'm presenting the stuff, I will give the impression of really loving it a lot.

It's amazing how much your attitude toward something is conditioned by what other people say about it, what other people's opinions are. If somebody who is very important starts to frown, your heart can sink. If you've done this a couple of times, you know this may not be the end of the world. He may have noticed that the girl has on a purple dress and he hates purple. Meanwhile you have to continue. You get yourself up. Some commercials require singing and dancing to present. It's like being in front of any audience. When you begin to lose your audience, there's cold feet, sweat.

He's not happy with the way the bear's moving. You don't know why he's unhappy. Clients have different styles. They can't articulate it. They begin to thrash around. You have to remain calm and figure out what's bothering him. Then you light on it and say, "We can change that." And he says, "Oh yeah? Then it's okay." Occasionally we present to people who are crazy.

Originally I was a copywriter. I sat in a room and it was very simple. I would go to the boss and he'd tell me what he wanted. I'd go back to my room and try to write it, and get mad and break pencils and pound on the wall.

Then finish it and take it in to him, and change it and change it, and then I'd go back and write it over again and take it in to him and he'd change it again, and I'd take it back. This would happen thirty or forty times and then we'd move to another man. He'd put his feet on the desk and change it again.

Now that the burden of work is greater, I take home less. I've gotten more and more good at erasing things from my mind. That's why I leave myself little notes on the typewriter. I just got back from a three-day week-end and I can hardly find the office. (Laughs.) I erased it completely from my mind. I think it's a sign of health. When you're doing creative work, you should think about it all the time. When you're doing administrative work, you should think about it as little as possible.

There's the contemplative mind and the business mind. The good businessman is always willing to make decisions on incomplete evidence. I came out of a whole contemplative mode. It was hard for me to learn that you have to make a decision. Advertising is terrific for spot decisions. I think I make more decisions in a week than my clients make in a year. I've changed a lot, I think.

Often the products are pretty much the same—which is why there's advertising. If the products were very different, you wouldn't need the skill you do. In some way, I think, advertising is very good for any writer, because of this whole image-making thing. Before, I had a tendency to get very word-involved. It's very like when you program computers. It's breaking everything down in this strange new way. Then you learn it and it becomes natural to you—seeing pictures instead of arguments.

I'm glad I didn't go into philosophy. I don't think I have the right personality for it. I think it involves talent. Also, it involves a language that fewer and fewer people can speak. Finally, you're speaking to yourself. Advertising is a more social business, which is also frustrating. I'm not sure I'm happy in advertising, but I don't think philosophy would have been heaven for me. I think I'd rather write—movies or books. For some reason I don't do that.

Advertising's a fashion business. There are five stages. "Who is this guy, John Fortune?" The second stage: "Gee, it would be great if we could get that guy, what's his name? John Fortune." The third stage: "If we could only get John Fortune." The fourth stage: "I'd like to get a young John Fortune." The fifth stage: "Who's John Fortune?" There are no old writers.

There's a tremendous threat from young writers. So much so that old writers just aren't around. When an older writer gets fired, he just doesn't get another job. I think there's a farm out in the Middle West or something where they're tethered. I don't know what happens to them.

You should start moving when you're about thirty-five. If you're not in a supervisory position around then, you're in trouble. By the time you're forty, you should be a creative director. That's the guy with a lot of people under him and nobody over him on the creative staff. But there's only room for a certain number of people who tell other people what to do.

They're all vice presidents. They're given that title for business reasons. Clients like to deal with vice presidents. Also, it's a cheap thing to give somebody. Vice presidents get fired with great energy and alacrity. (Laughs.) And they get jobs doing public relations for Trujillo or somebody. Or they go out and form their own company which you never hear of again.

There's a kind of cool paradox in advertising. There's a pressure toward the safe, tried and true that has worked in the past. But there's a tremendous need in the agency business for the fresh and the new, to differentiate this one agency from another. Writers are constantly torn between these two goals: selling the product and selling themselves. If you do what they tell you, you're screwed. If you don't do what they tell you, you're fired. You're constantly trying to make it, fighting. The struggle that goes on . . .

It becomes silly to some people, but poignant too. You see people fighting to save a little nuance in a formula commercial. There's a type called "slice of life." Somebody I know called it "slice of death." It is the standard commercial that starts out in the kitchen. Two people are arguing about a product. "How come you're getting your wash so white?" "I use this." "How can that be as good as this?" "Because it contains . . ." And she gives the reasons why it's better. It follows the formula. People are forced to write it because it's effective. But you see people fighting for some little touch they've managed to work in. So they can put it on their reel and get another job. Somebody will say, "Aha, look at the way it worked there." You want the thing to be better.

People at parties will come up and denounce me. There's a lot of paranoia about the power of advertising. They say we're being controlled, manipulated. Sometimes I enjoy playing the devil's advocate, so I'll exaggerate it: "We take human needs and control them." (Laughs.) I have an active fantasy life—not during the workday, because it's coming at me so fast. Many of my fantasies have to do with the control of society. Very elaborate technological-type fantasies: a benign totalitarianism controlled by me.

Actually, my career choice in advertising, which I've drifted into, is connected with the fantasy of power. I have a sense of slowly increasing power, but the limits are very frustrating. I feel I want to do more, but I feel restraints within the system and myself. I think I hold myself back more than the system does. The system is easy to work within if you're willing to, if you're smart enough . . .

What would our country be like without advertising? I don't know. (Laughs.) It would be a different country, I think.

POSTSCRIPT: *At a pub in mid-Manhattan frequented by advertising people, he said, "I have a recurring dream in which I'm a stand-up comedian. I'm standing on a stage with a blue spotlight on me, talking. I begin by telling jokes. Gradually, I begin to justify my life. I can't quite see the audience. The light becomes more and more intense. I can't remember what I say. I usually end up crying. This dream I've had maybe three, four times."*

ARNY FREEMAN

He is a dapper sixty-three. He appears a good twenty years younger. He has been a character actor—"I am a supporting player"—in New York for almost thirty years. He has worked in all fields: on Broadway, off-Broadway, radio, television, and "a few pictures here and there.

"And suddenly you become—a friend of mine audi-

tioned for a TV commercial. They said they wanted an Arny Freeman-type. He said, 'Why don't you call Arny?' They said, 'No, no, no, we can't use him. He's been used too much!' I was overexposed in TV commercials.

"I didn't do commercials until about '62, '63. Actors didn't do commercials. Beautiful blondes, Aryan models, six feet three, did commercials. A friend of mine told me, 'They're starting to look for people who look like people.' This one time I went down, they were looking at people all day. I happened to hit them right. One of the guys said, 'He has a French quality about him.' It was for Byrrh, a French apéritif, which is similar to Cinzano."

I did this commercial in '64. A thing called Byrrh* on the Rocks. I have a citation. They have festivals for commercials. Isn't that laughable? (Laughs.) It won five international awards—in Cannes, in Dublin, in Hollywood, in New York, in London. The goddamn thing was a local commercial. I walk in the bar and ask for Byrrh on the rocks. Everybody turns and laughs and looks at me. The bartender ... It was played in every station, day and night.

This commercial became so successful that I couldn't walk down the street. I now know what it's like to be famous, and I don't want it. I couldn't walk down the street. I'd be mobbed. People would grab me, "Hey, Byrrh on the rocks! You're the guy!" They'd pin me against the wall and the guy would say to his wife, "Hey, look who I got here!" I once got out of the subway at Times Square and a guy grabbed me and slammed me against the wall. (Laughs.) Crowds of people gathered around. My wife was terrified. They were all screaming, "Byrrh on the rocks!" Because of that little TV box.

They don't know your name but once they see your face, you're so familiar, you belong in their home. It really was terrifying, but I enjoyed it very much. It was great. It was like being a short Rock Hudson. (Laughs.) Sure, there's a satisfaction. I like a certain amount of it. I enjoy having people say complimentary things. I'm a gregarious person. I stop and tell them anything they want to know about making commercials, about the business and so on. But at times it does interfere with your life.

* Pronounced "beer."

I took a vacation. I went down to San Juan. There's nobody in San Juan but New Yorkers. I wouldn't go to the beach. The minute I stepped out, somebody would say, "Hey! Hey! Don't I know you? Ain't you the guy . . . ?" In the early days of live TV they couldn't figure out where they knew you from. Some guy would say, "Hey, you from Buffalo?" I'd say, "No." "Well, goddamn, there's a guy in my home town looks just like you." I'd say, "Did you ever watch 'T Men in Action' or 'The Big Story' on TV?" "Oh yeah! You're the guy!"

I came out of a movie house one day. I hadn't gone more than a few feet when two guys moved in on me, pushed me against the wall. I thought I was being held up. They flashed badges. They were detectives. One said, "Would you mind coming back into the lobby?" I said, "What for?" "We'd like to talk to you." So they moved me back and there was a woman, screaming, "That's him, he's the one!" Somebody had stolen her purse in the movie house and she fingered me. I played a gangster on TV in those days. The boss would say, "Hey, Shorty, do this." And I'd say, "Yeah boss." They were all alike. I asked the woman if she had seen 'T Men in Action' on Thursday. This was Saturday. "Oh, my God," she said, "That's where I saw you." (Laughs.) The dicks couldn't do enough. They drove me home in their car.

People still come up to me, even to this day. They're generally very polite. They say, "Excuse me, I don't mean to impose, I just want to tell you that I enjoy your commercials very much." Every once in a while I run into somebody who says, "I saw you in *The Great Sebastian*,"* or, "I saw you in *Cactus Flower*." But everybody doesn't go to the theater. Everybody has television.† People ask

* A play in which he appeared, starring Alfred Lunt and Lynn Fontanne.

† From *Notes on a Cowardly Lion* (New York: Alfred A. Knopf, 1969), John Lahr's biography of his father Bert Lahr, the highly gifted clown: "Advertisements for potato chips have made more people aware of his face than ever before. He invented a catchword for the product—'de-lay-cious'—turning his comedy easily from art to marketing. Cab drivers stop their cabs to yell. 'Bet you can't eat just one.' Grandmothers accost him like one of their own to ask if he really eats potato chips. These commercials, amounting to work more easily measured

for my autograph on the street, anywhere. Quite often someone will say he saw me in such and such a play. But it's really the commercials.

I'm a working actor. If you want to work, you have to do everything. To me, acting is a craft, a way of life. I have never been obsessed with the sickening drive inside to become a star. Possibly it's because I came into it very late in life. I was thirty-seven years old when I became a professional actor. I was a little more realistic about life. I knew the percentage of somebody who is five feet six and a half inches tall, who is dark and ethnic looking. The chances of becoming a star were quite remote. I've conditioned myself not to want it, because the odds against it are too great.

Since I came to New York, I've never been out of work. I've had only one relatively poor period, because my face became too familiar in television commercials. Where it got kinda lean, you begin to wonder if maybe you've gotten too old or whether you're worn-out. Through all these years, I went from one thing into another. I'd finished a play, there'd be a movie. In-between there'd be TV plays, there'd be commercials. I've signed with an office, all they do is TV commercials. Financially I'm not concerned. I have a little better than a hundred grand in the market. I want to go live in Mexico, but who wants to stop working?

"When I first came to New York I did what everybody else did. You took your pictures, you got your eight-by-ten glossies, and you called up or you wrote a letter, and you made an appointment to see an agent or the casting director. I'd write a letter and I'd say, 'This is my picture. This is what I've done. I would appreciate an interview at your

in minutes than days, earns him $75,000 a year, far more than a season on Broadway. . . . He is proud to have survived and succeeded in this newest facet of show business, the television commercial. But he is perplexed. His laughter was meant for people, not merchandise. The paradox has been hard for him to resolve. Even though his commercials are excellent and he has devised many of their comic situations, he is suspicious, 'I wonder if these ads have been good for my career? Here's a strange thing, John: after all these years of struggle, the biggest success I've had is in these trite commercials. It's stupid.' "

*convenience.' Invariably I'd get a letter back saying,
'Come in on such-and-such a date.' After you've done
that, you'd drop a note saying, 'I'm just reminding you,
I'm back in town, I'm available.' Now it's all done through
agents.*

"I've never submitted to any kind of cattle call. Some
agents will call all the actors they know and send them
down. So there's hundreds of actors scuffling, trying to get
in. I have an appointment at a given hour. I'm ushered
in and treated with respect. What governs your getting that
job—so many things over which you have no control. Often they say, 'Gee, he's fine for the part.' They get a different star and you're put into juxtaposition to him. Suddenly they say, 'Instead of using Arny, we're gonna get a
big fat guy.' These are the vagaries of the business. You
learn to live with them. With a financial cushion it's easier,
I suppose." (Laughs.)

If you're not a star, there is humiliation and degrada-
tion—if you allow it to happen to you. People who do the
hiring can be very rude at times. You don't find that too
much in the theater, because the theater still has a certain
nicety to it. You find it in TV commercial casting. They're
deluged. Many people, having seen the commercials, say,
"Hell, I could do that." You take a guy playing a truckdriver. So a truckdriver says, "Hell, I can do that." It's always been an overcrowded field simply because there was
never enough work for actors. Residuals, that's the thing
that's kept actors going through the years when there
wasn't any work.

I recently auditioned for a thing I'll know about Monday. We go to Florida to shoot. It's a comedy thing. He's
the king of gypsies and he's talking about this particular
rent-a-car system of trucks. There was a fella ahead of me
who had a great handlebar mustache and a big thick head
of hair. He looked like the most gorgeous gypsy in the
world. (Laughs.) My only hope is that this guy couldn't
read—and he couldn't. So I went in there with all the confidence in the world, 'cause I do all these cheesy accents.
My agent called that they were all excited. I'll know on
Monday.

I have one I'm shooting Tuesday for a bank. They
called up and said, "Do you happen to have a derby?" I
have one but I've never had the nerve to wear it. So I went

to the audition with the derby on, and I had a pin-striped gray suit with a weskit. I was exactly what they wanted. I vacillate from little French or Italians, little maître d's to an elegant banker to a wild gypsy. These accents—in radio they called it "Continental."

Thursday I went up to Syracuse, another fella and I. We did a commercial for a little home snow plow. We're out in this freezing, bitter cold. We spent from eight in the morning till five at night out in the snow. We were neighbors. He was shoveling snow and I came out of my garage, very dapper, with a derby on. I flip up the garage door and bring out my little machine and push the button and it starts. I do a debonair throw with the scarf. As I pass him with my little motorized snow cleaner, he looks up and I give him an up-yours, one-upmanship. And that's the commercial. We had a hell of a good time all day long. You would think it'd be murder in the cold snow, but we enjoyed it very much. The difference between this and theater is it's over in one day and it's more pinpointed. But it's still acting.

I used to think to myself, This is not a life. A man ought to be something more important, ought to be a doctor or a lawyer or something that does something for other people. To be an actor is to be a selfish person. It's a matter of ego, I think. Many actors make the mistake of thinking this is life. I have in recent years found my work somewhat meaningful. So many people have stopped me on the street and said, "I can't tell you how much I enjoy what you've done." If, for a moment or two, he can turn on his TV set and see you in a show or a commercial and it makes him a little happier—I think that's important.

I think of myself as someone who's rational, who isn't wild—except when I get certain comedic things to do. It is something bigger than life. It's still rooted in truth, but it's just a little bit larger. Rather than play comedy with a capital C, I love to find the qualities in a person, in a character, that are alive and human—even in a commercial.

RIP TORN

*He came to the big city from a small town in East Texas.
Because of some manner, inexplicable to those who hire
actors, he has been declared "troublesome." Though he
has an excellent reputation as an actor, he has—to many
producers and sponsors—a "reputation" as a person.*

*"I have certain flaws in my make-up. Something called
rise-ability. I get angry easily. I get saddened by things
easily. I figured, as an actor, I could use my own kind of
human machinery. The theater would be the place for my
flaws to be my strengths. I thought theater was kind of a
celebration of man, with situations that reflected man's
extremely comic and extremely tragic experiences. I say,
'Yeah, I can do that. That's the way I see life.' Since I
feel, I can use my feelings at work. In a lot of other types
of work I can sweat—I sweat as an actor—but I can't use
my feelings. So I guess that's why I became an actor. But
I found out that's not what they want. (laughs.) They
want you to be their Silly Putty."*

Actors have become shills. I remember doin' a television
show, oh, about ten years ago—I haven't worked on network television for about eight years. I was smokin' a
cigar. I was playing a Quantrell-type character, so I had a
long Cuban cigar. I got up on a horse and we had to
charge down a hill. It was a long shot. The director and
the producer both hollered, "Cut! Cut! What're you doin'
with that cigar in your mouth?" I said, "I don't naturally
smoke cigars, but I'm doing it for the role. They didn't
have cigarettes during the Civil War." They said, "You
don't understand." I said, "Oh, now I do understand. But
this isn't a cigarette program." The sponsor was Pontiac.
But this show had resale value. They didn't want a Civil
War character smoking a cigar because they might resell
it to a cigarette company and my act might damage their
commodity. They insisted I get rid of the cigar. We're
nothin' but goddamned shills.

An actor is used to sell products primarily. There's good
money in that. More than that, actors have become shills

for politicians, even for some I like. I remember one of them talking of actors as political commodities. They want an actor to be the boss's boy.

I don't have any contempt for people who do commercials. I've never been able to get even that kind of work. A friend of mine gave me a name, somebody to see. She said, "You'll have to shave your beard." This was long before beards and long hair were "in." I said, "It's only a voice-over, what difference does it make?" She said, "You won't get in." So I went up to read a Brylcreem commercial. There must have been forty people in the control booth. There usually are about five. It was as if everybody from all the offices of the agency were there. I didn't get the job. They came to look at the freak. I went around and read about three or four commercials. They liked what I did, but I never got any work.

I don't know, maybe you don't bow to them correctly. If I could learn that certain kind of bow, maybe I'd try it. It's like the army. There's a ruling in the army called "insubordination through manner." You don't do anything that could really be said, "I'm gonna bring that man up on company punishment. I'm gonna throw the book at 'im." It's his manner. He'll be saying, "Yes sir" and "No sir." But there's something within his corporal being makes you say something in his manner is insubordinate. He doesn't really kiss the golden spot in the right way. There's something about him. In a horse you say, "He hasn't quite been broken." He doesn't quite respond immediately to command or to the reins.

Years ago, when I worked in Hollywood someone said, "You don't understand. This town is run on fear. You don't appear to be afraid." Everyone has some kind of fears. I don't think the antithesis of love and happiness is hatred. I think it's fear. I think that's what kills everything. There's nothing wrong with righteous anger. But if you speak straight to them, even the sound is strange. I don't know how to deal with this ... I went to a party. A big producer gave it. It was alongside the pool. Must have been 150 people there. They had a diving board up in a tree. I remember when I was a kid, I could dive off a thing like that and do a double flip. Somebody said, "You never did that in your whole life." I said, "I guess I could do it now." He said, "That could be arranged." They got me some trunks. I said, "We might as well make a bet on

this, I'll bet you a dollar." I should have bet him a grand.
All the people at this party watched me. I got up there
and I did it. The guy very angrily gave me a dollar and
nobody would speak to me the rest of the night. It was as
if I'd done some offensive thing. He was some bigwig and
had meant to humiliate me. By showing him I wasn't bullshitting, I had committed some social gaffe. I should have
taken the insult and said, "I guess you're right." I was
never able to do that.

A few years later, I was reading a Pan Am commercial.
The man who wrote it came out of the control booth and
said, "I remember you. I remember you around that pool
in Hollywood. You thought you were pretty big in those
days, didn't you? You don't remember *me,* do you?" I
guess he was one of those who didn't talk to me that
night. He said, "You may not think artistry hasn't gone
into the writing of this material. I want to tell you that
twenty lines of this commercial has more thought, more
artistry, more time spent, more money spent than is spent
on your usual Broadway play." I said, "I believe you."
Then he said, "Give us a voice level, please." I said, "Pan
Am flies to—" He cut me off. "When you say that world
'Pan Am'—" I said, "I'm just giving you a voice level. I'm
not giving you a performance yet." So I tried again. And
he said, "Not much better." He just wanted to cave my
head in. Do you think he was getting even for my social
gaffe? (Laughs.) Me being me?

Who's running things now? The salesman. You must be
a salesman to reflect that culture, to be a success. People
that write commercial jingles make more money than people that write operas. They're more successful by somebody's standards. That somebody is the salesman and he's
taken over. To the American public, an actor is unsuccess-
ful unless he makes money.

At my grandfather's funeral, one of my uncles came
forward and said to me, "No matter what you've become,
we still love you. We would like you to know you have a
place with us. So why don't you stop that foolishness and
come home?" They look upon me as a failure.

The myth is: if you do commercials and you become financially successful, then you will do artistic work. I don't
know who's ever done it. People say, "You've had your
chance." I was offered over sixty television series. But I always look upon 'em as shills for products. I was always

told, "If you go ahead and do this, you will be able to have the theater. You will be able to do the roles you want to do." I know of no one who was able to do the other work he felt was his calling.

A lot of young actors come up and say, "I have respect for you because you never sold out." I've sold out a lot of times. We all have to make accommodations with the kind of society we live in. We gotta pay the rent. We do whatever we can. I've done jobs I wasn't particularly proud of. You do the best you can with that. You try to make it a little better for your own self-respect. That's what's changed in the nature of work in this country—the lack of pride in the work itself. A man's life is his work.

Why, you don't even have the kind of carpenters . . . He says, "Aw, fuck it." You know they're not even gonna countersink something when they should. They don't have the pleasure in the work any more. Even in Mexico, there was something unique about the road work. The curbing is not laid out by machine, it's handmade. So there's little irregularities. That's why the eye is rested even by the curbing in Mexico. And walls. Because it's craftsmanship. You see humanity in a chair. And you know seven thousand didn't come out in one day. It was made by some man's hands. There's artistry in that, and that's what makes mankind happier. You work out of necessity, but in your work, you gotta have a little artistry too.

EDDIE JAFFE

I can't relax. 'Cause when you ask a guy who's fifty-eight years old, "What does a press agent do?" you force me to look back and see what a wasted life I've had. My hopes, my aspirations—what I did with them. What being a press agent does to you. What have I wound up with? Rooms full of clippings.

Being called a press agent or a public relations man is really a matter of how much you get paid. You could say he's an advocate in the court of public opinion. But it's not really that deep. It's a person who attracts attention to his client. I project myself into another person's place. I say to them, "Why can't you do this?" Or that? Bringing up all the ambitions I'd have in their place. The one thing every press agent must do is get a client. If you don't get a client, you're not a press agent.

The occupation molds your personality. Publicity does that to people too. Calling an editor on the phone, asking favors, can be humiliating. Being refused a favor disturbs me, depresses me. That's why I could never resign myself to being a press agent. Many are not aware they're being turned down. They wouldn't develop colitis like I did. That's the way I act, emotionally, with my gut. That's why I went to the analyst.

He's been at it for forty-two years. He has worked for comedians, singers, strippers, industries, governments, evangelists, and families of dead gangsters. "Press agenting covers a multitude of sins."

When he first began, "I went around to these guys' offices. Most of them were gone. The landlord said, 'Hey kid, want to make ten bucks? Find out where they moved, they stuck us for rent.' About 1930, I looked in the phonebook under press agents, there were maybe eight or ten. Now there are pages of them. Here I was at the beginning of the industry and I wound up a little behind where I started.

"Some con men sold me a concession at Billy Rose's Fort Worth Frontier Centennial. I lost my inheritance, a couple of thousand bucks. That was '36. To avoid being arrested for vagrancy, I said, 'I'm a press agent.' They couldn't prove I wasn't. So I became a press agent."

While I was working a carnival in Norfolk, Virginia, I got a client, Adrienne the Psychic. The guy who owned the theater had a brother who was chief of detectives. He inspected the whorehouses and put a leaflet on every bed. I said, "Do you have any crimes you can't solve?" They'd just arrested a guy who confessed. He was in a jail fifty miles away. He gave me the guy's name. I went to the Rotarians and they said they'd have Adrienne as the guest of honor if she could solve the murder. So I coached Adrienne. She said, "Don't tell me. I'm a psychic." The editor of the paper was all set to give us the front page. A guy in the audience asked her the question. She gave the wrong initials and I didn't get a goddamn line. I got the name for her but she wouldn't take it. Some psychic!

I made a deal with Margie Kelly, the stripper. I took her to the World's Fair and arranged for her to call de Valera from the Irish Pavilion. I was going to get tremendous space in the *Daily Mirror*. Unfortunately the editor was Irish. He saw the spread: Stripper Margie Kelly Calls de Valera. He said, "I'm not gonna let any broad use Ireland and de Valea to get space." We didn't get a line.

I handled Margie Hart. I made her the poor man's Garbo. Margie was a redhead. So I went to Washington to petition the postmaster to show George Washington on the stamps with red hair. I was getting pages everywhere. When Margie was getting in the thousands, she didn't want to pay me. I had to sue her. So I decided to retire.

It was fun doing publicity for strippers. I got fantastic space for a girl named Babette Bardot. A college professor did a study of strippers. We announced that Babette was going to do a study of college professors, to find out what *their* hang-ups were. She wrote to the SEC asking permission for a public offering to sell stock in herself. She said she had exposed her assets very fully. We got quite a bit of space with the letter. I decided there's a direct relationship between sex and our economy. So I sent a stripper down to Wall Street. She said the economy's getting better because they mobbed her.

From strippers I got into a thing called Roller Derby: Hell On Wheels. By mistake we were booked in the same arena with a revival meeting. I tried to make a compromise—to have them go in jointly: Hell on Wheels and Save Your Soul. No go. I started getting into more conventional PR. I've handled accounts from Indonesia to U.S. Steel.

During the first World's Fair I handled the Iceland Pavilion. We were opening the pavilion. I looked over the commissioner's speech: how much dried herring and goose feathers they import to the U.S. each year. I said, "This won't get you in the papers." So I added a line. This was at the time of the Rome-Berlin-Tokyo Axis. So I said, "Here's to the Reykjavik-Washington Axis. Iceland is prepared to send troops any time to defend Washington. (Laughs.) We hope Washington feels the same way about us." That got in all the papers. It was forgotten for about two years. Cordell Hull gets a call one night from the *Mirror*, "Did you know the U.S. has a treaty to defend Iceland from the Germans?" Hull said, "What the hell are you talking about?" The *Mirror* had a headline about it. The Washington Treaty was based solely on my little publicity release.

Your ego affects the economics to publicity. I once handled Billy Daniels. I handled him when he was at the bottom of the ladder and when he was at the top. He said, "I'd like to make a new deal with you—pay you five percent of my income." He's getting four thousand dollars a day for ten days. My God, five percent of that is two thousand bucks. Great. But guys told me, "Billy Daniels! He hasn't paid his last six press agents." I said, "You don't understand. I'd rather not get two thousand dollars from Billy Daniels than get seventy-five bucks from a guy who pays me." It's the *idea* that you're making two thousand dollars. That's part of the magic, the lure of the thing.

I didn't really start making any money until I went to an analyst. He said, "You gotta come five days a week." I said, "I can't afford to." He said. "That's the first problem we'll solve." He went into the reasons for my not making any money. Being a publicity man is a confession of a weakness. It's for people who don't have the guts to get attention for themselves. You spend your whole life telling the world how great somebody else is. This is frustrating.

My dream was to establish a star, and from then on I would be taken care of. I would always get paid. The truth is: it's psychologically important for stars to get rid of people who helped them get where they are. The client is the child and the press agent's the parent. The child has to grow up and leave the nest. It's part of living. They're unknown, they need Eddie Jaffe. When they're known, they need Rogers and Cowan, who never dropped a coat in all the years they handled stars. They hold the client's coat. One reason they get the business is they get their client on the Hollywood party list. People have different needs at different times in their careers.

I was hired to cover maybe forty radio shows. The guy said, "Cover the 'Phil Baker Show.' " "What do I do?" He said, "You be the first guy there after the show's over and you say, 'Phil, that was great.' God help you if somebody gets there ahead of you." That's part of being a press agent for stars. That's what they need. They can afford it. And they're paying for it.

A gangster said, "I wish you'd help me. The papers are botherin' the hell out of me." I said, "Who's clean in your family?" He said, "My brother-in-law. He lost his arm and leg in the war, works as a clothing presser, and makes twenty-five bucks a week." I said, "Make him the official spokesman. They won't bother you. Your big danger is one of the mob will push a photographer and you'll have a picture in the paper." "How will we avoid that?" I said, "Very simple. Hire a Pinkerton. If anybody's gonna push a cameraman, the guy's in uniform. They can push. They're not a mob."

Punishment by publicity is more serious than punishment by law. If you were indicted tomorrow for a crime, the punishment through publicity is more severe than any jail sentence you might receive. Everybody has a lawyer, but very few have a public relations man.

I used to work for John Jacob Astor. I got a call from his lawyer saying he ran over somebody. So I called all the papers and said, "This is John Jacob Astor's press agent. I got a great story for you. He just hit a woman crossing the street." They said, "Why don't you get lost with that shit. He gets enough space." They didn't play the story at all. I tried to make them think I wanted in, so they didn't put it in.

I spent most of my life learning techniques that are of no value any more. Magazines, newspapers—print. I'm not oriented to television as I was to print. The biggest impact today is TV. This has helped reduce the need for press agentry. A client will come to me and say, "I want to be a star." In the old days, maybe I'd get her in *Life*. Today on the Carson show you could get more attention than I could have gotten her in a year. As press agentry becomes part of a bigger and bigger world it becomes more routinized. It's a mechanical thing today. It's no longer the opportunity to do stunts. They don't work any more. Much of what I've been doing all these years is not as potent as in the old days.

Most guys in my category have eight, ten clients. If you have less, you're in trouble. You can't depend on one or two, no matter how much they pay, 'cause you can lose 'em. One day I lost three clients that were paying me each over twelve thousand dollars a year. I lost Cinerama, Indonesia, and the Singer Company. This is thirty-six thousand dollars a year. I had years I made a hundred thousand. There's a law of making money. You never regard it as something temporary, and you live up to the scale. But

in this work, you don't build anything. If I had a little
candy store and I built it up to a bigger store, I might
have sold it for a quarter of a million dollars. Who do I
sell my clippings to?

RICHARD MANN

*He is fifty-three years old. He has been an installment
dealer for twenty years. "I sell credit. I'm not selling
goods. The firms I purchase from do that. I'm in business
for myself. I call on people. I sell them right in the home.
I bring merchandise to them." He puts in a seventy-hour
week.*

"Many people I had used to be in the ghetto, poor
blacks. When the riots came, all my accounts were on the
West Side.* Three of my customers were burnt out. I
tried to reach 'em by phone and I couldn't. I called many
of them up and asked them to send the money in by mail,
and they did. Many of them said, 'Richard, please don't
come. It's rough here.'

"When I used to walk by and hear some ten-year-old
Negro kid say a few choice words to me, I used to burn. I
couldn't stand it. I would pass a house where I'd see two
fifteen-year-old kids playing handball. I'd say, 'Should I go
or shouldn't I? Should I give it a pass?' I'd sit there and
burn. They may well have been just harmless kids. But
when I came down the stairs, they could be behind the
door.

"We sat for three days calling each other, installment
dealers, those who worked in that area. Could we go?
Could we go in pairs? Was it possible? I bought a lot of
accounts receivable from other men who were going out
of business. I had a little boy, black, about ten years old,
he used to go with me. His stepdad made these calls for
me on Saturday and Sunday. I collected quite a bit of it.
Little by little I moved out of the area. Now I'm out of it
completely.

"The areas I go to now are blue-collar and Southern

* The outbreaks in poor black communities following the
assassination of Martin Luther King.

*white suburbs—lower-middle-class white. My customers
now are mostly honkies. (Laughs.) A honky is someone
who is anti-black and he moved to the outskirts of town to
get away from the Negro. He hates all change, all progress. When his wife says, 'Bring some shirts for my husband,' I bring him three striped shirts with long collars.
He becomes furious. 'What the hell do you think I am,
some hippie punk? I don't wear shirts like that.' (Laughs.)
Save your white shirts, they're comin' back."*

I'm an offshoot of the old peddler. He bought a few
things, went out in the country with a horse and wagon
and sold it. His customers didn't have cash, so they paid
him in eggs. Many times people would say, "I can't pay
you anything," and he'd say, "You're good for the money,
I'll come every month or so."

Later on, as we become friendly, they have more confidence in me. They ask me to bring them things, electrical
appliances, household gadgets. If they want larger
items—if a customer wants to buy a kitchen set, table and
four chairs, she goes to the store, she picks it out. The
price is given to her, say $150. It's sent out and I'm billed
for the cost of that. I pay the bill and collect it from her.
I'm connected to the places that I bring the customer to.

A lot of these people need me. They need me psychologically. My wife has said, "You give your customers a hell
of a lot more than I get. I go to the store, I get a surly
clerk, I get a miserable manager." I go to these people, I
say, "Hello, Mrs. Smith. How's your husband. How's your
daughter-in-law?" I call her up, I tell her an off-color joke
once in a while. Most times you sell your personality.

If I'm really an enterprising entrepreneur, I see she
hasn't got an Osterizer, I see she needs drapes, curtains.
Or that her sofa's falling apart or that her carpet's wearing out. Or that I'm sitting in a broken chair. Or it's cold
outside and I know she's the type of a person who doesn't
shop on Michigan Avenue, and she hasn't bought her winter coat. I observe these things if I'm to be successful in
this business. I'm successful, I believe.

She's paying well, she's down to fifty dollars. You see
she hasn't got a four-slice toaster. So you bring it in.
"Here." Sweeten up the account. "We've got these beautiful toasters in. You've got a big family, six kids. How do
you make toast for 'em?" She says, "I had one and I had

trouble with it." Which is more truth than poetry, because many of these electrical appliances just fall apart.

If the toaster's twenty-nine dollars, now she owes me seventy nine—plus tax. Her payments haven't gone up. I'm just holding her for another three weeks. So I've got eight weeks of collections, eight ten-dollar payments. If she's slow in paying, I don't sell her anything. I'm trying to get out from under, to get what she owes me. If they're good customers, I want to keep 'em buying, continually owing me. The worst thing that can happen is for a good customer to pay up her bill.* Ach!! That's terrible! You can't ever get in to see her again. She pays you up for a reason: she doesn't want to buy from you any more.

The more she's in debt to you—

The better it is.

That $150 kitchen set may wind up setting her back $300?

No. She'll wind up paying $150 for that. When she buys on time, she pays one and a half percent carrying charge. This is all over, Sears, Ward's—it comes to nineteen percent a year. It's very difficult to figure out compound interest. It could drive you crazy.

You work on recommendations. You have a customer you get along with very well. She says, "Why don't you call on my nextdoor neighbor? She likes my drapes." I'm gambling. I gamble on a person's outside. I know nothing about their character. I gamble on what other people have told me. I have many losses.

I gave a bill to a collection lawyer this morning. She owed seventeen hundred dollars. I bought the account, discounted at ninety percent. I paid the man seventeen hundred less $170. That was four years ago. She was sup-

---

* Many years ago I conducted a radio news commentary program, whose sponsor was a credit clothing house. I was fired in one week. As the sponsor put it. "For Chrissake, his listeners barge into the store, payin' *cash* for everything! *Cash,* for Chrissake! I need that kind like a hole in the head. I want the element that buy on credit, no money down. What the hell do you think I'm in business for? Get rid of this guy, he's trouble."

posed to pay this out at the rate of twenty dollars a week. Lately she won't answer the door. She's called me a few choice names. She capped it off doing the worst thing she could, "You dumb Jew, I'm gonna give you two dollars a week and that's all." I threw the check she gave me and I said, "Forget it," and I walked out. I remembered that famous quote: "Free at last, thank God, I'm free of you, at last." (Laughs.) She used to make me sweat for this money—terribly. Used to make me feel in the position of a beggar.

I hate to collect. Collecting is a terrible, a horrible thing. I've always deprecated it. I know my children look down at it. To them it's demeaning, it's exploitive. So naturally I'm defensive about it. Actually, I just hate it. The people who say, "Boy! I'd like to have my husband have a job like that, go around collecting money all day long." I said, "I wish to hell your husband had a job like that! Give me a factory job instead of knocking on doors!" The strongest thing on me—I haven't got a muscle on me—is my knuckles. I can put that door through. From knocking on doors.

I've told my wife many a time, "When I come home at night, no matter if we've had a fight, come to the door and say, 'Hi,' and kiss me. Whatever you say after that, it's okay." Because all day long I knock on doors and say, "This is Dick" or "Mr. Mann," and all I hear is "Aw, shit!" I hear it through the whole house. (Laughs.) Can you imagine what happens to you, hearing this all day long? "Aw, shit!" Nobody loves a collector. They love a salesman. When you sell the merchandise, the honeymoon is on. But it's over when you come to collect.

I don't call people in advance when I visit. I start calling about fifteen minutes to eight. I get many people bitching about coming too early. I have to, because I have a lot of work. People who pay me on my account, I ask them if there's anything else they need: curtains, drapes, anything. I bring it to 'em the next week or two weeks, whenever I call. I finish about five. Saturday, I get up at six thirty and come home eight, nine at night. Another week, I sit down and make deadbeat calls. It's a miserable thing. My family used to leave the house when I made these calls. I could wind up throwing the phone against the wall. It's very, very discouraging.

"I used to work in a furniture store. Two years without a day off. So I decided to go in business for myself. You're never beholden to anybody. You always have a buck in your pocket. This is the easiest way, because you have no overhead. You don't have a store, you don't have employees. You pay no rent, no insurance . . ."

I couldn't sell you an automobile, but just about everything else. I've sold diamond rings, I've sole mink coats. I have people with beautiful homes. Many of my customers have good incomes. Why do they buy from somebody like me? There's a variety of reasons. A lot of them got a fart in their brain. They cannot go on shopping. They become confused by these large shopping centers. They're confused by the multitude, the plethora of things. It just overwhelms them. It's much easier to buy from somebody like me. If they want a coat, I bring two or three. If they want a ring, I bring one or two or three.

There's a customer who's shy. She would really like to tell people off, but when she goes into a large establishment, she's shy. She's overwhelmed by Marshall Field's, so she tells me off in no uncertain terms what she wants, how she wants it, and don't bring me this or that. It boosts their ego. In their house they are queen. I'm the one with the cap in the hand.

When I'm a salesman in a furniture store, I speak from a position of strength: We have this beautiful, gorgeous place that we built for you. Here is what we have. This is what they're using. When I come in, I can't say, "This is what *they're* using." I've been told a few times, "I don't care what *they're* using. It's what *I* want. I want white shirts."

It's a dying occupation. There are older men, sixty-five, seventy, who are just dabbling. They want to get out of it, so they sell their accounts. They're very good accounts 'cause they've had them twenty years. For me, it's a bonanza.

In the old days people in ethnic neighborhoods just got off the boat. They couldn't speak English. Young punks that were store clerks would look down upon them. The man who had a smattering of the language would go into the homes and people would welcome him with open arms. Here's a man they could occasionally tell off.

This whole business has fallen absolutely into disuse in

the past ten years. I know of no young man who's gone into it. To them, it's demeaning. I once asked my son to help me. His wife came over and told me she didn't want her husband to help me exploit people. She believes I exploit people. Of course, she believes anybody who makes a profit exploits people. So you ask, "What is not exploitation? One percent? Two percent? General Motors?" I don't feel I'm an exploiter. I'm a capitalist. I believe capitalism is the greatest economic system there is.

I'm in a hurry. I have obligations, I'm always trying to beat time. I'm dealing with people, most of them are dependent on their paycheck. It doesn't last past Saturday. If you don't come, you're not gonna get it. The people will honestly tell you, "I gave it to somebody else, the insurance man." Beating the clock. Deadbeats. There used to be a lot. Knock on the door, the flat was empty. You knock on the door, nobody answers, you know they're there. I'd like to kill somebody. (Laughs.) It's terrible. They have no respect. They don't give a damn. They're like anybody else.

(Sighs.) Yeah, I take my work home. I put in two, three hours on the phone at home. I don't care if I'm watching TV while I make a call. I'm disinterested in the call. DB* calls. "Mrs. Smith, you promised to send in one on the eleventh. It's now the eighteenth." I'm watching Dick Cavett at the same time.

I get so angry. I'd like to—I—I—I. (Laughs.) Sometimes it's lucky that I have an extension phone. I'd have torn it off the wall many times. You can't help it. I'm particularly choleric. Maybe there are people who take it better than I can. This one woman was making me eat crap for four years, to make me collect my money. I brooded about it for four years. Just making me absolutely crawl. I just—I just thought I'd like to hit her one.

The stories you hear from many salesmen that go into houses are figments of their imagination. About sex. Women paying off in that way. I've never seen it happen personally. Your real drive is to survive—get in the house, get out.

You go in. It's sort of a reflex action. They hear your name, go get the book and the money. I know exactly when they have the money or not. When she opens the

* Deadbeat.

door and turns around to go somewhere, you know she's got the money. If she stands there, blocking your way, you know she's broke. You say, "Oh, you have no money?" Or she tells you. You say, "Thank you very much, I'll see you next week." Or, "Are you short?" Some quick repartee. Then I drive elsewhere.

Saturday is the busiest day. I visit approximately seventy homes. There used to be men in the business who couldn't sleep on a Friday night. They knew they had this terrible pace on Saturday. Most men are home on Saturday. There's a rough and ready banter. Kidding around. I have Sunday off, unless I get very angry at a customer and go out to see her.

For a person like me who likes to talk and exchange ideas with people, it's very difficult to break away. I've been guilty many times of sitting down for too many cups of coffee. It's a question of absolutely driving yourself to get out. Collection isn't the only thing. I've got this book work. It's the most aggravating angle of the business. Keeping track of the payments, your sales tax, your income tax. I've got eight hours of book work ahead of me now, at home.

And you have to go out and do your shopping. On Christmas I'm shopping for a hundred people. I go to stores that are busy and wait to be waited on and am frustrated by every one of these decisions, as to what color, what size, and finding out they haven't got it. So I've waited forty-five minutes for nothing.

They give me a list of things. They want me to buy gifts. They want me to buy a 15-33 shirt for a son. The husband wears a 16½-34. They want a pretty color. They give you a choice and you have to decide. They're paying you to decide for them.

There are many people who can't make decisions. This is the trademark of most of the people I do business with. They tell you to get a pretty shirt. You say, "Pretty? What do you mean by that?" They say, "Well, what you think would be nice." They leave it up to you. You bring it and then they bawl the hell out of you if they don't like it. So they can tell you off. They do. And they're paying me for that service.

"I've had a duodenal ulcer. But it didn't come from this business. I had it when I was a furniture salesman. It was

*schlock furniture. A bait and switch type. Advertise some-
thing at a ridiculously low rate and then expect the salesman to switch the customer to something else. It's worked
on the TO system, turnover. The first man who greets the
customer warms him up a little. And then is commanded
to turn him over to a man who's introduced as the manager of the store—which makes a tremendous impression.
The greatest amount of things sold in this country right
now is bait and switch. Schlock."*

I'm tired. Because I'm not growing old gracefully. I resent the fact that I haven't got the coordination that I
had. I resent the fact that I can't run as fast as I used to.
I resent the fact that I get sleepy when I'm out at a night
club. I resent it terribly. My wife is growing old gracefully
but I'm not. I always have slept well.

There will always be room for this kind of occupation
as long as people want personal contact. We're all over
the world.

ENID DU BOIS

*She had been a telephone solicitor for a Chicago newspa-
per. She was at it for three months. "There are mostly females working there, about thirty. In one large phone
room. About four of us were black."*

I needed a job. I saw this ad in the paper: Equal Opportunity. Salary plus commission. I called and spoke ever so
nicely. The gentleman was pleased with the tone of my
voice and I went down for an interview. My mind raced
as I was on the train coming down. I'll be working on
North Michigan Avenue. It's the greatest street. I was
elated. I got the job right away. All we had to do was get
orders for the newspaper.

We didn't have to think what to say. They had it all
written out. You have a card. You'd go down the list and
call everyone on the card. You'd have about fifteen cards
with the person's names, addresses, and phone numbers.
"This is Mrs. Du Bois. Could I have a moment of your
time? We're wondering if you now subscribe to any news-

papers? If you would *only* for three short months take this paper, it's for a worthy cause." To help blind children or Crusade of Mercy. We'd always have one at hand. "After the three-month period, if you no longer desire to keep it, you can cancel it. But you will have helped them. They need you." You'd use your last name. You could alter your name, if you wanted to. You'd almost have to be an actress on the phone. (Laughs.) I was very excited about it, until I got the hang of it.

The salary was only $1.60 an hour. You'd have to get about nine or ten orders per day. If you didn't, they'd pay you only $1.60. They call that subsidizing you. (Laughs.) If you were subsidized more than once, you were fired.

The commission depended on the territory. If it was middle class, it would be $3.50. If it was ghetto, it would be like $1.50. Because some people don't pay their bills. A lot of papers don't get delivered in certain areas. Kids are afraid to deliver. They're robbed. The suburbs was the top territory.

A fair area, say, lower middle class, they'd pay you $2.50. To a lot of solicitors' dismay they'd kill some orders at the end of the week. He'd come in and say, "You don't get this $2.50, because they don't want the paper." We don't know if it's true or not. How do we know they canceled? But we don't get the commission.

If you didn't get enough orders for the week, a lot of us would work four and five hours overtime. We knew: no orders, no money. (Laughs.) We'd come down even on Saturdays.

They had some old pros, but they worked on the suburbs. I worked the ghetto areas. The old-timers really came up with some doozies. They knew how to psyche people. They were very fast talkers. If a person wanted to get off the phone they'd say, "No, they need you. They need your help. It's only for three short months." The person would just have to say, "Okay," and end up taking it.

They had another gimick. If they kept the paper they would get a free gift of a set of steak knives. If they canceled the order, they wouldn't get anything. Everybody wants something free.

There was a chief supervisor. He would walk into the office and say, "Okay, you people, let's get some orders! What do you think this is?" He'd come stomping in and holler, "I could pay all the bums on Madison Street to

come in, you know." He was always harassing you. He
was a bully, a gorilla of a man. I didn't like the way he
treated women.

I did as well as I wanted to. But after a while, I didn't
care. Surely I could have fast-talked people. Just to continually lie to them. But it just wasn't in me. The disgust
was growing in me every minute. I would pray and pray
to hold on a little longer. I really needed the money. It
was getting more and more difficult for me to make these
calls.

The supervisor would sometimes listen in. He had connections with all the phones. He could just click you in. If
a new girl would come in, he'd have her listen to see how
you were doing—to see how well this person was lying.
That's what they taught you. After a while, when I got
down to work, I wanted to cry.

I talked to one girl about it. She felt the same way. But
she needed the job too. The atmosphere was different here
than being in a factory. Everybody wants to work on
North Michigan Avenue. All the people I've worked with,
most of them aren't there any more. They change.
Some quit, some were dismissed. The bully would say they
weren't getting enough orders. They get the best liar and
the best liar stays. I observed, the older people seemed to
enjoy it. You could just hear them bugging the people . . .

We'd use one charity and would change it every so often. Different papers have different ones they use. I know
a girl does the same work for another paper. The phone
room is in the same building as the newspaper. But our
checks are paid by the Reader's Service Agency.

When I first started I had a pretty good area. They do
this just to get you conditioned. (Laughs.) This is easy.
I'm talking to nice people. God, some of the others! A few
obscenities. A lot of males would say things to you that
weren't so pleasant. Some were lonely. They'd tell you
that. Their wives had left them . . .

At first I liked the idea of talking to people. But pretty
soon, knowing the area I was calling—they couldn't afford
to eat, let alone buy a newspaper—my job was getting me
down. They'd say, "Lady, I have nine to feed or I would
help you." What can you say? One woman I had called
early in the morning, she had just gotten out of the hospital. She had to get up and answer the phone.

They would tell me their problems. Some of them

couldn't read, honest to God. They weren't educated enough to read a newspaper. Know what I would say? "If you don't read anything but the comic strips . . ." "If you got kids, they have to learn how to read the paper." I'm so ashamed thinking of it.

In the middle-class area, the people were busy and they couldn't talk. But in the poor area, the people really wanted to help the charity I talked about. They said I sounded so nice, they would take it anyway. A lot of them were so happy that someone actually called. They could talk all day long to me. They told me all their problems and I'd listen.

They were so elated to hear someone nice, someone just to listen a few minutes to something that had happened to them. Somehow to show concern about them. I didn't care if there was no order. So I'd listen. I heard a lot of their life histories on the phone. I didn't care if the supervisor was clicked in.

People that were there a long time knew just what to do. They knew when to click 'em off and get right on to the next thing. They were just striving, striving . . . It was on my mind when I went home. Oh my God, yeah. I knew I couldn't continue doing it much longer.

What really did it for me was one call I made. I went through the routine. The guy listened patiently and he said, "I really would like to help." He was blind himself! That really got me—the tone of his voice. I could just tell he was a good person. He was willing to help even if he couldn't read the paper. He was poor, I'm sure of that. It was the worst ghetto area. I apologized and thanked him. That's when I left for the ladies' room. I was nauseous. Here I was sitting here telling him a bunch of lies and he was poor and blind and willing to help. Taking his money.

I got sick in the stomach. I prayed a lot as I stayed there in the restroom. I said, "Dear God, there must be something better for me. I never harmed anyone in my life, dear Lord." I went back to the phone room and I just sat there. I didn't make any calls. The supervisor called me out and wanted to know why I was sitting there. I told him I wasn't feeling good, and I went home.

I came back the next day because I didn't have any other means of employment. I just kept praying and hoping and looking. And then, as if my prayers were answered, I got another job. The one I have now. I love it.

I walked into the bully's office and told him a few things. I told him I was sick and tired of him. Oh God, I really can't tell you what I said. (Laughs.) I told him, "I'm not gonna stay here and lie for you. You can take your job and shove it." (Laughs.) And I walked out. He just stood there. He didn't say anything. He was surprised. I was very calm, I didn't shout. Oh, I felt good.

I still work in the same building. I pass him in the hallway every once in a while. He never speaks to me. He looks away. Every time I see him I hold my head very high, very erect, and keep walking.

BOOK THREE

CLEANING UP

NICK SALERNO

He has been driving a city garbage truck for eighteen
years. He is forty-one, married, has three daughters. He
works a forty-hour, five-day week, with occasional over-
time. He has a crew of three laborers. "I usually get up at
five-fifteen. I get to the city parking lot, you check the oil,
your water level, then proceed for the ward yard. I meet
the men, we pick up our work sheet."

You get just like the milkman's horse, you get used to it.
If you remember the milkman's horse, all he had to do
was whistle and whooshhh! That's it. He knew just where
to stop, didn't he? You pull up until you finish the alley.
Usually thirty homes on each side. You have thirty stops
in an alley. I have nineteen alleys a week. They're called
units. Sometimes I can't finish 'em, that's how heavy they
are, this bein' an old neighborhood.

I'll sit there until they pick up this one stop. You got
different thoughts. Maybe you got a problem at home.
Maybe one of the children aren't feeling too good. Like
my second one, she's a problem with homework. Am I
doin' the right thing with her? Pressing her a little bit with
math. Or you'll read the paper. You always daydream.

Some stops, there's one can, they'll throw that on, then
we proceed to the next can. They signal with a buzzer or
a whistle or they'll yell. The pusher blade pushes the garbage in. A good solid truckload will hold anywhere from
eight thousand to twelve thousand pounds. If it's wet, it
weighs more.

147

Years ago, you had people burning, a lot of people had garbage burners. You would pick up a lot of ashes. Today most of 'em have converted to gas. In place of ashes, you've got cardboard boxes, you've got wood that people aren't burning any more. It's not like years ago, where people used everything. They're not too economy-wise today. They'll throw anything away. You'll see whole packages of meat just thrown into the garbage can without being opened. I don't know if it's spoiled from the store or not. When I first started here, I had nearly thirty alleys in this ward. Today I'm down to nineteen. And we got better trucks today. Just the way things are packaged today. Plastic. You see a lot of plastic bottles, cardboard boxes.

We try to give 'em twice-a-week service, but we can't complete the ward twice a week. Maybe I can go four alleys over. If I had an alley Monday, I might go in that alley Friday. What happens over the weekend? It just lays there.

After you dump your garbage in the hopper, the sweeper blade goes around to sweep it up, and the push blade pushes it in. This is where you get your sound. Does that sound bother you in the morning? (Laughs.) Sometimes it's irritating to me. If someone comes up to you to talk, and the men are working in the back, and they press the lever, you can't hear them. It's aggravating but you get used to it. We come around seven-twenty. Not too many complaints. Usually you're in the same alley the same day, once a week. The people know that you're comin' and it doesn't bother them that much.

Some people will throw, will literally throw garbage out of the window—right in the alley. We have finished an alley in the morning and that same afternoon it will look like it wasn't even done. They might have a cardboard carton in the can and garbage all over the alley. People are just not takin' care of it. You get some people that takes care of their property, they'll come out and sweep around their cans. Other people just don't care or maybe they don't know any better.

Some days it's real nice. Other days, when you get off that truck you're tired, that's it! You say all you do is drive all day, but driving can be pretty tiresome—especially when the kids are out of school. They'll run through a gangway into the alley. This is what you have to watch for. Sitting in that cab, you have a lot of blind spots around the truck. This is what gets you. You watch out that you don't hit any of them.

At times you get aggravated, like your truck breaks down and you get a junk as a replacement. This, believe me, you could take home with you. Otherwise, working here, if there's something on your mind, you don't hold anything in. You discuss anything with these guys. Golf, whatever. One of my laborers just bought a new home and I helped him move some of his small stuff. He's helped me around my house, plumbing and painting.

We've got spotters now. It's new. (Laughs.) They're riding around in unmarked cars. They'll turn you in for stopping for coffee. I can't see that. If you have a coffee break in the alley, it's just using a little psychology. You'll get more out of them. But if you're watched continually, you're gonna lay down. There's definitely more watching today, because there was a lot of layin' down on the job. Truthfully, I'd just as soon put in my eight hours a day as easy as possible. It's hard enough comin' to work. I got a good crew, we get along together, but we have our days.

If you're driving all day, you get tired. By the time you get home, fighting the traffic, you'd just like to relax a little bit. But there's always something around the house. You can get home one night and you'll find your kid threw something in the toilet and you gotta shut your mind and take the toilet apart. (Laughs.) My wife drives, so she does most of the shopping. That was my biggest complaint. So now this job is off my hands. I look forward to my weekends. I get in a little golf.

People ask me what I do, I say, "I drive a garbage truck for the city." They call you G-man, or, "How's business, picking up?" Just the standard . . . Or sanitary engineer. I have nothing to be ashamed of. I put in my eight hours. We make a pretty good salary. I feel I earn my money. I can go any place I want. I conduct myself as a gentleman any place I go. My wife is happy, this is the big thing. She doesn't look down at me. I think that's more important than the white-collar guy looking down at me.

They made a crack to my children in school. My kids would just love to see me do something else. I tell 'em, "Honey, this is a good job. There's nothing to be ashamed of. We're not stealin' the money. You have everything you need."

I don't like to have my salary compared to anybody

else's. I don't like to hear that we're makin' more than a schoolteacher. I earn my money just as well as they do. A teacher should get more money, but don't take it away from me.

ROY SCHMIDT

They call us truck loaders, that's what the union did. We're just laborers, that's all we are. What the devil, there's no glamour to it. Just bouncin' heavy cans around all day. I'm givin' the city a fair day's work. I don't want to lean on anyone else. Regardless if I was working here or elsewhere, I put in my day. We're the ones that pick up the cans, dump 'em in the hopper, and do the manual end of the job. There's nothing complex about it.

He is fifty-eight. His fellow crew members are fifty and sixty-nine. For the past seven years he has worked for the Sanitation Department. "I worked at a freight dock for two years. That was night work. It was punching me out. At the end of the week I didn't know one day from another. I looked for a day job and landed this."

In this particular neighborhood, the kids are a little snotty. They're let run a little too loose. They're not held down the way they should. It's getting a little wild around here. I live in the neighborhood and you have to put up with it. They'll yell while you're riding from one alley to another, "Garbage picker!" The little ones usually give you a highball, seem to enjoy it, and you wave back at 'em. When they get a little bigger, they're liable to call you most anything on the truck. (Laughs.) They're just too stupid to realize the necessity of the job.

I've been outside for seven years and I feel more free. I don't take the job home with me. When I worked in the office, my wife would say, "What was the matter with you last night? You laid there and your fingers were drumming the mattress." That's when I worked in the office. The bookkeeping and everything else, it was starting to play on my nerves. Yeah, I prefer laboring to bookkeeping. For one thing, a bookkeeping job doesn't pay anything. I was the lowest paid man there.

Physically, I was able to do more around the house. Now I'm too tired to pitch into anything heavy. I'll mow the lawn and I'll go upstairs and maybe catch a TV program or two, and I'll hit the hay. In the winter months, it's so much worse. After being outside all day and walkin' into a warm house, I can cork off in a minute. (Laughs.) The driver has some protection, he has the cab of the truck. We're out in the cold.

You get it in the shoulders and the arms. You have an ache here and an ache there. Approximately four years ago, I put my back into spasms. The city took care of it, put me in a hospital for a week. That one year, it happened twice to me—because of continual lifting. The way one doctor explained it to me, I may be goin' thirty days and it's already started. It's just on the last day, whenever it's gonna hit, it just turns you upside down. You can't walk, you can't move, you can't get up.

I wear a belt, sort of a girdle. You can buy them in any orthopedic place. This is primarily to hold me in. This one doctor says I'm fairly long-legged and I'm overlifting. The men I work with are average height. I'm six three, I was six four when I went in the army but I think I've come down a little bit. It's my own fault. I probably make it harder on myself with my way of lifting. I've been fairly well protected during the past four years. I haven't had any days off because of it. I wouldn't want to face it again, I'll tell you that.

It's a fifty-gallon drum you lift. I'd say anywhere from eighty pounds to several hundred pounds, depending on what they're loaded with. We lift maybe close to two hundred cans a day. I never attempted to count them. They surprise you every once in a while. They'll load it with something very heavy, like plaster.(Laughs.)

I always say you can read in a garbage can how a person lives. We have this Mexican and Puerto Rican movement in this area. You find a lot of rice and a good many TV dinners. They don't seem to care about cooking too much. I can't say that every family is like that. I never lived with 'em.

I wear an apron over this. By the time you get two or three days in these clothes they're ready for the washer. Working behind the truck, you never know what might shoot out from behind there—liquid or glass or plastic. There is no safety features on the truck. When these blades in the hopper catch it and bring it forward, it spurts out like a bullet. Two years ago, I was struck in the face with a piece of wood. Cut the flesh above the eye and broke my glasses. When I got to the doctor, he put a stitch in it. I had the prettiest shiner you ever seen. (Laughs.) It can be dangerous. You never know what people throw out. I've seen acid thrown out.

They tell you stay away from the rear of the truck when the blade's in motion, but if you did that throughout a day, you'd lose too much time. By the time the blade's goin', you're getting the next can ready to dump.

You don't talk much. You might just mention something fell out of the can or a word or two. Maybe we'll pull in an alley and they'll take five minutes for a cigarette break. We might chew the fat about various things—current events, who murdered who (laughs), sensational stories. Maybe one of the fellas read an article about something that happened over in Europe. Oh, once in a while, talk about the war. It has never been a heated discussion with me.

I'm pretty well exhausted by the time I get through in the day. I've complained at times when the work was getting a little too heavy. My wife says, "Well, get something else." Where the devil is a man my age gonna get something else? You just don't walk from job to job.

She says I should go to sixty-two if I can. I have some Social Security comin'. The pension from the city won't amount to anything. I don't have that much service. Another four years, I'll have only eleven years, and that won't build up a city pension for me by any means.

It'll be just day to day. Same thing as bowling. You bowl each frame, that's right. If you look ahead, you know what you're getting into. So why aggravate yourself? You know what we call bad stops. A mess to clean up in a certain alley. Why look ahead to it? The devil. As long as my health holds out, I want to work.

I have a daughter in college. If she goes through to June, she'll have her master's degree. She's in medicine. For her, it'll be either teaching or research. As she teaches, she can work for her doctorate. She's so far ahead of me, I couldn't . . .

I don't look down on my job in any way. I couldn't say

I despise myself for doing it. I feel better at it than I did at the office. I'm more free. And, yeah—it's meaningful to society. (Laughs).

I was told a story one time by a doctor. Years ago, in France, they had a setup where these princes and lords and God knows what they had floating around. If you didn't stand in favor with the king, they'd give you the lowest job, of cleaning the streets of Paris—which must have been a mess in those days. One lord goofed up somewhere along the line, so they put him in charge of it. And he did such a wonderful job that he was commended for it. The worst job in the French kingdom and he was patted on the back for what he did. That was the first story I ever heard about garbage where it really means something.

POSTSCRIPT: *Several months after the conversation he sent me a note: "Nick and I are still on the job, but to me the alleys are getting longer and the cans larger. Getting old."*

LOUIS HAYWARD

He is a washroom attendant at the Palmer House. It is one of the older, more highly regarded hotels in Chicago. He has been at this for fifteen years. For most of his working life he had been a Pullman porter. The decline in passenger train travel put an end to that. He is nearing sixty-two. "This work is light and easy. That's why I took it. I had a stroke. I might qualify for something better, but I feel I'm too old now."

It's an automatic thing, waiting on people. It doesn't require any thought. It's almost a reflex action. I set my toilet articles up, towels—and I'm ready. We have all the things that men normally would have in their cabinets at home: creams, face lotions, mouth washes, hair preparations. I don't do porter work, clean up. That's all done by the hotel. I work for a concession.

They come in. They wash their hands after using the service—you hope. (A soft chuckle.) I go through the old brush routine, stand back, expecting a tip. A quarter is what you expect when you hand the guy a towel and a couple of licks of the broom. Okay. You don't always get it. For service over and beyond the call of duty, you expect more. That's when he wants Vitalis on his hair, Aqua Velva on his face, and wants Murine for his eyes. We render that too, sometimes.

One thing that reduced our intake, that's when they stopped using the Liberty halves. I'm not talking about the Kennedy halves, they're not too much in circulation. They'd throw you a half. He don't have it in his pocket any more. Now he throws you a quarter. You'd be surprised the difference it makes. A big tip is the only thing that is uppermost in any attendant's mind, because that's what you're there for. You're there to sell service and you only have about a minute and a half to impress the person. The only thing you can do is be alert, to let the man know that you're aware of him. That's the way he judges you.

It builds his ego up a little bit. By the same token, he can be deflated by the right person. An attendant or a captain in a dining room or a doorman—I don't care who you are, if you're President of the United States or United States Steel, if you walk into any washroom, you like to be recognized. If you're with a client—"Hello, Mr. Jones"—that impresses the client. This guy really gets around. The washroom attendant knows him. I'm building him up. If he's been in before and is rude in one way or another, I can always be busy doing something else.

I can just separate the wheat from the chaff. I know live ones from almost lookin' at them from so-called deadheads. There's a bit of snob in me anyway. If you don't appeal to me the way I think you should, I'm not going to slight you, but there could be just a little difference in the attention you get.

Oh yes, there's been a change in fifteen years. Not in the size of the tip. That's pretty well standardized, a quarter. The clientele are different. I always felt that a good servant is a little snobbish. I don't enjoy waiting on my peers. I feel that if I'm gonna occupy a position that's menial, let it be to someone perhaps a cut above me. It's just a personal feeling. I'm not gonna let him feel that— the salesman or the person off the street. Now our customers are not too liberal. Most people who come to conventions today don't have big expense accounts any more. Everybody feels it all down the line.

It's open now to the public. Young black and white suddenly become aware of this washroom. It's just off the street. They're in here like flies. A lot of this stuff is new to them: "What is this, a barber shop?" It's free. Sometimes you think you're down in the subway. It's a parade, in and out. Some of 'em are real bad boys that are downtown. When they come in, you don't know if it's a rip-off or what it is. It has happened. Seven, eight years ago, it was not heard of. It never crossed anybody's mind.

They just don't know. I'm not talking about young people. Some of the older people, they come from downstate, a little town ... One other thing has changed in the past few years, the life style, in dressin'. Sometimes you make a mistake. You figure the wrong guy is a bum, and he's very affluent.

It has its ups and downs. You meet a few celebrities. It's always to your best advantage to recognize them. We got a lot of bigwigs from city hall for lunch. The mayor comes quite often. Judges ...

Most of the time I'm sitting down here reading, a paper or a book. I got a locker full of one thing or another. The day goes. I have a shine man in the back. At least you have someone to talk to. That takes a little of your monotony off it. Deadly sometimes.

I'm not particularly proud of what I'm doing. The shine man and I discuss it quite freely. In my own habitat I don't go around saying I'm a washroom attendant at the Palmer House. Outside of my immediate family, very few people know what I do. They do know I work at the Palmer House and let that suffice. You say Palmer House, they automatically assume you're a waiter.

This man shining shoes, he's had several offers—he's a very good boot-black—where he could make more money. But he wouldn't take 'em because the jobs were too open. He didn't want to be *seen* shining shoes. To quote him, "Too many pretty girls pass by." (Laughs.)

No, I'm not proud of this work. I can't do anything heavy. It would be hard to do anything else, so I'm stuck. I've become inured to it now. It doesn't affect me one way or the other. Several years ago (pause)—I couldn't begin to tell you how *menial* the job was. I was frustrated with myself—for being put in that position. The years piled up and now it doesn't even occur to me, doesn't cross my mind. I was placed in a very unusual position. It's very hard for me to realize it even now. It took a little while, but it don't take too long, really. Especially when you see other people doing it too. That's one thing that sped it along. If it were myself alone—but I see others doin' it. So it can't be so bad.

"I was a Pullman porter for God knows how many years. That's why I got into this so easily. When I was first employed, the porter status was very low. Everybody called him George. We got together and got a placard printed with our name on it and posted it on each end of the car: Car served by Louis M. Hayward. (Chuckles softly.) So we could politely refer everybody to this. When I first went on the road, the porter was the first accused of anything: wallet missing—the porter got it. (Dry chuckle.) A lot of them went on pensions. A pretty good pension— from a black man's standard. A white man might not think it's so hot. Others have jobs in banks—as messengers."

People are a lot more sophisticated today. It's so easy to say, "Is the shoe shine boy here?" Very few of 'em use that expression these days. They make very sure they ask for the shine *man*. This fellow I work with—I wouldn't call him militant, but he's perhaps a little more forward than I am—he wouldn't respond if you called him boy. He'd promptly tell 'em; "We don't have any shoe shine boy here. We only have men shining shoes."

The man I hand the towel to is perfectly aware of my presence. Sometimes he wants it to appear that he is unaware of you. You have to be aware of him whether he's aware of you or not. A very common ploy is for two men to come in discussing a big business deal. I stand with the towels and they just walk right by, talking about thousands of dollars in transactions. I'm to assume they're so occupied with what they're doing that they don't have time for me. They ignore me completely. They don't bother to wash their hands. (Laughs.) I laugh at them inside. The joke's on them as far as I'm concerned. Sometimes just for the hell of it, when they go back to the urinal, I'll have the water running: "Towel, sir?" "No, I gotta hurry and get back to eat." He's just come from the toilet. He hasn't bothered to wash his hands. (Chuckles.)

Truthfully, I don't carry my feeling of menial work quite that deeply that it hurts me. The only time I feel hurt is when I perform some extra service and don't get what I thought I deserved. I'm completely hardened now. I just take it in stride.

The whole thing is obsolete. It's on its way out. This work isn't necessary in the first place. It's so superfluous. It was *never* necessary. (Laughs.) It's just a hustle. Years ago, a black man at night spots and hotels would keep the place clean and whatever you could hustle there was yours. He did pretty good at it. Talked a little too much about how well he was doing. Well, people started to look into it. This could be an operation . . .

*The concessions took over?**

(A long pause.)

Uh—when did they start taking over?

(Softly) That I don't know. It happened in many cities. I've wondered about it myself. I—I don't know.

I heard the concession gets twenty-five cents from every attendant for every two towels handed out . . .

(A long pause.) That's what he told you?†

Yeah.

Well, that's a . . . (Trails off.)

Is that true?

I—I don't know. I don't question his word, but . . . (A

---

* There have been rumors through the past several years that the Syndicate controls these concessions. There is a natural reluctance on the part of attendants to discuss it. A similar phenomenon is the parking lot.

† "He" was another washroom attendant.

long pause.) I'll make an application for Social Security in a couple of months. I'll be sixty-two. I'm not gonna wait till sixty-five. I might not even be here then. I'll take what I got comin' and run. (A soft chuckle.)

I got it all pretty well figured out. I'll still work a little down here. That'll give me something. To sit down and do nothing, I don't look forward to that. There certainly is not gonna be that much money that I can afford to do it. (Laughs.) I'm not well off by any means. To say that I do not need much money now is not true. But I'm not gonna kill myself to get it. I could be a house man here, a waiter, but I can't handle it now.

"Years ago it was quite different than the way I'm spending my leisure time now. I spent a great deal of time up at the corner tavern with the boys. I don't go out much at night any more. Nobody does that's got his marbles. I read and watch television. If I want something to drink, I take it home with me. When I retire, I guess I'll be doing more of this same thing."

I always wanted to be a writer. My mother was a writer. Sold a couple of short stories. I enjoy reading— thought I might enjoy writing. I thought a little of her talent might rub off on me. Apparently it didn't. Her desire rubbed off on me, though. (Soft chuckle.) Just an idea . . . Most people like to say how rich and rewarding their jobs are. I can't say that. (As he laughs softly, he walks off toward the washroom.)

POSTSCRIPT: *He is a widower and has five grandchildren. He lives with his two unmarried sisters; one is working, the other is on a pension.*

LINCOLN JAMES

He works in a rendering and glue factory. He's been at it for thirty-six years. "A lot of people refer to me as a maintenance man. But I call it a factory mechanic."

Rendering is where you get the scrap—fat and bones—

from the butcher shops and cook them into a grease. We receive things people normally don't want. Years ago, we principally supplied soap factories. But today we make all different products from the residue. Tallows, glycerine, bone meal, poultry feed, fertilizer. The bones usually go to glue. Out of the marrow of the bones is where the glue comes from. People have no interest whatsoever in what they throw out. This rendering process takes it and makes millions of dollars off of it. They export this grease to foreign countries. That's our big business nowadays.

They bring it in by truck. It's unloaded on conveyors. Bones go one place, the fats go another. They take it through a cooking process and this is where we get the glue. It may start out like water, but when it cooks over and over, it gets almost like a syrup. It's just a thickening process.

I started out as a laborer. I became an oiler and from that to repairman. When I labored, I transported the meat and the bones after they were separated. Women were doing that at the time. Today it's automation. No women now. They were eliminated.

The odor was terrible, but I got used to it. It was less annoying when you stayed right in it. When you left for a week or so, a vacation, you had to come back and get used to the thing all over again. I've had people that say, "How do you stand it?" I say it's like anything else. I don't say you get exactly used to it, but it does get less annoying in time. It's not a stink, but it's not sweet either. It's a different odor altogether. Whenever meat lays around for a few days it smells like that. But once you cook it, it changes to a different odor. I can't explain . . .

I sometimes have a little fun with some of the guys. I say, "I work in one of the filthiest places in Chicago, I believe." Some of 'em work in tanneries and they say, "Your place is sweet smellin' besides a tannery." Some of the others kid me; "How do you survive it?" I say, "Did you know the percentage of stuff that we produce here you use it every day?" They says, "Oh? What?" I says, "You brush your teeth with toothpaste?" "Yes." "You have glycerine in your toothpaste. We produce that." They says, "Really?" "Do you eat chickens?" "Yes." "Well, we produce the poultry food, and this is the residue of some of the stuff you see laying around here looking so bad and smelling so bad." (Laughs.) They just look at me, mouth open.

I say, "I know you have in time past kissed good with lipstick." "Oh yeah." "Well, look man, we used to supply one
of the biggest lipstick factories of all the grease they use.
Now don't kiss no more girls." (Laughs).

I sometimes says, "I really don't think you know what's
happening." I'll tell 'em about soaps, the stuff they use to
fatten the chickens, the glue you use to lick the stamps to
go on your letter. (Laughs.) We manufacture here what
you use daily.

It's all purified, of course. (Pause.) But you just think
about what all this is. Could any part of this stink possibly
be used in an individual's life? You wonder sometime. But
you search it down and you find it do. Yes, yes. Many
other things, if you really knew from where it come, you
probably wouldn't be very interested. I had some years in
a packinghouse and I see some of the stuff manufactured
and I don't relish it too much myself. I happen to be
around and know what goes on.

You have to wear rubber gloves, but there'd still be an
odor to your hand. You had to wash it real good in order
not to smell it when you were eating lunch. The risk of infections and stuff are pretty great because of this contami-
nated stuff. They provide employees with tetanus shots every so often. They never had too many infections. Of
course, there was a few.

Accidents wasn't too frequent, but sometimes they got
burns. Oh yes, we've had some. If you puts the meat in
the pot and you would cook this meat until it was done,
then you drain the liquid off, you want to empty the tank.
Pull the residue out—why, we've had some guys get burns.
It seldom, if ever, get the face. It hits the chest, down to
the middle leg length. It lasted for months before some
employees were able to return to work.

I've known them to have six hundred people here. Now
they're down to less than three hundred due to automation. Where they used to have five people separating the
rubbish and things, they have only one or two doing it
now. I'm assigned to breakdowns on these hydraulic
pumps. If a lot of it goes bad overnight, I have to get 'em
going that day. It's not the same routine every day. You
never know.

This plant runs seven days a week, twenty-four hours a
day. They have a scheduled five-day week. But many of
them work six days and some of them seven days. Some-

times ten hours a day, sometimes twelve hours a day. In some instances, the overtime is compulsory. The equipment's gotta be used.

You speak of my working life? I like what I'm doing. I never been laid off in thirty-six years. I look forward to going to work. I'd be lost if I wasn't working. But I guess after you put in so many years . . .

Some of the younger help, they seems to have the attitude, "I won't be here long." They say, "How long you worked here?" I say, "Oh, somewhat longer than you all." They says, "I don't want nobody's job that long." They don't feel like coming to work, they take the day off. Saturday, Sunday, Monday, it don't make no difference. I would think they went out and had a big time. It doesn't seem to bother them to take a couple days off. Wherein it was a rare thing for me to lose a day, years back. I don't lose any time now.

I still think it's a wonderful thing to be employed. I don't know how I'd feel without it. (Pause.) But I'd like the experience. After so many years—I would just like the experience of not having to go to work. I look forward to retirement in another three, four years. I don't know what it would really turn out to be . . .

MAGGIE HOLMES

What bugs me now, since I'm on welfare, is people saying they give you the money for nothin. When I think back what we had to come through, up from the South, comin' here. The hard work we had to do. It really gets me, when I hear people . . . It do somethin' to me. I think violence.

I think what we had to work for. I used to work for $1.50 a week. This is five days a week, sometimes six. If you live in the servant quarter, your time is never off, because if they decide to have a party at night, you gotta come out. My grandmother, I remember when she used to work, we'd get milk and a pound of butter. I mean this was pay. I'm thinkin' about what my poor parents worked for, gettin' nothing. What do the white think about when they think? Do they ever think about what *they* would do?

She had worked as a domestic, hotel chambermaid, and as "kitchen help in cafes" for the past twenty-five years, up North and down South. She lives with her four children.

When it come to housework, I can't do it now. I can't stand it, cause it do somethin' to my mind. They want you to clean the house, want you to wash, even the windows, want you to iron. You not supposed to wash no dishes. You ain't supposed to make no beds up. Lots of 'em try to sneak it in on you, think you don't know that. So the doorbell rings and I didn't answer to. The bell's ringin' and I'm still doin' my work. She ask me why I don't an-swer the bell. I say; "Do I come here to be a butler?" And I don't see myself to be no doormaid. I came to do some work and I'm gonna do my work. When you end up, you's nursemaid, you's cook. They puts all this on you. If you want a job to cleanin', you ask for just cleanin'. She wants you to do in one day what she hasn't did all year.

Now this bug me: the first thing she gonna do is pull out this damn rubber thing—just fittin' for your knees. Knee pads—like you're workin' in the fields, like people pickin' cotton. No mop or nothin'. That's why you find so many black women here got rheumatism in their legs, knees. When you gets on that cold floor, I don't care how warm the house is, you can feel the cold on the floor, the water and stuff. I never see nobody on their knees until I come North. In the South, they had mops. Most times, if they had real heavy work, they always had a man to come in. Washin' windows, that's a man's job. They don't think nothin' about askin' you to do that here. They don't have no feeling that that's what bothers you. I think to myself; My God, if I had somebody come and do my floors, clean up for me, I'd appreciate it. They don't say nothin' about it. Act like you haven't even done anything. They has no feelin's.

I worked for one old hen on Lake Shore Drive. You remember that big snow they had there?* Remember when you couldn't get there? When I gets to work she says; "Call the office." She complained to the lady where I got the job, said I was late to work. So I called. So I said,

---

* It was the week of Chicago's Big Snow-In, beginning January 25, 1967. Traffic was hopelessly snarled. Scores of thousands couldn't get to work.

in the phone (Shouts), *"What do you want with me?* I got home four black, beautiful kids. Before I go to anybody's job in the morning I see that my kids are at school. I gonna see that they have warm clothes on and they fed." I'm lookin' right at the woman I'm workin' for. (Laughs.) When I get through the phone I tell this employer, "That goes for you too. The only thing I live for is my kids. There's nothin', you and nobody else." The expression on her face: What is this? (Laughs.) She thought I was gonna be like (mimics "Aunt Jemima"): "Yes ma'am, I'll try to get here a little early." But it wasn't like that. (Laughs.)

When I come in the door that day she told me pull my shoes off. I said, "For what? I can wipe my feet at the door here, but I'm not gettin' out of my shoes, it's cold." She look at me like she said: Oh my God, what I got here? (Laughs.) I'm knowin' I ain't gonna make no eight hours here. I can't take it.

She had everything in there snow white. And that means work, believe me. In the dining room she had a blue set, she had sky-blue chairs. They had a bedroom with pink and blue. I look and say, "I know what this means." It means sho' 'nough—knees. I said, "I'm gonna try and make it today, *if* I can make it." Usually when they're so bad, you have to leave.

I ask her where the mop is. She say she don't have no mop. I said. "Don't tell me you mop the floor on your knees. I know you don't." They usually hide these mops in the clothes closet. I go out behind all these clothes and get the mop out. (Laughs.) They don't get on their knees, but they don't think nothin' about askin' a black woman. She says, "All you—you girls . . ." She stop. I say, "All you *niggers*, is that what you want to say?" She give me this stupid look. I say, "I'm glad you tellin' me that there's more like me." (Laughs.) I told her, "You better give me my money and let me go, 'cause I'm gettin' angry." So I made her give me my carfare and what I had worked that day.

Most when you find decent work is when you find one that work themselves. They know what it's like to get up in the morning and go to work. In the suburbs they ain't got nothin' to do. They has nothin' else to think about. Their mind's just about blowed.

It's just like they're talkin' about mental health. Poor

people's mental health is different than the rich white. Mine could come from a job or not havin' enough money for my kids. Mine is from me being poor. That don't mean you're sick. His sickness is from money, graftin' where he want more. I don't have *any*. You live like that day to day, penny to penny.

I worked for a woman, her husband's a judge. I cleaned the whole house. When it was time for me to go home, she decided she wants some ironing. She goes in the basement, she turn on the air conditioner. She said, "I think you can go down in the basement and finish your day out. It's air conditioned." I said, "I don't care what you got down there, I'm not ironing. You look at that slip, it says cleanin'. Don't say no ironin'." She wanted me to wash the walls in the bathroom. I said, "If you look at that telephone book they got all kinds of ads there under house cleanin'." She said the same thing as the other one, "All you girls—" I said same thing I said to the other one; "You mean niggers." (Laughs.)

They ever call you by your last name?

Oh God, they wouldn't do that. (Laughs.)

Do you call her by her last name?

Most time I don't call her, period. I don't say anything to her. I don't talk nasty to nobody, but when I go to work I don't talk to people. Most time they don't like what you're gonna say. So I keeps quiet.

Most of her jobs were "way out in the suburbs. You get a bus and you ride till you get a subway. After you gets to Howard,* you gets the El. If you get to the end of the line and there's no bus, they pick you up. I don't like to work in the city, 'cause they don't want to pay you nothin'. And these old buildings are so nasty. It takes so much time to clean 'em. They are not kept up so good, like suburbs. Most of the new homes out there, it's easier to clean."

A commonly observed phenomenon: during the early

---

* The boundary line separating Chicago from the North Shore suburb, Evanston.

evening hour, trains, crowded, predominantly by young white men carrying attaché cases, pass trains headed in the opposite direction, crowded, predominantly by middle-aged black women carrying brown paper bags. Neither group, it appears, glances at the other.

"*We spend most of the time ridin'. You get caught goin' out from the suburbs at nighttime, man, you're really sittin' there for hours. There's nothin' movin'. You got a certain hour to meet trains. You get a transfer, you have to get that train. It's a shuffle to get in and out of the job. If you miss that train at five o'clock, what time you gonna get out that end? Sometime you don't get home till eight o'clock . . .*"

You don't feel like washin' your own window when you come from out there, scrubbin'. If you work in one of them houses eight hours, you gotta come home do the same thing over . . . you don't feel like . . . (sighs softly) . . . tired. You gotta come home, take care of your kids, you gotta cook, you gotta wash. Most of the time, you gotta wash for the kids for somethin' to wear to school. You gotta clean up, 'cause you didn't have time in the morning. You gotta wash and iron and whatever you do, nights. You be so tired, until you don't feel like even doin' nothin'.

You get up at six, you fix breakfast for the kids, you get them ready to go on to school. Leave home about eight. Most of the time I make biscuits for my kids, cornbread you gotta make. I don't mean the canned kind. This I don't call cookin', when you go in that refrigerator and get some beans and drop 'em in a pot. And TV dinners, they go stick 'em in the stove and she say she cooked. This is not cookin'.

And *she's* tired. Tired from doin' what? You got a washing dryer, you got an electric sweeper, anything at fingertips. All she gotta do is unfroze 'em, dump 'em in the pot, and she's tired! I go to the store, I get my vegetables, greens, I wash 'em. I gotta pick 'em first. I don't eat none of that stuff, like in the cans. She don't do that, and she says she's tired.

When you work for them, when you get in that house in the morning, boy, they got one arm in their coat and a scarf on their head. And when you open that door, she shoots by you, she's gone. Know what I mean? They want

you to come there and keep the kids and let them get out.
What she think about how am I gonna do? Like I gets
tired of my kids too. I'd like to go out too. It bugs you to
think that they don't have no feelin's about that.

Most of the time I work for them and they be out. I
don't like to work for 'em when they be in the house so
much. They don't have no work to do. All they do is get
on the telephone and talk about one another. Make you
sick. I'll go and close the door. They're all the same, everybody's house is the same. You think they rehearse it ...

When I work, only thing I be worryin' about is my kids.
I just don't like to leave 'em too long. When they get out
of school, you wonder if they out on the street. The only
thing I worry is if they had a place to play in easy. I always call two, three times. When she don't like you to
call, I'm in a hurry to get out of there. (Laughs.) My
mind is gettin' home, what are you gonna find to cook before the stores close.

This Nixon was sayin' he don't see nothin' wrong with
people doin' scrubbin'. For generations that's all we done.
He should know we wants to be doctors and teachers and
lawyers like him. I don't want my kids to come up and do
domestic work. It's degrading. You can't see no tomorrow
there. We done this for generation and generation—cooks
and butlers all your life. They want their kids to be lawyers, doctors, and things. You don't want 'em in no cafés
workin' ...

When they say about the neighborhood we live in is
dirty, why do they ask me to come and clean their house?
We, the people in the slums, the same nasty women they
have come to their house in the suburbs every day. If
these women are so filthy, why you want them to clean
for you? They don't go and clean for us. We go and clean
for them.

I worked one day where this white person did some
housework. I'm lookin' at the difference how she with me
and her. She had a guilt feeling towards that lady. They
feel they shouldn't ask them to do this type of work, but
they don't mind askin' me.

They want you to get in a uniform. You take me and
my mother, she work in what she wear. She tells you, "If
that place so dirty where I can't wear my dress, I won't
do the job." You can't go to work dressed like they do,
'cause they think you're not working—like you should get

dirty, at least. They don't say what kind of uniform, just say uniform. This is in case anybody come in, the black be workin'. They don't want you walkin' around dressed up, lookin' like them. They asks you sometimes, "Don't you have somethin' else to put on?" I say, "No, 'cause I'm not gettin' on my knees."

They move with caution now, believe me. They want to know, "What should I call you?" I say, "Don't call me a Negro, I'm black." So they say, "Okay, I don't want to make you angry with me." (Laughs.) The old-timers, a lot of 'em was real religious. "Lord'll make a way." I say, "I'm makin' my own way." I'm not anti-Bible or anti-God, but I just let 'em know I don't think thataway.

The younger women, they don't pay you too much attention. Most of 'em work. The older women, they behind you, wiping. I don't like nobody checkin' behind me. When you go to work, they want to show you how to clean. That really gets me, somebody showin' me how to clean. I been doin' it all my life. They come and get the rag and show you how to do it. (Laughs.) I stand there, look at 'em. Lotta times I ask her, "You finished?" I say, "If there's anything you gotta go and do, I wish you'd go." I don't need nobody to show me how to clean.

I had them put money down and pretend they can't find it and have me look for it. I worked for one, she had dropped ten dollars on the floor, and I was sweepin' and I'm glad I seen it, because if I had put that sweeper on it, she coulda said I got it. I had to push the couch back and the ten dollars was there. Oh, I had 'em, when you go to dust, they put something . . . to test you.

I worked at a hotel. A hotel's the same thing. You makin' beds, scrubbin' toilets, and things. You gotta put in linens and towels. You still cleanin'. When people come in the room—that's what bugs me—they give you that look: You just a maid. It do somethin' to me. It really gets into me.

Some of the guests are nice. The only thing you try to do is to hurry up and get this bed made and get outa here, 'cause they'll get you to do somethin' else. If they take that room, they want everything they paid for. (Laughs.) They get so many towels, they can't use 'em all. But you gotta put up all those towels. They want that pillow, they want that blanket. You gotta be trottin' back and forth and gettin' all those things.

In the meantime, when they have the hotel full, we put in extra beds—the little foldin' things. They say they didn't order the bed. They stand and look at you like you crazy. Now you gotta take this bed back all the way from the twelfth floor to the second. The guy at the desk, he got the wrong room. He don't say, "I made a mistake." You take the blame.

And you get some guys . . . you can't work with afightin' 'em. He'll call down and say he wants some towels. When you knock, he says, "Come in." He's standing there without a stitch of clothes on, buck naked. You're not goin' in there. You only throw those towels and go back. Most of the time you wait till he got out of there.

When somethin's missin', it's always the maid took it. If we find one of those type people, we tell the house lady, "You have to go in there and clean it yourself." If I crack that door, and nobody's in, I wouldn't go in there. If a girl had been in there, they would call and tell you, "Did you see something?" They won't say you got it. It's the same thing. You say no. They say, "It *musta* been in there."

Last summer I worked at a place and she missed a purse. I didn't work on that floor that day. She called the office, "Did you see that lady's purse?" I said, "*No*, I haven't been in the room." He asked me again, Did I . . . ? I had to stay till twelve o'clock. She found it. It was under some papers. I quit, 'cause they end up sayin' you stole somethin'.

You know what I wanted to do all my life? I wanted to play piano. And I'd want to write songs and things, that's what I really wanted to do. If I could just get myself enough to buy a piano . . . And I'd like to write about my life, if I could sit long enough: How I growed up in the South and my grandparents and my father—I'd like to do that. I would like to dig up more of black history, too. I would love to for my kids.

Lotta times I'm tellin' 'em about things, they'll be sayin', "Mom, that's olden days." (Laughs.) They don't understand, because it's so far from what's happening now. Mighty few young black women are doin' domestic work. And I'm glad. That's why I want my kids to go to school. This one lady told me, "All you people are gettin' like that." I said, "I'm glad." There's no more gettin' on their knees.

ERIC HOELLEN

I never heard a newsman, when we had severe winter weather, mention a janitor's name. He'll talk about a guy working out on a line, he'll talk about a guy doing outside work. But do you realize when it snows in the city of Chicago, the janitor's the man who gotta get there and keep the sidewalks clean? The weatherman on TV, that big bum, he don't say nothin'.

It's a low blow. They talk about heart attacks shoveling snow. In one of my buildings alone, I almost had a block of snow to shovel—plus the entrances, plus back porches. There's a lot of janitors that keel over in this cold weather. I get a big charge out of these TV weathermen. They'll talk about everybody in the world, "Take it easy. Don't work too hard." And this and that. But there's no mention of the guy that really has to get out there and remove the snow—by hand. And that's the janitor.

At Christmas time they always talk about janitors getting gifts. I have buildings. They have a mailman, right? I'm not knocking the mailman. He gets everything he deserves. He does a lot of walking in cold weather. But we *live* with these people. I've stayed in the hallway where I've worked every day and I've done these people favors. They'll hand the mailman a Christmas envelope and they won't even hand you a boo. This makes you feel like: What the hell is this? Did I offend this party? Didn't I do my work or something?

He's forty-three and has been a janitor for twenty-two years. "I got married in '50, got a janitor's job, and went to work the next day. My dad was with it when I was with it. For no college education you can't get a better job as far as paying is concerned. It's interesting. You got everything from electrical work to mechanical work—plus plumbing. You've got cleaning. The most is heat, though. You got the boiler room.

"Before the union was in, we had to paint, we had to do everything. They didn't get a half-decent wage at all.

Now we get a decent wage, we have health benefits, we started a pension plan.

"When you're on call it's twenty-four hours a day, seven days a week." He services five buildings, "about a hundred families I have to satisfy. I'm the good will ambassador between the owner and the tenants. I can either make a building or break it, depending on how you take care of it. Our main concern is to save the owner money."

When I first started out, we had hand fires. You gotta take a shovel and you open the door and you throw the coal in it. You put about ten, twelve shovels of coal. That would hold maybe, in good zero weather, two hours. To make a decent living, if you had three, four, five hand fires in your buildings, you just made one continuous circle from five thirty in the morning until banking time, about ten thirty at night. As soon as they pulled down, you had to heat 'em up, clean the fire and heat 'em up again. And hit 'em again. So I couldn't go nowhere. You had phone calls, man, that rang off the wall. They wanted heat, they wanted heat. I used to shovel two ton of coal a day.

A lot of people say, "What do you want to be a janitor for?" I say, "I haven't got no investment. I come and go as I please." I never got a fifteen-day notice yet—which means it's public relations. If the owner decides he wants to fire you, he has to give you a fifteen-day notice. And the union will replace you with somebody else.

There's two kinds of janitor work—high rise and walkup. High rise, your head man, he's more like an engineer. He carries the same union card I carry. Their job is mostly responsibility. They have helpers: cleaning men, repairmen. He makes contact with the tenants and he's responsible. He's got a clean job.

I carry on my jacket, it says: Hoellen, Building Engineer. But I'm a janitor. An engineer is just a word that people more or less respect. I don't care. You can call me a janitor. There's nothing wrong with a janitor. A lotta guys that work in high rises, he'll carry the same card as me but, man, he don't want to hear the word janitor. *He's* an engineer. He's even got "building engineer" written on his mailbox and his bells.

I have walkups mostly. I have buildings from forty

years old to a four-plus-one building.* This to me is a pain
in the ear. They're hard to keep straight. It's open, there's
parking underneath. They go hang something on the wall,
it falls off. Cabinets come off the wall. Zero weather came,
pumps all froze out. Whoever designed this building—!
Pump split wide open. Man, it flooded us out. A lady
came down the elevator, it didn't stop. When she hits bottom, water is in the elevator. It's lucky she didn't get elec-
trocuted.

Older buildings are less trouble than new ones—easier
to keep straight. In the new building, they're paying much
higher rent for less space. They want better service and
you can't blame 'em. These old cast-iron boilers they put
in long ago, they're repairable. You can't beat 'em. They'll
last a lot longer than these new ones.

My dad did the same kind of work, but he worked
harder than I do. Because of gas heat, I can sleep an
hour, maybe two hours later in the morning. He had to be
at that building opening doors at that boiler at five thirty
to get that heat up at six. If those radiators weren't clang-
ing at six in the morning, people were raising all kinds of
hay.

When I first started out, I had twenty-five porches of
garbage. Every morning I had to carry it. This building
was a six-story walkup. It was the only building I had.
When it came noon, by the time I got to the top, I was so
all-in and soaking wet from sweat that I had to sit there
and look out at the lake for a while and get my breath before I started on my way down.

You talk about heart condition. The janitor's got one of
the worst. He's gotta walk every day up and down stairs
carrying garbage. You carry a hundred, two hundred
pounds of garbage down. Going up, it's bad enough carrying something on your back. Coming down with two hundred pounds on your back, it gets heavier. It has never

---

* A realty phenomenon in Chicago: quickly constructed four-
story buildings, with an open parking lot as its ground floor.
The apartments are mostly one-room and two. Charges have
been made by community groups that the material is shoddy
and the buildings quickly deteriorate while the fast-buck
entrepreneurs take the money and run. Zoning changes, due
to these complaints, have, for the time being, discouraged
further construction of four-plus-ones.

bothered me. I have a real bad back, by the way. I've been in the hospital last year with a bad back. Shoveling coal and mopping is bad. If you have a lot of mopping, you're throwing your hips around. I tire out very easy because of my back. But I'm better in my job now.

A janitor on zero days, when the wind is blowin' and he has to go up those stairs in ice cold weather—a lot of janitors are up in age. You're talking about men fifty years old, fifty-five, up into there. He has to clean those porches off, he has to shovel the snow, and the ticker only takes so much.

Now I have a jeep. I plow the whole sidewalk. Instead of shoveling, I just push it off now. Almost all the janitors ... There's an ordinance that say's you're not allowed. A lot of rookies, especially, 'll give you trouble. You try to explain, "Man, I'm not hurting anybody. I'm going slow." "Get off the sidewalk." You'll get a ticket if you don't get off.

Today I can walk in the boiler room with clean trousers and go home with clean trousers. You check the glass, you're all set. That's the first thing you do. I check my fires and bring my garbage down right away. I take one of those big barrels on my back and I bring it up the flight of stairs and back down. I do this on three buildings and two have chutes.

Before air pollution we used to burn this. We burned it in the same boiler every morning. There was a city ordinance that it wasn't allowed, but yet they did that for years. Now we put it in the hallway. We bring it down and put it in drums and the scavenger hauls it out. We don't burn garbage any more. It helped you get the heat up in the morning, but it's a good thing they stopped. It's a little more work now, 'cause it was easier to throw it in the boiler than come out and stuff it in the barrel.

These cry babies we got, they're always hollering about something. I had a call one night about eleven o'clock. She said, "My pussy's caught in the door." (Laughs.) So I jumped up out of bed and said to my wife, "Someone's crazy or drunk or somebody's pulling a trick on me." I get my clothes all on and I'm ready to go out the door and my phone rings. She says, "Never mind, I got my pussy loose." She's talking about her damn cat. The next day I told her, "You know the way that sounded?" She says, "I thought about that afterwards." She got a big laugh out of it.

Ah, there's a lot of stuff. I'm not mentioning names, but this buddy of mine, I told him I got a couple of hot numbers on the third floor, students. And I says, "You can make out." (Laughs.) I says, "I'll go up first. When you see the blink at the window, come and knock, 'cause I'll have 'em all lined up." You know you can control electricity from the fuse, right? So I go down the boiler room and fuse box and turn the fuse, and the light in the window blinks off and on up there. Christ! he come runnin' up those stairs. He's bangin' at the door, "I know you're in there! I know you're in there!" I said, "Hey, I pulled a joke." He almost killed me; he chased me all the way down the steps.

As for making out with tenants, it's not like they say. Good-looking broads, if they're playing they ain't gonna monkey around with a janitor. 'Cause they know you're around the building and they're afraid you might say something. I'm not saying it's not done, but ninety-nine percent of the time you're not gonna make out in your own building.

I had a couple of girls, man, nearly crazy. One's a bunny. But she said, "I have to face you every day and I don't hold with making out in the building." I betcha I could go back and I'd make out. She's a very nice girl and everything.

Some people look down on us. A ditchdigger's a respectable man. A gravedigger's a respectable man. A garbage hauler, he's a respectable man—if he does his job. Now they're saying we're making money. They read in the papers the janitors got a raise. Thank God for the Janitor's Union.

We're making a lot more money than in my dad's time. Then they were living in basement apartments, where maybe a catch basin was in your kitchen. You live in a basement apartment, you start out when you're a young fella, you live in the apartment twenty years and when you get older, you're gonna feel it. Oh man, it's just damp.

I live in a townhouse now. I've been at this since '50, so I worked my bones around with the owners and got the okay for it, to live off the job. Actually, I live outside Chicago. I drive in in the morning.

I make a pretty good buck. I figure if I do my work

and do it honestly I should be entitled to whatever I make. For high-rise buildings, head man makes a thousand dollars a month and his apartment. You never heard of that stuff before. I've turned down high rises by the dozens. I can make more money on the side on walkup buildings.

Most tenants, I get along with 'em. The bad part about a tenant, they have no respect for your hours. Maybe my day starts when their day starts, but they want something done when they come home. My day is ending too. They'll call up and some will be sarcastic about it. "You have to come here when I'm home." That's not true. They can leave me the key, so I can do it on my own time. Some people don't trust you. If I'm gonna steal something, I'm not gonna steal from somebody I know, especially when they know I'm in there. If they can't trust me, I don't want to be around 'em.

They come home maybe around seven and you're sitting down to supper and they'll call. "I got a stopped up toilet. It was stopped up yesterday." I'll say, "Why didn't you call me? I could have had it fixed today while you were at work." "Well, I didn't have my key." Sometimes you get in a mood and you say, "Suffer then." (Laughs.) If I'm eating, I finish eating, then I go. But if it's a broken pipe and it's running into somebody else's apartment, you get on your high horse and you're over there right away.

Phone calls always go to your wife, and a lot of people are very rude. They figure your wife works. My wife is not on the payroll. They call her up and chew her out about something, "When will he get here?" She's just there, she's being nice enough to take my calls for me. A lot of the janitors now are getting machines to take their calls. They'll call you up and the machine says, "Leave your message." They'll say something silly and hang up. They'll see you on the street and tell you about it. They don't like an answering service. They want to make contact right there.

My wife gets tired of the calls. It's a pain in the neck. My mother lives with us since my dad passed away. She takes my calls for me. She's used to it. She's been doing it so long. She lets 'em talk if they have a complaint. She just lets 'em talk. (Laughs.) Some of 'em will demand. I just tell 'em, "I think you're very unreasonable. I'll see you in the morning." If they keep arguing, I just politely say, "That's it." And I hang up on 'em.

You just don't let it get the best of you. We've had janitors hang themselves. Since I've been out here, three hung themselves. They let it get the best of 'em. I asked this one guy, "Eddie, what on earth is wrong?"

He's up there fixing lights in this high rise and he's shaking all over. "These people are driving me crazy," he says. I read about this guy, Red, he blowed his brains out. People drive 'em batty. They want this, they want that. You let it build up inside—the heck with it. You do the best you can. If they don't like it . . .

You gotta watch. We have a business agent in the area and, oh man, there's too many guys lookin' for work. These people coming from Europe, Yugoslavs and Croatians. We're talking about young guys, thirty years old, twenty-five. They're nice guys. They talk broken, but you get to know 'em. They bowl with us and learn as quick as they can. A lot less young native-born are in it now. They'll take a job like a helper until they can find something better. A helper makes $640 a month, five-day week.

Back in the forties a janitor was a sort of low-class job. Nobody wanted it. But during the Depression, janitors were working. They had a place to live and they had food on the table. It was steady work. They had a few clothes on their back. Other people didn't.

Today a janitor is on the same level as the plant maintenance man. If I leave my work I would have no trouble walking into any plant and taking over as supervisor, maintenance electrical repair. I saw an ad the other day, it took my eye. They're paying twelve thousand and travel. To me it would be very interesting and easy. But I couldn't afford to take a salary of twelve thousand dollars. If I'm making more now, I want to better myself. My dad always said, "It's not what you make, it's what you save." (Laughs.)

Most of 'em will call me an engineer or they will kid me. 'Cause it's on my coat. I wear regular uniform clothes. Gray trousers, blue. I have different colors. I have green, blue, gray. Shirt and trousers to match and a jacket, sort of ski-jacket-like, with an emblem on it. I try to keep clean because nobody wants somebody dirty around. I'm not a sweeper. I'm like a stationary engineer. I've been out with lawyers. It's the way you conduct yourself. If you know nothing, keep your mouth shut. You learn a lot by keeping your mouth shut.

I got a boy married. I'm a grandfather. He's twenty, going on twenty-one. He was an honor student in math. I wanted him to go to IIT.* He run off and got married. A kid'll do what he wants to do. He hurt us real bad. He said, "Dad, why should I spend all your money and go to college. I can get a job driving a truck and make more money than a college graduate." I said, "There's two different kinds of work, though."

So he's working now as a janitor's helper. In a couple of months, he'll have a building himself and make eight hundred dollars a month and a free apartment. He'll probably pick up another building on the side and make another two hundred. And this is just a start for the kid. But I wish he'd a went into engineering. I don't know why, but I feel . . . (hesitates) . . . I believe in college. I didn't get a chance to go and I believe in it. Even if he comes back to janitoring, he's still got this in his head. College doesn't hurt anybody. He's saved me a lot of money and everything. He'll do all right for himself, but . . .

A college man is underpaid today. We have a janitor, a kid that eats with us every morning. This guy has all kinds of degrees in electrical engineering. He can't get a job. They want to pay him peanuts. He's making more money now.

I carry on the side a criminal investigator's badge. I can carry a gun whenever I want. I'm registered by the state, with the FBI and with the city police. You gotta be fingerprinted, you gotta be registered with Springfield. It's marked right on the card, it's volunteer.

I work for a detective agency because sometimes it's pretty rough at night. We go down holes, in basements. We stop a lot of burglaries, people robbing apartments. We can hold 'em for the police. We arrest 'em and we hold 'em. I've worked with the FBI. Watch out for Weathermen and stuff like that in the neighborhood.

I've worked with two or three young FBI men, very intelligent men, very respectable men. I really admire 'em and I love to help 'em. I'm all over the University of Chicago area, so I got it pretty well covered all around. They pass out pictures to watch for. You don't have no author-

* Illinois Institute of Technology.

ity, you just kind of see the area. This is for something like dope. We look through the garbage. They'll tell you what to look for.

Like some of these political kids?

Yeah, in a way. But they never bothered me with that. It's mostly like dope or something. They're not talking about a little pot party. About somebody selling it. We had a girl living in one of these buildings, she made trips to Mexico. She was crippled, she was in a wheel chair. They believed she was bringing it back and forth. I don't get involved because they don't let me get involved.

You report to them now and then . . . ?

Oh, yeah.

Do a lot of janitors do this?

No, no, no.

Is it because you're in a university area?

Well, yeah . . . (Quickly) They're not interested in the kids. They're interested in the guy bringing the stuff in. They might be watching him for a different reason altogether. There was a case where a kid didn't report for draft. They didn't want to arrest the kid or nothing. But they wanted to know where he was so . . .

All they told me is: "You know where he lives? Do you know where he moved?" So I tell them where they move. We saw him walking the street the other day and I called them and they said, "Find out where he moved." That's all. They don't want to arrest the guy, but I guess they want to talk to him. Oh, I don't know . . . what the hell, these draft dodgers.

The janitor knows more about the neighborhood than anybody, doesn't he?

He can, if he wants to get nosy, yeah. I enjoy my work. You meet people, you're out with the public. I have no boss standing over me. People call me Mr. Hoellen. Very

respectable. If I'm a good friend, they say Eric. I'm proud
of my job. I've made it what it is today. Up in the morning, get the work done, back home. Open the fires and
close 'em. (Laughs.)

WATCHING

FRITZ RITTER

He's the doorman at a huge apartment building on Manhattan's Upper West Side. "I would say about 180 apartments." It has seen better days, though signs of its long-ago elegance are still discernible. High ceilings, marble pillars, expansive lobby. The walls could stand a paint job. The floor's tile has had it; its patterns, hardly visible. We're seated on a divan in the lobby. He wears his uniform. He is bareheaded and is smoking a cigarette.

The neighborhood's not so good any more like it used to be. Used to be very nice, one of the best neighborhoods in the city—Nice restaurants, nice movies, and nice people. You know what I mean? I mean very high class. The times change and everything. You know what I mean? Sure. Don't you think so? Sure. There's still some good ones in this building, very nice ones. Mostly middle class, I would say. And some hippies too. But I think it will go down a bit more. You know?

I watch who comes in, goes out. If I see a stranger, I stop him and find out where he's going. We call upstairs, we have to announce him. In the nighttime now, twelve o'clock, you have the door locked. The old days, we had the doors open. I didn't have to stop nobody. Then it was opened twenty-four hours a day.

I worked forty-one years in this building. I started '31, '32, something like that. I worked twelve hours a day, six days a week. From seven to seven, nights. There was no

179

union then, no vacations, no nothing. Now we work five days and forty hours. That's much better.

In them days, the doorman was ... ohhh! You had to be dressed nice—white gloves and a stiff collar. And the white tie there, even like the waiters use, the head waiter. Nicer uniforms than this. In the summertime, gray uniform and white gloves, always gloves. You had to wear hats always. I had a problem one time with the boss. I didn't want to wear a cap. I don't know why. I always take it off. He comes by, I put it on. He goes away, I take it off. Off and on, off and on. But that's the way it is.

If tenants came by, you had to stand up. If you were sitting down, you'd stand up. As a doorman then, you couldn't sit like this. When I was first hired, I sat down with my legs crossed. The manager came over and he said, "No, sit down like this"—arms folded, legs stiff. If tenants came in, you had to stand up quick, stand there like a soldier. You only spoke when they spoke to you. Otherwise, don't say nothin'.

It was real high class, yes. Nice rugs on the floor, nice furniture. Oh, they all had maids. No maid could come in the front. You had to go all in the service, oh yeah. They were working Monday, Tuesday. The service cars would be up and down, up and down. Today they come in the front. They don't have many maids today like they had before.

When the house was high class, the tenants look down on me. When they used to see me on the street they'd make believe they didn't know me. There was a restaurant in here. I used to go there once in a while, they'd make believe they didn't see you. But it didn't bother me. Because I don't give a damn if they speak to me or not. Because I did my job a hundred percent. Even to this day, the old-timers, sometime they see you somewhere and they make believe you're not there. It's the truth. They think they're better. Years ago, sure they did. They wouldn't say nothin'. You couldn't say boo.

One time I felt lousy, I had hay fever. I was on the elevator, I say, low, "Good morning" to the man. And he says to me, "Don't you say good morning?" I say, "I *did* say good morning." 'Cause I had hay fever and I feel bad. He didn't spoke to me no more and he cut me off for Christmas. But I didn't care. It was about 1932, '33. See how people are.

I had good times here, don't get me wrong, very good times. Everyone dressed up, my dear man. They were dressed high as anything. There was movie stars living in this house. Sure. Singers, Metropolitan. Sure. Doctors, lawyers, bankers.

An elderly man walks by, erect, though with a slight touch of fatigue. He is carrying a doctor's black bag. Fritz calls out, "Good morning." The man nods, hardly looking our way. "He's an old-timer. He's been here thirty-five years, very nice man."

Times change. Today it's different. Today is every day more liberal. Today they discuss, they talk with you. Even the high-class ones change. Everybody change today, more friendly today. Today I make a joke, they take it. More on the equal side, more friendship. Before you couldn't do nothing. I see one time a doorman smokes a cigarette and the tenant went over to the manager and they fired 'im right out. They said, "Go"—just like that. You had no chance at all. Yesterday when payday was, they don't want you, you're through. They can't do that today no more. Today the man is better off.

But I would like to see the house the way it was. If a stranger come in today, I stop him. I ask where he's going. Some of 'em give me a little trouble, especially the Democrats, the black ones. I call 'em Democrats. I don't want to say colored or white or anybody—just Democrats. One time a guy says to me, "Didn't you ever see a colored man come in here?" I said, "Yes, but it's my job. I don't care what you do upstairs, but I have to ask where you're going, see?" When he came down, he said, "I'm awfully sorry. I didn't realize that." Seem with all this liberal stuff you have your ups and downs. I didn't have that years ago.

You never had to stop 'em before. I knew who they were. Years ago, they had more family life. Their friends come in or their brother or somebody you knew. Today is more open. They take apartments here, three, four guys, girls, and they have friends come in and you don't know who is who. You have to stop 'em. I have to tell 'em this is my job.

There's a lot of trouble around here. Pocketbook gets snatched, things like that. I used to work nighttime. There was a couch here. I slept there and the door was open in the summertime. Nobody came in, not a soul. Today you couldn't do that. When I was out of the service in 1945, it was pretty good. But in the last ten years you get a little trouble. You walk there in the street, you see it. Drinking, dope ... The uniform helps, yeah. If I would stay there with the suit on, they wouldn't respect me. But when they see a uniform, they know who I am.

A heavy-set blonde girl wearing slacks has entered the vestibule. It had started to rain several minutes before. It is now a downpour. She stands against the wall. She's obviously in a good humor. Fritz approaches her. She smiles at him and holds forth a half-pint. She offers it to him. She has a slight Spanish accent. He declines in a friendly manner. The rain slackens, she waves good-by and leaves.

"You need something?" she said. "I don't need something," I say to her. That would never happen years ago, no, no, never. You couldn't say things like this or "How are you?" I liked it. You didn't get in no trouble. They think today because you're friendly they got advantage, you know? Freshness.

The people, they all know me. When they go away here in the summertime, they give me the key and I take care of the apartment. Whatever, flowers. I don't care what's laying there, I wouldn't touch it. They know this. There could be whisky staying there, I wouldn't touch nothing. If they have a little money in there, I don't care what they got laying there, I wouldn't touch it. They know this. They respect me.

In forty-one years, if I took five days off for foolishness, I would be a liar. Oh, I never take off. I betcha I wasn't late five times in forty-one years. I'm very on the ball. I should get more money because I'm here a long time. A new guy comes in, he don't know nothing, he gets the same pay I do. But then the other way around; if they would have to pay me more, they would take the younger man and save money.

I don't care no more, because I'm sixty-five and maybe a year more and I will retire. I hope God is good to me, that I have my health. So long as I feel good, I work, because I have a nice job and I don't kill myself. I wouldn't like to take off now and sit on the bench here, with the older men here. I wouldn't like it every day, like friends of mine. I'm active, I like to do something.

I came to this country from Germany, there were no jobs. This is 1927. I was working in a candy factory. Christmas and Easter we worked. They lay me off. The money I saved up went to hell. So this job was steady. Even if I wanted to change, I couldn't change, because there was nothing. I was glad to have it. If I was to come to this country again, I would like to be a mechanic. Because today you have golden opportunity.

VINCENT MAHER

Each child has a dream. I had two. One was to be a marine and the other was to be a policeman. I tried other endeavors but I was just not cut out for it. I am a policeman. It is one of the most gratifying jobs in the world.

He is thirty-nine. He lives apart from his family—a wife and three children: two boys, fifteen and twelve, and a girl, fourteen. He presently directs traffic in Chicago's Loop. He had previously been a member of the Tactical Unit. Due to a personal grievance, he had resigned from the force. For a time, he worked as a bartender—disconsolately. "I had a deputy chief come in and a commander. They said, 'Vince, you're a cop. Get your fanny back on the job.' I came back on the job and I'm happy."

Two of his uncles had been on the force in New York City, as was his father, "until he lost his trigger finger in a railroad accident." As he reflects, past and present fuse.

I make an arrest on someone who commits a crime of violence. I have to resort to a physical type of arrest to subdue him, I might have to shoot the person. I'm chastised for being brutal. It's all right for him to do what he wants to do against myself or legitimate people, but in no way I can touch him. I don't see the justice.

I've been accused of being a bigot, a hypocrite, and a few other niceties. I'm a human being with a job. I judge people on face value. Just because a guy wears long hair doesn't make him a radical. Just because he's black—I'd

rather work in a black neighborhood. They need me more
than the white. White neighborhoods are not as involved
in actual crime, the dirtiness, as they are in poor neighborhoods. I don't mean blacks alone. There are Southern
whites that come up here, they live in jungles. So do the
Puerto Ricans.

The white man, he wants me to write an illegally
parked car or write the neighbor nextdoor for his dog def-
ecating on the grass. I don't dig this. This is not my kind.
I lived in a jungle, I've come from a jungle. In those early
days, nobody knew the word nigger. There was no hate.
You came and went as you pleased. I've seen kids come
out of a bad neighborhood, some become priests, some become policemen, others go to the penitentiary. I don't believe what some judges say: because of environment, this
is the way it is. I wasn't born with a silver spoon in my
mouth. I never finished high school. I finished the hard
way—Uncle Sam and I. I should be a crook because I
came out of a slum neighborhood? My dad was a Depression kid. I saw him when he was making four dollars a
week, supporting four kids and a wife. (Laughs.) That's
why I became a policeman.

I'm in traffic now—semi-retirement. (Laughs softly,
ruefully.) All I ever wanted was detective and I couldn't
make it. When I was on the Tactical Force, I just couldn't
wait. I used to work my days off. I felt I was really functioning as a police officer. I get out there and infiltrate, to
find out why, when, and where. We need an element to
get out there. I'm not saying it's the greatest thing in the
world, but it's necessary. It's a evil because crime is evil.
Why do these people who preach liberalism and pacifism
require walls around their houses? They need these buffers. That's what we are, buffers.

If there was a crime pattern working, we'd go out and
find out who, what, when, and cleaned it up. We would
roam the street as citizens, rather than marked as policemen. We'd wear neat and presentable suits. You can hear
a lot more when you're sitting in a group of hippies or
you're sitting in a restaurant. That's how I used to operate. I'd pick up information. Nobody knew I was a policeman.

I don't believe in entrapping. To entrap is to induce
someone to commit a crime. The prostitute was a great
source of information. This is funny, but I'd rather have a

prostitute working the street. This is her trade and it's been going since Adam and Eve. If I were President, I'd legalize it. As long as she's operating, I don't have to worry about someone being raped or a child being molested. They render a service as long as they're clean and don't hurt people.

I used to call the girls at two in the morning and say, "I need four or five for the night." And they'd say, "Okay Vince, we'll be here. Come back in about two hours." They'd all be lined up and I'd lock 'em up. I'd grab one of the broads off the street and I'd say, "Charlene, you'd better hustle because I'm coming back later and if I catch youse around—boom—you're gonna get nailed. The beef is on."

The good suffer for the faults of the bad. You get one hooker out there that's a bad one, starts jackrolling, working with a pimp, you've got a bad beef. As long as the broads are operating and nobody's hurt . . . If Sam wants to go out and get something strange. he's gonna go. I can't put a ball and chain on this man. His own conscience has got to be his guide.

I don't discriminate, black or white broads. They were good to me. They were my source of information. They can go places where my eyes and ears can't go. The best eyes and ears the policeman has got is the street, because the blue is known even when you don't have it on. So you send your other people out.

When they get pinched, they're not hurt so much. When they put up a twenty-five-dollar bond, they know I'm not gonna be in court and they get their money back and they're back on the street. They take the bust and it's a cover for them.

There was a gang of thieves in Old Town. At the time, there was sixty or seventy unsolved robberies. They were working in conjunction with prostitutes. They'd rob the trick. They would sometimes cut, beat, or shoot the victim. My two partners and I set out one night and I was the decoy. I was picked up by two prostitutes. I took on four guys in a gun battle. One guy stuck a shotgun in my stomach and it misfired. The other guy opened up on me with a .38. I killed the man with the shotgun, wounded the other guy, and took the other two. I *volunteered*. I was decorated for it and given a chance to make detective. But I didn't make it.

I'm human. I make mistakes like everybody else. If you want a robot, build machines. If you want human beings, that's what I am. I'm an honest cop. I don't think any person doing my job could face the stuff I face without losing your temper at one time or another. I've used the word nigger, I've used the word stump-jumpin' hillbilly, I've used vulgarity against 'em. It depends on the element.

I've never studied psychology, but I apply it every day of my life. You can go into an atmosphere of doctors and lawyers and educators and get a point across verbally. They understand. You can also work on the South or West Side,* where you can talk your fool head off and get nothing. They don't understand this nicety-type guy. So you walk with a big stick. Like the adage of a mule: He's a very intelligent animal, but in order to get his attention you have to hit him on the head with a stick. Same thing applies on the street.

You walk up to some of these people and they'll spit in your face. If you let them, then I've lost what I am as a policeman, because now I've let the bad overrule me. So I have to get physical sometimes. It isn't done in a brutal sense. I call it a corrective measure. You get these derelicts on the street. I've dealt with these people for years. You whack 'em on the sole of the foot. It isn't brutal, but it stings and he gets the message: he's not supposed to be sleeping on the street. "Get up!" You get him on his feet and say, "Now go on back to junk heaven that you live in and get some sleep." Someone coming down the street sees me use the stick on the sole of his foot is gonna scream that I'm brutal.

There were five gentlemen standing on the corner, all black. One guy stepped in front of my car, and said, "You white mother so-and-so, you ain't goin' nowhere." Bleep-bleep on the horn. I say, "Listen fella, move!" He didn't move. The challenge was there. I'm alone, I'm white. And he's one of these people that read in the magazines: Challenge the policeman. I got out of the squad car and I told him, "You . . ." (Hesitates.) I rapped to him in his tongue and he understood. I called him everything in the book. I said, "Get up off the curb or you're gonna go to jail." He made a very emphatic point of trying to take me physically. It didn't work. When his four buddies saw him go

* Black neighborhoods.

on the ground, I got the message across: I'm the boss on the street. If you're the jungle cat, I'm the man with the whip and the chain. If that's the way you want to be treated, I'm gonna treat you that way. If you want to be physical, mister, you better be an awful good man to take me.

From now on, I'd walk up and down that street and the guys'd say (imitates black accent), "Hiya mister po-lice, how ya doin'?" I don't care if you're yellow, pink, or purple, I'm a policeman and I demand respect. Not for me as an individual, but for what I represent. Unfortunately, the country's going the other way. They'll be throwing bricks and bottles at you and you'll be told don't do anything, they're merely expressing themselves.

Now this bit about advising people of their constitutional rights. I have been doing that for years. Nobody had to tell me to do it. I did it because I felt: Listen, baby, you open your big mouth and anything you tell me, I'm gonna use against you. I didn't come right out and say, "Sir, I must advise you of your constitutional rights." I didn't stand there and let them go bang-bang and stick-stick with a blade while I'm tellin' 'em. I'm just as much a policeman to the black man as I am to the white man, to the yellow man, to the liberal, to the conservative, to the hippie or whatever. I choose no sides.

I was respected as good cannon fodder. But where do I lack the quality of leadership? This is what bugs me. Is there something wrong with me that I can't be a leader. Who is to judge me? I've had guys on this job that have begged to work with me as a partner. If that doesn't show leadership . . .

Remember when you were a kid and the policeman took you across the street? What is he doing in essence? He's walking you through danger, is he not? Okay, I do the same thing. If I take you by the hand and walk you through Lincoln Park, nobody's gonna mess with you. But if I don't take you and walk you through the park, somebody's gonna mug you. I protect you from the dangerous elements. All these do-gooders that say, "Oh yeah, we respect you"—you have the feeling that they're saying yes with their mouth, but they're laughing at you. They don't respect me.

I'd love to go out on the college campus and grab some of these radicals. It's more or less a minority. When you apply logic and truth and philosophy, they cannot come back at you. You cannot fight truth. Who's being brutal? Before I make an arrest, I'll tell the guy, "You have a choice. You could be nice and we'll walk. If you become combative, I'm going to use physical force against you to compensate. In fact, I'm gonna have to break some bones. You forced the issue."

Oh yeah, the Democratic Convention. (A show of hurt appears, in the manner of a small boy's pout.) There was this radical garbage piece of thing, dirty, long-haired, not a human being in my book, standing by the paddy wagon. Not a mark on him. He spotted the camera and disappeared. In thirty seconds he came back. He was covered with all kinds of blood. He's screaming into the camera, "Look what they did to me!"

Lincoln Park. This group was comin' down on me. I'm by myself. They're comin' down the hill, "Kill the pig! Off the pig!" Well, I'm not a pig. There's only one of me and a whole mess of them. Well, *c'est le guerre*, sweetheart. I folded my arms, put my hand on my .38. I looked at them and said, "What's happening?" They stopped. They thought I was gonna pull out my weapon and start blowin' brains out. I didn't lose my cool. I'm a policeman, I don't scare. I'm dumb that way. (Laughs.) These kids were incited by someone to do something. They said, "Those guys up there with the cameras." I blame the media.

There's a picture in the Loop—*Sweet Sweetback's Badasssss Song*—it is strictly hate-white. Nobody pickets that. You can imagine an anti-Negro flick? These people can get away with anything they want. But if you try it, zero, you'll get nailed. The radicals and the black militants, they're the dangers. They could be standing here on the street corner selling this Black Panther thing. (Imitates black accent), "This magazine is fo' de black man." He wants to off the pig. And I'm standing there. How do you think I feel? You know what off the pig means? Kill the pig. I look at them and I laugh. I'd like to break his neck. But I'm a policeman, a professional. I know the element they are. They're like the Nazi was with the Germans. The SS. No good.

To me, when I was a kid, the policeman was the epitome—not of perfection—was a good and evil in combination, but in *control*. He came from an element in the neighborhood and he knew what was going on. To me, a policeman is your community officer. He is your Officer Friendly, he is your clergyman, he is your counselor. He is a doctor to some: "Mr. Policeman, my son just fell and bumped his head." Now all we are is a guy that sits in a squad car and waits for a call to come over the radio. We have lost complete contact with the people. They get the assumption that we're gonna be called to the scene for one purpose—to become violent to make an arrest. No way I can see that. I am the community officer. They have taken me away from the people I'm dedicated to serving—and I don't like it.

The cop on the corner took you across the street, right? Now, ten o'clock at night, he's still there on the corner, and he tells you to get your fanny home. He's not being nice. The next time he tells you, he's gonna whack you with the stick. In the old days, if you went home and told your dad the cop on the corner whacked you with a stick, you know what your father did? He whacked you twice as hard. He said, "You shouldn't've been there. The policeman told you to go home, go home." Today these kids defy you.

I handed one parent a stick. I said, "Lady, when I leave this room and you don't apply that stick to this young lady's mouth, I will. I'll also sign charges against you for contributing to the delinquency of this child. You don't know how to be a parent." If I was sitting at a table with my father and threw a temper tantrum, I got knocked on my rear end. When I was picked up I was told, "You eat it, 'cause it's there." The law is there. If you don't want the law and you don't like my country, get out.

Take an old Western town. I just saw a thing with Richard Widmark on TV, which I thought was great. A town was being ramrodded by baddies. So they got ahold of this gunfighter and made him their sheriff, and he cleaned up the town. A little hard, but he was a nice guy. He got rid of the element and they told him he could have the job for as long as he wanted it. Then the people that put him in got power and they became dirty. They wanted things done and he said no. He wound up getting killed. This is what I feel about me and these do-gooders. They get power, I'm in their way.

I'm the element that stands between the legitimate person and the criminal. Years ago, he wore a .45 and he was a gunfighter and he wasted people. Okay, I don't be-

lieve in killing everybody. But I do believe we've gone
overboard. They can shoot a guy like crazy but we cannot
retaliate. I'm a target for these people. Go ahead, vent
yourself. That's what I'm here for, a whipping boy. I'm
not saying life in itself is violent, but I deal in the violent
part of life.

There *is* a double standard, let's face it. You can stop
John Doe's average son for smoking pot and he'll go to
jail. But if I stop Johnny Q on the street and his daddy
happens to be the president of a bank or he's very heavy
in politics or knows someone, you look like a jerk. Why
did you arrest *him?* Do you know who he is? I could care
less who he is. If he breaks the law, go.

I made a raid up at the beach. The hippies were con-
gregating, creating sex orgies and pot and everything. The
word went out, especially about hitchhiking. Okay, we
used to raid the beach and lock everybody up, didn't care
who they were. One fella told me, "I'm gonna have your
job. My father is out on the lake with the mayor." I said,
"Fine, when you go to court bring your father *and* the
mayor. But as far as I'm concerned, mister, you're doing a
no-no, and you're going to jail."

We knew pot was involved. They were creating a disturbance. It was after eleven o'clock at night. You got
rules and regulations for one reason—discipline. I consider
the law as rules and regulations—in the military, on my
job, or as citizens. They were puncturing tires, breaking
antennas off cars, throwing bottles, fornicating on the
beach—everything! Hitchhiking was impeding traffic. So I
started locking them up for hitchhiking. All of a sudden,
lay off! The citizens made a peace treaty with them. I'm
the one who gets chastised! I did the job the citizens
wanted me to do, right? All of a sudden, "Hey, dummy,
lay off!"

Jealous? Never. No way. I'm not prudish in any way,
shape, or form. (Laughs.) I'm far from being a virgin.
You're not a marine to be a virgin, no way in the world.
But I don't believe in garbage. Sex is a beautiful thing. I
dig it. But to exploit it in such a fashion to make it garbage, that to me is offensive. Jealousy, no way. I look at
those people out there as I would be going to the zoo and
watching the monkeys play games. That doesn't turn me
on. They're all perverted people. I don't believe in perver-
sion. They're making it strictly animal. Monkeys in the

cage, boom, boom, boom, from one to the other, that's it. I believe in one man and one woman.

Do all long-haired guys bug you?

I don't want my sons to have it. Now, the sideburns I wear because I do TV commercials and stuff. I'm in the modeling field.

He moonlights on occasion—modeling, appearing in industrial films, selling insurance, and driving semi-trucks. "I'm not necessarily ambitious. I do it because I like it. I jump in a truck and I'm gone to Iowa, Ohio, Kentucky. It's a great kick for me."

But I don't like long hair. If it's your bag, do it, but don't try to force it on me. A long-hair person doesn't bother me, but when you see that radical with the mop and that shanky garbage and you can smell 'em a block away, that bothers me.

A few years ago there was this hippie, long-haired, slovenly. He confronted me. Don't ever confront me when I tell you to move. That's a no-no. To make a long story short, I—uh—(laughs) I cut a piece of his long hair off and I handed it back to him. With a knife. It was just a spontaneous reaction. He was screaming "brutality." Anyway, a couple of weeks later I was confronted by this nice-looking fellow in a suit, haircut, everything. He said, "Officer, do you recognize me?" He pulled out this cellophane packet and handed it to me, and there was his hair in it. (Laughs.) I said, "That's you?" And he said, "Yeah. You showed me one thing. You really care about people. I just had to go out and get a job and prove something to you." That kid joined the Marine Corps.

Sometimes I feel like a father out there. You don't really want to paddle your kid's rear end. It hurts you ten times more than it does him. But you have to put the point across, and if it becomes necessary to use a little constructive criticism . . . I will think of my father a lot of times. No way did he spare the rod on my rump. And I never hated him for it, no way. I loved him for it.

My sons adore me. My wife can't understand this. If they do something wrong in my presence—(mumbles) even though I don't live in that house—they get punished. My wife said, "You're so hard with them at times, yet they worship the ground you walk on." When I used the belt on them I'd always tell them why. They understand and they accept it. My oldest boy is now on the honor rolls at Notre Dame High School.

He gets a little stubborn. He'd confront me with things: "I want to wear my hair long." "You want to wear your hair long, get out of my house. You know what it represents to me. Till the day you are twenty-one and you will leave my jurisdiction, you will do as I tell you. You understand?" "Okay Dad, you're the boss." That's all there is to it. There's no resentment, no animosity. It's just an understanding that I lay the law down. There are rules and regulations.

But I'm not a robot, I think for myself. One thing bugs me. Burglary is a felony. If a burglar is trapped and becomes physical and is shot to death, that's justifiable homicide. Mayor Daley made an utterance—shoot to kill—and they—click—blew it up. I don't think he meant it literally.

I can't shoot an unarmed person. No way. Anyway, knowing people, they'll say, "Forget it, we're insured." So why should I get involved over an insurance matter? I would love to go after people who perpetrate robberies or hurt other people. A theft, granted it's a crime, but most of the people it hurts is the insurance company. Robbery is hurting a person.

I prefer going after robbery more than homicide. When a guy commits murder, he's usually done. He's caught and goes to the penitentiary or the chair. But a guy that commits robbery doesn't usually get caught the first time, second, third time. He's out there over and over again. I want to grab the guy that's hitting all the time, instead of the guy that's doing the one shot. I love risk and challenge. Driving a semi down the road is challenging. You never know what's going to happen. (Laughs.) Some guy passes you, cuts you off, you're jack-knifed. You blow a tire, you're gone. I don't like a boring life.

When I worked as a bartender, I felt like a nonperson. I was actually nothing. I was a nobody going nowhere. I was in a state of limbo. I had no hopes, no dreams, no ups, no downs, nothing. Being a policeman gives me the challenge in life that I want. Some day I'll be promoted. Somebody's gonna say, "Maher has had it for a long time. Let's give him something." Some sort of recognition. I've proven myself. I don't think it's necessary for a man to prove himself over and over and over again. I'm a policeman, win, lose, or draw.

I'm in this Loop traffic. I don't even consider this a job. It's like R&R, rest and recreation. My day today is like— (whistles) it's a no-no. It's nothing. I get up, I eat, and I blow the whistle. It's not very exciting. I'm looking at it now as a fellow who goes to the office and he's not very enthused. Because I wear a uniform people that are garbage will say I'm a pig. They don't look at me and say, "This is a human being." They look at my dress. I'm a representative of the law, of you, the citizen. You created my job, you created me. To you, I am a robot in uniform. You press a button and when you call me to the scene you expect results. But I'm also a man. I even have a heart. (Laughs.)

RENAULT ROBINSON

He is thirty. He has been a member of the Chicago Police Department for nine years. He is the founder of the Afro-American Patrolmen's League.

I became a police officer because of the opportunity it afforded a young black who didn't have a college education. I started out working in vice and gambling, a special unit in a black area. I worked in plain clothes, in undercover assignments—trying to stake out dice games, bookies, policy wheel operations, narcotics, prostitutes. I would write the report and another team would make the arrests. It was very easy for me to find these things in the community, because any black can find 'em. I really worked as a spy. At the time—I was twenty-one—I thought it was great to be a young police detective, being able to lock people up. A lot of young blacks are misdirected when they first join the force. I soon became disenchanted.

I watched the double standard at work, blacks being treated one way and whites the other. I learned one thing: whites control the vice and gambling in this city. They

make most of the money out of it and very few are arrested. The people being arrested are blacks.

My supervisor would say, "We need two policy arrests,
so we can be equal with the other areas." So we go out
and hunt for a policy operator. If our narcotics enforcement was down, we'd find an addict and we'd pressure
him to show us where his supplier was. We'd bust him.
We'd pay him some money so he could buy from another
supplier and we'd bust him too. Usually the addict had
one guy he didn't like. He was willing to trade the guy off
for fresh cash. The police department has a contingency
fund for these purposes. We'd pay the guy fifty or one
hundred dollars depending . . . We'd get a warrant, or if we
didn't have time we'd lock him up anyway. It would be
impossible to work without informers. How'd you know
there's a house of prostitution across the street? A policeman grabs a guy off the street: "I'm gonna pay you X
amount for information." These types come up to you
sometimes. They make a good living informing.

You arrest a narcotics peddler three or four times, you
know what he's doing. There's a way of putting him out of
business if you wanted to. If you think about the people
operating policy, bookies, narcotics—hundreds and hundreds are employed in these illegal trades. It's full-time
work. A lot of people would be out of business if they
broke these things up. What the police do is just enough to
let the public know they're out there. There's no fight between the professional criminals and the police. There's no
police brutality here. They know the police, they got the
bond money in their pocket or a lawyer who'll be down
there. We maintain an image, that's all. To look as though
we actively pursue organized crime. It's a farce. The fight
is with the normal citizen who goes astray once in a while.

A vice officer spends quite a bit of time in court. You
learn the judges, the things they look for. You become
proficient in testifying. You change your testimony, you
change the facts. You switch things around 'cause you're
trying to get convictions. You figure he's only a criminal,
so you lie about it. The judges are aware of it. The guy
who works in plain clothes is usually ambitious and aggressive and will take the time to go to court.

A lot of times for certain disorderlies, the policeman won't show up and the judge will throw the case out.
What he did was just inconvenience the guy. He didn't

even care about it. He just wanted to get the guy, sort of built-in I'm-gonna-punish-you kind of thing. He still gets his points.

About sixty percent of police-citizen conflict starts in a traffic situation. It's easier to stop a person on the pretext of a traffic violation than to stop him on the street. It's a lot easier to say, "Your tail light's out." "Your plate is dented." "You didn't make that turn right." You can then search his automobile, hoping you can find some contraband or a weapon. If he becomes irritated, with very little pushing on your part, you can make an arrest for disorderly conduct. These are all statistics which help your records.

Certain units in the task force have developed a science around stopping your automobile. These men know it's impossible to drive three blocks without committing a traffic violation. We've got so many rules on the books. These police officers use these things to get points and also hustle for money. The traffic law is a fat book. He knows if you don't have two lights on your licence plate, that's a violation. If you have a crack in your windshield, that's a violation. If your muffler's dragging, that's a violation. He knows all these little things.

They're sure the person who has stolen a car is probably driving, the person who is transporting stolen merchandise is in a vehicle, the person selling dope has it in his car. In their minds, the average black person driving down the street falls into one of these categories. (Laughs.) So if they stop the average black driver, in their mind the likelihood of finding five or six violations out of a hundred cars is highly possible. If you stop fifty cars, find five, stop a hundred, find ten. After you've stopped a thousand, you've got 950 people who are very pissed off, 950 who might have been just average citizens, not doing anything wrong—teachers, doctors, lawyers, working people. The police don't care. Black folks don't have a voice to complain. Consequently, they continue to be victims of shadowy, improper, overburdened police service. Traffic is the big entree.

If it's a bunch of kids, they get stopped automatically. If it's a black in a Cadillac, he gets stopped.* He's gotta

---

* Big Bill Broonzy, the late blues artist, frequently told the story of his visit to his mother, who lived in the outskirts of be selling dope or something. If it's a white woman and a black man in a car in a black community, they're automatically stopped, 'cause she's gotta be a whore. If it's a long-haired white kid, he's gonna be stopped, 'cause he's probably a communist.

It's not restricted to just the black community. There are a lot of white youths. Many of them know they were never stopped for violations before they let their hair grow long. Many whites know that before they put a bumper sticker on their car, PEACE IN VIETNAM, they were never stopped by the police.

The young black is the big police hang-up because his tolerance of police brutality has grown short. They say, "The new niggers don't respect us any more the way the old niggers used to. We used to holler at 'em and shout at 'em and kick 'em and they went along with it." Young niggers ain't going along with it and that's what bugs them more than anything in the world. That's why more young kids are being killed by police than ever before. They won't accept dehumanizing treatment.

You have to remove salesmanship from police work. Don't put me on a commission and say, "Every time you stop a guy, you get X amount of points." It takes a certain amount of points to reach a certain plateau. You can't go back to the boss and say, "I didn't see anything." He says, "I know they're out there. Go out and get 'em." So the policeman has to create a little something.

So many points for a robbery, so many points for a man having a gun. When they go to the scene and the man with the gun has gone, they'll lock up somebody anyway, knowing he's not the one. The record says, "Locked up two people for UUW"—unlawful use of weapons. The report will say, "When we got there, we saw these guys and they looked suspicious." They'll get a point even if the case is thrown out of court. The arrest is all that counts.

There are more cops in the black community than in the white. The eighth district, lily-white, is the largest in the city: thirty-two square miles, 237,374 people, all right? This district, black, five and a half square miles, has more police patrol than the eighth. The crime rate's

---

Little Rock, Arkansas. He was driving a Cadillac. A white policeman flagged him down. "Whose car is this, boy? Ain't yours, is it?" "No, sir. It belongs to my boss." "Okay."

highest in this area because we're unprotected. We've got more and more policemen here, yet the crime rate rises. Evidently something's wrong.

I worked in a white area on the West Side—briefly. Being black, in plain clothes, people might mistake me for a burglar and shoot me. It's better for me to be in a black area. Of course, people couldn't mistake me there. (Laughs.) Very few black officers work in white areas. They have a few, so they can say; "No longer are we segregated."

The majority of the policemen in the station where I worked were young whites. The older white officers were trying to get off the street, trying for a soft job in a station somewhere. They were tired. It's the young white officer who's in most of the black areas. They want to go there. It gives them the opportunity to be where the action is. They don't want to go to white districts because they're considered slow.

A large amount of young white officers are gung ho. It's an opportunity to make a lot of arrests, make money, and do a lot of other things. In their opinion, black people are all criminals, no morals, dirty and nasty. So the black people don't cooperate with the police and they have good cause not to. On the other hand, they're begging for more police service. They're overpatrolled and underprotected.

The young white guys turn out to be actually worse than their predecessors. They're more vicious. The average young white policeman comes from a working-class family, sometimes with less than a high-school education. He comes with built-in prejudices. The average young white cop is in bad shape. I think he can be saved if a change came from the top. If it could be for just eight hours a day. They may still hate niggers when they got off duty. They may still belong to the John Birch Society or the Klu Klux Klan. So what? They could be *forced* to perform better during the eight hours of work.

I myself didn't work with the young ones much. They were just too much. I worked with older, seasoned cops on the vice squad. They hated blacks, but we worked together, we drank together. They lived in Gage Park and on the Northwest Side,* so we didn't visit each other's

* Lower-middle-class white neighborhoods, where blacks are not welcome.

homes. One of them—he and I would talk frankly about how we felt. He'd say, "I don't like your people, but I can work around you. Maybe I'm wrong in feeling that way, but that's how I was brought up. I got basic feelings about my kids going to school with blacks and it can't be talked away. You can't talk me out of my fears." I respected him for his opinion and he respected mine. We got along.

Those who were enlightened had one major hang-up. If they did the right thing, they'd be ostracized by the other cops. A lot of these guys have mixed emotions, but they're neutralized. If they're by themselves, they perform quite well in the black community. But if they're with another white who wants to do it the rough way, and they object, their name go on the list—trouble makers.

The job makes those who aren't really bad bigots worse after a while. You could take a tender white boy, give him a badge and a gun, and man! he becomes George Wallace over night. You have to change the rationale by which they work. We must have a system where they get points for helping people rather than hurting them.

You can take the worst bigot in the world, and if he works in a steel mill, he can't take it out on anything but a piece of steel. If these white guys show they can't work with black folks, put 'em in an auto pound. Let 'em guard the lake, put 'em on factory detail. Don't take their job away from 'em. They gotta eat, they gotta feed their families.

About five years ago he organized the Afro-American Pa-trolmen's League "to improve relationships between the black community and the police. We felt, as policemen, we were the only organized group that could do something about it. Everything else seemed to be failing. We felt as black policemen we could effect a change. The police department would like to get rid of us. I'm still on the force. I don't know for how long. I got suspended a number of times. My losses totaled about fifteen thousand dollars."

He served a thirty-day suspension, "which will be an-other thousand." The charge: conduct unbecoming an offi-cer. He had been passing out League literature to black policemen at the station and was arrested on the spot for disorderly conduct. "White officers pass out leaflets all day long. There are twenty-four white groups and not one was ever arrested or bothered. If you go into any police station right now you'll find at least five or six different brochures on the bulletin board about organization activities."

He has been suspended for "traffic violations" numerous times. "I got five tickets, written the same day. It was impossible." He was recently fined two hundred dollars for parking illegally—a matter of tickets and arithmetic. He had been suspended for failing to follow the "proper medical role procedure." He has just been informed that dismissal charges have been instituted against him by the superintendent. The circumstance: He was attending a play at a local theater in the company of his wife and a colleague. He had been invited by the management to comment on the work; thus, his presence. Fifteen policemen sought to eject him and his party. They refused to leave. In court, the charge was disorderly conduct. His wife and his friend were acquitted, he was found guilty.

He has, for the second time, been assigned to the Traffic Division, pending charges. When the League was formed, he suddenly had been transferred from his plainclothesman job in the black area to the Loop.*

They seldom put young blacks in the Traffic Division. I directed traffic in the Loop for a short time. The white driver would say, "I want to turn down this street. My office is on this block." I'd say, "You can't turn down the street between four and six o'clock." He'd say, "Why the hell can't I? I'm a taxpayer." He'd argue, "I'm going to tell your boss, you son of a bitch." This wouldn't be stood for on the South Side. A black said something like that, he'd be knocked down or thrown in jail. They don't expect you as a black officer to do that in the Loop. I'd have been in trouble and I'd have been wrong. The citizen has a right to object. But that's only in the Loop or in white neighborhoods. Of course, if a black driver in the Loop said that, he'd have been locked up.

You aren't allowed to write tickets around city hall. You aren't allowed to write tickets on cars of people who own stores in the Loop. If a cop finds my car, I get a ticket if it runs out in one minute. In the Loop, they want you to give certain people fifteen minutes' courtesy parking. If you violate that rule, they stick you on some abandoned corner where you can't write tickets.

* His most recent assignment: guarding an alley behind police headquarters, "It's their way of trying to humiliate me."

I wrote fifty-three tickets around city hall and they moved me away. I wrote a list of tickets on another street and they moved me further away. I was actually ordered not to write tickets. I thought that was what I was supposed to do. The supervisor said, "Just don't write any tickets." The sign said: No Parking at Any Time. Courtesy parking isn't free. These people pay somebody for it.

We have a black officer who looks white and works in a white district. They don't know he's black. He'd come to our meetings and say, "You wouldn't believe the things they say. 'Give the whites the benefit of the doubt. If a guy says he left his license at home, drive by his house so he can get it. Don't misuse these people 'cause they'll just complain and we'll get hell. Don't give people a ten-dollar ticket for going shopping. It's only going to be five or ten minutes.'" In our area: "Give 'em tickets. Don't come back and tell me you didn't." Just outrageous double standards and nobody ever talks about it. The media always plays down the treatment blacks receive at the hands of the police.

Your average day? You'd go to roll call and sit through a half-hour of irrelevance. A guy is reading notices. Watch this, watch that. Up the tickets. John Doe got suspended for thirty days. Mr. John Doe has been given special parking privileges around his store. After that, you're given an assignment and a partner. That gets to be hairy, because most white guys are wondering what black they're gonna get with. The black guy wonders, Which one of these fools am I gonna get today?

They give you a different partner just about every day. You ride around, patrol the area, answer calls, write tickets—it gets pretty dull. You and him don't talk to each other for eight hours. The white guy feels, I'm with this black to put on a charade of integration. Black cop is saying to himself, The only reason I'm with this white cop is to protect his life while he's riding around in the black community. He messes with everybody and they put me with him to ward off the bullets. You say nothing to each other at all. Can you imagine that for eight hours?

Some of the guys wouldn't mind it much if they had to work with the same guy every day, 'cause they would get to know him. The problem is there are so few blacks and so many whites who don't want to work with them. So they keep rotating, and it's a different black with a different white every day.

The black community usually regards the black officer with suspicion. There are some black policemen that are just as bad as the white. As the years have gone by, more and more tend not to be that way. That was what was accepted. You were rated good as a policeman if you pushed people around. We're creating a new atmosphere. Deal with people on a human basis rather than a military one. There's a tremendous difference now in the attitude of black police.

ANTHONY RUGGIERO

He is an undercover investigator for a private agency. "My outfit has forty, fifty undercover agents. They have three surveillance teams, eight polygraph operators, and I don't know how many background investigators. And they got a good thirty guards. Mike, my supervisor, is the liaison man. Every time we're gonna make a move, we let him know. He's our contact. I report to Mike every day. We use a phone if something comes up quick.

"How would I describe my work? Different. Weird. At times, inconvenient. What they use us for is large thefts, continuous thefts of merchandise. Or if a client feels there's mismanagement, they'll put an undercover agent there, too. I've been doing this for two years and never had no problem. Undercover guys are the greatest actors in the world. You make a mistake and you're not allowed to come home. (Laughs.) If they knew I was undercover there, they woulda thrown me out of the window.

"It's a fast growing field of employment. Tremendous. Just pick up the papers, any day of the week, you can see it. There's a definite need for it. You take the department stores, they are being literally torn apart. It's three billion dollars a year in department stores. It's unreal.

"I like my work because you're not stuck in a lousy office. And I think people are very interesting. You get beautiful material . . . Pay's good, I got no complaints—Christmas bonus, three or four raises a year. I plan staying in it a long time. It's a very important field. This is

*one industry that affects all industries. Security. It's also
very helpful to the police department. We supply the police with a hell of a lot of information."*

*His wife, Diane, occasionally joins in the conversation.
A delightful little boy scrambles around and about the
apartment. There is an openhanded hospitality, as beer
and sandwiches are urged upon the guest.*

I've been on a case one day and I've been on a case eight
months. You never know how long you're gonna be there.
You put in an application for employment like you come
off the street. You're hired. It's set up. The plant manager
may be the only one in on it. Ninety percent of your job is
mobility, to be able to move around, like a porter or a
stock clerk. In the event of theft, you're put in the department where it's occurring.

In this one job I was a baker. They threw me in. You
have a training program. I was hired as a dough mixer.
They had a theft of butter. It sounds ridiculous but it ran
into quite a bit of money. Seventy cartons of butter was
being swiped on an average of once a week. This was
going on for six months to a year, which amounted to
something like four, five thousand dollars. This wasn't too
important. The problem was this company had a contract
with the city. It was well over a million-dollar contract
and they were worried about losing it. If the city sent an
order down to find out where the stuff was going.

After working in the mixing room about two or three
weeks, I was positive these guys were clean. I needed
more mobility, so I went on the sanitation gang. They're
the guys that clean up. I had only a week to bust this case
because I was going on a surveillance detail starting Monday. I did it in exactly one week.

We knew the butter was being taken out of the refrigerator. I stationed myself on top of the refrigerator, which
was a completely dark end of the room. I stayed up there
four days, eight-hour shifts. I sat, I walked around, there
was room. The ceiling was a foot over my head. Nobody
saw me.

I knew who had access to the refrigerator. I would see
them take the key. You'd time it. You look at your watch
and see what time he went and what time he came back.
I'd say to the guy I work for, "I have to go to the men's
room." I'd go up and check out the area. I had an idea it

was being done on the weekend because they usually found the butter gone on a Monday or Tuesday.

This one particular Friday he comes. This was like two o'clock in the morning. He takes the butter, brings it to an adjacent room, and then he left. I got the lot number, the serial number, wrote it down, and called my supervisor, "We got the guy, the case is over." He says, "Find out where he's gonna take it." That's where we ran into a problem. I never seen him actually take the butter out of the place.

On Monday our office sent down the polygraphers, the lie detector guys. They confronted him and explained to him that he'd have to take the test. Everything came out. He signed a confession. But he signed without any witnesses around. He didn't have any counsel. The confession, according to the union's lawyers, was useless. It was a big, drawn out affair. The union wanted the company to take him back. Meanwhile, he couldn't get unemployment because he was fired for theft. They won't give you unemployment for that. So it had to go to arbitration.

He was there, the union lawyer, I was there, the company's lawyer. He didn't have a leg to stand on. They fired him. When I got up and took the stand, my testimony destroyed the man. I never thought I'd finish a case in a week. I never thought I'd catch the guy. I met my deadline. I'm proud of that.

DIANE (suddenly interrupts): *You want it honestly? I can see sometimes where it really makes him feel bad. Where he really feels like the villain. Like the time that guy lost his job. (Addresses him) I couldn't talk to you for a couple of days.*

This one particular time she's talkin' about, it did. He was with the company twenty, twenty-five years. He was supposed to retire that September. Black man. And he just blew everything. He was out. That's it. We busted the guy. Nothing, after twenty-five years. He ain't got a job, he's not a kid anymore, what does he do?

DIANE: *What'd you say? In your own words, you said the employer was wrong. You're always stickin' up for the employer, but in this case you didn't. (Addresses me) He said, "The employer should have more rapport with the*

guy than that. He shoulda called him in and said, "What's
the problem? What do you need that extra money for?"
Maybe the guy's in a bind or something. You shouldn't
throw him out in the street." (To him) It was the first and
only time he ever met the man that owned the company,
right? He works for him for twenty-five years and never
saw his face for twenty-five years. You said, "He should
have some respect for the guy, as a man who put his life's
work into the business." All right, so he stole some lousy
butter. He should have found out the reasons. Apparently
he needed extra money for something, whatever it was,
right?

(He looks away for a moment. A slight pause.) First of
all, most people don't steal for money. These people are
not criminals, they're just like you and I. They feel they
can get away with somethin'. Whatever his reason was I
don't know. I don't think it was money. He was splittin' it
up with two other guys, so what the hell did he get out of
it?

I testified. Sure, it bothered me in that the guy lost so
much. I don't know if I was mad at the guy for bein' so
stupid to pull somethin' like this or what. The outcome
was bad. You picture a guy fifty years old, out after
twenty-five years. And if he's got kids, they're probably
married, maybe they have children. He's gotta go home
now and tell his wife, "I lost my job because I stole."

What happened to him?

I don't know. (A long pause.) My company doesn't like
the idea that you're gonna go out of your way to maybe
hurt somebody for a buck. I don't think they believe in
that. Contrary to popular opinion, we do more good for
people than damage. I wish I had a penny for every guy
that became a manager because of me. You report the
bad things, but you also report the good things. You've
got a good man here, this guy knows what he's doing. He
didn't go to college, but he knows his job—boom! I report
ability as well as mismanagement. We're complete. It's everything.

The thing I like is I could start on a case tomorrow and
there could be an office boy there and I could make that
son of a gun a manager within six months. If this kid's

got something on the ball. I could say, "Why don't you give him a better job? The other guy you got is a flunky, he's a loser." So he went to college, but he's not smart.

A lot of people say, "Oh, you're undercover," right away, "bustin' people by the dozen." How many people of all the cases I worked on, with the exception of one, every other case, was there any jail involved?

DIANE: *They can fire you.*

Yeah, but that's a far cry from servin' time in jail. (Muses) As soon as I go into a place, everybody's a suspect.

A long time ago I had this weirdo case. We had a client that was a big tire company that lost two hundred and some odd thousand dollars. They felt this one individual was stealin' 'em. He owned a bar, this guy. My job was to go to the bar and drink beer and eat sandwiches all night and get friends with this guy. (Laughs.) So I used to go every night. I got pretty friendly with this guy. He was sellin' hot jewelry and hot shoes, silverware you could buy, coats. But it never got down to tires. After two, three weeks, they pulled me off the case. I never found out what happened. I think if they woulda left me, I woulda found out, because the guy was mixed up in all kind of shady dealings.

The first night I walked in there, he comes over and says, "Are you a cop?" I said, "Jeez, I've been called a lot of things, I never been called that before." I got a little nervous. He was a big guy, big Polack, nine feet tall and a thousand pounds. That was the only time I was ever confronted. It was a raunchy neighborhood and anybody in their right mind wouldn't have gone in. I was clean. I never shoulda shaved.

I was called one weekend on a restaurant job. They felt it was being hit. The guys that were running it—at two o'clock they close it up—they were taking cases of beer and soda and putting it in shopping bags, and walking out with the joint. I had a beautiful spot to watch. I started at six. They close at twelve-thirty. They shut the lights out, they lock the door, and that's when they get their shopping bags and beer and soda and milk and everything. I sent in my report and that was it.

I was working on a very short case. They couldn't un-

derstand why all this stealing was going on. I found out
their top man was making $1.85 an hour. I said, "You
don't know why you have this theft problem?" (Laughs.)
Give a guy a halfway decent salary—$1.85 an hour!
What's he, kidding me or what? He said, "That's enough."
I worked there one day and they gave me something like
eighty dollars. They hired a lot of Spanish-speaking people, Puerto Rican, Bolivia, and all that. I said, "You can't
understand . . ."? He's smokin' a cigar and didn't say
nothin'. (Laughs.) They canceled the following day. The
big bosses were the ones that pulled the cork.

The surveillance I was on was hijacking. You follow a
truck all night, five days a week. You report all activities
of the truckdriver and anyone you encounter. You gotta
be a very good driver, you gotta have eyes like an eagle,
and you gotta be a quick talker if you're picked up by the
cops. Every time we had an encounter with the police,
they were very cooperative.

You got identification. They give you a card. The
only time I have identification on me is when I'm on surveillance. In undercover work you have nothing at all.
You may lose your wallet or the guy may fool around and
grab your wallet, pull out the card—hey, boom! it's all
over.

Before I was a placement manager in a personnel
agency. (Laughs.) The outfit I work for was one of my
accounts. I used to send people there for jobs. A lot of
guys went for it and a lot of guys didn't. Before they hire
you, you take a polygraph test. If they don't like the way
the results are, you're not hired. They're interested if you've
ever been a drug user, whether you ever stole anything—
in event you have to testify in court and you're cross-ex-
amined. Do you love your wife? They ask you that.

The guys who would shy away couldn't have made it
anyway. They're looking for a fairly honest person, a guy
not afraid to work—because you're put on cases involving
manual labor. Reliability is the key. You need someone to
show up for work, will do the reports and all this.

When I was in the personnel business, Wall Street was
dying. Eighty percent of our business was Wall Street—
brokerage houses, banks ... I got laid off. (Laughs.) I
knew these people were looking for someone, so I spoke
to Mike and the following week I was hired.

The recession isn't hurting this business, jeez, no! It's the fastest growing field in the past ten years. There's a need for it. If a person did something wrong twenty years ago or immoral, today's it's accepted, like nothin'. There's a moral decay since after the Second World War.

Take petty thefts. A guy'll take a salt shaker and then the other guy takes it. Years ago this was frowned down upon. Today it's the thing. If you don't take nothin', you're an idiot. You get five hundred people takin' fifty-cent ash trays, it's not fifty cents any more. It runs into money. That's what brought the need for these security outfits. Our company does a lot of polygraph. They have contracts with trucking firms.

DIANE: *Do they have to get the polygraph before they get the job?*

Sure, oohhh sure. Imagine they hire you to drive a truck loaded with a hundred million dollars worth of fur coats. Hey, you drive away, you're set for life. (Laughs.) The guy's out the money.

DIANE: *If you refuse, you don't get the job?*

I'm gonna hire a cashier, right. I want you to take a polygraph and you say no. I can say to you, "I don't want to hire you."

DIANE: *That's stupid.*

You don't *have* to take the test.

DIANE: *But you don't get the job.*

Yeah. Why wouldn't you want to take it?

DIANE: *Because I wouldn't. I want people to accept me as I am. I don't need a test to prove my honesty.*

Who said so?

DIANE: *I said so.*

It's your word against the employer's. He's got more to lose than you. He's gonna pay you X amount of dollars a week to do X amount of work. Maybe you're a loser, maybe you're a turkey.

DIANE: *That's the chance he takes.*

Why should he take a chance? You're gonna be guaranteed a week's salary. Shouldn't you guarantee a week's work?

DIANE: *I'd want to polygraph him.*

(Looks heavenward.) Everybody looks at the employer like he's the evil guy.

DIANE: *He is the evil guy.*

He is not, he wants to make a buck, just as much as you do.

DIANE: *He wants to make a buck on you, not the same as you.*

Of course. If he can't make a buck on you, you'd be out of a job. If my company wasn't makin' money on me, you think I'd be workin' there?

DIANE: *You always seem to think people are doin' you a favor and they're not. You're really doin' them a favor because they're makin' money on you.*

Of course. This is a capitalist society, whether you like it or not. It's not like goin' on welfare, you gotta work. There's nothin' wrong with it.

DIANE: *Big business uses people. They use people as long as they can.*

No news in that.

I been on this one case now about eight months. The problem is bad management, not theft. I started at the bottom and now I'm my own boss. Strange as it may seem, it's hampered my investigation like a son of a gun, 'cause I don't have the time to get around. I gotta answer this guy's question, take care of this and the other thing, I gotta know traffic. And I'll go higher than that. The guy who's on the case with me is today the merchandising manager of the company. He's still an undercover agent, and they don't know nothin' about it. (Laughs.)

The case is never gonna be solved. It's what we call preventive maintenance. Say an outbreak of thefts starts. Rather than call a UC man in after it started, they have a guy there all the time, who can report it constantly.

You and your friend may be at this company permanently.

I hope so.

DIANE: *He's got dental plans now with this one. You can get your teeth done and everything.*

When they claim losses on their income tax, they have to show the Internal Revenue that they're doing something to deter it. You can't go over to IRS and say we were robbed a million dollars last year. They'd say, "What kind of security you got?" Security is a tremendous break to the company. You could start a company tomorrow and put a UC man in there and you could be in business ten years and he could still be there and you know everything that's goin' on.

DIANE: *They have another agent workin' with him that is reporting on him. (Chuckles.)*

Yeah. What happened is this: Say I'm an agent and you're an employee. I'll go over to you and I'll say, "Hey, I seen a TV in there. I wonder what the chances are of gettin' that out." You as an employee would more or less go along or say, "You're crazy." But if you're an agent too, you're gonna feed me. You're gonna say, "Yeah, how the hell could we get it out of here?" And that's what happened. (Laughs.) As soon as I gave him the bait, this other guy says, "Right. What do you think we oughta do about it?" So I called up my office and I said, "This guy, Hal . . ." They said, "Forget it, he's one of our own men."

DIANE: *They finally told him, "Don't send us any more reports on him."**

So part of the work is provocative—you tempt . . . ?

You can't do that, it's against the law. I'm just providin' conversation. Entrapment is if I put a wallet on the floor, with a ten-dollar bill on it—forget it! Talkin' about it is just a line of conversation. It may lead anywhere.

You know what another problem is today? The upper echelon of the management hasn't the faintest idea of what's going on in the business. I report the likes and dislikes of the workers. A lot of 'em I get along with and I tell 'em, "The guys are right and the system's no good, it stinks, get rid of it." When I was workin' on another gig, it was 106 degrees in the goddamn place and they didn't have a water fountain. "Are you kiddin'?" I said. "The board of health comes down here, they'll close your joint up." All this little trivia, put them all together and it's no trivia any more. It's a big thing.

Are you ever called in on cases involving labor troubles?

No comment.

DIANE: *Oh, come on.*

I better not talk about it.

With friends, I say I'm an investigator and don't go into detail, 'cause you never know who you're gonna meet. When I go on a job, I suspect everybody and everything. Until they prove by their actions they're not doing anything, they're suspect.

This job has done more for me as far as understanding people is concerned than ever before. Some say, "That guy's a thief." I say, "What kind of a thief is he?" There are thieves and there are thieves. Why does a person steal?

---

* A note of One Worldism might be in order at this point. A news item: Bangkok, Thailand (UPI)—"Police battled a gang of bandits in southern Thailand Saturday. One bandit was killed. A police spokesman said the battle began when the bandit gang, disguised as policemen, challenged a group of policemen disguised as bandits."

If a guy steals a loaf of bread because his kid is hungry, you call this man a thief? There's a thief who's a junkie and there's a thief who just for the hell of it wants to see what he can get away with. Funny. My job's made me less suspicious of people. Constantly listening to conversations, you find that people aren't that bad, really. Regardless of what you read in the papers, people are pretty good. Everybody's the same, that's my discovery. I'm more tolerant of people now, right, Di?

DIANE: *Yeah, you come a long way.*

What do you mean?

DIANE: *He tended to see everything in black and white, no shades. You used to put people in categories, like into boxes. I think you've come out of that. Especially when you have to work on surveillance where his partners were colored guys and Puerto Ricans. He loved 'em.*

I'm one of the few white undercover guys in the agency. Most outfits prefer a guy that can speak two languages, particularly Spanish. Give you an idea, I was workin' for a big company and it was manual labor like I've never seen in my life. I used to come home and I was dyin'. There's a ramp where all the bosses used to walk on top, lookin' down at you, and you had to throw those boxes ...

DIANE: *Like a jail.*

That's exactly what it was. It was me and two other white guys. There was maybe six colored guys and everybody else was Spanish. I didn't know what the hell they were talkin' about and I was supposed to be investigatin'. I told my supervisor, "This is for a Spanish UC." He says, "Stay with it." I'm breakin' my ass, I'm dyin'. I never got nothin' out of there. I didn't even hear any good dialogue. It was a complete waste.

Things you pick up regarding narcotics. I was in on a bust. In the course of my work I come across this girl, she's pushin' pot, hash, pills. She's workin' her way through college. I saw her make sales and everything else. I notified the police. They said: Okay, they're gonna set

up a meeting between me and two narcs. And the narcs
bring their informer. They say, "Set up a buy." They want
me to introduce their informant to the girl. At the time of
the buy, they'll bust her. This is supposed to take place the
following day.

In the interim, these guys take it upon themselves to
give her a shakedown. They go into the store like gangbusters. She isn't there. They question manager, everybody, "Where is she? Where is she?" All this bullshit's
goin' on and I don't know nothin' about it. I'm still under
the impression I'm gonna set up this buy. The next morning a friend of mine says, "Did you hear what happened
to Jilly? Two detectives came yesterday and wanted to
bust her." I called my office, "Hey, Mike, what's with
these two guys? They tried to bust the broad and now I
gotta set up a sale. Are you kiddin' me?" He said, "Stay
away from her." She's still around.

People are really stupid. When I was on surveillance
during this hijacking case, we're workin' for a newspaper.
The guys deliverin' were sellin' papers on the side. The
newspaper was losin' a fortune. These guys knew they
were being tailed and they still continued the same shit.
People like that you have no sympathy for, they're stupid.
They deserve everything they get. There were fifty-two
indictments and twenty-five convictions.

I was with a cop, a retired cop, twenty years on the
force. We're sittin' in a car, surveillance—this newspaper
gig. It's three o'clock in the morning. Just then a truck
pulls up. He says, "You got a gun?" I say, "No, ain't you
got a gun, you're a cop." He says, "I turned mine in." I
say, "Shit, thanks." He says, "There's the truck we're
lookin' for." So he throws it into gear. We take off and
we're drivin' and drivin'. The truck's goin' about sixty.
We're right behind. He jams on the brakes and we're
squeakin'. He says, "Let's get 'em!" I says, "Larry, that's a
hot dog truck." This is a professional, twenty years on the
force. Plus my encounter with those two narcs, you can
see I don't have too much faith in professionals. They
leave something to be desired.

What I'm doin' now is just like a regular worker. The
only thing is listening to conversation, watching certain
movements of people. Without thinkin', people reveal their
innermost secrets and plots and everything. I was workin'
with a guy and he's tellin' me how they robbed televisions

out of a Hilton hotel. They were puttin' 'em in laundry bags with old clothes. Another guy was workin' for a drugstore and he was robbin' very expensive perfume—Chanel and all that. He's got boric acid, the boxes—and pourin' the boric acid out and puttin' the perfume in. And he's put 'em back on the shelf. He'd go back there at night and buy three or four tins of boric acid. (Laughs.) Forty dollars worth of perfume.

I'm constantly listenin'. We went to an affair, a dinner dance. In the bathroom I heard somethin' said and I'm listenin' and listenin'. The guy, he paid an X amount of dollars and the other guy hands him a little brown bag. And I wasn't workin', we were socializin'.

You're gonna have a lot more security. I think the neighborhoods are gonna instill their own police force, 'cause as far as cops are concerned, they're complete failures. Eventually every block association is gonna hire their own police department. I belong to an association and I got two patrolmen on my block, I'm payin' their salary and I have a voice in what they do and how they do it. More and more people will be under surveillance.

DIANE: *Innocent people will also be under surveillance, is that what you're trying to get at?*

Who the hell do you think is under surveillance? Criminals aren't under surveillance. The thefts you get in department stores is usually under ten dollars. They're not professional thieves. It's the everyday goodhearted American citizen who owns his own home—these are the people that are causin' the problem. You get a woman who's a sales clerk or a cashier and takes a three dollar blouse and sticks it in her pocket, she's not a criminal. She's a mother. She figures she can get away with it, so she takes it. So my job doesn't bother me, 'cause nothin' ever happens to these people really.

To write a report up every day about somethin' and to really tell 'em somethin' is rough. I'm up to the 178th report where I'm workin'. What the hell can I tell these people that I haven't told them already? So you gotta look for dialogue and make it sound interesting. You have to have a memory like an IBM machine. I usually use word association. I can remember what's said and I quote it. If you're quoting somebody you gotta be accurate, because you may be up on the stand.

The reason sex is in on this: say the manager's got a young girl working for him and he's goin' out with her. He may let her get away with theft. As far as this guy goin' out with the girl, the company doesn't give a shit. They just want to know where their money's goin', that's all.

Mike, the supervisor, reads all the reports. And he's got about twenty agents workin' for him. Mike was an agent for the FBI. Artie had his own business as a polygrapher. They're very savvy people. All you got is young guys as undercover. You're dealing mostly with young people. The bearded guys are our best agents. Who the hell would suspect 'em? Hair down, dress outrageously. A bunch of flunkies, they'll tell 'em anything. (Laughs.)

There's one thing I look forward to: to be licensed by the state and do it on my own at my own convenience. I would like to have a major concern call me up and say, "We have a problem. We'll give you X amount of dollars." And I'd say, "Call me next week. I'm busy this week. I'm goin' to Miami for the weekend." To be able to work on my own terms is what I'd like. Any private detective, he has one thing and only one thing—it's his wits.

(To his wife) You want to be an agent, Di? I can get you in. (Laughs.)

DIANE: *I couldn't do it. I can't lie. When I lie it shows all over my face. I can't even lie on the phone. When I'm callin' up sick at work, I can't even do it. (Laughs.) I make him.*

JILL FREEDMAN

We're in a studio in Greenwich Village, a steep flight of stairs above a small theater. It's in a state of some disorder; things are higgledy-piggledy—all save one. Singular care is evident in the matter of photographs, camera equipment, and the darkroom.

I took my first picture five years ago. I was taking pictures long before I had a camera. I always wanted to sit back and watch things. There are times where if I'd used the hidden camera I'd've had things that I don't have. But I'd never use it. I hate sneaky photographers. There's no respect.

Sometimes it's hard to get started, 'cause I'm always aware of invading privacy. If there's someone who doesn't want me to take their picture, I don't. When should you shoot and when shouldn't you? I've gotten pictures of cops beating people. Now they didn't want their pictures taken. (Laughs.) That's a different thing.

I hate cheap pictures. I hate pictures that make people look like they're not worth much, just to prove a photographer's point. I hate when they take a picture of someone pickin' their nose or yawning. It's so cheap. A lot of it is a big ego trip. You use people as props instead of as people. To have people say of the guy, "Oh, isn't he great?"—that's easy.

Weegee took a picture of that woman and daughter crying. The sister had just been burned in a fire. It's one of the most touching pictures in the world. Yet I know I could never have taken that picture. Especially shooting off the flash in their face at the time. And yet I'm glad that he took that picture. But that guy in My Lai—I couldn't have done it.

When I think of that guy taking those pictures. He was part of the army, too. He took a picture of those two children gunned down. He took a picture right before they were massacred, instead of running up to those kids. He just stood there and took the pictures. How could he? I don't think he had any moral problems at all. Just from what he said and those pictures. How is it possible to shoot two children being shot down without doing something?

There was a time when I was at this stock car race. With a bunch of motorcycle guys there. They were drinkin' and they were doin' that whole phony, masculine, tough guy shit. There were these two kids came by in a Corvair. They took these kids and stomped that car and they beat 'em up so bad. People were standing around lookin'. I was there with my camera. I had been shooting these motorcycle guys up till then. It was cool. But when they were beating up these guys, I found myself running up to the biggest guy, who was doing the punching. I grabbed his arm—one of the kids who was being beaten

up had a little camera and it was smashed to the ground. I
grabbed his arm and I was hollerin', "Stop it! Stop it!"
That's what I was doing. I was up all night mad at myself
that I didn't take that picture. Because that's where it's at:
a picture of people beating up on other people.

I was so mad. Why didn't I take the picture and *then*
grab the guy's arm? Because that picture is one of the reasons I take pictures. To show: Look at this. (Sighs.) But I
didn't. I would like to if it happens again. (A pause.) I
don't know what I'd do. I hope I can take it.

PAULINE KAEL

She is the film critic of The New Yorker.

Work is rarely treated in films. It's one of the peculiarities
of the movies. You hardly see a person at work. There
was a scene in *Kitty Foyle*, with Ginger Rogers. It wasn't
really well done, but it was so startling that people talked
about it. Any kind of work scene that has any quality at
all becomes memorable. The automat sequence in *Easy
Living*, the Preston Sturges film. It was done many years
ago, yet people still talk about it. It's amazing how rarely
work life gets on the screen.

Television now offers us this incredible fantasy on hospital work. In the movie *The Hospital* you really saw how a
hospital worked. (Laughs.) The audience recognized the
difference. They started laughing right from the very first
frames of that film. Because we all know the truth: Hospitals are chaotic, disorganized places where no one really
knows what he's doing. This pleased the audience as a
counterview of the television hospital's cleanliness and order.

Just think of Marcus Welby. All those poor, sad people
are going to this father figure for advice. You know actually that you go to a doctor, he tells you nothing. You're
sent to another doctor. The screen doesn't show how we
actually feel about doctors—the resentment because of the
money they make, the little help they give us.

Movies set up these glamorized occupations. When
people find they are waitresses, they feel degraded. No

kid says I want to be a waiter, I want to run a cleaning establishment. There is a tendency in movies to degrade people if they don't have white-collar professions. So people form a low self-image of themselves, because their lives can never match the way Americans live—on the screen.

I consider myself one of the lucky ones because I really enjoy what I do. I love my occupation. But I've spent most of my life working at jobs I hated. I've worked at boring office jobs, I never felt they were demeaning, but they exhausted my energy and spirit. I do think most people work at jobs that mechanize them and depersonalize them.

The occasional satisfaction in work is never shown on the screen, say, of the actor or the writer. The people doing drudge jobs enjoy these others because they think they make a lot of money. What they should envy them for is that they take pleasure in their work. Society plays that down. I think enormous harm has been done by the television commercial telling ghetto children they should go to school because their earning capacity would be higher.* They never suggest that if you're educated you may go into fields where your work is satisfying, where you may be useful, where you can really do something that can help other people.

When I worked at drudge jobs to support the family I used to have headaches all the time, feeling rotten at the end of the day. I don't think I've taken an aspirin or a pill in the last twenty years. The one thing that disturbs me on television is the housewife, who's always in need of a

---

* Several years ago, the University of Wisconsin produced a series of films (in which I was the interviewer) dealing with people who had achieved some form of recognition in their respective occupations. It was for showing before groups of ghetto children. The results of a survey indicated that the most admired subject was the lawyer-realtor-accountant, who spoke of his possessions—and showed them. He was astonishingly inarticulate—or inhibited—about his work. The least popular subject was a distinguished black sculptor, who in his studio enthusiastically talked of his work, and showed it in loving detail. The survey further revealed that the children were avid television viewers and remarkably knowledgeable about the commercials of the moment.

headache remedy from tension and strain. This is an incredible image of the American woman. Something terrible must be going on inside her if she's in that shape. Of course, she's become a compulsive maniac about scrubbing and polishing and cleaning—in that commercial.

Housewives in the movies and on television are mindless. Now it takes a lot of intelligence to handle children and it's a fascinating process watching kids grow up. Being involved with kids may be much more creative than what their husbands do at drudge jobs.

To show accurate pictures, you're going to outrage industry. In the news recently we've learned of the closing of industrial plants—and the men, who've worked for twenty years, losing out on their pensions. Are you going to see this in a movie? It's going to have to be a very tough muckraking film maker to show us how industry discards people. Are you going to have a movie that shows us how stewardesses are discarded at a certain age? And violate the beautiful pact that the airlines have with the movie companies, where they jointly advertise one another?

We now have conglomerate ownership of the movie industry. Are they going to show us how these industries really dehumanize their workers? Muckraking was possible when the movie companies were independent of big industry. Now that Gulf & Western, AVCA, Trans-America, these people own the movie companies, this is very tough. Are you going to do muckraking about the record industry, when the record from the movie grosses more than the film itself?

It's a long time since we've had a movie about a strike, isn't it? You get something about the Molly Maguires, which is set in the past, but you don't see how the working relationship is now. I'd be interested in seeing a film on Lordstown.

BOOK FOUR

BOOK FOUR

THE DEMON LOVER

What banks, what banks before us now
As white as any snow?
It's the banks of Heaven, my love, she replied
Where all good people go.

What banks, what banks before us now
As black as any crow?
It's the banks of Hell, my love, he replied
Where you and I must go.

> —"The Daemon Lover"
> Child Ballad #35

The Making

PHIL STALLINGS

He is a spot welder at the Ford assembly plant on the far South Side of Chicago. He is twenty-seven years old; recently married. He works the third shift: 3:30 P.M. to midnight.

"I start the automobile, the first welds. From there it goes to another line, where the floor's put on, the roof, the trunk hood, the doors. Then it's put on a frame. There is hundreds of lines.

"The welding gun's got a square handle, with a button on the top for high voltage and a button on the button for low. The first is to clamp the metal together. The second is to fuse it.

"The gun hangs from a ceiling, over tables that ride on a track. It travels in a circle, oblong, like an egg. You stand on a cement platform, maybe six inches from the ground."

I stand in one spot, about two- or three-feet area, all night. The only time a person stops is when the line stops. We do about thirty-two jobs per car, per unit. Forty-eight units an hour, eight hours a day. Thirty-two times forty-eight times eight. Figure it out. That's how many times I push that button.

The noise, oh it's tremendous. You open your mouth and you're liable to get a mouthful of sparks. (Shows his arms) That's a burn, these are burns. You don't compete against the noise. You go to yell and at the same time you're straining to maneuver the gun to where you have to weld.

You got some guys that are uptight, and they're not sociable. It's too rough. You pretty much stay to yourself. You get involved with yourself. You dream, you think of things you've done. I drift back continuously to when I was a kid and what me and my brothers did. The things you love most are the things you drift back into.

Lots of times I worked from the time I started to the time of the break and I never realized I had even worked. When you dream, you reduce the chances of friction with the foreman or with the next guy.

It don't stop. It just goes and goes and goes. I bet there's men who have lived and died out there, never seen the end of that line. And they never will—because it's endless. It's like a serpent. It's just all body, no tail. It can do things to you ... (Laughs.)

Repetition is such that if you were to think about the job itself, you'd slowly go out of your mind. You'd let your problems build up, you'd get to a point where you'd be at the fellow next to you—his throat. Every time the foreman came by and looked at you, you'd have something to say. You just strike out at anything you can. So if you involve yourself by yourself, you overcome this.

I don't like the pressure, the intimidation. How would you like to go up to someone and say, "I would like to go to the bathroom?" If the foreman doesn't like you, he'll make you hold it, just ignore you. Should I leave this job to go to the bathroom I risk being fired. The line moves all the time.

I work next to Jim Grayson and he's preoccupied. The guy on my left, he's a Mexican, speaking Spanish, so it's pretty hard to understand him. You just avoid him. Brophy, he's a young fella, he's going to college. He works catty-corner from me. Him and I talk from time to time. If he ain't in the mood, I don't talk. If I ain't in the mood, he knows it.

Oh sure, there's tension here. It's not always obvious,

but the whites stay with the whites and the coloreds stay with the coloreds. When you go into Ford, Ford says, "Can you work with other men?" This stops a lot of trouble, 'cause when you're working side by side with a guy, they can't afford to have guys fighting. When two men don't socialize, that means two guys are gonna do more work, know what I mean?

I don't understand how come more guys don't flip. Because you're nothing more than a machine when you hit this type of thing. They give better care to that machine than they will to you. They'll have more respect, give more attention to that machine. And you *know* this. Somehow you get the feeling that the machine is better than you are. (Laughs.)

You really begin to wonder. What price do they put on me? Look at the price they put on the machine. If that machine breaks down, there's somebody out there to fix it right away. If I break down, I'm just pushed over to the other side till another man takes my place. The only thing they have on their mind is to keep that line running.

I'll do the best I can. I believe in an eight-hour pay for an eight-hour day. But I will not try to outreach my limits. If I can't cut it, I just don't do it. I've been there three years and I keep my nose pretty clean. I never cussed anybody or anything like that. But I've had some real brushes with foremen.

What happened was my job was overloaded. I got cut and it got infected. I got blood poisoning. The drill broke. I took it to the foreman's desk. I says, "Change this as soon as you can." We were running specials for XL hoods. I told him I wasn't a repair man. That's how the conflict began. I says, "If you want, take me to the Green House." Which is a superintendent's office—disciplinary station. This is when he says, "Guys like you I'd like to see in the parking lot."

One foreman I know, he's about the youngest out here, he has this idea: I'm it and if you don't like it, you know what you can do. Anything this other foreman says, he usually overrides. Even in some cases, the foremen don't get along. They're pretty hard to live with, even with each other.

Oh yeah, the foreman's got somebody knuckling down on him, putting the screws to him. But a foreman is still free to go to the bathroom, go get a cup of coffee. He doesn't face the penalties. When I first went in there, I kind of envied foremen. Now, I wouldn't have a foreman's job. I wouldn't give 'em the time of the day.

When a man becomes a foreman, he has to forget about even being human, as far as feelings are concerned. You see a guy there bleeding to death. So what, buddy? That line's gotta keep goin'. I can't live like that. To me, if a man gets hurt, first thing you do is get him some attention.

About the blood poisoning. It came from the inside of a hood rubbin' against me. It caused quite a bit of pain. I went down to the medics. They said it was a boil. Got to my doctor that night. He said blood poisoning. Running fever and all this. Now I've smartened up.

They have a department of medics. It's basically first aid. There's no doctor on our shift, just two or three nurses, that's it. They've got a door with a sign on it that says Lab. Another door with a sign on it: Major Surgery. But my own personal opinion, I'm afraid of 'em. I'm afraid if I were to get hurt, I'd get nothin' but back talk. I got hit square in the chest one day with a bar from a rack and it cut me down this side. They didn't take x-rays or nothing. Sent me back on the job. I missed three and a half days two weeks ago. I had bronchitis. They told me I was all right. I didn't have a fever. I went home and my doctor told me I couldn't go back to work for two weeks. I really needed the money, so I had to go back the next day. I woke up still sick, so I took off the rest of the week.

I pulled a muscle on my neck, straining. This gun, when you grab this thing from the ceiling, cable, weight, I mean you're pulling everything. Your neck, your shoulders, and your back. I'm very surprised more accidents don't happen. You have to lean over, at the same time holding down the gun. This whole edge here is sharp. I go through a shirt every two weeks, it just goes right through. My coveralls catch on fire. I've had gloves catch on fire. (Indicates arms) See them little holes? That's what sparks do. I've got burns across here from last night.

I know I could find better places to work. But where could I get the money I'm making? Let's face it, $4.32 an hour. That's real good money now. Funny thing is, I don't mind working at body construction. To a great degree, I enjoy it. I love using my hands—more than I do my mind. I love to be able to put things together and see something in the long run. I'll be the first to admit I've got the easiest job on the line. But I'm against this thing where I'm being held back. I'll work like a dog until I get what I want. The job I really want is utility.

It's where I can stand and say I can do any job in this department, and nobody has to worry about me. As it is now, out of say, sixty jobs, I can do almost half of 'em. I want to get away from standing in one spot. Utility can do a different job every day. Instead of working right there for eight hours I could work over there for eight, I could work the other place for eight. Every day it would change. I would be around more people. I go out on my lunch break and work on the fork truck for a half-hour— to get the experience. As soon as I got it down pretty good, the foreman in charge says he'll take me. I don't want the other guys to see me. When I hit that fork lift, you just stop your thinking and you concentrate. Something right there in front of you, not in the past, not in the future. This is real healthy.

I don't eat lunch at work. I may grab a candy bar, that's enough. I wouldn't be able to hold it down. The tension your body is put under by the speed of the line . . . When you hit them brakes, you just can't stop. There's a certain momentum that carries you forward. I could hold the food, but it wouldn't set right.

Proud of my work? How can I feel pride in a job where I call a foreman's attention to a mistake, a bad piece of equipment, and he'll ignore it. Pretty soon you get the idea they don't care. You keep doing this and finally you're titled a troublemaker. So you just go about your work. You *have* to have pride. So you throw if off to something else. And that's my stamp collection.

I'd break both my legs to get into social work. I see all over so many kids really gettin' a raw deal. I think I'd go into juvenile. I tell kids on the line, "Man, go out there and get that college." Because it's too late for me now.

When you go into Ford, first thing they try to do is break your spirit. I seen them bring a tall guy where they needed a short guy. I seen them bring a short guy where you have to stand on two guys' backs to do something. Last night, they brought a fifty-eight-year-old man to do the job I was on. That man's my father's age. I know damn well my father couldn't do it. To me, this is humanely wrong. A job should be a job, not a death sentence.

The younger worker, when he gets uptight, he talks back. But you take an old fellow, he's got a year, two years, maybe three years to go. If it was me, I wouldn't say a word, I wouldn't care what they did. 'Cause, baby, for another two years I can stick it out. I can't blame this man. I respect him because he had enough will power to stick it out for thirty years.

It's gonna change. There's a trend. We're getting younger and younger men. We got this new Thirty and Out. Thirty years seniority and out. The whole idea is to give a man more time, more time to slow down and live. While he's still in his fifties, he can settle down in a camper and go out and fish. I've sat down and thought about it. I've got twenty-seven years to go. (Laughs.) That's why I don't go around causin' trouble or lookin' for a cause.

The only time I get involved is when it affects me or it affects a man on the line in a condition that could be me. I don't believe in lost causes, but when it all happened ... (He pauses, appears bewildered.)

The foreman was riding the guy. The guy either told him to go away or pushed him, grabbed him . . . You can't blame the guy—Jim Grayson. I don't want nobody stickin' their finger in my face. I'd've probably hit him beside the head. The whole thing was: Damn it, it's about time we took a stand. Let's stick up for the guy. We stopped the line. (He pauses, grins.) Ford lost about twenty units. I'd figure about five grand a unit—whattaya got? (Laughs.)

I said, "Let's all go home." When the line's down like that, you can go up to one man and say, "You gonna work?" If he says no, they can fire him. See what I mean? But if nobody was there, who the hell were they gonna walk up to and say, "Are you gonna work?" Man, there woulda been nobody there! If it were up to me, we'd gone home.

Jim Grayson, the guy I work next to, he's colored. Absolutely. That's the first time I've seen unity on that line. Now it's happened once, it'll happen again. Because everybody just sat down. Believe you me. (Laughs.) It stopped at eight and it didn't start till twenty after eight. Every-

body and his brother were down there. It was really
nice to see, it really was.

JIM GRAYSON

*A predominantly black suburb, on the outskirts of Chi-
cago. He lives in a one-family dwelling with his wife and
five-year-old son, whose finger paintings decorate a wall.*

*He is a spot-welder, working the third shift. His station
is adjacent to Phil Stallings'.*

*He is also a part-time student at Roosevelt University,
majoring in Business Administration. "If I had been white,
I wouldn't be doing this job. It's very depressing. I can
look around me and see whites with far less education who
have better paying jobs with status.*

*'My alarm clock goes off in the mornings when I go to
school. I come back home, take my shirt and tie off, put
my brief case down, put on some other suitable clothing.
(Laughs.) I go to Ford and spend the night there . . ."
(Laughs.)*

*As, on this late Sunday afternoon, he half-watches the
ball game on TV, turned down low, his tone is one of an
amused detachment. His phrases, at times, trail off . . .*

Oh, anything away from the plant is good. Being on the
assembly line, my leisure time is very precious. It's something to be treasured. I don't have much time to talk to
the family. I have to be a father, a student, and an assembly line worker. It's just good to get away.

On our shift we have lunch about seven thirty. A lot of
times I just read. Sometimes I just go outside to get away
from . . . I don't know if you've heard of plant pollution.
It's really terrible. Especially where I work, you have the
sparks and smoke. You have these fans blowing on us. If
you don't turn the fans down, the smoke'll come right up.

They don't use battery trucks. They should. They use
gasoline. Lots of times during lunch I never stay on the
floor. I usually go outside to get a breath of fresh air.
The further you are from the front door, the worse it is.
You can cut the heat with a knife, especially when it gets

up in the nineties. You get them carbon monoxide fumes, it's just hell.

Ford keeps its overhead down. If I had to go a few feet to get some stock, that would be the time I'm not working. So Ford has everything set up. If you run out, the truck'll come blowin' carbon monoxide all over your face. But it's making sure you'll never run out of work. I mean you're *really* tied down to the job. (Laughs.) You stand on your feet and you run on your feet. (Laughs.)

We get forty-eight minutes of break—thirty minutes in the morning and the other eighteen in the evening. You always go to the bathroom first. (Laughs.) It's three flights up. You come down, you walk to another part of the plant, and you walk up another three flights to get a bite to eat. On the line, you don't go to the washroom when you have to go. You learn to adjust your physical ... (Laughs.) For new workers this is quite hard. I haven't gotten used to it yet. I've been here since 1968.

The part of the automobile I work on is before it gets all the pretties. There's no paint. The basic car. There's a conveyorlike ... Mr. Ford's given credit for inventing this little ... (Laughs.) There is no letup, the line is always running. It's not like ... if you lift something, carry it for a little while, lay it down, and go back—while you're going back, you're actually catching a breather. Ford has a better idea. (Laughs.) You hear the slogan: They have a better idea. They have better ideas of getting all the work possible out of your worn body for eight hours.

You can work next to a guy for months without even knowing his name. One thing, you're too busy to talk. Can't hear. (Laughs.) You have to holler in his ear. They got these little guys comin' around in white shirts and if they see you runnin' your mouth, they say, "This guy needs more work." Man, he's got no time to talk.

A lot of guys who've been in jail, they say you don't work as hard in jail. (Laughs.) They say, "Man, jail ain't never been this bad." (Laughs.) That's the way I feel. I'm serving a sentence till I graduate from college. So I got six more months in jail. Then I'll do something else, probably at a reduction in pay.

If it was up to these ignorant foremen, they'd never get a car out. But they have these professional people, engineering time study. They're always sneakin' around with their little cameras. I can smell 'em a mile away. These people stay awake nights thinking of ways to get more work out of you.

Last night I heard one of the guys say we did 391 cars. How many welds are we supposed to put in a car? They have governmental regulations for consumer protection. We just put what we think ought to be in there and then let it go. (Laughs.) There are specifications, which we pay very little attention to.

You have inspectors who are supposed to check every kind of defect. All of us know these things don't get corrected. I was saying about buying a car, not too long ago. "I hope this buggy lasts till I get out of college." I can just look at a car and see all kinds of things wrong with it. You can't do that because you didn't see how it was made. I can look at a car underneath the paint. It's like x-ray vision. They put that trim in, they call it. The paint and all those little pretties that you pay for. Whenever we make a mistake, we always say, "Don't worry about it, some dingaling'll buy it." (Laughs.)

Everyone has a station. You're supposed to get your work completed within a certain area, usually around ten, maybe fifteen feet. If you get behind, you're in the hole. When you get in the hole, you're bumping into the next worker. Man, sometimes you get in the hole and you run down. The next worker up from you, he can't do his job until you get finished. If you're slowin' up, that starts a chain reaction all the way up the line.

Ford is a great believer in the specialization of labor, brings about more efficiency. Actually, I can be thinking about economics, politics, anything while I'm doing this work. Lotta times my mind is on schoolwork. There's no way I could do that job and think about what I'm doin', 'cause it's just impossible for me. The work is just too boring. Especially someone like myself, who is going to school and has a lot of other things on my mind.

"I get pretty peeved off lots of times, because I know I can do other work. They have their quota of blacks and they have just enough so you can't say they're prejudiced. I'm trying to graduate from college and I'd like to go into industry, where the money is.

"I have all sorts of qualifications for the kind of work I want, but none has been offered to me. In 1969 they ran an ad in the paper wanting a junior accountant. I have a

*minor in accounting, so I applied. They wanted a person
with good aptitude in mathematics and a high-school graduate. I had an associate arts degree from junior college
and two years of accounting. They took me to the head of
the department. He asked, "What makes you want this
type of work?" (Laughs.)*

You can compare the plant to a miniature United
States. You have people from all backgrounds, all cultures.
But most of your foremen are white. It seems a lot of
'em are from Alabama, Arkansas, a large percentage
Southern white. They don't hide their opinions. They don't
confront me, but I've seen it happen in a lot of cases. Oh
sure, they holler at people. They don't curse, cursing is
not permitted.

They'll do anything to get production. Foremen aren't
supposed to work on the line. If he works, he's taking
away a job from a union man. The union tries to enforce
it, but they do anything they want. Then they complain,
"Why didn't you get your people to come to work every
day?"

There's quite a bit of absentees, especially on Mondays.
Some guys just can't do that type of work every day. They
bring phony doctors' excuses. A lot of time, they get
the wife or girlfriend to call in: "Junior just broke his
leg." (Laughs.) "Your mother-in-law's cousin died and
you have to rush home." They don't send you home unless
it's an emergency. So lotta guys, they make up their own
lies. Monday's the biggest day. You'll have three days off
right in a row.

The company is always hiring. They have a huge turnover. I worked at Harvester for five years before I started
college. You would find guys there, fifteen years service,
twenty, twenty-five. You meet an old-timer here, you ask,
"How long you been here?" "About three years." (Laughs.)
I'm twenty-nine and one of the oldest guys around here.
(Laughs.)

Auto workers are becoming increasingly young and increasingly black. Most of the older workers are a lot
more—shall we say, conservative. Most of the older men
have seniority, so they don't have to do the work I do.
They put 'em on something easy. Old men can't do the
work I do. They had one about a year ago, and he had
three heart attacks. And they finally gave him a broom.

He was about forty. Yeah, forty, that's an old man around here.

I read how bad things were before the union. I was telling some of our officials, don't become complacent. There's much more work to be done, believe me. One night a guy hit his head on a welding gun. He went to his knees. He was bleeding like a pig, blood was oozing out. So I stopped the line for a second and ran over to help him. The foreman turned the line on again, he almost stepped on the guy. That's the first thing they always do. They didn't even call an ambulance. The guy walked to the medic department—that's about half a mile—he had about five stitches put in his head.

The foreman didn't say anything. He just turned the line on. You're nothing to any of them. That's why I hate the place. (Laughs.)

The Green House, that's where the difference of opinion is aired out. Ninety-nine percent of the time, the company comes out winning. If I have a problem, I go to the Green House about it. They might decide against me. They say, "This is it, period." I have to take the time off. Then I can write a grievance. It could be three weeks, three months, three years from now, they could say, "Back in 1971 you were right." So if a union doesn't want to push your particular grievance, you're at the mercy of the company.

They had a wildcat, a sit-down related to me. This particular foreman . . . I think it's jealousy more than anything. They don't like to see, you know—I'm going to school every day. I would bring my books and I'd read during the break. They'd sneak around to see what I'm reading. I seldom miss a day's work and I do my work well. But this guy's been riding me about any little thing. One night he said the wrong thing.

I was going on my break. You're supposed to wear your safety glasses all the time. They don't enforce these things. I took mine off just to wipe my forehead. He said, "Get your glasses on!" It's these nagging little things building up all the time. Always on my back. So I grabbed him, shook him up a little bit. And I went on to lunch. I came back and they were waiting for me. I was supposed to have been fired. I got the rest of the night and two days off.

These guys that worked with me, they didn't like it. So they sat down for a while. I'd already gone. They refused to work for about twenty minutes or so. Now this takes a lot of nerve for the guys to ... good guys. But oh, I definitely have to get away from this. (Chuckles, suddenly remembering.) One night, there was something wrong with the merry-go-round. We call it that 'cause it goes round and round. They had to call maintenance right away. About six guys came, white shirt, tie, everything. You shoulda seen these guys. On their hands and knees, crawling all over this line, trying to straighten it out. They wouldn't stop it.

Now I couldn't see myself—what kind of status would I have, with my white shirt and tie, crawling on my hands and knees with a crowbar, with grease all over ... ? It was pretty funny. Some of these guys who've been on a farm all their life, they say, "This is great, the best thing ever happened to me."

Phil Stallings said his ambition is to be a utility man. More variation to the job.

Well, that's a hell of an ambition. That's like the difference between the gravedigger and the one who brings the coffin down. So (laughs), he can have it. My ambition is higher than Phil's.

There's no time for the human side in this work. I have other aims. It would be different in an office, in a bank. Any type of job where people would proceed at their own pace.

Once I get into industrial relations—I got corporate law planned—then it won't be a job any more 'cause I will enjoy what I'm doing. It's the difference between a job and a career. This is not a career.

HOBART FOOTE

It's a trailer, off the highway along the Illinois-Indiana border. The quarters are cramped. He lives with his wife and two children: a boy fourteen and a girl thirteen. The dog wanders in and out aimlessly. The Holy Bible, old and scuffed, on a shelf, is the one visible book.

The clangor of trains, Gary-to-Chicago-bound, freights

off the sidings of the nearby steel mills, switching and coupling cars; it's pervasive, it trembles the trailer.

He is a utility man at the auto plant on the day shift. He has been there seventeen years. He is thirty-seven and looks older.

"I'm from Alabama, my wife and kids are Hoosiers. I was gonna work a few years and buy me a new car and head back south. Well, I met the wife now and that kinda changed my plans.

"I might've been working in some small factory down south or I might have gone to Detroit where I worked before or I might have gone to Kalamazoo where I worked before. Or else I mighta stuck on a farm somewheres, just grubbing off a farm somewhere. You never know what you woulda did. You can't plan too far in advance, 'cause there's always a stumblin' block."

From the word go, the clock radio goes off. About four thirty. First thing comes to my mind is shut my eyes just a few minutes. Yet I know I can't shut 'em for too long, I know I gotta get up. I hate that clock. We lay there and maybe listen to them play a few records. And she gets up about five minutes till. Of course, I say, "Get up! Get up! It's day, get up!" I tell you, after goin' on seventeen years, I don't want to be late. You're one minute late clockin' in, they dock you six.

I get up when the news comes on. Sometimes it's five to five, sometimes it's five o'clock. The assembly line starts at six. I go to the washroom, comb my hair. That's routine with me. I have to get every hair in place. Drink maybe a cup of coffee or half a cup of coffee. Maybe a whole piece of toast and sometimes I might eat two pieces of toast—depends on how I feel. In the meantime, I'm watchin' that clock. I say, "I gotta go, it's eight minutes after, it's nine minutes after. At twelve minutes after, I gotta leave here." You get in the car. You tell your wife, of course, you'll see her tonight. It's routine.

We do have a train problem, goin' from here to the assembly plant. I cross one set of tracks twice, then two other sets of tracks once each. Long freight trains, going from Chicago to Gary. I have waited as high as ten, twelve minutes. Then you're late.

If I see a train crossing, I keep going. It's a game you're playing. Watch the stop light, catch this light at a certain time and you got the next light. But if there's a train there, I take off down Cicero Avenue, watching the crossings. Then if I make her okay, you got a train just over at Burnham line, you got a train there you gotta watch for. But it's generally fast. (Takes a deep breath.) Well, these tensions ... It don't bother me, really. It's routine.

So we enter the plant. I generally clock in about five twenty-eight to five-thirty. You start seeing people you know. Pay starts at five thirty, but my boss don't say anything. Then I walk up the line and I got a bad habit of checking the log book. That's what the night foreman left for the day foreman: what happened the night before. I check what job is in the hole, what small part has to be put on. We work those jobs out of the hole. Maybe we put in a master cylinder or a headlight. If it needs any small parts, screws, clips, bolts—you know, routine.

Then I go into the locker room. Pull off my shoes, pull my pants and shirt off, put on my coveralls. Put my tools in: pliers, screw driver, trim knife. Then I come back up the line, routine every morning. Then I start checking the jobs. I'm what you call a trouble shooter in the crash pad area. Your general utility, which I am, get $4.49½. We got seventeen operations in the section and I can do all of it.

My routine in the morning's the same. I clean up cardboard. I tag up defective stock, put the damaged in the vendor. If my foreman tells me to take it over there, I take it over there. Of course, I don't take no hurry. After seventeen years, you learn to sort of pace yourself.

I like to work. Now two days this week have been kinda rough on me. I guess I come home grouchy. Absenteeism. When the men don't come to work, the utility men get stuck. One of us has got to cover his job until they bring a new man in there. Then we've got to show him the job.

I think one reason for our absenteeism over here right now is the second shift. We got this young generation in here. Lot of 'em single, and a lot of 'em ... They're not settled yet, and they just live from day to day. When they settle down, they do like myself. They get up and they have a routine. They go to work every day. I go to work here and I didn't feel like going to work, I shoulda stayed home. But I felt if I go to work, I'll feel better after a while. And I do.

I think a lot of it is in your mind. You get like what's

his name that works in the body shop—Phil Stallings. He's grown to hate the company. Not me. The company puts bread and butter on the table. I feed the family and with two teen-aged kids, there's a lot of wants. And we're payin' for two cars. And I have brought home a forty-hour paycheck for Lord knows how long.

And that's why I work. And those other people when they settle down one of these days, they'll be what we call old-timers. He'll want to work. Number one: the pay's good. Number two: the benefits are good. When I'm off work I draw $105 a week. And you don't get that everywhere.

The more settled a fellow gets, he quiets down. He'll set a pace. See, I set a pace. You just work so fast and you do just so much work. Because the more you do, the more they'll want you to do. If you start running, they'd expect you do a little bit more. If they catch you readin' the paper or some kind of old book or if he picks up some kind of wild magazine he comes into, they'll figure out how to break up this man's operation.

You get used to a job and you take short cuts. When you learn these short cuts, all of a sudden time standards: he's gonna come around and he's gonna time your job. They'll say you're working fifty six minutes out of the hour. I told foremen I won't do it all day and keep it up, 'cause it's too much of a strain. I mean, it's hard on a man, but the company says the man has time to do it.

"When I first started work, I was hangin' doors. That's the first time I got cut at the plant. I would say a man average gettin' cut, a minor cut, twice a week. At '54, I went over to drillin' doors for chrome. They have air drills now. Back then it was the big electric drills. Your hand swell up from holdin' the big drill.

"Then I got laid off. So I took off back south. I was called back to work at Ford's. I got a telegram. I worked ten nights puttin' off cars in boxcars and then they said you're laid off again. So it was a bunch of us came up here five and six hundred miles, just to work ten nights. So we went in to talk to the man from labor relations and the union rep, and I was put on the assembly line.

"We had the Depression in '58, I was laid off again. I got a job in a warehouse liftin' bags from sixty to a hundred pounds. Me and my partner were working at liftin'

from twenty-two hundred to twenty-four hundred bags a day. I lost twenty-five pounds in two weeks. Then I got my second call back to the Ford Motor Company.

I refused to do a job one time and I was fired. The window riser was in two pieces. You had to take a piece in each hand and stick it in the two holes in the door and hook it up inside. When you wasn't used to the job, you was cut in the arms. So I just told the foreman I wasn't gonna do it and I cussed him a little bit.

They took me up and said, "We don't need you any more." They say, "You're fired." Make you feel like you're through. Then the union rep, he starts talkin'. "What about this man's family? He's a good worker." And the foreman says, "Yeah, he's a good worker." They talk backwards and forward. Then they said, "We're gonna give you another chance." They tear a man down and threaten 'im and then they're gonna give him another chance. I guess they just want to make you feel bad.

I had a record, of different little things I'd done. You get disgusted, you get a little bored, you want to do somethin'. It was what you call horseplay. Or maybe you come in late. You build a record up. And when they take you in there for something, they pull this record out.

They felt I was gonna beg for my job. To which there has been people who have cried in labor relation. The company's gonna put 'em back to work, after they give 'em the day off. They dock you, what they call R and W, a reminder and warning. There's been people, they just sit there and they just fall apart—rather than fly back and cuss the foreman out.

I don't get mad like I used to. I used to call 'im, "Buddy, you SOB," in no uncertain terms. But now I'm settled down. After a long time, you learn to calm yourself down. My wife's shakin' her head. I do come home grouchy sometimes. But when you get mad, you only hurt yourself, you excite yourself. In the long run, you may say something the company may use against you.

My day goes pretty good on the average. Used to they didn't, but now I have a pace. Who I joke with, who I tease about did they have to sleep in a car that night. Just something to keep your day going. I'm always jokin'. We even go so far as to throw water on the fan. Something to break the monotony. Of course, you know who to do it to.

It's the same routine. But I can rotate mine just a little bit, just enough to break the monotony. But when it catches up with ya and all of a sudden it's real quiet, nobody says nothing—that makes the day go real long. I'll look at the watch pin on my coverall and see what time . . . you would look at your watch and it would be nine twenty. And you look at your watch again and it's twenty-five minutes of ten. It seems like you worked forever. And it's been only roughly fifteen minutes. You want quittin' time so bad.

I can be off a day and the colored guy that works here, he'll say to this one lady works over there, "Millie, sure was quiet over here." 'Cause I'm always teasin', keeping something goin'. We're teasin' one guy 'cause he's real short and his wife left him. And then they'll get off on the way some guy looks. Some guy looks a little funny and they'll wonder what happened to him. How did the other guy look? Maybe they'll tease 'im just because his nose is crooked. Or else the way he got his hair cut. It's just routine.

They have had no black and white fighting on the day shift. On the night shift they used to have it. I passed words with one not too long ago. It got pretty wild. I told him just what I thought. We kinda had to get something straightened out pretty fast. But there's no contact being made, because men's too smart for that. As they get older, they don't want no physical contacts. Because it's too easy to fall off the shelf, you could get hurt pretty bad.

What's most of the talk about?

Somebody's old lady. I'll be real honest about it, they're teasin' this guy about his old lady. All of a sudden, they're on you about your old lady. And the routine. Nothing serious. We make jokes with different black people. Like Jesse Jackson this, Jesse Jackson that. The black man makes jokes about George Wallace. But any other time, there's baseball, it's hockey, it's football.

We got drugs in the plant real bad. 'Specially on the night shift. They're smokin' or they're poppin' pills. When they're high, they got their sunglasses on. We been havin' a candy sale for Little League. One colored guy was buyin' a lot of candy from me. When they need all that dope, they can take somethin' sweet and it'll hold them over. This guy was buyin' that big eight-ounce milk chocolate bar from me.

He is active in the Little League activities of the trailer community. He is president, and "this crossbreed here, my wife, is president of the women's auxiliary. We're tied up six days a week at the ball park.

"When I first startin' umpirin', they would get on me. I even told one manager if he didn't shut his wife up, I was gonna send her out of the park. I did have that authority."

Used to daydream on the job, now I don't. My mind would be a long ways off. I just really was not conscious of what I was doin'. Like I been goin' to work in the mornin', when I go through the light, sometime I know it and sometime I don't. I don't know whether that light is red or green. I went through it. I had drived and yet my mind was somewheres else. Now it's jokin'. It used to be daydreamin'.

Comin' outa the plant when the sun's shinin', you kinda squint your eye. A lotta 'em wear sunglasses and I wondered why. Now I know. Because you got your fluorescent lights in there, and you open the door and there's the real bright light. You get used to it. It's that same routine. You speak to some of the guards, make a wisecrack about one of the guys, about his hair or mustache or he had himself taken care of so there'll be no more kids. I crack jokes about that. And then you come across the same set of tracks you cross in the morning. Get in the car, roll your window down, and you're not in a hurry to get home, because you're not timed to go home. If you get caught by a train, occasionally I'll stop for a milk shake or a cup of coffee.

I'm proud of what my job gives me. Not the job. I couldn't say I'm proud of workin' for the Ford Motor Car Company, but what makes it good is what the union and the company have negotiated over these period of years.

If a man's due any respect, he'll get respect. Got foremens in here I have no respect for whatsoever. Everyone is passing the buck. Management and they've got groups under them and it spreads out just like a tree. Some foremen is trying to make it big, want to go to the top, and they don't last too long. Respect . . .

You couldn't guess what I'd like to do. I'd like to farm.

But there is not a decent living unless you're a big-time farmer. Because you got these different companies like Libby's, they have these big farms now. Yeah, I would just like to farm. You set your own pace, you're your own boss. When it comes a little cloud and it comes a little rain, you quit. Wait till the sun comes out before you do the work. But here it's different. (He's intense: he feverishly acts out his job, moving his arms in the manner of a robot.) Lightning can strike and it can rain or be eighteen degrees below zero, and you're still in there, grindin.'

Suppose a car could be made by robots, and all the people were free to do what they most wanted for a living . . .

The land's runnin' out. Maybe they would like to have a service station or a grocery store or sit on the creek bank and fish or be a loafer or turn hippies or whatever or nothin'. I'd say it'd be thirty percent hippies in the country. They'd just give up.

It wouldn't be safe for you to walk out of your front door, because you'd have too many people with unoccupied minds. They got the money and that's all they care. They'll either have a gun, they'll either have dope, they'd be hot rodding. They'd be occupied with trouble. Because someone has got to work.

Thirteen more years with the company, it'll be thirty and out. When I retire, I'm gonna have me a little garden. A place down South. Do a little fishin', huntin', Sit back, watch the sun come up, the sun go down. Keep my mind occupied.

NED WILLIAMS

I done the same job twenty-two years, twenty-three years. Everybody else on that job is dead.

He has worked for the Ford Motor Company from 1946 to now. His wife is a seamstress. They have six children. In the parlor of his two-story frame house he acts out his life, his work. He cannot sit still. He moves about the room, demonstrates, jabs at the air in the manner of an old-time boxer. He has a quickness about him—for a moment, in the guest's mind, is the portrait of the agile little forward who led Wendell Phillips High School's basketball team to triumphs in the late twenties.

I started out on truck tires. I made sixty to eighty jobs a day, and this is all times six. We put in six days a week. A job's a whole truck. And six tires to a truck, plus spare. There was a trick to putting the rim in, so that it had a little click. You had to be very fine to know. So you would put this clip around and then you stand over it, and I would just kick it over—boom!—in there. This I had to learn on my own. Didn't nobody teach me this. I'd take this tire, roll it up. I'll lay it right beside. I'd come back, get another tire, put it on, get another tire, put it on . . .

He indicates a photograph on the end table. It is a young Ned Williams, smiling, surrounded by a whole wall of tires. He is wearing gloves.

After you mount it, you just don't leave them there on the floor. We had to put air in 'em, and then roll 'em on to little stalls. And these tires come on racks. I'd go get 'em, and you can't reach in the rack and grab any tire. You got 7/15s, you got 6/15s, you got 7/18s, you got 10/20s.

I could knock down five tires like that. Just take my left hand, guide 'em with my right. If you don't get production, you're out of there. I got my skill playin' basketball. Gotta speed it up. You had a quota, startin' time in the morning and another in the afternoon. At that time there was two of us, then they cut it down to one.

Bend and reach—like a giraffe. I had to jump all the time. Sometime I had to climb. I continually told 'em to lower the racks. They wasn't supposed to put but seventy-five on the racks. But they put 125, 140, 150. And it's up as high as you could get up on a ladder. A lot of times you pull a tire around like that (feverishly he relives the moment in pantomime)—it might go around your glasses, around your head. Some got hurt.

I wish I had a penny for every time I jumped. You really don't have time to feel tired. I'm tired, yeah, but I got a job to do. I had to do it. I had no time to think or daydream. I woulda quit. (Laughs.) Worked on the line till about two years ago.

I'm arrogant. Not too much now. Before I was. The only way I could object is—don't do it. When I get tired, I come in there with one of my mean days ... I didn't care if they let me go and they knew it. I was proud of my work. Just don't push me. I was born here.

For the first four hours I worked there I was gonna quit. I had been addressed just the wrong way. I just came out of the service. This foreman, he walked around like a little guard. Shoot me in the back, I was doin' the best I could. I had never been on an assembly line in my life. This thing's moving, going. You gotta pick it up, baby. You gotta be fast on that. He was like a little shotgun. Go to the washroom, he's looking for you, and right back.

He was pushing. Somebody's pushing him, right? After I went and ate, I felt pretty good. I said, "I'm gonna defeat him." I worked under him for ten years. That man sent me a Christmas card every Christmas. We had a certain layoff in 1946. He said, "I'm gonna get some job for you here." That's when I got into tires. See, I been here four hours now and he's on my back. I came back in the afternoon, after that he was love and kisses. I wanted to do a job really.

I had a sense of responsibility. I been to the Green House many times, though, man. That's for a reprimand. You goofed. How I goofed? Say I'm runnin' 400 jobs, 450. I can look at that sheet, and after you look at that paper so long you may read the same thing twice, right? I'd be reprimanded. It's fast work, but they didn't see it. You can do twenty years of right and one hour of wrong and they'd string you.

If somebody else is treated bad, I'll talk for him. Maybe he don't have sense enough. They say, "Tend to your own business." My business is his business. He's just like me. When a foreman says to me it's none of my business I say, "If I was in the same shoe, you'd try to do that to me, but you better not. No, they ain't never gonna get me till I'm down and dead."

Sometimes I felt like I was just a robot. You push a button and you go this way. You become a mechanical nut. You get a couple of beers and go to sleep at night. Maybe one, two o'clock in the morning, my wife is saying, "Come on, come on, leave it." I'm still workin' that line.

Three o'clock in the morning, five o'clock. Tired. I have worked that job all night. Saturday, Sunday, still working. It's just ground into you. My wife tap me on the shoulder. Tappin' me didn't mean nothin'. (Laughs.)

Sometimes I got up on my elbows. I woke up on a Sunday goin' to work. We were working six days a week then. I still thought it was another workday. My wife, she sees me go in the bathroom. "Where you goin'? Come back." I got washed up, everything. "Where you goin'? You got a girl this time of the morning?" I said, "What? What girl? I'm just goin' to work." She says, "On Sunday?" I said, "Today's Sunday? Jesus Christ!" A mechanical nut. Yet, honest to God, I done that more than once. Nineteen fifty-four, I know I done it twice.

I was sleeping in front of an American Legion post. I had more than a few drinks. This was Sunday. Somebody says, "Go home." I thought they said, "Go to work." Whoosh! I had a brand-new 1955 Montclair Merc and I whoosh! I cut out of there. I went out to the plant and drove all the way to the gate and got there, and I don't see no cars. I don't know what, baby.

It just affected all the parts of my life as far as that go. I'm looking at the fellas been here longer than me. They the same way, worse. I talk to 'em every day, and I hear fellas that got forty-two years, thirty-seven years, thirty-five years. Mechanical nuts.

The union does the best they can. But if the man has a record, there's nothin' union can do. They put the book on the table and he gets his time off, maybe a week, maybe three days, maybe three weeks. It's no paid vacation.

Some of the younger guys are objectin', oh yeah. They got nothin' to lose. Just like my boy I got hired out there. Some of 'em are twenty, twenty-two, ain't got no wife, so they don't worry about it. They don't show up on Monday, they don't show up on Tuesday. Take 'em to the Green House. Give 'em a week off, they don't care. If I could figure 'em out, I could be a millionaire and just sit on the porch out here. I could retire right now if I could figure 'em out.

If I had my life to live over again, it would be the first thirty-five years of my life. I didn't do nothin'. I don't like work, I never did like work. There's some elderly people here right now who looked at my mother and said, "I never thought that boy would work." My hands were so soft, like a sponge. Went to a manicurist twice a week. I always wore gloves at work. I didn't want to get my hands messed up.

I am a stock chaser now for the audit area. I get all the small parts you need, that I carry on a bicycle—like a mirror or chrome or door panels. I get 'em as quickies, 'cause I'm on the sell floor. This job is ready to go. Been doin' this last two years. Up front. There's hardly anybody there that's under twenty years' service. That's old folks home.

It's a cut in pay. I have what you call a nonpromotion job. It's easier work. I don't have to bend down now. It ain't right, but this is what you live under. I was a good worker, but I suffered that for this. Say you lose $1.20 a day. I come home and I can still play volleyball.

I don't feel tired, just older. I haven't talked in my sleep since I got off that job. I don't bring nothin' home now. I got the keys to the bicycle and that's it. (Laughs.) I don't worry about it till I get there.

Is the automobile worth it?

What it drains out of a human being, the car ain't worth it. But I think of a certain area of proudness. You see them on that highway, you don't look and see what model it is or whose car it is. I put my labor in it. And somebody just like me put their area of work in it. It's got to be an area of proudness.

TOM BRAND

He is plant manager at the Ford Assembly Division in Chicago. He has been with the company thirty years, aside from service in the Navy during World War II. At forty-eight, he exudes an air of casual confidence, ebullient, informal . . .

He came up from the ranks. "I was in the apprentice school in Detroit. Then I moved over to the Highland Park plant and was a leader in the milling department. I was eighteen. They were all women and they gave me a fit. All had kids older than me. 'Hey Whitey, come over here.' They kidded the life out of me." (Laughs.)

After the war he attended the University of Michigan and earned a degree in engineering. "Went to work for Ford Research." Various moves—test engineer into quality control, processing . . . five moves around the country: St. Louis, Twin Cities, back to Detroit, Chicago. "I've been here three years."

There's a plaque on the desk: Ford, Limited Edition. "That was our five millionth car. There are about forty-five hundred people working here. That's about 3,998 hourly and about 468 salaried." Management and office employees are salaried.

You're responsible to make sure the car is built and built correctly. I rely on my quality control manager. Any defects, anything's wrong, we make sure it's repaired before it leaves the plant. Production manager takes care of the men on the line, makes sure they're doing their job, have the proper tools and the space and time to do it in. But the quality control manager is really our policeman. Quality control doesn't look at every item on the car. Some by surveillance. You take a sample of five an hour. Some, we look in every car. They make sure we're doing what we say we're doing.

Okay, we've got to build forty-seven an hour. Vega, down in Lordstown, had a hundred an hour. They got trapped with too much automation. If you're going to automate, you always leave yourself a loophole. I haven't seen their picture. I want to show it to all my managers. Okay, we build 760 big Fords a day.

These things go out the door to the customer. The customer, he comes back to the dealer. The dealer comes back to us and the warranty on the policy. That's the money the Ford company puts out to the dealer to fix any defects. We listen better. If the customer comes in and says, "I have a water leak," the dealer'll write up an 1863 and the company pays for that repair. Everybody's real interested in keeping this down. We've been very fortunate. It's been progressively getting better and better and better. In December, we beat $1.91. It's unheard of for a two-shift plant to beat $1.91 in the warranty.

I'm usually here at seven o'clock. The first thing in the morning we have a night letter—it's from the production manager of the night shift. He tells us everything's fine or we had a breakdown. If it was a major problem, a fire, I'd be called at home. It's a log of events. If there's any problem, I get the fellas, "What can we do about this? Is it fixed?" It's eight o'clock in Detroit. I might get an early call.

Then I go out on the floor, tour the plant. We've got a million and a half square feet under the roof. I'll change my tour—so they can't tell every day I'm going to be in the same place at the same time. The worst thing I could do is set a pattern, where they'll always know where I'll be.

I'm always stopping to talk to foremen or hourly fellas. Or somebody'll stop me. "I got a suggestion." I may see a water leak, I say to the foreman, "Did you call maintenance?" Not do it myself, let him go do it. By the time I get back in the office, I have three or four calls, "Can you help me on this?" This is how you keep in contact.

Usually about nine thirty I've looked at our audit cars. We take eight cars, drive 'em, rewater 'em, test 'em, put 'em on a hoist, check all the torque, take a visual check. We look over the complete car for eight of 'em. Then there's forty more each day that we go and convoy and take an expanded audit look.

We usually have a manpower meeting, we'll go over our requirements for next week. In our cost meeting every Thursday afternoon, we have both shifts together. The operating committee meets usually every other day: my assistant plant manager; an operations manager, he has two production managers; a controller; an engineering manager; a quality control manager; and a materials manager, that's the eight key figures in the plant.

We have a doctor. We like him here at ten o'clock in the morning, so he overlaps into the night shift. There are four nurses and one standby. If there's an accident, they're the first one to go down. Is it carelessness? Is it our fault? Was there oil on the floor? Did they slip? Make sure everybody wears safety glasses. We provide them prescription lenses free—and safety shoes at a real good discount. If I went into the store to buy these, they'd probably run around $30. Here they're only $11.50. And we bought 257 earmuffs in the body shop where we do a lot of welding and in various areas where we have compressed air. Or big blowoff stations. The federal government says you must provide ear protection for anybody in a high noise level area. We baffled all those. Some of the fellas said, "I'm not gonna wear 'em." We said, "Either you wear 'em or you're not gonna work here." We've never had a hard of hearing comp case in all the years I've been with Ford.

We have a big project now on the spot-weld guns and manifolding of all our guns. The company's paid a lot of money. Earplugs and earmuffs. A fella wears 'em and if it's ninety degree temperature, okay, they get warm. I can appreciate that. I wouldn't like to wear 'em all day myself. So what we've done on the big blowers is put insulation that thick. You can stand right next to it. We're well within the noise level requirement. In the summertime, we have big 440 fans. They really move the air. It's much cooler in the plant than it is on a ninety degree day outside.

We had an accident about two years ago, a fella on the trim line. He slipped and he hit his head and he was laying on the conveyor. They shut the line down. It didn't start up again until the ambulance took him to the hospital. There isn't any car worth a human arm or leg. We can always make a car. But if somebody's hurt, an act of God—a human eye—my brother's got only one eye. That's why I'm a bug on safety glasses.

Three years ago, I had plenty of grievances. We had a lot of turnover, a lot of new employees. As many as 125 people would be replaced each week. Now with the economic situation, our last raises, and the seven days' holiday between Christmas and New Year's, this just changed the whole attitude. They found out it's a real good place to work. They're getting top dollar. Twelve paid vacation days a year, and they like the atmosphere. There was a lot of fellas would go in the construction industry about this time of the year. Less now.

I've had fellas come in to me and say, "I'm not satisfied. Can I talk to you about it?" I say, "Sure, come on in." You can't run a business sitting in the office 'cause you get divorced too much from the people. The people are the key to the whole thing. If you aren't in touch with the people they think, He's too far aloof, he's distant. It doesn't work. If I walk down the line, there'll be a guy fifty feet away from me. I'd wave, he'd wave back. Many of 'em I know by name. I don't know everyone by name, but I know their faces. If I'm in the area, I'll know who's strange. I'll kid with one of 'em . . .

(Indicates identification tag on his shirt.) These are a real asset because we have a lot of visits from Detroit. They come in and somebody says, "Go see George Schuessler; he's the chassis superintendent." He may kind of forget. So he'll look and see the name. We have a lot of new managers in the turnover. When they brought me in from Twin City, this was a real assist for me to have them walk in and say: "Good morning, Tom, how are you?" I've had a lot of 'em call me Mr. Brand—men I've known before in the other places. I said, "Look, has it changed since I moved from that office to this office?" So it's worked. All the salaried people have tags, not the girls.

Not guys on the line?

We were thinkin' about it, but too many of 'em leave 'em home. It was a job gettin' 'em to bring their glasses every day and the key to their locker. Some are forgetful, some have a real good sense of responsibility. Others do a good job, but don't want the responsibility. We've asked some of 'em, "How would you like to be a foreman?" "Naw, I don't want any part of being a foreman. I want to be one of the boys."

We've got about forty-five percent black in the plant. I would say about twenty-five percent of the salaried are black. We've got some wonderful ones, some real good ones. A lot of 'em were very militant about three years ago—the first anniversary of Martin Luther King's—about the year I got here. Since that time we haven't had any problem. Those that may be militant are very quiet about it. They were very outspoken before. I think it's more calmed down. Even the younger kids, black and white, are getting away from the real long hair. They're getting into the shaped and tailored look. I think they're accepting work better, more so than in years previous, where everything was no good. Every manufacturer was a pollutant whether it be water, the air, or anything. "The Establishment's doing it." I don't hear that any more.

"My dad worked for Ford when they started in 1908. He got to be a superintendent in the stock department. They called 'em star badges in those days. One day jokingly I took his badge with the star on it and left him mine. I almost got shot. (Laughs.) My brother worked for Ford.

*My son works at the Twin City plant. He's the mail boy.
In the last two summers he's been working in the maintenance department, cleaning the paint ovens and all the
sludge out of the pits. He said, 'You got the best job in
Chicago and I got the worst job in Twin City.' (Laughs.)
He was hourly then, dirty work. Mail boy, well, that's salaried. He's going to school nights. He's learning a lot."*

On Tuesdays at two thirty is the 1973 launch meetings,
new models. It's March and the merry-go-round conveyers
are already in. It's a new type of fixture. This is where we
build all the front ends of the car. Between Christmas and
New Year's we put in the foundation under the floor. Usually every other year there's a model change. Next year
everything goes. Sixty-eight hundred parts change.

*"My boss is the regional manager in Detroit. He has seven
assembly plants. Over him is the assistant general manager. Over him is our vice president and general manager.
Assembly is one division. There's the Glass Division,
Transportation Division, Metal-stamping Division . . .*

Assembly's the biggest division. We're the cash register
ringers. The company is predicated on the profit coming off
this line. Knock on wood, our plant maintenance people
do a remarkable job. When we get 'em off the line they go
to the dealer and to the customer. And that's where the
profit is.

When I'm away I'm able to leave my work behind. Not
all the time. (Indicates the page boy on his belt) Some
nights I forget and I suddenly discover at home I've got
the darn thing on my belt. (Laughs.) We just took a four-
teen-day Caribbean cruise. They sent me a telegram: "Our
warranty for December, $1.91. Enjoy yourselves." That's
better than some single-shift plants in quality.

I don't think I'll retire at fifty. I'm not the type to sit
around. Maybe if my health is good I'll go to fifty-seven,
fifty-nine. I enjoy this work very much. You're with people. I like people. Guys who really do the job can spot a
phony. When I walk out there and say good morning, you
watch the fellas. There's a world of difference if they really know you mean it.

Doing my job is part salesmanship. I guess you can
term it human engineering. My boss, so many years past,

used to be a real bull of the woods. Tough guy. I don't believe in that. I never was raised that way. I never met a guy you couldn't talk to. I never met a man who didn't put his pants on the same way I do it in the morning. I met an awful lot of 'em that think they do. It doesn't work. The old days of hit 'em with a baseball bat to get their attention—they're gone.

If I could get everybody at the plant to look at everything through my eyeballs, we'd have a lot of the problems licked. If we have one standard to go by, it's easy to swing it around because then you've got everybody thinking the same way. This is the biggest problem of people—communication.

It's a tough situation because everybody doesn't feel the same every day. Some mornings somebody wakes up with a hangover, stayed up late, watched a late, late movie, missed the ride, and they're mad when they get to work. It's just human nature. If we could get everybody to feel great . . .

WHEELER STANLEY

"I'm probably the youngest general foreman in the plant, yes, sir." He was invited to sit in the chair of the plant manager as Tom Brand went about his work. "I'm in the chassis line right now. There's 372 people working for us, hourly. And thirteen foremen. I'm the lead general foreman."

He grew up in this area, "not more than five minutes away. I watched the Ford plant grow from when I was a little boy." His father is a railroad man and he is the only son among four children. He is married and has two small children.

He has just turned thirty. He appears always to be "at attention." It is not accidental. "I always had one ambition. I wanted to go in the army and be a paratrooper. So I became a paratrooper. When I got out of the army, where I majored in communications, I applied at Illinois Bell. But nobody was hiring. So I came out here as an hourly man. Ten years ago. I was twenty."

I was a cushion builder. We made all the seats and trim. I could comprehend it real easy. I moved around considerably. I was a spot-welder. I went from cushion to trim to body shop, paint. I could look at a job and I could do it. My mind would just click. I could stand back, look at a job, and five minutes later I can go and do it. I enjoyed the work. I felt it was a man's job. You can do something with your hands. You can go home at night and feel you have accomplished something.

Did you find the assembly line boring?

No, uh-uh. Far from boring. There was a couple of us that we were hired together. We'd come up with different games—like we'd take the numbers of the jeeps that went by. That guy loses, he buys coffee. I very rarely had any problems with the other guys. We had a lot of respect for each other. If you're a deadhead when you're an hourly man and you go on supervision, they don't have much use for you. But if they know the guy's aggressive and he tries to do a job, they tend to respect him.

I'm the kind of guy, if I was due for a raise I'm not gonna ask for it. If they don't feel I'm entitled to it, they're not gonna give it to me. If they think I'm entitled to it, they'll give it to me. If I don't deserve it, I'm not gonna get it. I don't question my boss, I don't question the company.

When I came here I wanted to be a utility man. He goes around and spot relieves everybody. I thought that was the greatest thing in the world. When the production manager asked me would I consider training for a foreman's job, boy! my sights left utility. I worked on all the assembly lines. I spent eighteen months on the line, made foreman, and eighteen months later I made general foreman—March of '66.

A lot of the old-timers had more time in the plant than I had time in the world. Some of 'em had thirty, thirty-five years' service. I had to overcome their resentment and get their respect. I was taught one thing; to be firm but fair. Each man has got an assignment of work to do. If he has a problem, correct his problem. If he doesn't have a problem, correct him.

If an hourly man continued to let the work go, you have to take disciplinary action. You go progressively, depending on the situation. If it was me being a young guy and he resented it, I would overlook it and try to get him to think my way. If I couldn't, I had to go to the disciplinary route—which would be a reprimand, a warning.

If they respect you, they'll do anything for you. If they don't, they won't do nothin' for you. Be aggressive. You have to know each and every man and know how they react. I have to know each and every one of my foremen. I know how they react, all thirteen.

There's a few on the line you can associate with. I haven't as yet. When you get familiarity it causes—the more you get to know somebody, it's hard to distinguish between boss and friend. This isn't good for my profession. But I don't think we ever change much. Like I like to say, "We put our pants on the same way." We work together, we live together. But they always gotta realize you're the boss.

I want to get quality first, then everything else'll come. The line runs good, the production's good, you get your cost and you get your good workmanship. When they hire in, you gotta show 'em you're firm. We've got company rules. We've got about seventeen different rules here at Chicago Ford Assembly that we try to enforce from the beginning.

The case begins with a reprimand, a warning procedure. A lotta times they don't realize this is the first step to termination. If they've got thirty years' service, twenty years' service, they never realize it. There's always a first step to termination. If you catch a guy stealing, the first step *is* a termination. In the case of workmanship, it's a progressive period. A reprimand, docked time—three days, a week. Then a termination.

You mean discharge?

Discharge. This isn't always the end. You always try to correct it. It's not directly our responsibility to discharge. It's a labor relations responsibility. We initiate the discipline and support the case for a discharge.

Guys talk about the Green House ...

I never call it a Green House. This is childish. It never seemed right to me: "I'll take you to the Green

House." You wanted to tell a guy in a man's way, "If you don't do better, I'll take you to the office." Or "We'll go to labor relations to solve this thing." It sounds a lot more management. Not this: "I'm gonna take you to the Green House."

When you worked on the line, were you ever taken to the . . . office?

No. I didn't take no time off and I always did my job well, wore my glasses and everything. I don't think I've missed three days in the last five years. My wife likes to nag me, because if she gets sick I pick up my mother-in-law and bring her over, "You stay with my wife, she's not that bad. I'm going to work."

Dad never missed work. He worked hard. He used to work a lot of overtime. He'd work sixteen hours. They'd say, "He gets his wind on the second shift." He started off as a switchman. Now he's general yard master. He's been a company man all his life. I always admired him for it.

Do you feel your army training helped you?

Considerably. I learned respect. A lotta times you like to shoot your mouth off. You really don't know how to control your pride. Pride is a good attribute, but if you got too much of it . . . when it interferes with your good judgment and you don't know how to control it . . . In the army, you learn to shut up and do your job and eat a little crow now and then. It helps.

There's an old saying: The boss ain't always right but he's still the boss. He has things applied to him from top management, where they see the whole picture. A lot of times I don't agree with it. There's an instance now. We've been having problems with water leaks. It doesn't affect the chassis department, but it's so close we have to come up with the immediate fix. We have to suffer the penalty of two additional people. It reflects on your costs, which is one of my jobs. When the boss says pay 'em, we pay 'em. But I don't believe our department should be penalized because of a problem created in another department. There's a lot of pride between these departments.

There's competition between the day shift and the night shift. Good, wholesome competition never hurt.

Prior to going on supervision, you think hourly. But when you become management, you have to look out for the company's best interests. You always have to present a management attitude. I view a management attitude as, number one, a neat-appearing-type foreman. You don't want to come in sloppy, dirty. You want to come in looking like a foreman. You always conduct yourself in a man's way.

I couldn't be a salesman. A salesman would be below me. I don't like to go and bother people or try to sell something to somebody that they don't really want, talk them into it. Not me. I like to come to work and do my job. Out here, it's a big job. There's a lot of responsibility. It's not like working in a soup factory, where all you do is make soup cans. If you get a can punched wrong, you put it on the side and don't worry about it. You can't do that with a five-thousand-dollar-car.

There's no difference between young and old workers. There's an old guy out here, he's a colored fella, he's on nights. He must be fifty-five years old, but he's been here only five years. He amazes me. He tells me, "I'll be here if I have to walk to work." Some young guys tell you the same thing. I don't feel age has any bearing on it. Colored or white, old or young, it's the caliber of the man himself.

In the old days, when they fought for the union, they might have needed the union then. But now the company is just as good to them as the union is. We had a baseball meeting a couple of nights ago and the guys couldn't get over the way the company supported a banquet for them and the trophies and the jackets. And the way Tom Brand participated in the banquet himself.

A few years ago, it was hourly versus management—there was two sides of the world. Now it's more molded into one. It's not hourly and management; it's the company. Everybody is involved in the company. We've achieved many good things, as baseball tournaments, basketball leagues. We've had golf outings. Last year we started a softball league. The team they most wanted to beat was supervision—our team. It brought everybody so much closer together. It's one big family now. When we first started, this is '65, '66, it was the company against the union. It's not that way any more.

What's the next step for you?

Superintendent. I've been looking forward to it. I'd be department head of chassis. It's the largest department in the plant.

And after that?

Pre-delivery manager. And then production manager and then operation manager is the way it goes—chain of command. Last year our operation man went to Europe for four months. While he was gone I took the job as a training period.

And eventually?

Who knows? Superintendent, first. That's my next step. I've got a great feeling for Ford because it's been good to me. As far as I'm concerned, you couldn't ask for a better company. It's got great insurance benefits and everything else. I don't think it cost me two dollars to have my two children. My son, he's only six years old and I've taken him through the plant. I took him through one night and the electricians were working the body hoists. He pushed the button and he ran the hoist around and he couldn't get over that. He can now work a screw driver motor. I showed him that. He just enjoyed it. And that's all he talks about: "I'm going to work for Ford, too." And I say, "Oh, no you ain't." And my wife will shut me up and she'll say, "Why not?" Then I think to myself, "Why not? It's been good to me."

I like to see people on the street and when they say, "I got a new Ford," I ask how it is. You stop at a tavern, have a drink, or you're out for an evening, and they say, "I've got a new Ford," you like to be inquisitive. I like to find out if they like the product. It's a great feeling when you find someone says, "I like it, it rides good. It's quiet. Everything you said it would be."

Have you heard of Lordstown, where the Vega plant is?

I like to read the *Wall Street Journal*. I'd like to invest some in Wall Street. I'd like to learn more about the stock market. Financially, I can't do it yet—two small children

... I read the entire Lordstown article they had in there. I think the union was unjustified. And I think management could have done a better job. A hundred cars an hour is quite excessive. But again, you're building a small car and it's easier to set a line up. But I understand there was some sabotage.

I think the president of the union is only twenty-nine years old. I imagine he's a real hardheaded type of individual. He's headstrong and he wants his way. If I was working with him, we'd probably be bumpin' heads quite a bit. I've been known to be hardheaded and hard-nosed and real stubborn if I have to be.

"I won a scholarship at Mendel High School, but I couldn't afford the books. At the time, my family was pretty hard up. So I went to Vocational High and it was the biggest mistake I ever made. I was used to a Catholic grammar school. I needed Catholic schooling to keep me in line 'cause I was a pretty hot-tempered type."

I'm the type of guy, sometimes you gotta chew me out to let me know you're still around. If you didn't, I might forget and relax. I don't like to relax. I can't afford it. I like to stay on my toes. I don't want to get stagnant, because if I do, I'm not doing anybody any good.

(He studies his watch. It has all the appurtenances: second, minute, hour, day, month, year . . .)

I refer to my watch all the time. I check different items. About every hour I tour my line. About six thirty, I'll tour labor relations to find out who is absent. At seven, I hit the end of the line. I'll check paint, check my scratches and damage. Around ten I'll start talking to all the foremen. I make sure they're all awake, they're in the area of their responsibility. So we can shut down the end of the line at two o'clock and everything's clean. Friday night everybody'll get paid and they'll want to get out of here as quickly as they can. I gotta keep 'em on the line. I can't afford lettin' 'em get out early.

We can't have no holes, no nothing.

If a guy was hurt to the point where it would interfere with production, then it stops. We had a fella some years ago, he was trapped with body. The only way we could get him off was to shut the line off. Reverse the belt, in order to get his fingers out. We're gonna shut the line to see that he don't get hurt any more. A slight laceration or something like that, that's an everyday occurrence. You have to handle 'em.

What's your feeling walking the floor?

Like when I take the superintendent's job, if he's going on vacation for a week. They drive what they call an M-10 unit. Their license plate is always a numeral 2, with a letter afterwards: like 2-A, 2-D—which reflects the manager's car. When he's on vacation and I take his job, all his privileges become mine for a week. You're thirty years old and you're gonna be a manager at forty. I couldn't ask for nothing better. When I take the car home for a week, I'm proud of that license plate. It says "Manufacturer" on it, and they know I work for Ford. It's a good feeling.

Tom Brand has returned. Wheeler Stanley rises from the chair in soldier-like fashion. Brand is jovial. "In traveling around plants, we're fortunate if we have two or three like him, that are real comers. It isn't gonna be too long that these fellas are gonna take our jobs. Always be kind to your sweeper, you never know when you're going to be working for him." (Laughs.) Wheeler Stanley smiles.

GARY BRYNER

He's twenty-nine, going on thirty. He is president of Local 1112, UAW. Its members are employed at the General Motors assembly plant in Lordstown, Ohio. "It's the most automated, fastest line in the world." A strike had recently been settled "for a time."

He had just come from a long negotiating session. It was one of many for him during the past twenty months of his presidency. We're in a restaurant along the highway. It's part of a complex of motels and shopping centers, somewhere between Youngstown and Warren. The area is highly industrial: steel, auto, rubber. "Lordstown was a crossroads. People have migrated from cities around it . . .

*I live in Newton Falls, a little town of six thousand. Ten
minutes from General Motors."*

*After graduating from high school in 1959, he "got a
job where my father worked, in Republic Steel." He was
there four years—"dabbled with the union, was a steward.
I was the most versatile guy there. (Laughs.) I started on
the track gang, I went into the forging department, a
blacksmith's helper. Then, a millwright's helper. Then a
millwright until I was laid off in '63." He worked at another factory in Ravenna for three years. "That's where I
really got involved in the union." In 1966 he "went to
General Motors at Lordstown."*

Someone said Lordstown is the Woodstock of the workingman. There are young people who have the mod look,
long hair, big Afros, beads, young gals. The average age is
around twenty-five—which makes a guy thirty over the
hill. I'm a young union president but I'm an old man in
my plant.

Sixty-six, when they opened the complex for hiring,
there was no Vega in mind. We built a B body, Impalas
and Capris and wagons and whatnot—the big family car.

I took on a foreman's job, some six or seven weeks and
decided that was not my cup of tea. The one thing they
stressed: production first, people second. One thing sticks
in my mind. They put us in an arbitration class in labor
relations while we were training. It was a mock case, an
umpire hearing. All the people mocking were company
people. We had a guy who was the umpire. We had attorneys for management and union. The guy who was supposed to be discharged was there. We had to write down
whether we thought the guy was innocent or guilty. I was
the only guy of some thirty-odd foremen-to-be who
thought the guy was innocent and should have been paid
all his money. The others wanted to be pleasing in the
eyes of the people that were watching. I took it seriously
and really felt the guy was innocent. So I said, "Thank
you, but no thank you." I took off the shirt and tie. All
foremen wear shirts and ties. They've become somewhat
liberal now at General Motors. Foremen can wear colored
shirts and any kind of tie.

I went back as an assembly inspector—utility. I relieved
six or seven guys. I was able to get around and talk to a
lot of people. I was very dissatisfied the way things were

going. People being pressured, being forced to run. If a guy didn't do it they fired his butt. It was a mail-fisted approach by management because everybody was new. The way they treated us—management made more union people in 1966 and 1967 than the union could ever have thought of making.

When the plant first opened, it wasn't young people they drew from. It was people who had been in the community, who gave up jobs to come to GM because it was new. It was an attractive thing back in '66 to be one of the first thousand hired. I was twenty-three. I thought of it as security. I'm the 136th in a plant of seventy-eight hundred. You got the best jobs. You had the most seniority. A lot of the tradesmen hired had ten years of it, maintenance men, pipe fitters, millwrights, plumbers.

After so many hundreds were hired other people didn't want to come in and work the second shift or take lesser paying jobs, because they had already established themselves somewhere else. So that's when kids got hired right out of high school. This was in early '67. There was a drastic turnover in our plant. A guy would come in and work a week or two on his vacation, quit, and go back to the job he had. Standing in line, repetitively doing a job, not being able to get away, this wasn't for them. The young people were perfect—management thought. They were—boom!—dropped into it. But they wouldn't put up with it either.

That was '67. You go on to '68, '69, and they had sped up the line. They had started out at sixty cars an hour. Then they went on to a model 6, two models. We had a Pontiac, what is it called?—Firebird. And a B body on the same line. That presented difficulties. On top of it, '72 is not '66. There was a lot of employment then. Now there isn't. The turnover is almost nil. People get a job, they keep it, because there's no place else.

I don't give a shit what anybody says, it was boring, monotonous work. I was an inspector and I didn't actually shoot the screws or tighten the bolts or anything like that. A guy could be there eight hours and there was some other body doing the same job over and over, all day long, all week long, all year long. Years. If you thought about it, you'd go stir. People are unique animals. They are able to adjust. Jesus Christ! Can you imagine squeezing the trigger of a gun while it's spotted so many times? You

count the spots, the same count, the same job, job after
job after job. It's got to drive a guy nuts.

So what happened? A guy faced up to the facts. If he
was going into the service, he didn't give a damn what
was going on. He was gonna leave anyway. If he were
young and married, he had to do one thing: protect his
pace. He had to have some time. The best way is to slow
down the pace. He might want to open up a book, he
might want to smoke a cigarette, or he might want to
walk two or three steps away to get a drink of water.
He might want to talk to the guy next to him. So he started fighting like hell to get the work off of him. He
thought he wasn't obligated to do more than his normal
share. All of a sudden it mattered to him what was fair.

Fathers used to show their manliness by being able to
work hard and have big, strong muscles and that kind of
bullshitting story. The young guy now, he doesn't get a
kick out of saying how hard he can work. I think his
kick would be just the opposite: "You said I had to do
that much, and I only have to do *that* much. I'm man
enough to stand up and fight for what I say I have to do."
It isn't being manly to do more than you should. That's
the difference between the son and his dad.

Father felt patriotic about it. They felt obligated to
that guy that gave him a job, to do his dirty work.
Whereas the young guy believes he has something to say
about what he does. He doesn't believe that when the
foreman says it's right that it's right. Hell, he may be ten
times more intelligent as this foreman. If he believes he's
working too hard, he stands up and says so. He doesn't
ask for more money. He says, "I'll work at a normal pace,
so I don't go home tired and sore, a physical wreck. I
want to keep my job and keep my senses."

My dad was a foreman in a plant. His job was to push
people, to produce.

He quit that job and went back into a steel mill. He
worked on the incentive. The harder you work, the more
he made. So his knowledge of work was work hard, make
money. Maybe my father taught me something without
even knowing it. My father wasn't a strong union advocate.
He didn't talk management, he was just a workingman.
He was there to make money.

The almighty dollar is not the only thing in my estima-
tion. There's more to it—how I'm treated. What I have to

say about what I do, how I do it. It's more important than the almighty dollar. The reason might be that the dollar's here now. It wasn't in my father's young days. I can concentrate on the social aspects, my rights. And I feel good all around when I'm able to stand up and speak up for another guy's rights. That's how I got involved in this whole stinkin' mess. Fighting every day of my life. And I enjoy it.

Guys in plants nowadays, their incentive is not to work harder. It's to stop the job to the point where they can have lax time. Maybe to think. We got guys now that open a paper, maybe read a paragraph, do his job, come back, and do something else. Keeping himself occupied other than being just that robot that they've scheduled him to be.

When General Motors Assembly Division came to Lordstown, you might not believe it, but they tried to take the newspapers off the line.* The GMAD controls about seventy-five percent of the assembly of cars produced for the corporation. There's eighteen assembly plants. We're the newest. Their idea is to cut costs, be more efficient, take the waste out of working, and all that kind of jazz. To make another dollar. That's why the guys labeled GMAD: Gotta Make Another Dollar. (Laughs.)

In '70 came the Vega. They were fighting foreign imports. They were going to make a small compact that gets good milage. In the B body you had a much roomier car to work on. Guys could get in and out of it easily. Some guys could almost stand inside, stoop. With the Vega, a much smaller car, they were going from sixty an hour to a hundred an hour. They picked up an additional two thousand people.

When they started up with Vega, we had what we call Paragraph 78 disputes. Management says, On every job you should do this much. And the guy and the union say, That's too much work for me in that amount of time. Finally, we establish work standards. Prior to October, when GMAD came down, we had established an agreement: the

* "It's not a group of people. It's a division within a corporation. The plant manager came from Van Nuys, California. Production managers came from the South, and one came from the East. They came here with the ideas of how to make a faster buck through the backs of the workers, as I see it."

guy who was on the job had something to say. When GMAD came in, they said, He's long overdue for extra work. He's featherbedding.

Instead of having the guy bend over to pick something up, it's right at his waist level. This is something Ford did in the thirties. Try to take every movement out of the guy's day, so he could conserve seconds in time, to make him more efficient, more productive, like a robot. Save a second on every guy's effort, they would, over a year, make a million dollars.

They use time, stopwatches. They say, It takes so many seconds or hundreds of seconds to walk from here to there. We know it takes so many seconds to shoot a screw. We know the gun turns so fast, the screw's so long, the hole's so deep. Our argument has always been: That's mechanical; that's not human.

The workers said, We perspire, we sweat, we have hangovers, we have upset stomachs, we have feelings and emotions, and we're not about to be placed in a category of a machine. When you talk about that watch, you talk about it for a minute. We talk about a lifetime. We're gonna do what's normal and we're gonna tell you what's normal. We'll negotiate from there. We're not gonna start on a watch-time basis that has no feelings.

When they took the unimates on, we were building sixty an hour. When we came back to work, with the unimates, we were building a hundred cars an hour. A unimate is a welding robot. It looks just like a praying mantis. It goes from spot to spot to spot. It releases that thing and it jumps back into position, ready for the next car. They go by them about 110 an hour. They never tire, they never sweat, they never complain, they never miss work. Of course, they don't buy cars. I guess General Motors doesn't understand that argument.

There's twenty-two, eleven on each side of the line. They do the work of about two hundred men—so there was a reduction of men. Those people were absorbed into other departments. There's some places they can't use 'em. There's some thinking about assembling cars. There still has to be human beings.

If the guys didn't stand up and fight, they'd become robots too. They're interested in being able to smoke a cigarette, bullshit a little bit with the guy next to 'em, open a book, look at something, just daydream if nothing else. You can't do that if you become a machine.

Thirty-five, thirty-six seconds to do your job—that includes the walking, the picking up of the parts, the assembly. Go to the next job, with never a letup, never a second to stand and think. The guys at our plant fought like hell to keep that right.

There was a strike. It came after about four or five months of agitation by management. When GMAD took over the plant, we had about a hundred grievances. They moved in, and where we had settled a grievance, they violated 'em. They took and laid off people. They said they didn't need 'em. We had over fourteen hundred grievances under procedure prior to the strike. It's a two-shift operation, same job, so you're talking about twenty-eight hundred people with fourteen hundred grievances. What happened was, the guys—as the cars came by 'em—did what's normal, what they had agreed to prior to GMAD. I don't think GM visualized this kind of a rebellion.

The strike issue? We demanded the reinstitution of our work pace as it was prior to the onslaught by General Motors Assembly Division. The only way they could do it was to replace the people laid off.

In that little book of quotes I have: "The workingman has but one thing to sell, his labor. Once he loses control of that, he loses everything." I think a lot of these young kids understand this. There's some manliness in being able to stand up to the giant. Their fathers' was in working hard. There's a substantial number of people that are Vietnam war vets. They don't come back home wanting to take bullshit from foremen who haven't seen as much of the world as he has, who hasn't seen the hardships.

Assembly workers are the lowest on the totem pole when it comes to job fulfillment. They don't think they have any skill. Some corporate guy said, "A monkey could do the job." They have no enthusiasm about pride in workmanship. They could care less if the screw goes in the wrong place. Sometimes it helps break the monotony if the screw strips. The corporation could set up ways to check it so when the product goes to the consumer it should be whole, clean, and right. But they've laid off inspectors. 'Cause they could give a shit less. Inspectors are like parasites—they don't produce, they don't add something. They only find error. That error costs money to fix, so . . . they laid off, I don't know how many inspectors per shift. They want quantity.

When they got in the fight with us, there was an enormous amount of repairs to be done because the people refused to do the extra work. That was one thing that shocked the hell out of General Motors Assembly Division. Management was shipping defective parts, safety as well as trim and show items, paint, chrome, and that kind of stuff. Our guys were taking down serial numbers on every job they could get their hands on. Where they knew the product was defective, we made records of it. We constantly badgered the international union to blast the hell out of them. We did vocally, across the bargaining table. They finally had to let up on the thing.

The biggest polluter is the thing we produce, the automobile. The livelihood that puts bread on your table. I don't know if the people in the plant question it. I wouldn't want to see all the automobiles banned because they pollute the air. Yet I realize what the hell good is my livelihood if the air's gonna kill me anyway. There are so many priorities that have to be straightened out. I think all this smog control is tokenism, simply that. I heard a plant manager today, he says, "Until the guy learns how to adjust himself in driving the car, there will always be emission. But once he learns how to put his foot on the gas, we'll pass the standards." It's just another gosh damn gimmick. They're not really fighting air pollution, they're not concerned.

I've never gotten into a rap session with that kind of thing because they keep us busy fighting. Every year we've had a potential strike on our hands. In six years I've put out six strike letters. There are so many things to do. You major on the minors and minor on the majors. That major being pollution, the minor being our money.

In some parts of the plant, cars pass a guy at 120 an hour. The main line goes at 101.6. They got the most modern dip system in paint. They got all the technological improvements. They got unimates. But one thing went wrong. (Chuckles.) They didn't have the human factor. We've been telling them since we've been here: We have a say in how hard we're going to work. They didn't believe us. Young people didn't vocalize themselves before. We're putting human before property value and profits.

We're still making 101 cars an hour, but now we have the people back GMAD laid off. They tried to create a speed-up by using less people. We stopped 'em.

"Ten to twelve percent of our people are black or Span-ish-American. Most of the seniority people are whites. The best jobs go to the white people. To me, General Motors is a bunch of bigots. The young black and white work-ers dig each other. There's an understanding. The guy with the Afro, the guy with the beads, the guy with the goatee, he doesn't care if he's black, white, green, or yellow. The older guys still call each other niggers and honkies. But that doesn't happen with the younger set here. You see them eating their lunch. You see them riding in the same car. You see them date the same kind of girls, going to the same kind of places.

"I think they're sympathetic to students. They tend to be friends with the guy that's in college. They're not iso-lated. We have some going to school part-time and work-ing.

"Our women have been here only a year. Right now they're more interested in learning how the union func-tions and how to get more restrooms. They work on the line just like the men. It's been a good thing for our union. It has finally dawned on the guys that if a woman comes here to work, she's able to go on that job. In '66 and '67 the jobs were so physically demanding that a woman couldn't have done them. They had to be made more nor-mal. I think women really helped our union.

"Drugs are used here. Not so much hard stuff—they use grass, some pills. Young people are on drugs, especially marijuana, like their parents are on alcohol. There's some-thing else to drugs. It has to do with monotony, it has to do with society. Until you show the kids a better way of life, they're gonna stick on the grass."

The guys are not happy here. They don't come home thinking, Boy, I did a great job today and I can't wait to get back tomorrow. That's not the feeling at all. I don't think he thinks a blasted thing about the plant until he comes back. He's not concerned at all if the product's good, bad, or indifferent.

Their idea is not to run the plant. I don't think they'd know what to do with it. They don't want to tell the company what to do, but simply have something to say about what *they're* going to do. They just want to be treated with dignity. That's not asking a hell of a lot.

I weave in on both sides of the assembly line. From the right side, the passenger's side, to the driver's side. Talking to guys. You get into a little conversation. You watch the guy, 'cause you don't want to get in his way, 'cause he'll ruin a job. Occasionally he'll say, "Aw, fuck it. It's only a car." It's more important to just stand there and rap. I don't mean for car after car. He'd be in a hell of a lot of trouble with his foreman. But occasionally, he'll let a car go by. If something's loose or didn't get installed, somebody'll catch it, somebody'll repair it, hopefully. At that point, he made a decision: It was just a little more important to say what he had on his mind. The unimate doesn't stand there and talk, doesn't argue, doesn't think. With us, it becomes a human thing. It's the most enjoyable part of my job, that moment. I love it!

The Driving

BOOKER PAGE

*He drives his own cab in Manhattan. He is sixty-one. It is
early evening—the end of his day. A heavy man, he has
plopped into a chair, visibly exhausted. As he tugs off his
shoes, wiggles his toes, he sighs, "Oh, my feet!"*

*He has been a cabdriver for about a year. For thirty
years he had been at sea, 1942–1972. Once during that
time, "I was ashore for a year. My brother and me bought
a diner. I was very glad to get rid of it. I went to sea
again." Years ago he had worked in an auto body shop.
He quit because "I've always enjoyed seeing ships, always
hoped I'd be able to go to sea."*

I'm using muscles I haven't used before. Sometimes I have
to stop the cab and get out and walk a while, just to
stretch out. Sitting for ten, eleven hours a day got me so
that I'm all cramped up. I have to take soap, hot water,
my wife rubs my feet, my ankles, 'cause my muscles are
actually sore. I don't get no exercise at all like I usually do.

I was a cook and baker on a ship, a freighter. My last
ship, I was making runs to India and South Africa. It
wouldn't take me too much to do my work. I walked
around on deck all day. I enjoyed it. I was getting my
exercise. I put on twenty pounds since I been in the cab.

I promised my wife I'd quit the sea. One time when my
ship came back from India she came down by bus and
drove eighteen hours, but just stayed overnight around
Savannah. She asked me to give it up because she was just
tired of being alone. I said, "Give me one more year," because we'd been saving and had plans of what we wanted
to do. This Indian run lasted two years. I gave my youth
to the sea and I come home and gave her my old age.

It used to be that every seaman ran away to sea. 'Cause
he's a drunk, a wastrel, running away from his family.
You found the scum that went to sea. Today you find
some college graduates. We have on board two or three

young fellas that are studying to be doctors. They made the trip to get some extra money. Seamen are mostly young now. It's better than when I first went to sea. Where once a fella was glad to eat his three meals a day and get paid and get drunk, the young man feels they're not paying him enough. Sometimes he has a chip on his shoulder.

The big topic at sea is still exploits with women. Because there's always loneliness. A traveling salesman, he has a means of picking up a phone. But a seaman is one month, two, three months before he'll get a letter from his wife. I used to phone my wife three, four times every trip. In Calcutta I waited five hours to get a phone call through. If I didn't get it through one night, I'd call again and wait three, four hours the next morning. The feeling you get, just hearing her voice ... I'd stand on the phone and just actually choke up. My wife would be crying on the other end and I'd say, "Woman, listen, I'm spending too much money on this phone call. Stop crying." (Laughs.) But it was just so happy.

"My wife and I always loved each other. Matter of fact, we liked each other. Everything we do, we do together. Even when I get up at night to go pee, she gets up and dances with me to the bathroom. The family that pees together stays together. (Laughs.) I take water pills for my weight and it runs me to the bathroom four times a night. She'll walk ahead of me and I'll put my arms around her waist and we'd fox trot up the hallway. It could be two, three o'clock in the morning, it doesn't matter."

It's impossible to pay for the loss of family life. The time away is like being in jail. I used to tell my wife that when the whistle blew, even if we're still tied up in dock, I was automatically three and four thousand miles away. The lines are goin', the gangway's goin'—even though I'm only a few feet from the dock, I'm separated. I would put myself in suspended animation, knowing nothing's going to bother me until I come back. No matter where I went, how many times I called her on the phone, I was never home. Even though I would reach two, three American ports, it was no more than to touch my wife. We're losing so much, giving up so much of family life. You should be compensated for it. But no one forces you to go to sea. It gets in your blood . . .

Some of the major ports like Calcutta, Karachi, we stay eight days, twelve days picking up cargo. I'd stay aboard ship. I'd go to movies almost every night 'cause I don't drink, I don't smoke, I don't gamble. I was just a poor ass seaman. (Laughs.) I'd do other things, naturally. (Laughs.) There's always women. (Laughs.)

"Women-chasing was my weakness. You can love your wife, but a man is like a dog. He'll chase anything with a skirt on it. Drop the skirt, he'll still chase. I've never cared for women singly. There's always two or three at a time. I found in traveling the most beautiful women are less sexy than others. In India, they're beautiful, delicate. Chinese women, delicate—like a piece of porcelain. In bed? Nothing. In these countries, you find a great deal of prostitutes, because they need it for survival. The seaman doesn't meet the better class, the families. His time is limited."

I love nature. I'm so fed up with man's so-called superiority. I've seen things happen at sea. I've seen a beautiful day change in minutes to a storm so hazardous you can't describe it unless you see today's pictures on TV. More strength and terrible power's been exerted in five minutes than man has concocted in all his atom bombs. Storms that would lift the ship up and toss it like a match. Think of the power, think of the weight and strength of nature. Man with all his egotism . . .

I can't think of the sea now, I'm so busy with a cab. It keeps you so occupied with traffic that you can't think of anything else. The only time I think of the sea is when I'm going up the East Side and I see a ship in the harbor or hear a ship blow. It's only a fleeting moment . . .

It's like changing a life. It's like being born again into something else. I'm talking to people every day, meeting different people. They'll get in a cab and discuss all their problems. I've had people talk over certain things that should be kept in the family. I had a man get in one time, said, "Get me away quick before I kill the sonofabitch." Him and his partner fell out in business and he was overwrought, he had to get him a drink. He got off in two blocks and gave me a dollar.

You must be alert every moment to everything that happens. You can't relax yourself while you're driving. I've got this brand-new cab and I got three dents in it already, as careful as I am.

Oh, I'm so tired. My bottom gets so . . . Oh, every muscle aches in my body. It's my legs and feet, ankles and so forth. I figure in another few months I'll be able to sit up, stand up, do anything else. I'll be used to it then. But right now, I'm so . . . My pedaling the gas and brake, gas and brake, all the time . . . At sea I never had no aches and pains. Then it was just blahs. You'd get tired of the same monotony, day in and day out. The only time I think about the sea is at home or going in my cab in the morning.

Right now my outlook is making as much money as I possibly can. To make back what I put into the investment of buying a cab. It'll take about four years. I don't stay out after dark, but I put in eleven hours a day. I make good money, but I just have to keep going right now.

No matter how much you love your wife, the sea is drawing you . . . I have so much love for the sea, my whole dream is I want to buy a schooner and live aboard and then charter—in the West Indies. That's what my wife and I are both planning for. A cab is just a steppingstone to a car wash and then a car wash will be a means of buying my boat. Even at my age, I haven't given it up. Nothing's going to stop me. That's how much I love the sea. If I get a schooner, that'll be tops, that'll be it. I'll have both my loves: my wife and my sea. I would like to die at sea and be buried at sea, and then spread out at sea . . .

LUCKY MILLER

I hate to admit that driving a cab is no longer the novelty to me that it once was. It has its moments, but it's not the most ideal job in the world as far as determining one's attitude is concerned.

He is twenty-six. He has been a cabdriver for four years. "My original intention was to drive for a couple of years.

It's the sort of job where I could have flexible hours while I was going to school." He had begun as a part-time driver, but he now puts in a forty-hour week. "During the past four years I've been going to school off and on. More off than on.

"Drivers are more transient now than they used to be. I'd say there's well over fifty percent turnover every year. Companies are always hiring and don't care what you do. I suspect the younger part-time drivers outnumber the older ones."

Cabdrivers can no longer be stereotyped. One time the popular conception was of the balding, pot-bellied, cigar-chomping, middle-aged man, who'd drive like a bat out of hell and yell at all the other drivers that they had their hands up their asses. There are as many different types of cabdrivers, with as many different dispositions, as there are among the entire human race.

I've always known the city quite well. I figured it was a way of meeting a lot of interesting, live, colorful people. Oh, sometimes you get an occasional fella or woman who's a little high and they're more talkative ... When I first started, I used to work till eleven at night. I drive strictly days now, from about seven thirty in the morning to maybe five in the evening. A driver doesn't get live wires during the day. They're mostly drab businessmen with nothing much to say, who don't have much to discuss other than the weather. But it's a lot safer.

I'm sorry to say I've gotten to the point where I don't initiate conversations any more. Ninety percent of them would come to dead ends. These businessmen are preoccupied with whatever policy they're trying to sell or whatever advertising they're trying to put together in their heads.

Business isn't nearly as good as it was four years ago. We used to get a lot of expense account fares. We don't get nearly as much now. They'd ask for receipts. They'd tip about the average. I think a lot of them would tip better, yet they fear if they're too generous the company might react. I'd say a fare that runs eighty cents, a twenty-cent tip is sufficient. For long trips, we don't expect as great a percentage.

Whether it's a long day or a short day depends on my meter and tips. A good day is about forty-five on the meter and ten in overs, as we call tips. I get about forty-eight percent of the meter. It averages to about thirty or thirty-three a day, or about four dollars an hour. I usually clear about $125 after taxes. No driver declares the tips he actually makes.

I don't react violently to getting stiffed—which means not receiving a tip. A lot of drivers do. I realize there are some people who are barely just able to afford cabs, who really can't afford to tip. People who live in fairly rough neighborhoods, who are afraid to walk the streets and feel much safer taking a cab. There are others, who may have recently immigrated, who aren't familiar with the custom. Puerto Ricans generally tip. Mexicans don't, as a rule. Apparently Mexican cabdrivers don't expect to get tipped. A matter of custom. I don't feel I'm the one to familiarize them. Some other driver will, one way or another. I can say for sure that the best tippers are not people who live on Lake Shore Drive, or the businessmen. They're generally the blue-collar people I pick up in the neighborhoods.

A lot of drivers, they'll agree to almost anything the passenger will say, no matter how absurd. They're angling for that tip. I'm not just going to nod my head in agreement with someone I don't agree with, just for the sake of getting a tip. After five years I can handle myself pretty well in downtown traffic. A lot of drivers wind up with ulcers. They're the most likely candidates for a heart attack. Driving a cab tends to shorten your life span—if one does it for a career—especially if the driver spends most of his time downtown.

And the fumes and the traffic. That driver is breathing in the exhausts all day. This applies specifically to drivers of Checker cabs.* The ventilating system in this type of car is not constructed for the convenience of the driver. The vents are right in back of the engine. So we're breathing in fumes from our own engines, as well as those of the other cars and trucks.†

The company doesn't give a damn about the conditions

* In Chicago, the Yellow Cab Company and the Checker Cab Company, under one ownership, use the above described type of car, and comprise most of the cabs in the city.

† "Most truckdrivers are generally quite courteous. They'll drive as far to the right as possible, so if they're moving slowly other traffic can get around them."

of their cabs. Some of them are pretty wretched, low brakes, bald tires, bad valves, most anything. These cabs are given to part-timers. I see new drivers driving these junks day after day and breaking down with them. A cab has to break down five or six times before something is done about it. They're dangerous. Neither the company nor the union gives a damn about us. As far as they're concerned, we're machines—as wretched as the cabs.

A person who's driving a cab a number of years tends to become hardened. I hate having to turn somebody down. On the other hand, I think of the reality. I may have sixty, seventy dollars on me at the end of a good day. The money itself is expendable, but my life isn't. I read of incidents in which drivers have been shot even after surrendering their money. This may sometimes happen in the case of junkies. I think most guys who hold up cabdrivers are junkies. They can't control themselves. It's not that they're malicious people, it's just that they've got this habit and they're desperate. It's fear. It's fear that results in a lot of cabdrivers passing up black people. This includes black drivers.

On the right sun visor of every cab is a sign that says, "Not for Hire." All we have to do is pull that visor down. When I'm ready to check in, even when I'm downtown, I throw the visor down. Then I'll ask where he's going, black or white. If the fare's going in my direction, fine. Generally people understand. They know the real reason—I'm scared. Most people are aware that you have to lie.

After you've been driving a cab for a while, you can sort of tell—like a sixth sense—what his attitude is, whether or not he's going to give you trouble. But you can't always tell, that's the point.

There's appearance. The attire, such as the leather jacket and shades and this sort of menacing expression. I think it's probably just a front. A lot of these fellas are just covering up. In their everyday life they feel themselves being really shit upon and they just have to feel that they're somebody. And this is their way of manifesting it. Much as I hate to say it, I sometimes pass them up. Now if a guy is wearing an attire that is really far out—a brightly colored dashiki sort of thing or an unusually large natural—I'll pick him up.

I was robbed once. The fella was dressed in a non-descript sort of fashion: white sport shirt, brown slacks, just medium-thick Afro. It happened last year. I picked him up downtown, in the afternoon, about three o'clock. Brought him out south. On the way, we had a very amiable conversation. So it came as a complete surprise. When we got out there, he pulled a gun on me. First he got out of the cab and came around to my window to pay. It was a hot day so I had my windows open. I'd never suspected he'd draw a bead on me.

He came around the window and said, "Give me your money or I'll kill you." Naturally I gave him everything I had—about sixty-five. I gave him my changer and all the bills in my wallet. Funny thing, he didn't demand my wallet. I just pulled out the bills and gave them to him. He ran into the alley. I wasn't about to chase him. I was frozen, my mind was a blank. I was like paralyzed. Oh, wow! I just sat there for about ten minutes. Then I realized how close I had come to being wiped out.

I must admit that one incident sort of changed my attitude, made me a little more wary of who I was picking up thereafter. Before that incident, I didn't really give anyone that thorough a going-over. A person would hail a cab and I'd pick them up. Now I really find myself deliberating: should I or shouldn't I?

I don't find myself getting into as many conversations. I'm not sure that's due to a change in my own attitude or that of the public generally. It may be a bit of both. It's especially true of women passengers, the younger ones. They have this fear—of not talking to strange men. People are just becoming more uptight.

People on the verge of a break up . . .

"One time I picked up a woman who wanted to go out to this landing strip at O'Hare. She said her people were being held captive on the landing strip. 'My countrymen . . .' She appeared to be an actress right out of one of those foreign intrigue films, very slender, with blonde hair, very expensively dressed. In this very thick Polish accent. I explained I couldn't drive out to the landing strip. The passenger terminal was the best I could do. 'That's not good enough,' she hopped out. I had a feeling as soon as

*she got in I wouldn't be taking her anywhere, except maybe Chicago State.**

There's been an occasion when I wish I could tell people I was something else than a cabdriver. I feel there's a lot more I could be doing than just shuttling people from place to place for a price. Older guys with families, they have no choice. I wouldn't want to raise a family as a cabdriver. At this point, I'm not exactly sure what I'm going to do. I had been intending to teach. But with the glut on the market, I don't think by the time I get my B.A. I'll stand much of a chance. I'm thinking of the field of mental health—if by the time I get my degree I still have my own sanity. (Laughs.)

WILL ROBINSON

He's forty-seven. He has been a Chicago bus driver for twenty-seven years. He works the swing shift, which allows him a two-and-a-half-hour break in the middle of the day. He prefers it to the straight run because "going eight hours straight out there is kinda rough."

During this Sunday conversation, his wife, on occasion, speaks her mind.

"It was a nice job in the beginning. As the time goes along, it gets harder. I was in the second bunch of blacks that was hired. Nineteen forty-five. The job was predominantly white. We had all kinds of facilities in the barn: we had pool tables, we had a little library, we even had a restaurant there. As more blacks came in, they started taking these things away. Now you don't have anything to do but go in, check in for your run, check out, and go home."

His wife recalls, "When the job was first given to blacks, it was a prestige job."

"This was right after the war. It was a giant step coming from the Depression into a good job. I can remember when a black man, working on CTA,† instead of wearing a dress suit on Sunday, they'd wear their uniforms because

---

* An institution for the mentally disturbed.

† Chicago Transit Authority

*it was a prestige thing. It was a little Eisenhower jacket. I
wore it on social occasions. I lost the sense of that, oh,
about twenty years ago. It had status once. Not so today.*

You have your tension. Sometimes you come close to
having an accident, that upsets you. You just escape
maybe by a hair or so. Sometimes maybe you get a dis-
gruntled passenger on there, and starts a big argument.
Traffic. You have someone who cuts you off or stops in
front of the bus. There's a lot of tension behind that. You
got to watch all the time. You're watchin' the drivers,
you're watchin' other cars. Most of the time you have to
drive for the other drivers, to avoid hitting them. So you
take the tension home with you. And most of the runs are
long runs. From one end of the line to the other would be
about an hour and twenty minutes. Most of the drivers,
they'll suffer from hemorrhoids, kidney trouble, and such
as that. I had a case of ulcers behind it.

In the beginning you had to punch transfers, we had
to make change, we had to watch traffic. We had to do all
this at the same time and drive. We had the tension when
people who look suspicious would get on the bus. You had
the tension as whether this was a stickup.

Then we'd have people get on the bus and pay their
fare just like any other passenger, but all the time they're
a spotter, see? They're watching everything that goes on.
If there's anything you do wrong, two or three days later
you're called into the office. I was called in about a year
ago. (Laughs.) We have the fare boxes. As the people
drop their money there's a little lever there, and you're
supposed to continuously hit this lever so that the money
can go down into the bottom. I was called in. Some spotter on the bus said I didn't make the money go down—
which was very erroneous. I'd forced a habit of just steady
hitting this all the time. There's a little door that lets the
money go through. It's spring operated. Once so much
money gets in there the weight'll make the door open anyway and it'll fall down. There's nothing you can do
about it anyway. Once the money goes down all you can
do is see it.

They will report if any passengers are getting by you
without paying. They check up on the transfers that you
issue—if you give someone a transfer with too much time
on it, or if you accept a transfer that's too late. A spotter

will get on the bus and give you a transfer that's late, purposely, to see if you'll observe it.

Then you have the supervisors on the street. They're in automobiles. If you're running a minute ahead of time, they write you up and you're called into the office. Sometimes they can really upset you. They'll stop you at a certain point. Some of them have the habit of wanting to bawl you out there on the street. That's one of the most upsetting parts of it.

If you're running hot, ahead of time, they're afraid you're gonna miss some passengers. If I go out there and run three or four minutes hot, then the guy in back of me, he's the one that gets all the passengers. You got a guy in front of you two or three minutes ahead, you gotta carry the whole street. It's pretty tough.

They call these checkpoints. On my run I have three, four checkpoints between one terminal to the other. You'll never know when they'll be there. Most of 'em are in little station wagons. If you come late to a checkpoint, there isn't much they can do about it. They allow you time for being late, with traffic conditions. But they say there's no excuse for running ahead of time. They'll suspend you for a day or two, whatever the whims of the superintendent. He's the guy who has the say in the garage. If he decides to suspend you for a week, you lose a week's work. If you're caught running ahead of time, within about six months you'll get whatever he feels he wants to give you.

The union, as far as that goes, it's nothing. That's why we was on strike. It was as against the union as against the Company. You don't have any court of appeals. We had this wildcat about the buses not having good tires on the back. No threads, slick. That's a hazard to us. It's also endangering the lives of the passengers. During rainy weather or snowy weather, that's when we're really into it. We don't have any traction whatsoever. That's why I got off the Outer Drive. On those slippery mornings, you go into skids. That was one of our grievances. They promised there would be good tires on the buses. But it's still the same.

I'm too young to get a pension and too old to be a checker, which is a safer job for yourself and the passengers. After you get a certain age, you don't have the reflex you have when you're younger. I think when a man gets up a certain age, they should give him the easier job. My doctor told me to quit driving. (Laughs.) But there's nothing left for me to do, so I have to keep on driving. The earliest retirement age is sixty-two. I'll be eligible to retire in about fifteen years. That means I'd have had to work forty-two years.

We should have a contract where we can retire after twenty-five years' service. Service instead of age. When it came up before us, the pensioners didn't go along. We got to negotiate a new contract, the absentee pensioners, livin' in Florida, have the right to vote on it. They automatically vote against anything that's progressive. They're practically all white. The only thing they vote in favor of is the pension plan, because as it goes up for us, it goes up for them.

A fella worked with me that was eligible for a pension. He was so ill, his private doctors said he couldn't work. He had a terrible case of bleeding ulcers. The company doctors said he could work. So he died fighting for his disability.

Mrs. Robinson remembers the early days: "They even had some kind of incentive. They used to give Will shirts if he didn't have an accident. They'd give 'em all kinds of things to at least show they were aware that the men were trying to be good drivers. On Christmas, on Thanksgiving Day, they would give them turkeys. Now nothing! When the whites were there, their families would come up to the barn and have dinner. I used to go up there with Will when I first met him, I'd have lunch, sit around, play the piano. It was like a recreational center for the neighborhood. But not now. Nothing, since it's all black."

He brings matters up to date. "Now, after a certain hour, if you're out of uniform, you can't get in. During my breaks, I come home, take a nap, go back to work. One time, during your break, you didn't have to go home. You'd have lunch, recreation right there. We had lockers. You could get yourself a shower and change of clothes. They took all the lockers away. Now you just check out and leave . . .

"When you work that straight run, you get only a thirty-minute break. That's just enough time to grab a bite, to wash, and get back to work. That's why I don't work those straight runs any more. At the terminals,

there's no facilities for washrooms, toilets. Some of our drivers use the back door of the bus if it's a deserted area. If they really are in need to go, they say, 'Go to a filling station.' But you're not supposed to leave your bus with passengers on it. There's a Clark station, we had trouble with the guy. He'd always tell us the washroom was out of order. From what I heard, the CTA didn't give no money for drivers to use the washroom."

MRS. ROBINSON: *Will was written up once, because I got on the bus and we were talking about something. They didn't know what kind of conversation it was, but they called him into the office. (Laughs.)*

It wasn't known she was my wife. I remember one morning, the bus was crowded and there was a lady standing right up over me. She was asking questions and talking all the way downtown. She was a stranger in town. A couple of days later, I was called in the office and they said I was holding a conversation with a passenger. It was one of the passengers wrote this in. Passengers can write you up. You have to spend your own time to go in there and answer the complaint.

Friday evening I had a little incident happen. It's upsetting. The traffic was very heavy. Sometime the light'll change before you can get all through. You'll stop short so you don't block the other traffic going in the other direction. I was a little far out in the street, but I stopped still, so the other traffic could go in their direction. There's an automobile on the left side of me, he was farther out than I was. The people who was crossin' the street couldn't get past him, period. They had to go around him and then come in front of the bus to get across. One guy comes up to the bus window and says, "Why the hell don't you move it back?" He didn't say anything to the white fella in the auto who was really blocking everything. He had to say it to me. I knew what the reason was.

I think young bus drivers will kind of change things around. I don't think they're gonna go along with it too long. I think eventually something will blow up right there in the garage—with this superintendent. I don't think they'll take quite as much as the older ones, because if they get fired, they have a better chance of making it.

MRS. ROBINSON: *When the strike was called, it was the younger drivers. The older driver, he'll play down these harasses, because he's gotta keep up these mortgage notes. They're really afraid.*

The younger ones led the strike and practically all the leaders were fired.

MRS. ROBINSON: *I can always tell when Will's had a bad day. He's got a nervous twitch. I don't think he's even aware of it. I think Will is a very proud man, and he wants me to look upon him as a man. This is one reason I stopped riding his bus. I didn't want him humiliated in front of me by the inspectors. He wants to talk back like a man. He'd be more likely to do that if I'm on the bus than he would be if I'm not there. I know if he goes too far, he doesn't have a job. So Will doesn't tell me much that happens. Much of it would be humiliating, so we don't talk too much about the job. I just have to feel and tell by his attitude when he's had an exceptionally hard day. (She leaves the room.)*

(He is obviously weary.) You're trying to make schedules and at the end of the line you only get a ten-minute layover. Some guys'll stretch out on the long seat and relax, some will read a paper, and some will sit there and maybe smoke two or three cigarettes. I smoke more than I ever did. In that short time, I may have to run about three blocks to the washroom, a filling station over there. It looks like you gotta smoke two or three cigarettes before you can ease the tension after that run.

A lot of guys want to sit around and talk after they get off from work. I just want to get out of there and head home. All I do now is get up in the morning, go there, and I don't be thinking about that. Like a machine, that's about the only way I can feel.

FRANK DECKER

He had been hauling steel "out of the Gary mills into Wisconsin. They call this a short haul, about 150 miles in ra-

dius." He had been at it since 1949 when he was nineteen
years old. "I figure about 25 hundred trips. Sounds monotonous, doesn't it?"

*Most steel haulers are owner-operators of truck and
trailer. "We changed over to diesel about fifteen years
ago. Big powerful truck. You lease your equipment to the
trucking companies. Their customers are the big steel corporations. This is strictly a one-man operation."*

*Since the wildcat strike of 1967 he's been an organizer
for the Fraternal Association of Steel Haulers (FASH.)
"Forty-six months trying to build an association, to give
the haulers a voice and get 'em better working conditions.
And a terrific fight with the Teamsters Union."*

*Casually, though at times with an air of incredulousness,
he recounts a day in the life of a steel hauler.*

I'll go into the steel mills after supper. Load through the
evening hours, usually with a long waiting line, especially
years ago before the Association started. We'd wait as
high as twelve, fifteen hours to get loaded. The trucking
companies didn't charge the corporations for any waiting
time, demurrage—like they did on railroad cars.

We get a flat percentage no matter how much work we
put in. It didn't cost the trucking company anything to
have us wait out there, so they didn't charge the steel outfits anything. They abused us terribly over the years. We
waited in the holding yard behind the steel mill. The long-
est I've ever waited was twenty-five hours.

You try to keep from going crazy from boredom. You
become accustomed to this as time goes by—four hours,

* "The long hauler, if they give him a pickup to go over to
Detroit from Chicago, he feels it's a waste of time, no trip at
all. He wants to load New York. He'd leave Chicago, drop a
drop in Cleveland and a drop in Pittsburgh, and peddle the
rest of it off in New York. Once a dispatcher told Jim—he's
a little over fifty, been long haul for twenty-five years—'We
have a little box here, not a load, weighs thirty-five hundred
pounds, do me a favor, pick it up.' Jim says, 'I don't have room
for this box and it's goin' the other way, I'll pick it up next
time I'm in New York.' He was heading for St. Louis. It takes
a certain kind of individual that thinks in thousands of miles
so casually, as you and I'll pick something up from my neighbor here next week."

eight hours, twelve hours. It's part of the job to build patience. You sit in the cab of the truck. You walk a half mile down to a PX-type of affair, where you buy a wrapped sandwich in cellophane or a cup of coffee to go. You sit in the mill by the loader's desk and watch the cranes. You'll read magazines, you'll sleep four hours, you'll do anything from going nuts. Years ago, there was no heat in the steel mills. You had to move around to keep from freezing. It's on the lakefront, you know.

Following the '67 wildcat strike, the trucking companies instituted a tariff that said four hours we give the steel mill for nothing, the fifth hour we begin to charge at $13.70 an hour. We get seventy-five percent of that or ten dollars. And when we deliver, they got four free hours at our point of delivery. So we start every day by giving away eight potential free hours. Besides your time, you have an investment ranging from fifteen to thirty thousand dollars in your truck and trailer that you're servicing them free. The average workingman, he figures to work eight hours and come home. We have a sixteen-hour day.

If I were to go in the mill after supper, I'd expect to come out maybe midnight, two o'clock in the morning. The loading process itself is fifteen to thirty minutes. Once they come with the crane, they can load the steel on it in two or three lifts. Maybe forty-five to fifty thousand pounds.

We protect it with paper, tie it down with chains and binders, tarp it, sign our bills, move toward the gate. It takes you fifteen to twenty minutes to get to the front gate. I must weigh in empty and weigh out loaded. Sometimes, even though you're all loaded, tarped down and everything, you get on the scale and you're off-weight. If you scale in at twenty-five thousand pounds empty and you come out weighing seventy-two thousand pounds, you're five hundred, six hundred pounds off the billed weight. You have to go back and find out who made a mistake. Let's say it's over the one percent they'll allow. They have to weigh everything again and find out that some hooker made a paper mistake. That's happened many times to haulers. Prior to '67, we never got paid a penny for it.

Years ago, we ran through city streets, alongside streetcars, buses, and what have you. It was a two-hour run from the mills of Gary to the North Side of Chicago.

Some seventy-six traffic lights. Every one of them had to be individually timed and played differently. If you have to stop that truck and start it, it's not only aggravating and tiring, but you'd wear out the truck twice as fast as you would if you made those lights. It was a constant thing of playing these lights almost by instinct.

This is all changed with the expressways. It's just as if automation had entered the trucking business. Now you pull out of U.S. Steel in Gary and you don't have a light until you drop off at the expressway in the city of Milwaukee. It's a miracle compared to what it used to be. So much easier on yourself, on your equipment.

A stop at the Wisconsin state line, a place to eat. Big trucks stop there. Maybe meet a bunch that have been in the steel mill all night. Coffee-up, tell all the stories, about how badly you're treated in the steel mill, tell about the different drunks that try to get under your wheels. Then move towards your destination and make the delivery at seven o'clock in the morning. We're talking about thirteen hours already. My routine would be to drop two days like this and not come home. Halfway back from Milwaukee take a nap in the cab at a truck stop. You use the washroom, the facilities, you call your dispatcher in Gary, and pick up another load. Went home for a day of sleep, wash up, get rejuvenated, live like a human being for a day, come back to the mill after supper, and be off again. During the last ten years almost everybody bought a sleeper truck. It has facilities behind the seat. If you were to get a hotel room every night you were on the road, why, you'd be out of business shortly.

On weekends, if you're lucky enough to be home, you're greasing the truck and repairing it. It's like a seven-day week. There's nobody else to do the work. Years ago, the rate of truck repair was five dollars an hour. Today it's eleven, twelve dollars an hour. You do ninety percent of the work yourself, small repairs and adjustments.

I would make two round trips to Milwaukee and pass within four blocks of my house and never go home. You can't park a big truck in the neighborhood. If the police have anything to do with it, you can't even park on an arterial street more than an hour. It's a big joke with truckdrivers: We're gonna start carrying milk bottles with us. Everywhere we go now, there's signs: No Truck Parking. They want you to keep that thing moving. Don't stop around here. It's a nuisance; it takes up four spaces, which we need for our local people. You're an out-of-town guy, keep moving.

If I chose to park in the truck terminal, I'd have an eight-mile ride—and I don't think I'd be welcome. The owner-operator, we're an outcast, illegitimate, a gypsy, a fella that everybody looks down on. These are words we use. We compare ourselves to sailors: we sail out on the highways. The long-distance hauler is gone for a week, two weeks, picking up a load at one port, delivering it to another port.

You get lonely not talking to anybody for forty-eight hours. On the road, there's no womenfolks, unless there's a few waitresses, a couple of good old girls in the truck stop you might kid around with. They do talk about women, but they don't really have the time for women. There's a few available, waitresses in truck stops, and most of them have ten thousand guys complimenting them.

There's not much playing around that goes on. They talk of women like all guys do, but it's not a reality, it's dreaming. There's not these stories of conquest—there's the exceptional case of a Casanova—because they're moving too much. They're being deprived of their chance to play around. Maybe if they get more time, we'll even see that they have a little more of that. (Laughs.)

Truckers fantasize something tremendous. When they reach a coffee stop, they unload with all these ideas. I've seen fellas who build up such dreams when they come into a truck stop they start to pour it out, get about three minutes of animated description out of it, and all of a sudden come up short and realize it's all a bunch of damn foolishness they built up in their minds. It's still that they're daydreaming from the truck. He builds a thing in his mind and begins to believe it.

You sit in a truck, your only companionship is your own thoughts. Your truck radio, if you can play it loud enough to hear—you've got the roar of the engine, you've got a transmission with sixteen gears, you're very much occupied. You're fighting to maintain your speed every moment you're in the truck.

The minute you climb into that truck, the adrenaline starts pumping. If you want to have a thrill, there's no comparison, not even a jet plane, to climbing on a steel truck and going out there on the Dan Ryan Expressway. You'll swear you'll never be able to get out the other end of that thing without an accident. There's thousands of cars and thousands of trucks and you're shifting like a maniac and you're braking and accelerating and the object is to try to move with the traffic and try to keep from running over all those crazy fools who are trying to get under your wheels.

You have to be superalert all the time. Say I'm loaded to full capacity, seventy-three thousand pounds. That's equivalent to how many cars—at four thousand pounds a car? I cannot stop. I got terrific braking power. You have five axles, you'll have fourteen tires on the ground, you got eight sets of brakes. You have to anticipate situations a block ahead of you. You're not driving to match situations *immediately* in front of you. A good driver looks ahead two blocks, so he's not mousetrapped into a situation where he'll have to stop—because you can't stop like a car's gonna stop. You're committed. It's like an airplane crossing the ocean: they reach that point of no return. Your commitment's made a hundred, two hundred yards before you reach the intersection. It's really almost impossible.

You have to get all psyched up and keep your alertness all the time. There's a lot of stomach trouble in this business, tension. Fellas that can't eat anything. Alka-Seltzer and everything. There's a lot of hemorrhoid problems. And there's a lot of left shoulder bursitis, because of the window being open. And there's a loss of hearing because of the roar of the engine. The roar of the engine has a hypnotic effect. To give you an idea of the decibel sounds inside a cab, nowadays they're beginning to insulate 'em. It's so tremendous that if you play the radio loud enough to hear above the roar and you come to a tollgate and stop, you have to turn it down it's screaming so loud. You could break your eardrums. And the industrial noises in the background . . . I'm sure his hearing's affected. There was a survey made of guys that transport cars. You've heard the loud metal noise, where the different parts of the gates comes together. They found these fellas have a great loss of hearing. It's one more occupational hazard. There has been different people I've worked with that I've seen come apart, couldn't handle it any more.

"I'll tell you where we've had nervous breakdowns, when we got in this '67 thing, the wildcat. We've had four people associated with us in Gary have had nervous breakdowns. And at Pittsburgh, they've had several. The tension of this labor thing, forty-six weeks, is real strong. The tension's even greater for a guy with a family to support. . ."

There seemed an unusual amount of fellas having problems with their family, with the wife in particular. They're average guys with their wives going through the change and so forth. Really, that's an awful problem for the wife, because she has to raise the kids, she has to fight off the bill collectors on the phone. She can't even count on her husband to attend a graduation, a communion, any kind of social function. She's just lucky he's home Christmas and New Year's. He's usually so darn tired that he'd much rather be home sleeping than getting ready to go out Sunday night.

Sure, truckers eat a lot of pills. It's a lot more prevalent than I thought. I heard fellas say they get a better price on bennies if they buy them by the thousand. We know a lot of individuals we consider hopheads off on benzedrine. A couple of guys I know are on it, even though it's on the weekends when they don't need to stay awake. It's become a habit.

The kids call 'em red devils. In trucking, they call it the Arkansas Turnaround—or whatever your destination is. A lot of 'em are dispensed by drugstores on prescription for weight control. So their wife gets the pills and the old man ends up usin' 'em to keep awake, because they're a benzedrine base. It'll be the little black ones or the little red ones . . .

They'd like to pick up the kids, hitchhikers, if it weren't for the prohibitions. I think the biggest transporters of hippies would be the owner-operators, because they want company. For years you didn't see a hitchhiker, but now with the hippie, with kids traveling across the country, every interchange has got a bunch of long-haired, packsacked kids hitchhiking from one end of the country to the other. It's a reborning . . .

It's a strange thing about truckers, they're very conservative. They come from a rural background or they think of themselves as businessmen. But underneath the veneer they're really very democratic and softhearted and liberal.

But they don't *realize* it. You tell 'em they're liberal and you're liable to get your head knocked off. But when you start talking about things, the war, kids, when you really get down to it, they're for everything that's liberal. But they want a conservative label on it. It's a strange paradox.

In the steel mill, the truckdriver is at the absolute bottom of the barrel. Everybody in that mill that is under union contract has some dignity, has some respect from management. If he's the fella that sweeps the floor, he has job status. The man in the crane, if there's no work for his crane, he doesn't have to do anything. If the fella that pushes the broom in Warehouse Four, if he's got everything groomed up, they can't tell him, "No, you go and do another job."

Now comes the steel hauler. Everybody in that mill's above somebody, from top management down. At the bottom of the ladder, there's the hooker on your truck. He wants to feel that he's better than somebody. He figures I'm better than this steel hauler. So you get constant animosity because he feels that the corporation looks down on this steel hauler, and he knows he can order him around, abuse him, make him wait. It's a status thing. There's a tremendous feeling.

The first couple of years when I got abused, I howled and I yelled and I did my dance: "You can't do this to me." After a few years, I developed a philosophy. When I scream, it gives them pleasure, they can put it to me. They're sadists. So the average steel hauler, no matter how abused he is, you always give them that smile and you leave it go over your head. You say to yourself: One day my time will come. If you don't take this philosophy, you'll go right out of your mind. You cause an incident, you're barred from the mill. It's such a competitive business that you dare not open your mouth because your company will be penalized freight—and you get it in the neck. You try to show 'em a cockiness like you could care less.

Over a number of years, your face becomes familiar. It breaks the ice. The loader considers you an old-timer, he has some identity with you. You might find, on rare occasions, friendship. The loader is the foreman on the shift for truck loading. He has a desk in between all the piles of steel and he lays out the loads that are gonna be placed on the truck. If the hookers see the loader's giving you respect, they'll accept you.

The newer people get the most grief, do the screaming, and get the worst treatment. Younger fellas. The fella that comes into this business that's over forty takes his life's savings and buys a truck because somebody told him there's big money to be made and he wants to get in his own business. If you last the first five years, you last the worst hardships. Success means you survive. If you don't make a dime on your investment, but you're still in business after five years, we say he's a regular. Those first five years is your biggest nut to crack. You don't know the ropes, you don't know how to buy and service your truck reasonable, you make all the mistakes. Fifty percent turnover in our business every year. They drop out, lose their trucks. That's the only reward: In your mind, you feel you're in business.

There's been a change since the '67 wildcat. It spread across the country like wildfire. We're respected in a lot of places now because they know we stand up and fight for our rights. As much as it was a money problem, it was a problem of dignity.

"Ninety percent of the fellas were Teamster Union members, but you'd never know it. Outside of the dues money they take out of your check, they did absolutely nothing. They did less than nothing. We know that a few telephone calls by high Teamster officials to steel mill officials could have changed our picture completely. If they would call up and say, 'Look, you're abusing our people and if you don't straighten it out we're gonna do something about it.' They could put one man down there at U.S. Steel, for instance, and say, 'I'm a Teamster official. We're asking you guys not to load in this mill until they treat you fairly.' In twenty-four hours we'd be getting loaded out there so fast we couldn't keep our hat on our head.

"But they're establishment. They're interlocked with the steel mills and the trucking companies. They don't even know who their members are. Our guess is between twenty and thirty thousand steel haulers. Nobody can come up with the figures. A Teamster official was maybe a truckdriver twenty-five or thirty years ago. Fought the good fight, built the union, got high on the hog. So many years have passed that he doesn't even know what a truck

*looks like any more. He now golfs with his contemporaries
from the trucking companies. He lolls about Miami Beach
at the Hollywood Hotel that they own. To him, to have to
deal with a truckdriver is beneath his station. It's awfully
hard when you get to the union hall to talk to a Teamster
official. They're usually 'busy.' That means they're down at
the Palmer House, at the Steak Restaurant. It's a hangout
for 'em."*

Truckdrivers used to spend ninety percent of their time
bitchin' about how they got screwed at the mill, how they
got screwed by the state trooper. Troopers prey on truckdrivers for possible violations—mostly regarding weight
and overload. It's extremely difficult to load a steel truck
legally to capacity. If you're a thousand pounds over, it's
no great violation but you have to get around the scales.
At regular pull-offs, they'll say: Trucks Must Cross Scales.

You pull in there and you find, lo and behold, you're
five hundred or a thousand pounds over. You've got to
pay a ticket, maybe twenty-five dollars, and you have to
move it off. This is a great big piece of steel. You're supposed to unload it. You have to find some guy that's light
and break the bands on the bundle and transfer sheets or
bars over on the other truck. Occasionally it's something
that can't be broke down, a continuous coil that weighs
ten thousand pounds. You work some kind of angle to get
out of there. You wish for the scale to close and you close
your eyes and you go like hell to try to get out of the
state. You have a feeling of running a blockade in the
twenties with a load of booze. You have a feeling of
trying to beat the police. Or you pay the cop off.

Most state troopers consider truckers to be outlaws,
thieves, and overloaders. The companies and the union
don't try to upgrade our image. They don't go to the police departments and say, "Stop abusing our members."

Everybody's preying on the trucker to shake him down.
The Dan Ryan is unbelievable. They're working deals you
couldn't believe, that nobody would care about, because
they're out of state truckers. Who cares what happens to
them? What would you think of a trucker coming up the
Dan Ryan for the first time? He's coming from Pittsburgh
with an overload. He approaches the South Side of the
city and it says: All Trucks Must Use Local Lanes. But
the signs aren't well enough marked and he's out in the

third lane and gets trapped. He can't get over because of the other cars, he goes right up the express lane. Well, there's cops down there makin' their living off these poor guys. They pull him over and they say, "Hey buddy, you're out where no trucks are supposed to be. We're gonna have to lock you up." They go through their song and dance about they're horrified about how you've broken the law, endangering everybody. And they're hinting around that maybe you want to make a deal.

Maybe you don't want to make a deal? Oh, you have to make bond and appear in court, that's twenty-five dollars. If you've got an out-of-state chauffeur's license, they'll take your chauffeur's license. So if you're going to come up with a ten, he'll hold court right there and he'll tell you never do it again. But if you're gonna be ha_ _eaded—I'm gonna fight this thing—he'll say, "Okay, we're gonna take you in the neighborhood out here and we're gonna park your truck and we're gonna take you over to the station in a squad car." I can't swear to it, but there's a story goin' around that these cops are working with the people in the neighborhood. So you park your car out on those streets. While you're at the station making bond you come back and there ain't much left to your truck. The tires are gone, the cab's been broken into, the radio's gone. That's what happens to thousands of truckdrivers.

Thg cops tell you, "You get back on your truck any way you know how." Because they don't want to be there when you see your truck. You take a cab over there and there you stand. Now you call the copper, this official paragon of law and order, and he tells you, "How am I gonna find out who wrecked your truck and stole everything off?" A truck tire costs a hundred dollars. You're liable to come back from the station, trying to fight your ticket, to have four hundred-dollar bills gone right off the trailer.

Why the devil do you do it, right? There's this mystique about driving. The trucker has a sense of power. He has a sense of responsibility too. He feels: I know everything about the road. These people making mistakes around me, I have to make allowances for them. If the guy makes a mistake, I shouldn't swear at him, I shouldn't threaten him with my truck. You say, "That slob can't drive. Look at that dumb woman with her kids in there. Look at that drunk." *You've* got status!

Every load is a challenge and when you finally off-load it, you have a feeling of having completed a job—which I don't think you get in a production line. I pick up a load at the mill, going to Hotpoint in Milwaukee. I take a job and I go all through the process. You have a feeling when you off-load it—you see they're turning my steel into ten thousand washing machines, into a hundred farm implements. You feel like your day's work is well done when you're coming back. I used to have problems in the morning, a lot of heartburn, I couldn't eat. But once I off-loaded, the pressure was off. I met the deadline. Then I could eat anything.

The automobile, it's the biggest thing in the country, it's what motivates everybody. Even that model, when they drape her across the hood of that car ... In the truck stop, they're continually talking about how they backed into this particular place in one swing. The mere car drivers were absolutely in awe. When you're in that truck, you're not Frank Decker, factory worker. You're Frank Decker, truck owner and professional driver. Even if you can't make enough money to eat, it gives you something ...

There's a joke going around with the truckdrivers. "Did you hear the one about the hauler that inherited a million dollars?" "What did he do with it?" "He went out and bought a new Pete."* "Well, what did he do then?" "He kept running until his money ran out." Everybody knows in this business you can't make no money. Owning that big Pete, with the chrome stacks, the padded dashboard, and stereo radio, and shifting thirty-two gears and chromed wheels, that's heaven. And in the joke, he was using up the inheritance to keep the thing on the road.

You have to figure out reasons to keep from going crazy, games to try to beat yourself. After a number of years, you begin to be a better loader. They come with a thirty-thousand-pound coil. If you set it down on the truck three inches forward or backward of where it's supposed to be, you're misloaded. So there's a challenge every time you load. Everybody's proud of that. At the truck shop they'll flash a weight ticket: "Take a look at that." They've loaded a balanced load.

* "That's a Peterbilt, the Cadillac of trucks. It's a great, big, long-nosed outfit. The tractor alone costs 30,000 dollars."

Now as we approach '67, I've about had it. I'm trucking seventeen years. There's nothing left to do. I never dreamt that our hopes of getting together some day was gonna come true. It was just a dream. I'll finish out the year, sell off my truck and trailer, and I'm gonna build a garage up at the Wisconsin-Illinois state line. I'm gonna service trucks in there. The guys needed a garage where they could get work done. The commercial garages—you got a bunch of amateurs working on your truck. To be an owner-operator, you gotta be a mechanic. I had a three-car garage when I was seventeen. So I was gonna build this garage ...

But I met an old-timer I'd seen around for years. This was at Inland Steel on a Thursday night. One of my last hauls—I thought. We sat for about six hours waiting to get loaded. He said to me, "Did you hear about the rumble going on down in Gary?" He showed me this one-page pamphlet: "If you're fed up with the Teamsters Union selling you out and all the sweetheart contracts and the years of abuses, go in front of your union hall Monday morning at ten o'clock. We're gonna have a protest."

Friday I talked to everybody. "We're finally gonna do something. We've been talkin' about it for years ..." I couldn't get anybody to talk to me. "Ah, hell, that's all you ever talk about."

Well, Monday morning I went out to Gary. There was twenty guys picketing. We didn't get much help through the day. We decided to go to the steel mills and intercept our people, who were coming in from all over the country with their trucks. You got the picture? Ninety percent of the guys didn't know where the union was at. For years, they paid dues as an extortion. They're hurting. Most of 'em are one paycheck away from the poorhouse. So we went there and tried to tell 'em, "Park your truck and come and picket." Well, it turned into something because the time was ripe. Everybody knew something had to happen.

"We picketed for eight days on the mills. It built till we had five hundred, six hundred guys—most of 'em from out of town. Parked their trucks all over town. We hung on them gates. Sometimes we'd get down to two, three guys and we thought it was all over. But there's a new carload of guys come in from Iowa or from Detroit or from Fre-

mont, Ohio, or something. They'd heard about this rumble that was going on and they came to help.

"We picketed the steel mills and we talked to any steel haulers that come in, told them not to load, to join the picket line. Some of the haulers tried to run you down. You'd have to jump for your life. Other guys would come up and they wouldn't know what to do. They recognized a lot of faces. We met each other in truck stops for years. You know the guy—Tom, Dick, or Harry. But you never knew much more about him than just a service stop. We began to build relationships down here with these guys we'd seen for years, but we didn't know where they lived or anything else. They'll say, 'What kind of truck you drive again?' They recognize you by your truck, see?

"So we're having meetings. The guys call from Detroit. They shut down Armco Steel or Great Lakes Steel. Then we heard they're picketing at Pittsburgh and finally they're picketing in Philadelphia. And then we heard they blew up two trucks with dynamite in New Jersey. The Jersey crowd, they're always rough. It spread clear from here to the east coast. And it went on for nine weeks.

"Steel mills got injunctions out against us. They took us into court and locked us up and everything else. The Teamsters helped the steel mills and the carriers to try to get us back to work. They come out in cars: a company official, a Teamster official, a marshal—pointing out who we were to serve papers on. They were working together.

"Everybody's telling everybody: 'They'll go back to work. They're all broke. They can't last more than a couple of weeks.' But we hung on and we hung on, you know. (He swallows hard, takes a deep breath.) Some of the guys didn't go home at all. We raised money by going around asking truck stops and truck dealers and tire dealers to donate money and help us. A lot of 'em were dependent on us and knew we were poor payin' and knew that maybe if they helped us out we could start gettin' in better shape and start to pay our bills."

Truckdrivers are known as an awful lot of deadbeats. They live off credit and lay on everybody. Deprive their family, two legs ahead of the bill collectors, charge fuel at the new guy's station that's givin' credit to everybody and then, when they run up a big bill, they'll go by. All to keep that truck going. I don't think they're worse responsible than anybody else. But they get in a position like a businessman: you owe everybody and his brother and you start writin' paper and you try to survive. You get in deeper and deeper and deeper . . .

So we formed an organization—the Fraternal Association of Steel Haulers, FASH. We organized like hell, leading up to the contract time again. We went on a nationwide strike because we didn't hardly scratch the door the first time. This time we asked the Teamsters Union to represent us, which they never did before. Fitzsimmons* promised in the agreement he'd set up a committee to meet with us. He sent us the very thieves that had locals where the steel haulers had members. These guys had vested interests to keep things the way it was. We met with 'em a couple of times and saw they weren't about to do nothin'.

"So we demanded Fitzsimmons meet with us—not that we thought he'd do anything. He's nothing but a dirty old man shuffling along and filling a hole for Hoffa. But we did feel we could get recognition if we'd meet with him. Nothing doing. He wouldn't even talk with us. He sent a big bully, that's Hoffa's right hand, the head of the goons, guy with a prison record as long as your arm. He started tellin' us all he's gonna do for the steel haulers. We said, 'You ain't doin' nothin' for us.' We told him we didn't have to listen to his boloney. He said, 'What do you want?' We told him we want the International to give us charters for steel locals. We want to have elections and we want to elect our own people. We want autonomy. And then we told him, 'We want you and your crooked pals to stay ten miles away from any of our halls.' He said he'd take the message back, and that's where it stands now.

'We'd become aware, checking our rates with the Interstate Commerce Commission and the Department of Labor, about their misuse of our pension fund. A nine-hundred-million-dollar pension fund that got about a billion finagled away. That's our pension. We don't have the freightside driver's feeling for good old Jimmy Hoffa. They don't care how much he steals. That ain't us. That's

---

* Frank Fitzsimmons, president of the Teamsters Union.

our *pension money in that fund. He belongs in jail, a lot of 'em do."*

In January '70, we went out on strike to reinforce our demands for recognition. We filed with 167 companies that employed steel haulers under Teamster contract. When the hearings began in Pittsburgh, there were thirty-seven lawyers from the carriers and Teamsters and two of our attorneys—one guy and another guy helping out. The hearings lasted sixteen days. It cost the Teamsters $250,-000 for their legal costs. There was ten thousand pages of testimony. The National Labor Relations Board ruled against us. We think it was a politically inspired ruling. Nixon was playing footsie with Fitzsimmons.* We were fighting the mills, the union, the carriers, the President. Who else is there left?

I talked with a fella who sold trailers. He said, "You guys are nuts. You've taken on all these big people. You don't have a chance." But there's just one thing—we feel that we're a revolution. There's people's power here and truck power. And there's a lot of people in the Teamsters Union watchin' us. If they start to see that we don't get our heads busted, that we're tough enough to lead, they're gonna come out of the woodwork. *They* all want to know where their pension money went. What's wrong is that they're all scared.

We did extremely well till this last strike. We didn't make it in the strike. There were some defections in our ranks. They voted to go back to work. We were about gonna grab that brass ring when we dropped it. So there's been a lot of disillusionment on the part of a lot of guys. But we gained so much in these three years that a lot of guys are stickin'.

We're treated with quite a bit more respect, I'll tell ya, than we were before 1967. Sure, we're havin' problems. The Teamsters are trying to get the carriers to blackball us, trying to control the steel haulers. But they know they've lost us. We have membership stickers on the trucks. The sticker alone sometimes gets 'em loaded twice

* The conversation took place before Jimmy Hoffa was granted a pardon by President Nixon and long before the Teamsters Union came out in support of the Committee for the Re-election of the President.

as fast. What they'll say, "You better load that guy, he belongs to that outfit and you don't load him you're gonna have to pay for it." We got a good reputation.

Our people are very cynical. They are always suspicious of leadership sellin' 'em out. They've seen the Teamsters. They gotta pay their dues whether they're workin' or not. So they turn on us. They're supercritical—every little thing. Between the day the strike started until March '68, I didn't pull a load of steel—that's eight months I didn't draw a penny. I been, since then, on a fifty-dollar-a-week salary, full-time for FASH, out of the Gary office. Had one guy tell me, "You only get fifty dollars a week, but that's how Hoffa started." Had another guy tell me, "I wouldn't have anybody that dumb working for fifty dollars a week to represent me." The cynicism is unbelievable.

First thing they figure, These guys are after soft, cushy jobs. They're after Hoffa, they're after the same thing we've been taken advantage of. What you have to do is rebuild confidence. These people don't trust nobody. They don't even trust themselves no more. "You're workin' in a crooked system and you gotta be a crook." So the guy figures, I wouldn't do it for anybody else, why this guy? Another typical thing is: It won't work. You can't beat 'em. They're too big. The Teamsters are too big. The steel mills are too big. Everything's against us. If you fight it, you get hurt.

You gotta re-educate 'em, you gotta climb up on the cross every day. What you build, eventually, unfortunately, is a following that will follow you no matter what you do. That's why you end up with Hoffa, with them sayin' "I don't care if Jimmy stole a million dollars, he's okay with me." It's a shame that people are that much sheep.

We're not getting the grass-roots backing we'd like to have. They're too busy, they go to their families. Sometimes I wonder why I'm in this thing. But it's rewarding. There's nothing like dealing with people, dealing with situations. It's like a crash course to educate yourself. It's something I really enjoy doing because it's something I thought should have been done all these years. After eighteen years of trucking, a change to do this work . . .

If I thought I could hand-tailor a job that I'd like to do, it's this job I'm doing right now. I never worked so hard at anything in my life. Most of this forty-six months has been seven days a week. I get weary but I never get tired of doing the job. I'm enjoying every minute of it. We're up against a lot of big people, big corporations. It has the feeling of playing chess with the top contender. It can affect people's lives, even people that don't even know.

If you win, the stakes are high. It's not just whether you're gonna make a buck. All of a sudden, you feel catapulted into these levels of decision-making that I never dreamed I'd ever reach. All of a sudden, you're no longer the guy smiling and putting up a front and waiting all the time in the truck. All of a sudden, you found your own sense of self-respect. The day's finally here. Now.

The Parking

ALFRED POMMIER

He is forty-nine and has been a parking lot attendant for about thirty years. He bears a remarkable resemblance to the late Jimmy Rushing, the blues singer. "They call 'em car hikers, they call 'em jockeys. They call me Lovin' Al, the Wizard, One-Swing Al—I'm known from Peking to Hong Kong, from the West Coast to Pecos." We're seated in a car on this wintry afternoon, each of us puffing away at a fifteen-cent cigar.

It is a flat parking lot "'cause you don't have no floors to go. We have forty, fifty cars, lots of room to park. When you come eleven o'clock, you can't get in. You take two, you check out three. You gotta just work around 'em, and people squawkin', 'May I get my car?' 'We're workin' on it.' 'Why you got so many cars?' 'Sorry, lady.' But it's easier than a garage, where there's too many men and always somethin' goin' on."

He is one of two attendants. He's worked at this corner fifteen years, six days a week. "When it rains, it gets a little hard. When it's cold, it gets very hard, 'cause you gotta wipe the snow off the windshield. Hard on everybody, you gotta get home, get rubbed down by my wife or your girl friend. It tells on me the next morning. I'm not gettin' any younger.

"I don't know who owns the lot. You never know. You ask no questions, who owns this or that. They never have us in the office. We get our check where we work. Never see who owns it. It's big business. But you have to make your tips to make your salary 'cause the union get you only what—$1.95? If I wouldn't make no tips, I couldn't survive."

There's always people trying to get something for nothing, saying their car was hit when it wasn't. Some people get very arrogant and talking that they may get their lawyer. Oh yeah, we have a lot of people that have holy feelings about their car. It don't have a scratch but they check it

297

and go around it. So I go around with 'em. There were no scratches, but it was good exercise.

Another guy, he'll pull in, get his ticket, and leave. Then he comes back and goes around the car. I'll say, "Why don't you go around when you come in?" He'll say, "I went around just in case you hit it." I say, "If I'd a hit it, you got to see if it's fresh or it's old. 'Cause we don't have to tell you no story if we hit your car. The company'll pay you. We don't have no jive about that. Me and George who work here, we don't hit cars."

If I should hit a car, I wouldn't say I have no bad feelin' about it. Things can happen. When you talk to a man nice or a lady nice, then you calm 'em down. If you have a hot temper, then it's just a big argument. I had only one real serious argument in thirty years, me and a manager. Never had another scrap with anyone. So that's not a bad record for feelings. I've had customers that have called me names. Once I had this guy from Texas, I asked him, "Will you please pull it over?" But he was a Texan, he jumped out of the car, not pulling up, and he called me an m-f. And I called him one in exchange. He finally pulled up and that was the end of that. You got a temper and another guy got a temper, you got to have the police to come get one of you off or both of you off—or the ambulance. So why not cool it?

We had a lady come in about six months ago. She wanted her car in the same spot. I said, "Sorry lady, can't put it in a certain spot." She said, "I want it in *that* spot." She came back and I had it in *that* spot. She said, "Thank you." I said, "Okay, lady." She came back again and we was filled up. She wanted *that* spot again, and I said, "No, I'm filled, lady. I can't get you *that* spot. I can't get you *any* spot." She didn't give you a tip and she wanted extra service. Okay, if she pay her parking and just get parked, that's all right. We have regular customers, we don't worry about tips every day. They tip once a week. We give them what we call soigné service. Those who don't, we still have to give 'em service, but it ain't soigné.

We got a lot of fancy Cadillac cars don't tip. The workingman is the best tipper. He works all day, he'll give you a quarter or a half a dollar. But you get some people ridin' a big Cadillac and fancy dress, he'll give you a thin dime. But he'll pull that car in again and if we have the FULL sign, that's it for him. We have to wave him away. He puts up a beef, but if you don't answer him, you don't have no argument.

I have one big irritation. When people see you getting a car and you got two or three pulls—claim checks—and there might be eight people goin', you're trying to pull the easiest cars to make room to get the other people—they think you're not giving 'em service. There's a whole crowd and you might not know either one of 'em, you're tryin' to make it easy all around. There's no need in movin' the same car over to get the car that's easier to move out. They still can't get across the street because traffic is blocked, so what's the cause of all the confusion?

They think you're tryin' to ignore them. You're tryin' to make it easy, but they see you get the other guy and they paid first. When a show breaks up, people panic. "I'm first." "I gotta get home." "I gotta catch a plane." Two men can't handle no fifteen people at one time. Somebody has to wait. A lot of people go get their own car. They may hit a car or scratch it and then they want to put it on the attendants.

You can't go too fast in the parking lot. I once worked five-, six-floor garages. I was much younger then. I'd get in that Cadillac or that Buick or that Volkswagen, whatever is in there, and I'd go around them floors. As you get older, you learn more. There's a lot of young guys drive fast, which I don't do no more. It's a very good feeling if you're a young man.

In my younger days I used to be a wizard, I used to really roll. I could spin a car with one hand and never miss a hole. When I got in a new car, I thought it was *my* car. It was a customer's car and I was only going upstairs. I *know* it wasn't mine, 'cause at that time I didn't even own a car. And when I owned a car, I couldn't own over a hundred-dollar car. So it was a great feelin' to drive anybody's new car. When I'd take that car to drive, I thought it was just a dream car.

It is a very big feeling about a man when he drives in with that car and he get out and he might be in his tuxedo. As a younger man, when a customer'd come in, I'd say, "Gee, that's a beautiful car, sir." I'll just go sit in that car, maybe I'll just back it up a couple of times. 'Cause we was never supposed to take the car off the premises, which I never did myself. 'Course, when you got five or six men there, it might be one might go off.

I was sittin' in that guy-with-the-tuxedo car. He got out of it, him an' his girl friend goin' night clubbing. And that car smelling real good with cologne and the windows be up. And I just be looking in that car, you know, the music be up. I'd pull back in the lot, back to the front, maybe I'll go back in the stall. I'd say, "Why can't I be a rich man, get me a lot of money, get me a new car?" 'Cause I rode an old car for eighteen years. The feeling of sitting in that rich man's car, that's a great feeling. Different feeling between the workingman's car and the rich man's car. It's something strong in your mind that someday you may get one. It was a hundred to one that you would get it unless somebody will you something or you would be a stickup man.

As I get older now, a car's a car. I'm drivin' a '65 Pontiac. I know it's seven years old, but it's mine. I have to enjoy it. Sure I'd love to have a new car, but I can't afford it with three babies. I don't need to be dreamin' of a Cadillac which I know I can't get. There's no need of me dreamin' for an Imperial Chrysler which I know I can't get. I used to dream about cars very bad. The last five or six years I haven't dreamed too much about cars. 'Cause I know I got other things to do for my kids.

I used to be a chauffeur and it was a dream for me driving, too. I'd drive him to his office and when I drop him off, the car was mine. (Laughs.) I might not have to pick him up for a couple of hours. If I go south or ride around the Loop, I take the chauffeur's cap off, put my hat on. It's mine. You always feel the chauffeur drivin' the rich man's car is the one really enjoyin' it more than the rich man.

I quit chaufferin'. I make more money in a parking lot with tips and salary. When people ask what I do, I tell 'em I park cars just like my other job. Only thing you got is a white collar, that's okay with me. Working behind a typewriter, that's fine. You're a doctor, that's cool. I got man friends, teachers. We meet sometimes, have a drink, talk. Everything is normal. Everybody got a job to do. My friends never feel superior to me. They'll say, "I'll go downtown and park with Lovin' Al."

After twenty-five, thirty years I could drive any car like a baby, like a woman change her baby's diaper. I could handle that car with one hand. I had a lot of customers would say, "How you do this? The way you go around this way?" I'd say, "Just the way you bake a cake, miss, I can handle this car." A lotta ladies come to you and a lot of gentlemen come to you, say, "Wow! You can drive!" I say, "Thank you, ma'am." They say, "How long you been doin' it?" I say, "Thirty years. I started when I'm sixteen and I'm still doin' it."

All day is my car. I drive my car to work, and when I get out of my car, it's a customer's car. When I leave work at night, I'm in my car. When I get to work in the morning, it's the customer's car. All my waking hours is cars. When I go out, my wife drives. I get in the back seat and play with the kids. I drove all week, I tell her, why don't you drive? If I have an argument on the job, I never discuss it with my wife because she has enough problems, with the kids. And I'm too bushed.

How long would I continue? I would say I would go another four years, maybe five. 'Cause I know I can't continue walking any more. If I ever decide to quit parking cars, I think I could get me a watchman job. Maybe I might be a cashier or pick up tickets at a theater. I know I won't retire in the parking lot, 'cause they don't pay any retirement money. The walking is pretty bad on your feet. Every day, I should say I take a good sixty times goin' and sixty times comin' back.

The way I felt about cars when I was young, I used to love to park 'em. Now when they're comin' in so busy, I say, "Where are all the farmer's goin'?" Saturday's the roughest day, because people are comin' in from all angles. Oh, the thrill been gone, oh, fifteen years. I do my work because I know I have to work. Every now and then I have to rub myself down or my wife rubs me down with alcohol. I might last another four, five years at most.

I was so good when I was nineteen, twenty. A guy bet me five dollars that when a certain car came in I wouldn't make a hole. I had one hand and I whipped it into that hole, and I did it three times for him. Another guy said, "You're too short to reach the gas pedal." I said, "No, I can even push the seat back and I can sit and swing that car in with one swing"—when I was younger. I had one customer, he was a good six feet seven and I'm only five feet three. He said, "You better pull the seat up." It looked like I was sittin' in the back seat and I was barely touchin' the brake. I whipped his car in the hole. He said, "You mean to tell me, short as you are, you put the car in that hole there?" I said, "I never move anybody's seat." I may pull myself up and brace from the wheel, but I never miss that hole. I make that one swing, with one hand, no two hands. And never use the door open, never park a car with the door open. Always I have my head inside the car, lookin' from the backview mirror. That's why they call me Lovin' Al the Wizard, One-Swing Al. They used to call me the Chewin' Gum Man. I used to chew twenty-five sticks of gum a day. Now I smoke cigars. (He and I puff away in silence for several moments.)

I was one of the best. I didn't care where the hiker was from, you coulda bet money on me. They'd say, "Lover, you never miss." I say, "When I miss, I slip and I don't slip often." (Laughs.) I didn't care how big the car was, I didn't care how little it was, I never missed my swing.

I did it for years, since I was nineteen till I got about twenty-seven. Then I started driving normal, like anybody else. That was my most exciting years, when I was nineteen and twenty. Then I got around twenty-seven, I could sense it. I felt slowing down. I was like a prize fighter, he turn in his gloves at thirty. Car hiker, he goes to fifty, sixty. I intend to quit parking cars when I get to fifty-four, fifty-five. I'm pretty good now and I'm forty-nine. I can still wheel good, yeah, pretty good. Lovin' Al, signing off . . .

The Selling

JOHNNY BOSWORTH

He is one of seven salesmen, working for a car dealer in a middle-class suburb on the outskirts of a large city. He is twenty-seven, married, and has a small child. His wife, he implies, comes from a well-to-do family, while "I'm a country boy. I wasn't able to finish school. Our family was kinda big and didn't have the money that most families do."

His hair is styled, his dress is modish, and his mustache is well-trimmed Fu Manchu. In the apartment: a hi-fi set, a small TV set, several cassettes, a variety of sound, and a small poodle running about. Though he doesn't drink, he suggested to his guest, who was reaching for Cutty Sark, Chivas Regal. "Until a couple of months ago, I was a greaser. My hair was slicked back. My wife insisted . . ." (She had worked as a Playboy bunny.)

He has been a car salesman for four years, though "I've been selling since I was fourteen. Door to door, magazines, pots and pans, anything."

If you hit a person's logic, you've got 'im. Unless you've got a dingaling. Everybody can sell an idiot. An idiot, Jesus, I wish I had fifty thousand of 'em a day, because you can sell 'em the world. You can sell 'em the Brooklyn Bridge.

I don't stand around on pins and needles like a lot of guys there, afraid to do this, afraid to do that. If I think it's gonna benefit me, I'm gonna do it. You never know unless you try. My office is different than anyone else's. I try to fix it up, to make it look more comfortable instead of like a butcher room, which is what they refer to an office, the closing room, the box. I got a nice desk from Dunhill. I bring my own TV down so customers can watch. I've got radios, different gadgets, trinkets, whatnots. Books, magazines, *Playboy*. I just try to make it a little presentable.

I'm not really a good salesman. The product sells itself.

303

The only thing that makes me good is I try to put myself in the customer's place. If I was to purchase a car, I know how I'd want to be treated. I wouldn't want to be pushed.

I threw a man out a couple of weeks ago. I just walked in the door and there's a guy standing there. He says, "Hey!" I says, "Excuse me, can I help you?" He says, "How much is this car?" He's pointing to a Dart Swinger. I said, "Let me check the book." He says, "What do you mean, check the book?" I says, "Sir, I don't have the prices of all the cars in my head." He says, "All right, check the book." You know, rude attitude. So I checked the book and gave the guy a price. He says, "You gotta be kiddin'!" I give him the price, which is two hundred dollars over cost, which is very fair. I say, "That's what the car costs, sir."

I figured I got nothing with this guy going. There's already a personality clash. I proceeded to the back and get my coffee, and this guy walks back. There's cars all over the floor. He points to another one and says, "How much is that car?" I says, "Again, sir, you mean the car there or one like it? Give me an idea of what kind of car you want. Let me help you." He says, "I didn't ask you. I asked the price." I says, "Okay, if that's your attitude. The price is on the window." He says, "Boy, you guys are all alike, you're a bunch of jagoffs." I said, "What?" He said, "You heard me, you punk, you're all a bunch of jagoffs." So I walked over to him and I said, "Look, pal, all I do is come here and work. I'm gonna treat you like a gentleman as much as I can. You're gonna treat me the same. Otherwise you and I aren't gonna get along." So he says, "You mother-this, you mother-that," started calling me names and everything else. So I said, "Please, go to my boss and maybe he'll fire me." The guy says, "Aaahhh, I oughta punch your head in." When he said that I said, "You got two seconds to hit that door." He said, "What are you talkin' about?" So I grabbed him and pushed him out the front door.

I went to my boss and said, "You heard the disturbance out there. Do what you want to do, but that's the way it is." He said, "You were wrong. You shoulda punched him and knocked his teeth out." I get along real good with my boss. I go play golf with him. This guy has time to be a human being.

A long-haired kid comes in and they don't wait on him

because they figure he's a dreck. That's the term they use. "Dreck" means nothing. The Jewish people brought most of the expressions in here. I jump on these kids. I try to sell 'em. Most of the long-haired kids here, their father's a doctor or a lawyer or a teacher. They got money. They're not hard to please. If the kid likes the car, all you have to do when the parent comes in is hit them with a little bit of logic. The kid usually wants a fast, souped-up car, a convertible more or less, with four-speed engine, all high performance. He wants the car to look real sharp. You go along with him some way, but I try to get him away from the four-speed because it's the worst thing in the world on a car. When you trade the car in, it loses $500 if it's a four-speed. You lose $250 in value if it's a stick shift.

I hit them with a little logic, too. Is your mother and father gonna go for this? The insurance is gonna run a little higher. When the parents come in, you gotta go with them. You tell 'em it's okay to have a big engine, because it's no worse than a six-cylinder. A six-cylinder will go 80 miles an hour, that's enough to get killed. The big engines, they go 100 to 140, but there's no place you can do it in the city anyway. You just try to suit both parties. I learned that from life. You have to bend.

Factory people are much easier to sell. A doctor calls up and he's a little arrogant sometimes. I want this, I want that, my buddy can get it three hundred dollars cheaper, so you better give me a good deal or forget it. They call you on the phone and want you to quote a price and everything else. That's all fine and good, except you know their buddy can't give 'em anything three hundred dollars cheaper. I know the prices of all the cars. That's one of the hardest things to get across to people, that we've all gotta make a living.

The blue collar is easier to sell, not so much because he's dumb, because a lot of 'em are lots smarter than some of these psychiatrists. They're more down-to-earth. They can't afford to take time out and go shopping, where a doctor and a lawyer, he can take off two or three weeks at a time. The guy that works in the factory nine times out of ten, you put 'em in the car that day. If you give him a car to drive home, give him a certain amount of money for his trade-in that he's content with, you've got a sale. He doesn't care about the profit you're making.

If you're a real good salesman, you can put 'em in the

car that *you* want and just forget about the car *they* want.
You can sell 'em the Brooklyn Bridge. Of course, I'm not
that type of salesman. I'm not that far advanced. I study
people, I'm still learning.

I like people. If it's a hippie, I ask him, "Do you smoke
grass? Do you take dope? Do you like this type of music?"
I try to find out things to make 'em relax. I also keep
askin' questions that they'll answer yes. Get them in the
habit of saying yes. When you say, "Will you give me the
order?" they'll say yes rather than no because they haven't
said no for a long time. "Do you like baseball? You like
the way they play it today?" "Yeah." Whatever it takes to
get 'em to say yes. A woman, you ask about fashions. Get
'em in the habit of saying yes.

Would you like to sell the Brooklyn Bridge?

No, because that would be taking advantage of someone. This may be hard to believe, but I don't enjoy taking
advantage of people. Most of the salesmen in this business,
they tell you it's a cutthroat world, you gotta screw your
brother before your brother screws you. I disagree with
that. I've been screwed many times myself because I've
helped other people. They've turned around and just
kicked me in the head. Rather than rebel and say I hate
the world, I chalk it up to experience.

Black people, they're the easiest to sell, the easiest in
the world. If you can make them think they're gettin'
somethin' for nothin', oh, they grab it quick. You give
them a sharp car, man, that shines and glistens, make the
neighbors think them as really big strong people, rich and
all that, they eat it up. You can sell 'em one, two, three.

Worst person in the world to sell is a pipe smoker. Pipe
smoker comes in, I let him go to someone else. They'll sit
there all day, kill your time. They all think they're ge-
niuses. They think this pipe is a symbol. And they keep
asking you all these questions. They picked up a book before they came and they learned a couple of words—you
know, transmission or engine or cubic inches. They try to
be a professor. I just tell 'em, "Look, did you come here
to buy a car or did you come in to match wits with me?"
'Cause I'll match my IQ with Einstein. I happen to have a
very high IQ.

And Orientals, they're another. They want something

for nothing, for sure. Everybody thinks that the Jewish guy is hard to sell. Sure, he wants a break, he wants everything cheap. But he's realistic. These Orientals and Indians, they want everything for nothing. They want to buy for less than the dealer paid for it. A Jewish person, you say, "It cost me a thousand dollars, I'll give it to you for twelve." They want it for eleven fifty, fine, eleven fifty. But you tell an Oriental, "Here it is, in black and white, it cost a thousand. I'll give it to you for ten fifty." He'll say, "No, no, no. I want it for nine fifty. I want it for less than you paid for it."

The black guy doesn't care what you paid for it. He's concerned with what he can afford. Can you keep the payments for around fifty dollars a month? Can he afford it, that's all. But you know who I'd rather sell to more than anybody? The professional people. It's a challenge, and I like challenges.

"I've always wanted to be the best in whatever I did. I would tell people, remember something as you go through life: Bosworth is Best. I even had cards printed up with that, just to joke with guys at the pool hall. Anything they could do I could do it better. That's why I got into automobiles, the challenge."

Say I've been working at this place twenty years, okay? Most people's jobs, after twenty years you got seniority. You're somebody. After twenty years at this job, I go in tomorrow as if I started today. If I don't sell X amount of cars a month, I've gotta look for another job. It's not because they're bad people, but they're in business. If you got a bad egg, you get rid of it. I don't like it. I'm young, I'm healthy, I'm strong, I can do just about anything. But for my family, I'd like a little more security.

People are out to gain whatever they can. If sometimes it means stepping on someone, they don't think too much about it. I wouldn't say they're necessarily out to take advantage of others. They're just out for personal gain. Me, I don't like to step on people. I've had money. I've had opportunity. I could've been a gigolo. I could've married a Jewish girl, her father is a multimillionaire. I took a pass. I'm not a goody-goody, because I've been in jail, I fought, I stole.

The only one that could be a threat are the people who can cost you your job. Because that would threaten my family. They can kill me. I could care less if they killed me. I like my work. I have to like it, I must like it. Otherwise I'd be miserable. It's not what I'd like most to do, but I like it. If you're not happy, you can't sell. You have to be ready: let's sell, sell, sell. You're all gung ho.

Most people in the business drink. Mostly they talk about wine, women, and song. In some places they talk about horses, which doesn't interest me in the least. I'm not gonna bet on four-legged animals. Most of my friends—or acquaintances—are people I've known for a long time. We play Monopoly, we go to the movies, go to a play like *Fiddler on the Roof*. I don't play pool with 'em, cause I refuse to play for nothin'. It took me a long time to get good at that game. If anybody wants to beat me, it's gonna cost 'em money. I like gambling. I like playing cards for money.

Selling cars is a gamble. Every customer that walks in there, they've got a twenty-dollar bill or a fifty-dollar bill in their pocket. It's up to you to get it out of their pocket. The only way to get it out is to sell 'em a car. It's a gamble. If I had more education I'd be a little better at it. I wish to God I could turn back the clock and go back to school. That's why it's a challenge to sell a man that's been educated, been through college. I can make him come to me instead of me going to him. They see it my way.

Could the world survive without my work? No. There has to be a saleman. Oh, if a man put his mind to it—and I've thought about it myself—that could all be computerized. All a salesman does is find a car that suits you, which has the best features and which has the worst. All that can be put into a computer and you'd have a questionnaire that people would answer. The only thing that would require a salesman is the price. Ninety-nine out of a hundred people are price-conscious. That's all they care about. You could sell 'em a bag of potatoes if the price was right. You could sell 'em a 1948 Chevy if the price was right.

How do you feel about Ralph Nader?

Pardon me?

How do you feel about Ralph Nader?

We could do without him. He's taken the choice away

from the people. He doesn't give them the choice of having head restraints or belts. Or having emission control systems. He took that choice away. Carbon monoxide, all that poisonous stuff, leave that to the manufacturers that know such things and what it would cost to build all that new equipment. I think he's an alarmist. Chicken Little or whatever. He's driving my wife crazy. She's afraid to breathe air and everything, 'cause of him.

Sure, cars could be much better if it wasn't for the oil companies and the gas companies. They could run on air, they could run on water—or electric. There's no end to what they could do right now, but they won't.

My wife's been wanting a Volkswagen for two years and she'll wait two hundred before she gets one. It's an unsafe car. That's why I watch commercials—to see if I can find something I can use in my next sales meeting with a customer. I watch how TV commercials affect people who watch it with me.

I wish the public would realize that I'm a human being, too. You meet some guy at a party and its, "Aw, you guys are all alike." "Watch out for him," blah, blah, blah. I tell 'em, "Stick it in your keester." The public thinks the automobile salesman is a rat. Some of the customers are the real animals. Why must they wait? Why can't they be number one? "How come I'm not getting good gas mileage?" They beat a car to death and they wonder why it doesn't perform for them. All they do is make you eat your guts out. Then they'll go right down the street and they'll do it to another guy and they'll wonder: Is everybody a rat? And *they're* the rat.

They don't have to be animals. It's the whole system that makes 'em animals. Everybody goes on strike, they want more money. The wife needs more money to buy groceries because groceries are higher because the delivery is on strike, the trucks are on strike, the factories are on strike, everybody is on strike. The car salesman can't go on strike. I have no union. I go on strike, I say, "I'm not gonna do this." They say, "See if they want to hire you down the street."

I've been fired from this place five times because of my mouth. And they call me back every time. They realize they were wrong. You can't hate a man for being honest. Jesus, I feel if you can't be honest, what's the sense in doing anything?

BOOK FIVE

APPEARANCE

SAM MATURE

He has been a barber for forty-three years. For twenty-one years he has owned a shop at the same locale, an office building in Chicago's Loop. "A master barber may have a couple of other barbers that are better barbers than he is, but they call him master because he's the boss."

Long hair is nothin' new. We had some fancy haircuts them days the same as we have today. I did a bit of musicians and they had long hair. But not like the hippie. I have no objections as long as they keep it clean, neat, a little light trim. But you know what gets me? A fella's got a son in college, he's got long hair, which he's in style. Here's the old man, he wants to get long hair. And he's the average age fella in the fifty age bracket. He wants to look like his son. Now that to me is ridiculous. Happens quite often. The fella'll come in and he'll say, "I'm gonna let my hair grow, Sam, because my daughter or my wife ..." Daughters and women tell their husbands how to cut their hair. The guy's been married for twenty-five years. I don't see the sense in him changing. We still like what they call the he-man cut. Businessman haircut. Not all this fancy stuff. It's not here to stay.

It hurt the barber quite a bit. I know about nine barbers went out of business in this area alone. A man used to get a haircut every couple weeks. Now he waits a month or two, some of 'em even longer than that. We used to have customers that'd come in every Friday. Once

313

a week, haircut, trim, everything. Now the same fella would come in maybe every two months. That's the way it goes.

We used to have five chairs here. Now there's only three of us. We used to have a manicurist here that works five days a week. Now she works one day a week. A lot of people would get manicured and fixed up every week. Most of these people retired, moved away, or they passed away. It's all on account of long hair. You take the old-timers, they wanted to look neat, to be presentable, and they had to make a good appearance in their office. Now people don't seem to care too much.

You take some of our old-timers, they still take their shampoo and hair tonic and get all fixed up. But if you take the younger generation today, if you mention, "Do you want something on your hair?" they feel you insulted them. I had one fella here not too long ago, I said, "Do you want your hair washed?" He said, "What's the matter? Is it dirty?" (Laughs.) A young guy. An older person wouldn't do that.

In the city of Chicago a haircut's three dollars with the exception of the hair stylin' shops. They charge anything they want. It runs up to as high as twelve dollars. We don't practice it. The three of us can do it but we usually don't recommend it. We have to charge a man so much money. I don't think it's considerate, that kind of price for a haircut.

In stylin', you part his hair different, you cut his hair different. Say you got a part and you don't want no part. You comb it straight back, you're changing his style. Say his part's on the right side. All right, you want to change his style, you part the part to the left side. Then you wash his hair and you cut him down and redress his hair over again. *That's* hair stylin', I actually never went much for that myself.

When I came here twenty-one years ago, I had a separate chair here in the little room, in which I cut all ladies' hair. We'd run about six or seven or eight cuts a day in women's hair. I love to cut women's hair. At one time I won second prize cutting ladies' hair, which was back in 1929. The wind-blown haircut. Their hair was all combed forward. It was like a gush of wind hits you in the back of the head and blew your hair forward. Today young girls don't know what it is. I think it's a lot easier than cutting men's hair. They're less trouble, too.

"Most of your new barbers today, actually there isn't too many taking it up. Take these barber colleges. It used to be three, four hundred students. Not any more. You maybe get five or six there. Not only that, the tuition has gone up so high. It cost me $160. Now it would run you about six hundred dollars or better. Young barbers today, unless they go in for hair styling, it isn't enough money in it.

"So many of them, they get disgusted for the simple reason that it takes so long to be a barber. When I took up barberin', it took six months. Today you have to apprentice for almost three years before you can get your license. You work for a lot less—about thirty dollars less a week than a regular barber would get."

You can't think of other things while you're working. You concentrate on the man's hair or you'd be talkin' to him whatever he wants to talk about. A barber, he has to talk about everything—baseball, football, basketball, anything that comes along. Religion and politics most barbers stay away from. (Laughs.) Very few barbers that don't know sports. A customer'll come in, they'll say, "What do you think of the Cubs today?" Well, you gotta know what you think. You say, "Oh, they're doin' swell today." You have to tell 'em.

Fans today in sports are terrific, hockey, all those things. That counts in bein' a barber. You gotta know your sports. They'll come in, "What do you think of that fight last night?" Lotta sports barber has to watch on TV or hear about it or read about it. You gotta have somethin' to tell him. You have to talk about what he wants to talk about.

Usually I do not disagree with a customer. If there is something that he wants me to agree with him, I just avoid the question. (Laughs.) This is about a candidate, and the man he's speaking for is the man you're not for and he asks you, "What do you think?" I usually have a catch on that. I don't let him know what I am, what party I'm with. The way he talks, I can figure out what party he's from, so I kind of stay neutral. That's the best way, stay neutral. Don't let him know what party you're from cause you might mention the party that he's against. And that's gonna hurt business.

I disagree on sports. Fans are all different. TV plays a good role, especially during ball games, real good. All the shops should have TV because the customer, he wants to look at something, to forget his office work, forget the thing he has in his mind that he has to do. Watchin' TV relaxes his mind from what he was doin' before he came in the shop.

A lot of people sit down and relax. They don't want to have anything to do, just sit there and close their eyes. Today there is less closin' their eyes. We had customers at one time that if they couldn't go to sleep, they wouldn't get a haircut.

Customers call me by my first name—Sam. I have customers twenty years old that call me Sam. I call the customer Mister. I never jump to callin' a man by his first name unless a man tells me himself, "Why don't you call me Joe?" Otherwise I call him mister.

About tips. Being a boss, sometimes they figure they don't have to tip you. They don't know that the boss has to make a living same as anybody else. Most of your master barbers, they don't bank on it, but they're glad to get whatever they get. If a man, through the kind heart of his, he wants to give me something, it's all right. It's pretty hard to keep a person from tipping. They tip a bellhop, they tip a redcap, they tip a waiter.

If bosses in these shops would agree to pay the barber more, I'd say ninety percent of them wouldn't do it. They'd rather the customer to help pay this barber's salary by tipping him. I'm in favor of not tipping. I'd just as soon pay the man ten dollars more a week than have him depend on that customer. This way he knows that he's got that steady income. In the old days you kind of depended on tips because the salary was so small. If you didn't make the extra ten dollars a week in tips you were in bad shape.

I'll tell ya, by tipping that way it made me feel like I was a beggar. See? A doctor you don't give him a tip. He's a professional man. You go to a dentist, you don't give him a tip because he fixed your tooth. Well, a barber is a professional man too. So I don't think you should tip him.

When I leave the shop, I consider myself not a barber any more. I never think about it. When a man asks me what I do for a living, I usually try to avoid that question. I figure that it's none of his business. There are people who think a barber is just a barber, a nobody. If I had a son, I'd want him to be more than just a barber.

What's gonna happen when you retire?

They're gonna be just another barber short.

"Barbers that work on the outskirts of downtown are different. Outskirt barbers are more chummy with their customers because they're friends. They go bowling, they go fishing, they go hunting together. Here you see a fella, an executive, maybe every two weekends, then you don't see him any more, and you don't know where he lives. The outskirt barber has more authority than we would here."

EDWARD AND HAZEL ZIMMER

Mr. Edward is a beauty salon in a suburb close to a large industrial city. "She works with me. Twenty years we've been here almost. They demand more from a hair stylist and you get more money for your work. You become like a doctor becomes a specialist. You have to act accordingly—I mean be Mr. Edward."
   At a certain point she joins the conversation.

Some people go to a barber shop, you get an old guy, he hasn't kept up to date with the latest styles, newest cuts. They're in a rut. They cut the same thing no matter what's in. A barber should be a hair stylist himself. There's some male beauty shops, they deal more in your feminine men and actors. Most actors prefer going to a beauty shop because a barber might just give you the same old cut and you might look like the janitor down the street or the vice president of a bank. Appearance is importance.

There are beauty operators, there's hairdressers, and there's hair stylists. A hair stylist is more than a beauty operator. Anybody can fuzz up hair, but you ask them, "Do I look good in this Chinese look which is coming in now, Anna May Wong?"—they don't know.

You have to sense the value of your customer. If the jewelry is a little better and she's accustomed to services, such as maids, her husband makes a good dollar. If you're getting a woman with five kids and her husband's a cabdriver—which is no fault in that—she is not the kind that's gonna come in here every week. Or the little lady down the street, who lives with her cats and dogs or even her husband, who doesn't care. They say, "Just set it nice. I can't wash my hair because of my arthritis." They're not fussy. You say to the beauty operator you employ, "You take Mrs. Brown because she's not fussy." You pick out the fussy one that's been around, they've been to Acapulco, Hawaii. They expect a little more from you than the beauty operator. Then you become the stylist. You have to know which customers are for whom and which are not.

The name counts. Kenneth does Mrs. Kennedy's hair—Onassis. I never saw Jacqueline Kennedy's hair when it looked anything worthwhile. Sometimes she wears a wig. Just because she came to him, this put him on a pedestal. If the Queen of England came to my place, I'd have to hire fifteen more people. They'd all come flocking in. A social thing.

The hairdresser cashes in on some of it. You'll never get this in the smaller beauty shops. You have to be a hair stylist to attract ones with money. A hair stylist can get fifteen dollars for a haircut, whereas the beauty operator, she'll get only three. Now your hairdresser is in the middle.

What makes a man become a hair stylist is different from what makes a woman become one. For women it's an easy trade. They learn this when they are twelve years old, making pin curls at home. But a man, it takes a little different approach. Jacqueline Kennedy, in a book her maid or someone wrote, said, when security police found out that two employees in the White House were homosexual, she ordered them fired. She said, "I don't want my sons to be exposed to this type of people because they're liable to grow up to be hairdressers." Not all hairdressers are homosexually inclined. Some enjoy the work more if you enjoy women.

The most important thing for a hairdresser, male, he has to dominate the woman. You can sense when you're not dominating the customer. She can tell you, "I want two rollers here." She becomes the stylist and all you become is the mechanical thing with the fingers.

In the field of beauty work, you got to have personality. I'd say one-fifth is personality. Be able to sell yourself. Your approach, your first word, like, "Good morning, the weather we're having." A man has to have a personality where he's aloof. He has to act like—without a word: Don't tell me, I'm the stylist. You expect more from Mr. Edward and you get it. If a woman needs a hair style, he says, "Madame, what you need is a little more color. I will fix it up." He doesn't do it. He will call his assistant. And he will tell her, "I want curls here, I want this, I want that." And she says, "Yes, Mr. Edward." I don't dirty my hands with the chemicals. I'm the stylist. Your symbol right there, the male. You're giving yourself a title. Otherwise, you're gonna be nothing but a flunky. Being a male, it's important you must have this ego.

Everybody expects the hairdresser to be a prototype, to have a black mustache, slick Hollywood-type or feminine. I could spot one a mile away sometimes if they're feminine. On the other hand, I know someone you'd never know he was a hairdresser. He's owned five shops at one time, a married man with a family and he's bald. I'm not gonna hide the point that I'm a beauty operator.

I used to go to a tavern around here. I met this guy. He didn't know I knew he was a cop. He knew I was a hairdresser. He was drunk. He says to me, "You're a queer." I says, "How could you tell by looking at people?" He says, "The way you twist your mouth." I said, "You're drunk and you're a cop." He says, "How do you know I'm a cop?" I says, "Just the way you look and act." Right away, he says, "Aaahhh!" I said, "If you didn't have a gun, how much authority would you pull around here? Anybody can do your job. You can't do mine. It takes skill." Right away he avoided me. He was an idiot. I do a lot of policemen's wives' hair. I always mention that he called me a queer. This other woman's husband says, "Wait'll I see him, I'll bash him in the face."

After an interval in the army he met his wife at a dance. She was working in a beauty parlor. "I said, 'I think I'll be a hairdresser.' She says, 'You wouldn't last two days.' I says, 'Hell I won't.' " *He studied beauty culture.* "I had my suitcase and my white jacket. I felt like an idiot. I saw

*these feminine young men dancing around, and these little
old ladies waiting for me. They lay down and undress and
you gotta rub their back and around their chest. What you
learn in beauty school is nothin'. You don't learn how to
handle people. My father-in-law always says, 'You do
nothing but a lady's work.' But it's hard work, psychologically hard. You gotta perform a little better than a female."*

Hair stylists, even if they're married, are called Miss
This or Miss That. They don't seem to go much for the
last name. Mr. Alexander of Paris or Mr. André. Mr. Edward. That should go over bigger than Eddie's Beauty
Shop. It's a little flat, see? Sometimes these young fellas
who are on the feminine side lean on a feminine name. He
calls himself Mr. Twinkie or something. This fella we had
working here, he tried to hide the fact that he was feminine. He called himself Mr. Moran.

HAZEL: The name became important when the male entered the business. They built a reputation on their name.
They use it rather than call a salon by some idiotic or
nondescriptive name. A woman might call the shop Vanity
Fair or Highlight. For a man, it's more important that he
retains his name.

What are you called?

HAZEL: Hazel.

EDWARD: She's just called Hazel.

HAZEL: I worked for Mr. Maurice in Florida and all of
us were known as Miss. He renamed me Miss Rena because he didn't like Hazel.

Do you feel less when you're called by your first name?

HAZEL: Never. I never felt inferior to any of my customers. Even though sometimes they try to make you feel that
way. I think I would quit a long time ago if I ever felt
any inferiority.

EDWARD: I would not stand humiliation. It's not openly when a woman gets hostile against you and says, "If you're a hair stylist, you're below me." Many wealthy people will hire a hair stylist and haul them around and they will carry their suitcases. It really looks la-de-da, you might say elite, where she's going to the airport with her hairdresser and her poodles and her dressmaker all following after her like the Queen of Sheba. This is a form of humiliation. But the guy don't care. She's paying him well and he builds his name. And she's using his image to make herself.

HAZEL: The less important or average-intellectual customer is the one that tries to humiliate you more. Where she can suddenly go to the hairdresser weekly. These kind of people try to depress your importance. She'll ask for something that you may not have heard that term. So she'll say, "Oh, you don't know!" But people who have been around, if they don't like what you do, they go to another place. It's the average-intellectual individual who's apt to come in and show her importance and try to decrease yours. I'm very good at putting them in their place.

EDWARD: There was some humiliation when I was newer. I didn't rub hard enough. "Oh, just don't bother any more! Just have Hazel do it." The beginning hairdresser could be very embarrassed by a customer. The customer says, "Oh, just leave my hair alone! Comb this out for me, get this idiot away from me!" Because the person was green. There are times when the woman will take the comb and say, "Give me that thing!" This is an insult. When she says, "This is good enough!" and you're not happy with it. Some hairdressers will blow their fuse and throw the comb on the floor and say, "I wouldn't touch you with a fourteen-foot pole." Verlaine was like that. He threw customers out of the door with wet hair. He was eccentric that way.

But I still feel we are servants. A servant to the public, like a doctor. Not a servant that does housework. I didn't mean in that class. Just because you're a great hair stylist, win prizes—anybody can buy a trophy and put it in his window. But he becomes a star, arrogant. Some people say, "I won't take this crap any more." If they give you a hard time, all you say, "Look lady, I'm sorry, this is the

way I think it should be. If I can't please you, you'll have
to find someone else." But you don't argue and throw
brushes around like some of these guys. You may see ads
in papers for hairdressers: No stars, please.

We hired this one guy, he was going to hair coloring
school. He was using our place to practice with his hair
colors. One day he took a very prominent customer of
ours. He colored her hair red. She's out in the car crying.
She says, "I can't go home like this. My husband'll kill
me." I said, "I thought you wanted to be a redhead." She
says, "All I asked for was a rinse." I brought her back. By
this time he was packing his bag. I didn't have to fire him.
He just simply walked out. He took a woman and being
another genius, he's gonna make something of her. You
don't take it upon yourself.

You have to put in a thousand hours in beauty school
to get your license. The average hair stylist, dresser,
beauty operator has an equal amount of schooling as a
practical nurse. You have to know blood, you have to
know diseases. You have to know everything that pertains
to the human body so you can understand why hair grows.

Styles are basically the same since the bob. What can
you do with hair? It's like cooking chop suey. By adding
more mushrooms or less. Styles repeat themselves over
and over again, like women's clothes. You always go back
to something.

We used to get fifty dollars for a permanent. Like sil-
ver-blonding. Years ago, a wife wouldn't think of going to
a grocery store with blond hair. 'Cause what is she? A
show girl? Light hair only went with strippers, prostitutes,
and society women. In order to silver-blond in those days,
you would use a lot of ammonias and bleaches and the
woman would have to come back two or three times before it got light enough to be a silver blonde. This cost
fifty, sixty dollars a treatment. So the average *hausfrau*
and her husband, he'd say "What are you workin' as a cigarette girl or something? You're a mother, you got four
kids, you're insulting me in church, you look like a
hoozy." But today all girls look like hoozies.

HAZEL: They had commercialized it and came out with
all these gadgets, and put work that should be done in a
shop into home. You can buy a comb that cuts hair. You
can buy a permanent. They should have strictly remained

professional. The manufacturers got greedy and they commercialized hairdressing, whereas they make it so easy it can be done at home. So you can't command the prices you did a number of years ago. Today they sell these kits, and if you can read you can do it. It has hurt the poorer sections mostly. More wealthier neighborhoods, it hasn't hurt them bad. Most of these women, they don't want to take the time.

Once in a while a hairdo will disturb me because I feel I didn't do it quite right. I'll brood over it for a little while. I like to feel I've done the best on each one every day. Once in a while I'll flunk. (Laughs.)

EDWARD: You feel like a doctor who has a patient who died on the operating table. You're concerned. What went wrong? Why didn't I get that right? A beauty operator wouldn't care. I enjoy the work. I'd do it again even if I made less money.

We have lost young people in the beauty shop. The average person we work on is over twenty-five. The oldentime mother would never stand to see her daughter with that straight gappy look. She looks like a witch on Halloween night. Today it's the style for young people.

I have a girl come in the shop: how can I straighten her hair? There was one time, a woman with hair like that, she was something on a broom. Even her mother would say, "Why the hell don't you go to the beauty shop and get the hair out of your mouth?" Today you can't tell a child . . .

In my opinion, the men are getting more feminine and the women are getting more masculine. If a boy and a girl walk down the street together and his hair is as straight as hers, he'll get a permanent at home. The one with the straight hair is usually the girl and the one with the wavy hair is the guy.

It's due to our permissive society. There was a time once, September rolled around, they were forced to go to the barber shop or beauty parlor and get it clipped for school. Otherwise, the teacher sent them home. Today you have a whole society where a young man can go on the street, raise a beard, wear crazy clothes, he can wear one shoe off and one shoe on, and no one bothers to look at him.

HAZEL: It has regressed.

Do you disagree with customers on occasion?

EDWARD: I often disagree with customers—depends on
who she is and what authority she has. I lost a customer
once because she was from Germany and this other customer happened to be from a very, very pronounced
Jewish family. She said she wouldn't buy a Volkswagen
because of what they did to our people. And the woman
said, "What did I do? I was a child." Next thing you
know, she called her a Nazi. So here I'm bound to lose
one customer. The one I favored, the one I hoped I didn't
lose, was the one that paid the most money and had the
most service. But I felt sorry for the other girl. I took
sides only for monetary reasons.

JEAN STANLEY

*She sells cosmetics and perfumes in a department store. It
is a suburban Connecticut branch of the city's most
fashionable establishment. The patrons are, for the most
part, upper middle class.*

*Though it has been her five-day-a-week job for the last
seven years, she had been at it, on and off, for thirty
years. "I was home for about twenty years. I went back to
work when the children were in high school."*

*Her husband is a buyer in textiles. Though he has an
excellent record and reputation, his position is tenuous,
due to the industry's impersonal drive for young executives. They have three children, all of whom have gone to
college.*

I sell cosmetics to women who are trying to look young.
They are spending more on treatment creams than they
did years ago. I can remember when lipstick at two dollars was tops. Now they have lipsticks that sell for five.
Appearance. Many times I think, thirty dollars for this little jar of cream. I know it doesn't have that value. But in
the eye of that woman, it has that value. A cosmetic came
out that was supposed to smooth out the wrinkles for

five or six hours. It puffs out the skin. The wrinkles would return. We criticized it. But a woman came in one morning, she said, "I'm going for a job interview and I'm past forty. I want to look nicer." I felt differently about selling it to her. It might bring her a job.

They say everything comes out of the same pot. (Laughs.) There isn't a cream that's worth forty, fifty dollars. But when you see the enthusiasm of the women who purchase these things (laughs), you don't want to make them feel discouraged. They're beginning to show lines and wrinkles. They know their husbands are out in the business world with young women who are attractive. They're trying to look nice, to keep their husbands interested. So cosmetics have their place, I think.

There is always the competition of keeping their husbands interested. You see the fear in their faces—becoming lined. They all discuss this: "Look at me. I look terrible." They will talk about seeing it on television—the cream that erases lines. Television is the thing that has brought all this. More anxiety.

Customers ask your advice. They rely on you. If you've worked in one of these places for a number of years, you have a following. People come in and wait for you actually. You become a little bit of a friend. They can speak to a stranger more than they can to an acquaintance. They may tell you some little tragedy or something. You learn a lot about people when you're with the public all day. There are so many lonely people. So many women between the ages of forty and seventy.

You're supposed to try and sell a certain brand. Many stores work that way. We suggest the brand we know about most. Many women come in and they'd like to see an Arden, a Lauder, or a Rubenstein product, and you show it to them. If they ask for a definite brand, you don't try to sell them another. I'm not aggressive. I don't want to send a customer home with a bag full of things and when she gets home she feels, Why did I buy this? You try to feel the customer out. I stress the saving: "How much would you like to spend?"

Years ago, women that sold cosmetics and perfumes made more money on the average than they do now. You could earn much more than girls working in an office. Today you hardly earn as much. The companies are spending so much money on advertising. Perhaps they feel the girl will sell much more and earn more, that way. (Laughs.) They don't put it into salaries, I know that much. They have tremendous advertising budgets. We work on salary plus commission. One of my children who's sold said, "The lowest common denominator is the salesclerk on commission." (Laughs.) It brings out their greed and their disregard for their fellow workers.

I'm not paid by the store. I'm paid by the cosmetics company. The company expects you to sell their merchandise. You send them a monthly report. There are ten of us in my department. Each one represents a different company. Out here in the suburbs you represent more than one company. You might have two or three cream lines; four, five, or six perfume lines. You have a tremendous amount of stock to take care of, reports to send in. You have to have an auditor help you with your income tax. (Laughs). You have salaries from so many different companies.

The extra work, making out reports, is done in your own home, on your own time. The Revlon report can be eighteen inches, with numerous items on it. You can't work on these reports when you get home at night. Your eyes become a little blurred. (Laughs.) You're a little weary. You have to do it on Sunday. You spend the whole day on it.

There's another hazard to the job. (Laughs.) You get no health insurance or anything like that. The companies don't cover you for hospitalization. I have to carry my own. You can't get in on a pension plan either. A woman that just retired worked in this section fifteen years. If she worked directly for the store, she could have retired with a little pension. She retired with nothing. I will get nothing.

The company I represent gives you five days a year sick leave. If you're sick more than five days, you don't get paid. The one year I was sick, I didn't get paid for the few days over. There are department store unions, but if you're in the pay of someone else, it's . . . no man's land. Years ago, when earnings were greater, I could have retired with something. Now I won't.

My manager is very friendly with me. She knows she's secure with me. I'm going to stay just where I am. It's been seven years and I've been here every day. When we get to the age where we have to ... (trails off). I can be dismissed at will. We have no protection.

You stand on your feet all day. Years ago, there was a rule that there had to be a stool in the back of each counter. I don't see that enforced any more. There aren't any stools around. I think everyone's feet feel tired at the end of the day. We have college kids that come in, especially before Christmas. They complain more about being tired than the older women.

The managers seem afraid to tell the young people what doesn't go. They're not as willing to work. A little less courtesy, too. Maybe it's a good sign, in a way. Maybe they feel this is nonsense, all the thank you's and the please and everything. The same thing with their appearance. There's a certain independence they're showing. But in showing their independence they look like all the others. (Laughs.)

When you have children that are going through college for years, it takes money. (Laughs.) That the reason many women go back to work, their children's schooling. We have widows, women who were caught in the Depression, who couldn't go into professions. So we turned to selling.

Stores like ours that carry high-priced merchandise have make-up for black women. Many buy light make-up. They think they'll look better. You have to be very careful when you're selling a black women. Some like a strong fragrance. Some, because they're black, will not buy a strong fragrance. These are middle-class women. The prejudice behind the counter—I can't begin to tell you. They use the words. You wonder how it's ever going to be resolved. Sometimes you get discouraged with humanity.

There are other things you'd like to be doing. I was interested in teaching but the Depression ... You would have liked to do something more exciting and vital, something you felt was making a contribution. On the other hand, when you wait on these lonely old women and they leave with a smile and you feel you've lifted their day, even a little, well, it has its compensations.

DR. STEPHEN BARTLETT

He is a dentist who has practiced for nineteen years in an upper-middle-class suburb just outside Detroit. He is forty-six, divorced. It was a late start for him; he enrolled at dental school at the age of twenty-eight.

He comes from Tennessee. "I worked for three years in the mines, digging thirty-inch coal" for his brother, who was an operator. "I was in one cave-in." He drove a truck. He worked in the world of outdoor advertising: "There was a lot of corruption, a lot of the under-the-table bit. That took all the fun out of it for me."

One day a week he teaches at a hospital in the city. He rides a motorcycle to and from his office, which is five blocks from his home.

Dentistry is very precise. No matter what you do, sometimes things just don't go right. One of the big diseases dentists have is stress. It's physically hard because you're in an uncomfortable position most of the day. With techniques today, young fellows are sitting down. I wish I'd sit down more, but I'm not accustomed to it. So I stand most of my day.

The mouth you work on usually is not in an ideal condition. If the patient is not cooperating, moving their mouth or salivating a lot, it's hard to get the job done. You're nervous. If you're not satisfied when you've completed your work, nobody else knows, but you do. You're your own worst critic.

The patients are in a tense position too. There is stress on both sides. The consciousness of pain is always with you. There are two categories of people: those that are more scared of the needle than the drill, who don't want Novocain, and those more scared of the drill. If you get those who don't want Novocain, you're under more stress, because the equipment today is high powered, fast. All they have to do is jerk once on you and they've damaged themselves.

You don't make money unless you have your hand in somebody's mouth. It's not like any other business where you can get income by being away. Any time you're not working on a patient, you're losing money. Your overhead continues.

What appeals to me here is that I can practice the dentistry I like. I couldn't be happy practicing in an area where a guy comes in and says, "Come on, doc, pull it, it hurts." Rather than pull a tooth, we could fix it with endodontics or root fill or put a gold crown on it. You don't have to really lose your teeth. When someone loses teeth, it's a traumatic experience. It's getting more so with all the TV ads. With toothpaste and mouthwashes and all this, people are getting a lot more conscious of their teeth.

I insulted a girl last night, a young, beautiful child. I noticed the corners of her mouth turned down a little bit. I asked if I could see her teeth. I wanted to see what kind of work she had there. She was missing a lot of teeth. The mouth closes like a person who's a denture wearer, and she will get old before her time. That's one of the first things I look at.

I went to see *Fiddler on the Roof*. When I saw a close-up of Topol and his teeth, he had partials. To me, this made him human. Did you know that Clark Gable for a number of years had only one tooth here in front? And no one saw it. When you're close to it, it's your life.

Teeth can change a person's appearance completely. It gives me a sense of satisfaction that I can play a role. The thing that bugs me is that you work hard to create, let's say, a good gold bridge. It requires time, effort, and precision. Before I put them in place, I make the patient look at them. An artist can hang his work on the wall and everybody sees it. No one sees mine except me. A dentist is creative too. It requires a certain skill, a certain art. If you do a good job, damn it, you're proud of it. And you want other people to appreciate it.

I don't think a patient knows whether you're a good dentist or a bad one. They know one of two things: he didn't hurt and I like him or he's a son of a bitch. It's strictly a personality thing. I tried to change my personality when I first started in and I did myself more damage than good. My first cards I had printed when I became a dentist were S. Harrison Bartlett. It was ridiculous, I dropped it. I'm not a formal type. I tell jokes, I make notes and remember things of interest to them. I try to say

something personal to each of my patients. I don't antago-
nize people.

I've had some patients who did not stay with me. There
are some people who are used to deference. This is not
my way. They're always demanding. If you run a little
late, they get upset—or if you don't hand them the napkin
properly. They get irritated and raise their voice or they
try to tell you what they want done and what they don't
want done. Damn it, when they're in my office, I'm the
boss.

Some tried to put me down when I was trying to establish myself. It hasn't bothered me for a number of years.
Some people are chronically late, and that's all right. But
if you're late with them once, they're upset. Sometimes
they call up a half-hour before the appointment and say,
"I forgot." I make adjustments now. My girl has a list of
people who can come in immediately. So when somebody
doesn't show, we start down the list. Otherwise, that's time
lost which cannot be made up.

I have people who pay me once a year for income tax
purposes, or they're waiting to clip coupons. I have people
that drive Cadillacs but can't pay their dental bills. It's not
because they don't want to. Dentistry is one of the first areas in business cut back in a recession, that people tend to
ignore, unless they have a toothache.

When a person walks into the office, it's an instinct.
You know who's gonna pay and who isn't gonna pay. I've
never used a collection agency. I should, 'cause I have an
awful lot on the books. But this bothers me. I don't want
to do it.

My life is entirely different since my divorce. If someone told me of these opportunities as a married man, I
would have called them a liar to their face. It is really unbelievable. The banter. When you're in a dental chair,
you're under stress, I don't care who you are. As a consequence, your guard is down. People reveal more of themselves and their true nature than at other times.

Fantasies about women come before and after work.
The schedule is set up that you're operating against time.
You have a half-hour to get this done. Now in the evening
or going back over the day I might think, "Goddamn, she
was good looking!" Or, "I wonder what she meant when
she said that?" Or, you know, "Hmm!" Draw your own
conclusions.

I like girls. And women. I'm called a dirty old man lots of times in a joking situation. That's part of my image too. But you don't eat and play where you work, this bit. I not only work here, I live here. So I'm very careful. Reputation is very important in a small community such as this one.

Dentistry as a whole feels its a second-class citizen. I know a lot of dentists who wanted to be physicians and couldn't get into medical school, so they went to dental school. I personally don't feel second-class because I spend every third month in the emergency room of the hospital. Believe me, medical men don't know the first thing in the world about dentistry.

People say, "Oh, he's a dentist." That doesn't bother me. When I first got my D.D.S. and I was a new doctor, hell yes, I was very proud and I wanted everybody to recognize that. Remember, I was older when I got out than most fellas, so it doesn't bother me as it might the others.

I wouldn't be a physician if they gave it to me, to be honest with you. I don't know any profession in the world that is better than dentistry. You're your own boss, you set your own hours, you can go anywhere in the world and practice. You don't have the burden of life and death over your head at every decision. Your working conditions are ideal. Okay, they're physically hard, but there's nothing wrong with that.

There are supposed to be peak years for a dentist, I've been told. I don't know what they are. My predecessor was an old man, his hands were shaking and all this bit. I know that will be a factor in time to come. But I think if you keep your image up-to-date, you'll decrease the age factor. I've seen many young men who are old and I don't propose to go that route.

DOC PRITCHARD

We're in a Manhattan hotel near Times Square. It is an old, established place of some three hundred rooms. Its furnishings are quite simple, unpretentious. There are permanent guests as well as transients.

He is a room clerk, on the 8:00 A.M. to 2:00 P.M.

*shift, five days a week. He's been at this work twenty-two
years. "I not only room people, I do cashiering, checking
out, cashing checks, all that sort of thing. The day goes
pretty fast. Before you can say, 'Jack Robinson,' it's time
to go home. (Laughs.) It's difficult at times." (Laughs.)*

I begin at eight in the morning. I have to have a smile on
my face. Some mornings that's a little difficult. The first
thing you run into is people checking out from the night
before. You might get a slight lull and then people begin
arriving. They're like little bees. You're concentrating on
what you're doing. It's a little difficult to have that smile
all the time. I have one particular girl who says to me,
"What? No smile this morning?" So I smile.

Clerks are really underpaid people. It is one of the
lowest paid jobs in the United States. I think they should
put out more money for a good hotel clerk. If you get a
fellow on the front desk who has got a good personality
and can get along with people and he's on his toes, I mean
really serving the guests, I mean really getting out there
and encouraging them to come back—the hotel has to be
halfway decent too. Then I think you've got a clerk that's
worth two hundred dollars a week.

They don't get that. It's difficult sometimes for them to
get along with just one job. A great many of 'em moonlight. Or they work a couple extra nights in another hotel.
A great many actors went into this. They did it just to eat
between jobs. This was before the unemployment check.
Many show people worked in hotels. They'd do it until the
next part came along. Then they'd quit. So nobody really
cared.

I doubt if a hotel clerk really commands a heck of a lot
of respect. I've had people talk to me just like I was some
sort of dog, that I was a ditchdigger, let's say. You figure
a fellow who comes to work and he has to have a cleanly
pressed suit and a white shirt and a tie on—plus he's gotta
have that big smile on his face—shouldn't be talked to in
a manner that he's something so below somebody else.

It affects me. It gives you that feeling: Oh hell, what's
the use? I've got to get out of this. Suddenly you look in
the mirror and you find out you're not twenty-one any
more. You're fifty-five. Many people have said to me,
"Why didn't you get out of it long ago?" I never really
had enough money to get out. I was stuck, more or less.

In a lot of hotels, the cashiering is done by a certain person and the rooming is done by the clerk. Here I do everything. At times I even act as manager, because if the manager's out, you have to take hold. There's a good deal of bookkeeping. It can get quite confusing. I've had fellows from universities come in. I would try to break them in. They couldn't make head nor tail out of being a room clerk. The one thing you must remember: Forget what happened yesterday and let tomorrow take care of itself. It's today you're working. Everything you do has to come under this date. So many look back two days and post back two days and this is how we get fouled up. (Laughs.)

There's pressure when you're doing it all. There is tension, quite a bit of tension. On a busy day I'll go home and it takes me about an hour and a half to unwind. I just want to sit there and pick up a book or a paper or something. Just get away from it all.

My legs are quite tired. I'm on my feet the whole time. In doing these jobs I don't have much of a chance to sit down. You're moving back and forth and pivoting most of the time. You're not in a large area. You're turning and pivoting. Ofttimes through the day I take a walk in front of the desk.

The thing I don't like about it is you're trapped—in a small area eight hours a day. You're behind the desk. We had a grill on our desk and I asked them to take it away, because I felt like I was in jail. The other side is open, wide open, where you can talk with the guests. But this cage was near the cash. I told it to more than one guest. There's a glass there now and a sign: Please go to the front.

"When I broke in, it was shortly after World War II. Hotels were much busier. I've worked most of 'em. I've even worked resort hotels. You might work two or three months, then you got to trudge out and look for another job. I'd rather work in a commercial house like this. Here you got things set winter through summer."

You see a lot. I'm not a nosy person. I don't care what another person is doing. It's none of my business. I've found out that people who do worry about what a guest is doing, nine times out of ten they're wrong. Especially

when you're dealing with people in the arts. Many times
it's pertaining to business, has nothing to do with what
that person who thinks like Archie Bunker thinks is going
on. I've got enough to worry about what I do without
worrying about what somebody else does.

The clerk in a hotel is rarely tipped. The bellboys,
rather, get all the tips. A fellow that comes into the hotel
to do a little cheating will always tip the bellboy heavily.
The boy can't help him at all, in any way, shape, or form.
It's the clerk who watches his mail, watches his messages,
and watches who comes in and out to see him. It's really
the clerk who covers for him. But he never seems to realize that. If the manager wishes that he be ejected from the
hotel, it's the clerk who can save him. The bellboys
couldn't do a thing for him.

The clerk knows what's going on. The fellow relies on
the bellboy to keep his mouth shut. The bellboys never
keep their mouth shut. The first guy they tell is the clerk,
when they come back—if the clerk doesn't already know
it. (Laughs.) Occasionally you will get people who seem
to know their way around. They will throw the clerk a
couple of bucks or a five-dollar bill now and then.

We're not getting any young blood. There's no incentive. I don't blame 'em—to be tied up in one spot. There's
not as many hotels as there used to be. A great many of
the two-hundred-, three-hundred-room houses are being
torn down or they're turned into office buildings. All that's
left are a few old stand-bys. There's the big hotels, mon-
strosities. There is no homey feeling. You're just a lonely
traveler. If you go down to the bar, you don't know who
the hell you're gonna run into. Your information clerk will
probably be a nineteen-year-old college girl or boy. He
doesn't know a thing about hotels. He could care less. He
wouldn't even have an idea what you did for a living.
These hotels are going to be missed.

Everybody's in a rush: "Will you *please* hurry up with
my bill? I'm in a hurry. I gotta catch a plane." It's a
shame, because we could live in such a relaxed society . . .

I'm getting a little older. Can't take it the way I could
twenty years ago. Sometimes you just sit and ponder the
day. You get a lot of laughs. (Laughs.) A fellow walked
in one morning, he wanted to know if I had seen his wife.
He took a picture out of his pocket and held it up. He
said, "If you see her, tell her I was looking for her." It

was a picture of a nude woman. (Laughs.) You get a lot of laughs.

I have about nine years to go until sixty-five. My hope is that I'll be in good condition, so I can do two or three days work at least in hotels. I know I'll miss people. You always have the idea that you're gonna better yourself. You think, Gee, I wonder if I could write a book or just exactly what I could do. I think I could have done a lot better than just being a clerk.

HOTS MICHAELS

"Do you have a favorite tune? Here's an oldie." He plays "As Time Goes By." The piano bar is fairly crowded. The drinking is casual. It is early evening at the downtown hotel. Once it was a favorite gathering place for the city's sporting crowd, politicians, and strangers looking for action. It will be razed this year to make way for a modern high rise.

He started here in 1952. He refers to a mutual friend, who has since died. "Chet and I began the whole thing. The first piano bar was in this hotel. Now every tavern and saloon has one." There is a jukebox in the room. Its loudness envelops all during the piano breaks.

He works five nights a week, from five-thirty to "around midnight. If there's a crowd, I keep going. I might play many hours in a row. I take a break when it's empty." There are frequent phone calls for him, interrupting the conversation.

Piano playing is incidental to this place. It's kind of background music for talking. Businessmen talking deals. Out-of-town visitors. Occasionally you get some people interested in hearing a certain type of song, and you entertain them. I never took any lessons. I play strictly by ear. I'm lucky I can read titles. (Laughs.)

Over the years I get to know people. They'll hit the piano bar and we'll talk back and forth. A second group will move in, strangers. They might be from small towns and they want to know what's happening. You have close contact with people. This petrifies some piano players, so they play with bands. I never played with a band because I wasn't qualified.

Late business is a thing of the past. People don't stay down as late as they used to after work. The local people will have their drinks and go home. At one time they stayed down five, six hours. And they don't come down like they used to. They have places out in the suburbs. And I think there's a little bit of fear. I'll see people check into the hotel, come down and sit around the piano bar. They're really afraid to leave the hotel. It's the strangest thing. Myself, I feel very safe. Evidently my work at the piano bar will be ended. Nothing is forever.

I hate to see it end. I'll dread the day it comes, because I enjoy the action. I enjoy people. If I were suddenly to inherit four million dollars, I guarantee you I'd be playin' piano, either here or at some other place. I can't explain why. I would miss the flow of people in and out.

You're kind of a listening board here. Sometimes they tell me things I wish they'd keep to themself. Personal, marriage problems, business. I get about twenty calls a night. A wife looking for a husband to bring something home. In a cute way she's trying to find out if he's here or some place else. If he doesn't show up in an hour, I'll be hearing. (Laughs.) I cover up constantly. They tell me things I'd just as soon not know. (Laughs.)

Some people think I run an answering service. We kid about it. They'll get ahold of me and say, "Is so-and-so there? Do you know where he might be? If you get ahold of him, will you have him call this number?" A bartender hears the same stories. Saloons are full of lonely people trying to fill an empty hour or two. Waiting for a train . . .

There's only a few things that separate you from the masses of workers. Through this business I have met some dignitaries. Where else could a piano player meet President Truman or Bob Hope or people like that? I'd never do it if I were a steam fitter or a plumber. There's nothing wrong with their line of work. They probably make more than a piano player—except that I happen to be where people gather. It's a good feeling. We're fighting for a little bit of status, one way or the other.

Every minute of my life I deal with a drinking public. I'm not knocking it, they pay my salary. But you have to treat them a certain way after they have a few martinis. They change that rapidly. It doesn't bother me unless they get rough. If he offends somebody around the bar, some wild vulgarity, I get up and get him out. Just by being nice. Most people you can talk to. It's much more difficult with a woman who is drinking. She can be difficult. You can't put your hands on her.

They're never discourteous to me, directly. What gets me is the lack of courtesy to waitresses and bartenders. People could be a little kinder to 'em. Not "Hey you, give us a drink over here!" Of course, we're dealing with drinking people, so you have to put up with it. If someone happens to be rude to me, I don't get mad. It rolls right off me. I just think, Poor souls. (Laughs.) You can't show your troubles in this business. The customer is allowed to have troubles. That's why we're here.

Generally the customer is always right. But if he's out of line ... I have seen brutal racial vulgarity right in this hotel. People from a certain part of the country would talk abusive to black waiters. Aw, brutal. Back in 1952, '53, Chet and I would step in. When that happened he either pays his check right away and gets out or he does an about-face: "Can't you see I'm joking?" I'm a person who gets involved—sometimes too much. It's best not to get involved in everything.

I get a straight salary. I was never what you'd call a tip man. I don't know why. I worked at the piano bar and there was nothing but money around. Men on expense accounts. But I never made the tips others in this industry made. We had all those wonderful years, but I never saw any of it. Why, I don't know. (Laughs.)

It might be sort of an independence I have. Sometimes people feel they would offend by tipping me. Here's your city guy sitting at the piano and he's dressed rather well. He seems to be getting along with the crowd. Maybe they feel he doesn't need it. Most of the people in town, the really big spenders, the sporty class, I knew too well. They started tipping me, but the first thing you know I'm the person's friend and that's the end of the tip. I know piano players that keep aloof. They'll walk out of the room on a break. They stay away from people on their own time. It's good psychology.

I couldn't do that. Naturally anyone would want to make a little extra money. But it wasn't the target in my

life. I was never a hustler. There's ways of hustling people
for tips. You can put a bowl on the piano, put a few dollars in it. There's also a verbal way. A fella is hitting you
for a few tunes. He keeps it up. There's ways of kidding
him: "God, that's a five-dollar number, that one." But it
just doesn't run in me. If they want to give it to me, fine.
If they don't, all right. They're gonna get the same action.

I play along whether it's noisy or quiet. It doesn't
bother me if people talk or are loud. It's part of the game.
I never had a strong ego. I sometimes wish I did. I can
play all the melodies, but I'm not really a good piano
player. I wish I were. I never touch a piano until I walk in
here. I don't have a piano at home. My father was a talented musician. In our home there was always a piano.
Everybody played, my father, my mother, my brothers,
my sister, myself.

I consider myself a whisky salesman. The amount of
money spent in this room pays me. I encourage people in
a nice way to have a good time. I usually take a break
only when business dies down. But you might as well be
there while you have visitors. That way it helps the bartender. I never thought of myself as an artist. I know my
limitations. It's a business. It's all show biz.

I shudder to think of retirement. The most frightening
thing to me will be the day I say, "I'm going down to St.
Petersburg and buy a little home." I know everything in
life ends. It's not growing old that worries me, but what
would I do? When it gets quiet here, your mind strays and
you start thinking of many things. I find myself talking
about the future but I'm always thinking about the past.

TEDDY GRODOWSKI

*He's an elevator starter at a large office building. He had
operated a car, "but they became automated." He had
previously worked in a factory. "Man, I had to sweat,
buffing, polishing. This is a clean job. I really enjoy it.*

*"You could say I work at least five and a half hours on
my feet out of eight. See what I'm wearing? Those are
good shoes, arch support, cushion. Oh, you gotta.*

"I went two years of high school but I coulda gone

*four. It was my fault. But what are you gonna do? You
can't cry over spilt milk."*

Some of these starters, they won't do nothin'. I told 'em,
"One good piece of ass and one day's work would kill you
guys." They never done hard work. They were always on
the cars. They were squawking that they work hard opening doors for people. That was a pleasure to me, 'cause
you get to know people. You get to know their habits.

Certain persons get on at the same time and I know just
where they're goin'. This one woman, I'd catch her every
time, at ten or ten thirty. She wouldn't tell me where she
was goin'. She'd always get off at the fourteenth floor. See,
the main washroom's on the fourteenth floor. (Laughs.)

I'm security too. Anybody takes anything out, they
gotta get a pass. Somebody look suspicious, you ask 'em
where they're going—in a polite way. You just watch the
car, see where they're going, and don't say no more.
Sometimes by lookin' at a person you can tell what character he is. Any time they go to the board I always say,
"Can I help you?" I won't say any more. When they see
you're watchin' 'em, they'll go right down again. That's all.

A lot of people come in here, they go to that board,
they won't even ask you, 'cause they're afraid. Some of
these buildings, the guy says, "There's the directory." I try
to help. It don't hurt. You mention a room number, I
would give you that room number. 'Cause every time they
change that directory I try to study that board. It makes
me look like a genius when somebody asks me something.

A person goes on a vacation or they're out on a business trip, I tell 'em, "You were gone." They'll say thanks
that you were thinkin' about 'em. Remembering people's
names, that means a lot. They let you know if they want
to be called mister or missis. I respect these guys with
their high positions. If they want you to call 'em by their
first name, they'll tell you.

I found out executives are the really good ones. They'll
kid around. Even the ordinary people, they'll kid around
with you. Someday, if I don't talk to 'em, they'll say,
"What's the matter, you mad or somethin'?" If I don't
smile, people will want to know if I'm sick or what happened. You gotta always have somethin' goin'. I always
tell 'em in the morning, "Have fun." Next time I see 'em,
"Hurry back." When it's bad out, I always say, "Did you

order this weather?" They like this kidding around. They say it cheers up their day. I'm not hard to get along with nobody.

I got a picture with Dirksen.* We open the door when he come in and just as he shook my hand, this photographer—I got it home, two of 'em, colored pictures. He come right up and shook my hand. Daley came in: "Hello, there." He thanked me for takin' him up. You know who else I met there? Sonny and Cher. They were dressed like hippies. I didn't know who they were, so somebody told me. It could happen any time. When I see a celebrity, I go home and tell my wife about it. She'll tell all her friends and relatives. She'll say who I saw. I don't want to retire. I'd be lost if I had to stay home and don't see the public all day long.

POSTSCRIPT: *"Today we have no friends since TV came out. One time, before TV, friends come to your house. You say, 'Come over,' and as soon as they come over, they stick their nose in that TV. Forget about it! I'll tell you, I bought a Hammond organ. I'm takin' organ lessons. Soon's I get home, before I have my dinner—two cans of beer. Then I'll eat. Then I'll practice the organ. TV? Forget it."*

TIM DEVLIN

He suffered a nervous breakdown and was in the hospital for three months. He's been out for a year. "I'm thirty years old and I sometimes feel fifty." (Laughs.)

Right now I'm doing work that I detest. I'm a janitor. It's a dirty job. You work hard. When I'm at work I wear a uniform, gray khaki pants and a gray shirt. It's baggy pants. It's what you see a lot of janitors wearing. This is the kind of work I used to think niggers would do or hillbillies or DPs. You don't associate with people like that. Now I'm one of them.

"You're a bum"—this is the picture I have of myself.

*The late U. S. Senator Everett Dirksen of Illinois.

I'm a flop because of what I've come to. There's five of us at work here. It's a housing project. Three can barely speak a word of English. They're DPs. They work very hard and don't complain. They're perfectly content, but I'm not. It's a dead end. Tonight I'm gonna meet a couple of friends at a bar. I haven't seen them for a long time. I feel inferior. I'll bullshit 'em. I'll say I'm a lawyer or something.

When you meet somebody at a party they ask, "What do you do?" I bullshit 'em. I tell 'em anything. Their minds are like a computer. "I'm a CPA." Oh, he's gotta make at least eighteen-thousand a year. He's a success. If I said I was an electrician, they'd think I make nine dollars an hour. If you say, "I'm a janitor"—ooohhh! You get this feeling that you are low. It's a blow to my ego. Who wants to be a janitor? They even call them maintenance engineers.

I don't have any interest in furthering myself, but I just can't see myself doing this the rest of my life. I almost get to the point that I ought to be on welfare. I ought to chuck it all and just not do anything. My whole outlook on work is different than it was. I'd be free if I could say I'm a janitor . . . If I could only say, "I'm Tim Devlin and I enjoy what I'm doing!"

I've had college training and I'd been in sales almost eight years. I was right off the assembly line: In life you become a success to get ahead; money is the key to judge people by. That was my childhood thing—the big office, the big car, the big house. I was doing as good as I wanted to be. I could have done much better.

I fell in love and thought it was the most beautiful experience in the world. Shortly after I was married I found out that my wife—I'm not blaming her—was interested in money. She was judging me against other people my age. Was I a financial success? I put in long hours. I got this feeling I was just a machine. I felt at the end of the week, Here's the money. Now do you love me? Am I a better man?

I was selling a photocopy machine for $1,250. My commission was $300. The total value of the machine was $480. I thought, Jesus Christ, there's something wrong here. If it costs $480, why can't it be sold for $480—for as small a margin of profit as possible, not for as much profit as possible? I'm looking toward a utopian society, ain't I? I didn't feel proud of myself.

I was one of their soldiers. I read the sales manuals. If the customer says this, you say that. Turn him around, get him in the palm of your hand, and—boom!—get him to sign on the dotted line. You give him bullshit. You wiggle, you finagle, you sell yourself, and you get him to sign. Pow! you won a round. The next day is another round. What the hell am I doing? I don't enjoy it. My marriage is turning sour. I'm making good money. I have a company car. This is what my wife wants, but I feel bad. I begin to question things. It blew the whole marriage.

I never talk about it to anyone. People would think I'm a communist or I'm going crazy. A person that's making money shouldn't question the source of it. I always kept it to myself. This was the American Dream. This is what my father was always pounding into my head.

I learned this angle thing from my father. He was always trying for some gimmick to make a lot of money. He didn't want to spend the rest of his life as a tradesman. He was always trying to open up a business or a franchise. He lost every dime he made. He believed in the American Dream. We should examine this dream. If I sell a machine that's worth $480 for $1,250, is that the American Dream?

When I got divorced it hit me bad. I went through a crisis. I blamed the system, I blamed the country, I blamed God. This is where the nervous breakdown came in. I just didn't give a shit any more. I didn't want to see anyone any more. I didn't want to hear someone tell me, "Yeah, next week I'm gonna get a promotion to district manager." Big deal. I don't give a goddamn if he's gonna be President of the United States. I'm cynical. This is what I'm carrying around with me.

When I was selling, my friends looked up to me. One worked in a bakery. Another was driving a cab and delivering pizza. They were thinking. "Maybe I ought to go into sales." A salesman! You wear a suit every day, you drive a company car. Now they call them account executives. A CTA bus driver may make more money, but you have a white shirt, a tie . . . My sisters are all married to white-shirts.

A lot of people are considered failures but it's not their fault. I don't know exactly what I want to do. I don't want to go back in the rat race. Will it be the same thing again? I've had offers to go back into sales—to be a con artist. But I've gotten turned off. I think I missed the boat. If I could do it all over again, I would have gone into the field of mental health, really finding out what makes people tick. I would love to find out why people think it's important to be a success.

I do want to make it financially. But the only thing open for me would be sales work again. I'm not twenty-one any more. My God, I'd have to start off with maybe a hundred and a quarter a week. That really isn't any money. That's just enough to put a roof over your head. If I do apple polishing, I might make assistant manager in ten years—and maybe a lot of titles along the way. I'm afraid that's the only way open for me now. I guess I could buy stock, get remarried, and be part of what the system's all about. But I really question the system . . .

COUNTING

NANCY ROGERS

At twenty-eight, she has been a bank teller for six years. She earns five-hundred dollars a month.

What I do is say hello to people when they come up to my window. "Can I help?" And transact their business, which amounts to taking money from them and putting it in their account. Or giving them money out of their account. You make sure it's the right amount, put the deposits on through the machine so it shows on the books, so they know. You don't really do much. It's just a service job.

We have a time clock. It's really terrible. You have a card that you put in the machine and it punches the time that you've arrived. If you get there after eight-forty-five, they yell and they scream a lot and say, "Late!" Which I don't quite understand, because I've never felt you should be tied to something like a clock. It's not that important. If you're there to start doing business with the people when the bank opens, fine.

I go to my vault, open that, take out my cash, set up my cage, get my stamps set out, and ink my stamp pad. From there on until nine o'clock when the bank opens, I sit around and talk to the other girls.

My supervisor yells at me. He's about fifty, in a position that he doesn't really enjoy. He's been there for a long time and hasn't really advanced that much. He's supposed to have authority over a lot of things but he hasn't really kept informed of changes. The girls who work under him don't really have the proper respect that you think a person in his position would get. In some ways, it's nice. It's easier to talk to him. You can ask him a question without getting, "I'm too busy." Yet you ask a question a lot of times and you don't get the answer you need. Like he doesn't listen.

We work right now with the IBM. It's connected with the main computer bank which has all the information about all the savings accounts. To get any information, we just punch the proper buttons. There are two tellers to a cage and the machine is in between our windows. I don't like the way the bank is set up. It separates people. People are already separated enough. There are apartment houses where you don't know anybody else in the building. They object to your going into somebody else's cage, which is understandable. If the person doesn't balance, they'll say, "She was in my cage." Cages? I've wondered about that. It's not quite like being in prison, but I still feel very locked in.

The person who shares my cage, she's young, black, and very nice. I like her very much. I have fun with her. She's originally from the South. She's a very relaxed type of person. I can be open and not worry I might offend her. I keep telling her she's a bigot. (Laughs.) And she keeps saying, "There are only three kinds of people I dislike—the Italians, the Polacks, and the Jews." (Laughs.) I'll walk up to her and put my hands on her shoulder and she'll say, "Get your hands off me, white girl, don't you know you're not supposed to touch?" It's nice and relaxed kind of—we sit around and gossip about our boyfriends, which is fun.

A lot of people who work there I don't know. Never talk to, have no idea who they are. You're never introduced. I don't even know who the president of the bank is. I don't know what he looks like. It's really funny, because you have to go have okays on certain things. Like we're only allowed to cash up to a certain amount without having an officer okay it. They'd say, "Go see Mr. Frank." And I'd say, "Who's that? Which one? Point him out." The girl who's the supervisor for checking kept saying, "You don't know who he is? You don't know who he is? He's the one over there. Remember him? You waited on him." "Yeah, but I didn't know what his name was. Nobody ever told me."

I enjoy talking to people. Once you start getting regular

customers, you take your time to talk—which makes the job more enjoyable. It also makes me wonder about people. Some people are out working like every penny counts. Other people, it's a status thing with them. They really like to talk about it. I had a man the other day who was buying stock. "Oh well, I'm buying fifty-thousand dollars worth of AT&T, and I'm also investing in . . ." He wouldn't stop talking. He was trying to impress me: I have money, therefore I'm somebody.

Money doesn't mean that much to me. To me, it's not money, it's just little pieces of paper. It's not money to me unless *I'm* the one who's taking the money out or cashing the check. That's money because it's mine. Otherwise it doesn't really mean anything. Somebody asked me "Doesn't it bother you, handling all that money all day long?" I said, "It's not money. I'm a magician. I'll show you how it works." So I counted out the paper. I said, "Over there, at this window, it's nothing. Over there, at that window, it's money." If you were gonna think about it every minute: "Oh lookit, here's five-thousand dollars, wow! Where could I go on five-thousand dollars? Off to Bermuda—" You'd get hung-up and so dissatisfied of having to deal with money that's not yours, you couldn't work.

People are always coming in and joking about—"Why don't you and I get together? I'll come and take the money and you ring the alarm after I've left and say, 'Oh, I was frightened, I couldn't do anything.' " I say, "It's not enough." The amount in my cash drawer isn't enough. If you're going to steal, steal at least into the hundreds of thousands. To steal five or ten thousand isn't worth it.

It's joked about all the time. Sometimes it's kidded about if you do have a difference. Maybe I was paying out a hundred dollars and two bills stuck together and I gave him $110 instead. A lot of times people have come back and said, "I think you gave me ten dollars too much." Like they didn't want me to get in trouble. "She won't balance today and here I am sitting with ten dollars she doesn't have." It's really nice to know people are honest. Quite a few are. Anyway, we're bonded, we're insured for that. The bank usually has a slush fund for making up differences one way or the other.

I've never been held up. We have a foot alarm, one that you just trip with your toe. At the other place, we had a button you push, which was immediately under the counter. Some people, you get a funny feeling about. Like I don't think that's his passbook, it's probably stolen. Most of the time you're never right. (Laughs.)

One of the girls who works here was held up. She just gave the man the money he wanted. (Laughs.) Which is all you can do. She went up to our head teller to get more money. She said, "Mr. Murphy, I was just held up." He said, "Oh sure, uh huh, ha, ha, ha." She said, "No really I was." (Laughs.) He said, "Ooohhh, you really were, weren't you?" (Laughs.) Like wow! I don't think they ever caught the person. She didn't give him all that money. She just gave him what she had in one part of the drawer and didn't bother to open the other drawers, where most of that cash was stored.

I really don't know what I'd do. I don't think I'd panic too badly. I'd be very nervous and upset, but I'd probably do exactly what the man wanted. If possible, trip the alarm, but that's not going to do much good. I'd give him the money, especially if he had a gun in his hand or even giving the slight implication ... Money's not worth that much. The bank's insured by the government for things like that, so there's no real ... It'd be exciting, I guess.

A lot of younger girls who are coming in now, they get pushed too fast. If you've never done it before, it takes time just to realize—you have to stop and think, especially if it's busy. Here I am doing three different things. I am taking money out of these people's accounts and putting part of it into checking and he wants part of it back, plus he wants to cash a check, and he asks for a couple of money orders. You got all these things that you have to remember about—that have to be added and subtracted so everything comes out right.

You force yourself into speeding up because you don't want to make people wait. 'Cause you're there for one reason, you're there to serve them. Lots of times there's somebody you know back there and you want to get rid of these people so you can talk to him. (Laughs.)

In a lot of cases, as far as males, you're gonna be asked out. Whether you accept or not is something else. I met quite a few people in the bank who I've gone out with. Sometimes relationships work out very nicely and you become good friends with these people and it may last for years. My social life is affected by my job, oh sure. A cus-

tomer coming in and saying, "I'm giving a party next
week, would you like to come?"

Some places kind of frown on it. But most of them
have no control. One fella I met at the bank, he was from
an auditing firm, who I went out with for a short while.
He said, "Don't tell anybody. We're not supposed to go
with anybody from the bank we work for." That's weird,
for a job to carry over into your private life.

Banks are very much giving into desexualizing the
women who work there, by putting uniforms on them.
Trying to make everybody look the same. In one way it's
nice, it saves on clothes. In another way, it's boring. Putting on the same thing almost every day is—ech!! Some
I've seen aren't too bad, but in some places they're very
tailored and in drab colors. Uptight is the only word I
can think of to describe them. The place I worked before,
it was a navy-blue suit and it was—blach!! (Laughs.)

Most bank tellers are women because of the pay scale.
It's assumed that women are paid a little bit lower than
men. (Laughs.) There are only two men that work in the
area, aside from my supervisor. The head teller, who's
been there for years and years and years, and a young fella
in charge of all the silver. For most men it's a job that
doesn't offer that much kind of advancement. You'd have
to be the type that would really just enjoy sittin' back and
doing the same thing over and over again. A transaction is
a transaction is a transaction.

Some days, when you're aggravated about something,
you carry it after you leave the job. Certain people are
bad days. (Laughs.) The type of person who will walk in
and says, "My car's double-parked outside. Would you
hurry up, lady? I haven't got time to waste around here."
And you go—"What???—" You want to say, "Hey, why
did you double-park your car? So now you're gonna blame
me if you get a ticket, 'cause you were dumb enough to
leave it there?" But you can't. That's the one hassle. You
can't say anything back. The customer's always right.

Certain people who are having a bad day themselves
feel they must take it out on you: "What are you doing
there?" "Why are you checking that?" "Why did you have
to do that?" You calmly try and explain to them, "That's
what's required." You can't please 'em. They make sure
you're in as nasty a mood as they are. (Laughs.)

We have quite a bit of talk during coffee breaks.

There's speculation: "Do you think this is what happened?" There was a girl who was let go this week. Nobody was told as to the why or wherefore. Nobody really still knows. They keep coming through the bank saying, "We don't want rumors started about such-and-such." But they don't explain it. She doesn't exist any more totally. She's no longer here.

The last place I worked for, I was let go. I told the people I worked with, "If anybody asks tell them I got fired and give them my phone number." One of my friends stopped by and asked where I was at. They said, "She's no longer with us." That's all. I vanished.

When it happened, it was such an abrupt thing. I hadn't really expected it. I was supposed to be an example so that these things wouldn't occur any more. One of the factors was a man I wasn't getting along with. He worked out at the desk. He was—how can I put it?—he was a very handsy person. He was that way towards everybody. I didn't like it. He'd always pick out a time when you were balancing or you were trying to figure something out. You didn't want to be interrupted. At other times, you wouldn't mind, you'd laugh it off.

The reason I was given for being fired was that I was absent too much and had been tardy too often. But I think there was really another reason. The girl who was supervisor was leaving and I was next in seniority. I just don't think they were going to let me go further.

With her the job was everything, it was her whole life. She would stay there till seven in the evening if something went wrong, and come in on Saturdays if they asked her to. When I was done—I'm sorry, I was done for the day.

And I was very open about being different. It started when one of the girls had brought in a little sticker-thing for Valentine's Day. I thought they were cute. So I had just taken a couple of hearts out of one and put it on my name sign on the window, 'cause I liked it. There was never anything really said except "How come that's there?" And I said, " 'Cause I like it." A lot of customers'd come in and say, "Wow! She had hearts on her window, she must be a nice girl." It gave them an opportunity to have something to say instead of just feeling they didn't know you and didn't quite know what to say. I think the bank didn't care for that too much. They want everybody to be pretty much the same, kind of conservative, fitting into the norm. I think that was the real reason I was let go.

I think a lot of places don't want people to be people. I think they want you to almost be the machines they're working with. They just want to dehumanize you. Just like when you walk in in the morning, you put the switch on and here you are: "I am a robot. This is what I do. Good morning. How are you? May I help you?" I hate having to deal with people like that.

In some way, I feel my job's important. Especially when you work with people who are trying to save money. It's gratifying for them when they give you the stuff and you mark in their book and there it is—wow! I've accomplished this. And you say, "I'm glad to see you again. You're really doing well." Most of these people here work in restaurants downtown and are secretaries. Lower middle class and a lot of blacks come in this bank. They're a lot more friendly than some of your other people, who are so busy trying to impress one another.

They don't even recognize you. It's like I'm almost being treated as a machine. They don't have time to bother. After all, you're just a peon. I had a black man come up to my window and say, "It's really nice to see somebody working in a place like this who's even halfway relevant." And I thought—wow! (Laughs.) I had my hair up like in little ponytails on the side and just had a pullover sweater and a skirt on and wasn't really dressed up. I was very taken aback by it. It's the first compliment I had in a long time. It's nice to be recognized. Most places, it's your full name on the window. Some places just have Miss or Mrs. So-and-so. I prefer giving my whole name so people can call me Nancy. (Laughs.) They feel a little more comfortable. Certain officers you refer to by their first names. Other people you don't. Some people you would feel kind of weird saying, "Hey, Charlie, would you come over here and do this for me?" Other people you'd feel strange calling them by their proper name. All men who sit at the desk in the office you refer to as Mister. Okay, he's a vice president, he must be called Mr. So-and-so. Whereas you're just a teller. Therefore he can call you by your first name. Smaller banks tend to be more friendly and open.

When I tell people at a party I work for a bank, most of them get interested. They say, "What do you do?" I say, "I'm a teller." They say, "Oh, hmm, okay," and walk away. I remember getting into a discussion with one person about the war. We were disagreeing. He was for it. I wasn't getting angry because I thought he has his right to his point of view. But the man couldn't recognize that I had the right to mine. The thing finally was thrown at me: "What do you mean saying that? After all, who are you? I own my own business, you just work in a crummy bank." It doesn't compute. Like, unless you're capable of making it in the business world, you don't have a right to an opinion. (Laughs.)

My job doesn't have prestige. It's a service job. Whether you're a waitress, salesperson, anything like that—working directly for the public—it's not quite looked on as being prestigious. You are there to serve them. They are not there to serve you. Like a housemaid or a servant.

One of the girls said, "People who go through four years of college should have it recognized that they have achieved something." A man said, "Don't you think someone who becomes an auto mechanic and is good at it should also be recognized? He's a specialist, too, like the man who goes to be a doctor." Yet he's not thought of that way. What difference? It's a shame that people aren't looked at as each job being special unto itself. I can't work on a car, yet I see people who can do it beautifully. Like they have a feel for it. Some people can write books, other people can do marvelous things in other ways . . .

FRED ROMAN

I usually say I'm an accountant. Most people think it's somebody who sits there with a green eyeshade and his sleeves rolled up with a garter, poring over books, adding things—with glasses. (Laughs.) I suppose a certified public accountant has status. It doesn't mean much to me. Do I like the job or don't I? That's important.

He is twenty-five and works for one of the largest public accounting firms in the world. It employs twelve hundred people. He has been with the company three years. During

*his first year, after graduating from college, he worked for
a food chain, doing inventory.*

The company I work for doesn't make a product. We
provide a service. Our service is auditing. We are usually
hired by stockholders or the board of directors. We will
certify whether a company's financial statement is correct.
They'll say, "This is what we did last year. We made X
amount of dollars." We will come in to examine the books
and say, "Yes, they did."

We're looking for things that didn't go out the door the
wrong way. Our clients could say, "We have a million dollars in accounts receivable." We make sure that they do,
in fact, have a million dollars and not a thousand. We ask
the people who owe the money, "Do you, in fact, owe our
client two thousand dollars as of this date?" We do it on a
spot check basis. Some companies have five thousand individual accounts receivable. We'll maybe test a hundred.

We're also looking for things such as floating of cash. If
a company writes a check one day and deposits money the
next day, it tells you something of its solvency. We look
for transfers between accounts to make sure they're not
floating these things—a hundred thousand dollars they
keep working back and forth between two banks.
(Laughs.)

We work with figures, but we have to keep in mind
what's behind those figures. What bugs me about people in
my work is that they get too wrapped up in numbers. To
them a financial statement is the end. To me, it's a tool
used by management or stockholders.

We have a computer. We call it Audex. It has taken the
detail drudgery out of accounting. I use things that come
out of the computer in my everyday work. An accountant
will prepare things for keypunching. A girl will keypunch
and it will go into the monster. That's what we call it.
(Laughs.) You still have to audit what comes out of the
computer. I work with pencils. We all do. I think that's
'cause we make so many mistakes. (Laughs.)

You're an auditor. The term scares people. They believe
you're there to see if they're stealing nickels and dimes out
of petty cash. We're not concerned with that. But people
have that image of us. They think we're there to spy on
them. What we're really doing is making sure things are

reported correctly. I don't care if somebody's stealing money as long as he reports it. (Laughs.)

People look at you with fear and suspicion. The girl who does accounts receivable never saw an auditor before. The comptroller knows why you're there and he'll cooperate. But it's the guy down the line who is not sure and worries. You ask him a lot of questions. What does he do? How does he do it? Are you after his job? Are you trying to get him fired? He's not very friendly.

We're supposed to be independent. We're supposed to certify their books are correct. We'll certify this to the Securities Exchange Commission, to the stockholders, to the banks. They'll all use our financial statements. But if we slight the company—if I find something that's going to take away five hundred thousand dollars of income this year—they may not hire us back next year.

I'm not involved in keeping clients or getting them. That's the responsibility of the manager or the partner. I'm almost at the bottom of the heap. I'm the top class of assistant. There are five levels. I'm a staff assistant. Above me is senior. Senior's in charge of the job, out in the field with the client. The next level is manager. He has over-all responsibility for the client. He's in charge of billing. The next step is partner. That's tops. He has an interest in the company. Our owners are called partners. They have final responsibility. The partner decides whether this five hundred thousand dollars is going to go or stay on the books.

There are gray areas. Say I saw that five hundred thousand dollars as a bad debt. The client may say, "Oh, the guy's good for it. He's going to pay." You say, "He hasn't paid you anything for the past six months. He declared bankruptcy yesterday. How can you say he's gonna pay?" Your client says, "He's reorganizing and he gonna get the money." You've got two ways of looking at this. The guy's able to pay or he's not. Somebody's gotta make a decision. Are we gonna allow you to show this receivable or are we gonna make you write it off? We usually compromise. We try to work out something in-between. The company knows more about it than we do, right? But we do have to issue an independent report. Anyway, I'm not a partner who makes those decisions. (Laughs.)

I think I'll leave before I get there. Many people in our firm don't plan on sticking around. The pressure. The constant rush to get things done. Since I've been here, two

people have had nervous breakdowns. I have three bosses
on any job, but I don't know who's my boss next week. I
might be working for somebody else.

Our firm has a philosophy of progress, up or out. I
started three years ago. If that second year I didn't move
from SA–3, staff assistant, to SA–4, I'd be out. Last
June I was SA–4. If I hadn't moved to SA–5, I'd be
out. Next year if I don't move to senior, I'll be out. When
I make senior I'll be Senior–1. The following year, Senior–2. Then Senior–3. Then manager—or out. By the
time I'm thirty-four or so, I'm a partner or I'm out.

When a partner reaches fifty-five he no longer has direct client responsibility. He doesn't move out, because
he's now part owner of the company. He's in an advisory
capacity. They're not retired. They're just—just doing research. I'm not saying this is good or bad. This is just how
it is.

It's a very young field. You have a lot of them at the
bottom to do the footwork. Then it pyramids and you
don't need so many up there. Most of the people they get
are just out of college. I can't label them—the range is
broad—but I'd guess most of them are conservative. Politics is hardly discussed.

Fifteen years ago, public accountants wore white shirts.
You had to wear a hat, so you could convey a conservative image. When I was in college the big joke was: If
you're going to work for a public accounting firm, make
sure you buy a good supply of white shirts and a hat.
They've gotten away from that since. We have guys with
long hair. But they do catch more static than somebody in
another business. And now we have women. There are
several female assistants and seniors. There's one woman
manager. We have no female partners.

If you don't advance, they'll help you find another job.
They're very nice about it. They'll fire you, but they just
don't throw you out in the street. (Laughs.) They'll try to
find you a job with one of our clients. There's a theory behind it. Say I leave to go to XYZ Manufacturing Company. In fifteen years, I'm comptroller and I need an audit. Who am I gonna go to? Although their philosophy is
up or out, they treat their employees very well.

Is my job important? It's a question I ask myself. It's
important to people who use financial statements, who buy
stocks. It's important to banks. (Pause.) I'm not out com-

batting pollution or anything like that. Whether it's important to society ... (A long pause.) No, not too important. It's necessary in this economy, based on big business. I don't think most of the others at the firm share my views. (Laughs.)

I have a couple friends there. We get together and talk once in a while. At first you're afraid to say anything 'cause you think the guy really loves it. You don't want to say, "I hate it." But then you hear the guy say, "Boy! If it weren't for the money I'd quit right now."

I'd like to go back to college and get a master's or Ph.D. and become a college teacher. The only problem is I don't think I have the smarts for it. When I was in high school I thought I'd be an engineer. So I took math, chemistry, physics, and got my D's. I thought of being a history major. Then I said, "What will I do with a degree in history?" I thought of poli sci. I thought most about going into law. I still think about that. I chose accounting for a very poor reason. I eliminated everything else. Even after I passed my test as a CPA I was saying all along, "I don't want to be an accountant." (Laughs.) I'm young enough. After June I can look around. As for salary, I'm well ahead of my contemporaries. I'm well ahead of those in teaching and slightly ahead of those in engineering. But that isn't it ...

When people ask what I do, I tell them I'm an accountant. It sounds better than auditor, doesn't it? (Laughs.) But it's not a very exciting business. What can you say about figures? (Laughs.) You tell people you're an accountant—(his voice deliberately assumes a dull monotone) "Oh, that's nice." They don't know quite what to say. (Laughs.) What can you say? I could say, "Wow! I saw this company yesterday and their balance sheet, wow!" (Laughs.) Maybe I look at it wrong. (Slowly emphasizing each word) *There just isn't much to talk about.*

FOOTWORK

JACK SPIEGEL

He is an organizer for the United Shoe Workers of America.

"*About sixty percent in the industry are women. In some shops it goes as high as seventy percent. A great many are Spanish-speaking and blacks. It's low paying work. The average wage in the shoe industry today is a little over a hundred dollars a week. There are all kinds of work stoppages. Even conservative workers are militant in shops.*

"*Traditionally the shoe industry has been on piecework. We discourage it and, in many cases, struggle with our own people. They can pick up twenty-five, thirty percent over their time week. But we don't accept the philosophy that you've got to work till you drop.*

"*Small shops are going out of business because they can't compete with the giants. There's been a lot of mergers in the shoe industry. Importation has cut into a third of the shoes being sold in our country. Shoes are brought in from Spain, Japan, Italy ... The average wage in this country is $2.60. In Italy it is $1.10*

"*The same manufacturers who exploit here open up factories there, bring the shoes in here, finish 'em in some places, and put a "Made in America" label on them. The consumer thinks he's getting a break. They get it a little cheaper, but the quality and workmanship may not be as good.*

"*Up to about twelve years ago, we had about a quarter of a million workers. There are now less than 170,000.*

In the next ten, fifteen years it may diminish to less than fifty thousand. What happened to watchmaking may happen to us. It's happened to textiles, too, where half the workers have lost their jobs in the past twenty years.

"*If some measures aren't taken by the government to tax those who send money out and establish those factories in other countries, and take jobs away from people here, it will be good-bye to the American shoe industry. Those in their sixties will retire. Those who are still able to work will find it more difficult.*"

ALICE WASHINGTON

She works in the warehouse of the Florsheim Shoe Company. She is an order filler. "When I first started it was hard, but after nine years you get used to it." She is secretary-treasurer of the union local. "I have five children at home."

You go to different aisles or bins, you just pull out shoes according to your order. You have your AS orders* and your regular orders. You have rushes. You'd get an order in a folder for about two hundred to seven hundred pair of shoes. Oh, just all different types of orders.

I am walking all day long. Usually we work two hours overtime, which is until six o'clock. We work five hours on Saturday. All day long I'm on my feet. I've thought about it seriously and I'm gonna sit down and try to figure out just exactly how many miles I do walk within a week. To me, it's about fifty miles a day. (Laughs.)

I feel the exercise is good for me but it hasn't done anything for me. (Laughs.) After listening to doctors and different books that you read, they say walking is very healthy for you. Yeah? Do I look like I lost weight? That's what's disgusting. (Laughs.)

It's not only the walking. It's the reaching, the bending. I mean, you get a great amount of exercise in all areas. Say, for instance, you wanted 20292. I know it's in Zone Three or Four. Say your size is 8½ B. Maybe 8½ B is ex-

* Assorted stock.

tremely high. I have to reach up and get a ladder. Or maybe it's very low. I have to bend down and bring the shoe out.

You push around a rack all day. It's a big steel rack, which normally holds 208 pairs of shoes. You complete your rack. You count your shoes. You make out your ticket. Some orders are very hard to fill, calling for odd sizes. I had two orders today that gave me a complete headache. If you put your mind to it and try to get those orders out, it's nerve-racking. Some days I'm not as tired as I should be. There are other times when I get *absolutely* tired.

Right now I'm having a lot of trouble with my feet. Cement is bad on your feet anyway. The whole building is cement floor. I wear crepe-soled shoes. You can't wear anything too flat. You have to have something slightly elevated to keep your heel up off the floor. You have a lot of young girls coming in and they say, "Don't you ever complain about your feet? My feet are killing me." We have complained, yes. The management would say, "Get yourself the right-type shoe."

Most of the young girls are on the bonus system—piecework. You're out there trying to make extra money besides the average rate. That's a dull, steady pace all day long. Entirely too much. The other day we had a big rouse-up. Who's getting the best orders, who's not? Naturally they want the big orders where they can make their bonus money at the end of the month. Me myself, I'll never go for it. I know in the long run I wouldn't be able to keep up with it. I'm just there to do a day's work.

I've often thought about a sit-down job, but I don't know. Maybe it's because I'm used to this. I have worked in checking. You check for mistakes after the picker has picked the shoes. You sat down all day long. Truthfully, I prefer walking. The sitting down seemed to bother my back.

She started working at seventeen as a chambermaid in a South Carolina motel. At eighteen she married. She worked in New York for three years, "at a business school. Part-time, six to ten. I was doing switchboard and comptometry. We had got in this bookkeeping machine. I worked the IBM, the comptometer, and the switchboard. I had time to get myself with it.

"When I came to Chicago I was looking for the type of office work I had been doing in New York. The places where I was applying, they wanted speed—so they said. I tried not to feel my color had anything to do with it. I went to a place downtown two, three times. I knew that switchboard as well as anybody. I watched her train a girl and I could hardly keep my hands out from showing the girl how to do it, by me knowing it so well. When I took the test for the job, the woman who was training me was so nasty, for no reason. She got me so upset, so nervous. I had to look at her two or three times. I said, 'No, I won't lose my temper. I'm trying to get a job.' After the examination was over, she said, 'If we have an opening we'll let you know.' (Laughs.) It couldn't be nothin' but by color. (Laughs.) You hate to feel that, but ... I couldn't find anything. I have these children to support, so I was hired at the warehouse and have been here ever since."

I used to work overtime almost every day, but after my oldest son went off to college, I stopped. I could sort of rely on him to take care of the smaller kids. I take the bus home or, if I'm lucky, I catch a ride with some of the fellas that travel the same route. Every evening I fix dinner and see about the homework and that they've done things I told them to do before I leave in the morning. On Wednesday, I wash. We have a laundry room. I walk back and forth, washing, and I'm cooking all the time. Do you realize the walking that is done? On Wednesday evenings, I don't get to bed until about eleven o'clock. Some mornings I'm so tired. (Laughs.) But once I get up and wash my face and get stirred around, I'm in pretty good shape.

If you stop and daydream, you're losing a lot of time picking up your shoes. When you hit that floor in the morning you say, "Well, I'm gonna get started with it and I'm gonna get through with it." If you constantly work and don't pass off the time, messin' around, the time goes by. You turn around and look at your watch, Oh my goodness, it's break time—or it's lunch time or it's time to go home.

During lunch we kid around with each other. We like to have a little fun. That takes the drudgery out of knowing you gotta hit the floor again. And to keep you from feeling tired. We discuss different things that we hear on the news, just things in general. Our main conversation is discussing the kids. If my child does something funny or bad, I tell it. If my co-workers' children do something, they tell it.

We get along very well with the office workers. Every time I go in, I always give them a good morning and I always try to have something funny to say. I don't feel less than they do. In fact, we have a young lady, she's in the office and she wants to come out on the floor because she's not making enough money. You don't make as much in the office as you would working in a factory.

For all that walking, I should be making at least five dollars an hour. I'm able to save very little, and I do mean very little. You have to pay rent, lights, and telephone bill. You have to clothe your children, you have to feed them. It's very hard. If you get a nickel or two, something comes up and you have to spend it. My son just got off to college. Every time he picks up the telephone, this has got to be done, that has to be done . . . it's rough.

How long will I be able to hold up at this? That is my main worry. That's the reason I never bothered about the bonus. I knew as I became older I wouldn't be able to continue. So I just worked along the pace that I was working. When I punch that clock in the morning I have a certain amount of work to get out because I'm being paid a day's work. But to rip and run like these younger children . . . You have your nineteen-, twenty-year-olds—there's two of us that are up in age—these younger ones, they go partying and everything else and—boom!—right back to work the next morning. Me? I can't do that.

Oh, sometimes I become very disgusted with myself and I say to myself, "Do I always have to walk like this?" Maybe I should strike out and do something else before I get too old. Age is a great barrier after you wait nine years and try to strike out and do something else. I say, "I can't give up now. I have children in school." So . . . (a heavy sigh) it runs through my mind, I become very discouraged sometimes.

(Her face is transformed; she glows.) I would like to work with children, small children. I have thought several times of trying to set up a nursery, even if I didn't start with but one or two children. That's what I'd really like. I have thought about it very seriously. About two, three years ago, I mentioned it to some of the girls on the job. It's not what you would charge a person, it's just the idea of helping. This mother had to get out there. Believe me, it's many of us that have to get out here. I mean *have* to get out and come a great distance and——have you ever gotten on a bus and see a mother with arms swinging and two, three children holding on to each hand, and she's trying to get to that job? I'd like to work with children. That has been my real hopes in life.

JOHN FULLER

He has been a mail carrier since 1964, though he's worked in the post office for twenty-six years. "Back in '47 I was a clerk at the finance window. I had a break in the service and came back as a truckdriver. I was a little confined. Bein' a carrier gives me more street time where I'm meeting more of the public." He is forty-eight years old.

I'm doing a job that's my life ambition. When I was in school, you said in the yearbook what you're most likely to be. I did say mailman. First thing came to my mind. As a kid, when I was coming up, I didn't have any idea this would wind up as my chosen profession. It has.

This is a profession that everyone has looked up to and respected. They always say, "Here comes the mailman"—pony express or something. This always brought a gleam to everybody's eye. Everyone likes to receive mail. I feel it is one of the most respected professions that is throughout the nation. You're doing a job for the public and a job for the country.

It's getting to a point where it's payin' now. Used to be they didn't pay 'em much. Everyone thought the mailman was making much more than he makes, "Aw, you got a good job, you're makin' lots of money." What it takes to live, you're barely scraping it, just barely getting along.

You find that most people in the post office have two jobs. Some of 'em have three jobs. I have had two most of the time. Now I only have one. My wife, she's working. If she wasn't, I don't know how we'd make it.

Now the top is eleven thousand dollars. This is just the last couple of years, they'd progressed to that status. For quite a while, the top was only in the seven thousand bracket. A mailman, breaking in, he makes somewhere along $3.60 an hour. This is subs. They progress somewhere about seven cents a year.

Everybody in the post office are moonlighting. We have a lot of men in the post office and their wives also in the post office. There are more women carriers today. And they're doing a bang-up job. It's a fabulous job for a woman. At the eleven-thousand-dollar bracket after eight years, it's a nice piece of change for a woman.

My day starts at four o'clock. I hit the floor. At five thirty I'm at work. We pull mail from the cases that the night clerks have thrown. I start casin', throwin' letters. At my station we have fifty-three carriers. Each one has a pigeonhole that his mail goes in. You are constantly pulling mail out of these pigeonholes.

I have one big office building downtown and a smaller one. Each firm is a case. As you work on a case, you get to know the people who get personal mail. You throw it to that firm. I have sixty different outfits in the building that I service. Downtown is much easier than the residential district. You could have about 540 separations in the residential. I know about ninety percent of the people in the office building. We are on a first name basis.

I make two trips a day. The mail is relayed by truck. I get over to the building, I unsack it and line it up according to various offices. Then I start my distribution, floor by floor. We have twenty-three floors in this building. I take the elevator up to the fifteenth, and as I go up, I drop the mail off on each floor. Then I walk down and make the distributions. Later, I get the upper floors.

The various people I meet in the building, we're constantly chatting, world affairs and everything. You don't have a chance to go off daydreaming. My day ends about two o'clock. During the day I might feel sluggish, but at quitting time you always feel happy.

I worked residential six months and flew back downtown. (Laughs.) Quite a bit more walking there. I had one district that covered thirty-two blocks. In a residential district you have relay boxes. It's a large brown box, which you probably see settin' on a corner next to the red, white, and blue box. You have a key that will open this. You have maybe three relay boxes in your district. You can run about twenty-five miles a day. If I had a pedometer, I'd be clocked around ten on this job.

Walking is good for you. It keeps you active. You more or less feel better. The bag's on my shoulder with me at all times. It varies from two pounds to thirty-five—which is the limit you're supposed to carry. The shoulder's not affected. Just keep goin', that's all.

Constantly you walk. You go home and put your feet in a hot basin after. That feels good. About twice a week, you give 'em a good soakin'. When I'm home, I keep 'em elevated, stay off 'em as much as possible, give 'em a lot of rest. I wear out on the average about three or five pairs of shoes a year. When I first started the bag, seemed like I was carryin' a ton. But as you go along, the bag isn't getting any lighter but you're getting accustomed to it.

When I come home, I walk in the door, turn the one-eyed monster TV on, take my uniform off, sit on the couch to watch a story, and usually go to sleep. (Laughs.) Around six, seven o'clock, my wife comes home. "You tired?" "Somewhat." So I watch TV again with her and eat dinner. Nine thirty, ten o'clock, I'm ready for bed.

If you've got a second job, you get off at two, hustle and bustle off to that second job. You get off from there eight, nine o'clock and you rush home, you rush to bed. Sleep fast and get up and start all over again. I've had a second job up until last year. I tried to get away from walkin' on that one. To find something wherein I was stationary in one spot. But most of my part-time jobs have always been deliveries. I was on the move at all times. If I hadn't been on the move, I would probably be asleep on the job. Moving about on my feet kept me awake.

Most things a carrier would contend with is dogs. You think he won't bite, but as soon as you open the door the dog charges out past the patron and he clips you. This is a very hectic experience for the mailman. On a lot of residential streets, you have dog packs roaming, and a lot of times you don't know whether the dog is friendly or not. You try to make friends with him in order that you won't be attacked. In some cases, he'll walk your district with you. He'd walk this block with you. When you reach the corner, he'd turn back and go home. (Laughs.) You got a vicious dog, he chases after you.

(Sighs.) There's more dogs nowadays. Yes, they have dogs that's always out. Oh, I've been attacked. (Laughs.) I've had several instances where dogs have made me jump fences. One was over in a vacant lot. I was about a hundred yards from him. I was doing steps and coming down. I'm watching him, and he's evidently watching me. As I pass this lot, here he comes, It's a middle-class white area. The woman, she was walking down the street. She musta knew the dog. She called him by name and shooed at him. Shot mace at him. (Laughs.) She come up and said, "I'm sorry he's bothering you." She spoke to him and told him to go and he went off.

Most people have the mailman pretty well timed as to what time he'll be around. You have old lady pensioners. You have ADC. They're constantly waiting for checks. They're always waiting. If they miss you on this block, they will run around to the next block. "Mailman, you got my check?" (Laughs.) You know it's not there 'cause you know what you have. "Look in the bag again. It might be mixed up with somebody else's mail." You look anyway to make 'em feel good. You know who are getting checks. Therefore you have to be ready for 'em. Interesting life.

I'll work until retirement. I have the years of service but I don't have the age. Last year they made a special package. We could get out at twenty-five years of service and fifty-five years of age. I need seven more years. Retirement pays anywhere from $250 to $300 a month. Not much. That's why quite a few of 'em didn't go.

With thirty years of service, you can go up to seventy years of age. If the retirement's right, I'll not be here. At retirement, I'll be looking for another job where it wouldn't be life and butter. This other job would be just a supplement. I'm thinkin' about goin' in business for myself. So when I reach my reclining years I wouldn't have to work so hard.

Ever talk about your day's work with your wife?

No. She has enough problems of her own.

CONRAD SWIBEL

He is a gas meter reader. He has been at it for about a year. He is twenty-four, married. "I have a kid comin' July twenty-eighth. The first one. It'll be pretty exciting."

Reading gas meters, it's kind of a strenuous business. You have to do a lot of running around. Today I had a real bad book. It was crummy, 'cause I did Wilmette,* kinda the older homes. The houses are on an acre, half-acre plots, and you do a lot of walking. They call it juice if you got a good day. You got a juice book, a real good book. Today I didn't have a juice book. If I have all outside meters, I can read a hundred meters, which is a hundred homes, in an hour. I was doing maybe thirty-five in an hour today.

With the big homes, half of them will be in Florida. They have beautiful homes. I'd like to own a home like that, yeah. You usually go to the back door. I'll ring the doorbell, then I'll knock. I knock too loud, she'll get on me. If I just ring the doorbell and don't knock, they'll say, "Why didn't you knock?" You get it all the time. If I knock, I get it. If I don't knock, I'll get it. Maybe eight out of ten homes, their doorbells don't work. Sometimes they're good enough to put a little sign up: Doorbell doesn't work, please knock.

You have the blue shirt with the gas company on a patch. During the wintertime they give you a badge, with your ID picture and all that. That helps you get in. They try to keep us on the same route so people will get used to you. People are suspicious.

They have some colored people who work for the gas company. They'll have the police called in on 'em almost every day they're out there. They'll have an older woman and she'll say, "Oh my God, a colored person!" She'll think he's breaking into the house. They have these big Afros. I have a nice face, so they don't bug me. The colored gas meter readers get followed all the time when they go down in the basement—which slows you up. They ask, "You read it that quick? Come back here and read it again." Wow, I read it, leave me alone.

In Evanston I do the colored section and the white section. Maybe five out of ten colored homes would have dogs, where eight out of nine or ten white homes would have dogs. The worst ones are the schnauzers and the poodles. They'll bite you in the knee or in the leg. Almost every time you'll go into a house, they jump on ya and

* An upper-middle-class suburb north of Chicago.

sniff ya and if you do three hundred homes a day, it gets aggravating.

I've been bit once already by a German shepherd. And that was something. It was really scary. It was an outside meter the woman had. I read the gas meter and was walking back out and heard a woman yell. I turned around and this German shepherd was comin' at me. The first thing I thought of was that he might go for my throat, like the movies. So I sort of crouched down and gave him my arm instead of my neck. He grabbed a hold of my arm, bit that, turned around. My arm was kinda soft, so I thought I'd give him something harder. So I gave him my hand. A little more bone in that. So he bit my hand.

I gave it to him so he wouldn't bite my throat. I didn't want him to grab hold of my face. He turned around again and by that time—they usually give you a three-cell flashlight, a pretty big one—I had that out and caught him right in the mouth. And he took the flashlight away from me. I jammed it in his mouth and he just ripped it away. I jumped a six-foot fence tryin' to get away from him, 'cause then I had my senses back. It was maybe in five seconds this all happened.

Were you badly hurt?

No. Just a hole right here in my arm. (Indicates a livid scar.) I was cussin' pretty good, too. She was tryin' to call the dog back, which made me turn around. Otherwise he'd probably got me in the back. I'm just glad I turned around.

You can usually tell if a dog's gonna bite ya. You're just waitin' for him to do somethin' and then you can clobber him. The gas company'll stay behind you in that kind of thing. That's the biggest part of a dog's day, when the gas man comes. (Laughs.)

I've gone into houses where the woman will say, "Let me grab the dog. I don't want you to give him a hard time." I've had one house where I was trying to make friends with the dog. He was a schnauzer. I started to walk away because it was just barking its little fool head off. It just fell over on its side. I thought it had a heart attack. She said, "He usually relapses from barking too much." She gave me a glare like it was my fault.

Usually they'll say, "Don't hit the dog." If it's bad

enough, I usually hit him in the head with the flashlight, to knock it away. Then they'll say, "Why did you hit it? The dog's not gonna bite you." I say, "It's jumping on me, it's scratching me." And she says, "All it's doing is scratching you?" It's weird. It's not biting me, it's scratching me. (Laughs.) So that's okay.

When nobody's looking. . . ?

You kick him down the stairs usually. (Laughs.) Usually the dog will follow you down the stairs or back up. That'll give you a good chance, 'cause the dog'll try to pass you. So you would kick him down the stairs. (Laughs.) Even if he just follows you down the stairs you try to get him for the one you missed a couple of houses back. Many people will report you if you abuse a dog. But what about *me?*

People complain to the company for jumping over their fence or going across their grass. I usually don't jump fences any more unless I'm in a hurry. The boss is usually nice about it. It'll get to him and he'll say, "Okay, it won't happen again." They mark down a code nine in the book: Do not cross the lawn or do not jump the fence. Older people that take care of their lawns don't like nobody to cross their lawns—which is kind of weird.

I got a good letter one time, not that I've gotten bad ones. I really deserve maybe six to ten letters. Maybe a woman was crippled in the house and I'll waste five, ten minutes of my time, and I'll say, "I'll give you a cup of coffee." And they'll say, "Thanks a lot," and I'm on my way. What would it hurt to write in and say this guy really helped me out?

They don't want to be bothered to come to the door. They'd rather have something else to do than answer the doorbell and let the gas man in. Why can't they say, "I don't want to admit you in my home at the present time cause it's dirty?" I can tell you something. Most of the houses are dirty, they're filthy. They stink. I have one woman, she's got fifteen cats and she's got 'em down in the basement. I'll walk down there and walk right out without reading the gas meter. Yeah, white middle class. Even in Wilmette, high class. The outside of the house is kept nice, beautiful, but when you get inside, when you get into the heart of it, it's filthy.

One guy was reading gas meters for eight years. He went to buy furniture. The next day he was supposed to read the gas meter at the store. He wanted me to go in because he didn't want the salesman to see him, to know that he was a gas meter reader. He was embarrassed. It doesn't really matter what kind of job you do, as long as you're working.

The meter readers is the bread of the whole company. Without these people being billed and having the money come into the gas company, the other employees wouldn't get paid. You have to know how to read a meter, 'cause if you make a mistake, it could be maybe the guy would pay another hundred dollars more. It's kinda tricky. There's four dials. The company gives you a high and a low. Let's say 3000 for the low and 5000 for the high. It's usually about 4000, right dead in the middle. You have to go there and make sure they're using the middle. I can read a meter from twenty, thirty feet away.

There's a guy been reading meters for eight or nine years now and he's getting old. I can't see doing it for eight years. I'd probably age incredibly. Because I'm bad with putting on weight anyway, and with this running I do. My wife bought me one of these walk-a-mile meters that you can put on your belt, little Japanese thing. I found out I walk about eight, ten miles a day. So I don't have to worry about getting a heart attack for quite a long time. (Laughs.)

I usually start reading meters at nine o'clock and with an eight-hour day I'm usually done by noon. I'm pretty quick. You learn to pace yourself. Usually if they keep you on a book long enough, you can tell if the people are home and which is a good home to miss, 'cause if the people give you a bad time, you say, "We'll catch you in a couple of months." If they took maybe a little too much time to peek through the window, I'm off. I'm rushed and they're rushed.

My boss and the boss before him were meter readers and they would have the same book as I had. What was usually an eight-hour day took them four hours, so they're not gonna rat on me. Five years ago, they were doing the same thing. It's more or less going through the ranks. Like you're a private, then private first class. You have to go up that way.

When I get home I'm usually calling out numbers to

myself. Usually four numbers. Like the last house I read: 2652. I'll be home and I'll be going 2652, 2652, 2652. It'll just be going through my mind: 2652. Like a song you hear too much.

"When I was a little kid I wanted to be a baseball pitcher. I went through Little League, Pony League, and went to college for a year and a half, when I got drafted. Baseball would have been nice. Good yearly sum." (Laughs.)

The gas company's really been good with the pay. Out of every two weeks I'll make about $250 clear after taxes—which isn't bad. For being there a year, that's real good—and working half a day. Every couple of months they'll put in a nickel or a dime more. You don't even have to ask 'em.

We're starting to get young guys in now. The older you get, the more chance you have of being promoted. Over twenty-six we'll say as being old. We have from eighteen, nineteen, twenty. They start flourishing at twenty, twenty-one. What they're trying to do is get married people. They don't want to hire eighteen, nineteen-year-olds. Because they have a thing called curbing, where a guy could sit in his car and mark the numbers down themselves. Take an estimate reading. The computer would catch him, but it would maybe take three, four months. By that time, the guy would have six, eight hundred bucks and he'll go work in a gas station or whatever. They just want somebody with responsibilities.

There's big rumors going around that they'll be able to call your phone number and it'll divert to the gas meter, and the reading will come through on the telephone. I hope by that time I'll be in a different field. But I like it for now.

Sometimes they'll ask you if you want something to drink or a Coke. Then I'll sit around and talk to the people, 'cause if they're nice enough to offer me a cookie or a coke, I'll say, "Sure" (laughs), and shoot the breeze for five or ten minutes. I wish it would happen more often. Then I'd probably get done at the normal time. I would probably take my time a bit more. Usually I have to go outside and get the hose going and sneak a drink of water that way. If they caught me, they'd wonder what I was doing. Most people are just preoccupied or overwhelmed with what they have to do, rather than bother with me. Maybe they have their laundry to do.

The big subject of conversation with us is dogs and women. "You shoulda seen this one in a bathing suit, real cute." If you have a nice cute chicken, that kinda brightens up your whole day. If they're younger women and they're nice looking, we have a code we put on the card. We put a Q—that stands for cutie. Then the guy'll stop and read the house for sure. But they've never gotten down to the nitty-gritty.

There's been times when the little boy would let you in and say, "Go down in the basement." I don't do this no more. When I first started, I didn't know any better. So I went down and the woman was doing her laundry nude. It shocked me as much as it shocked her. I had one woman answer the door nude. She told me later she thought it was her girl friend. I thought I was the electric meter man instead of the gas meter man when I opened the door. (Laughs.) Completely confused. Nothing's happened physically yet. One of these days it will.

I do this one Jewish party in Skokie. The women there, I wouldn't say they're pretty wild, but they're older and when they see a young man come in the house, wants to read their gas meter, you know. (Laughs.) It's that kind of thing. It would depend on the women. I wouldn't . . .

If you see a nice lady sitting there in a two-piece bathing suit—if you work it right and they'll be laying on their stomach in the sun and they'll have their top strap undone—if you go there and you scare 'em good enough, they'll jump up. To scare 'em where they jump up and you would be able to see them better, this takes time and it gives you something to do. It adds excitement to your day. If you startle 'em they'll say, "You could've said something earlier, rather than just jumping up behind me yelling, 'Gas man'!" You have to make excitement for yourself.

Usually women follow you downstairs to make sure that maybe you're not gonna take nothin'. It definitely is a reflection. Of course, if she's wearing a nice short skirt, you follow her back up the stairs. (Laughs.) It's to occupy your day, you know? To pass the time of the day.

BRETT HAUSER

He is seventeen. He had worked as a box boy at a super-market in a middle-class suburb on the outskirts of Los Angeles. "People come to the counter and you put things in their bags for them. And carry things to their cars. It was a grind."

You have to be terribly subservient to people: "Ma'am, can I take your bag?" "Can I do this?" It was at a time when the grape strikers were passing out leaflets. They were very respectful. People'd come into the check stand, they'd say, "I just bought grapes for the first time because of those idiots outside." I had to put their grapes in the bag and thank them for coming and take them outside to the car. Being subservient made me very resentful.

It's one of a chain of supermarkets. They're huge complexes with bakeries in them and canned music over those loud-speakers—Muzak. So people would relax while they shopped. They played selections from *Hair*. They'd play "Guantanamera," the Cuban Revolution song. They had *Soul on Ice*, the Cleaver book, on sale. They had everything dressed up and very nice. People wouldn't pay any attention to the music. They'd go shopping and hit their kids and talk about those idiots passing out anti-grape petitions.

Everything looks fresh and nice. You're not aware that in the back room it stinks and there's crates all over the place and the walls are messed up. There's graffiti and people are swearing and yelling at each other. You walk through the door, the music starts playing, and everything is pretty. You talk in hushed tones and are very respectful.

You wear a badge with your name on it. I once met someone I knew years ago. I remembered his name and said, "Mr. Castle, how are you?" We talked about this and that. As he left, he said, "It was nice talking to you, Brett." I felt great, he remembered me. Then I looked down at my name plate. Oh shit. He didn't remember me at all, he just read the name plate. I wish I had put "Irving" down on my name plate. If he'd have said, "Oh yes, Irv-

ing, how could I forget you. . . ?" I'd have been ready for
him. There's nothing personal here.

You have to be very respectful to everyone—the customers, to the manager, to the checkers. There's a sign on
the cash register that says: Smile at the customer. Say
hello to the customer. It's assumed if you're a box boy,
you're really there 'cause you want to be a manager some
day. So you learn all the little things you have absolutely
no interest in learning.

The big things there is to be an assistant manager and
eventually manager. The male checkers had dreams of
being manager, too. It was like an internship. They enjoyed watching how the milk was packed. Each manager
had his own domain. There was the ice cream manager,
the grocery manager, the dairy case manager . . . They
had a sign in the back: Be good to your job and your job
will be good to you. So you take an overriding concern on
how the ice cream is packed. You just die if something
falls off a shelf. I saw so much crap there I just couldn't
take. There was a black boy, an Oriental box boy, and a
kid who had a Texas drawl. They needed the job to sub-
sist. I guess I had the luxury to hate it and quit.

When I first started there, the manager said, "Cut your
hair. Come in a white shirt, black shoes, a tie. Be here on
time." You get there, but he isn't there. I just didn't know
what to do. The checker turns around and says, "You
new? What's your name?" "Brett." "I'm Peggy." And
that's all they say and they keep throwing this down to
you. They'll say, "Don't put it in that, put it in there." But
they wouldn't help you.

You had to keep your apron clean. You couldn't lean
back on the railings. You couldn't talk to the checkers.
You couldn't accept tips. Okay, I'm outside and I put it in
the car. For a lot of people, the natural reaction is to take
out a quarter and give it to me. I'd say, "I'm sorry, I
can't." They'd get offended. When you give someone a tip,
you're sort of suave. You take a quarter and you put it in
their palm and you expect them to say, "Oh, thanks a lot."
When you say, "I'm sorry, I can't," they feel a little put
down. They say, "No one will know." And they put it in
your pocket. You say, "I really can't." It gets to a point
where you have to do physical violence to a person to
avoid being tipped. It was not consistent with the store's
philosophy of being cordial. Accepting tips was a cordial

thing and made the customer feel good. I just couldn't understand the incongruity. One lady actually put it in my pocket, got in the car, and drove away. I would have had to throw the quarter at her or eaten it or something.

When it got slow, the checkers would talk about funny things that happened. About Us and Them. Us being the people who worked there. Them being the stupid fools who didn't know where anything was—just came through and messed everything up and shopped. We serve them but we don't like them. We know where everything is. We know what time the market closes and they don't. We know what you do with coupons and they don't. There was a camaraderie of sorts. It wasn't healthy, though. It was a put-down of the others.

There was this one checker who was absolutely vicious. He took great delight in making every little problem into a major crisis from which he had to emerge victorious. A customer would give him a coupon. He'd say, "You were supposed to give me that at the beginning." She'd say, "Oh, I'm sorry." He'd say, "Now I gotta open the cash register and go through the whole thing. Madame, I don't watch out for every customer. I can't manage your life." A put-down.

It never bothered me when I would put something in the bag wrong. In the general scheme of things, in the large questions of the universe, putting a can of dog food in the bag wrong is not of great consequence. For them it was.

There were a few checkers who were nice. There was one that was incredibly sad. She could be unpleasant at times, but she talked to everybody. She was one of the few people who genuinely wanted to talk to people. She was saying how she wanted to go to school and take courses so she could get teaching credit. Someone asked her, "Why don't you?" She said, "I have to work here. My hours are wrong. I'd have to get my hours changed." They said, "Why don't you?" She's worked there for years. She had seniority. She said, "Jim won't let me." Jim was the manager. He didn't give a damn. She wanted to go to school, to teach, but she can't because every day she's got to go back to the supermarket and load groceries. Yet she wasn't bitter. If she died a checker and never enriched her life, that was okay, because those were her hours.

She was extreme in her unpleasantness and her consideration. Once I dropped some grape juice and she was squawking like a bird. I came back and mopped it up. She kept saying to me, "Don't worry about it. It happens to all of us." She'd say to the customers, "If I had a dime for all the grape juice I dropped . . ."

Jim's the boss. A fish-type handshake. He was balding and in his forties. A lot of managers are these young, clean-shaven, neatly cropped people in their twenties. So Jim would say things like "groovy." You were supposed to get a ten-minute break every two hours. I lived for that break. You'd go outside, take your shoes off, and be human again. You had to request it. And when you took it they'd make you feel guilty.

You'd go up and say, "Jim, can I have a break?" He'd say, "A break? You want a break? Make it a quick one, nine and a half minutes." Ha ha ha. One time I asked the assistant manager, Henry. He was even older than Jim. "Do you think I can have a break?" He'd say, "You got a break when you were hired." Ha ha ha. Even when they joked it was a put-down.

The guys who load the shelves are a step above the box boys. It's like upperclassmen at an officer candidate's school. They would make sure that you conformed to all the prescribed rules, because they were once box boys. They know what you're going through, your anxieties. But instead of making it easier for you, they'd make it harder. It's like a military institution.

I kept getting box boys who came up to me, "Has Jim talked to you about your hair? He's going to because it's getting too long. You better get it cut or grease it back or something." They took delight in it. They'd come to me before Jim had told me. Everybody was out putting everybody down . . .

BABE SECOLI

She's a checker at a supermarket. She's been at it for almost thirty years. "I started at twelve—a little, privately owned grocery store across the street from the house. They didn't have no cash registers. I used to mark the prices down on a paper bag.

"When I got out of high school, I didn't want no secretary job. I wanted the grocery job. It was so interesting for a young girl. I just fell into it. I don't know no other work but this. It's hard work, but I like it. This is my life."

We sell everything here, millions of items. From potato chips and pop—we even have a genuine pearl in a can of oysters. It sells for two somethin'. Snails with the shells that you put on the table, fanciness. There are items I never heard of we have here. I know the price of every one. Sometimes the boss asks me and I get a kick out of it. There isn't a thing you don't want that isn't in this store.

You sort of memorize the prices. It just comes to you. I know half a gallon of milk is sixty-four cents; a gallon, $1.10. You look at the labels. A small can of peas, Raggedy Ann. Green Giant, that's a few pennies more. I know Green Giant's eighteen and I know Raggedy Ann is fourteen. I know Del Monte is twenty-two. But lately the prices jack up from one day to another. Margarine two days ago was forty-three cents. Today it's forty-nine. Now when I see Imperial comin' through, I know it's forty-nine cents. You just memorize. On the register is a list of some prices, that's for the part-time girls. I never look at it.

I don't have to look at the keys on my register. I'm like the secretary that knows her typewriter. The touch. My hand fits. The number nine is my big middle finger. The thumb is number one, two and three and up. The side of my hand uses the bar for the total and all that.

I use my three fingers—my thumb, my index finger, and my middle finger. The right hand. And my left hand is on the groceries. They put down their groceries. I got my hips pushin' on the button and it rolls around on the counter. When I feel I have enough groceries in front of me, I let go of my hip. I'm just movin'—the hips, the hand, and the register, the hips the hand, and the register ... (As she demonstrates, her hands and hips move in the manner of an Oriental dancer.) You just keep goin', one, two, one, two. If you've got that rhythm, you're a fast checker. Your feet are flat on the floor and you're turning your head back and forth.

Somebody talks to you. If you take your hand off the item, you're gonna forget what you were ringin'. It's the feel. When I'm pushin' the items through I'm always hav-

ing my hand on the items. If somebody interrupts to ask
me the price, I'll answer while I'm movin'. Like playin' a
piano.

I'm eight hours a day on my feet. It's just a physical
tire of standing up. When I get home I get my second
wind. As far as standin' there, I'm not tired. It's when I'm
roaming' around tryin' to catch a shoplifter. There's a lot
of shoplifters in here. When I see one, I'm ready to run
for them.

When my boss asks me how I know, I just know by the
movements of their hands. And with their purses and their
shopping bags and their clothing rearranged. You can just
tell what they're doin' and I'm never wrong so far.

The best kind shoplift. They're not doin' this because
they need the money. A very nice class of people off Lake
Shore Drive. They do it every day—men and women.
Lately it's been more or less these hippies, livin' from day
to day . . .

It's meats. Some of these women have big purses. I
caught one here last week. She had two big packages of
sirloin strips in her purse. That amounted to ten dollars.
When she came up to the register, I very politely said,
"Would you like to pay for anything else, without me embarrassing you?" My boss is standing right there. I called
him over. She looked at me sort of on the cocky side. I
said, "I know you have meat in your purse. Before your
neighbors see you, you either pay for it or take it out."
She got very snippy. That's where my boss stepped in.
"Why'd you take the meat?" She paid for it.

Nobody knows it. I talk very politely. My boss doesn't
do anything drastic. If they get rowdy, he'll raise his voice
to embarrass 'em. He tells them not to come back in the
store again.

I have one comin' in here, it's razor blades. He's a very
nice dressed man in his early sixties. He doesn't need these
razor blades any more than the man in the moon. I've
been following him and he knows it. So he's layin' low on
the razor blades. It's little petty things like this. They're
mad at somebody, so they have to take their anger out on
something.

We had one lady, she pleaded with us that she wanted
to come back—not to have her husband find out. My boss
told her she was gonna be watched wherever she went.
But that was just to put a little fright in her. Because she

was just an elderly person. I would be too embarrassed to come into a store if this would happen. But I guess it's just the normal thing these days—any place you go. You have to feel sorry for people like this. I like 'em all.

My family gets the biggest kick out of the shoplifters: "What happened today?" (Laughs.) This is about the one with the meat in her purse. She didn't need that meat any more than the man in the moon.

Some of 'em, they get angry and perturbed at the prices, and they start swearin' at me. I just look at 'em. You have to consider the source. I just don't answer them, because before you know it I'll get in a heated argument. The customer's always right. Doesn't she realize I have to buy the same food? I go shopping and pay the same prices. I'm not gettin' a discount. The shoplifters, they say to me. "Don't you want for something?" Yes, I want and I'm standing on my feet all day and I got varicose veins. But I don't walk out of here with a purse full of meat. When I want a piece of steak I buy a piece of steak.

My feet, they hurt at times, very much so. When I was eighteen years old I put the bathing suit on and I could see the map on my leg. From standing, standing. And not the proper shoes. So I wear like nurse's shoes with good inner sole arch support, like Dr. Scholl's. They ease the pain and that's it. Sometimes I go to bed, I'm so tired that I can't sleep. My feet hurt as if I'm standing while I'm in bed.

I love my job. I've got very nice bosses. I got a black manager and he's just beautiful. They don't bother you as long as you do your work. And the pay is terrific. I automatically get a raise because of the union. Retail Clerks. Right now I'm ready for retirement as far as the union goes. I have enough years. I'm as high up as I can go. I make $189 gross pay. When I retire I'll make close to five hundred dollars a month. This is because of the union. Full benefits. The business agents all know me by name. The young kids don't stop and think what good the union's done.

Sometimes I feel some of these girls are overpaid. They don't do the work they're supposed to be doin'. Young girls who come in, they just go plunk, plunk, so slow. All the old customers, they say, "Let's go to Babe," because I'm fast. That's why I'm so tired while these young girls are going dancin' at night. They don't really put pride in

their work. To me, this is living. At times, when I feel
sick, I come to work feelin' I'll pep up here. Sometimes it
doesn't. (Laughs.)

I'm a checker and I'm very proud of it. There's some,
they say, "A checker—ugh!" To me, it's like somebody
being a teacher or a lawyer. I'm not ashamed that I wear
a uniform and nurse's shoes and that I got varicose veins.
I'm makin' an honest living. Whoever looks down on me,
they're lower than I am.

What irritates me is when customers get very cocky
with me. "Hurry up," or "Cash my check quick." I don't
think this is right. You wait your time and I'll give you my
full, undivided attention. You rush and you're gonna get
nothin'. Like yesterday, I had two big orders on my counter and I push the groceries down, and she says, "I have
to be somewhere in ten minutes. Hurry up and bag that."
You don't talk that way to me or any other checker.

I'm human, I'm working for a living. They belittle me
sometimes. They use a little profanity sometimes. I stop
right there and I go get the manager. Nobody is gonna
call me a (cups hand over mouth, whispers) b-i-t-c-h.
These are the higher class of people, like as if I'm their
housekeeper or their maid. You don't even talk to a maid
like this.

I make mistakes, I'm not infallible. I apologize. I catch
it right there and then. I tell my customers, "I over-
charged you two pennies on this. I will take it off of your
next item." So my customers don't watch me when I ring
up. They trust me. But I had one this morning—with this
person I say, "How are you?" That's the extent of our conversation. She says to me, "Wait. I want to check you." I
just don't bother. I make like I don't even know she's
there or I don't even hear her. She's ready for an argument. So I say, "Stop right there and then. I'll give you a
receipt when I'm through. If there's any mistakes I'll correct them." These people, I can't understand them—and I
can't be bothered with their little trifles because I've got
my next customer that wants to get out . . .

It hurts my feelings when they distrust me. I wouldn't
cheat nobody, because it isn't going in my pocket. If I
make an honest mistake, they call you a thief, they call
you a ganef. I'm far from bein' a ganef.

Sometimes I feel my face gettin' so red that I'm so aggravated, I'm a total wreck. My family says, "We better

not talk to her today. She's had a bad day." They say, "What happened?" I'll look at 'em and I'll start laughin', because this is not a policy to bring home your work. You leave your troubles at the store and vice versa. But there's days when you can't cope with it. But it irons out.

"When you make a mistake, you get three chances. Then they take it out of your pay, which is right. You can't make a ten-dollar mistake every week. It's fishy. What's this nonsense? If I give a customer ten dollars too much, it's your own fault. That's why they got these registers with the amounts tendered on it. You don't have to stop and count. I've never had such mistakes. It happens mostly with some of these young kids."

Years ago it was more friendlier, more sweeter. Now there's like tension in the air. A tension in the store. The minute you walk in you feel it. Everybody is fightin' with each other. They're pushin', pushin'—"I was first." Now it's an effort to say, "Hello, how are you?" It must be the way of people livin' today. Everything is so rush, rush, rush, and shovin'. Nobody's goin' anywhere. I think they're pushin' themselves right to a grave, some of these people.

A lot of traffic here. There's bumpin' into each other with shoppin' carts. Some of 'em just do it intentionally. When I'm shoppin', they just jam you with the carts. That hits your ankle and you have a nice big bruise there. You know who does this the most? These old men that shop. These *men.* They're terrible and just *jam* you. Sometimes I go over and tap them on the shoulder: "Now why did you do this?" They look at you and they just start *laughin'.* It's just hatred in them, they're bitter. They hate themselves, maybe they don't feel good that day. They gotta take their anger out on somethin', so they just *jam* you. It's just ridiculous.

I know some of these people are lonesome. They have really nobody. They got one or two items in their cart and they're just shoppin' for an hour, just dallying along, talkin' to other people. They tell them how they feel, what they did today. It's just that they want to get it out, these old people. And the young ones are rushin' to a PTA meeting or somethin', and they just glance at these people and got no time for 'em.

We have this little coffee nook and we serve free coffee.

A lot of people come in for the coffee and just walk out. I have one old lady, she's got no place to go. She sits in front of the window for hours. She'll walk around the store, she'll come back. I found out she's all alone, this old lady. No family, no nothin'. From my register I see the whole bit.

I wouldn't know how to go in a factory. I'd be like in a prison. Like this, I can look outside, see what the weather is like. I want a little fresh air, I walk out the front door, take a few sniffs of air, and come back in. I'm here forty-five minutes early every morning. I've never been late except for that big snowstorm. I never thought of any other work.

I'm a couple of days away, I'm very lonesome for this place. When I'm on a vacation, I can't wait to go, but two or three days away, I start to get fidgety. I can't stand around and do nothin'. I have to be busy at all times. I look forward to comin' to work. It's a great feelin'. I enjoy it somethin' terrible.

THOMAS RUSH

We're in a modern bungalow in a middle-class black community. It is an area of one-family dwellings with front lawns well-trimmed and cars carefully parked. An air of well-being pervades in this autumn twilight.

He is a lead skycap for one of the major airlines—"supervisor of passenger service. I make out the work schedule, who's going to work upstairs in the lobby, who's going to work downstairs, who's going to work the baggage claims area. I direct all the skycap traffic."

He's been at it since 1946. "When I came home from the service I was gonna go in the police department. While waiting for the call, I applied for a job at the airport and got it. The following day I was called by the police academy. My mother didn't want me to be a policeman. My wife didn't want me to be a policeman. So I said, 'What the heck, I'll just stay here and see what happens.' I've been here ever since." He is fifty-seven years old.

I've walked hundreds of miles on this job. I haven't really had too much problem with my feet. But I do get tired, very tired. (Laughs.) I'm wearing a knee supporter. One day I went to the check-in counter with a passenger that had excess baggage. As I turned to walk away, my knee just snapped. I went around first aid and she bandaged it for me. It comes and goes.

When I first started you carried all baggage by hand. Later, when we worked for individual airlines, you got two-wheel carts. Some fellas can put as many as eighteen to twenty bags on a cart. I've done it many times, but I don't do it any more. 'Cause I'm a little old now. I don't press myself.

The skycap came into being with the jet aircraft. We were called porters, redcaps. The man you meet now at the curb cannot be a dummy. He has to read tickets, he has to sell tickets. He has to get someone to take hotel reservations. You'd be surprised at the things people ask you to do.

We have to do a lot more than the general public thinks. They think of us as a strong back and a weak mind. They don't realize that what we're doing is the same thing they get when they walk to a counter. All the agent does is look at his ticket and check his bag. We have schedules in our pockets. I know if there's a meal on the plane. I know if there's cocktails, movies, and so forth. No one has to tell me this. From memory I know most flights on my shifts—where they go, what time they go, when they arrive.

We're the first and the last people to meet the passengers. We meet them when they get out of their cars or cabs and we meet them at baggage claim. Old people, especially, are anxious to talk to anybody that's working for the airlines. They want to be reassured. I tell them silly little stories: "You're not going to get the thrill you get on a roller coaster. There ain't nothin' gonna happen. Just relax and enjoy it. When you come back, I want you to look me up."

I look at everybody at eye level. I neither look down nor up. The day of the shuffle is gone. I better not see any one of the fellas that works for me doing it. Not ever! You do not have to do anything but be courteous and perform your job. This is all that is necessary. That perpetual grin I just don't dig. I have been told that I don't smile,

period. I said, "I don't think it's necessary." I smile when I
have something to smile about. Otherwise I don't. If I
make the passenger happy, that's all that's necessary.
I don't have a problem with people. Maybe it's the way I
carry myself. I'm strictly business at work. People just
don't run over me.

I had a sailor one night who walked up to me and said,
"Boy, where can a man get a drink?" I took him down to
the end of the terminal, under the steps, and cracked
him in the mouth. He was half-drunk and I didn't try to
hurt him. I said, "Now what were you telling me a few
moments ago?" He said, "Can't you take a joke?" I said
"Okay, boy, you can get a drink across the street." I just
thought I'd teach him a lesson. I was much younger then.
It was about twenty years ago.

The skycap makes a good living. If he didn't, he
wouldn't stay. We have fellas here with all kinds of degrees. They make more money doing what they're doing.
It's just that simple. Most fellas here are from forty-six
years old and up. You can't get this job and be a young
man. There are no openings. There will be an opening
when somebody retires or dies. I haven't known anyone to
quit and I've been here twenty-six years.

I wouldn't have a job that didn't make tips. But I would
not be a cab-driver. I would not be a waiter. I never
wanted to be a Pullman porter. These people here have a
dignity all their lives.

Yet I think I'm grossly underpaid in salary, because of
what we really do. There are fellas here that sell three or
four thousand dollars worth of seats a week. They don't
come anywhere close to making the salary that agents
make, that are doing absolutely nothing by way of selling.
We have people at the ticket counters who make two hundred dollars a month more than the average skycap. I'd
say the average skycap sells a thousand dollars a month
more than this man.

There are many people that will leave at the spur of the
moment. Salesmen, especially. There's no reservation or
anything. He just comes to the airport and wants to know
what airline has what flight going as soon as possible to his
destination. It's up to you to sell him your line. I don't
think our value is recognized. At the quarterly meeting the
company tells us how important we are, but they don't say
that on the UG-100s, when it comes to salary raises.

But we make it on tips. Every time I walk through that door I get money. And don't you think these people know I'm making money? I think most agents have a little animosity towards skycaps because they feel we're doing quite well. The ramp service man makes something more than five dollars an hour. He's the guy who puts the baggage in the pressurized cabins, brings them into the claiming area, and puts them on the belt. I take 'em and the man gives me four dollars. (Laughs.) He does all the work out in the cold and here comes Tom gettin' money. (Laughs.)

Supervisors don't bother us. If a supervisor comes to me and tells me he wants skycaps to do something and I say no, there isn't anything he can say about it. Would I ever want to be a supervisor? Of course not. He doesn't make as much money as I make. (Laughs.)

We prefer not to have a union. We make more money than most people out there. We get more benefits than the guys on the ramp, and they have a union. They're not dressed like we are, either. They wear dungarees and things. We don't wear that crap. We wear a uniform, we wear a suit. We're the elite of the fleet. (Laughs.)

POSTSCRIPT: *"Every one of the fellas on my shift own their own home. All our wives are good friends. We go around each other's homes occasionally. My wife is in the process of organizing the other wives into a stock buying club.*

"The house next door is a skycap's. Next door to him is a salesman. And next to him is a policeman, whose wife owns a beauty shop. This neighborhood has changed for the better. The house over there was always falling down and they never cut the grass. A white police lieutenant had it. He never painted it. Everything was peeling. Look at it now, all remodeled. Most people are surprised when they come out here. I wonder why. (Laughs.) Isn't that house gorgeous? It looks five hundred times better than when the lieutenant had it."

GRACE CLEMENTS

*She is a sparrow of a woman in her mid-forties. She has
eighteen grandchildren. "I got my family the easy way. I
married my family." She has worked in factories for the
past twenty-five years: "A punch press operator, oven un-
loader, sander, did riveting, stapling, light assembly ..."
She has been with one company for twenty-one years,
ARMCO Corporation.*

*During the last four years she has worked in the luggage
division of one of the corporation's subsidiaries. In the
same factory are made snowmobile parts, windshield de-
frosters, tilt caps, sewer tiles, and black paper speakers for
radios and TV sets.*

*"We're about twelve women that work in our area, one
for each tank. We're about one-third Puerto Rican and
Mexican, maybe a quarter black, and the rest of us are
white. We have women of all ages, from eighteen to sixty-
six, married, single, with families, without families.*

*"We have to punch in before seven. We're at our tank
approximately one or two minutes before seven to take over
from the girl who's leaving. The tanks run twenty-four
hours a day."*

The tank I work at is six-foot deep, eight-foot square. In
it is pulp, made of ground wood, ground glass, fiberglass, a
mixture of chemicals and water. It comes up through a
copper screen felter as a form, shaped like the luggage
you buy in the store.

In forty seconds you have to take the wet felt out of
the felter, put the blanket on—a rubber sheeting—to draw
out the excess moisture, wait two, three seconds, take the
blanket off, pick the wet felt up, balance it on your shoulder—there is no way of holding it without it tearing all to
pieces, it is wet and will collapse—reach over, get the hose,
spray the inside of this copper screen to keep it from plug-
ging, turn around, walk to the hot dry die behind you,
take the hot piece off with your opposite hand, set it on
the floor—this wet thing is still balanced on my shoulder—put the wet piece on the dry die, push this button

that lets the dry press down, inspect the piece we just took off, the hot piece, stack it, and count it—when you get a stack of ten, you push it over and start another stack of ten—then go back and put our blanket on the wet piece coming up from the tank . . . and start all over. Forty seconds. We also have to weigh every third piece in that time. It has to be within so many grams. We are constantly standing and moving. If you talk during working, you get a reprimand, because it is easy to make a reject if you're talking.

A thirty-inch luggage weighs up to fifteen pounds wet. The hot piece weighs between three to four pounds. The big luggage you'll maybe process only four hundred. On the smaller luggage, you'll run maybe 800, sometimes 850 a day. All day long is the same thing over and over. That's about ten steps every forty seconds about 800 times a day.

We work eight straight hours, with two ten-minute breaks and one twenty-minute break for lunch. If you want to use the washroom, you have to do that in that time. By the time you leave your tank, you go to the washroom, freshen up a bit, go into the recreation room, it makes it very difficult to finish a small lunch and be back in the tank in twenty minutes. So you don't really have too much time for conversation. Many of our women take a half a sandwich or some of them don't even take anything. I'm a big eater. I carry a lunch box, fruit, a half a sandwich, a little cup of cottage cheese or salad. I find it very difficult to complete my lunch in the length of time.

You cannot at any time leave the tank. The pieces in the die will burn while you're gone. If you're real, real, real sick and in urgent need, you do shut it off. You turn on the trouble light and wait for the tool man to come and take your place. But they'll take you to a nurse and check it out.

The job I'm doing is easier than the punch presses I used to run. It's still not as fast as the punch press, where you're putting out anywhere to five hundred pieces an hour. Whereas here you can have a couple of seconds to rest in. I mean *seconds*. (laughs.) You have about two seconds to wait while the blanket is on the felt drawing the moisture out. You can stand and relax those two seconds—three seconds at most. You wish you didn't have to work in a factory. When it's all you know what to do, that's what you do.

I guess my scars are pretty well healed by now, because I've been off on medical leave for two, three months. Ordinarily I usually have two, three burn spots. It's real hot, and if it touches you for a second, it'll burn your arm. Most of the girls carry scars all the time.

We had two or three serious accidents in the last year and a half. One happened about two weeks ago to a woman on the hydraulic lift. The cast-iron extension deteriorated with age and cracked and the die dropped. It broke her whole hand. She lost two fingers and had plastic surgery to cover the burn. The dry die runs anywhere from 385 degrees to 425.

We have wooden platforms where we can walk on. Some of the tanks have no-skid strips on to keep you from slipping, 'cause the floor gets wet. The hose we wash the felter with will sometimes have leaks and will spray back on you. Sometimes the tanks will overflow. You can slip and fall. And slipping on oil. The hydraulic presses leak every once in a while. We've had a number of accidents. I currently have a workman's comp suit going. I came up under an electric switch box with my elbow and injured the bone and muscle where it fastens together. I couldn't use it.

I have arthritis in the joints of some of my fingers. Your hands handling hot pieces perspire and you end up with rheumatism or arthritis in your fingers. Naturally in your shoulder, balancing that wet piece. You've got the heat, you've got the moisture because there's steam coming out. You have the possibility of being burnt with steam when the hot die hits that wet felt. You're just engulfed in a cloud of steam every forty seconds.

It's very noisy. If the tool man comes to talk to you, the noise is great enough you have to almost shout to make yourself heard. There's the hissing of the steam, there's the compressed air, a lot of pressure—it's gotta lift that fifteen pounds and break it loose from that copper screen. I've lost a certain percentage of my hearing already. I can't hear the phone in the yard. The family can.

In the summertime, the temperature ranges anywhere from 100 to 150 degrees at our work station. I've taken thermometers and checked it out. You've got three open presses behind you. There's nothing between you and that heat but an asbestos sheet. They've recently put in air conditioning in the recreation room. There's been quite a little discussion between the union and the company on this. They carry the air conditioning too low for the people on the presses. Our temperature will be up to 140, and to go into an air-conditioned recreation room that might be set at 72—'cause the office force is happy and content with it—people on the presses almost faint when they go back. We really suffer.

I'm chairman of the grievance committee.* We have quite a few grievances. Sometimes we don't have the support we should have from our people. Sometimes the company is obstinate. For the most part, many of our grievances are won.

Where most people get off at three, I get off at two o'clock. I have an hour to investigate grievances, to work on them, to write them up, to just in general check working conditions. I'm also the editor of the union paper. I do all my own work. I cut stencils, I write the articles, copy the pictures. I'm not a very good freehand artist (laughs), so I copy them. I usually do that in the union office before I go home and make supper. It takes about five hours to do a paper. Two nights.

(Laughs.) I daydream while I'm working. Your mind gets so it automatically picks out the flaws. I plan my paper and what I'm going to have for supper and what we're gonna do for the weekend. My husband and I have a sixteen-foot boat. We spend a lot of weekends and evenings on the river. And I try to figure out how I'm gonna feed twenty, twenty-five people for dinner on Saturday. And how to solve a grievance . . .

They can't keep the men on the tanks. We've never been able to keep a man over a week. They say it's too monotonous. I think women adjust to monotony better than men do. Because their minds are used to doing two things at once, where a man usually can do one thing at a time. A woman is used to listening to a child tell her something while she's doing something else. She might be making a cake while the child is asking her a question. She can answer that child and continue to put that cake together. It's the same way on the tanks. You get to be au-

---

* It is a local of the UAW.

tomatic in what you're doing and your mind is doing something else.

I was one of the organizers here (laughs) when the union came in. I was as anti-union in the beginning as I am union now. Coming from a small farming community in Wisconsin. I didn't know what a union was all about. I didn't understand the labor movement at all. In school you're shown the bad side of it.

Before the union came in, all I did was do my eight hours, collect my paycheck, and go home, did my housework, took care of my daughter, and went back to work. I had no outside interests. You just lived to live. Since I became active in the union, I've become active in politics, in the community, in legislative problems. I've been to Washington on one or two trips. I've been to Springfield. That has given me more of an incentive for life.

I see the others, I'm sad. They just come to work, do their work, go home, take care of their home, and come back to work. Their conversation is strictly about their family and meals. They live each day for itself and that's about it.

"I tried to get my children to finish vocational school. One of the girls works for a vending machine company, serving hot lunches. She makes good. One of the daughters does waitress work. One of the girls has gone into factory work. One of the boys is in a factory. He would like to work up to maintenance. One girl married and doesn't do any work at all. My husband is a custodian in a factory. He likes his work as a janitor. There's no pushing him.

"This summer I've been quite ill and they've been fussin' about me. (Laughs.) Monday and Tuesday my two daughters and I made over sixty quarts of peaches, made six batches of jam. On Wednesday we made five batches of wild grape jelly. We like to try new recipes. I like to see something different on the table every night. I enjoy baking my own bread and coffee cake. I bake everything I carry in our lunch."

My whole attitude on the job has changed since the union came in. Now I would like to be a union counselor or work for the OEO. I work with humans as grievance committee chairman. They come to you angry, they come to you hurt, they come to you puzzled. You have to make life easier for them.

I attended a conference of the Governor's Commission on the Status of Women. Another lady went with me. We were both union officers. Most of the women there were either teachers or nurses or in a professional field. When they found out we were from labor, their attitude was cold. You felt like a little piece of scum. They acted like they were very much better than we were, just because we worked in a factory. I felt that, without us, they'd be in a heck of a shape. (Laughs.) They wouldn't have anything without us. How could we employ teachers if it wasn't for the factory workers to manufacture the books? And briefcases, that's luggage. (Laughs.)

I can understand how the black and the Spanish-speaking people feel. Even as a farmer's daughter, because we were just hard-working poor farmers, you were looked down upon by many people. Then to go into factory work, it's the same thing. You're looked down upon. You can even feel it in a store, if you're in work clothes. The difference between being in work clothes going into a nice department store and going in your dress clothes. It is two entirely different feelings. People won't treat you the same at all.

I hope I don't work many more years. I'm tired. I'd like to stay home and keep house. We're in hopes my husband would get himself a small hamburger place and a place near the lake where I can have a little garden and raise my flowers that I love to raise . . .

DOLORES DANTE

She has been a waitress in the same restaurant for twenty-three years. Many of its patrons are credit card carriers on an expense account—conventioneers, politicians, labor leaders, agency people. Her hours are from 5:00 P.M. to 2:00 A.M. six days a week. She arrives earlier "to get things ready, the silverware, the butter. When people come in and ask for you, you would like to be in a position to handle them all, because that means more money for you.

"I became a waitress because I needed money fast and you don't get it in an office. My husband and I broke up and he left me with debts and three children. My baby was six months. The fast buck, your tips. The first ten-dollar bill that I got as a tip, a Viking guy gave to me. He was a very robust, terrific atheist. Made very good conversation for us, 'cause I am too.

"Everyone says all waitresses have broken homes. What they don't realize is when people have broken homes they need to make money fast, and do this work. They don't have broken homes because they're waitresses."

I have to be a waitress. How else can I learn about people? How else does the world come to me? I can't go to everyone. So they have to come to me. Everyone wants to eat, everyone has hunger. And I serve them. If they've had a bad day, I nurse them, cajole them. Maybe with coffee I give them a little philosophy. They have cocktails, I give them political science.

I'll say things that bug me. If they manufacture soap, I say what I think about pollution. If it's automobiles, I say what I think about them. If I pour water I'll say, "Would you like your quota of mercury today?" If I serve cream, I say, "Here is your substitute. I think you're drinking plastic." I just can't keep quiet. I have an opinion on every single subject there is. In the beginning it was theology, and my bosses didn't like it. Now I am a political and my bosses don't like it. I speak *sotto voce*. But if I get heated, then I don't give a damn. I speak like an Italian speaks. I can't be servile. I give service. There is a difference.

I'm called by my first name. I like my name. I hate to be called Miss. Even when I serve a lady, a strange woman, I will not say madam. I hate ma'am. I always say milady. In the American language there is no word to address a woman, to indicate whether she's married or unmarried. So I say milady. And sometimes I playfully say to the man milord.

It would be very tiring if I had to say, "Would you like a cocktail?" and say that over and over. So I come out different for my own enjoyment. I would say, "What's exciting at the bar that I can offer?" I can't say, "Do you want coffee?" Maybe I'll say, "Are you in the mood for coffee?" Or, "The coffee sounds exciting." Just rephrase it enough to make it interesting for me. That would make them take an interest. It becomes theatrical and I feel like Mata Hari and it intoxicates me.

People imagine a waitress couldn't possibly think or have any kind of aspiration other than to serve food. When somebody says to me, "You're great, how come you're *just* a waitress?" *Just* a waitress. I'd say, "Why, don't you think you deserve to be served by me?" It's implying that he's not worthy, not that I'm not worthy. It makes me irate. I don't feel lowly at all. I myself feel sure. I don't want to change the job. I love it.

Tips? I feel like Carmen. It's like a gypsy holding out a tambourine and they throw the coin. (Laughs.) If you like people, you're not thinking of the tips. I never count my money at night. I always wait till morning. If I thought about my tips I'd be uptight. I never look at a tip. You pick it up fast. I would do my bookkeeping in the morning. It would be very dull for me to know I was making so much and no more. I do like challenge. And it isn't demeaning, not for me.

There might be occasions when the customers might intend to make it demeaning—the man about town, the conventioneer. When the time comes to pay the check, he would do little things, "How much should I give you?" He might make an issue about it. I did say to one, "Don't play God with me. Do what you want." Then it really didn't matter whether I got a tip or not. I would spit it out, my resentment—that he dares make me feel I'm operating only for a tip.

He'd ask for his check. Maybe he's going to sign it. He'd take a very long time and he'd make me stand there, "Let's see now, what do you think I ought to give you?" He would not let go of that moment. And you knew it. You know he meant to demean you. He's holding the change in his hand, or if he'd sign, he'd flourish the pen and wait. These are the times I really get angry. I'm not reticent. Something would come out. Then I really didn't care. "Goddamn, keep your money!"

There are conventioneers, who leave their lovely wives or their bad wives. They approach you and say, "Are there any hot spots?" "Where can I find girls?" It is, of course, first directed at you. I don't mean that as a compliment, 'cause all they're looking for is females. They're not looking for companionship or conversation. I am quite adept at understanding this. I think I'm interesting enough that someone may just want to talk to me. But I would philosophize that way. After all, what is left after you talk? The hours have gone by and I could be home resting or reading or studying guitar, which I do on occasion. I would say, "What are you going to offer me? Drinks?" And I'd point to the bar, "I have it all here." He'd look blank and then I'd say, "A man? If I need a man, wouldn't you think I'd have one of my own? Must I wait for you?"

Life doesn't frighten me any more. There are only two things that relegate us—the bathroom and the grave. Either I'm gonna have to go to the bathroom now or I'm gonna die now. I go to the bathroom.

And I don't have a high opinion of bosses. The more popular you are, the more the boss holds it over your head. You're bringing them business, but he knows you're getting good tips and you won't leave. You have to worry not to overplay it, because the boss becomes resentful and he uses this as a club over your head.

If you become too good a waitress, there's jealousy. They don't come in and say, "Where's the boss?" They'll ask for Dolores. It doesn't make a hit. That makes it rough. Sometimes you say, Aw hell, why am I trying so hard? I did get an ulcer. Maybe the things I kept to myself were twisting me.

It's not the customers, never the customers. It's injustice. My dad came from Italy and I think of his broken English —*injoost*. He hated injustice. If you hate injustice for the world, you hate more than anything injustice toward you. Loyalty is never appreciated, particularly if you're the type who doesn't like small talk and are not the type who makes reports on your fellow worker. The boss wants to find out what is going on surreptitiously. In our society today you have informers everywhere. They've informed on cooks, on coworkers. "Oh, someone wasted this." They would say I'm talking to all the customers. "I saw her carry such-and-such out. See if she wrote that on her check." "The salad looked like it was a double salad." I don't give anything away. I just give myself. Informers will manufacture things in order to make their job worthwhile. They're not sure of themselves as workers. There's always someone who wants your station, who would be pretender to the crown. In life there is always someone who wants somebody's job.

I'd get intoxicated with giving service. People would ask

for me and I didn't have enough tables. Some of the girls are standing and don't have customers. There is resentment. I feel self-conscious. I feel a sense of guilt. It cramps my style. I would like to say to the customer, "Go to so-and-so." But you can't do that, because you feel a sense of loyalty. So you would rush, get to your customers quickly. Some don't care to drink and still they wait for you. That's a compliment.

There is plenty of tension. If the cook isn't good, you fight to see that the customers get what you know they like. You have to use diplomacy with cooks, who are always dangerous. (Laughs.) They're madmen. (Laughs.) You have to be their friend. They better like you. And your bartender better like you too, because he may do something to the drink. If your bartender doesn't like you, your cook doesn't like you, your boss doesn't like you, the other girls don't like you, you're in trouble.

And there will be customers who are hypochondriacs, who feel they can't eat, and I coax them. Then I hope I can get it just the right way from the cook. I may mix the salad myself, just the way they want it.

Maybe there's a party of ten. Big shots, and they'd say, "Dolores, I have special clients, do your best tonight." You just hope you have the right cook behind the broiler. You really want to pleasure your guests. He's selling something, he wants things right, too. You're giving your all. How does the steak look? If you cut his steak, you look at it surreptitiously. How's it going?"

Carrying dishes is a problem. We do have accidents. I spilled a tray once with steaks for seven on it. It was a big, gigantic T-bone, all sliced. But when that tray fell, I went with it, and never made a sound, dish and all (softly) never made a sound. It took about an hour and a half to cook that steak. How would I explain this thing? That steak was salvaged. (Laughs.)

Some don't care. When the plate is down you can hear the sound. I try not to have that sound. I want my hands to be right when I serve. I pick up a glass, I want it to be just right. I get to be almost Oriental in the serving. I like it to look nice all the way. To be a waitress, it's an art. I feel like a ballerina, too. I have to go between those tables, between those chairs ... Maybe that's the reason I always stayed slim. It is a certain way I can go through a chair no one else can do. I do it with an air. If I drop a fork, there is a certain way I pick it up. I know they can see how delicately I do it. I'm on stage.

I tell everyone I'm a waitress and I'm proud. If a nurse gives service, I say, "You're a professional." Whatever you do, be professional. I always compliment people.

I like to have my station looking nice. I like to see there's enough ash trays when they're having their coffee and cigarettes. I don't like ash trays so loaded that people are not enjoying the moment. It offends me. I don't do it because I think that's gonna make a better tip. It offends me as a person.

People say, "No one does good work any more." I don't believe it. You know who's saying that? The man at the top, who says the people beneath him are not doing a good job. He's the one who always said, "You're nothing." The housewife who has all the money, she believed housework was demeaning, 'cause she hired someone else to do it. If it weren't so demeaning, why didn't *she* do it? So anyone who did her housework was a person to be demeaned. The maid who did all the housework said, "Well, hell, if this is the way you feel about it, I won't do your housework. You tell me I'm no good, I'm nobody. Well, maybe I'll go out and be somebody." They're only mad because they can't find someone to do it now. The fault is not in the people who did the—quote—lowly work.

Just a waitress. At the end of the night I feel drained. I think a lot of waitresses become alcoholics because of that. In most cases, a waiter or a waitress doesn't eat. They handle food, they don't have time. You'll pick at something in the kitchen, maybe a piece of bread. You'll have a cracker, a litle bit of soup. You go back and take a teaspoonful of something. Then maybe sit down afterwards and have a drink, maybe three, four, five. And bartenders, too, most of them are alcoholics. They'd go out in a group. There are after-hour places. You've got to go release your tension. So they go out before they go to bed. Some of them stay out all night.

It's tiring, it's nerve-racking. We don't ever sit down. We're on stage and the bosses are watching. If you get the wrong shoes and you get the wrong stitch in that shoe, that does bother you. Your feet hurt, your body aches. If you come out in anger at things that were done to you, it would only make you feel cheapened. Really I've been keeping it to myself. But of late, I'm beginning to spew it out. It's almost as though I sensed my body and soul had had quite enough.

It builds and builds and builds in your guts. Near crying. I can think about it ... (She cries softly.) 'Cause you're tired. When the night is done, you're tired. You've had so much, there's so much going ... You had to get it done. The dread that something wouldn't be right, because you want to please. You hope everyone is satisfied. The night's done, you've done your act. The curtains close.

The next morning is pleasant again. I take out my budget book, write down how much I made, what my bills are. I'm managing. I won't give up this job as long as I'm able to do it. I feel out of contact if I just sit at home. At work they all consider me a kook. (Laughs.) That's okay. No matter where I'd be, I would make a rough road for me. It's just me, and I can't keep still. It hurts, and what hurts has to come out.

POSTSCRIPT: *"After sixteen years—that was seven years ago—I took a trip to Hawaii and the Caribbean for two weeks. Went with a lover. The kids saw it—they're all married now. (Laughs.) One of my daughters said, "Act your age." I said, "Honey, if I were acting my age, I wouldn't be walking. My bones would ache. You don't want to hear about my arthritis. Aren't you glad I'm happy?"*

JUST A HOUSEWIFE

> Even if it is a woman making an apple
> dumpling, or a man a stool,
> If life goes into the pudding, good
> is the pudding,
> good is the stool.
> Content is the woman with fresh life
> rippling in her,
> content is the man.

> —D.H. Lawrence

THERESE CARTER

We're in the kitchen of the Carter home, as we were eight years ago. It is in Downers Grove Estates, an unincorporated area west of Chicago. There are one-family dwellings in this blue-collar community of skilled craftsmen—"middle class. They've all got good jobs, plumbers, electricians, truckdrivers." Her husband Bob is the foreman of an auto body repair shop. They have three children: two boys, twenty-one and fourteen, and one girl, eighteen.

It is a house Bob has, to a great extent, built himself. During my previous visit he was still working at it. Today it is finished—to his satisfaction. The room is large, remarkably tidy; all is in its place. On the wall is a small blackboard of humorous familial comment, as well as a bulletin board of newspaper clippings and political cartoons.

On another wall is the kitchen prayer I remembered:

> *Bless the kitchen in which I cook*
> *Bless each moment within this nook*

Let joy and laughter share this room
With spices, skillets and my broom
Bless me and mine with love and health
And I'll ask not for greater wealth.

How would I describe myself? It'll sound terrible—just a housewife. (Laughs.) It's true. What is a housewife? You don't have to have any special talents. I don't have any.

First thing I do in the morning is come in the kitchen and have a cigarette. Then I'll put the coffee on and whatever else we're gonna have for breakfast: bacon and eggs, sausage, waffles, toast, whatever. Then I'll make one lunch for young Bob—when school's on, I'll pack more—and I get them off to work. I'll usually throw a load of clothes in the washer while I'm waiting for the next batch to get up out of bed, and carry on from there. It's nothing really.

Later I'll clean house and sew, do something. I sew a lot of dresses for Cathy and myself. I brought this sewing machine up here years ago. It belongs here. This is my room and I love it, the kitchen.

I start my dinner real early because I like to fuss. I'll bake, cook . . . There's always little interruptions, kids running in and out, take me here, take me there. After supper, I really let down. I'm not a worker after supper. I conk out. I sit and relax and read, take a bath, have my ice cream, and go to bed. (Laughs.) It's not really a full day. You think it *is?* You make me sound important. Keep talking. (Laughs.)

I don't think it's important because for so many years it wasn't considered. I'm doing what I'm doing and I fill my day and I'm very contented. Yet I see women all around that do a lot more than I do. Women that have to work. I feel they're worthy of much more of a title than housewife.

If anybody else would say this, I'd talk back to 'em, but I *myself* feel like it's not much. Anybody can do it. I was gone for four days and Cathy took over and managed perfectly well without me. (Laughs.) I felt great, I really did. I knew she was capable.

I'll never say I'm really a good mother until I see the way they all turn out. So far they've done fine. I had somebody tell me in the hospital I must have done a good job of raising them. I just went along from day to day and they turned out all right.

Oh—I even painted the house last year. How much does a painter get paid for painting a house? (Laughs.) What? I'm a skilled craftsman myself? I never thought about that. Artist? No. (Laughs.) I suppose if you do bake a good cake, you can be called an artist. But I never heard anybody say that. I bake bread too. Oh gosh, I've been a housewife for a long time. (Laughs.)

I never thought about what we'd be worth. I've read these things in the paper: If you were a tailor or a cook, you'd get so much an hour. I think that's a lot of boloney. I think if you're gonna be a mother or a housewife, you should do these things because you want to, not because you have to.

You look around at all these career women and they're really doing things. What am I doing? Cooking and cleaning. (Laugh.) It's necessary, but it's not really great.

It's known they lead a different life than a housewife. I'm not talking about Golda Meir or anybody like that. Just even some women in the neighborhood that have to work and come home and take care of the family. I really think they deserve an awful lot of credit.

A housewife is a housewife, that's all. Low on the totem pole. I can read the paper and find that out. Someone who is a model or a movie star, these are the great ones. I don't necessarily think they are, but they're the ones you hear about. A movie star will raise this wonderful family and yet she has a career. I imagine most women would feel less worthy. Not just me.

Somebody who goes out and works for a living is more important than somebody who doesn't. What they do is very important in the business world. What I do is only important to five people. I don't like putting a housewife down, but everybody has done it for so long. It's sort of the thing you do. Deep down, I feel what I'm doing is important. But you just hate to say it, because what are you? Just a housewife? (Laughs.)

I love being a housewife. Maybe that's why I feel so guilty. I shouldn't be happy doing what I'm doing. (Laughs.) Maybe you're not supposed to be having fun. I never looked on it as a duty.

I think a lot. (Laughs.) Oh sure, I daydream. Everybody does. Some of 'em are big and some of 'em are silly. Sometimes you dream you're still a kid and you're riding your bike. Sometimes you daydream you're really someone special and people are asking you for your advice, that you're in a really big deal. (Laughs.)

I have very simple pleasures. I'm not a deep reader. I can't understand a lot of things. I've never read—oh, how do you pronounce it, Camus? I'm not musically inclined. I don't know anything about art at all. I could never converse with anybody about it. They'd have to be right, because I wouldn't know whether they're right or wrong. I go as far as Boston Pops and the Beatles. (Laughs.) I have no special talents in any direction.

I just read a new Peter De Vries book. I can't think of the name of it, that's terrible. (Suddenly) *Always Panting.* I was the first Peter De Vries fan in the world. I introduced my sister to it and that was the one big thing I've ever done in my life. (Laughs.) Now I'm reading *Grapes Of Wrath.* I'm ashamed of myself. Everybody in the family has read that book and I've had it for about fifteen years. Finally I decided to read it because my daughter raved about it.

There is a paperback copy of The Savage God *by A. Alvarez nearby. I indicate it.*

I just started a little bit about Sylvia Plath and I decided I would read this book. *Ms.* magazine has an article about her. Sure I read *Ms.* I don't think it's unusual just because I live around here. I don't agree with everything in it. But I read it. I read matchbox covers too. (Laughs.)

I think Woman's Lib puts down a housewife. Even though they say if this is what a woman wants, it's perfectly all right. I feel it's said in such a snide way: "If this is all she can do and she's contented, leave her alone." It's patronizing.

I look on reading right now as strictly enjoyment and relaxation. So I won't even let myself pick up a book before ten o'clock at night. If I do, I'm afraid I might forget about everything else. During lunch time I'll look through a magazine because I can put it down and forget about it. But real enjoyable reading I'll do at night.

I'd feel guilty reading during the day. (Laughs.) In your own home. There are so many things you should be doing. If I did it, I wouldn't think the world's coming to an end, but that's the way I'm geared. That's not the time to do it, so I don't do it.

When I went to school a few years ago it was very startling around here. Why would an older woman like me be wanting to go back to school? They wouldn't say it directly, but you hear things. I took some courses in college English, psychology, sociology. I enjoyed going but I didn't want to continue on and be a teacher. I still enjoyed being at home much more. Oh, I might go back if there was anything special I'd like.

I enjoy cooking. If it was a job, maybe I wouldn't like doing it. As low on the totem pole as I consider being a housewife, I love every minute of it. You will hear me gripe and groan like everybody else, but I do enjoy it.

I'll also enjoy it when the kids are all gone. I always had the feeling that I can *really*—oh, I don't know what I want to do, but whatever that would be, I can do it. I'll be on my own. I'm looking forward to it. Just a lot of things I've never taken the time to do.

I've never been to the Art Institute. Now that might be one thing I might do. (Laughs.) I've grown up in Chicago and I've never been there and I think that's terrible. Because I've never gotten on the train and gone. I can't spend all that time there yet. But pretty soon I'll be able to.

I haven't been to the Museum of Science and Industry for ten years at least. These things are nothing special to anybody else, but to me they would be. And to sit down and read one whole book in one afternoon if I felt like it. That would be something!

When the kids leave I want it to be a happy kind of time. Just to do the things I would like to do. Not traveling. Just to do what you want to do not at a certain time or a certain day. Sewing a whole dress at one time. Or cooking for just two people.

That's what makes me feel guilty. Usually when kids go off and get married the mother sits and cries. But I'm afraid I'm just gonna smile all the way through it. (Laughs.) They'll think I'm not a typical mother. I love my kids, I love 'em to pieces. But by the same token, I'll be just so happy for them and for myself and for Bob, too. I think we deserve a time together alone.

I don't look at housework as a drudgery. People will complain: "Why do I have to scrub floors?" To me, that isn't the same thing as a man standing there—it's his livelihood—putting two screws together day after day after

day. It would drive anybody nuts. It would drive me wild.
That poor man doesn't even get to see the finished product. I'll sit here and I'll cook a pie and I'll get to see everybody eat it. This is my offering. I think it's the greatest
satisfaction in the world to know you've pleased somebody. Everybody has to feel needed. I know I'm needed.
I'm doing it for them and they're doing it for me. And
that's the way it is.

JESUSITA NOVARRO

*She is a mother of five children: the oldest twelve, the
youngest two. "I went on welfare when my first husband
walked out on me. I was swimming alone, completely
cuckoo for a while. When I married this second man, I
got off it. When he started drinking and bringing no
money home, I had to quit my job and go on welfare
again. I got something with this welfare business and I
don't like it."*

*She is working part-time as an assistant case aide at a
settlement house in the neighborhood. The director "says
I'm doing real good and can have a job upstairs with a little bit more money. It's only four hours, because in the afternoon I want to be with my children. They're still
small."*

*She has just come home from the hospital where she
was treated for a serious illness. On this hot August afternoon—it is over a hundred degrees—the blower in the
kitchen isn't doing much good. The three children in the
house are more fascinated by technology—the tape recorder—than the conversation, though they are listening . . .*

I start my day here at five o'clock. I get up and prepare
all the children's clothes. If there's shoes to shine, I do it
in the morning. About seven o'clock I bathe the children.
I leave my baby with the baby sitter and I go to work at
the settlement house. I work until twelve o'clock. Sometimes I'll work longer if I have to go to welfare and get a
check for somebody. When I get back, I try to make hot
food for the kids to eat. In the afternoon it's pretty well

on my own. I scrub and can and cook and do whatever I have to do.

Welfare makes you feel like you're nothing. Like you're laying back and not doing anything and it's falling in your lap. But you must understand, mothers, too, work. My house is clean. I've been scrubbing since this morning. You could check my clothes, all washed and ironed. I'm home and I'm working. I am a working mother.

A job that a woman in a house is doing is a tedious job—especially if you want to do it right. If you do it slipshod, then it's not so bad. I'm pretty much of a perfectionist. I tell my kids, hang a towel. I don't want it thrown away. That is very hard. It's a constant game of picking up this, picking up that. And putting this away, so the house'll be clean.

Some men work eight hours a day. There are mothers that work eleven, twelve hours a day. We get up at night, a baby vomits, you have to be calling the doctor, you have to be changing the baby. When do you get a break, really? You don't. This is an all-around job, day and night. Why do they say it's charity? We're working for our money. I am working for this check. It is not charity. We are giving some kind of home to these children.

I'm so busy all day I don't have time to daydream. I pray a lot. I pray to God to give me strength. If He should take a child away from me, to have the strength to accept it. It's His kid. He just borrowed him to me.

I used to get in and close the door. Now I speak up for my right. I walk with my head up. If I want to wear big earrings, I do. If I'm overweight, that's too bad. I've gotten completely over feeling where I'm little. I'm working now, I'm pulling my weight. I'm gonna get off welfare in time, that's my goal—get off.

It's living off welfare and feeling that you're taking something for nothing the way people have said. You get to think maybe you are. You get to think, Why am I so stupid? Why can't I work? Why do I have to live this way? It's not enough to live on anyway. You feel degraded.

The other day I was at the hospital and I went to pay my bill. This nurse came and gave me the green card. Green card is for welfare. She went right in front of me and gave it to the cashier. She said, "I wish I could stay home and let the money fall in my lap." I felt rotten. I was just burning inside. You hear this all the way around you. The doctor doesn't even look at you. People are ashamed to show that green card. Why can't a woman just get a check in the mail: Here, this check is for you. Forget welfare. You're a mother who works.

This nurse, to her way of thinking, she represents the working people. The ones with the green card, we represent the lazy no-goods. This is what she was saying. They're the good ones and we're the bad guys.

You know what happened at the hospital? I was put in a nice room, semiprivate. You stay there until someone with insurance comes in and then you get pushed up to the fifth floor. There's about six people in there, and nobody comes even if you ring. I said, "Listen lady, you can put me on the roof. You just find out what's the matter with me so I can get the hell out of here."

How are you going to get people off welfare if they're constantly being pushed down? If they're constantly feeling they're not good for anything? People say, I'm down, I'll stay down. And this goes on generation to generation to generation. Their daughter and their daughter and their daughter. So how do you break this up? These kids don't ask to be born—these kids are gonna grow up and give their lives one day. There will always be a Vietnam.

There will always be war. There always has been. The way the world is run, yes, there will always be war. Why? I really don't know. Nobody has ever told me. I was so busy handling my own affairs and taking care of my children and trying to make my own money and calling up welfare when my checks are late or something has been stolen. All I know is what's going on here. I'm an intelligent woman up to a certain point, and after that ... I wish I knew. I guess the big shots decided the war. I don't question it, because I've been busy fighting my own little war for so long.

The head of the settlement house wants me to take the social worker's job when I get back to work. I visit homes, I talk to mothers. I try to make them aware that they got something to give. I don't try to work out the problems. This is no good. I try to help them come to some kind of a decision. If there's no decision, to live with it, because some problem doesn't have any answer.

There was one mother that needed shoes, I found shoes for her. There was another mother that needed money because her check was late. I found someplace for her to borrow a couple of dollars. It's like a fund. I could borrow a couple of dollars until my check comes, then when my check comes I give it back. How much time have mothers left to go out and do this? How many of us have given time so other mothers could learn to speak English, so they'll be able to go to work. We do it gladly because the Lord gave us English.

I went to one woman's house and she's Spanish speaking. I was talking to her in English and she wouldn't unbend. I could see the fear in her eyes. So I started talking Spanish. Right away, she invited me for coffee and she was telling me the latest news . . .

I would like to help mothers be aware of how they can give to the community. Not the whole day—maybe three, four hours. And get paid for it. There's nothing more proud for you to receive a check where you worked at. It's yours, you done it.

At one time, during her second marriage, she had worked as an assembler at a television factory. "I didn't care for it. It was too automatic. It was just work, work, work, and I wasn't giving of myself. Just hurry it up and get it done. Even if you get a job that pays you, if you don't enjoy it, what are you getting? You're not growing up. (Taps temple.) Up here."

The people from the settlement house began visiting me, visiting welfare mothers, trying to get them interested in cooking projects and sewing. They began knocking on my door. At the beginning, I was angry. It was just like I drew a curtain all around me. I didn't think I was really good for anything. So I kind of drew back. Just kept my troubles to myself, like vegetating. When these people began calling on me. I began to see that I could talk and that I did have a brain. I became a volunteer.

I want to be a social worker. Somebody that is not indifferent, that bends an ear to everybody. You cannot be slobberish. You cannot cry with the people. Even if you cry inside, you must keep a level head. You have to try to help that person get over this bump. I would go into a house and try to make friends. Not as a spy. The ladies have it that welfare comes as spies to see what you have. Or you gotta hide everything 'cause welfare is coming.

There is this fear the social worker is gonna holler, because they got something, maybe a man or a boyfriend. I wouldn't take any notes or pens or paper or pencils or anything. I would just go into the house and talk. Of course, I would look around to see what kind of an environment it is. This you have to absorb. You wouldn't say it, but you would take it in.

I promised myself if I ever get to work all day, I'm going to buy me a little insurance. So the next time I go to the hospital I'll go to the room I want to go. I'm gonna stay there until it's time for me to leave, because I'm gonna pay my own bill. I don't like to feel rotten. I want my children, when they grow up, they don't have to live on it. I want to learn more. I'm hungry for knowledge. I want to do something. I'm searching for something. I don't know what it is.

BOOK SIX

THE QUIET LIFE

DONNA MURRAY

She has been binding books for twenty-five years. Among her clients have been the University of Chicago, the Arboretum, the Art Institute, and private collectors. Her reflections are somewhat free associative in nature.

"I didn't even really become a bookbinder. It happened because we had so many books. I inherited this great big library from my father, and John* had many, many art books that were falling apart. We had acres of books, and I thought this was the thing to do: I'll put these books together and make them fit. So I began a sort of experiment and I enjoyed it very much. I became a bookbinder because I had nothing else to do."

At first no one taught me. I wasn't doing much of anything. Then a *marvelous* woman, who's a brilliant artist, gave me a *marvelous* frame that her father made for her, for sewing books and that sort of thing. So I learned to sew books. They're really good books, it's just the covers that are rotten. You take them apart and you make them sound and you smash them in and sew them up. That's all there is to it.

I have a bindery at home, it's kind of a cave, really. It's where you have your gear—a table where you work, a cutter, a press, and those kinds of things. You have a good screw press, a heavy one that presses the books down. A

---

* Her husband, an artist and professor of art at a local branch of the state university.

binder's gear is principally his thumbnail. You push, you use your thumbnail more than anything else.

I mustn't pose as a fine binder because I'm not. That's exhibition binding, gold tooling. You roll out this design and you fill it with egg white. Then you cover it with pure gold leaf. I enjoy restoration very much—when you restore an old book that's all ragged at the back. You must make a rubbing of the spine. The spine's all rotten, so you put that aside and you turn back the pages *very carefully*. That's what I enjoy most of all.

Obviously I don't make much money binding books, but it's very cozy work. Carolyn* and I did simple, necessary things for the university. We bound precious pamphlets in a way that preserved them. Incunabula—books printed before 1500. Architectural works and something of the Latin poets.

Those made of vellum are usually just rotten in the back. Vellum's a wild thing, the hide of a calf or a lamb. It's treated with acid. The pages are falling apart. You take them out if you can and wash them, deacidify them in a certain solution. Then you fold them together and press them in your press.

Some of my private customers have very splendid collections, beautiful bindings you'll never see again. I have very specific, lovely clients. One, who's no longer living, had a magnificent collection of Stevenson and Dickens, first editions.

I go to the house and take my equipment, oils and paints and a certain binder's paste. And a painter's drop cloth. There's a beautiful Oriental rug, and indeed you may not drop anything on it. You set up a card table and book ends and that's about it, really.

We calculate the books. We make a point of being sure that the books go back exactly where they were before. We look at each book and pull it out and test it for tears. Almost everybody pulls books out by their tops, and they're always broken. Torn from beautiful leather bindings. In dusting books, you never touch them inside. The dust only goes to the top. People who pull them out with the idea of dusting them—it's just ridiculous. It only destroys the book.

My assistant takes the cloth for me, and then we line up

* Carolyn Horton, her mentor.

the books. She dusts the tops. You always dust from the spine out, cleaning the book. Then you use the *marvelous* British Museum formula, potassium lactate. It's swabbed on the books to put back in the leather the acids that were taken out, that were in the hide in the beginning. They've been dried out completely and all the salts have been destroyed. So we swab all the leather goods with this potassium lactate. A very little swab, and let it sink in. Then these books are polished and put back on the shelves. It preserves books that could never exist in this climate after five years.

It's an arduous thing, but I suppose it's important because if that kind of thing didn't happen, the books would just disintegrate. Father's library did. Especially in the city with its very high potency of sulphur dioxide, which eats up the books. The hideous air, the poisonous air of the city. People love to have whole sets of Dickens or Mark Twain or Dumas—the kinds of popular acquisitions in our mother's age, when they filled up their shelves. The books in Chicago are disintegrating to a most appalling degree in comparison to the books of the same issue in Lake Forest.* It's been going on for years. It destroys them. It eats them up. Terrible.

I usually arrive at about ten thirty. I work as long as it pleases me. If I fill up the table and the books are oiled, I often leave at four or six. I might work for one client two or three weeks. In the case of Mrs. Armour's books, it was a matter of six months. She had a superb collection stored in the old house. It took two days to unpack the crates. Her mother was a collector of exceedingly marvelous taste. It was undeniably one of the most beautiful collections of books I've ever seen. Not only in the binding, but in the selection. It was kind of wonderful to be there at that moment.

I wouldn't want to bind anything that was flimsy. You have to think of what's inside. If you're binding a book about a big idea—Karl Marx! (laughs)—you obviously would accommodate a binding, wouldn't you? The idea of the binding should reflect what's inside. The books at the Arboretum are among the most interesting. Some of them are sixteenth- and seventeenth-century books, marvelous herbals. Beautiful, beautiful books. Flower papers. There

* A far North Shore suburb of Chicago; its most upper U.

is no special way you relate your own taste, your reflections.

If they're the *marvelous* trees of Japan—oh dear, oh dear. I was reared in California where I saw the redwoods that are now being systematically destroyed. And there's some redwood trees in Japan that relate to what you're thinking, oh dear (softly). You must be very clever with a binding and give it the dignity it deserves. Because the pages are so full of stunning, *fantastic* things that say, This is life. So what do you do with a binding like that? I don't know. You just give it a strength. If it's leather or it's cloth or it's paper, you give it strength, an indication of what is inside.

I only enjoy working on books that say something. I know this is an anathema to people who insist on preserving books that are only going to be on the shelves forever—or on coffee tables. Books are for people to read, and that's that. I think books are for the birds unless people read them.

That's what I discovered when I worked in Florence after the big flood. I came in the summer. John and I lived there and he worked there during his first sabbatical. I loved that city so much. And when someone from the Biblioteca Nazionale asked me to come . . .

It would be *darling* to look into books when you're working on them, lured by them—but obviously you can't. You'd never finish your work. I can read books on my own time. I feel very strongly about every book I pick up. It's like something alive or—or decadent, death. I wouldn't for one moment bind *Mein Kampf*, because I think it's disgusting to waste time on such an obscenity. Are you offering me a million dollars to bind that? Of course not.

I adore the work. It's very comforting. The only thing that makes me angry is that I'm almost all the time on the outside rather than on the inside. I'd like to be reading them. But I do think working in my house and being comfortable and doing something you feel is beneficial—it is important, isn't it?"

"I'm just a swabber. (Laughs.) I'm not an artist. I just use aniline dyes, so they won't be hurting the leather. Aniline's a natural dye, and that's about it. It isn't very skilled work. It's just knowing what books need, if you want to preserve them. It's just something you do. A mechanic takes care of a tire, and he knows . . .

Oh, I think it's important. Books are things that keep us going. Books—I haven't got much feeling about many other things. I adore the work. Except sometimes it becomes very lonesome. It's nice to sit beside somebody, whether it's somebody who works with you or whether it's your husband or your friend. It's just lovely, just like a whisper, always . . . If you were really brainy, you wouldn't waste your time pasting and binding. But if you bind good books, you make something good, really and truly good. Yes, I would like to make a good book hold good and I would like to be involved in a pact that will not be broken, that holds good, which would really be as solid as the book.

Keeping a four-hundred-year-old book together keeps that spirit alive. It's an alluring kind of thing, lovely, because you know that belongs to us. Because a book is a life, like one man is a life. Yes, yes, this work is good for me, therapeutic for old age . . . *just keep going* with the hands . . .

NINO GUIDICI

We're behind the counter of a corner drugstore. It is a changing neighborhood. To the east are upper-middle-class high rises; to the west are the low-income people. Along the big street that divides, the transient young are among the most visible. "It's hard to believe I spent forty years on this street." He has been a pharmacist since 1926. He is seventy years old.

In the bins to the rear of the counter are shelved thousands of bottles allocated according to the name of each large drug firm. "It's been estimated there are 5,000 to 7,500 varieties of pills. When I'm stuck—in the old days I wasn't—we go to the Red Book. It lists the names and tells you who makes it and how much it is."

The corner drugstore, that's kinda fadin' now. The small store is on its way out. Can't do the volume. In the old days they took druggists as doctors. How many come in today and say, "I have an earache, what would you recommend?" Or, "My child has a cold." Gone with the wind. Still, the customer's the same as when I got started. Like that man that came in. He wants a paper tonight. He said, "Be sure and save me a paper." He's a regular. If I forget it I might as well forget to fill a prescription. It's a big mistake. Still very personal with me.

All we do is count pills. Count out twelve on the counter, put 'em in here, count out twelve more . . . Today was a little out of the ordinary. I made an ointment. Most of the ointments come already made up. This doctor was an old-timer. He wanted something with sulfur and two other elements mixed together. So I have to weigh it out on the scale. Ordinarily I would just have one tube of cream for that.

Doctors used to write out their own formulas and we made most of these things. Most of the work is now done in the laboratory. The real druggist is found in the manufacturing firms. They're the factory workers and they're the pharmacists. We just get the name of the drugs and the number and the directions. It's a lot easier. In the old days you filled maybe twenty, twenty-five prescriptions a day by hand. Nowadays you can fill about 150. This time of the year they're most antibiotics, because people are having colds.

In the old days we just used simple drugs, simple ointment base like vaseline, lanolin and mixed them together. They didn't have the properties that you find today. You're really an order filler now. (Laughs.) I'm not knockin' the pharmacist, but it's got so highly developed . . . We just dispense, that's all.

I like it better this way. If you had to make up everything and the physician had to write down a prescription with all the ingredients, you could hardly exist in this economy. Everything is faster, it's better. People wouldn't get relief out of medicine in them days like they get today.

"In the days I went to pharmacy school, you only went two years. Now it's six. In my day, they'd give you basic metals and salts. You knew certain salts were good for a cough and you mixed it with distilled water and that's how you'd make your medicine. The young ones know a lot more chemistry. They're much better educated than we were. They're prepared to go to the manufacturing end of

it. Young kids in high school, they learn how to make things which I don't know anything about. (Laughs.) LSD and all that. These kids know more about how to make dangerous drugs than I do. (Laughs.)"

When I first started out, you dispensed very little medicine for children after they were seven or eight. We didn't have ointments to fix up pimply faced kids with acne and things like that. Now, some children have a little pimple and they're sent to a skin man. We fill a lot of ointments for 'em. We sell a lot more cosmetics than we did. That used to be a small part of the business. Now it's at least fifty percent. I'd say about twenty percent come in for prescriptions. The other just come in for their everyday needs.

People come in the store and, unless I know who the person is, I'm pretty near afraid to wash out their hand. The laws tell you to tell them to go to a doctor. Gee whiz, here's a guy ain't got thirty-five cents. I had a butcher over here, he's cut his artery with a knife. Boy, he was bleeding like the devil. Tell him to go to a doctor? He'd bleed to death. I stuffed it with rags. Jeez, the guy pretty near died on top of it. It was all right. I might have saved him, but you don't get credit for anything like that. Suppose he died in the back room. Boy. I try to give first aid. Then you try to tell 'em to get a tetanus shot. Jeez, nine times out of ten you're talking to somebody who can't afford it. I've taken things out of people's eyes. I've always been pretty good at that. Others tell me, "Boy, you're crazy."

His colleague, Grace Johnson, enters and puts on her white gown. She has been a pharmacist for thirty years. "There was only three of us girls in my class of 360 men. The men customers always hesitated coming to me. I would always know what a man wanted because he would avoid me. (Laughs.) When I started in my father's store, I'd be compounding something in the back and he'd call me out. The men would turn around and walk out. They thought I had two heads. Women have always accepted me.

"When I say I'm a pharmacist—ooohhh!!! Oh, that's marvelous! You must really be a brain or something. The

idea of a woman pharmacist. It's like being a woman doctor. But I don't think a pharmacist really gets credit enough for what we do, as a liaison person between the patient and the doctor. If the doctor makes a mistake and we don't catch it, they can sue us. They don't sue the doctor because they stick together.

"The big change in thirty years is in the merchandise. We have such a variance today. Whoever heard of selling a radio in a drugstore? (Laughs.) And whoever heard of these thousands of drugs? A pharmacist once said to me that if the atom bomb were dropped on this neighborhood in the middle of the night, no one would know it (laughs), because ninety-nine percent of the people take Seconal, Nembutal, right? They just automatically pop them in their mouths, if they need them or not. Almost everybody is on some drug. Everybody has a nerve problem today, which is the tensions we live in."

I enjoy working. (Laughs.) I like to be around people. I coulda quit work five years ago. It's not that I don't like home, but it's monotonous to sit around. With your Social Security and what taxes I pay, I'm just as well off if I didn't work. But I like to come down. I'm not saying I love people, but you miss 'em. Some days you go home and say, "Oh gee, I've seen so much today. So many guys drove me nuts," and that and that trouble. I like that. The minute you don't see anybody and you're not talkin' to people . . .

Jeff, the manager, who is thirty, interjects: "I don't know anybody who doesn't like to be away from work—except Nino."

A lot of people, it's drudgery to go to work. Not me. I don't say I love work, I don't say I hate work. I do it. It's a normal thing for me than just not doing anything. I figure that I'm kinda needed. If you don't show up, you might be putting somebody out a day. If I took off and walked down the street for an hour, I like to hear him say, "Where in the heck have you been? Gee whiz, it was busy. I needed you." Some fellas would call that a bawlin' out and get mad. I wouldn't. If you come down and they'd say, "We really didn't need you," I might as well quit. I like to feel kinda needed. It kinda feels good. You say, well, you're of some value.

A lot of people just can't wait to get sixty-five and quit. They're just tickled to death. I don't know what for. Then they get home, and I've seen wives, they're sorry their husbands are home and more or less in the way. The average man at home, like myself, when he's through doing this kind of work, there's not really much I can do now. That's why you like to feel wanted.

"I first started workin' in drugstores when I was twelve years old." He had lived in a small town in southern Illionis. His father, a stone cutter, had died in his young years. *"I'd open the store, sweep up the sidewalk, mop the floor."* In Chicago he attended pharmacy school while working at night. *"I used to see my father work hard and people on farms and miners work awful hard for a few dollars a week. I was getting the same amount of money just standing around waiting on people, saying hello. To me that seemed an easy way to make money."*

I never wanted to own my own store. I had chances, but I stopped and I figured. I'd have to pay interest on the loan. I couldn't run it by myself. I didn't want my wife workin' twelve hours a day. A lot of my friends, their wives got in and they pitched and worked hard and they got someplace. They're welcome to it. It wasn't my philosophy.

I've been boss all right. I managed stores. I used to see girls on the soda fountains at five, six dollars a week. That was the going pay. I'm the kind of guy, I couldn't ask anybody to work for nothing. To be a success, you have to take a lot of advantage of help. Don't get me wrong. I'm not saying that to be successful you have to be a rat, but you have to do things—I realized long ago I wasn't that type of man. Not that I'm such a good man. I'm not a good person, but I don't want to ask people to do things I wouldn't do.

"I got quite a bit of colored trade right here, people who work in the neighborhood. They tell me, 'You know why I'm buying here? They rob me in my home neighborhood.' It's the truth. In the old days, I worked out there. I know they take advantage of the poor people in those stores."

I know I'm not going to be a millionaire. To make a lot of money you have to have a lot of ambition. With me, as long as I pay the rent, eat, go to a ball game, go to the race track, take the old lady out once in a while, and the bills are paid—well, what else do you need? I want to have enough money where I wouldn't have to be a bum on the street or where I wouldn't have to take a gun and hold somebody up to get a dollar. It's a wonderful feeling to go out and earn the amount of money that it takes for you to live on. That's my opinion—maybe it's as stupid as a hundred thousand dollars, and there's nothin' more stupid than a hundred thousand dollars—but it's my opinion.

I never cared about being rich. I know that sounds silly. I have a friend, he says, "I never seen a fella like you, who don't care for money." That's a lie. I like money. I know you gotta have a certain amount of it. But how much does a guy need to live? I have a kid brother, he's a go-getter. He can buy and sell me half a dozen times. It isn't that I'm lazy. I'm kind of a dreamy guy, you'd say.

I think I've succeeded. If they didn't want me any more, retirement wouldn't bother me. I'd go to the ball game, I'd go to the track, I'd do a little fishing. There was a little time in my life when I was kinda worried. There used to be an ad in the papers: Pharmacist—do not apply over forty. I was forty-five when that happened. I thought, this is getting to be a young man's game. But I was lucky. Nothing ever happened.

If I had to do it all over again, I'd be a doctor. I took pre-medics. Then I thought, Oh, four more years is just too rough. But I can't complain. I've been lucky. I haven't contributed anything to the world. There's a few men who do. They're men who are intelligent and probably could have made all kinds of money. But they spend their whole lives in educating. They gave their whole lives to society. You don't read about them going on big trips. You don't see 'em so much in the society column. We have some awful ignorant men too. It's funny how they get to be the head of nations. It's crazy, right?

I've been selfish, like the average man. Probably just thought of myself. Takin' it easy, havin' a good time, eat and sleep. There are so few men that have been really good, I can't name 'em. My work's important to me, but it's such a little thing. It's not important to the world.

Ms. JOHNSON: *Of course it is, Nino. You're very important. How many times have you corrected the doctor on things he's written? As far as this store is concerned, you're more than important. (To the others) People love him. He has a terrific following. They bring their babies in, they bring their grandchildren in to meet him.*

JEFF: *Seventy percent of the people come in here because of Nino.*

I don't know about that. Look around—at the people who do great things for humanity.

Ms. JOHNSON: *Oh Nino, you do something for humanity every day you stand there.*

(Abashed, he looks heavenward.) Oh listen to that, will ya? Oh my gosh. Jeez.

POSTSCRIPT: *There was talk of an old colleague who has since died. He was the strict one. "Some of our worst arguments was on account of me not being strict enough. Somebody'd come in and say, 'I can't sleep tonight.' He wouldn't give 'em anything unless they had it in writing. They'd walk around the block and come back to me. I'd say, 'I know you, you're solid. Oh sure, here's one or two. I would take a chance on humanity. I don't think that's a sin."*

EUGENE RUSSELL

He is occasionally seen on the streets of the city, walking or on a bicycle. What distinguishes him, aside from his casual work clothes, is a wide belt, from which hangs a case containing the tools of his trade—pliers, wire cutters, and scrapers of various kinds. He is a piano tuner and has been at it professionally for fifteen years.

"I am a piano technician. He is a dedicated piano tuner. (Laughs.) Piano tuning is not really business. It's a dedication. There's such a thing as piano tuning, piano rebuilding, and antique restoration. There's such a thing as scale

*designing and engineering, to produce the highest sound
quality possible. I'm in all of this and I enjoy every second
of it.*

*"I was a musician for many years, a jazz clarinetist.
Played a lot of Dixieland. Every piano I came to was just
a little bit unsatisfactory to work with. I've been tuning
since I was fourteen years old, more to satisfy the aesthetic part of playing than actually commercializing on it."*

His wife Natalie joins in the conversation.

EUGENE: Every day is different. I work Saturdays and
Sundays sometimes. Monday I'm tuning a piano for a record company that had to be done before nine o'clock.
When I finish that, I go to another company and do at
least four pianos. During that day there's a couple of
harpsichords mixed in. In the meantime, I'll check with
my wife, who stands near the phone. I might see a fill-in
sometime in-between. By the time I get through it's pretty
dark.

I've been known to go entirely asleep and continue to
tune the piano—and no one would know. (Laughs.) If
I'm working on some good Steinways, my day goes so fast
I don't even know where it's gone. But if I'm working on
an uninteresting instrument, just the time to tune it drags
miserably. There's something of a stimulus in good sound.

I had a discussion with another tuner, who is a great
guitar man. He said, "Why are we tuners?" I said, "Because we want to hear good sounds." I went into a young
student's home and rebuilt an old upright, restrung it. It
sounded lovely. A week later he wanted to sell the piano.
I said, "Why?" He said, "I've heard the sound I want to
hear."

It doesn't have to be a grand. It can be a spinet, it can
be an old upright, it can be an antique piano from the late
1700s—maybe a harpsichord. They all have to be tuned as
often as possible.

The nature of equal temperament makes it impossible
to really put a piano in tune. The system is out of tune
with itself. But it's so close to in tune that it's compatible.
You start off with a basic A-440 and you tune an octave
down and then tune a relationship of that combination of
tunes. Go up a fifth, down a fourth. Go through a circle
of fifths within a given octave. When you get that to bal-

ance out in fourths and fifths, you take it in thirds, in sixths—so that it's balanced. Then you go out in the rest of the octaves and tune the rest of the piano. All you have to be able to do is count beats.

NATALIE: It's an electronic thing now. Anyone in the world can tune a piano with it. You can actually have a tin ear like a night club boss. I have no ear at all, but with one of these electronic devices, I could tune a piano.

EUGENE: It's an assist, but there's no saving of time. You get to a point where you depend on it like a crutch. Somebody using it for a long time may think it's valuable.

I don't think anyone can teach you to tune a piano. I'd say practice more than training. You go in, you get your feet wet, and you just practice, practice and practice until it becomes a natural thing with you.

NATALIE: Gene has one of these extraordinary ears. It's as close to absolute pitch as I think any human ear can be. Any sensible boy can really learn to tune contemporary instruments, but very few people have learned to do what Gene does. We know of only three other technicians in the country who do what he does with antique instruments, and two of them are retired. Sometimes he has to make the machinery, make the tools. He's worked on virginals and very, very early harpsichords. It's really a lost art. It doesn't seem to be the thing that attracts young men. Gene has had a series of apprentices, but they lack patience.

EUGENE: There are fewer younger men in tuning because you don't make money fast enough in the beginning. Most people in it are musicians, who are having a hard time and are looking for something in their idle time. There's as much piano tuning as there ever was. It's strange, but during a recession or depression, the piano tuning business goes ahead. People have more leisure time and they want to develop their artistic capabilities. And they want their pianos tuned. A piano can last for several generations if it's properly cared for. It isn't like a car that becomes obsolete next year. It's possible for a piano to keep going for two hundred years. Old people are going into things they

know are ageless. Most of the older musicians are going
into piano tuning because you can make a living at the
age of a hundred. In fact, the older you get, the mellower.

NATALIE: He doesn't mind a bit when he's called a piano
tuner. But little kids are very status-minded. When people
say Billy's father tunes pianos, my child wants to go up
and kick them. Almost anybody's father, if he has normal
intelligence, could tune a piano. But no one can do what
Gene does. We're terribly proud of him. My child is very
clear and precise about the nature of his daddy's work.
We think that's rather nice, too. I had no idea until I was
a teen-ager just precisely what my daddy went off on a
train to do every day. Presumably it was legal. (Laughs.)
That was all I knew. But Billy knows and he's proud.

EUGENE: It's immaterial to me what I'm called. If anyone
wishes to call me a piano tuner, it's perfectly all right with
me. I am not the slightest bit status conscious.

NATALIE: Oh, but he's had some very strange experiences
with high rises. We'd decided Gene must carry his tools in
an attaché case. When he's gone in for a club date in a
dinner jacket to play at someone's party, he's treated with
great courtesy. But when he walks in with his tool kit,
dressed like Doolittle the Dustman (laughs), they look at
you and wonder. What is he really?

EUGENE: Oh yes, I have to check through security in
some of the high rises. I sign my name and where I'm
going and what time I got there, and when I come back
through security, I sign out and everything. If I had a
business suit on and an attaché case, I could go on the elevator directly.

I realize these buildings have to have security, so I forget my personal feelings. Although once in a while I resent
the idea of going down into the basement. Sometimes you
have to go to the receiving room and sign in. It wastes so
much time. It takes forever to get where you're going on
a service elevator. I have gone to an apartment as a guest
on an elevator. But as soon as I have that tool chest in my
hand, I have to take the service elevator. It's the *same*
doorman. Oh, once in a while I get mad . . .

NATALIE: My son and I are buying him an attaché case for Christmas. We're afraid he'll lose his temper one day and something foul may happen.

"I've been stopped by the police and they'll ask me, 'What've ya got in 'atcase?' And I'll say, 'A do-it-yourself burglar kit.' And they'll say, 'Dump your case out.'" I had this metal cylindrical tube, which I keep blueprints in. They actually stood fifteen feet away with drawn guns while I took the cap off to show them there was nothing in it. (Laughs.)

"I walk along with my work clothes, with my tool chest. They'll pull up. 'Whatcha got inna case?' 'Tools.' 'What kind of tools?' 'Working tools. They're for my business.' They don't ask you what your business is. They want to see your tools. After I show them the tools, they'll say, 'What business are you in?' 'I'm a piano technician.' 'Are ya sure?' 'Yes, I'm sure.' 'Where do you live?' 'Up the street.' 'Show us where ya live.' I brought them over and they had me dump all my tools out on the lawn. They looked it over very carefully and they said, 'I think you'd better come down to the station.' 'I don't think I'd better.' 'You could very easily break into houses with these.' 'I know that, but I never have and I have no reason to break in a house. These are legitimate tools for a legitimate business, which keeps me going very nicely.' 'You show us where you live.' So they ring the buzzer and they holler, 'Does Eugene Russell live here?' 'Yes, he lives here.' 'We were just checking out.' And good-by. I know it was a routine checkout so it didn't bother me. There was no reason to be angry."

EUGENE: It's a competitive business. If you've got a plum and some other technician wants it, he'll go after it. I can't do that. There's plenty for everybody. I try to keep my fee to at least ten dollars an hour. Somebody who's been a customer of mine for many years asks, "How much do you want?" I always say, "You know." They look at what the check was before and that's what they pay.

NATALIE: Gene is terribly modest, which is why I'm being so terribly pushy. There's a technician we know who has two shops. He would call Gene in to redo the unsatisfactory work he did for his customers. But he's a marvelous merchant. He's terrific, an absolute whiz of a businessman. Gene didn't tell you, but he's also a dealer on a very small scale. With keyboard instruments, buying and selling them. Right from our home, from the kitchen, I buy them and sell them. It is more cutthroat than you would believe, especially the antique business.

EUGENE: Square grand pianos and things like that. I have a lovely old square grand with an organ built into it, unusual—

NATALIE: I do an awful lot of work just as a piano broker right here in the kitchen. Bill tells me a piano's for sale and people call him and want to buy them. That phase of the business is exceedingly cutthroat. Oh, frightfully.

When you're a broker, you don't take title to the merchandise, you don't warehouse it, you don't usually move it. It's like dealing in securities. And I don't always collect because I'm not a businessman. We buy old instruments too, and Gene restores them and we sell them. We work in our home. Anywhere, garage . . .

EUGENE: I don't see any possibility of separating my life from my work.

NATALIE: Because we are—as the French say—of an age, so many people say, "Mrs. Russell, how did you and your husband hit on such a lovely retirement business? What did he do before he retired? Is he a retired army-type?" They think it's something adorable. What a sweet old couple to open an antique shop, who's gotten into this sweet little old-fashioned craft sort of business.

EUGENE: Sort of a hobby, they think. Because it's so enjoyable. I get a big kick out of it, because there are so many facets. Other people go through a routine. At a certain time, they punch a clock . . . Then they're through with it and *then* their life begins. With us the piano business is an integral part of our life.

NATALIE: Oh yes, yes, yes. He obviously does it with a great deal of relish and enthusiasm. We have the feeling that millions of people are putting in time at work they don't especially adore. And they look forward when they retire to opening a little antique business or something else that they will truly delight in. Because that's the great American fantasy. They say all Americans secretly want to own a night club. I never did. But I'm not very American. I worked in them and so did Gene, and perhaps that's why. Another myth is that all American girls want to be stewardesses or girl singers. I don't think that's true—not if you've done either. (Laughs.) But apparently the most middle-class American dream is opening up a dear little antique shop, somewhere safe and pleasant. We know several dealers who live a divine life. They're moneyed people and it's a perfectly adorable little hobby for them. They're never in their shop. You see the same merchandise year after year. Nothing's moving. If you think of an antique shop as a source of income, you can't approach it that way. It's cutthroat—frightfully. It doesn't mean you have to be crooked to succeed, but there's a tremendous amount of it. Gene knows the field and he can spot fakes.

(Laughs lightly.) I'm less of a scientist than Gene, less of an engineer. More of a business person, yes. But I rather like it. Frankly, I'll tell you something. When I retire, if we can ever afford to, I'm sure not going to go into the music business or the antique business. No.

EUGENE: I don't think I'll ever retire. I'm like the window washer who was asked, "Do you enjoy washing windows?" He said, "No, I don't." They said, "Why don't you quit your job?" He said, "What else is there to do?" (Laughs.) I love that.

(Quickly.) Of course, I enjoy my work. And I know others in the field have a high opinion of me.

NATALIE: When we got married, he was working with a band, though he had a shop. I started apartment hunting. I said he was a merchant or that he was a technician because everybody said, "My God, don't tell them your husband's a musician. You'll never get an apartment." There's a strong prejudice against musicians. They think they're birds of passage, perhaps, or that he'll give drunken parties. There's still an aura of sinfulness about it.

EUGENE: Everything we do in our lives has something to

do with respectability. What it appears to someone else is not too important as long as we do a good job and as long as we do it honestly. It's the real life. If you're using people and you gain by exploitation—I couldn't live that way.

I've never really had anybody put me down. There seems something mystic about music, about piano tuning. There's so much beauty comes out of music. So much beauty comes out of piano tuning. I start working at chord progressions . . .

NATALIE: He's learning Bach.

EUGENE: I know enough chords to get the sounds that I want to hear out of it. I was tuning a piano for a trombone player who once played for Jan Savitt. As I was tuning, I played around with Savitt's theme song, "Out of Space." I got those big augmented eleventh chords progressing down in ninths. It's a beautiful thing. He came dashing in the room. "Where did you hear that? How did you know it?" I hear great big fat augmented chords that you don't hear in music today. I came home one day and said, "I just heard a diminished chord today."

I have a mood of triumph. I was sitting one day tuning a piano in a hotel ballroom. There was a symposium of computer manufacturers. One of these men came up and tapped me on the shoulder. "Someday we're going to get your job." I laughed. "By the time you isolate an infinite number of harmonics, you're going to use up a couple of billion dollars worth of equipment to get down to the basic fundamental that I work with my ear." He said, "You know something? You're right. We'll never touch your job." The cost of computerized tuning would be absolutely prohibitive. I felt pretty good at that moment.

BROKERS

MARGARET RICHARDS

She has been a realty broker for the past five years. Widowed, she has two grown children. "This is a new career." She worked in her younger days, "before I took something like twenty years out to raise a family." She works for a firm, along with twenty-seven colleagues. "It's very aggressive, in the nicest sense of the word. Good thinking, new thinking. They believe in advertising. I think we're performing a great service in the area."

She has lived in this area for thirty-four years. Her husband was a banker, from whom she inherited a comfortable income. "My family will eat and be housed and be clothed whether I sell real estate or not." It is an upper-middle-class enclave of suburbs to the north of a large industrial city.

"To qualify as a broker, you go to school and take the state exam. You have to understand surveys, you have to understand mortgages, you have to understand title charges, closing costs. You have to understand about zoning."

Being a realtor is something I enjoy very much. It probably has something to do with being nosy. The niftiest part is to be in on the ground floor of this decision making. A house is the largest investment a family can make. They say college education has taken that over, it's gotten so expensive. Well, number two is to buy a house. It becomes pretty vital in the lives of these people.

There has not been a good image in the past of realtors. Do you suppose it fell in with the same thing as a used car

salesman? Somebody who is just buying and selling? Yet
they always ask your advice. Nothin's so bad about that.
(Laughs.) About neighborhoods, schools, parks. The most
rewarding thing for me personally is to work with young
people buying their first house. You find out just how important a fireplace is. Who needs a basement? (Laughs.)
"We really don't have to have a garage, but we've got to
have a fireplace." (Laughs.) That kind of thing.

One of the nicest parts is the continual influx of people
from all over the country, all ages. It would be easy to
stagnate in a village, where you only see people of similar
backgrounds. I find it stimulating to be exposed to someone that isn't cut out of the same piece of cloth as I am.

I thought. Why not try real estate? Houses, I love. I'm
probably a frustrated architect at heart. (Laughs.) I started as a secretary and then went into the sales end of it.
It's infinitely more lucrative. The commission is six percent
of the first fifty thousand dollars and five percent on anything above that. Always meeting new people, always
meeting new situations, that's the kicker.

This is a very competitive area. There are a good many
seasoned, highly professional realtors in this area. So you
do step on each other's toes. It's seldom intentional. If
somebody picks up the Sunday paper and reads an ad
about a house listed with me and they call me, I can tell
in two minutes whether they've been looking for houses
with someone else. If they don't volunteer the information,
I'll ask them. I encourage them to call their own realtor.
If they're working with one who has given them good service, has given them time, for heaven's sake, stick with
him or her. My time is too valuable to spend with people
who are shopping with other brokers. The odds are not so
good there. I will do my best for anybody who sticks with
me. I'll give them my very best service and I'm entitled to
their loyalty.

As we get into integration, that kind of thing, realtors
take the stand that they represent buyers and sellers. They
do not have a stand to take themselves. A realtor is hired.
It's not up to him to educate you about who you want to
sell your house to or who you shouldn't. There's a feeling
that realtors ought to take a more active stand. Our position is: he owns it, we don't. We simply represent him—
within the framework of the law, of course. I have never
been instructed not to sell to a black family or to a Jewish

family. I'm not naïve. I'm sure there must be cases. But it has not happened to me. Our average house is fifty thousand dollars apiece, so you're limited right there.

This Sunday I will hold a house open from one to four. It will be advertised in the newspaper. I will be there to answer questions. Individuals who are looking for a house will undoubtedly come. Other brokers will bring their clients. I'm representing the seller. We cooperate. Hopefully the owners of the house will not be there from one to four. It's better for them. That's a hard experience for an owner—somebody walking through and saying, "Why did she ever pick this color for the living room?" You're there taking the names of people going through. Watching the house, showing it to its best advantage. Although I don't hesitate to point out what I think are bad features.

About twenty years ago there were many part time ladies in this field. Ladies who had lunch with friends and somebody said, "I'm looking for a house." So you found them a house and that was your contribution and your workday. This is frowned upon and no longer condoned. If you're going to hold a realtor's license, you declare this is your occupation and you're doing nothing else. I think that's good. Men who are supporting their families doing this should not be undermined by the ladies luncheon realtor.

A woman realtor makes very good sense. Women know more about kitchens than men. (Laughs.) By and large, it's the woman who buys the house. Most men, in my experience, let the wife decide, as long as the price is right and the schools are okay and he can get to the train. She's going to be spending the time in it. What pleases her pleases him. Naturally a woman can better understand a woman's needs and find what she's looking for.

You've got business transfers. These are an active thing. Maybe the guy's been promoted and comes in from Connecticut. They lived in a very attractive thirty-five-thousand-dollar house and, boy, they can spend sixty thousand now. They begin to cry a little when they see what they're gonna get for sixty thousand dollars. (Laughs.) It isn't as pretty as the thirty-five-thousand-dollar home they left in Connecticut. Status is important when they first come looking. They're apt to get over that when they see that some of the best areas have ugly stucco houses. But they're close to the schools, close to the beach, there's good transportation, and good things going on for the kids. Status goes out the window. They want to know if there are children on the block. We don't get many questions about ethnic groups. Status goes out the window.

Of course you get tensions. I just had a three-thousand-dollar deal fall apart. It didn't look good from the beginning, that's the only thing I can say about it. (Laughs.) It's been listed with me for six months. Another broker brought in an offer on it. I actually didn't spend more than eight or ten hours on this deal. But if you compound the time I've spent holding this house open, writing ads, showing it, answering phone calls, writing letters—yeah, yeah, it's a lot of time, yeah.

Some days are just like lightning. This last year, from the first of April until the middle of August, I had one Sunday at home. I can't show a house much before ten or eleven o'clock on a Sunday morning. But I'd be showing three or four houses between eleven and one. Then I'd be going to a house I'd be holding open maybe from two to five. Then somebody'd come in, they'd like to look at others. First thing you know it's seven thirty and I'd be dragging in. It can be very tiring.

On these open house mornings when you're going into house after house, there's an old trick. You go in on the first floor and then you go to the second floor, instead of going to the basement. From the second floor you can go down two flights to the basement. Then you just have to come up one. If you go to the basement first, you've got to *climb* two flights. (Laughs.) It keeps you in shape. (Laughs.) It's very important when you're showing a house that you be spry, that the stairs may not seem too high. If you go clombering, breathing heavy up the stairs, she may think, "How am I going to get my laundry up those stairs?" So . . .

I hear people say this is just like selling cars, nothing to it. I think there's a great deal to it. To me, the most exciting thing in the world is picking up the phone and having someone say, "Some friends are coming to town. Can you help them?" I hear some realtors say, "I hate showing somebody the first time." What that really means is: I hate meeting them, feeling uncomfortable. I'm excited about that couple I haven't seen. I'm excited about seeing them and getting to know them. I think it's fun. As long as I can make those stairs. (Laughs.)

JAMES CARSON

He has been a yacht broker for forty-one years. "I perform essentially the same service as a real estate broker. I locate yachts for customers. Every sale I make takes approximately 170 hours of effort. I can show the same yacht to twenty people before I have a buyer. The average number of yachts I sell a year is twenty. I've sold roughly eight hundred since I've been in the business."

He sells used yachts, valued at fifteen thousand dollars or more. "I don't have a showroom. It is where the yacht is at the moment. In the summertime they're usually in harbors. In the wintertime they're put in storage. I don't like to sell 'em if they're more than ten years old.

"There's salesmen that sell new yachts and they're dealers. They work right from the factory and they're required to buy so many yachts. I tried that and gave it up. It's not for me. You're on a treadmill. To keep your dealership you have to sell X number of new yachts a year. If there's a recession, the bank takes away most of the dealer's money. It's a pretty rough business. The dealer, unless he has a loyal manufacturer, can get in big trouble. I've seen many of 'em take on a dealership and then have the factory selling yachts right in his territory through a phony dealership. This ends up in bitterness and law suits. All that glitters is not gold when you sell yachts."

I find unfortunately, after forty-one years in this business, that up to eighty percent of the people take advantage of a situation. (Laughs.) It's a sour way to look at humanity, but it's the way I have found it.

Most of the time the seller calls me. Or else I'm a yacht locator. A buyer calls and says, "I'm looking for a thirty-four-foot Tartan sloop." This is what starts me off on my 170-hour search. I maintain my own file system. My radius is about three hundred miles. Some of these people want you to pay their fare back and forth. I could go broke flying people around the country.

I had a brother-in-law, when he was bored on a Sunday afternoon, he'd go look at houses. There was no intention of buying one, but he took up a lot of the real estate broker's time. In my younger days, when I was naïve, I spent a good deal of time not only showing yachts but taking people out for a two-hour cruise on the lake. Also feed 'em at the yacht club. They'd walk away without a thank you and you'd never see 'em again. That's human nature. Now I don't take anyone out on a yacht unless there's a deposit subject to inspection.

The seller pays the commission. It's a fixed price—seven percent. That's what I started with forty-one years ago and that's what I'll end with. Others charge ten percent. I make a living out of it. I feel that maybe I should charge more, but I'm getting ready to fold up and that's it.

I usually have the seller on a written contract. Sometimes this is not possible. Sometimes a customer calls up and says, "What have you got in a forty-two-foot half-cabin cruiser." I'll say, "I just got a listing over the phone." He'll say, "Let's go out and look at it." We'll go out to the yacht and the owner has a key hidden somewhere. I've never met the man. So maybe by the end of the day I'll have a deposit check and no contract to sell. I've been burned here, too. Buyer and seller get together . . .

There's a wide variety of people who buy yachts. He could be a carpenter, could be a doctor, any average man on the street. I've sold yachts to every class of workman. I'd say ninety-nine percent of our yachts are financed. The banks handle boat paper over a five-year period. But they want at least twenty-five percent down. It's just like automobiles. Practically everyone you see has got a loan on it.

When I started in this business, right up through World War II, bankers were scared of anyone that was improvident enough to own a yacht and also need money. They felt like J. P. Morgan—if you had to question the cost of the yacht, you shouldn't buy it. They thought a workingman had no right to buy it unless he could write a check for the full amount. But afterwards the banks solicited business. They have quite a bit of yacht paper now. There's every price class, there's a yacht. Some yachts go up to a million dollars, and you can buy a small sailboat for a couple hundred.

These big ones are rare. There's not too many people willing to splurge that kind of money on a yacht. When I first started out, the average wealthy man would buy a yacht, oh, seventy-five to one hundred, two hundred feet. There was a whole fleet of these yachts right on the Great Lakes. Some of them employed as high as sixteen men in a crew. After World War II and the tax situation, the 165-foot yachtsman owned a 52-foot yacht that could be run with one man instead of sixteen. Then they started putting yachts under corporations and charging them off. This kind of phased out when they were hounded by Internal Revenue.

The 1970 recession was so bad that it cost me over four thousand dollars. I had to go into my own savings to carry me through the year. The first thing they can do without is a yacht. People stopped buying yachts six months before the '70 crash. I guess they had inside information. I could tell it from the resistance to sales. You get along with a three-year-old automobile, you get along with a five-year-old yacht.

Oh, the yacht is a serious status symbol. A lot of the wealthier class people live right smack against Lake Shore Drive in those high rises overlooking Belmont Harbor. It's almost impossible to get a yacht in that harbor. They have a long waiting list. I'm sure those people sit in their apartments and say, "Oh yes, that's my yacht over there." Some of the yachts aren't even used, just kept as status symbols, pure and simple. They want to say, "I got a yacht."

They jump about five feet at a time, for status. First they'll start with an outboard, which I know nothing about. They'll come to me usually at thirty feet. They'll sell the thirty-footers, and want a thirty-five. They'll jump up five feet at a time until they get up to sixty or seventy feet. And that's it. There wasn't much jumping in '70, I'll tell you that.

There's two classes of buyers. One who's never had a yacht before, who you have to shepherd along. You baby-sit with him until you're confident he's well versed in the handling of the yacht. You can't give him the key and walk away and have him get in trouble in the lake. I'm emotionally involved with the man, I'm responsible for him. There's just purely selfish motives, too. Any bad publicity on the lake is bad publicity for yachting and bad publicity for the broker. I've got to see that he's safe.

You get involved with people that are overnight experts in boat construction. At first I used to argue with 'em. But now I just sit there and smile. You're a dummy, you just don't know anything. You just let them tell you. Doesn't matter any more. I regret this work. If I had to do it over again, I wouldn't do it. I'd be an engineer, a construction designer.

There's some fine men in this field. I don't think there have ever been used car dealers in the yacht business. The yachting fraternity is quite a gossipy clique. It doesn't take too long to get around if a fella throws a lot of curves. If you establish a good reputation, which I hope I have, that gets around too.

Sometimes you feel like you're appreciated and needed. Other times they make you feel like you're a parasite. What burns me up is after you've worked real hard on selling the man's yacht and showed it to a great number of people and you get ready to close the deal, he says, "I don't think I owe you seven percent." "Why not?" "You made only one phone call and this fella bought it." They don't know how many hours, how many months, how many days and years you sit there hoping something will happen. And the overhead goes on.

The frustration, the humiliation—but that's in any business, isn't it? Some of the people you trust the most want to chisel you the most. Your biggest danger is when you get to like a person. You become less businesslike than you should be. You don't get him signed up. You think, Well, I just can't ask the man. I've been a guest at his house, I've wined him and dined him and we're on a first name social basis. But when you sit down at the table you're got a different man entirely. Two different people. You find this out too late. You've got a law suit on your hands.

I had one man I thought so highly of, it was remarkable. He's an ex-Air Force pilot, had been a bombing pilot. And God, he's good looking, tall, slender, most gracious smile. He's a WASP, if you know what I mean. He looked like he could be an elder in any church in the country. And he had a very sociable wife. If you wanted somebody to represent the upper crust yachtsman, he would be the one. My God, how he disappointed me.

I sold the man his first yacht. I knew him for years and admired him. He traded in this yacht on a great big expensive diesel. His son, who was a teen-ager, was throwing wild parties on the boat. His wife was afraid something was bound to happen. She said, "We're going to sell it and get out of yachting entirely." They put the pressure on me constantly to sell the boat. Finally I got him a buyer. I had done a good job and got him a hell of a good price for it. (Sighs.) After all these years, I didn't—like a damn fool—if my attorney told me once he told me a thousand times, "Never trust anyone when it comes to business."

(Takes a deep breath.) The buyer got a forty-thousand-dollar loan at the bank, which I arranged. And the bank hands my old friend a cashier's check for forty thousand dollars. I said, "Charlie, what about my commission?" It came to over twenty-eight hundred dollars. He looked at me real blank. He glances at his coat pocket where he'd keep his wallet and said, "Oh, I forgot my checkbook." He didn't have to finish the sentence. I knew I was in trouble with this man, 'cause I had nothing in writing.

He brought in eight hundred dollars in cash and said, "This is unreported. You don't have to show it on your books. Internal Revenue will never know anything about it. I'm doing you a favor." I said, "You're trying to beat me out of two thousand bucks and put me in a penitentiary. Boy, you're the biggest surprise to me that I've ever had. I thought you were the *ne plus ultra* of everything a yachtsman would represent. You are the biggest phony I have ever met." He's president of a big coal and oil company. Top flight. It makes you wonder if you're too bright. God, to get hurt by a man like this.

You think a yacht broker is all smiles, and everything is milk and honey. You have your select circle of friends. And you just wonder how bright you are when you establish that circle. You just can't trust people. Regardless whether they're street cleaners or bank presidents, you can never tell when they're gonna throw that curve at you.

(A long pause.) The sooner I retire, the better. I'm getting to sixty-five and I'm just fed up. I can't roll with the punches like I used to. They bother me more than they used to. So I feel—what for? I should have quit years ago. Oh, I don't know what I'm gonna do. You know these people your whole life. You have no social life other than yacht broking. I don't know if I have anything to sell. Maybe you'd find some retired man that's looking for occupational therapy, that would keep him busy and would bring in about a thousand a month? (A dry chuckle.)

DAVID REED GLOVER

We're in the offices of Reed Glover and Company, a brokerage firm on La Salle Street, along Chicago's financial district. "My father was a founding partner. There are twelve partners. We have about twenty salesmen, who also handle the customers' accounts. These salesmen are otherwise known as customers' men.

"Our firm was founded in 1931 by my father, Reed Glover. He had been a banker in a downstate town. He felt an investment firm was needed to serve the small community banks. Now there are fifteen thousand bankers, mostly in the middle states, who receive our letters. After having been on the list for forty years, many of them get around to calling us. I'd say we're medium sized.

I'm forty years old. I started in the securities business in 1954, the only job outside the army I've had. I believed we were in a new era. I thought the founding partners of my firm were hampered by a Depression-era psychology, that they didn't understand there could no longer be a severe collapse in stock prices. The senior brokers were considered old fogies and stodgy for their unwillingness to go along with some of this new thinking. There has been a great chastening among younger men.

What happened in 1968 and 1969 is that a great many large firms overexpanded. Worse than that, they recommended stocks which were unsound. I'm talking now about the conglomerates. You've heard about the Four Seasons nursing homes, about electronic stocks. This became the rage. When the downturn occured in '69 and '70, many of these firms went out of business. They forgot that there really isn't a new era. The business cycle is not going to vanish. You must be prepared for adversity as well as prosperity. I realize now there are certain principles that must be adhered to.

There have been many times of personal questioning about my occupation. The worst time came when I approached the magic mark of forty. (Laughs.) During that time we were in the heart of the bear market (laughs), and this is a highly emotional business. When the market is on its way up, you have a feeling of well-being and fulfillment, of contributing to the welfare of others. When the market is going down, this is a rather unfortunate line to be in. When you're dealing with an individual's money it's a terrific responsibility.

The individual of means is exposed to so many people in the brokerage business that it's quite a compliment to have him turn to you for investment service. The rule I've always gone by is that I expect to have my brother-in-law's account and my roommate in college. But it seems everybody has a roommate in college or a brother-in-law who's in this business. So I don't really use my social acquaintances for purposes of business. My closest friends are with many of the brokerage firms. At social gatherings we don't discuss the market, other than in an amusing rather than a serious way.

I'm amazed how rarely the individual customer will find fault with the broker. Along with that, there's no written contract in our business. If the stock goes down, the customer's word is his only pledge. They all pay. This is an honorable business.

When you're dealing with a person's money and investments, you deal with his hopes and ambitions and dreams. More people are becoming sophisticated in understanding that they can actually own part of a corporation like General Motors simply by placing an order for an intangible item like a stock certificate.

It's quite easy to look around and say this is a parasitical business. All you're doing is raking off your cut from the productivity of others. That is, I think, an erroneous view. Frankly, I've wrestled with that. It comes down to this: the basis of this country's strength and prosperity is the finest economic system that's ever been devised, with all its inequities and imperfections. Our system depends on a free exchange of publicly owned assets, and we're part of the picture.

If there were no stock market, I think the economy would be stifled. It would prevent the growth of our companies in marketing the securities they need for their expansion. Look at Commonwealth Edison. It came out just the other day with a million shares. Without a stock market, the companies wouldn't be able to invest their capital and grow. This is my life and I count myself very fortunate to be in this work. It's fulfilling.

RAY WAX

He has been a stockbroker on Wall Street for several years. He lives in an upper-middle-class suburb on the outskirts of New York City. He is married, has two grown children.

"I really believed when I was growing up that somehow I would score. As a kid—I was no more than twelve—I'd get up at five o'clock in the morning and go to an open market where they sold cakes in an open stall. It was so goddamned cold you had to cut the goddamned cakes with mittens. I made four, five dollars a day. That was a lot of money in those days. I worked. I felt good about it.

"I was a golf caddy at fourteen. I used to carry two sets of golf bags for eighteen holes for $2.50. I guess its a ten-dollar bill today. You really earned your pay when you went through eighteen holes. If the caddy master liked you, maybe you did thirty-six holes.

"I felt even though there was money in the house, I was supposed to work. I was supposed to earn something. It was one of the things you had to do. If you did, it was supposed to make you feel good. I was a good caddy and I felt good about it. I felt that somewhere along the line someone would recognize that I had that special gleam. Horatio Alger—which is a crock of shit."

For twenty years he engaged in all sorts of enterprises and "I was generally successful. Then I lost interest or I thought the promise had gone out of it and I went on to something else. In the late fifties I had exported cars to South America. I was doing a million dollars a year and sort of ran out of steam. My one virtue was I didn't rip anybody off. For a while I thought I could live in South America. And I found out that the whole world was rigged. They didn't want me to do anything legit."

What kept you from becoming a millionaire?

"I just wasn't ... I wasn't facile enough. I was bright

enough to do the things I had to do to make a good living, but I really didn't come up with a big score. And . . . (Pause.) Well, there was a limit to what I was prepared to do to make money in a crazy way. But that's no good. You're supposed to do everything you have to do to make money. I guess at some point there's a limit. You either demean yourself or change yourself or something happens where you become something else. Later, when I owned a hotel, the only way I could survive is if I let a pimp put four broads in the bar. I passed. I couldn't do it. I eventually lost the hotel.

He became a land speculator. "*I kinda ran out of money, because land takes a lot of money. I became a real estate broker in self-defense. I began to peddle land. I sold land to builders. I realized they were just one cut above running a candy store. Within a couple of years I was building houses and building them better than anybody's ever built them before. I really had some kind of responsibility to build a house that was a good house. Until I began to run out of land . . .*"

I loved building houses. It's really a marvelous thing. You work with people that work with their hands. When the carpenters come in to work, goddamn it, they're good. When the bricklayers came in, they gotta know their job. I had a roofer, a Norwegian or whatever the hell he was—when he went up on that fuckin' roof and he bucked that stuff there, man, you knew you were gonna have the best roof you ever had on a house. I didn't cheat on the house. I sold my own houses, wouldn't turn them over to an agent. I enjoyed doing that more than anything I ever enjoyed in my life. I don't know why I didn't continue it.

I was kind of driven. I had to go on doing something else. I couldn't see myself building a development of fifty, a hundred houses, little boxes. I couldn't get the kind of plots where I could put five, six houses on one or two acres, to build a house with enough nuances. The challenge went out of it after a while.

I invested in a hotel. It had 101 keys. I got fascinated with hotels, the operation of it, how it was put together, who came, who went. I came out with a quarter of a million and I built my own hotel—alongside the World's Fair grounds. We did the biggest job of any motel at the fair. In two years the fair was a shambles. The area was a desert, death. I walked away with a whole skin, but gave the hotel back to the bank.

While I was fiddlin' around with the hotel I began to play the market. I got lucky at some point and made about a hundred thousand dollars. That convinced me I could make this my way of life. I thought it would be a nice way to live. I began to study to be a stockbroker. I passed the exam. You learn the ethical side of the business, what you can and can't do. It's all mumbo jumbo.

The New York Stock Exchange has 1,066 members. I always think of it as the Norman Invasion. These are William the Conquerors. The 1066 is one of the greatest clubs in that world. A seat on the exchange costs anywhere from a hundred thousand dollars in bad times to a half a million in good times. These guys didn't pay that price of admission without deciding that they're gonna take care of each other, protect their own. They're the guardians of all the stock. They're the specialists. They dole out these stocks to each other and they have the edge. They become the bookies on all the stocks. This is the only wheel in town.

I really thought of the market as a sort of river. Money running to the sea. I figured all I had to do is just stand on that bank and lower a bucket every once in a while and take a little bit of that out. I didn't care how much these gentle gentiles, with those little briefcases under their arms, took back to Larchmont or how much went up to Westport. I figured they're gonna let me lower my bucket. But they don't let anybody lower a bucket.

I'm afraid the work of a stockbroker is superfluous. He did have a function at one time, when little people were allowed in the market and given a chance to share in part of the goodies. The market really is a game played by very skilled people, who accumulate stocks at low levels so they can be distributed at high. The market is rigged. Knowledgeable people buy certain stocks, whether they have intrinsic value or not, and at some later hour the public is told these stocks represent good values and should be purchased. By the time Joe Blow goes in, the people who've created this atmosphere go out. For every dollar made in the market, a dollar has been lost. The pros make it, the 1066 boys.

The brokerage firms need some people to make this whole machine work. Somewhere in this pattern of things is the stockbroker. Here's where I come in. We're all hooked in. I'm watching every transaction. Everything that happens in the market I see instantaneously. I have a machine in front of me that records and memorizes every transaction that takes place in the entire day. It's called a Bunker-Ramo. It's really a television screen that reproduces the information from a master computer that sits in New Jersey. Within a fraction of a second, when I press for the symbol I want, it goes to the central computer and it automatically comes back. When I take my hand from the machine, the screen in front of me is already reproducing the information.

I watch eighteen million, twenty million shares pass the tape. I look at every symbol, every transaction. I would go out of my mind, but my eye has been conditioned to screen maybe two hundred stocks and ignore the others. I pick up with my eyes Goodrich, but I don't see ITT. I don't follow International Tel, I'm not interested in that. I don't see ITT, but I do see IBM. There are over thirty-two hundred symbols. I drop the other three thousand. Otherwise I'd go mad. I really put in an enormously exhausting day.

It's up at six thirty, I read the *New York Times* and the *Wall Street Journal* before eight. I read the Dow Jones ticker tape between eight and ten. At three thirty, when the market closes, I work until four thirty or five. I put in a great deal of technical work. I listen to news reports avidly. I try to determine what's happening. I'm totally immersed in what I'm doing. For the amount of work and intelligence I bring to this job, I'm not being properly compensated. I make a routine living now. The only compensation is like me against the machine. I'm trying to use my intelligence against the wheel. I'm a fuckin' John Henry fightin' this goddamned steel drill, and I'll probably die with my hammer in my hand. (Laughs.) Because I don't want to buy the package. Maybe I'm wrong, but I want to get there my own way. It's very difficult, that's God's truth.

The market moves to destroy you. It says, Play it your way, sucker, buy the package. Believe in the American Dream, buy the hundred time multiple, believe in IBM, and if you doubt it, God help you. Don't ever question what you're doing.

*"People go to the race track. When there's fifty thousand
people at the track, 49,990 are there to lose money. It's
kind of a self-flagellation. There's maybe ten people in
that park who are pros, who've been there at six in the
morning and clocked the horses, who've felt the turf and
talked to the jockeys or stable boy. They're the professional
gamblers. They're there for just one reason—to make
money. The 49,990 other slobs, they're there to lose. I
don't have to tell you about horses."*

People who go into the market are committed to losing
money. They don't blame the broker. They don't blame
the machine, which is rigged against them. The moment
you buy a stock, you're hooked. You're gonna pay a commission on the way in or on the way out. Normally that's
a sizable percentage. The stock has to move up at least a
point and a quarter for you to get even. If you bought a
stock at $50, it has to move to $51.35 before you'd get
even. You're being humped before you even get around
the corner. The moment you buy that stock, you're a
loser.

What I try to do to justify my existence is to understand
how it works. I took courses. I took in every lecture. I
subscribed to services. I do charting. I'm almost like that
gambler who clocks the horse at six in the morning on the
workout when they blow that horse out. But I'm really on
the outside lookin' in. Somebody else has rigged the race
and knows who's gonna win it. And somebody else knows
what stock's gonna go. I'm sure every stock has a group
that decides when they're gonna go and when they're
gonna get off. All you can hope to do when you see that
train moving—there's the theory of the moving train . . .

When the train begins to move, all you can do is see it
move and hope to get on. You don't know when the train
slows down until after the big boys have jumped off.
You're gonna get on ten points after they did and get off
ten points after they did. If you can discern the direction
of the train . . .

Maybe if I was twenty, twenty-five years and I just
came out of Harvard Business School and I believed this
bullshit, which is packaged and wrapped . . . Wall Street,
Madison Avenue. The people even look the same. They
really believe in their invulnerability. They believe their
own success story. I don't believe it. (A rueful chuckle.)

That's a hell of an argument to be a broker. In a crazy way I do a service. I try to give such customers as I have a rational explanation for an investment. I try ... (Sighs wearily.)

"Look, we've got eighty billions of dollars worth of money floating around in Europe. It's nonconvertible. We've fucked every country in the world. We've got every central bank in the world with dollars up to their ass. They can't do anything with it. We said to 'em, "We're the Texans." The world belongs to Connally. He told 'em in effect, 'Live with that money. We've bought your companies, we've taken over your economies, we've given you dollars that are spurious. Don't blow the whistle on us, because the whole fuckin' sky is gonna come down, Chicken Little. Maybe two, three years from now, if the spirit moves us, we may talk about the convertibility of the dollars into gold. In the meantime, Fuck ya. Put those dollars in our treasury notes, buy our stocks, do somethin' with 'em. But don't come back to me to redeem 'em, because they're worthless.' We fucked the world.

"I've seen 'em do this. I buy gold, I buy silver. It's the only thing that's real. You can't buy gold in this country. We don't dare. If we let Americans buy gold, everybody'd be diggin' up his fuckin' back yard and buryin' gold bullion in it. 'Cause he knows the fuckin' thing's real."

(A long pause.) I try to perform a function that has some meaning. I try to take somebody's money and not make shit out of it. If a banker's taking your money and giving you five percent and he's earning twelve percent on it, there should be a better way for the little man to participate. He should do a hell of a sight better than giving it to an insurance company or a bank. It shouldn't be that rigged. He should have a chance to get a fair return on that money. He's worked for it. Somebody else shouldn't be able to use that money and get a twelve percent return while paying the little guy five in front.

The real money made in the market is being made by people with real wealth. I'll say, "If you give me five thousand dollars, I can make you a ten percent return. If we're pretty good, maybe I can get you twenty percent. If it's a smash, maybe we'll double it." But the only way you're gonna make a million dollars is to start with a million dollars.

*"People who have made money in the market have consist-
ently had money. The great wealth in this country has
bought Johnson & Johnson, has bought IBM. They never
sold a share. To this day, sixty-six percent of the stock is
owned by people that never sold a share. They bought
General Motors in 1930 they never sold it. They didn't
put it in the banks at four percent return. They live on the
return. They never sell the principle."*

I'm trying to use my intelligence, which I've exercised
in other businesses. But it's like wrestling with an octopus.
Too many things that I can't control are happening. I can
tell you what happened after the fact, but it's very difficult
to tell you before the fact. The market never really repeats itself exactly in the same way day after day. There
is similarity over the years. Jesse Livermore, a legend,
went broke three times. But he was so valuable to the
Street, he created so much excitement that the fraternity,
the 1066 club, gave him the money to put him back in
business. His manipulation in the market, his activity,
created additional sales every day. Other people became
excited and involved. Yet this man, with all his experience,
continually got wiped out. He was bucking something bigger than he was. Ultimately he was destroyed and killed
himself. He lost touch with even the reality he knew.*

It's really an illusion. It's only real because enough people believe it's real. The whole market is based on a premise—potential growth. You can put any kind of multiple
on a stock. If a stock earns a dollar a year, it sells for a
hundred. It's selling at a hundred times its earning capacity. If you believe the stock is a reflection of some future
experience, that you can invest in a hundred times its
earning capacity and that you will subsequently benefit, you

---

* "Livermore said, 'I own what I believe to be the controlling
stock of IBM and Philip Morris.' So I asked, "Why do you
bother with anything else?' He answered 'I only understand
stock. I can't bother with businesses.' So I asked him, 'Do
men of your kind put away ten million dollars where nobody
can touch it?' He looked at me and answered, 'Young man,
what's the use of having ten million if you can't have big
money?' "—Arthur Robertson's recollections in *Hard Times*
(New York: Pantheon Books, 1970.)

qualify as a true believer. But the moment you question that premise, the whole thing collapses like a house of cards. You have to buy this whole crazy fiction or there would be no market.

"IBM, Eastman Kodak, Xerox, these are called growth stocks. And they're held by every major institution, every pension fund, every university. This is the backbone. Nobody questions the basic premise that these stocks will continually get better. Polaroid over the past four years has had an earning growth of minus eleven. But because they've got a camera that is unique, they pretend they will expand at an infinite rate. As long as you believe that, you can pay 130 for Polaroid, as it was today. You'll pay anything as long as you believe this American Dream that growth is forever. But the people who make this market, at some bad hour they're gonna sell Polaroid at 130 to shnooks like you and me. And they're gonna pick it up again at 65 and start the whole process all over. They've done it continually."

Some people know me over a period of years and have allowed me to handle their business. I've created new business on solicitation, depending on how good my track record is. The function of a broker is to try to get his account to trade. The real money is never made by selling stock. A broker's lifeblood, the only money he makes, is by generating commissions. Most money is made by getting people to turn their portfolios, their stocks, over three, four, five times a year. If you're really unethical—cynical, the milder word—you may get 'em to turn their stocks over ten times a year or fifteen times. There's a name for it.

Brokers merely are ribbon clerks. They're order takers. They do very little if it's a big house. It's a profession that's in its decline. Everything is being committed to computer, to systemized tapes. These are houses now on the Street that say, "Don't you ever make a decision. We have a computer that tells you what to do to your customer, to buy and to sell." At some point the function of a broker may be relegated to some girl who sits at a phone and repeats what the computer has told the customer to buy and to sell. I see Wall Street being reduced to kind of a supermarket. The biggest houses will be swallowing the others. You'll wind up with four or five houses and not many more than half a dozen.

There are houses that guarantee if you utilize the machine, you'll get five or ten trades a year out of your customers. They'll put him in a stock and they'll take him out. Beautiful. But in actual practice, when the market goes sour, the machine breaks down. It can't take care of the vagaries. The machine can't account for an economic crisis or a world depression. The machine can't account for an unemployment rate that exceeds six percent. The machine can't account for a military adventure in Vietnam. It's a robot. It can do what the programmed tape tells it to. But it can't account for the extraordinary world we live in.

People like me start out with a feeling that there's a place for them in society, that they really have a useful function. They see it destroyed by the cynicism of the market. A piece of worthless stock can be given glamour and many people may be induced to buy it. Excitement, public relations. The people can be wiped out with the absolute cynicism that brings those who conceived it to the top.

Can you imagine? I really felt I could buck this machine. When I began, I was sure I could win. I no longer have that confidence. What's happening is so extraordinary. It's so much bigger than I am.

I'm just trying to go along for the ride. I have little to do with it. They believe the game because they know how the cards are gonna be dealt. I don't believe the game because I know the cards are stacked. After being told about fiscal responsibility, they know the treasury's gonna spew out all kinds of dollars, and all kinds of money's gonna be made available to the corporations for them to put in the market. This is a contradiction. This is where the thing breaks down.

I can't say what I'm doing has any value. This doesn't make me too happy. If I could learn in some way to live with the wheel—but I can't. If I make an error and it costs the customer money, it's as though it were my money. This is extraordinary. The average broker lives to generate commissions and he goes home as though he were selling shoelaces or ties. He doesn't carry the goddamn market with him. I carry it like it was a monkey on my back. Man, I wake up in the middle of the night remembering what I did right or wrong. That's no good. But I really can't make it happen.

When I built the houses, I hired a bricklayer, I hired the roofer, I determined who put the goddamned thing together. And when I handed somebody a key, the house was whole. I made it happen. I can't do it in the market. I'm just being manipulated and moved around and I keep pretending I can understand it, that I can somehow cope with it. The truth is I can't.

The broker as a human being is being demeaned by the financial community. His commissions are being cut. I joined the Association of Investment Brokers—we number about a thousand members as against forty thousand brokers—which tries to think of itself as though it were the Pilots Union. The terrible thing is we don't fly planes. We handle the fuckin' phone and punch out digits on something that translates from a computer. We pretend we have status in the community, but we're expendable.

The brokerage firms just cut our commission again, while they increased their own rate by forty-two percent. The SEC approved a new set of commission rates. The SEC is just an arm of the stock exchange. They put their people in it. Like every regulatory agency, it serves the exchange and pisses on the public. The commissions for the houses are larger, but I make no more than I made before. This happened in every firm on the Street. It's as though they went out and played golf together and agreed on it.

In this rip-off, we're treated with contempt by the members of the stock exchange. You're being told you're not a useful member of society. They're really saying, "If you make too big a noise, we're gonna have a girl take the orders and the machine'll do the rest. You're better off to let us make your decisions. Don't attempt to use your intelligence. Don't attempt to figure out what's happening, if you know what's good for you."

Oh, I'll continue to cope. (Laughs.) I'll continue to struggle against the machine. I'll continue with my personal disillusionment. (Laughs.) Oh, I'd like one morning to wake up and go to some work that gave me joy. If I could build houses all over again, I would do it. Because when it's finished, somebody's gonna live in it, and the house is gonna be built and it's gonna be there after I'm gone. (Pause.) Ahhh, fuck it!

BUREAUCRACY

STEVE CARMICHAEL

"I'm a coordinator. I'm project management." He works
*for the Neighborhood Youth Corps. Though it is federally
funded through the OEO, he is employed by the city.
"Two of our agencies were joined together about six
months ago. A further step toward institutionalizing the
poverty program."* He heads a department of nine people.
*"We take young people of poverty income families and as-
sist them through work experiences, those who've dropped
out of school, and thereby better their potential of obtain-
ing a job."*

He is twenty-five, has a wife and one child.

When I was with VISTA my greatest frustration was
dealing with administrators. I was working in a school and
I saw the board of education as a big bureaucracy, which
could not move. I was disdainful of bureaucrats in Washington, who set down rules without ever having been to
places where those rules take effect. Red tape. I said I
could replace a bureaucrat and conduct a program in relationship to people, not figures. I doubt seriously if three
years from now I'll be involved in public administration.
One reason is each day I find myself more and more like
unto the people I wanted to replace.

I'll run into one administrator and try to institute a
change and then I'll go to someone else and connive to get
the change. Gradually your effectiveness wears down.
Pretty soon you no longer identify as the bright guy with
the ideas. You become the fly in the ointment. You're crit-

icized by your superiors and subordinates. Not in a direct manner. Indirectly, by being ignored. They say I'm unrealistic. One of the fellas that works with me said, "It's a dream to believe this program will take sixteen-, seventeen-year-old dropouts and make something of their lives." This may well be true, but if I'm going to believe that I can't believe my job has any worth.

I may be rocking the boat, though I'm not accomplishing anything. As the criticism of me steps up, the security aspect of my job comes into play. I begin to say, "Okay, I got a recent promotion. I earned it." They couldn't deny anybody who made significant inputs. Now I'm at a plateau. As criticism continues, I find myself tempering my remarks, becoming more and more concerned about security.

I'm regarded as an upstart. I'm white and younger than they are. (Laughs.) They're between thirty and forty. They might rate me fair to middlin' as a person. They might give me a sixty percent range on a scale of a hundred percent. As a supervisor, I'd be down to about twenty percent. (Laughs.) I think I'm a better supervisor than they give me credit for. They criticize me for what criticism they may have of the entire program—which is about the way I criticized my supervisor when I was in their position. He became an ogre, the source of blame for the failings of the program. The difference is I don't patronize my staff the way he did. They make a recommendation to me and I try to carry it out, if I feel it's sound. I think it's built up some of their confidence in me.

My suggestions go through administrative channels. Ninety percent of it is filtered out by my immediate superior. I have been less than successful in terms of getting things I believe need to be done. It took me six months to convince my boss to make one obvious administrative change. It took her two days to deny that she had ever opposed the change.

We've got five or six young people who are burning to get into an automotive training program. Everybody says, "It takes signatures, it takes time." I follow up on these things because everybody else seems to forget there are people waiting. So I'll get that phone call, do some digging, find out nothing's happened, report that to my boss, and call back and make my apologies. And then deal with a couple of minor matters—Johnny ripped off a saw today

... certain enrollees are protesting because they're getting gypped on their paychecks.

So we're about a quarter to five and I suddenly look at my desk and it's filled with papers—reports and memos. I have to sort them out before a secretary can file 'em. Everybody'll leave at five o'clock, except for me. Usually I'm there until six o'clock. If I did all the paper work I should, my sanity would go. Paper work I almost totally ignore. I make a lot of decisions over the phone. It hits you about two months later when somebody says, "Where's the report on such and such? Where's the documentation?"

"I had a lot more hope once. When I came out of VISTA I wanted to work in education. I wanted a decent paying job, too. I started out here at ten thousand dollars a year. That's good when you consider I had no experience in the field and was only twenty-three. I didn't realize how much it meant when you said you were a VISTA. I didn't think it was that phenomenal.

"I had four years of college in business administration. I worked for Illinois Bell, a fairly decent job. But this was not for me. I had too much energy. I got into business because it was easy. After working awhile, all my beliefs in the corruption of private industry were substantiated. (Laughs.) That turned me off. What's left? Social service. I quit, hightailed to Washington, and I was accepted in VISTA four days after I got my induction notice. (Laughs.) They got me a 2-A deferment, and miraculously I was not tripping rice paddies.

The most frustrating thing for me is to know that what I'm doing does not have a positive impact on others. I don't see this work as meaning anything. I now treat my job disdainfully. The status of my job is totally internal: Who's your friend? Can you walk into this person's office and call him by his first name? It carries very little status to strangers who don't understand the job. People within the agency don't understand it. (Laughs.)

Success is to be in a position where I can make a decision. Now I have to wait around and see that what I say or do has any impact. I wonder how I'd function where people would say, "There's a hotshot. He knows what he's talking about." And what I say became golden. I don't know if it would be satisfying for me. (Laughs.) That might be more frustrating than fighting for everything you want. Right now I feel very unimportant.

POSTSCRIPT: *"While I was waiting for this job I was advised to see my ward committeeman. I was debating. My wife was pregnant. I had virtually no savings. I was gonna get a ten-thousand-dollar job. What was I gonna do? I was all set to work as a taxicab driver. Then I said, 'I'm going to be a bricklayer. Just come home at night, take a bath, relax.' I was prepared to call my uncle, who's a mason. I knew he could connect me, that's the irony. I was decrying a system that forced me to go to my ward committeeman to get a city job, but I was going to call my uncle to get me at the head of the line to get in the masons union. (Laughs.) One sytsem was just as immoral as the other. By a stroke of luck, my application cleared city hall without my having to go through politics. To this day I'm politically unaffiliated. I don't know how long that will last. I may have to go to an alderman to get my promotion cleared.*

"My goal for the last two years is to be a university professor. He works only nine months a year. (Laughs.) He can supplement his income. What's a comfortable income? We started at fifteen thousand dollars—my wife and I—as our goal. We're up to about twenty-five thousand now. If I have another kid, the goal'll go to thirty thousand. The way I look at the university professor— aside from his capacity to influence other people—is that the business world often uses him as a consultant. Not bad.

LILITH REYNOLDS

It's hard for me to describe what I'm doing right now. It may sound like gobbledygook. It's hard to understand all the initials. It's like alphabet soup, We just went through a reorganization, which is typical of government. Reorganization comes at a rapid rate these days. My job has changed not only in name but in status.

She has worked for the federal government for nine years. "I work for the OEO. I was assistant to the regional director. I was what's called the regional council liaison person.

There's something called the Inter-Agency Regional Coun-
cil, which is made up of five agencies: OEO, HEW, Wel-
fare, Labor, Transportation, and Housing. This group
meets once a month.

"Agencies don't really want to coordinate their efforts.
They want to operate their programs their way and the
hell with the others. OEO has been unique in that we've
funded directly to communities without going through
other government structures.*

"The regional councils are really directed from Wash-
ington. They're told what to do by the Office of Manage-
ment and Budget. They are just a little political thing. One
of the big pushes was to make better contact with the six
governors of the region and the mayors—from appoint-
ments secretary to planning staffs to budget departments.
Getting the money you need for the programs you want,
getting it down to the people. We spent most of our time
doing that.

It's amazing how little information there really is
around. How systematically it's kept from getting around.
Some of the Spanish-speaking community groups got fairly
good at harassing the regional director. They wanted answers to questions. How many Spanish-speaking people
are employed in our office? That wasn't hard—two. How
many are employed by agencies to which we were giving
grants? How many people are being served by the programs we're funding? These were legitimate questions. The
way we went about getting the answers was ridiculous. We
just couldn't come up with the statistics. We made an educated guess. It's hard to change the rules. People take the
course of least resistance.

There's a theory I have. An employee's advancement
depends on what his supervisor thinks of him, not on what
the people working for him think. The regional director's
job depends on his friendship in Washington. So the best
thing for him to do is not challenge the system, not make
waves. His future depends on being nice to the people who

* "The Nixon administration has accelerated the movement
toward patient, prudent evaluation, particularly in the Office
of Economy Opportunity . . . Prominent among the victims
was the OEO, flagship of old ways but also home of the new"
(Jack Rosenthal, *New York Times,* February 4, 1973).

are making the decisions to make the cuts that are hurting his employees. So he's silent. But the people down here, the field representatives, who know what's going on, make waves. So the director tries to get rid of the most troublesome.

At our office there's less and less talk about poor people. It's mainly about how we should do things. I don't know if this was always so. It's just more obvious now. Local politicians have more and more say in the programs. In Chicago, Mayor Daley runs it. In other cities, it depends on the power structure. We talk more of local institutions these days, not of poor people.

I have been very active in the union.* We've frequently confronted management with problems we insisted they solve. We tried to get them to upgrade the secretaries. They're being underpaid for the jobs they're doing. Management fought us. We've tried to have a say in policy making. We've urged them to fund poor groups directly. Management fought us.

For instance, the union has backed the Midwest Poor People's Coalition. We tried to get funds directly to the Chicago Indian Village and a poor group in Indiana. Almost always, the agency has balked. We've attacked management because they're just not carrying out the Economic Opportunity Act.

The employees should help make policy, since they're closest to what's going on. It's probably the same as in auto plants. A lot of times workers can make better decisions about production than managers. The managers aren't down there often enough to know what's going on.

Your education prepares you to go into a job and accept what you're told as being correct. I worked several years for the Social Security Administration. It has a fantastic number of rules and regulations. For a long time I believed they were correct and it was my job to carry out these rules. After I got to OEO it became more and more obvious to me that a lot of these rules were wrong, that rules were not sacrosanct. I think this is happening to workers all over. They're challenging the rules. That's what we're in the process of doing.

Through the union people have been bringing up ideas

* American Federation of Government Employees.

and management is forced more and more to listen. They hadn't taken us very seriously up to now. But we just got a national contract which calls for union-management committees. I think our union has challenged management a lot more than most government unions. That's largely because of the kind of people OEO has attracted. They believe in being advocates of the poor. They believe in organizing people to challenge the system. It's a natural carryover to organize a union which also challenges the system.

I'm among the top fifteen people in the decision making process in the office. As the union became more aggressive—it was on the issue of the Indians, the director tried to fire our president—I got into a big hassle. We developed thirty-three charges against the director and made a mass mailing to all community agencies, to all the grantees, to all the senators and congressmen in the region. After that, I was no longer assistant to the regional director. (Laughs.)

That's another typical thing in government. When management wants to get rid of you, they don't fire you. What they do is take your work away. That's what happened to me. He didn't even tell me what my new job would be. They sent somebody down to go through my personnel file "My God, what can we do with her?" They had a problem because I'm a high-grade employee. I'm grade 14. The regional director's a 17. One of the deputy directors told me, "You're going to be economic development specialist." (Laughs.)

I'm very discouraged about my job right now. I have nothing to do. For the last four or five weeks I haven't been doing any official work, because they really don't expect anything. They just want me to be quiet. What they've said is it's a sixty-day detail. I'm to come up with some kind of paper on economic development. It won't be very hard because there's little that can be done. At the end of sixty days I'll present the paper. But because of the reorganization that's come up I'll probably never be asked about the paper.

It's extremely frustrating. But, ironically, I've felt more productive in the last few weeks doing what I've wanted to do than I have in the last year doing what I was officially supposed to be doing. Officially I'm loafing. I've been working on organizing women and on union activities. It's been great.

If they would let me loose a little more, I could really do something. We've got plenty of statistics to show incredible sex discrimination. Black women have the lowest average grade. White women have the next lowest. Then black men. Then white men. I'm sure these are the statistics for our whole society. We believe that in organizing women we can make changes in all directions. We've already started to do that.

There's no reason why we can't carry this to the community action agencies. Many of them deal with welfare mothers, with all kinds of households headed by women. If women knew more about their rights, they'd have an easier time. If we could get into the whole issue of law suits, we'd get real changes. My office is trying to stop us.

When you do something you're really turned on about, you'll do it off-hours too. I put more of myself into it, acting like I'm a capable person. When you're doing something you're turned off on, you don't use what talents you have. There are a lot of people in our office who are doing very, very little, simply because their jobs are so meaningless.

Some of these jobs will appear meaningful on paper. The idea of the antipoverty program is exciting. But people are stifled by bureaucratic decisions and non-decisions. When you're in the field and get into sticky situations with politicians, you can't count on your office to support you. You'll be punished—like having your job taken away from you. (Laughs.)

Since I've been doing what I want to do, my day goes much faster. When I was assistant to the regional director, an awful lot of my time was taken up with endless meetings. I spent easily twenty or more hours a week in meetings. Very, very nonproductive. Though now I'm doing what I want to do, I know it's not gonna last.

I have to hide the stuff I'm doing. If anybody walks into the office, you have to quick shove the stuff out of the way. It's fairly well known now that I'm not doing any official work, because this huge controversy has been going on between the union and the director. People are either on one side or the other. Most people who come in to see me are on the union side. I'm not hiding the fact that I'm not doing any official work.

I hide the stuff because I feel a little guilty. This is probably my Protestant upbringing. I've been work oriented all my life. I can't go on drawing a paycheck doing what I want to do—that's my conditioning. My dad worked in a factory. I was taught work is something you *have* to do. You do that to get money. It's not your life, but you must do it. Now I believe—I'm getting around to it (laughs)—you should get paid for doing what you want to do. I know its happening to me. But I still have this conditioning: it's too good to be true.

I've had discussions with friends of mine to the right and to the left of me. The people to the left say you shouldn't take any part in a corrupt system. To give them your time and take money from them is a no-no. People to the right say you have no right to take the taxpayers' money for doing nothing. You're not doing official work, therefore you shouldn't be paid for it.

I feel much less guilty about this than I would have a year ago. I have less and less confidence that management people should be telling me what to do. They know less than I do. I trust my own judgment more. I believe that what I'm doing is important.

What would be my recommendation? I read Bellamy's *Looking Backward,* which is about a utopian society. Getting paid for breathing is what it amounts to. I believe we'd be a lot better off if people got paid for what they want to do. You would certainly get a bigger contribution from the individual. I think it would make for exciting change. It'd be great.

The reasons people get paid now are wrong. I think the reward system should be different. I think we should have a basic security—a decent place to live, decent food, decent clothing, and all that. So people in a work situation wouldn't be so frightened. People are intimidated and the system works to emphasize that. They get what they want out of people by threatening them economically. It makes people apple polishers and ass kissers. I used to hear people say, "Work needs to be redefined." I thought they were crazy. Now I know they're not.

DIANE WILSON

She works for the OEO. "This is a section called PM&S. I can't for the life of me ever remember what it means* Sometimes they change it. They reorganize and you get another initial. (Laughs.)

"I'm a processing clerk. There are three of us in this one department. We send grants to grantees after field reps have been out to see these poverty-stricken people. The grantees are organizations of the poor. Maybe the Mobilization Center in Gary, where I live—Grand Rapids Poverty Center, something for senior citizens, a day care center. They give 'em all names.

"We mail 'em out forms to sign so they can get the money from Washington. When they return the forms to us there's another process we go through. We have a governor's letter and a package in an orange folder that we send out to him. He has to give his consent. We have a little telegram we type up. He approves it or he doesn't. We send it on. That makes it official. There's a thirty-day waiting period. After that time we send out the package to Washington . . .

You wish there was a better system. A lot of money is held up and the grantees want to know why they can't get it. Sometimes they call and get the run-around on the phone. I never do that. I tell the truth. If they don't have any money left, they don't have it. No, I'm not disturbed any more. If I was just starting on this job, I probably would. But the older I get, I realize it's a farce. You just get used to it. It's a job. I get my paycheck—that's it. It's all political anyway.

A lot of times the grantee comes down to our audit department for aid. They're not treated as human beings. Sometimes they have to wait, wait, wait—for no reason. The grantee doesn't know it's for no reason. He thinks he's getting somewhere and he really isn't.

They send him from floor to floor and from person to

* Personnel, Management, and Service.

person, it's just around and around he goes. Sometimes he leaves, he hasn't accomplished anything. I don't know why this is so. You can see 'em waiting—so long. Sometimes it has to do with color. Whoever is the boss. If you're in the minority group, you can tell by their actions. A lot of times they don't realize that you know, but this has happened to you.

So this person was standing out there. He had come to offer something. He was from out of state. The secretary told this boss he had someone waiting. He also had someone in the office. He could've waited on the grantee and got him on his way quick. But he closed the door in the young man's face and the young man stood there. That went on for about forty-five minutes. The secretary got tired of seein' the man standin' there, so she said, could she help him? Was it somethin' he just wanted to give the man? He told her yes. She took it, so he wouldn't stand there. That was all he was gonna do, give it to him. I thought this was awfully rude. This boss does this quite often. I don't know if he does it on purpose. I know if it's an Indian or a black or a Latin he does this.

Life is a funny thing. We had this boss come in from Internal Revenue. He wanted to be very, very strict. He used to have meetings every Friday—about people comin' in late, people leavin' early, people abusin' lunch time. Everyone was used to this relaxed attitude. You kind of went overtime. No one bothered you. The old boss went along. You did your work.

Every Friday, everyone would sit there and listen to this man. And we'd all go out and do the same thing again. Next Friday he'd have another meeting and he would tell us the same thing. (Laughs.) We'd all go out and do the same thing again. (Laughs.) He would try to talk to one and see what they'd say about the other. But we'd been working all together for quite a while. You know how the game is played. Tomorrow you might need a favor. So nobody would say anything. If he'd want to find out what time someone came in, who's gonna tell 'em? He'd want to find out where someone was, we'd always say, "They're at the Xerox." Just anywhere. He couldn't get through. Now, lo and behold! We can't find *him* anywhere. He's got into this nice, relaxed atmosphere ... (Laughs.) He leaves early, he takes long lunch hours. We've converted him. (Laughs.)

After my grievances and my fighting, I'm a processing clerk. Never a typist no more or anything like that. (Laughs.) I started working here in 1969. There was an emergency and they all wanted to work overtime. So I made arrangements at home, 'cause I have to catch a later train. Our supervisor's black. All of us are black. We'll help her get it out so there won't be any back drag on this. Okay, so we all worked overtime and made a good showing.

Then they just didn't want to give us the promotion which was due us anyhow. They just don't want to give you anything. The personnel man, all of them, they show you why you don't deserve a promotion. The boss, the one we converted—he came on board, as they call it, after we sweated to meet the deadline. So he didn't know what we did. But he told us we didn't deserve it. That stayed with me forever. I won't be bothered with him ever again.

But our grievance man was very good. He stayed right on the case. We filed a civil rights complaint. Otherwise we woulda never got the promotion. They don't want anybody coming in investigating for race. They said, "Oh, it's not that." But you sit around and see white women do nothin' and get promotions. Here we're working and they say you don't deserve it. The black men are just as hard on us as the white man. Harder. They get angry with you because you started a lot of trouble. The way I feel about it, I'm gonna give 'em all the trouble I can.

Our boss is black, the one that told us we didn't deserve it. (Laughs.) And our union man fighting for us, sittin' there, punchin' away, is white. (Laughs.) We finally got up to the deputy director and he was the one—the white man—that finally went ahead and gave us the promotion. (Laughs.) So we went from grade 4 clerk-typist to grade 5 processing clerk.

We had another boss, he would walk around and he wouldn't want to see you idle at all. Sometimes you're gonna have a lag in your work, you're all caught up. This had gotten on his nerves. We got our promotion and we weren't continually busy. Any time they see black women idle, that irks 'em. I'm talkin' about black men as well as whites. They want you to work continuously.

One day I'd gotten a call to go to his office and do some typing. He's given me all this handwritten script. I don't know to this day what all that stuff was. I asked him, "Why was I picked for this job?" He said his secretary was out and he needs this done by noon. I said, "I'm no longer a clerk-typist and you yourself said for me to get it out of my mind. Are you trying to get me confused? Anyway, I can't read this stuff." He tells me he'll read it. I said, "Okay, I'll write it out as you read it." There's his hand going all over the script, busy. He doesn't know what he's readin', I could tell. I know why he's doing it. He just wants to see me busy.

So we finished the first long sheet. He wants to continue. I said, "No, I can only do one sheet at a time. I'll go over and type this up." So what I did, I would type a paragraph and wait five or ten minutes. I made sure I made all the mistakes I could. It's amazing, when you want to make mistakes, you really can't. So I just put Ko-rect-type paper over this yellow sheet. I fixed it up real pretty. I wouldn't stay on the margins. He told me himself I was no longer a clerk-typist.

I took him back this first sheet and, of course, I had left out a line or two. I told him it made me nervous to have this typed by a certain time, and I didn't have time to proofread it, "but I'm ready for you to read the other sheet to me." He started to proofread. I deliberately misspelled some words. Oh, I did it up beautifully. (Laughs.) He got the dictionary out and he looked up the words for me. I took it back and crossed out the words and squeezed the new ones in there. He started on the next sheet. I did the same thing all over again. There were four sheets. He proofread them all. Oh, he looked so serious! All this time he's spendin' just to keep me busy, see? Well, I didn't finish it by noon.

I'm just gonna see what he does if I don't finish it on time. Oh, it was imperative! I knew the world's not gonna change that quickly. It was nice outside. If it gets to be a problem, I'll go home. It's a beautiful day, the heck with it. So twelve-thirty comes and the work just looks awful. (Laughs.) I typed on all the lines, I continued it anywhere. One of the girls comes over, she says, "You're goin' off the line." I said, "Oh, be quiet. I know what I'm doin'. (Laughs.) Just go away." (Laughs.) I put the four sheets together. I never saw anything as horrible in my life. (Laughs.)

I decided I'd write him a note. "Dear Mr. Roberts: You've been so much help. You proofread, you look up words for your secretary. It must be marvelous working for you. I hope this has met with your approval. Please call on me again." I never heard from him. (A long laugh.)

These other people, they work, work, work, work and nothing comes of it. They're the ones that catch hell. The ones that come in every day on time, do the job, and try to keep up with everybody else. A timekeeper, a skinny little black woman. She's fanatic about time. She would argue with you if you were late or something. She's been working for the government twenty-five years and she hadn't gotten a promotion, 'cause she's not a fighter.

She has never reported sick. Some days I won't come. If it's bad outside, heavy snow, a storm, I won't go. You go the next day. The work's gonna be there. She thinks my attitude is just terrible. She's always runnin', acts like she's scared of everybody. She was off *one* day. She had a dental appointment. Oh, did the boss raise hell! Oh, my goodness! He never argues with me.

The boss whose typing I messed up lost his secretary. She got promoted. They told this old timekeeper she's to be his secretary-assistant. Oh, she's in her glory. No more money or anything and she's doing two jobs all day long. She's rushin' and runnin' all the time, all day. She's a nervous wreck. And when she asked him to write her up for an award, he refused. That's *her* reward for being so faithful, obedient.

Oh, we love it when the bosses go to those long meetings, those important conferences. (Laughs.) We just leave in a group and go for a show. We don't care. When we get back, they roll their eyes. They know they better not say anything, 'cause they've done nothing when we've been gone anyhow. We do the work that we have to do. The old timekeeper, she sits and knits all that time, always busy.

I've been readin'. Everything I could on China, ever since he made that visit. Tryin' to see how people live and the ideas. It changed me a lot. I don't see any need for work you don't enjoy. I like the way the Indians lived. They moved from season to season. They didn't pay taxes. Everybody had enough. I don't think a few should control everything. I don't think it's right that women lay down and bear sons and then you have a few rich people that tell your sons they have to go and die for their country.

They're not dying for their country. They're dying for the few to stay on top. I don't think that's necessary. I'm just tired of this type of thing. I just think we ought to be just human.

ORGANIZER

BILL TALCOTT

My work is trying to change this country. This is the job I've chosen. When people ask me, "Why are you doing this?" it's like asking what kind of sickness you got. I don't feel sick. I think this country is sick. The daily injustices just gnaw on me a little harder than they do on other people.

I try to bring people together who are being put down by the system, left out. You try to build an organization that will give them power to make the changes. Everybody's at the bottom of the barrel at this point. Ten years ago one could say the poor people suffered and the middle class got by. That's not true any more.

My father was a truckdriver with a sixth-grade education. My uncle was an Annapolis graduate. My father was inarticulate and worked all his life with his hands. My uncle worked all his life with his mouth and used his hands only to cut coupons. My father's problem was that he was powerless. My uncle's problem was that he was powerless, although he thought he was strong. Clipping coupons, he was always on the fringe of power, but never really had it. If he tried to take part in the management of the companies whose coupons he was clipping, he got clipped. Both these guys died very unhappy, dissatisfied with their lives.

Power has been captured by a few people. A very small top and a very big bottom. You don't see much in-between. Who do people on the bottom think are the powerful people? College professors and management types, the local managers of big corporations like General Motors.

What kind of power do these guys really have? They have the kind of power Eichmann claimed for himself. They have the power to do bad and not question what they're told to do.

I am more bothered by the ghetto child who is bitten by rats than I am by a middle-class kid who can't find anything to do but put down women and take dope and play his life away. But each one is wasted.

"I came into consciousness during the fifties, when Joe McCarthy was running around. Like many people my age—I'm now thirty-seven—I was aware something was terribly wrong. I floundered around for two years in college, was disappointed, and enlisted in the army. I was NCO for my company. During a discussion, I said if I was a black guy, I would refuse to serve. I ended up being sent to division headquarters and locked up in a room for two years, so I wouldn't be able to talk to anybody.

"At San Francisco State, I got involved with the farm workers movement. I would give speeches on a box in front of the Commons. Then I'd go out and fight jocks behind the gym for an hour and a half. (Laughs.) In '64, I resigned as student body president and went to Mississippi to work for SNCC. I spent three years working in the black community in San Francisco.

"At that point, I figured it was time for me to work with whites. My father was from South Carolina. We had a terrible time when I visited—violent arguments. But I was family. I learned from that experience you had to build a base with white people on the fringe of the South. Hopefully you'd build an alliance between blacks and whites . . ."

I came to East Kentucky with OEO. I got canned in a year. Their idea was the same as Daley's. You use the OEO to build an organization to support the right candidates. I didn't see that as my work. My job was to build an organization of put-down people, who can *control* the candidates once they're elected.

I put together a fairly solid organization of Appalachian people in Pike County. It's a single industry area, coal. You either work for the coal company or you don't work. Sixty percent of its people live on incomes lower than the government's guidelines for rural areas.

I was brought in to teach other organizers how to do it. I decided these middle-class kids from Harvard and Columbia were too busy telling everybody else what they should be doing. The only thing to do was to organize the local people.

When I got fired, there were enough people to support me on one hundred dollars a month and room and board. They dug down in their pockets and they'd bring food and they'd take care of me like I was a cousin. They felt responsible for me, but they didn't see me as one of them. I'm not an Appalachian, I'm a San Franciscan. I'm not a coal miner, I'm an organizer. If they're gonna save themselves, they're gonna have to do it themselves. I have some skills that can help them. I did this work for three years.

The word organizer has been romanticized. You get the vision of a mystical being doing magical things. An organizer is a guy who brings in new members. I don't feel I've had a good day unless I've talked with at least one new person. We have a meeting, make space for new people to come in. The organizer sits next to the new guy, so everybody has to take the new guy as an equal. You do that a couple of times and the guy's got strength enough to become part of the group.

You must listen to them and tell them again and again they are important, that they have the stuff to do the job. They don't have to shuck themselves about not being good enough, not worthy. Most people were raised to think they are not worthy. School is a process of taking beautiful kids who are filled with life and beating them into happy slavery. That's as true of a twenty-five-thousand-dollar-a-year executive as it is for the poorest.

You don't find allies on the basis of the brotherhood of man. People are tied into their immediate problems. They have a difficult time worrying about other people's. Our society is so structured that everybody is supposed to be selfish as hell and screw the other guy. Christian brotherhood is enlightened self-interest. Most sins committed on poor people are by people who've come to help them.

I came as a stranger but I came with credentials. There are people who know and trust me, who say so to the others. So what I'm saying is verifiable. It's possible to win, to take an outfit like Bethlehem Steel and lick 'em. Most people in their guts don't really believe it. Gee, it's great when all of a sudden they realize it's possible. They become alive.

Nobody believed PCCA* could stop Bethlehem from strip mining. Ten miles away was a hillside being stripped. Ten miles away is like ten million light years away. What they wanted was a park, a place for their kids. Bethlehem said, "Go to hell. You're just a bunch of crummy Appalachians. We're not gonna give you a damn thing." If I could get that park for them, they would believe it's possible to do other things.

They really needed a victory. They had lost over and over again, day after day. So I got together twenty, thirty people I saw as leaders. I said, "Let's get that park." They said, "We can't." I said, "We can. If we let all the big wheels around the country know—the National Council of Churches and everybody start calling up, writing, and hounding Bethlehem, they'll have to give us the park." That's exactly what happened. Bethlehem thought; This is getting to be a pain in the ass. We'll give them the park and they'll shut up about strip mining. We haven't shut up on strip mining, but we got the park. Four thousand people for Pike County drove up and watched those bulldozers grading down that park. It was an incredible victory.

Twenty or thirty people realized we could win. Four thousand people understood there was a victory. They didn't know how it happened, but a few of 'em got curious. The twenty or thirty are now in their own communities trying to turn people on.

We're trying to link up people in other parts of the state—Lexington, Louisville, Covington, Bowling Green— and their local issues and, hopefully, binding them together in some kind of larger thing.

When you start talking to middle-class people in Lexington, the words are different, but it's the same script. It's like talking to a poor person in Pike County or Mississippi. The schools are bad. Okay, they're bad for different reasons—but the schools are bad.

The middle class is fighting powerlessness too. Middle-class women, who are in the Lexington fight, are more alienated than lower-class women. The poor woman knows she's essential for the family. The middle-class woman thinks, If I die tomorrow, the old man can hire

* Pike County Citizens' Association.

himself a maid to do everything I do. The white-collar guy is scared he may be replaced by the computer. The schoolteacher is asked not to teach but to baby-sit. God help you if you teach. The minister is trapped by the congregation that's out of touch with him. He spends his life violating the credo that led him into the ministry. The policeman has no relationship to the people he's supposed to protect. So he oppresses. The fireman who wants to fight fires ends up fighting a war.

People become afraid of each other. They're convinced there's not a damn thing they can do. I think we have it inside us to change things. We need the courage. It's a scary thing. Because we've been told from the time we were born that what we have inside us is bad and useless. What's true is what we have inside us is good and useful.

"In Mississippi, our group got the first black guy elected in a hundred years. In San Francisco, our organization licked the development agency there. We tied up two hundred million dollars of its money for two years, until the bastards finally came to an agreement with the community people. The guy I started with was an alcoholic pimp in the black ghetto. He is now a Presbyterian minister and very highly respected."

I work all the way from two in the morning until two the next morning seven days a week. (Laughs.) I'm not a martyr. I'm one of the few people I know who was lucky in life to find out what he really wanted to do. I'm just havin' a ball, the time of my life. I feel sorry for all these people I run across all the time who aren't doing what they want to do. Their lives are hell. I think everybody ought to quit their job and do what they want to do. You've got one life. You've got, say, sixty-five years. How on earth can you blow forty-five years of that doing something you hate?

I have a wife and three children. I've managed to support them for six years doing this kind of work. We don't live fat. I have enough money to buy books and records. The kids have as good an education as anybody in this country. Their range of friends runs from millionaires in San Francisco to black prostitutes in Lexington. They're comfortable with all these people. My kids know the name of the game: living your life up to the end.

All human recorded history is about five thousand years old. How many people in all that time have made an overwhelming difference? Twenty? Thirty? Most of us spend our lives trying to achieve some things. But we're not going to make an overwhelming difference. We do the best we can. That's enough.

The problem with history is that it's written by college professors about great men. That's not what history is. History's a hell of a lot of little people getting together and deciding they want a better life for themselves and their kids.

I have a goal. I want to end my life in a home for the aged that's run by the state—organizing people to fight 'em because they're not running it right. (Laughs.)

BOOK SEVEN

THE SPORTING LIFE

EDDIE ARROYO

There was an accident at the track today and I don't know really how the boy came out. At Hawthorne today. His horse fell and he just sailed. I don't know if he was conscious or not. The ambulance picked him up.

He is a jockey, unmistakably, and has been at it for about six years. He's had a good share of win, place, and show at race tracks out East, in the South, as well as in his home territory, Chicago. For "better than six months" of the year, he's a familiar man on a horse at Hawthorne, Arlington, and Sportsman's Park. "The first couple of years I rode, I didn't miss one day. I'd finish in Florida and took a plane and rode here the next day or whenever a track was open. I worked ninety-nine percent of the year."

He is twenty-eight. Though born in Puerto Rico, he's considered a Chicago home town boy, having attended high school and junior college here. "They said I was too small to be a baseball player, so why don't you try to be a jockey? I read how much jockeys made, so I figured I'll give it a try. Now that I've become a jockey, you're always worried about playin' ball and gettin' hurt. You have to be at such a peak that you're afraid to do anything else. So I quit anything else but riding.

"To the people it's a glamorous job, but to me it's the hardest work I ever held in my life. I was brought up tough and I was brought up lucky. Keeps me goin', I love it. I like the glamour, too. Everybody likes to read about themselves in the papers and likes to see your name

471

*on television and people recognize you down the street.
They recognize me by my name, my face, my size. You
stick out like a basketball player. I think we're all self-cen-
tered. Most of us have tailor-made clothes and you can
see it—the way you carry yourself."*

I been having a little problem of weight the last three
weeks. I've been retaining the water, which I usually don't
do. I'm not losing it by sweating. My usual weight's about
110, with saddle and all. Stripped naked, I'm about 106½.
Right now I weigh 108. If I try to get to 106, I begin to
feel the drain, the loss of energy. But you waste so much
energy riding that I eat like a horse. Then I really have to
watch it.

I've learned to reduce from other riders who've been
doing it for twenty-some years. They could lose seven
pounds in three hours, by sweating, by just being in the
hot box. All the jockeys' rooms have 'em. Or you can take
pills. It weakens extremely. It takes the salt out of your
body and you're just not completely there.

Riding is very hazardous. We spend an average of two
months out of work from injuries we sustain during the
year. We suffer more death than probably any other sport.
I was very late becoming a jockey, at twenty-two. They
start at sixteen usually. At the age of sixteen, you haven't
enough experience in life to really see danger. At twenty-
two, you've been through harder times and you see if you
make a wrong decision you might get yourself or somebody else hurt. When you're sixteen you don't really care.

I been lucky until last year, almost accident-free. My
first accident last year came in February, when I broke
the cartilage in my knee in a spill, warming up for a race.
The horse did somethin' wrong and I fell off of him and
he run over me—my knee—and tore the ligaments in my
ankle, broke my finger, bruises all over. About three
months later I fell again. I had a concussion, I had lacer-
ations in the temple, six stitches, and I had a fracture in
the vertebrae in my back. (Indicates a scar.) I just did
this Saturday. A horse threw me out of the gate right
there on my nose. I had all my teeth knocked out.
(Laughs.)

*His mother, who is serving coffee, hovers gently nearby.
As she listens, her hand tentatively goes toward her cheek.*

The universal gesture. Toward the end of the evening she confides softly concerning her daily fears. She hopes he will soon do other things.

The most common accident is what we call clippin' of another horse's heels. Your horse trips with the other horse's heels, and he'll automatically go down. What helps us is the horse is moving at such a momentum, he falls so quick, that we just sail out into the air and don't land near the horse. We usually land about fifteen feet away. That's what really helps.

You put it off as casual. If I were to think how dangerous it is, I wouldn't dare step on a horse. There's just so many things that can happen. I'll come home with a bruise on my arm, I can't move it. I have no idea when it happened. It happened leaving the gate or during the race. I'll pull a muscle and not know it happened. I'll feel the pain after the race. Your mind is one hundred percent on what you're doing. You feel no pain at that moment.

I'd say the casualty rate is three, four times higher than any other sport. Last year we had nine race track deaths, quite a few broken backs, quite a few paralyzed . . .

A real close friend of mine, he's paralyzed. Three days after I fell, he fell. Just a normal accident. We all expected him to get up and walk away. He's paralyzed from the waist down. It's been a year and some months. We had a benefit dinner for him. Gettin' money out of those people—track owners—is like tryin' to squeeze a lemon dry.

He gets compensation if he's a member of the Jockeys' Guild or the Jockeys' Association. Of the two thousand or more jockeys, about fifteen hundred belong to the guild. I'm the representative here in Chicago. The guild comes up with fifty dollars a week and the race track gives us fifty.

Only fifty bucks compensation! We don't have a pension plan. We're working on one, but the legislature stops us. They say we're self-employed. They put us in the same category as a doctor. There are old doctors, but there are no old jockeys.

Some tracks still object to the guild. A lotta time the tracks get so hazardous that we refuse to ride on 'em. They usually wait till two or three riders fall, then they determine the track's hazardous. Sometimes nothin' happens to riders, other times they break bones. The rains, the cold weather, sometimes it freezes and there are holes. It's plain to see it's just not fit for an animal or a human being to work on these conditions.

Bones break a little casual. You get used to it, a finger ... What most breaks is your collarbone. I fractured it. I could name you rider after rider, that's the first thing that goes, the collarbone.

I prep horses for a race. Three days before, I'll go a half mile with the horse I'm gonna ride, or three-eighths of a mile. The owner wants me to get the feel of the horse. I do this day in and day out through the year. So I'm a good judge of pace. He knows I'm not gonna let a horse go three seconds too fast. He might loose all his energies out, and when the race comes up he's empty. I'll average two or three in the morning. Most of the time I'll just talk to the man and he'll tell me, "How did my horse run the other day?" or "I'm gonna ride you on this horse and he likes to run this way." I don't work for one man. I ride for anyone that wants me.

If I ride within the first four races, I have to be back at twelve-thirty. The first race is two-ten. They want you at least an hour and a half before. You have about a good thirty, forty-five minutes to get dressed, get your weight down, get prepared, read up on the charts of the horses that are gonna ride that day, plus your own. You look for speed.

You know their records, because more or less you rode against them before or rode them themselves. Does he like to go to the front? Does he like to come from behind? Does he like to stay in the middle? Does he like to go around? Does he like to go through? Then the trainer will tell you how he likes his horse rode. If he's a good trainer, he'll tell you the habits of the horse, even if they're bad habits. A bad habit are horses that lug in, that like to ride around instead of inside, that don't break too good. It makes it more dangerous—and a little more difficult to win races. There's more ways of getting beat.

You have only a minute and ten seconds sometimes to do everything you have to do. The average race is three-quarters of a mile, and they usually are a minute and ten or a minute, eleven. You make the wrong decision, that's the race. You really don't know where you're gonna lay or how the horse is gonna react from one race to the other. Your first thing is to get him out of the gate. You have to look for position. Where can I be? There's ten, twelve other horses that would like to have the same position. There's maybe six horses that want to go into the lead. The other six might come from behind. You can't be all in the same place at the same time. You have to wiggle your way around here and there.

You ride around, you find the race is half-over. If you're layin' near the leaders, you're gonna wait a little later to move. If you're way back there, you have to move a little earlier, because you have a lot of catching up to do. Here's what makes riders. You must realize there are other jockeys as capable as you are in the race. So you must use good judgment. You have to handicap which horses are gonna do what in front of you. Which ones are gonna keep runnin' and vacate that space that you can flow through. Or which are stoppin' and you have to avoid.

You must know the other jockeys, too. They all have habits. I know jockeys I can get through and jockeys that don't let you. I have a habit. I've been known as a front running rider, that I can save a horse better. I got a good judge of pace when I'm in front. But I feel I'd rather ride a horse from behind. A horse is competitive. It's his nature to beat other horses. That's all they've been taught all their lives. Usually at three years old they start going in pairs. When they start gettin' ready in the morning workouts, we're matchin' 'em up against each other. You can see the little babies, two year olds, they are trying to beat each other, just their instinct. One tries to get in front of the other, just like a little bitty game. One will get so much in front and he'll wait. The other will get in front. And they'll go like that. They're conditioned to it.

Sure the animal makes a difference, but if you have two horses alike you have to beat the other rider. You have to wait for his mistakes or his habit. I've learned patience. I know other people's habits a lot better than mine. I'm sure they know mine a lot better than they know theirs.

If a jockey's in trouble and he hollers for help, that other rider has to do everything in his power to help—whether it's gonna cost him the race or not. One possibility: there's horses all around him, he's in the middle, he can't control his horse. So he's gonna run into another horse, he' gonna clip the other horse's heels. If he does this, he's gonna fall, and the people behind him are gonna fall over him. That's what happened today.

You see him or he hollers "I can't hold my horse!" You just move out, let him out, so he can take his horse wide. Most jockeys'll do this even if it'll cost 'em the race. Not all. Some that are just interested in winning ... They're frowned on. They have very little friends among other riders. You don't give them the benefit of the doubt. I know a lot of riders that had me in trouble and I've asked for help, and I felt they coulda done a lot more than they did. No conscience. At the same time, they been in trouble and I did everything possible to help. I had to stop ridin' a horse to protect another rider. What's worse is seein' another rider make a mistake and you have to protect him. You *have* to do it.

People of the racing world are a close fraternity. "We work together, we travel together. The whole shebang moves over from one state to another. We automatically seek each other out. We're good friends."

The wages consist of ten percent of the horse's purse. If it's $4,500, you get about $450. About ten percent of the win. The smallest purse here is $2,500, so you win $250. You get a straight wage for place or show. For second place, it would be fifty or fifty-five. Third money is forty, forty-five. For the out money, fourth or under, it's thirty, thirty-five dollars.

We have agents. My agent works only for me. I pay him twenty-five percent of my gross earnings. It's quite a bit, but he's worth it. An agent is very important in a jockey's success. He gets your mounts. He has the right to commit you to ride a horse and you have to abide by it. He tries to get you on the best horse he can. He has to be a good handicapper. He has to be a good talker. And he has to be trustworthy, that the owners can trust him. There's an awful lot of information related from the trainer to the agent to the jockey, which you wouldn't want someone else to find out. Some agents are ex-jockeys, but not too many. They're connected with racing, father to son and so on. Racing has a habit of keeping their own.

You go to the barn and start as a hot walker. He's the one that walks the horse a half-hour, after he's been on the track for his training, while he drinks the water.

About every five minutes, you gotta do about two or three swallows. Then you keep with him until he's completely cooled down, until he's not sweating any more. You do this every day. You might walk six, seven horses, which starts building your legs up. We all started this way. There's no short cuts.

From walkin', I became a groom—one that takes care of horses. That's a step up. He usually takes care of three or four horses all day. He cleans them, he massages their legs and their body, takes care of the stalls.

I went from groom to exercise boy, another step higher. Now you're riding a horse. You first start walking, getting used to the reins, getting used to the little bitty saddle. You might walk for a week around shed row. They usually pick an old horse, that's well-mannered. From then, you graduate to goin' on the track.

The first day you go to the track it's really hilarious. Because there's somethin' about a galloping horse there's no way to prepare for it. No matter how much exercise you do, you're not fit. I went clear around this mile and an eighth track. When I got up to the back side where they pulled me up, my legs were numb. I couldn't feel any more. I jumped off the horse, there was nothin' there to hold me up. I went down right to the ground. I sat there a half-hour, right where I landed. They made a lot of fun out of it. It happens to everybody.

Some days I'll ride seven, eight. Some days two or three. You feel it at the end of the day. Sometimes I come home, I just collapse. I could sleep right through the next day. You're lucky when you have horses that want to run. Other times you have to do all the work. It's easier to have a free-running horse. You don't have to do very much but kinda guide him along and help him when the time comes. But if you get a horse that doesn't want to run, you're pretty tired after three-quarters of a mile.

To be a jockey you must love the horse. There's a lot of times when I lose my patience with him. There's just certain horses that annoy you. There's no two alike. They have personalities just like you and I do.

Distant-U, the filly, she's beautiful. She's a little lady. She looks like a lady, petite. Except she's a little mean, unpredictable. I've gotten to like her and I know how she likes to be rode. I don't know if she knows me, but I know her, exactly what she likes me to do. The horse can tell it right away. When I sit there with confidence she'll be a perfect lady. If you don't have confidence, the horse takes advantage of it.

Willie Shoemaker's the greatest. He has the old style of the long hold. He has a gift with his hands to translate messages to the horse. He has the gift of feeling a horse's mouth. But it's a different style from ninety percent of us. We've gone to the trend of the South American riders. They ride a horse's shoulder instead of a horse's back. They look a hundred percent better. Most riders have now changed over, mixed the two together.

Latin American riders are dominating the sport. They're hustlers and they've had it tougher than American riders. They come from very, very poor people. They have a goal they want to reach, bein' the tops. The American rider, he's satisfied makin' a livin', makin' a name for himself. He's reached a plateau and he's stayed there. While the other fella is just pluggin' away . . .

There's some prejudice from riders, but most jockeys become very good friends after they get to know each other. But most is from the officials. I couldn't believe it. The stewards are prejudiced against Spanish riders. I have not felt it because I was brought up here. Home town boy makes good. But the Spanish ones . . . two riders commit the same infraction, one's penalized, the other isn't. One's Spanish, the other isn't. Once in a while, okay, but it's repeated again and again. It has a prejudice.

Sometimes I feel people don't treat you as they should. Other times they treat you a little too well. They get a little pesty. Lotta times you want to be by yourself. They don't realize I spent fifteen minutes combin' my hair and they come along and the first thing they do is muss it up. They'll put their arm around you and buy you a drink, and you can't drink. You have to ride the next day. You turn the drinks down and right away, they'll say, "This kid is too good for me." If I was gonna accept every drink that was offered to me, I'd be as big as a balloon."

I have a lot of friends who are horse players, but I've never been approached by undesirables, gangsters. I've been approached by other riders. I'd say racing has changed a little bit from the days when they were notorious. Riders now make enough money where they don't have to cheat. Any race I win, I'm gonna make two, three hundred dollars. For me to take a chance of losing my license, it don't make sense. A rider is more apt to take it when the money isn't there.

It's incredible to see jockeys as honest as they are, for the conditions they come from. If you could see conditions on the back side, the way people have to live. The barn area, it's bad now like it was twenty years ago. The filth I had to live in, the wages I had to work for, the environment I was with, with alcoholics and whatnots. To come out of there . . . I was twenty-two, I was set in my ways. But friends of mine, when they were thirteen, fourteen years old, lived through this and made good citizens of themselves. It's *incredible* to believe that people could come out of there and become great athletes and great individuals. You figure, they'd be no good.

The guild is workin' for better track conditions, better rooms for where we ride at. I think only four or five tracks have jockey quarters that are clean and livable. Here's an organization, they're bettin' a million dollars a day and you get a newspaperman come in and interview you. You're embarrassed to have him walk in there. It's filthy. We drag all that mud in from the track. You figure they would have someone to keep it clean. They don't. The same furniture . . . there hasn't been much change.

In the barn, we have the tack rooms, where the grooms and the hot walkers live. A hot walker earns sixty dollars a week. He can't afford an apartment, he lives in the tack room. They have two cots. It's almost like a stall. You can put a horse in there if you wanted. A groom makes about $100. The exercise boys earn a little more, about $150. So they usually get apartments. I really don't know what the average jockey gets. I average around sixty thousand a year. I don't know if we average more than three or four years. I have no idea how long I'll continue. I wish I could ride another ten years, but . . . My ambition is to win the Kentucky Derby. It's still the most honored stake of all. I've come awful close two or three times to riding in it. I'm riding for Mr. Scott now. Say he comes up with a colt that's a two-year-old that I ride and I'll ride him next year and this horse works his way to the Derby. I have worked my way up there with him. Mm-hmm, could happen.

Through experience you know what to do. Whether the stick will make him run, whether hand riding, whether hittin' him on the shoulders, hittin' 'em on the rear, whistling or talkin' to 'em. You try everything. If one doesn't work, you try the other.

I'm pretty relaxed now, but when I first started riding—the night before a big stake I'd get very little sleep. You lost two, three pounds from just nervousness, just by going to the washroom and thinking about it. Especially when you run one of the favorites. You have to fight this. I have to really get rid of the butterflies or I'm really gonna make a big mistake. Actually just mind over matter. Concentration.

What I've learned as a jockey sometimes drives me crazy. I've gotten where I could look at animals and see personalities in them. Most of what I've learned is patience. It comes with love of the horses. A lot of times a horse will do something that could even get me hurt. At first you want to hit him, correct him. But then you realize he's just an animal. He's smart but not smart enough to know that he's hurting himself and is gonna hurt you. He's only doin' it because it's the only thing he knows how to do.

Let me tell you somethin'. Animals got traits from humans. You put a nervous person around a nervous horse and he becomes a nervous horse. It's helped me to understand humans, too. By understanding the horse, the animal himself, his moods, his personality, his way of life, his likes, his dislikes—humans work the same way—you have to accept them for what they are. People do things because it's the only way they know. You try to change them to your way of thinking, but you have to accept people the way they are.

POSTSCRIPT: *"I would like to see the sport treated differently. I would like to see the politicians out of it. I would like to see the states own all the tracks. People that own the tracks now are draining them . . ."*

STEVE HAMILTON

He is a well-traveled relief pitcher, having been with the Washington Senators, New York Yankees, San Francisco Giants, and Chicago Cubs. "I live in the foothills of the

*Cumberland Mountains. Morehead, Kentucky, is a town
of only four thousand. I'm not a hero there 'cause everybody knows everybody."*

*It is Saturday evening in the late August of 1971.
We're in Chicago at a downtown hotel. His team, the San
Francisco Giants, in first place but slipping fast, had lost
this afternoon to the Cubs.*

Several times I'd go downtown in Manhattan and somebody'd stop me and say, "Aren't you Steve Hamilton?"
This made me feel all puffed up. It made me feel good
that people knew me. Whether guys admit it or not, I
think most of them feel good when they're recognized.
They feel they're something special. Everybody gets a kick
out of feeling special. I think that's one part of this game.

I've never been a big star. I've never done anything outstanding. I feel I've been as good as I can be with the
equipment I have. I played with Mickey Mantle and now
I'm playing with Willie Mays. People always recognize
them. Yogi Berra, people always recognize him. Yogi has
a face you couldn't forget. But for someone to recognize
me!

*"I signed with the Cleveland Indians in 1958, with their
farm club. Back and forth in the minors." He was working
on a master's degree. A scout signed him up. "I told them
I was twenty-one. I was really twenty-three. He felt I
wouldn't have a good chance if I was twenty-three, so I
went along with him. Now I give my right age. I'm
thirty-six." (Laughs.)*

Age is very important in baseball. If you've got two
prospects of equal ability, one kid's twenty and I'm
twenty-three, they're gonna take the boy that's twenty.
They think they're gonna have him longer. That's why it
was important to the scout that I be twenty-one. Scouts
get some money back if you make the big leagues. Most
of us in baseball who are thirty are considered old men.
Lotta times when Larry Jansen* wants me to get in the
bull pen he'd say, "Pappy . . ." (Laughs.) I don't feel old,
but in baseball I'm ancient.

The average time in the big leagues is two to four

* At the time he was pitching coach for the Giants.

years. When you consider that only one of about seventy that sign a contract even make the big leagues, that's a very short life. In the minors, guys'll play eight, nine years. He's getting really nothing. He makes about five thousand dollars a year. If he hangs on long enough, he may make ten thousand. But he has no winter job and he becomes an organization man. They figure he can help young players. And age is passing by . . .

In the minor leagues we spent a lot of hours riding in buses, and they were so hot and you didn't have too many stops to eat. You ate poorly because you had bad meal money. We got $1.50 a day. But you were young. When I was with a class B league, I got a long distance call. My wife went to the hospital in labor. It was the first baby. I had to get home. The ticket was forty-some dollars. We didn't have it between us (laughs)—the manager, everybody. I got there a day late. I thought baseball players made so much money. (Laughs) That's why I wanted to play it, loving the game too.

To be perfectly honest with you, I'm ready to quit. I feel I don't want to play any more. I'm losing the desire. I suppose I can play for several more years, but I don't quite have the same spring in my legs. I'd be the first to admit it. My arm is good, because I never did throw hard. I was never a power pitcher. I was always a curve ball pitcher, control. You don't lose it this quick. But I'm tired of traveling. I'm tired of the hours and I'm losing the zest. When this happens it's time to leave.

People say we're lucky we have airplane travel. It means they can schedule more games. We play 162 games now. Before, we played 154 in the same amount of time. Now we play more night games. Last night we played a game in St. Louis. It was over about ten forty. We had to get dressed and take a forty-five-minute bus ride to the airport. We took our short fifty-five-minute flight to Chicago. We had another thirty-five-minute bus ride from the airport to downtown. We got in here last night around two o'clock. The bags were late coming in. They had a mix-up. Three thirty, we're still waitin' up for our bags. It adds up to a real long night, when we had to play a game today.

There's a rule that says if there's a flight one hour and a half or less, you can schedule a night game and a day game the next day. The old umpire who said, "You can't beat them hours"—that was another time. (Laughs.) Another thing, when you travel by train, you don't worry so much about crashes. Everybody—in the back of their mind—thinks about it. There's a little bit of worry, especially in bad weather. We were coming into Milwaukee last year and while we were bouncin' around, comin' in for a hairy landing, Pete Ward said, "Babe Ruth never hit sixty home runs traveling like this." (Laughs.) The tension's really rough. On the train they were relaxed. They talked, they slept. When they came in, they didn't go from one bus to another. I don't think conditions are that much better now.

A longer season, more games scheduled, and longer spring training. We start playing exhibition games right away. Here again, a night game last night, a day game today, a doubleheader tomorrow. We were to have an off-day Monday, but they scheduled an exhibition game Monday night in Minnesota with the Twins. (Laughs.) Then we get on a plane after *that* game and travel all the way to San Francisco to play the next day. (Laughs.)

What's the purpose of this exhibition game?

Money. (Laughs.) Willie Mays once played for Minneapolis and they're capitalizing on his name. The Giants are guaranteed so much money and Calvin Griffith* is gonna make a bundle. It's gonna hurt us, because we need the rest. Here we are in the pennant race and we're tired. We're goin' rather badly. We were lookin' forward to the day off. Maybe you just want to sleep all day, or just relax and get away from it. But we're playing Monday night just to make extra money for someone. It kinda hurts.†

For a day game I get to the park about ten. We sign anywhere from one to two dozen baseballs every day. When I was with the Yankees, we signed six dozen each

---

* Owner of the Minnesota Twins.

† The Giants, in first place at the time of this conversation, blew the pennant. In 1972 the Chicago White Sox and the Oakland Athletics, battling for first place, played a nineteen-inning game. It was August 11. On the following night they played another extra inning game. On the following night, the Sox traveled to Chicago and played as exhibition game with the Cubs.

day. We used to hate that. People in the front office have friends they want to give them to. I don't know where all these balls go. Six dozen a day! Eighty-one days! That's a lot of baseballs! (Laughs.)

On the road, ball players are great bargain hunters. Nobody wants to pay the retail price for anything. So we spend time going to our little wholesale places. In each town it's different. In New York it's sweaters. In Los Angeles it's suits. In Atlanta it's shoes. I'll read quite a bit. That's primarily what I do when I'm on the road. My roommate's a great movie fan.

People criticize pitchers. But in the past few years the baseball's hotter. It's wound tighter and can go further. Anybody can hit a home run now. Everybody swings for the fence, and you're more nervous about throwing a strike. Old-timers say they just reared back and threw the ball. Now you get wild because you're hesitant about throwing that ball over the plate. So that makes the game longer.

There's not much talk about the craft any more. Say, you've got a fella who's an outfielder. He's learned in the minors that there are certain ways you catch a ball. You've got to learn which base to throw it to. You've got to know how to scoop up a ball. Nobody comes to see a fellow because he's a good outfielder. What he comes to do is hit. He'll come out early in the batting cage and he'll hit and hit and hit. He won't shag flies, he won't catch fungoes. It's not important to him. There's no status in catching a fly ball. I'm sure that's the way it is with a lot of jobs. You work on the things that bring you the most fame and fortune.

The average fan can't understand it. They think you're overpaid and you've got great working hours. They read about the superstars and huge salaries. For most of us the money's not that great, when it's only for a short time and it doesn't really help you when you're out of baseball. There are only six hundred of us, and we're the tops in our profession. To play baseball you've got unique skills. There's a great to-do about our salaries, but no one questions the income of the six hundred top lawyers or top insurance men—the kind who own the ball clubs. I've always wondered about that.

You can be traded any time they want to trade you. There's no guarantee. You may just move your family and you get traded again. You've got seventy-two hours to go from one club to another. We feel the player should have some say-so over where he goes and where he leaves. Let's say a kid comes up from the minors. He's here a month and they ship him back. He's brought his whole family with him ...

"I have two girls and a boy. In about six months we're gonna have another one. If you don't take your family to spring training, there's six weeks right there. Before they come and join me in the season, there's about five more weeks. They're here for about three months in the summer. But I'm gone for a month and a half.

"I miss my family. My wife had to be head of the household. She has to do everything. If the sewer breaks down, if the commode doesn't work, she has to take care of it. She pays all the bills. She does it all. I'm not the head person any more."

In the last ten years baseball has changed a lot. We're getting more college boys. When I first went into the game, they used to get on me, call me "professor," because I had a college education. Today more of 'em are thinking about what they're gonna do when they get out of baseball. Sometimes they're criticized for being too conscious about later life. It's crazy not to. I've seen guys over thirty playing minor leagues. They'll play baseball in the summertime and work nonskilled labor in the wintertime. They've got no future at all. There's nothing they're trained to do. You'd be amazed at the number of ballplayers that have no means of income and are in bad shape. Most of 'em are old-timers and some of 'em are pretty famous.

You hear so much about welfare. How do you get around it? They've criticized our Players' Association for not helping old ballplayers. Why should the onus be on the modern player? Why not the owners? They played for them. They made the money for them.

"I was players' representative with the Yankees for five years. I was the American League rep for four of those five years. In the early years, someone took the job because no one else wanted it. There was a big problem. We really had no permanence. To keep the Players' Associa-

tion in turmoil, all you had to do is keep trading player reps. I couldn't prove it, but I know player representatives' life expectancy was fairly short. We were always in a state of confusion."

You always hated to say anything against the owners because you were made to feel you were lucky to be playing baseball. You should be thankful for it. Never mind you're not getting a fair shake, you're lucky to be there and you shouldn't ever, but never, criticize the major league owners or the administration. One of the first things my coach in college told me when I went into pro baseball: "Don't be a clubhouse lawyer."

A clubhouse lawyer was a troublemaker. Don't make waves, man. Don't rock the boat. Just go play, do your job, and be happy, you hear? That stuck with me. I was a good boy. There were very few clubhouse lawyers. They were branded right away as being loud-mouthed hotheads who didn't care about the game. It seems to me a person who speaks out against injustice is not a clubhouse lawyer. He's just exercising his rights.

"The good of the game" is what you hear so much about. Everything owners do is for "the good of the game." They talk about baseball as a sport. But they move teams around from city to city strictly for money. A new team in Seattle two years ago cost the people about five million dollars. It sold for a tremendous amount. Here's a club that's supposed to be losing a lot of money. Yet there was an interested buyer. No club in baseball loses money. Every club makes money. I don't see how you could call it a sport. It's big business.

Company ownership has replaced the individual owner. This became apparent to me when we signed the first agreement with the owners. There wasn't one baseball team that was called, say, the Boston Red Sox. It was Golden West and CBS and Charles Finley Enterprises. They're all parts of corporations. This is how they make money. It's a super tax write-off. There's no way that any club that's part of a corporation can lose money. Finley's Oakland team is part of his insurance company. The Yankees are CBS. The Giants are part of a land corporation. It's impersonal.

A lot of owners don't really want to know players. Then you become more than a name. You become more than a piece of paper they can trade or sell or release. They insist on knowing you as a thing. It's easy for them to manipulate. But when you become involved with somebody, it's difficult. The only way to run a successful baseball operation is to treat the players as things.

Or as children. This bed check, watching players. Why would you check on men over twenty-one? Call their room, make sure they're in bed? It makes you feel funny. You're an adult and yet they do this to you. Your phone rings. You're asleep. Say it's twelve thirty. You've gone to sleep at eleven. They call, "Hey, are you in?" (Laughs.) You wake up out of a deep sleep. Okay, now you can't go to sleep until four in the morning. (Laughs.)

Blacklist? I have no proof, but—Clete Boyer was one of the best defensive third basemen in baseball. He was released by Atlanta for criticizing the management. You've got teams in the pennant race who can use him. He wasn't picked up by a single club. I've a hunch there's collusion between managements. He's now playing in Hawaii. If this wasn't a blacklist, there never was one.

The association has helped us in contracts. I'm not a businessman, so they really rip me up. Now we have someone to help us. The minimum was five thousand dollars in the beginning. Then it was seven thousand until three years ago. Then it went up to ten. It's going up to $13,500 next year. This was a super battle. When you consider how much the cost of living's gone up, it's not out of line. And you don't stay long in baseball. You've got to recognize it.

You've got a lot more freethinking players today. They never thought much of it before. We all had the attitude: Don't question it. There are a lot of guys trying to take your job and they're all pretty good, so you're lucky to be here. If you're a big star, you don't worry about it because you're making a hundred thousand dollars a year. You could care less. I don't blame 'em. If I have $125,000 a year and lived in one town, I'd be more reluctant to criticize a ball club. The owners treat the star very well because he's their meal ticket. Those guys usually don't kick. But a lot of that's changing now. Today ballplayers are more concerned with helping each other. The young fellow is more aware also of world events and what's going on. We talk a lot more of social problems.

"When I first started in the Southern Association in 1960, they didn't even allow black players. We were lily-white. Now the relationship is pretty good, but I couldn't say there's no racism. I had a player take me out to the field this year and say, "Now there's a real nigger." It appalled me. I felt afterwards that I didn't say anything to him. I just walked away. I'm as guilty as he was."

With some guys, winning is everything. It's the whole ball of wax. If you don't win, it's a waste. I do my best, but if you judge your life on winning, you're hurtin'. I know we play for money. These guys say, "If I don't win, I don't make any money." But if I go out and play, there's a certain satisfaction in knowing I've done as good as I can. No matter how hard I try, I could never be a Sandy Koufax. But if I can be as good as Steve Hamilton, I feel I've been successful.

I might tell you things about myself I really don't want to know. When I was in the minor leagues I used to hope guys in the big leagues would do bad, so I could get up there. I didn't know the guys. Some days it'd bother me. I used to wonder if it was right. I used to wonder if it was sinful. It's almost like saying, I don't know whether I've got the ability, but if he fails, I'll have a chance. I have seen guys really happy when other people do bad on their own team because it makes them look better. It's a sign that he's insecure. It's a bad thing to see. I can't say I ever rooted against a pitcher.

I see guys that come back—you watch 'em come in the clubhouse. Nobody recognizes 'em. The fans don't know 'em any more. I set back and watch the front runners come and grab ahold of the guys that are doin' good and are big stars. They want to grab ahold of their shirt tail. I've seen too many guys get a false sense of importance. People always saying good things about you and treating you like you're something special. You start believing you're something special. Now they're out of baseball. They feel, "I was great." But nobody remembers them. It doesn't make any difference what your name is. I've seen people really have a hard time coping with it.

You find out people no longer want to be associated with you when you're no longer in the limelight. I've seen these people come into the locker room at Yankee Stadium. And I've seen 'em quit coming. When we went to sixth place then to last, I didn't see 'em around at all. Last year we got back to second place. I saw them comin' back. (Laughs.) Yeah, here they come again, the front runners.

A lot of ex-players go into insurance or as car salesmen. I've talked to two or three of 'em: "Yeah, because I was big, it got me in to see a lot of people." Today things are tighter and what you were doesn't mean that much. When I get out of baseball I feel sure I will teach and coach. This is what I want to do. I do lots of Christian work in the wintertime.

(Sighs.) Once you start getting recognized it becomes important to you. I didn't used to feel that way. One day when we were coming off the plane, a guy asked me if I was the traveling secretary. That's not good. (Laughs.) When I came over to the National League, nobody asked for my autograph, because I had gray hair. It started to bother me. (Laughs.) I put stuff on my hair and it went sort of medium-brown. But I don't like it and I'm letting it grow out. I just figure it was me. I don't feel right. My legs still hurt, my arms didn't feel any better. (Laughs.)

Recognition, fame—I think of all the time I stood outside my house in Charlestown, Indiana, a two-tone brick, and I threw a baseball where the different colors met. I hit it over and over and over again. We caught flies where it got too dark to see, just hours and hours and hours and hours ... that's what most of us have done.

BLACKIE MASON

"I'm a space cadet, a space thief. I've always shied away from the term 'public relations counsellor,' the old Madison Avenue cliché. You lay back and extol the virtues of others. Some of the people you're talking about have no talent, some are great. I got into publicity accidentally. I wanted to be a night club comedian. I didn't go to a school of journalism. My education came from life, from the streets of the city."

You hit the pavement, gettin' out, pluggin' every day. If I don't hit a newspaper office once a day I feel I've missed something. I'm not a great one to sit at typewriters and do slick releases. I have to go out and see the fruit of my work—to see my client get out of the second sports page onto the front sports page. Or see my fighter work his way up. What little success I enjoy I owe to boxing.

Today there's nothing more exciting than a world's heavyweight championship bout. You've been working with one guy for six hard weeks. It's now the night of the fight. There's a certain drama, there's a certain vibrancy. Suddenly a spotlight hits one end of the arena and you see the champeen coming down. Right before your eyes, everything you've toiled for. Millions are gonna be watching this guy. You know him better than anybody sitting out there. You've ate with him, you've slept with him, you know his inner thoughts, you know the magazines he likes to read, you know what type of food he likes. You see he and the challenger come down the aisle. That's when you get goose pimples.

I worked in the camps with the late Rocky Marciano. It's a very important function during the reign of a heavyweight champion. I was the buffer. There were tours of newspapermen that would come up every day. I had to be fully prepared to answer all questions. Why does Rocky put his left shoe on first? Is he superstitious? How many rounds has he boxed, total? What kind of food does he like to eat? People like Ed Sullivan call me and say they want Marciano on his show. I would be able to adjudge, to see that he cannot leave the camp on this and that day. Sullivan came up and did it right from camp. It's a momentous job.

I worked with a sullen, belligerent Sonny Liston, who had a disdain for a newspaperman. He would cause you aggravation because you never knew what he was gonna say. I worked with Muhammad Ali. When he says, "I am the greatest," he is among the greatest. Ali is his own press agent. When I worked in camp with him, I felt I was being paid for nothing. He did all the work. He made it easy for me. He would take over a press conference and forget about you. You would not have to sit there and coach him. He would take over and say, "Gentlemen, you have twenty minutes." They would ask him one question and he would not stop talking until I would get up and say, "Gentlemen, that's it for the day."

I'm up at seven. At a quarter after eight I'm in my auto-

mobile heading for the Loop. I'm kind of morose. I'm not
one of those cheerful risers that get up singing arias and
operatics and tell funny jokes in the morning. I begin to
feel better when I hit the fringes of Chicago. The tempo
grabs me. I'm hittin' the jungle. The Loop is my domain.
I'm away for three days and I'm a lost soul. When I
prowl, I'm within my realm. These are my, my, my people.

I don't really begin to function until the afternoon.
That's when I can rip and tear. That's when I'm strongest
and the adrenaline begins to flow. I'm punching, punching.
I'm calling up different media: "I've got a great angle for
you." This goes on all afternoon. I'm getting constant,
constant phone calls, people asking for my clients for appearances. I'm beginning to feel like a theatrical agent.

Just today, the phone rings. Muhammad Ali. "Hello
there, you little white devil you." This came out of the
blue. This gave me a buoyed up feeling. I suddenly felt
this day was worthwhile. He took time to call me and converse with me. "Are you coming out to this fight?" So on
and so forth.

I have a certain tempo. You come from your rounds at
the paper. You have seven, eight messages waiting. You
have lunch, come back—more messages waiting. You go
across the street for a cup of coffee—there's more messages. Some days you come in and there are no messages.
Who have you offended? Who have you hurt? I can't afford to hurt anybody. It's part of my work. You come hat
in hand. You're like a peddler. You're fighting. A client
doesn't want to see slick releases. He wants to see the
tearsheets from the papers. You fight and you fight like
mad.

You're afraid of telling the particular individual what he
really stands for. You want to, but you've got to suppress
this because he holds the destiny of your future livelihood.
It frustrates me. You want to have a feeling of independence.

People are always calling you up. A divorce case? "Can
I get a lawyer?" "Can I keep it out of the paper?" You go
and do big favors and you never see them people again.
When you ask them for a favor, these people will always
give you that one cliché: "If I could do it for you, I
would. But, gee, I don't know." I don't say they're obligated, but it's a hurt feeling. To have somebody say to

you, "I'll never forget you, Blackie, for what you did for me." You see these people later and you get the feeling they're trying to avoid you. I get the feeling they give me a cold hello.

You say to yourself, That's the story of my life. Why can't I be like that individual? Use a guy, then walk away. You felt like you've been used and totally discarded for what you have just done. I'm sensitive. It stays with me, and then I find myself becoming vindictive. I only hope this man comes to me for a favor again and I'll hurt him bad. These situations have turned me into that kind of an individual. I came out of a tough neighborhood and a favor was the big thing. We believed in the buddy system. Too many people I've met are constantly using you as a stepping stone.

There's been a change in the element in twenty-seven years, since I broke in. The people now are a different breed. They are the Madison Avenue-PR-type. The Brooks Brothers suit, attaché case, and let the cookie crumble if it will and all these clichés. These three-hour lunches. Big corporations have these people knifing each other, backstabbing, jockeying for position. Oh, it's become very commercial, cold and impersonal. It's now: "We'll have an eyeball to eyeball confrontation," and they come in with structures and surveys. This leaves me very confused. It must be impressive to a board, when somebody walks in with facts and figures and so on and so forth. I can take pride without going through this phony rigamarole.

How do I feel about my work? I wouldn't be doing anything but. I'm happiest in this field of endeavor. If somebody took me out of this and offered me twenty-five thousand dollars a year more—"You're the manager of a men's clothing department"—I would say no. I'd be miserable. I'd be like a caged lion, pacing. I'd growl at everybody, because the money wouldn't be worth it. I do not want to demean the man that sells clothing, because these people are necessary too. But I could never visualize a challenge selling a man a tie for three dollars, ringing that cash register, and saying, "I accomplished something today." Within thirty days I would be taking psychiatric treatment. I would be cornered. This would not be my cup of tea.

When a fighter walks in, or a basketball player, you say, "I'm gonna sell that guy." You pick up the papers and you see the results of the work you put in. There's the challenge. This work is meaningful. It gives me happiness.

I think I'm the last of the breed. I'm the last of the real hustlers. I can accomplish what I want with you in an hour. I don't have to sit over four martinis. Nor can I deal with an account who says, "Get me a broad." The era I came out of—the great teachers—they're all gone now. I learned from the greatest of them all, the late Jack Kearns. He was my mentor, God rest his soul. He said to me many, many times, "Kid, you're a throwback to the old days. But there's one thing you haven't got—larceny. I gotta teach it to ya." Well, I never took a full course. That's why I haven't made the big score. I do the best I can. I gotta be me.

JEANNE DOUGLAS

She is a professional tennis player. She is twenty-two. She travels nine months of the year as a member of the Virginia Slims Professional Women's Circuit. "It's Women's Lib, you've come a long way baby. Yeah. There's been quite a discussion about a cigarette company sponsoring a sporting event. What can you say? Some of the girls smoke, some don't. It's just a way of promoting tennis. We're not promoting smoking."

When the women organized their own circuit, they were blacklisted by the United States Lawn Tennis Association. "The officials of USLTA are very well-to-do businessmen, who've never paid their way to Wimbledon. I always paid my way. It's like the tournament is run for them, not the players." The schism occurred because "women's prize-money was less than half of the men's. For Forest Hills men were getting six thousand dollars and the women would get sixteen hundred. Billie Jean* is Women's Lib. She hit the roof." It was touch and go until Philip Morris came along. "They own Virginia Slims. They couldn't advertise on TV any more, so they put money into Virginia Slims tennis circuit."

The circuit: Long Beach to Washington D.C., to Miami

* Billie Jean King.

to Richmond. "People in town come out. Married couples. The blue collar will come maybe once a week. The upper class comes every night. Tennis is spreading. But I'm getting tired of living out of a suitcase and having my clothes wrinkled. That I hate. I love playing tennis.

"I started playing when I was eleven years old. My whole family plays. We're a huge tennis family. My uncle was like ten in the United States. My mom took it up after she was married. She got ranked twenty-fifth in southern California, which is one of the best places to play tennis. She works in a pro shop at our tennis club. She pushed me and I really resented it at first. But she made me play to the point where I was good enough to like it."

It's pure luck that I was born when I was born. Now there's professional tennis. There wasn't before. It's a business now. Just like a dentist. You go at it training-wise, exercises, running. Match-wise, girls are now cheating. (Laughs.)

It's not maybe really cheating. We have umpires and linesmen. The other day an umpire made a call against my opponent. It was very close. He called it "out." I'm not gonna go against the umpire. Maybe in amateur days I would say, "Hold it. I thought that was good." I may have said, "Play two, take it over." I'm not gonna do that now and nobody's gonna do it. When you were amateur, you were more open. Winning now is everything.

The first time I encountered it, I was just out for the juniors.* It was doubles. There was no way we were gonna beat the others, they're world class players. Okay, I hit the ball down the center. On a clay court it kicks the back line. It's taped. You can see it shoot off. It's the first game of the whole match and they spend five minutes looking at the mark. "It's out! It's out!" My partner says, "If it's that close, let's play two." No. This was typical of the whole match. They were top players. It wasn't even gonna be close. But nobody's giving away one little inch.

Players tend to be more superficial now. Before you were more friendly. You'd write back and forth and have a good time. Now you don't have good friends. You're on the court and people are just having fits, losing tempers. People are now so competitive for money you just don't

_____
* Juniors are eighteen and under.

want to get involved personally. You get on the court and how can you beat your best friend type of thing. Kind of a lonely life.

I want to be good, and this is the only way. But when there is money, the competition is so tough. There are like sixty-five women in the world, beating their heads against the wall every week, just playing against each other just week after week after week. It's really a hard life and getting a little shaky. Quite a few girls have gone home. The tops are getting the glamour—Billie Jean says, "We're the ones who bring the crowds."

That's why I've got to keep improving. I'll never be a tennis bum. We have them among the girl players, too. Someone who's not making it and just won't let go. They go to tournaments ... They're kinda down on themselves. It's a sad life to be not advancing. When I stop improving I'll go into something else. Something better—like about six-foot-three. (Laughs.)

"I grew up fast, I was very awkward. I really didn't like the game. My mom paid me twenty-five cents an hour to play. There's five children in my family. We all play tennis. My oldest brother's been number one for UCLA two years in a row. He's twenty-third in the United States.

"We subscribe to World Tennis *magazine. You see pictures of people in Wimbledon. I said, "I'd never see those people in my life." I got pretty good and I started to travel. I was on the Junior Wightman Cup Team for three years. I quit school—I was gonna major in design at UCLA—and went to Australia, South Africa, France, Italy, and I played in Wimbledon. Financially it was tough. You pay your own way. You get token prize money. Then Virginia Slims came up. It's just lucky timing.*

"My mom wanted it for me because she never could play tennis. She's been to all the teas and just felt she accomplished nothing with her life. I go to these houses and stay with these housewives and it blows my mind that all they do is plan dinner and take care of the kid. They don't do anything, these ladies. I do want to get married and have a family, but I do want to do something."

There's zero social life. I get romantically involved about twice a year and wreck my tennis to death. There's this French girl who was like number three in the world a couple of years ago. When she's having a great love life she's just playing fantastically.

My brother goes on the circuit too. We compare notes all the time. It's different for men. The townies come out. It never ceases to amaze me how they can sit and watch a tennis match in ninety degrees heat with false eyelashes on, make-up, hair spray, and not one drop of sweat. The guys pick 'em up. It's harder for girls to go out on a one-night. It's gotten to a point where I only go out with guys that I've met before. You can be friendly and have a good time, but you hate to be put-upon. I'm just not that kind of girl. I'm not a prude, but I'm not going to bed with some guy just while I'm in town.

Male athletes are just big studs. The girl tennis players used to laugh. A couple of Australians got this little game they play. They'd pick up girls and they'd rig it up so one guy would watch from the next room—and give points. They kept track. They made it a contest. These townies had no idea what these guys were pulling off. They would just pick up one girl after another after another. It was a mechanical-type thing.

Through tennis I've met fantastic people. When I'm home I teach fantastically wealthy people in Rolling Hills. They live behind gates, they have guards, they have private courts. I'm teaching a man who owns his own jet, and he's giving me a ride home from New York so I don't have to pay the airfare type of thing.

I have a sponsor, he's paying my way. Last year I barely made it. My mom has paid for all of my tennis. A lot of parents support the girls, work. It's much better with a sponsor. Last year, before each tournament, I calculated how far I had to get and my next plane ticket and everything. I was so uptight. We have to pay our own airfare.

Why can't Virginia Slims pay your fare?

They can't afford it at this time. The only thing we're guaranteed is to be able to play in the tournament. And maybe win prize money.

Suppose you don't win?

You just lose. You don't get anything. You get hospitality. My sponsor gets paid back everything he spent. After he's gotten paid back, we split fifty-fifty. This year I made my five hundred dollars profit so far, so I'm way ahead of the game. One girl has a sponsor who gets ninety percent of every prize money check she gets until he's paid back. At the time I was so excited. But now it's coming out where it's not such a good deal.

My sponsor's a race track driver. I'm so impressed with him. He's been written up in *Time* magazine. He's such an unbelievable man, and he's so impressed with me.

If I go out with guys that aren't sports-minded, I feel like a jock. The whole conversation, there's nothing to go on. You go out with a baseball player or something, you carry on a normal conversation. But this one guy can't get it out of his mind. A female athlete is just so new. It's just like a kid growing up to be an astronaut. This was never before. It's amazing how little girls come up and ask for your autograph. They say, "Oh, I want to grow up and be a Virginia Slims tennis player, just like you." That just blows my mind. One of the greatest things happened to me. I was at a basketball game and someone asked me for an autograph. I mean, I'm not a Billie Jean King.

I meet these fantastically wealthy people I would never have a chance to meet before. A dentist, he goes to a cocktail party, who's gonna talk about your teeth? If you're a tennis pro, everybody can talk. There's a common bond. It's kind of neat to be able to talk to someone instead of having a feeling like a housewife: How do I ever talk to Billie Jean?

In a way it's an ugly wealth, too. Gaudy diamond rings, impressing each other. At Miami Beach I stayed at the Jockey Club. I lucked out, and three of us got to stay like on an eighty-five-foot yacht. They all had such disrespect for each other, but they had respect for us. It's something money couldn't buy.

Before Virginia Slims I was interested in a lot more things. I wanted to travel and learn languages. I can speak Spanish and a little French. Every country I've been in, I stayed in people's homes. You talk to them and find out much more about a country. Now it's making money.

I'm really trying to zero in and make a business out of it, 'cause all of a sudden it's big business. It never occurred to me before. So I'm trying to change my ways. I'd like to be able to endorse some rackets or shoes, do commercials, make a lot of money. I'm not a materialist like my father. He hasn't been in favor of tennis. He'd always say, "Okay, when are you going to be a secretary and make some money?" He's like a sunny day friend. When I'm winning—great! He loves publicity. I'm his daughter. But if I'm losing, "Be a secretary, get the money." He can't even see the way he changes. I couldn't care less about him. I want to be independent. Money means freedom.

If I get married and have a daughter, I would push her into something, like my mom did me. I think kids should be pushed. Okay, pushed is a crummy word. Kids should be guided. I stayed at a house a couple of weeks, the kids were fat. They didn't do anything after school, just watch TV. It's like they were dying. I would prefer athletics. I would push her to the point where she's good. And if she still didn't like it, I wouldn't push her.

"Junior tennis is like a world of its own. The parents usually take the kids, because they can't drive. This is like stage mothers. There's like tennis mothers. There's quite a few fathers that are obnoxious, too. These people sit on the sidelines and coach from behind the baseline. My mom's never come out to see me, though she's watching my little sister . . ."

My second brother, who had a scholarship to Long Beach State, does not enjoy competition. He plays an hour a day just to make my mom happy. If he was serious, he'd be really good. He goes out and enjoys playing, and he won't get upset. He'll come home and my mom will say, "How'd you do?" He'll say, "I lost four and four. I should have won." She'll say, "Why didn't you win? Why didn't you start coming to the net?" And he'll just laugh and say, "I didn't think of it." It upsets my mom. He isn't that keen to win. He just enjoys playing. This I don't understand, because I'm very competitive.

My little sister, who's ten years old, she was on the cover of *Tennis World* when she was four. She's great. She's been playing since she was two. She's done clinics all over California, with my coach. Usually you begin about five or six. So I started kind of late. I'm thirteen years older than she is, but she has more incentive. She knows exactly where she can go. She's number one in the Ten and Under.

She has not lost a match in her eight years—ever. She started playing tournaments when she was seven years old. It's going to be interesting to see how my little sister takes defeat . . .

ERIC NESTERENKO

He has been a professional hockey player for twenty years, as a member of the Toronto Maple Leafs and the Chicago Black Hawks. He is thirty-eight. He has a wife and three small children.

"I lived in a small mining town in Canada, a God-forsaken place called Flinflan. In the middle of nowhere, four hundred miles north of Winnipeg. It was a good life, beautiful winters. I remember the Northern Lights. Dark would come around three o'clock. Thirty below zero, but dry and clean.

"I lived across the street from the rink. That's how I got started, when I was four or five. We never had any gear. I used to wrap Life magazines around my legs. We didn't have organized hockey like they have now. All our games were pickup, a never-ending game. Maybe there would be three kids to a team, then there would be fifteen, and the game would go on. Nobody would keep score. It was pure kind of play. The play you see here, outside the stadium, outside at the edge of the ghetto. I see 'em in the schoolyards. It's that same kind of play around the basket. Pure play.

"My father bought me a pair of skates, but that was it. He never took part. I played the game for my own sake, not for him. He wasn't even really around to watch. I was playing for the joy of it, with my own peers. Very few adults around. We organized everything.

"I see parents at kids' sporting events. It's all highly organized. It's very formal. They have referees and so on. The parents are spectators. The kids are playing for their parents. The old man rewards him for playing well and doesn't reward him for not doing so well. (Laughs.) The father puts too much pressure on the kid. A boy then is

*soft material. If you want a kid to do something, it's got
to be fun.*

*"I was a skinny, ratty kid with a terrible case of acne. I
could move pretty well, but I never really looked like
much. (Laughs.) Nobody ever really noticed me. But I
could play the game. In Canada it is part of the culture. If
you can play the game, you are recognized. I was good almost from the beginning. The game became a passion
with me. I was looking to be somebody and the game was
my way. It was my life."*

*At sixteen, while in high school, he was playing with
semi-pro teams, earning two hundred dollars a week. At
eighteen, he joined the Toronto Maple Leafs.*

There's an irony that one gets paid for playing, that play
should bring in money. When you sell play, that makes it
hard for pure, recreational play, for play as an art, to exist. It's corrupted, it's made harder, perhaps it's brutalized,
but it's still there. Once you learn how to play and are accepted in the group, there is a rapport. All you are as an
athlete is honed and made sharper. You learn to survive in
a very tough world. It has its own rewards.

The pro game is a kind of a stage. People can see who
we are. Our personalities come through in our bodies. It's
exciting. I can remember games with twenty thousand
people and the place going crazy with sound and action
and color. The enormous energy the crowd produces all
coming in on the ice, all focusing in on you. It's pretty
hard to resist that. (Laughs.)

I was really recognized then. I remember one game: it
was in the semi-finals, the year we won the Stanley Cup. I
was with Chicago. It was the sixth game against Montreal.
They were the big club and we were the Cinderella team.
It was three to nothing, for us, with five minutes left to
go. As a spontaneous gesture twenty thousand people
stood up. I was on the ice. I remember seeing that whole
stadium, just solid, row on row, from the balcony to the
boxes, standing up. These people were turned on by us.
(Sighs.) We came off, three feet off the ice . . . (Softly)
Spring of '61.

When Toronto dropped me I said, "I'm a failure."
Twenty-two, what the hell does one know? You're the boy
of the moment or nothing. What we show is energy and
young bodies. We know our time is fleeting. If we don't

get a chance to go, it makes us antsy. Our values are instant, it's really hard to bide your time.

Violence is taken to a greater degree. There is always the specter of being hurt. A good player, just come into his prime, cracks a skull, breaks a leg, he's finished. If you get hit, you get hit—with impersonal force. The guy'll hit you as hard as he can. If you get hurt, the other players switch off. Nobody's sympathetic. When you get hurt they don't look at you, even players on your own team. The curtain comes down—'cause it could have been me. One is afraid of being hurt himself. You don't want to think too much about it. I saw my teammate lying there—I knew him pretty well—they put forty stitches in his face. I saw him lying on the table and the doctors working on him. I said, "Better him than me." (Laughs.) We conditioned ourselves to think like that. I think it's a defense mechanism and it's brutalizing.

The professional recognizes this and risks himself less and less, so the percentage is in his favor. This takes a bit of experience. Invariably it's the younger player who gets hurt. Veterans learn to be calculating about their vulnerability. (Laughs.) This takes a little bit away from the play. When I was young, I used to take all sorts of chances just for the hell of it. Today, instead of trying to push through it, I ease up. It takes something off the risk. The older professional often plays a waiting game, waits for the other person to commit himself in the arena.

The younger player, with great natural skill, say Bobby Orr, will actually force the play. He'll push. Sometimes they're good enough to get away with it. Orr got hurt pretty badly the first couple of years he played. He had operations on both knees. Now he's a little smarter, a little more careful, and a little more cynical. (Laughs.)

Cynicism is a tool for survival. I began to grow up quickly. I became disillusioned with the game not being the pure thing it was earlier in my life. I began to see the exploitation of the players by the owners. You realize owners don't really care for you. You're a piece of property. They try to get as much out of you as they can. I remember once I had a torn shoulder. It was well in the process of healing. But I knew it wasn't right yet. They brought their doctor in. He said, "You can play." I played and ripped it completely. I was laid up. So I look at the

owner. He shrugs his shoulders, walks away. He doesn't
really hate me. He's impersonal.

Among players, while we're playing we're very close.
Some of the best clubs I've played with have this intimacy—an intimacy modern man hardly ever achieves. We
can see each other naked, emotionally, physically. We're
plugged into each other, because we need each other.
There have been times when I knew what the other guy
was thinking without him ever talking to me. When that
happens, we can do anything together.

It can't be just a job. It's not worth playing just for
money. It's a way of life. When we were kids there was
the release in playing, the sweetness in being able to move
and control your body. This is what play is. Beating somebody is secondary. When I was a kid, to really *move* was
my delight. I felt released because I could move around
anybody. I was free.

That exists on the pro level, but there's the money aspect. You know they're making an awful lot of money off
you. You know you're just a piece of property. When an
older player's gone, it's not just his body. With modern
training methods you can play a long time. But you just
get fed up with the whole business. It becomes a job, just
a shitty job. (Laughs.)

I'm not wild about living in hotels, coming in late at
night, and having to spend time in a room waiting for a
game. You've got a day to kill and the game's in back of
your mind. It's hard to relax. It's hard to read a good
book. I'll read an easy book or go to a movie to kill the
time. I didn't mind killing time when I was younger, but I
resent killing time now. (Laughs.) I don't want to *kill*
time. I want to *do* something with my time.

Traveling in the big jets and going to and from hotels is
very tough. We're in New York on a Wednesday, Philadelphia on a Thursday, Buffalo on a Saturday, Pittsburgh
on a Sunday, and Detroit on a Tuesday. That's just a terrible way to live. (Laughs.) After the game on Sunday, I
am tired—not only with my body, which is not a bad kind
of tiredness, I'm tired emotionally, tired mentally. I'm not
a very good companion after those games.

It's a lot tougher when things are going badly. It's more
gritty and you don't feel very good about yourself. The
whole object of a pro game is to win. That is what we sell.
We sell it to a lot of people who don't win at all in their

regular lives. They involve themselves with *their* team, a winning team. I'm not cynical about this. When we win, there's also a carry-over in us. Life is a little easier. But in the last two or three years fatigue has been there. I'm sucked out. But that's okay. I'd sooner live like that than be bored. If I get a decent sleep, a bit of food that's good and strong, I'm revived. I'm alive again.

The fans touch us, particularly when we've won. You can feel the pat of hands all over. On the back, on the shoulder, they want to shake your hand. When I'm feeling good about myself, I really respond to this. But if I don't feel so good, I play out the role. You have to act it out. It has nothing to do with pure joy. It has nothing to do with the feeling I had when I was a kid.

'Cause hell, nobody recognized me. I didn't have a role to play. Many of us are looking for some kind of role to play. The role of the professional athlete is one that I've learned to play very well. Laughing with strangers. It doesn't take much. It has its built-in moves, responses. There is status for the fans, but there's not a whole lot of status for me. (Laughs.) Not now. I know it doesn't mean very much. I shy away from it more and more. When I'm not feeling good and somebody comes up—"Hello, Eric"—I'm at times a bit cold and abrupt. I can see them withdrawing from me, hurt. They want to be plugged into something and they're not. They may make a slurring remark. I can't do anything about it.

I'm fighting the cynicism. What I'd like to do is find an alter-life and play a little more. I don't have another vocation. I have a feeling unless I find one, my life might be a big anticlimax. I could get a job, but I don't want a job. I never had a job in the sense that I had to earn a living just for the sake of earning a living. I may have to do that, but I sure hope I don't.

I have doubts about what I do. I'm not that sure of myself. It doesn't seem clear to me at times. I'm a man playing a boy's game. Is this a valid reason for making money? Then I turn around and think of a job. I've tried to be a stockbroker. I say to a guy, "I got a good stock, you want to buy it?" He says, "No." I say, "Okay." You don't want to buy, don't buy. (Laughs.) I'm not good at persuading people to buy things they don't want to buy. I'm just not interested in the power of money. I found that out. That's the way one keeps score—the amount of money you earned. I found myself bored with that.

I've worked on construction and I liked that best of all. (Laughs.) I'd been working as a stockbroker and I couldn't stand it any more. I got drunk one Friday night and while I was careening around town I ran into this guy I knew from the past. He said for the hell of it. "Why don't you come and work on the Hancock Building with me?" He was a super on the job. The next Monday I showed up. I stayed for a week. I was interested in seeing how a big building goes up—and working with my hands.

A stockbroker has more status. He surrounds himself with things of status. But the stockbroker comes to see me play, I don't go to see him be a stockbroker. (Laughs.)

The real status is what my peers think of me and what I think of myself. The players have careful self-doubts at times. We talk about our sagging egos. Are we really that famous? Are we really that good? We have terrible doubts. (Laughs.) Actors may have something of this. Did I do well? Am I worth this applause? Is pushing the puck around really that meaningful? (Laughs.) When I'm not pushing that puck well, how come the fans don't like me? (Laughs.) Then there's the reverse reaction—a real brashness. They're always rationalizing to each other. That's probably necessary. It's not a bad way to handle things when you have no control over them. Players who are really put together, who have few doubts, are usually much more in control. If you're recognized by your peers, you're all right.

I still like the physicality, the sensuality of life. I still like to use my body. But the things I like now are more soft. I don't want to beat people. I don't want to prove anything. I have a friend who used to play pro football, but who shares my philosophy. We get into the country that is stark and cold and harsh, but there's a great aesthetic feedback. It's soft and comforting and sweet. We come out of there with such enormous energy and so fit. We often go into town like a couple of fools and get mildly drunk and laugh a lot.

Being a physical man in the modern world is becoming obsolete. The machines have taken the place of that. We work in offices, we fight rules and corporations, but we hardly ever hit anybody. Not that hitting anybody is a solution. But to survive in the world at one time, one had to stand up and fight—fight the weather, fight the land, or fight the rocks. I think there is a real desire for man to do that. Today he has evolved into being more passive, conforming . . .

I think that is why the professional game, with its terrific physicality—men getting together on a cooperative basis—this is appealing to the middle-class man. He's the one who supports professional sports.

I think it's a reflection of the North American way of life. This is one of the ways you are somebody—you beat somebody. (Laughs.) You're better than they are. Somebody has to be less than you in order for you to be somebody. I don't know if that's right any more. I don't have that drive any more. If I function hard, it's against a hard environment. That's preferable to knocking somebody down.

I come up against a hard young stud now, and he wants the puck very badly, I'm inclined to give it to him. (Laughs.) When you start thinking like that you're in trouble, as far as being a pro athlete is involved. But I don't want to be anybody any more in those terms. I've had some money, I've had some big fat times, I've been on the stage.

It's been a good life. Maybe I could have done better, have a better record or something like that. But I've really had very few regrets over the past twenty years. I can enjoy some of the arts that I had shut myself off from as a kid. Perhaps that is my only regret. The passion for the game was so all-consuming when I was a kid that I blocked myself from music. I cut myself off from a certain broadness of experience. Maybe one has to do that to fully explore what they want to do the most passionately.

I know a lot of pro athletes who have a capacity for a wider experience. But they wanted to become champions. They had to focus themselves on their one thing completely. His primary force when he becomes champion is his ego trip, his desire to excel, to be somebody special. To some degree, he must dehumanize himself. I look forward to a lower key way of living. But it must be physical. I'm sure I would die without it, become a drunk or something.

I still like to skate. One day last year on a cold, clear, crisp afternoon, I saw this huge sheet of ice in the street. Goddamn, if I didn't drive out there and put on my skates. I took off my camel-hair coat. I was just in a sort of jacket, on my skates. And I flew. Nobody was there. I was free as a bird. I was really happy. That goes back to when I was a kid. I'll do that until I die, I hope. Oh, I was free!

The wind was blowing from the north. With the wind behind you, you're in motion, you can wheel and dive and turn, you can lay yourself into impossible angles that you never could walking or running. You lay yourself at a forty-five degree angle, your elbows virtually touching the ice as you're in a turn. Incredible! It's beautiful! You're breaking the bounds of gravity. I have a feeling this is the innate desire of man.

(His eyes are glowing.) I haven't kept many photographs of myself, but I found one where I'm in full flight. I'm leaning into a turn. You pick up the centrifugal forces and you lay in it. For a few seconds, like a gyroscope, they support you. I'm in full flight and my head is turned. I'm concentrating on something and I'm grinning. That's the way I like to picture myself. I'm something else there. I'm on another level of existence, just being in pure motion. Going wherever I want to go, whenever I want to go. That's nice, you know. (Laughs softly.)

GEORGE ALLEN

Head coach and general manager of the Washington Redskins. One word, if but one were chosen, describes him: intense. One aim, if but one were chosen explains him: to win. An air of monasticism as well as industry pervades. He is Parsifal seeking the Holy Grail each Sunday afternoon of the season.

We're at the headquarters of the professional football team. It is an enclave in Virginia, some twenty-five miles outside Washington. It has the appearance of a successful industrial complex. Aside from blackboards, chalked with arcane diagrams, there are plaques on the walls of the offices bearing the recurring encomium: "... for the unselfish sacrifice while serving with outstanding leadership, vision, ability...." Most striking are two silver discs under

*glass: it is the Fiftieth Anniversary American Legion Award
for God and Country.*

*The conference room, in which the frequently interrupt-
ed conversation took place (his secretary, besieged by
callers, in person and on the telephone, beckoned him out
every few minutes,) has the feel of "clout." The enormous
table should be the envy of any board of directors. He appears harried by the pressures of the moment. Tomorrow
the training camp opens in preparation for the forthcoming
season.*

I took the job and walked out in the middle of this woods.
I call it our Shangri-La. We've got everything we need
here to win. And we're going to improve it. We're putting
in a hundred yards of Astroturf, and they're replacing the
cinder track with a synthetic track, tartan. There will be
no distractions.

We've been working in the off-season as much as twelve,
fourteen, fifteen hours a day. When the season begins, it's
seven days a week, morning, noon, and night. To get
ready for football.

I like to make notes at home and go over things. I take
a pad and a pencil and carry it around with me all the
time. I want to read, things that have to be done.

Among the books in his office were The Encyclopedia of
Football, Best Plays, *several by himself, including* Defense
Drills, How to Train a Quarterback, The Complete Book
of Winning Football Drills, *as well as the* Football Register, *the* Congressional Directory *for the 92nd Congress,*
Outstanding Young Men in America, *and* What the Executive Should Know About the Accounting Statements.

You have to put a priority on everything you do each
day. If you don't, you won't finish it. If you enjoy your job,
it isn't work. It's fun. If you detest going to work, then
you're looking for ways to beat the clock. I'd rather come
to the Redskin Park and do my thing, so to speak, than I
would play golf. Golf is a fine sport, but it's too time-
consuming. I don't have that time schedule.

When you get so engrossed in your job during the season it has to come ahead of your family. I'm fortunate
that I have an understanding wife, who's a good mother.
My children have now kind of accepted that routine.

They've been brought up with it and it's just the way I am. It may be a mistake. It should be that your family and church come first. But I think that during the season there's so much to be done. I am even working right up to the kickoff to figure out a way that we can still win.

Everything we do is based on winning. I don't care how hard you work or how well organized you are, if you don't win, what good is it? It's down the drain. You can have a tremendous game plan, but if you lose the game, what good was the plan?

One of the greatest things is to be in a locker room after a win. And be with the players and coaches and realize what's been accomplished, what you've gone through. The rewards are not necessarily tangible. It's the hard work and the agony and the blood and sweat and tears.

When you lose, it's a morgue. That's the way it should be, because you've failed. Once in a while you'll see some tears. I don't think there's anything wrong with crying. I think it's good, it's emotional. I think when you put a lot of yourself into something it should take a lot out. Some people can lose and then go out and be the life of the party. I can't. The only way you can get over a loss is to win the next week.

Grantland Rice, who was one of our great sports writers, said it didn't matter if you won or lost, it was how you played the game. I disagree completely. The main thing is to win. That's what the game is for. Just to go out and play and then say, "Well, I didn't win but I played the game, I participated"—anybody can do that. You have to be number one, whether it's football or selling insurance or anything.

Most coaches aren't too business-minded. I'm the general manager of the Redskins, so I have to be a little more aware of business than just a coach. I'm more interested in how we can get more income in, to use that to help us win. So we can spend more money. Anything you can learn on accounting or business is helpful. We're an organization.

Each player is part of a whole team. A football team is a lot like a machine. It's made up of parts. I like to think of it as a Cadillac. A Cadillac's a pretty good car. All the refined parts working together make the team. If one part doesn't work, one player pulling against you and not doing his job, the whole machine fails.

Nobody is indispensable. If he can't play, we let him know that he's not going to be with us. "Do you want to play somewhere else?" We try to improve and replace some of the parts every year.

The only time you relax is when you win. If you lose, you don't relax until you win. That's the way I am. It's a state of tension almost continuously.

Allen's Ten Commandments*

1. Football comes first. "During the off-season, I tell my players that their family and church should come one, two, with football third. But during the six months of the season, the competition in the NFL is so tough that we have to put football ahead of everything else."

2. The greatest feeling in life is to take an ordinary job and accomplish something with it. . . .

3. If you can accept defeat and open your pay envelope without feeling guilty, you're stealing. "You're stealing from your employer and from yourself. Winning is the only way to go. . . . Losers just look foolish in a new car or partying it up. As far as I'm concerned, life without victories is like being in prison."

4. Everyone, the head coach especially, must give 110 percent. . . . "The average good American pictures himself as a hard worker. But most persons are really operating at less than half-power. They never get above fifty percent. . . . Therefore, to get one hundred, you must aim for 110. A man who is concerned with an eight-hour day never works that long, and seldom works half that long. The same man, however, when challenged by a seventeen-hour day, will be just warmed up and driving when he hits the eighth hour. . . .

5. Leisure time is that five or six hours when you sleep at night. "Nobody should work all the time. Everybody should have some leisure. . . . You can combine two good things at once, sleep and leisure."

6. No detail is too small. No task is too small or too big. "Winning can be defined as the science of being totally prepared. I define preparation in three words: leave nothing undone. . . . Nowadays there is . . . no difference

* From interview by Bob Oates, *Los Angeles Times*, July 9, 1970.

between one team and another in the NFL. Usually the winner is going to be the team that's better prepared. . . ."

7. You must accomplish things in life, otherwise you are like the paper on the wall. "The achiever is the only individual who is truly alive. There can be no inner satisfaction in simply driving a fine car or eating in a fine restaurant or watching a good movie or television program. Those who think they're enjoying themselves doing any of that are half-dead and don't know it. . . ."

8. A person with problems is dead. "Everybody has problems. The successful person solves his. He acknowledges them, works on them, and solves them. He is not disturbed when another day brings another kind of problem. . . . The winner . . . solves his own problems. The man swayed by someone else is a two-time loser. First, he hasn't believed in his own convictions and second, he is still lost."

9. We win and lose as a team. . . .

10. My prayer is that each man will be allowed to play to the best of his ability.

IN CHARGE

WARD QUAAL

We're at Tribune Square, Chicago. We're in the well-appointed office of the president of WGN-Continental Broadcasting Corporation—"the most powerful broadcast medium in the Midwest." He has been battling a slight sinus condition, but his presence is, nonetheless, felt.

"I'm responsible for all its broadcasting properties. We have radio and television here. We have a travel company here. We have a sales company here. We have the Continental Productions Company here. We have radio and television in Minnesota and translator systems in northern Michigan, Wisconsin, as well as Minnesota. We have cable television in Michigan and California. We have television in Denver. We have sales companies in New York and Tokyo. I operate sixteen different organizations in the United States and Japan."

My day starts between four thirty and five in the morning, at home in Winnetka. I dictate in my library until about seven thirty. Then I have breakfast. The driver gets there about eight o'clock and oftentimes I continue dictating in the car on the way to the office. I go to the Broadcast Center in the morning and then to Tribune Square around noon. Of course, I do a lot of reading in the car.

I talk into a dictaphone. I will probably have as many as 150 letters dictated by seven-thirty in the morning. I have five full-time secretaries, who do nothing but work for Ward Quaal. I have seven swing girls, who work for me part-time. This does not include my secretaries in New

York, Los Angeles, Washington, and San Francisco. They get dicta-belts from me every day. They also take telephone messages. My personal secretary doesn't do any of that. She handles appointments and my trips. She tries to work out my schedule to fit these other secretaries.

I get home around six-thirty, seven at night. After dinner with the family I spend a minimum of two and a half hours each night going over the mail and dictating. I should have a secretary at home just to handle the mail that comes there. I'm not talking about bills and personal notes, I'm talking about business mail only. Although I don't go to the office on Saturday or Sunday, I do have mail brought out to my home for the weekend. I dictate on Saturday and Sunday. When I do this on holidays, like Christmas, New Year's, and Thanksgiving, I have to sneak a little bit, so the family doesn't know what I'm doing.

Ours is a twenty-four-hour-a-day business. We're not turning out three thousand gross of shoes, beans, or neckties. We're turning out a new product every day, with new problems. It's not unusual for me to get a phone call on a weekend: "What are your thoughts on it, Mr. Quaal? Would you speak out on it?" I'm not going to hide my posture on it. I'm going to answer that. This may mean going into the studio to make a recording. Or I may do a tape recording at home. Or maybe I'll just make a statement. I am in a seven-day-a-week job and I love it!

"I grew up in a very poor family. Not only did no one come to us for advice, we went to other people for advice. We wondered what we were going to do for the next dollar. We did manage during the Depression. But I know others who didn't extricate themselves from these difficulties. I won't forget them. A letter from one of those individuals asking for help is just as important to me as a suggestion from the chairman of the board of the Chase Manhattan Bank. They get the same weight. They get a personal letter from me. He didn't write to my assistant, he didn't write to my secretary. He wants to hear from Ward Quaal."

When I come to the Broadcast Center, I'll probably have about five or six different stacks of mail. One stack is urgent and should be acted upon before I make any phone calls. Once I handle that, which usually takes about fifteen, twenty minutes, I start the important phone calls. In-between these phone calls and others of lesser importance, I get into the other mail. On a typical day we'll get thirteen hundred pieces of first-class mail addressed to me personally. Every letter is answered within forty-eight hours—and not a form letter. There are no form letters. If they write to the president of the company, they don't want to hear from the third vice president. They hear from the president. Mail and the telephone, that's the name of the game in this business.

I imagine your phone calls are not long in nature?

No, they're not long in nature. I have this ability—I learned this when I was an announcer years ago, and we were feeding six networks out of here. I could listen to all these channels with earphones and I knew when to say the right cue at the right time. I can still do that.

"In high school I wanted to be a good football player, a good basketball player, a good baseball player. I managed to be captain of every team on which I ever played. At the end of my freshman year my coach said, 'There's a shortage of people to do oratory and declamatory work.' He said, 'We've just simply got to have somebody with your voice. If you would do this, I would excuse you from football practice a couple of nights a week.' I won the oratorical and declamatory championship for the state of Michigan. On the night of the finals in Ishpeming, which were broadcast, the chief engineer of a radio station, a Polish gentleman, called my mother and told her I'd be a network announcer someday.

"I started working during my freshman year in high school as an announcer at WBEO in Marquette. I worked from 10:00 A.M. to 10:00 P.M. and got $17.50 a week. At the same time, I drove a commercial milk truck from four in the morning to eight, and I got $22.50 a week for that. The two jobs gave me money to go to the University of Michigan. I have great pride in my university. I was chairman of the Alumni Fund and its Development Council.

"I won the job as a Detroit radio announcer at thirty-five dollars a week, while still a student. I hitchhiked or took a bus every day from Ann Arbor to Detroit. On the

*campus I was promotion manager of the yearbook. I was
sports and feature writer for the* Michigan Daily. *I was on
the freshman football team, baseball team, and basketball
team. And I was president of the fraternity. All at one
time. Shows you can do it if you work hard enough.*

*"When I applied for admission at the university, I was
asked what my goal was after graduation. I said, 'The announcing staff of WGN.' I finished my last exam June 8,
1941, and I started at WGN the next day."*

I had no desire to be an announcer forever. I wanted to
become general manager. I think this is something anybody can do. The number one thing in any business is to
go get a background, so you can show your people you
can do anything they can do. My people today know I can
announce any show they could, I can write a script, I can
produce a show, I can handle a camera. If I still had the
voice, I would enjoy being back on the air again.

I've had to develop a team effort with all people. I prefer being called Ward rather than Mr. Quaal. Ninety percent of the people do call me by my first name. The young
women of the organization do not, although I certainly
would not disapprove of them calling me Ward. The last
thing I want to be is a stuffed shirt. I'm trying to run this
organization on a family basis. I prefer it to be on the informal side.

I've always felt throughout my lifetime that if you have
any ability at all, go for first place. That's all I'm interested in. That doesn't mean I'm trying to be an autocrat.
Lord knows I'm not a dictator. I try to give all my colleagues total autonomy. But they know there's one guy in
charge.

Of course, you have to be number two before you become number one—unless you're born into something. I
was born into a poor family. I had to create my own
paths. Sure, I've been second vice president, first vice president, and executive vice president. But I had only one
goal in life and that was to be president.

A fellow like Ward Quaal, he's one of the old hands
now. That doesn't mean I'm going to vegetate. I intend to
devote more time to our subsidiaries and to develop young
people who come forth with new ideas. I don't look for-

ward to retirement. I feel I have many useful years ahead of me. When the time comes to step aside, I won't regret it at all. I have a lot of writing to do. I'll have so much to do.

You're more of a philosopher-king than a boss ...

I think that is true. When I came here sixteen years ago, August first, I never had any desire to be a czar. I don't like to say I ruled with an iron hand, but I had to take charge and clean up the place. I am the captain calling the signals and every once in a while I call the right play and we're pretty lucky.

I don't feel any pressure, though my family says I sometimes show it. I'm not under tension. I go to bed at night and I sleep well. The company is doing well. My people are functioning as a team. The success story is not Ward Quaal. It's a great team of people.

POSTSCRIPT: *"On a typical day we get about seven hundred phone calls. We average eighty a day long distance." I estimated that during the time of this conversation, there were about forty phone calls for Ward Quaal.*

DAVE BENDER

It is a newly built, quite modern factory on the outskirts of a large industrial city. Scores of people are at work in the offices. Sounds of typewriters and adding machines; yet an air of informality pervades. He has come into his private office, tie askew; he's in need of a shave. We have a couple of shots of whisky.

"*I manufacture coin machine and vending machine parts—components. We also make units for amusement devices. We don't know what they're gonna do with it. We have ideas what they might. I have about two hundred employees. I never counted. They're people. We have tool and die makers, mold makers, sheet metal, screw machine, woodwork, painting, coil winding. You name it, we got it.*"

I just stay in the background. Myself, I like making things. I make the machinery here. I'm not an engineer, but I have an idea and I kind of develop things and—(with an air of wonder)—they *work*. All night long I think about this place. I love my work. It isn't the money. It's just a way of expressing my feeling.

When we started here we were strictly in the pinball game part business. I kept adding and adding and adding and never stopped. Finally I got into the jukebox end of it. Of course, slot machines came in and then slot machines went out. Never fool with Uncle Sam. When they said no slot machine parts, they meant it and I meant it too. I don't want them checking up on us. You can live without it. We make so many different things. A little of this, a little of that. Not a lot of any one thing.

I made a machine that makes plastic tubes. It becomes like a parasite. It runs through 250 feet a minute, five tubes at a time. I made it with a bunch of crazy ideas and junk I found around the place. I can sell that machine for twenty thousand dollars. If I dress it up and put flowers on it, you can sell it for much, much more.

I was a no-good bum, kicked out of high school. I went up to a teacher and I said, "If you don't pass me, I'll blow your brains out." I stole a gun. (Laughs.) I was kicked out. It was my second year. I did some dirty things I can't talk about. (Laughs.) When I was thirteen years old I took a Model T Ford apart and put it together again in the basement. I did some crazy things.

When I talk to people about plastic I take the position *I'm* the plastic and how would I travel through the machine and what would I see. Maybe I'm goofy. In business I take the position: where would I be if I were the customer? What do I expect of you? Some people are natural born stinkers. I try to find a way to get to them. You can break down anybody with the right method.

I sell all I make. I don't know what to do with 'em. (Laughs.) They use 'em for packaging. I work with wood, plastic, metal, anything. I work with paper. Even at home. Sunday I was taking paper and pasting it together and finding a method of how to drop spoons, a fork, a napkin, and a straw into one package. The napkin feeder I got. The straw feeder we made already. That leaves us the spoon and the fork. How do we get it? Do we blow the bag open? Do we push it open? Do we squeeze it down?

So I'm shoving things in and pushing with my wife's hair clips and bobby pins and everything I can get my hands on. I even took the cat's litter, the stuff you pick up the crap with (laughs), even that to shove with the bag, to pull it open. This is for schools, inexpensive packaging. It sells for about a penny a package. Plastic. In a bag, the whole darn thing. So what can I tell you?

Everybody is packaging the stuff. Their method is antique. My method is totally automatic. I know what my competitors are doing. I never underestimate 'em, but I'm ten steps ahead of 'em. I can meet them any way they want. But not to cut their heart out. We all have to make a living.

"I started this whole damn thing with forty dollars. In 1940. I borrowed it. In 1938 I was a big dealer. I was the greatest crap shooter in the world. (Laughs.) I was makin' rubber parts and plunger rods for the pin games. Then the war broke out in '41. Where do you get the rods? I took a hacksaw and went to the junkyards. Remember the old rails that went up and down on the beds? I cut that out and made plunger rods. I did some crazy things.

"I started with a couple of people. I made fifteen dollars a week for myself and I didn't even have that. Oh boy, oh boy, oh boy, I tried everything. Making work gloves. I was eighteen. I went into the coal business. I borrowed two hundred dollars from my brother. Suddenly I had four trucks. I got sick and tired of coal and gave my father the keys for the four trucks and I said, 'Pa, it's your business. You owe me zero.' What else did I do? Oh God, making things. Making a factory. I love making.

"Business to me is a method of engineering. Even in advertising. I've always wondered why they don't get people for what they really are. Like this Alka-Seltzer commercial. I operate business the same way—in getting to the people. What are we other than people?"

Even during the war, I never took advantage of a price. I used to sell something for thirty-five cents. During the war I still sold it for thirty-five cents. A customer said, "Dave, I'll never forget you." They're liars. They did forget soon afterward. I never took anybody. I built my busi-

ness on that. My competitors came and they went and I'm
still at it. I'm bigger now than ever.

I hope to be going public. So I have to show an in-
crease. That's the name of the game. I have workers been
here twenty-seven, twenty-eight years. I feel I owe them
something. I don't know how to compensate them. At
least if I go public, I can offer them stock. I'd like to re-
pay people. This is a way of saying thank you.

I was offered all kinds of deals which I turned down—
by big vending companies. It would be beautiful for me. I
walk away with a million many times over. So what?
What about these poor devils? I'll fire 'em all? Huh?

To them, I'm Dave. I know the family. I know their
troubles. "Dave, can you give me a dollar?" "Dave, how
about some coffee?" I'll go to the model maker and talk
about our problem and we'll have a shot of whisky. Ask
him how his wife's feeling. "Fine." He wants to put something for his home, can I make it? "Sure." They all call
me Dave. When they call me Mr. Bender I don't know
who they're talking to. (Laughs.)

I love mechanics. All my fingernails are chopped off. I
washed my hands before you came in. Grease. Absolutely.
I get into things. You stick a ruler here or a measure here.
I want this, I want that. "Frank, you chop this up. Put
this in the mill. Cut that off." I got three, four things happening at one time.

I'm here at six in the morning. Five thirty I'll leave.
Sometimes I'll come here on Sunday when everybody's
gone and I'll putter around with the equipment. There
isn't a machine in this place I can't run. There isn't a thing
I can't do.

They tell me it don't look nice for the workers for me
to work on the machine. I couldn't care less if I swept the
floors, which I do. Yesterday some napkins fell on the
floor from the napkin feeding machine. I said to the
welder, "Pick up the napkins." He says, "No, you pick it
up." I said, "If you're tired, I'll pick it up." So I'm pickin'
em up.

The workers say: "You're the boss, you shouldn't do
this. It's not nice. You're supposed to tell us what to do,
but not to do it yourself." I tell 'em I love it. They want
me more or less in the office. I don't even come in here. If
I do it's just to get my shot of booze with my worker and
we break bread, that's all. When they call me Mr. Bender,

I think they're being sarcastic. I don't feel like a boss to 'em. I feel like a chum-buddy.

I know a lot of people with money and I have very little to do with them. They're a little bit too high falutin' for me. I think they're snobs. They're spoiled rotten, their wealth. I won't mention names. I was born and raised poor. I had zero. I'm a fortunate guy. Whatever I got I'm thankful for. That's my life. I just like plain, ordinary people. I have a doctor friend, but outside of being a doctor, he's my swear-buddy. We swear at each other. A guy who works in the liquor store is my friend. Some of the workers here are my friends.

You're the boss of these people . . .

(Hurt) No, I just work here. They say, "Dave you should give us orders. You shouldn't be pickin' up napkins." Oh, don't misunderstand me. I'm not the easiest guy in the world. I swear at 'em. I'm a stubborn son of a gun. When I finally get my idea straight, I'm rough. I know what I want, give me what I want. But I do have enough sense to know when to leave 'em alone.

Don't you feel you have status in being a boss?

Ooohhh, I hate that word! I tell people I don't want to hear another word about who I am or what I am. I enjoy myself eleven hours a day. When I get home, I take my shoes off, get comfortable, pinch my wife's rear end, kiss her, of course, and ask her what she did today. I try not to take my problems home. I have problems, plenty, but I try to avoid it.

Saturdays and Sundays are the worst days of the week. It's a long weekend because I'm not here. I bum around, see movies, go to somebody's house, but I'm always waiting for Monday. I go away on a vacation, it's the worst thing in the world. (Laughs.) My wife got a heart attack in Majorca, Spain. She was in the hospital. I was there six weeks. It was the first real vacation I ever had. I finally went fishing. Here I am drinking wine, eating oranges and cheese, tearing the bread on the boat, had the time of my life. I told my wife it took her heart attack to get me to enjoy a vacation. (Laughs.)

Retire? Hell no. I'd open up another shop and start all

over again. What am I gonna do? Go crazy? I told you I love my work. I think it's some form of being insecure. I've always worried about tomorrow. I worried and I fought for tomorrow. I don't have to worry about tomorrow. But I still want to work. I *need* to.

Today I worked all day in the shop with the model maker, two tool makers, and a welder. I don't have neat blueprints. I don't have a damn thing. All I have is this. (Taps at his temple.) I'll take a piece of paper. I can't even make drawings. I'm measuring, taking off three-eights of an inch or put on two inches here. It's the craziest piece of iron you ever saw. I never saw anything like this in my life. But I saw it working the other day.

When I get it fabricated it'll be a packaging machine. You'll see arms going up and down, gears working, things going, reelers and winders, automatic everything. I know it could be patented. There's nothing like it. It's unique. This is all in my mind, yes sir. And I can't tell you my telephone number. (Laughs.)

I never tell people I'm the boss. I get red and flustered. I'm ashamed of it. When they find out—frankly speaking, people are parasites. They treat you like a dirty dog one way, and as soon as they find out who you are it's a different person. (Laughs.) When they come through the front door—"I want you to meet our president, Mr. Bender"—they're really like peacocks. I'd rather receive a man from the back door as a man. From the front door, he's got all the table manners. Oh, all that phony air. He's never down to earth. That's why I don't like to say who I am.

A man comes in and I'm working like a worker, he tells me everything. He talks from the bottom of his heart. You can break bread with him, you can swear. Anything that comes out of your heart. The minute he finds out you're in charge, he looks up to you. Actually he hates you.

My wife's got a friend and her husband's got a job. If only they stopped climbing down my back. I do so many wrong things. Why don't you tell me to go to hell for the things I do? I deliberately see how far I can push them. And they won't tell me to go to hell, because I'm Dave Bender, the president. They look up to me as a man of distinction, a guy with brains. Actually I'm a stupid ass, as stupid as anybody that walks the street.

Yet what the hell did we fight for? A goddamned empty

on top of nothing? A sand pile? King of the Hill means you stood there and you fought to get on top of an empty hill. But it did satisfy your ego, didn't it? We do these crazy things. It doesn't have to be a financial reward. Just the satisfaction.

I'm making a machine now. I do hope to have it ready in the next couple months. The machine has nothing to do with helping humanity in any size, shape, or form. It's a personal satisfaction for me to see this piece of iron doing some work. It's like a robot working. This is the reward itself for me, nothing else. My ego, that's it.

Something last night was buggin' me. I took a sleeping pill to get it out of my mind. I was up half the night just bugging and bugging and bugging. I was down here about six o'clock this morning. I said, "Stop everything. We're making a mistake." I pointed out where the mistake was and they said, "Holy hell, we never thought of that." Today we're rebuilding the whole thing. This kind of stuff gets to me. Not only what was wrong, but how the devil do you fix it? I felt better. This problem, that's over with. There's no problem that can't be solved if you use logic and reason the thing out. I don't care what it is. Good horse sense is what it's known as. With that you can do anything you want—determination, you can conquer the world.

ERNEST BRADSHAW

"I work in a kind of bank, in the auditing department. I supervise about twenty people. We keep an eye on the other areas. We do a lot of paper checking to make sure nobody inside is stealing. It's kind of internal security." The company is a large one—about five thousand employees.

He's been at this job a year. He started there two and a half years ago as a clerk. "You always feel good about a promotion. It means more money and less work." (Laughs.) He is twenty-five, married. His wife is a teacher. There are two blacks aside from himself in the department.

You have control over people's lives and livelihood. It's good for a person who enjoys that kind of work, who can dominate somebody else's life. I'm not too wrapped up in seeing a woman, fifty years old, get thrown off her job because she can't cut it like the younger ones. They moved her off the job, where she was happy.

Some people can manage and some people can't manage. I figure I can manage. But it's this personal feeling— it just doesn't seem right for me to say to this woman, "Okay, I'll rate you below average." She has nobody to support her. If she got fired, where would a woman fifty years of age go to find a job? I'm a good supervisor. I write it up the way it's supposed to be written up. My feeling can't come into play. What I do is what I *have* to do. This doesn't mean I won't get gray hairs or feel kind of bad.

At first they doubted my word, being black and being young. The woman was white. They told me to document my feelings. They didn't know if it was a personality prejudice or black against white. So I documented it. I showed this point and that point . . . So they said okay. They knew I didn't particularly care for doing it. They knew my feelings. I told them she was a good woman. They said, "You can't let personal feelings come in. We'll give her about five months to shape up or ship out." She was put on probation.

That's the thing you get in any business. They never talk about personal feelings. They let you know that people are of no consequence. You take the job, you agree to work from eight thirty to five and no ifs, ands, or buts. Feelings are left out. I think some of the other supervisors are compassionate, as I think I am. But they take the easy way out. You take a person that's minimal, you rate him as average. He'll get a raise in six months. When you write a person as minimal, the person won't get a raise and he's subject to lose his job. Everybody takes the easy way out and just puts down a person's average. This takes away all the pressures. I felt it has to be one way; be truthful about a person 'cause it's gonna come up on 'em sooner or later. I look at people as people, person to person. But when you're on a job, you're supposed to lose all this.

If it's a small organization, you don't need anything like that. You don't need appraisals. Everybody knows everybody. In a larger company people become pawns. These big corporations are gonna keep on growing and the people become less and less. The human being doesn't count any more. In any large corporation it's the buck that counts.

In this case, we could've moved her to an area in which the job wasn't as demanding. Someplace where she'd never have to worry about firing and not worry about somebody like me watching her. Give her a job that she has a potential for, where she can do her optimum, where she could have a slower pace. Why put her where you have so much youth and speed?

I don't see this job as status. Okay, I got twenty people under me. That's not status to me. Status is being the man at the top. Not just to be another pawn. You're not at the bottom level. You're on the step right above it. But there are fifty more above you. So there's really no status to this job.

But what does the guy at the top do? He's chairman of the board. I don't know if that's a particularly nice feeling to have—five thousand people under you, two billion dollars in assets, and a handful of men watching it. What are they doing while you're gone? Being up there is something I couldn't ever envision.

After spending two years in the service he had worked in a neighborhood realty office. "Managed property, screened out people who were acceptable and who weren't. The neighborhood changed to where it was pretty rough, so I decided it was advantageous to leave.

"I hadn't planned on making this a permanent thing. Just stay here six months and go back to school full-time, accounting. But I got married, so I had to remain. I'm undecided now. I have a few business courses, but I stopped taking them and just work on the humanities. See if there's anything there I'd prefer to business."

I'm usually at the desk by eight o'clock, half an hour before work starts. Getting set up for the day, writing programs, assigning different jobs to different people. When they come in we take a head count. You see who's late and who's not. You check around and make sure they start at eight thirty and not go in the washroom and powder their nose for fifteen minutes. You make sure when

they go for breaks they take fifteen minutes not twenty.
You check for lunch hours, making sure they take forty-
five minutes and not an hour. And that they're not supposed to make personal telephone calls on the bank's
phone. All you're doing is checking on people. This goes
on all day.

The job is boring. It's a real repetitive thing. I don't
notice the time. I could care less about the time. I don't
really know if it's five o'clock until I see somebody clean
up their desk. At five I leave for school. It's always the
same. Nothing exciting ever happens.

It's just this constant supervision of people. It's more or
less like you have a factory full of robots working the machinery. You're there checking and making sure the machinery is constantly working. If it breaks down or something goes wrong, you're there to straighten it out. You're
like a foreman on the assembly line. If they break down,
replace them. You're just like a man who sits and watches
computers all day. Same thing.

Just like Big Brother's watching you. Everybody's
watching somebody. It's quite funny when you turn and
start watching them. I do that quite a bit. They know I'm
watching them. They become uneasy. (Laughs.)

A man should be treated as a human, not as a million-
dollar piece of machinery. People aren't treated as good as
an IBM machine is. Big corporations turn me off. I didn't
know it until I became a supervisor and I realized the
games you have to play. When you were a clerk, you
didn't have no worries. You just had to do your job. You
just had to worry about signing in on time and signing out
on time. You just knew you had a job to do and to do it.

I won't be there forever at the place. Working in a
bank, there's no thrill in that. I didn't run home and say,
"Ma, I'm working for a bank now. Isn't that wonderful?"
I'm still searching. I do move around. I never sit at the
desk. That's one thing I could never do is just sit. Maybe
that's what my next job will be, something where I can
move around. Maybe a salesman . . .

Quite a few people stay after work. I look at 'em every
day when I walk out the door. (Laughs.) I'm not that
way. They are the older generation. They stay there just
to make sure the work is all caught up. I can't see that.
The older ones are much more dedicated than the younger
ones. I can't ever envison a time where we'll go back to a

period where when a man starts out in a business he's dedicated to it for the rest of his life. I can't envision a man staying with a company forty years. That's over with.

A man can go to school for three years and change his profession any time he gets good and ready. He might be a clerk pushing papers all day, but he also goes to this computer school. And he'll probably go to another corporation, where he'll get better pay. A lot of men of the last generation are just content with their jobs. They never look for any other place.

I promised I'd never let myself get an ulcer. Money isn't worth that. But that woman really bothered me. She was nice, gentle. But it was something I had to do and I told her it had to be done. I told her people had been carrying her all along and just marking her average. She sat about two desks away from me and I was helping her most of the time. Her pay wasn't going up or anything. I think she appreciated me telling her.

PETER KEELEY

"I sell draperies. I've done that for many years. In the past I've manufactured them. It was my business. It's no longer my business. I sell the product I used to make. It was a come down when I went broke. I don't believe it is today. I believe it is an adjustment to age. I think it's a victory. There's many men in the same condition, have given up and just rotted. Quite a few of my old friends. Not me."

He is sixty-five years old.

"Originally, I started selling in New England. Broad silks. Small stores, hardheaded New England Yankees. It was quite an education. If you can sell them, you can sell anybody. In 1941 they moved me to Pittsburgh for forty dollars a week. I became branch manager. I was quite successful—until the present day."

The company I was running the business for sold out to a corporation on the west coast—a merger. I was dropped. It was company policy: no man older than forty-five. Everybody was merging. A lot of people got dropped by the wayside. I didn't bounce. That hurt my ego. It hurt me in twenty directions. I got cold feet, scared. It was a year ago, November. I was sixty-four. Many friends drop you, many people don't know you. You have to fight your own way—which I've done all my life. I'm damn well adjusted now.

I brought this branch from about a hundred thousand dollars a year to a million and a half. There was no great shakes over that. I was frantically, insanely mad. (Laughs.) I spent four months going insane. Another month, I probably would burn the building down and kill myself. I blamed everything on everybody.

These days I'm drawing $128 a week for a company I'm handling inventory for. And purchasing. He has a seventy-thousand-dollar inventory, about a hundred thousand yards. No fabric can come in, be cut, go out without me knowing it. I work very hard until about noon.

I run a little business of my own and make about three hundred dollars a month—a decorating business, a tiny company. A few jobs here and there. I work on this a couple of hours in the afternoon. I very seldom go out to lunch.

I call my customers cold turkey. I look in the book and call ten people: "Do you want draperies or don't you?" You'd be surprised. (Laughs.) It's like the guy that said to twenty girls, "Would you go to bed with me?" Nineteen said no, but one said yes. (Laughs.)

I use a telephone directory, I read the paper. Here's a new office building. I'll call the builder, the architect, or the company that's gonna manage it. I get a lead off that. Usually I get nowhere. All of a sudden you get that one guy and you have him. General Electric, a nationwide corporation, right? They got my name out of the Yellow Pages: Kee of Pittsburgh. The head porter—they now call him superintendent of maintenance—this janitor called me up and said, "This is General Electric. We want to have our offices decorated." They didn't know me from Adam. It was a lead out of a phonebook. That's one way.

I say, "This is Kee of Pittsburgh. My name's Pete Keeley. May I speak with the doctor?" You never talk to him, he's busier than a dog with fleas. So you talk to the nurse. "How about your draperies? I want to make some money off you. I can make about forty bucks on it. But you'll be satisfied." That's a good pitch. Either she'll think you're crazy or she'll say, "Okay, come on up." I never say I'm the cheapest. He can go to Penny's, you can go to Sears and get it cheaper, but you won't get me. I just cannot sell a cheap fabric. It always had to be the best. We're talking now about very small stuff, very small business. (Laughs.) I can get the job, maybe one out of ten, one out of twenty. That's enough. If I got 'em all, I wouldn't be talking to you. I'd own the building. I pick up about five a month. I've never used the stereotype approach. "My name is Pete Keeley. I'm Kee of Pittsburgh. I want to make some dough off you."

I try to pick carefully. I just feel it. I won't take a dentist who's been there forty-five years and cleans his drapes every five years. That's not the guy to approach. When I hear of new buildings, I may drive by and get the list off the front.

All my life, everytime I make a cold call, I've had cold feet. Whether I call the president of General Motors—as I have in the past—or on a little mama-and-papa store, the same butterfly, always. If you make enough calls and make the butterfly fly away, you're gonna hit. One out of ten, twenty. Like the old guy that sells doughnuts. If he makes enough calls, he's gonna sell a doughnut.

They hang up on me many times. A baseball player doesn't bat more than .300. When he hangs up on me, I say, "Look, Kee, what did you do wrong with this guy? Theoretically you're a genius in selling." Then I'll say to myself, "I did nothing wrong. I'm a genius. This guy's a dumb son of a bitch."

I've never felt humiliated. I got into a fistfight once with the head buyer of a store in Boston. He was a very nasty son of a bitch. He told me I was overpriced and no damn good. He and I resented back and forth, right there on the fifth floor. It ended in the elevator. The merchandise man separated us. The only time I got mad at a buyer. A lousy buyer is a buyer who won't buy from you, but there's no physical combat. We both got arrested. (Pause.) Maybe he did humiliate me. (A longer pause.) The more I think about it . . . It's the only time of my life I ever resorted to violence—in selling.

It's been a very bad year emotionally. I worried a lot, I sweat a lot of blood, and spent a lot of sleepless nights. Because of this let-out, this comedown. I felt it. I knew it was comin'. I knew the policy of this coast company. I didn't do anything about it. I should have. It's a shock to an egotist. All of a sudden you find you're not the smartest guy in the world. (Laughs.)

It's much easier to say, "Mr. Keeley resigned from X Company," than it is to say, "Mr. Keeley was dropped by X Company." (Pause.) Just like that, they dropped me. They handed me a couple of checks. "We regret this, Mr. Keeley, and thank you, good-by." That was it.

I should have made the change myself when I had the opportunity. When a man has a responsible position, there are many offerings open to him. When he's out of it, these offerings disappear. They're gone. To look for another job when you have a job is not too difficult. But when you haven't got one, to look for a job—that was my mistake. I felt I failed bitterly. It came close to destroying me.

I have no regrets. I never met a man yet that didn't make mistakes. I feel I'm a tremendous success—to a point. Monetarily I'm no success. But mentally I'm a tremendous success. At sixty-five I'm still selling. I can't help it. You can't give up something you love. I'm doing it to keep my mind awake and clear. I'm doing it to keep myself alive.

"The word sell is the key to my life. I was a scared boy. I couldn't even talk on the phone. I'd sweat blood, I'd perspire, I'd fall down, I'd have to go to the bathroom. I'd walk around the building twenty times and smoke two packs of cigarettes. I never had the nerve to go in. I was a complete introvert. But the minute I found out people liked me and I liked them, I started selling. It's the best thing that ever happened to me. You have to like every slob that ever was. There's something in every guy."

I ran up against an unbeatable fact with a large corporation—age. Competence didn't enter into it. Nothing entered into it. No, uh-uh. I don't look forward to retirement. It would kill me. There is no such thing as retirement. It's a slow death.

Maybe I'm still trying to prove something. I've had a very bad stock in life. I went to grammar school four years late. I finished high school at night eleven years late. I went two years to college, twelve years late. I was trying to catch up. I've had to prove a lot of things later than other people did. Every man has to have a victory in something. To me, my life's a victory. Now at this moment I can sell you whatever I want to sell you. But I still have something to prove ... and I'm not sure what it is.

LOIS KEELEY

Peter Keeley's daughter. She is a schoolteacher. She has been seated nearby, listening to her father's reflections.

My dad lost his business the year I was married. (To him) I remember you coming home and sitting on the bed. You had to fire all those people. He had to post a notice: their employment was terminated. It was the end of Kee of Pittsburgh. I'd never seen a man cry. That really frightened me. Nineteen fifty-six. I thought my father was the wisest man that ever lived. He was always telling me how I could do all these things. He used to help me with math. I used to dread those sessions at the kitchen table when my father would help me. Actually I resented it. I wondered, Could I ever be as intelligent, as successful as he was?

I was a sophomore in college when everything went down the drain. I never thought it would happen. It was like the end of the world. We had those great plush years. I remember the house. The kid's say, "Is that *your* house?" The schools we went to, Palm Springs, inviting your friends down for the weekends, swimming pools, fancy dresses. It was all tied up with my father. Finally I had to face my father being a real person.

And when it happened a year ago, his discharge, I knew it. My mother told me on the phone, "Please come home. Something's wrong." I knew it, but it was a strange feeling. My father's work was the key, my father's success was the key to how we lived.

LARRY ROSS

The corporation is a jungle. It's exciting. You're thrown in on your own and you're constantly battling to survive. When you learn to survive, the game is to become the conqueror, the leader.

"I've been called a business consultant. Some say I'm a business psychiatrist. You can describe me as an advisor to top management in a corporation." He's been at it since 1968.

I started in the corporate world, oh gosh—'42. After kicking around in the Depression, having all kinds of jobs and no formal education, I wasn't equipped to become an engineer, a lawyer, or a doctor. I gravitated to selling. Now they call it marketing. I grew up in various corporations. I became the executive vice president of a large corporation and then of an even larger one. Before I quit I became president and chief executive officer of another. All nationally known companies.

Sixty-eight, we sold out our corporation. There was enough money in the transaction where I didn't have to go back in business. I decided that I wasn't going to get involved in the corporate battle any more. It lost its excitement, its appeal. People often ask me, "Why weren't you in your own business? You'd probably have made a lot of money." I often ask it myself, I can't explain it, except . . .

Most corporations I've been in, they were on the New York Stock Exchange with thousands and thousands of stockholders. The last one—whereas, I was the president and chief executive, I was always subject to the board of directors, who had pressure from the stockholders. I owned a portion of the business, but I wasn't in control. I don't know of any situation in the corporate world where an executive is completely free and sure of his job from moment to moment.

Corporations always have to be right. That's their face to the public. When things go bad, they have to protect themselves and fire somebody. "We had nothing to do with it. We had an executive that just screwed everything up." He's never really ever been his own boss.

The danger starts as soon as you become a district manager. You have men working for you and you have a boss above. You're caught in a squeeze. The squeeze progresses from station to station. I'll tell you what a squeeze is. You have the guys working for you that are shooting for your job. The guy you're working for is scared stiff you're gonna shove him out of his job. Everybody goes around and says, "The test of the true executive is that you have men working for you that can replace you, so you can move up." That's a lot of boloney. The manager is afraid of the bright young guy coming up.

Fear is always prevalent in the corporate structure. Even if you're a top man, even if you're hard, even if you do your job—by the slight flick of a finger, your boss can fire you. There's always the insecurity. You bungle a job. You're fearful of losing a big customer. You're fearful so many things will appear on your record, stand against you. You're always fearful of the big mistake. You've got to be careful when you go to corporation parties. Your wife, your children have to behave properly. You've got to fit in the mold. You've got to be on guard.

When I was president of this big corporation, we lived in a small Ohio town, where the main plant was located. The corporation specified who you could socialize with, and on what level. (His wife interjects: "Who were the wives you could play bridge with.") The president's wife could do what she wants, as long as it's with dignity and grace. In a small town they didn't have to keep check on you. Everybody knew. There are certain sets of rules.

Not every corporation has that. The older the corporation, the longer it's been in a powerful position, the more rigid, the more conservative they are in their approach. Your swinging corporations are generally the new ones, the upstarts, the *nouveau riche*. But as they get older, like duPont, General Motors, General Electric, they became more rigid. I'd compare them to the old, old rich—the Rockefellers and the Mellons—that train their children how to handle money, how to conserve their money, and how to grow with their money. That's what happened to the older corporations. It's only when they get in trouble that they'll have a young upstart of a president come in and try to shake things up.

The executive is a lonely animal in the jungle who doesn't have a friend. Business is related to life. I think in our everyday living we're lonely. I have only a wife to talk to, but beyond that ... When I talked business to her, I don't know whether she understood me. But that was unimportant. What's important is that I was able to talk out loud and hear myself—which is the function I serve as a consultant.

The executive who calls me usually knows the answer to his problem. He just has to have somebody to talk to and hear his decision out loud. If it sounds good when he speaks it out loud, then it's pretty good. As he's talking, he may suddenly realize his errors and he corrects them out loud. That's a great benefit wives provide for executives. She's listening and you know she's on your side. She's not gonna hurt you.

Gossip and rumor are always prevalent in a corporation. There's absolutely no secrets. I have always felt every office was wired. You come out of the board meeting and people in the office already know what's happened. I've tried many times to track down a rumor, but never could. I think people have been there so many years and have developed an ability to read reactions. From these reactions they make a good, educated guess. Gossip actually develops into fact.

It used to be a ploy for many minor executives to gain some information. "I heard that the district manager of California is being transferred to Seattle." He knows there's been talk going on about changing district managers. By using this ploy—"I know something"—he's making it clear to the person he's talking to that he's been in on it all along. So it's all right to tell him. Gossip is another way of building up importance within a person who starts the rumor. He's in, he's part of the inner circle. Again, we're back in the jungle. Every ploy, every trick is used to survive.

When you're gonna merge with a company or acquire another company, it's supposed to be top secret. You have to do something to stem the rumors because it might screw up the deal. Talk of the merger, the whole place is in a turmoil. It's like somebody saying there's a bomb in the building and we don't know where it is and when it's going to go off. There've been so many mergers where top executives are laid off, the accounting department is cut by sixty percent, the manufacturing is cut by twenty percent. I have yet to find anybody in a corporation who was so secure to honestly believe it couldn't happen to him.

They put on a front: "Oh, it can't happen to me. I'm too important." But deep down, they're scared stiff. The fear is there. You can smell it. You can see it on their faces. I'm not so sure you couldn't see it on my face many, many times during my climb up.

I always used to say—rough, tough Larry—I always said, "If you do a good job, I'll give you a great reward. You'll keep your job." I'll have a sales contest and the men who make their quota will win a prize—they'll keep their jobs. I'm not saying there aren't executives who instill fear in their people. He's no different than anybody walking down the street. We're all subject to the same damn insecurities and neuroses—at every level. Competitiveness, that's the basis of it.

Why didn't I stay in the corporate structure? As a kid, living through the Depression, you always heard about the tycoons, the men of power, the men of industry. And you kind of dream that. Gee, these are supermen. These are the guys that have no feeling, aren't subject to human emotions, the insecurities that everybody else has. You get in the corporate structure, you find they all button their pants the same way everybody else does. They all got the same fears.

The corporation is made up of many, many people. I call 'em the gray people and the black—or white—people. Blacks and whites are definite colors, solid. Gray isn't. The gray people come there from nine to five, do their job, aren't particularly ambitious. There's no fear there, sure. But they're not subject to great demands. They're only subject to dismissal when business goes bad and they cut off people. They go from corporation to corporation and get jobs. Then you have the black—or white—people. The ambitious people, the leaders, the ones who want to get ahead.

When the individual reaches the vice presidency or he's general manager, you know he's an ambitious, dedicated guy who wants to get to the top. He isn't one of the gray people. He's one of the black-and-white vicious people— the leaders, the ones who stick out in the crowd.

As he struggles in this jungle, every position he's in, he's terribly lonely. He can't confide and talk with the guy working under him. He can't confide and talk to the man he's working for. To give vent to his feelings, his fears, and his insecurities, he'd expose himself. This goes all the way up the line until he gets to be president. The president *really* doesn't have anybody to talk to, because the vice presidents are waiting for him to die or make a mistake and get knocked off so they can get his job.

He can't talk to the board of directors, because to them he has to appear as a tower of strength, knowledge, and wisdom, and have the ability to walk on water. The board of directors, they're cold, they're hard. They don't have any direct-line responsibilities. They sit in a staff capacity and they really play God. They're interested in profits. They're interested in progress. They're interested in keeping a good face in the community—if it's profitable. You have the tremendous infighting of man against man for survival and clawing to the top. Progress.

We always saw signs of physical afflictions because of the stress and strain. Ulcers, violent headaches. I remember one of the giant corporations I was in, the chief executive officer ate Gelusil by the minute. That's for ulcers. Had a private dining room with his private chef. All he ever ate was well-done steak and well-done hamburgers.

There's one corporation chief I had who worked, conservatively, nineteen, twenty hours a day. His whole life was his business. And he demanded the same of his executives. There was nothing sacred in life except the business. Meetings might be called on Christmas Eve or New Year's Eve, Saturdays, Sundays. He was lonesome when he wasn't involved with his business. He was always creating situations where he could be surrounded by his flunkies, regardless of what level they were, presidential, vice presidential . . . It was his life.

In the corporate structure, the buck keeps passing up until it comes to the chief executive. Then there ain't nobody to pass the buck to. You sit there in your lonely office and finally you have to make a decision. It could involve a million dollars or hundreds of jobs or moving people from Los Angeles, which they love, to Detroit or Winnipeg. So you're sitting at the desk, playing God.

You say, "Money isn't important. You can make some bad decisions about money, that's not important. What is important is the decisions you make about people working for you, their livelihood, their lives." It isn't true.

To the board of directors, the dollars are as important as human lives. There's only yourself sitting there making the decision, and you hope it's right. You're always on guard. Did you ever see a jungle animal that wasn't on guard? You're always looking over your shoulder. You don't know who's following you.

The most stupid phrase anybody can use in business is loyalty. If a person is working for a corporation, he's supposed to be loyal. This corporation is paying him less than he could get somewhere else at a comparable job. It's stupid of him to hang around and say he's loyal. The only loyal people are the people who can't get a job anyplace else. Working in a corporation, in a business, isn't a game. It isn't a collegiate event. It's a question of living or dying. It's a question of eating or not eating. Who is he loyal to? It isn't his country. It isn't his religion. It isn't his political party. He's working for some company that's paying him a salary for what he's doing. The corporation is out to make money. The ambitious guy will say, "I'm doing my job. I'm not embarrassed taking my money. I've got to progress and when I won't progress, I won't be here." The schnook is the loyal guy, because he can't get a job anyplace else.

Many corporations will hang on to a guy or promote him to a place where he doesn't belong. Suddenly, after the man's been there twenty-five years, he's outlived his usefulness. And he's too old to start all over again. That's part of the cruelty. You can't only condemn the corporation for that. The man himself should be smart enough and intuitive enough to know he isn't getting anyplace, to get the hell out and start all over. It was much more difficult at first to lay off a guy. But if you live in a jungle, you become hard, unfortunately.

When a top executive is let go, the king is dead, long live the king. Suddenly he's a *persona non grata*. When it happens, the shock is tremendous. Overnight. He doesn't know what hit him. Suddenly everybody in the organization walks away and shuns him because they don't want to be associated with him. In corporations, if you back the wrong guy, you're in his corner, and he's fired, you're guilty by association. So what a lot of corporations have done is when they call a guy in—sometimes they'll call him in on a Friday night and say, "Go home now and come in tomorrow morning and clean out your desk and leave. We don't want any farewells or anything. Just get up and get the hell out." It's done in nice language. We say, "Look, why cause any trouble? Why cause any unrest in the organization? It's best that you just fade away." Immediately his Cadillac is taken away from him. His phone extension on the ,WATS line is taken away from him.* All these things are done quietly and—bingo! he's dead. His phone at home stops ringing because the fear of association continues after the severance. The smell of death is there.

We hired a vice president. He came highly recommended. He was with us about six months and he was completely inadequate. A complete misfit. Called him in the office, told him he was gonna go, gave him a nice severance pay. He broke down and cried. "What did I do wrong? I've done a marvelous job. Please don't do this to me. My daughter's getting married next month. How am I going to face the people?" He cried and cried and cried. But we couldn't keep him around. We just had to let him go.

I was just involved with a gigantic corporation. They had a shake-up two Thursdays ago. It's now known as Black Thursday. Fifteen of twenty guys were let go overnight. The intelligent corporations say, "Clear, leave tonight, even if it's midweek. Come in Saturday morning and clean your desk. That's all. No good-bys or anything." They could be guys that have been there anywhere from a year to thirty years. If it's a successful operation, they're very generous. But then again, the human element creeps in. The boss might be vindictive and cut him off without anything. It may depend what the corporation wants to maintain as its image.

And what it does to the ego! A guy in a key position, everybody wants to talk to him. All his subordinates are trying to get an audience with him to build up their own positions. Customers are calling him, everybody is calling him. Now his phone's dead. He's sitting at home and nobody calls him. He goes out and starts visiting his friends, who are busy with their own business, who haven't got time for him. Suddenly he's a failure. Regardless what the

* Wide area telecommunications service. A prerogative granted important executives by some corporations: unlimited use of the telephone to make a call anywhere in the world.

reason was—regardless of the press release that said he resigned—he was fired.

The only time the guy isn't considered a failure is when he resigns and announces his new job. That's the tipoff. "John Smith resigned, future plans unknown" means he was fired. "John Smith resigned to accept the position of president of X Company"—then you know he resigned. This little nuance you recognize immediately when you're in corporate life.

Changes since '42? Today the computer is taking over the world. The computer exposes all. There's no more chance for shenanigans and phoniness. Generally the computer prints out the truth. Not a hundred percent, but enough. It's eliminated a great deal of the jungle infighting. There's more facts for the businessman to work from, if the computer gives him the right information. Sometimes it doesn't. They have a saying at IBM: "If you put garbage in the computer, you'll take garbage out." Business is becoming more scientific with regard to marketing, finance, investsments. And much more impersonal.

But the warm personal touch *never* existed in corporations. That was just a sham. In the last analysis, you've got to make a profit. There's a lot of family-held corporations that truly felt they were part of a legend. They had responsibilities to their people. They carried on as best they could. And then they went broke. The loyalty to their people, their patriarchy, dragged 'em all down. Whatever few of 'em are left are being forced to sell, and are being taken over by the cold hand of the corporation.

My guess is that twenty corporations will control about forty percent of the consumer goods market. How much room is there left for the small guy? There's the supermarket in the grocery business. In our time, there were little mama-and-papa stores, thousands and thousands throughout the country. How many are there today? Unless you're National Tea or A & P, there's just no room. The small chains will be taken over by the bigger chains and they themselves will be taken over ... The fish swallows the smaller fish and he's swallowed by a bigger one, until the biggest swallows 'em all. I have a feeling there'll always be room for the small entrepreneur, but he'll be rare. It'll be very difficult for him.

The top man is more of a general manager than he is an entrepreneur. There's less gambling than there was. He won't make as many mistakes as he did before in finance and marketing. It's a cold science. But when it comes to dealing with people, he still has to have that feel and he still has to do his own thinking. The computer can't do that for him.

When I broke in, no man could become an executive until he was thirty-five, thirty-six years old. During the past ten years there've been real top executives of twenty-six, twenty-seven. Lately there's been a reversal. These young ones climbed to the top when things were good, but during the last couple of years we've had some rough times. Companies have been clobbered and some have gone back to older men. But that's not gonna last.

Business is looking for the highly trained, highly skilled *young* executive, who has the knowledge and the education in a highly specialized field. It's happened in all professions and it's happening in business. You have your comptroller who's highly specialized. You have your treasurer who has to know finance, a heavily involved thing because of the taxation and the SEC. You have the manufacturing area. He has to be highly specialized in warehouse and in shipping—the ability to move merchandise cheaply and quickly. Shipping has become a horrendous problem because costs have become tremendous. You have to know marketing, the studies, the effect of advertising. A world of specialists. The man at the top has to have a general knowledge. And he has to have the knack of finding the right man to head these divisions. That's the difficulty.

You have a nice, plush lovely office to go to. You have a private secretary. You walk down the corridor and everybody bows and says, "Good morning, Mr. Ross. How are you today?" As you go up the line, the executives will say, "How is Mrs. Ross?" Until you get to the higher executives. They'll say, "How is Nancy?" Here you socialize, you know each other. Everybody plays the game.

A man wants to get to the top of the corporation, not for the money involved. After a certain point, how much more money can you make? In my climb, I'll be honest, money was secondary. Unless you have tremendous demands, yachts, private airplanes—you get to a certain point, money isn't that important. It's the power, the status, the prestige. Frankly, it's delightful to be on top and have everybody calling you Mr. Ross and have a plane at your disposal and a car and a driver at your disposal. When you come to town, there's people to take care of you. When you walk into a board meeting, everybody gets up and says hello. I don't think there's any human being that doesn't love that. It's a nice feeling. But the ultimate power is in the board of directors. I don't know anybody who's free. You read in the paper about stockholders' meetings, the annual report. It all sounds so glowing. But behind the scenes, a jungle.

I work on a yearly retainer with a corporation. I spend, oh, two, three days a month in various corporate structures. The key executives can talk to me and bounce things off me. The president may have a specific problem that I will investigate and come back to him with my ideas. The reason I came into this work is that all my corporate life I was looking for somebody like me, somebody who's been there. Because there's no new problems in business today. There's just a different name for different problems that have been going on for years and years and years. Nobody's come up yet with a problem that isn't familiar. I've been there.

Example. The chief executive isn't happy with the marketing structure. He raises many questions which I may not know specifically. I'll find out, and come back with a proposal. He might be thinking of promoting one of his executives. It's narrowed down to two or three. Let's say two young guys who've been moved to a new city. It's a tossup. I notice one has bought a new house, invested heavily in it. The other rented. I'd recommend the second. He's more realistic.

If he comes before his board of directors, there's always the vise. The poor sonofabitch is caught in the squeeze from the people below and the people above. When he comes to the board, he's got to come with a firm hand. I can help him because I'm completely objective. I'm out of the jungle. I don't have the trauma that I used to have when I had to fire somebody. What is it gonna do to this guy? I can give it to him cold and hard and logical. I'm not involved.

I left that world because suddenly the power and the status were empty. I'd been there, and when I got there it was nothing. Suddenly you have a feeling of little boys playing at business. Suddenly you have a feeling—so what? It started to happen to me, this feeling, oh, in '67,

'68. So when the corporation was sold, my share of the sale was such . . . I didn't have to go back into the jungle. I don't have to fight to the top. I've been to the mountain top. (Laughs.) It isn't worth it.

It was very difficult, the transition of retiring from the status position, where there's people on the phone all day trying to talk to you. Suddenly nobody calls you. This is psychological . . . (Halts, a long pause.) I don't want to get into that. Why didn't I retire completely? I really don't know. In the last four, five years, people have come to me with tempting offers. Suddenly I realized what I'm doing is much more fun than going into that jungle again. So I turned them down.

I've always wanted to be a teacher. I wanted to give back the knowledge I gained in corporate life. People have always told me I'd always been a great sales manager. In every sales group you always have two or three young men with stars in their eyes. They always sat at the edge of the chair. I knew they were comers. I always felt I could take 'em, develop 'em, and build 'em. A lot of old fogies like me—I can point out this guy, that guy who worked for me, and now he's the head of this, the head of that.

Yeah, I always wanted to teach. But I had no formal education and no university would touch me. I was willing to teach for nothing. But there also, they have their jungle. They don't want a businessman. They only want people in the academic world, who have a formalized and, I think, empty training. This is what I'd really like to do. I'd like to get involved with the young people and give my knowledge to them before it's buried with me. Not that what I have is so great, but there's a certain understanding, a certain feeling . . .

MA AND PA COURAGE

During the Thirty Years' War, Anna Fierling, known as "Mother Courage," survives as a small entrepreneur, following the army. She sells her beer, shoes, and sundries to the soldiers. She speaks:

"If there is too much virtue somewhere, it is a sure sign that there is something wrong. Why, if a general or a king is stupid and lands his people in a mess, they need desperate courage, a virtue. And if he is slovenly and pays no attention, they must be as clever as snakes, or else they are done for."

—Bertolt Brecht,
Mother Courage and Her Children

GEORGE AND IRENE BREWER

It is a grocery and gift store. "We got a sign out front: 10,000 items. We got all your cigarettes, ice creams, novelties. All your paints, crayons, school supplies. Drugs—not prescription, just your headache—remedies, alcohols, peroxide, and your bandages. Then we go into jewelry, which is now just costume. Before, we used to have diamonds. But the clientele didn't care for 'em. We have sundry, your hair goods, your sewing things, needles, threads, and buttons. Greeting cards ... Ma, pa stores are foldin' fast because they don't have enough variety. Like chain stores, where they can get everything and anything they want.

"We started out toys and hobbies. Then I put milk in. I said, 'Honey, that's gonna be the ruin of us. We're gonna become a slave to it.' Then they started hollerin' for bread. Then they wanted lunch meat. Then they wanted

541

canned goods. So it became the old country general store."

They have owned the business for fourteen years. "Before that," says George, "my folks had it since 1943." He has since expanded it. We're in the living quarters behind the store: five rooms, including one for "meditation." There are all manner of appliances and artifacts including a player piano. To the rear is a two-car garage.

Their fourteen-year-old daughter is minding the store. Their eldest daughter, twenty-one, lives elsewhere. Their son, nineteen, has been in the army three years. A dog, "mixed terrier," wanders in and out.

It is one of the oldest blue-collar communities in Chicago: Back Of The Yards. Though the stockyards have gone—to such unlikely places as Greeley, Colorado, and Clovis, New Mexico—the people who live here are still working-class. But there have been changes. "This used to be an old-time Polish, Lithuanian neighborhood. Now it's more young, mixed, Puerto Ricans, hillbillies. Blacks are movin' closer, nothing here yet, but closer. It's not as clannish as it used to be. In the old days if you offended one, you'd have the whole block mad at you. Now it don't matter. The next will come in and take the place of him."

IRENE: We used to know ninety-five percent of our customers by name. Now it's hardly anyone we know by name any more. You could walk down the street at six in the morning and you'd see these Polish women out with their brooms and they'd be washin' the concrete down, fixin' the alleys. You don't see too much of this any more.

GEORGE: The personal touch. "How's the kids?" "How's this one?" "How's that one?" "Work going okay?" "Sorry to hear you lost your job." All this sort of thing—gone.

It's more of a transient deal, even though they live in the neighborhood. They're so flighty you don't know who's livin' where. You can't even trust somebody who's come in for six months, because they just up and turn that fast. We would cash checks and give 'em credit and carry 'em along. As the area changed, you'd get stuck with bad debts. So we've eliminated cashin' checks due to the fact that we have thirteen hundred dollars worth of bad checks. We allow a little bit of credit to old stand-bys for about a week.

IRENE: If we take a chance and cash a check that does bounce, we find 'em walkin' on the other side of the street. They don't want to acknowledge they're in the neighborhood—for a measly five dollars. The people, they've changed in such a way it's unbelievable. We had magazines and books, but we took 'em out two years ago because the theft was so bad.

GEORGE: We had thirteen hundred dollars of books stolen in the last three months of the last year we handled books. A lot of cases with food. Women would open their purse and drop lunch meat in it. I caught a guy one evening puttin' two dozen eggs in his Eisenhower jacket.

IRENE: I was standin' at the bread rack there. I see this guy tryin' to stuff the *second* dozen eggs down his jacket, with a zipper and to the waistline. (Laughs.) He was havin' a tough time gettin' that second dozen in. I said, "Hey, hon, some guy's stealin' two dozen eggs back here." George's runnin' around and all the other customers are lookin' at one another. No one knows who's got the eggs.

GEORGE: I'm runnin' around one way and he's comin' around the other. I said, "Where is he?" He said, "Here I am." (Laughs.) He gave 'em back. The customers would come in and tease and say to Irene, "Hey, you want to search? I got eggs." (Laughs.)

IRENE: Nylons were stolen. Now we'll lock the door after eleven and only let the ones we know in. Forget it, there isn't many that you know any more. We were always open to midnight, all through the years. We used to work in the store to two, three in the morning and leave the door open. Now we can't wait to bolt the door at night, it's so bad. I take a chance when I open it. It's hard to tell any more by looks who's all right and who isn't. Some of 'em are the worst lookin' people but they're really all right when you get talkin' to 'em.

GEORGE: The worst lookin' hippie things that come in the door are so polite and some of 'em, the ones that are very well dressed, are so ignorant. When the folks had this store, it was all family. This is not too much a ma and pa

area any more. The ones that are left close at six. They're
scared to death.

IRENE: We've had several holdups. It was around eleven-
fifteen at night, three young people came with ski masks
over their face. Two guys and a girl.

GEORGE: I'm checkin' out and they put the gun to the side
of my head. I said, "Aw, go to hell." I thought it was the
kids in the neighborhood horsin' around. I look up—they
backed us around the jewelry counter. The front part was
more expensive stuff, high-class, diamonds, gold rings.
They scooped off the cheap costume jewelry off the back
shelf. I said, "Damn it, leave me somethin' for the next
time you come in." They said, "Okay, okay," and they
backed off. (Laughs.) We've had several holdups since
then. I don't worry too much about it.

IRENE: When Martin Luther King was killed, you can
imagine the tension. I was alone here. People were panicky.
They were announcing on the radio and television that people should be off the street at eight o'clock at night. The
stores were forced to close. Our youngest was nine and
was instigator of our selling a lot of food that night. She
would say, "We may not be here tomorrow because
there'll be a riot tonight and they might come in the
neighborhood. You better get all you can get. Stock up
now." She was half-hysterical and she put the fear in everyone else. They cleaned out the refrigerators, all the food.
I couldn't ring it up fast enough. The police came by three
times tellin' me to close the store. We really made a haul
that night.

   When she was three years old she'd come out in the
store. We had girlie books on the rack. The guy would
stand here lookin' at *Playboy*. She'd come up behind him
on a ladder and hold a crucifix in front of him. That was
too much for him. He had to fold the book. (Laughs.)

GEORGE: We used to open at six in the morning. One day,
one mother come in hollerin' I shouldn't sell Johnny penny
candy on the way to school. Next day, another mother
come: Susie shouldn't have bubble gum because she's got
fillin' in her teeth. Another come. So I says, "Listen, I'm
not gettin' fringe benefits of bein' married to you. If you

can't handle your children—I'm doin' this for your convenience so you can get things for your breakfast. I won't open till they're in school." So now I don't open till around ten-thirty.

There usually isn't that much sleep. We used to average two, three hours. That went on for ten years that way. Now we get on the average of four hours. Sometimes you have time to eat breakfast. In the morning I mop the floors, haul fifteen, twenty cases of soda from the basement, throw it in the cooler. For the first three hours you have your variety of salesmen, your bread men and your milkmen. You might open with a $200 bank in the morning. By two in the afternoon, you've paid out $197 and taken in $6. Then your evening trade starts. We switch hours between meals. I wouldn't say we're tired at the end of the day, we just drop. (Laughs.)

Seven days a week. Sundays we're open from 7:00 to 10:00 A.M., close to go to church, have dinner, and reopen at four to midnight. We started goin' out for dinner because they would come to the window (mimics high-pitched voice): "I gotta have a greeting card." "I need a quart of milk." We couldn't eat our dinner in peace.

IRENE: Some people think ownin' a store is real easy. All you have to do is stand there and sell it. They say, "What's your old man doin', sleepin'?" He hardly ever sleeps. Movin' all the stock, the refrigerator's blocked up, cleanin' all those drains, he hauls all the groceries home, cuts up boxes moving all the time.

GEORGE: I usually say to her, "Hi, good-by." That's the extent of our conversation.

IRENE: After twelve o'clock we unwind for an hour, but we're so exhausted we fall asleep. It's always been a rough life, but we've made a decent living out of it and raised three children and have never gone without.

"Our boy was almost the ruination of us. He supplied the whole neighborhood with everything and anything they wanted. He could never say no. The kids pressured him: 'You get me that or we'll beat you up.' He was haulin' the soda out as fast as we could bring it in. We almost went bankrupt with the boy. When he was in his first year high

school he had nothin' on his mind but army. So when he reached the age we signed papers for him."

GEORGE: Chain stores don't bother me. People gotta have a place where they can run for a loaf of bread, a dozen eggs, or somethin' for a snack, a pint of ice cream or a bottle of soda. Instead of goin' in the chain store and standing in line. The cold indifference. They still get the personal touch here, the chatter back and forth, the gossip and the laughter.

IRENE: George and I like to kid with the customers. He horses around with the women and flatters them, no matter what they look like. I'll kid the guys.

GEORGE: A new customer come in, she got shocked. I said, "Still love me like you never did?" She said, "I beg your pardon. I love only my husband." (Laughs.) We have a standard joke. People come in and buy a box of Kotex, we'd say, "Use it here or take it with you?" They'd get all shook up. (Laughs.)

IRENE: Prophylactics, there's another joke. A man would come in at night and say, "Is your husband here?" I'd just know, and they'd turn so red, like a woman askin' a man for Kotex.

What I notice is a big change in the people's attitudes. They come in and they may look grouchy. I'd say, "Hi, how are you?" They used to answer, "Hi." Now they look at you like I'm nuts. They think you're crazy because you say hello to them. It's more like a big city now than a small neighborhood. People are kind of cold.

Years ago, every Halloween we'd give about five hundred dollars worth of toys away. We'd have several kids out front. We would drop ballons from the upstairs windows with tickets in 'em. They would turn the tickets in and get prizes. When the neighborhood changed, the parents would start grabbin' the balloons and steppin' on the kids. So we just cut it out.

GEORGE: Actually, this is a gold mine. We're on the main drag. People on this side of the street don't want to send the children on the other side. Your main trade here is all the little darlings who want "one of dem, one of dese, one of dose." Penny candy. They come in, three cents, and it takes them twenty minutes to make up their minds.

IRENE: They say, "How do you have the patience to stand and wait on those kids?" It's really difficult, but if you allow yourself to get uptight, you look bad in front of your customers. So we just shrug our shoulders.

We've seen people now that are married and divorced who were in grammar school when we came in, have got two and three children. They were miserable little kids and George taught most of 'em manners. They'd come in: "Gimme change for a dollar." He'd teach 'em to say, "Could I please have change for a dollar?" Some of 'em, you wonder where the teachings are at home.

GEORGE: One of the things in a ma, pa store you have to put up with—mothers use it as a baby sitter. It's much easier for a mother to give the child a penny and go to the store. It takes a kid ten minutes to walk to the store, ten minutes in the store, and ten minutes back. Mom says, "You're a good boy, here's another penny." So for two cents an hour they got a baby sitter. In the course of the day you'll have the same monster in eight, ten times a day. A penny at a time.

IRENE: It's unbelievable what we go through. All through the years we've had all sorts of telephone calls during the night. Not so much any more, because we don't have our name in the book like we used to. We had so many goofy calls. They call and ask if we have Prince Albert and I say yes and they'd say, "Let the poor guy out of the can." Those kind of jokes. Oh, a lot of people will stand around waitin' for papers and they talk about bingo and they complain about the blacks who take all their parking areas. We have to hear all that.

GEORGE: They used to hang around more. But now I don't allow anybody to drink soda or eat food in the store. I put the opener outside. Keep it movin'. Otherwise, it'd be just a regular hangout. It'd get pretty crowded.

IRENE: They come in in droves, six, seven teen-agers at a time. One or two might buy and the rest circulate through

the store and they'll rob you blind. You have to sort 'em
out right away. "How many want to buy? The rest of you
leave, please." You have to be a little rude.

GEORGE: When I first came in here, some of the punks,
we call 'em, some of the neighborhood rowdies, I'd pick
out a leader of the group. I'd take 'im down to the health
club where I was workin' out. I'm in condition, liftin'
weights. You take these young guys who think they're real
tough, you put 'em through calisthenics and their bodies
would ache for a week. (Laughs.) The next time they'd
have a little more respect for you. Now I got into karate
and I worked up to a black belt. They found out about
that and they got a healthy respect for me. (Laughs.)

IRENE: A lot of people come in and make comments:
"How come you're drivin' such an old car? What's the
matter? You got so much money you're hoarding it. You
can't buy a new car?" Then we would buy a new car: "Oh
boy, you're really makin' it off us poor people." There's no
pleasin' 'em nohow.

When prices go up, people come in the store and they
throw the items on the counter and they blame us. Eggs
go up ten cents a dozen and they act like it's us that raised
them. Actually, we make two cents on a gallon of milk.
You can't tell them that. They can't understand that anyone could make so little. They say, "Now you're a buck
richer." They're so used to having items raised that the resentment is much more. They slam the door and they cuss
at you. They gotta blame somebody so they blame us.

GEORGE: When we first opened the store, our insurance
was $398 a year. Now it's jumped to $1,398. They say
you're in too high a risk area. Your lights have went up,
your gas, your utilities. Your mark-up on your profit has
decreased. Like Hostess cakes—they raised an item a
penny, it costs you a penny more. You're getting a less
percentage on the return. At one time, you were makin' a
twenty-two percent mark-up with a five percent overhead—which would leave you a seventeen percent profit.
Now they squeeze you down to a twelve percent mark-up
if you're lucky. With costs up, your overhead is ten percent, now you're workin' on two percent profit. Instead of

coming out of the hole, you're going into the hole. It's impossible to survive unless you're doing something else on the side.

"We've been turned in for everything. We had a raid here. It was a set-up deal. A couple of crooked cops had some guy bring in cans of lunch meat. The guy said he's goin' out of business and he had a couple cases. I got a good price off of him. I set it in the aisle. About a half an hour later in walks these two guys. 'That's stolen merchandise. What else you got that's stolen?' They went through the house. 'We're gonna have to take your television. We're gonna have to take this. This is stolen. That's stolen. We know how things are. Give us a thousand dollars and we'll leave you alone.'

"We were new at this thing and got scared. So I went out and borrowed the money and gave it to these guys. I took the license number of their car and reported it. They put us through a lie detector test. They didn't want to believe us. We had to go to the police show-up and things like that. During this time cop after cop was comin' in raiding us with search warrants, just harassment, one thing after another. All the time, we were waitin' to identify these guys at the show-up.

"The phone'd ring all night long, with heavy breathing and all. They worked on the family and stuff like that. We had health inspectors, building inspectors, fire inspectors, all the harassments of the city that you could get. Just because we turned in a couple of cops. They were hushing it up all down the line."

Irene interjects: *"One day, nine or eleven plainclothesmen come in and started goin' through the store, tearing stuff out and everything. He has a search warrant that we had a printing press and we're supposed to be printing false credit cards and false ID cards. They tore the place upside down, up in the attic, in the basement. What really took the cake, they came in looking for these pornography books. They said some woman in the neighborhood reported us that we were selling to children. They put me in a state of shock. What we were selling were those coin saver books. We had 'em behind the counter and let the kids go through 'em. It was a thing seven or eight years ago. It was part of harassment. We had it all."*

"By the time we went down to IID,* we just dropped it. We said we couldn't identify 'em. Then everything quieted down."

GEORGE: Of course you're always lookin' for a buck on the side. Years ago fireworks were illegal. It was a beautiful setup. The police were shakin' down the peddler on the street and bringing' it in here and sellin' it to me. (Laughs.) I would turn around and sell 'em on the counter—on the open counter. Sky rockets, Roman candles, the whole works. They would get calls that we were sellin' illegal fireworks. They'd call us and say, "We gotta make a raid on you. Put everything away." So they'd come in and say, "I don't see nothin', do you, Joe?" "No, I don't see nothin'." (Laughs.)

It's such a rat race. We were becoming stagnant in the area. We were getting to be puppets. We were ruining our sense of being. We were ruining our vocabulary. What do you hear in here? "You got dat?" "You got dis?" "You got dose?" You find yourself talking like the trade that comes in, especially with the area degenerating as it is. You begin to feel like you're not progressing in life.

"We decided we had to do something to enlighten ourselves. To be mentally active besides physically active. So we got into the psychic field. I did palmistry before. We went to hypnosis classes. Irene went into more development in hand reading and I was teaching hypnotic principles. She's a staff member at the psychic center."

Irene interjects: "We're both ordained as reverends by the IGAS—International General Assembly of Spiritualists. It's a nondenominational church. George takes people in that have hang-ups and problems. In the meditation room here."

GEORGE: The work is confining. In our spare time, between midnight and six in the morning, I built the whole upstairs. Made the attic into the girls' dorm. We own the building, us and the finance company. (Laughs.)

IRENE: The tension is so great—you got to watch 'em all

* Internal Investigation Division of the Chicago Police Department.

the time. Turn your back, they're fillin' their pockets. We've had people fake injuries here and try to collect. By the end of the day you're talkin' to yourself.

GEORGE: This is where the psychic center has helped a lot. We can come in here and just lay down for fifteen minutes and bein' able to relax. It's equal to an hour's sleep of somebody else's time.

I hope we won't be doing this forever. If we can unload it, we have hopes to get into the psychic field, in a resort area, a rest home, retreat type of thing, where people can develop finer awareness of theirself.

The only kind of family that can survive in a ma, pa store is where everybody pitches in and helps at all times. And have their little kingdom of their own.

POSTSCRIPT: *There is a sign on the wall of the apartment: "Great Spirit, grant that I may not criticize my neighbor until I've walked a mile in his moccasins."*

REFLECTIONS ON IDLENESS AND RETIREMENT

BARBARA TERWILLIGER

She is in her thirties. She has an independent income and is comfortably well-off. During her less affluent days she had worked as an actress, as a saleswoman, engaged in market research, and had assorted other occupations.

It can be splendid not to work for a while, because it changes the rhythm. You can reflect on what you've done. There's no feeling of being indolent. I like being by myself for long periods of time and do not need an occupation. After two months, though, it doesn't work for me. I begin to feel the need for a *raison d'être.* Unless I'm in love. If I should be in love, after months I would begin to feel parasitic and indolent.

What's love got to do with it?

Oh well, love is a woman's occupation. (Laughs.) It's a full-time occupation if you're married. Since I'm not married, I'm talking about a love affair. If you have any sort of ego, you can't make a love affair a justification for life.

About work and idleness ...

You raise the subject of guilt.

(Slightly bewildered) I did?

I have come to some conclusions after having been free

552

economically from the necessity of work. To be occupied is essential. One should find joy in one's occupation. A great poet can make love and idleness fructify into poetry, a beautiful occupation. He wouldn't think of calling it work. Work has a pejorative sound. It shouldn't. I can't tell you how strongly I feel about work. But so much of what we call work is dehumanizing and brutalizing.

I've done typing as a young girl. I've worked in places where the office was like a factory. A bell rang and that was time for a ten-minute coffee break. It was horrifying. Still, most people are better off—their sanity is maintained in anything that gives their life some structure. I disliked the working conditions and I disliked the regimentation, but I enjoyed the process of typing. I was a good typist. I typed very fast and very accurately. There was a rhythm and I enjoyed that. Just the process of work. It's movement. There's something enlivening ... A blank piece of paper, your hands on the keys. You are making something exist that didn't exist before.

I tried to pay very much attention to the words I was typing down. I care about language. Some of the words were repugnant to me. If I were having to type some porno stuff or having to say, "Dry cereal is the best thing to feed one's kids night and day, they're going to flourish eating Crunchy Puffs," I wouldn't have been able to do it. But the process gave me satisfaction. There weren't very many erasures. It was neat.

I really feel work is gorgeous. It's the only thing you can depend upon in life. You can't depend on love. Oh, love is quite ephemeral. Work has a dignity you can count upon. Work has to be a game in order for it to be well done. You have to be able to play in it, to compete with yourself. You push yourself to your limits in order to enjoy it. There's quite a wonderful rhythm you can find yourself involved in in the process of any kind of work. It can be waxing a floor or washing dishes ...

I worked for an employment agency, doing placements. They divided the girls into placeables and unplaceables. I was usually drawn to the unplaceables. These were girls who seemed to me to have some sort of—maybe, inchoate—creative gifts. They wanted jobs where they could feel as individuals. The girls whose hair was not in place, who looked untidy, who weren't going to be that easily accepted. There were some eccentricities involved. I would spend most of my time with them. I would make phone calls to—God forgive—advertising agencies, radio stations.

If you concentrated on the placeables, you made money. These were the girls who came off the production line of high schools, particularly the Catholic schools. They seemed to be tractable young girls. They went into banks as filing clerks in those days. You called the banks and you had your card file and you sent the girl over to the job. You could be a mass production worker yourself, working these girls into the system. There were no tough corners, nothing abrasive. One of my colleagues made two hundred dollars a week shoveling people into these slots. I wasn't doing what the other girls at the desks were doing. I found myself haunted at night by the unplaceable girls. The unplaceable girls were me. If I failed them, I was failing myself. I couldn't make any money. I quit in three weeks. They probably would have fired me anyway.

They were pretty intense weeks. I suffered a lot. I needed the money. I was living on practically nothing. My girls were losers. I found it unbearable to reject them. You say, "We have nothing for you," and send them away. Your time is money, you work on commission. There was a code on the application blank, so you could give the girl the brushoff and she'd never know why.

There were a couple of times I found jobs for the unkempt girls, whose stockings were baggy. And there was even some pleasure in placing those sweet naïve girls, who wanted nothing better than to work in banks, and they were grateful. Even there, the process—being part of something, making something happen—was important. That's the difference between being alive and being dead. Now I'm not making anything happen.

Everyone needs to feel they have a place in the world. It would be unbearable not to. I don't like to feel superfluous. One needs to be needed. I'm saying being idle and leisured, doing nothing, is tragic and disgraceful. Everyone must have an occupation.

Love doesn't suffice. It doesn't fill up enough hours. I don't mean work must be activity for activity's sake. I don't mean obsessive, empty moving around. I mean creating something new. But idleness is an evil. I don't think man can maintain his balance or sanity in idleness. Human beings must work to create some coherence. You do it only through work and through love. And you can only count on work.

BILL NORWORTH

It is a suburb to which many old railroaders have retired. We're in a modern brick bungalow. Outside is a flower garden, lovingly tended. Inside are flowers in vases, statuettes of religious figures, plastic covers on the furniture; on one wall, a cross, on another, the legend: God Bless Our Home, and on the kitchen wall, a framed verse:

> My house is small
> No mansion for a millionaire
> But there is room for love
> And room for friends
> That's all I care.

"I put in fifty-three years with the railroad and I thought that was plenty. I worked right from the bottom to the top for the Northwestern." *From 1917 to 1922 he worked in a roundhouse at Spring Valley, Illinois, his home town. From 1922 to 1944 he was a railroad fireman. From 1944 until the day of his retirement, August 30, 1970, he was a locomotive engineer. He is president of his local of the Brotherhood of Railroad Engineers. For twenty years he was secretary-treasurer.*

At times his wife joins in the reflections.

A diesel's a lot easier than steam. It's a lot better job. Diesels can handle more cars, more tonnage. Diesel'll pull anything. They move, they can run. They don't take the know-how that you had to have with a steam engine. Steam engine was more of a challenge. Those men weren't well educated, but still had the know-how. They could get more out of an engine than a man that had a college degree. It was all pride.

When they got the diesel and got rid of the firemen, they had to make 'em engineers overnight almost. They're savin' themselves a penny, but it cost 'em, in my imagination, a dollar afterwards. 'Cause they've got men now goin' over the road that never even worked as a fireman on that territory, that hardly spent any time on the road.

Most of the diesel work, it's electrical. If it breaks down, they can't fix it. You've gotta send for somebody. In the old days with a steam engine, why, it was up to you to get that engine in. If something you could see was wrong, why, you could do nearly all the repairs yourself or put grease or oil or what was needed to bring it in. With the diesel, you got your throttle and a brake, same as an automobile. I think it's easier than driving an automobile. You're on rails. On an automobile, you gotta watch curves and all that. That's truthful.

Diesel's very clean. In the old days, with the steam engine, you had steam leaks and all that. And in the wintertime there was times you could almost go over the road and barely see any crossings, with the steam leaking around the cylinders. Diesel, you could sit in a business suit. Same as this room. It's almost soundproof. With a diesel, all you are is like a bump on the log up there up front.

In the old days, I'd say nine out of ten of the firemen come from small towns. 'Cause they were about the only ones that had a strong back and a weak mind. (Laughs.) When I first started, they used to have the boomer fireman. A boomer'd be a man, he'd have the cantaloupe run down in Texas and the coal rush in Illinois and the ore season up in Escanaba and the wheat harvest out on the coast. They'd just go, and when business would slow up, why, he'd put his little suitcase and be on to the next place.

That's when the company'd really get a break. They were experienced men. In the rush season, if they didn't have these boomers and had to hire new men, they'd say it used to cost 'em two thousand dollars to make a fireman. Until you knew what you were doing. When a boomer come up, he had about five, ten years' experience, and you were getting it for nix. I had a half-brother who was a boomer. He got drowned in Cordova, Alaska—gold mining. Boomers were single. They'd all know where the season work was, where they were gonna be hirin', and would write to the master mechanic and be Johnny on the spot. They're not doing that work any more.

The engineer, fireman, and brakeman was in the cab. Not much conversation, it was usually mostly business—as to the right of way, see around every turn, every curve. It was your duty if the curve was on your side to look the train over, see if there was any hot boxes or anything dragging. 'Cause it didn't take very long for somethin' to pop, where it could be disastrous, and if you're not on the job, why . . .

I was in what they call a pool. That's all extra work. When you leave home, say you go to Clinton, Iowa. Well, you'd stay there and maybe they'd ship you to Belvidere, Illinois, to go back to Nelson, Iowa, or back to Clinton. They had to start you home on your sixth day. You could come home and you take ten hours' rest and be on your way again, maybe for another six days. I'd say two-thirds of your time was away from home.

You were very glad to get a little more than eight hours sometimes. Plus the time you clean up and get something to eat and then try to leave the meal settle down a little bit, instead of going to bed with a full stomach, why, you only had about four hours left before they'd be after you again. When you got up, even if it was three o'clock in the morning, and you figured this might be twelve, sixteen hours before you could get any more to eat, why, steak and potatoes or ham and eggs, you filled up all the empty spots you had down there. (Laughs.) It was seven days a week till I retired. There was no holidays. You just got your turns.

MRS. NORWORTH: *You had to raise the children mostly by yourself. He'd be gone as long as six days. You didn't know when he's coming back. We're married forty-two years and, up until the time he retired, he was still gone every other night or every couple of days. You're alone quite a bit.*

It was seven days a week. There was no holidays. At the pool you'd just wait your turn when they'd have an extra train. We had as high as forty-five crews in a pool. For a long time you laid over without even gettin' paid. It's about maybe in the last twenty years where they started payin' you after sixteen hours. If you were, say, in Clinton sixteen hours, you'd go on what they call penalty time. If you were there twenty-four hours, you got eight hours' pay. Then they could run you back again, add another sixteen hours, and not have to pay you another cent.

MRS. NORWORTH: *You had to sit around the house waiting for the phone to ring, oh yes. If you went somewhere, you'd have to call and give them the number, in case they'd need you. Then you'd have to hurry home to get ready to go to work. It's about two, three in the morning, get up, eat breakfast, and go to work.*

Actually, the extra board was just as bad. If you were on a regular job or in the pool or laid off—you got sick or something—they'd have a board there with extra men. I couldn't leave the house for long, figuring something's gonna show up. If you miss the call, you're in for insubordination and you've got to see the master mechanic. Yeah, if you missed your call they'd put you on the bottom again. They got no more pools today, but they've still got an extra board.

Stock trains, cattle. Sunday was your big day for bringing in your Monday market. Oh, there was a lotta days when I seen thirteen hundred cars come out of Clinton. Monday morning, that's when you'd start with your empties back to Clinton. Sometimes you were there until the next Sunday to bring in another stock train, without any pay.

You usually tried to find a rooming house, tried to get a room as reasonable as you could. They had rooming houses where widows would have maybe two or three cots in a room. There was about a hàlf a dozen homes in town and an old hotel there used to have an old comedian, a cook called Charlie. We used to kid him about the pancakes, claimed. "You'd hit the dog in the hind end with a broom and then you'd sweep out the griddle." (Laughs.)

MRS. NORWORTH: *Mostly nights they'd be gone. And you couldn't make a date with anyone or a party because you'd know you'd never make it. That night he'd be gone. It took two years to get together at this one couple's house. One would be in and the other would be out or the other in and he'd be out. A lot of our friends that were with the railroad, it was the same way. Someone would invite us to dinner and I would tell them, "If you don't mind and wait it might be the last minute or so I could tell you." Because we didn't know when he'd get in. You didn't know what time they'd come home.*

He liked the job, so it was all right. But it was kinda lonely to raise your children. It was kinda hard. Sometimes there'd be a wreck and he'd call up and say, "I won't be home for two, three days." Or if there was a big storm.

We have three daughters. I said, if we had a son, I'd never let him be a railroader, 'cause he'd never be home. Once a railroader gets it in his blood that's all he's got, nothing.

When the diesels came, they cut off the firemen and they gave 'em a little service pay. After a while they started needin' 'em, but very few of 'em come back. They got a few on the suburban trains. You gotta have a fireman now. That's the state law.

There's a lot less engineers now, maybe sixty percent of what used to be. At one time we had seventeen passenger trains to the coast, Northwestern did. Now you don't have a passenger train, outside of a suburban job. All freight. In the old days, they used to have stock cars. That's a thing of the past. We used to have milk trains. That's a thing of the past.

In the old days, we're in a little town, Spring Valley, the Rock Island goes through there, down in the bottom of the valley, and the town's kinda on a hill, and the train would be going through there whistling for the crossing there. It carried, oh, a mile or two, the echo'd come up through there. That was a . . .(he pauses) . . . really a nice feelin'.

MRS. NORWORTH: *We used to live on top of the hill and the roundhouse and the track was right down below this big hill and you could hear the trains goin' by. I still like to hear the sound of an engine. It's sort of fascinating to hear a train. You don't hardly hear 'em any more. They're all freights. But I think trains are nice.*

The little kids, if they could see the engineer, or if you'd wave at 'em, why, they really had somethin'. The man waved at 'em. When you're on a train like that, why, you got certain places where women or somebody would come out in person and give you a highball. And that's a nice feeling. A lot of it's gone now.

MRS. NORWORTH: *And when they'd walk the streets of the town, they knew you by your coveralls and your cap and your handkerchief. The minute you'd see 'em, you knew they were railroaders.*

They were the aristocrats at one time, but that time's gone now. You had to know somebody to get a job, even as a fireman. From the younger ones that I worked with, that were hired after this, I don't think they coulda stuck in the old days. A lotta days you'd shovel thirty ton of coal. Yeah.

MRS. NORWORTH: *He came out of there black as coal. I went on a train with him once and I had on a black chiffon dress, believe it or not, and as I rode up in the cabin, and when I got off there, I was as black as the dress. Oh, it was oh!!! And then he'd usually get prickly heat from all the fire.*

It wasn't too bad. You learned to like shoveling thirty ton of coal. There's ways where the shovel would hit the door and it isn't carryin' it all in. There's tricks in all the trades. You have the shovel do a lot of the work instead of your back.

Everyone I knew, ninety-nine out of a hundred figured they were getting a good day's pay for a good day's work. Now these guys, if they don't get the world with a fence around there—they'll work when they want to. In the old days, when it was two, three o'clock in the morning and it was twenty below zero, you've got to go to work somehow. But not now. Hell, I was there thirty years before we ever got a vacation.

Our major grievance was trying to get a vacation. At the start, we had a lot of grievances. In the old days, they had oil lamps. With the old oil lamps you had to go down and fill that lamp and clean it for your headlight. I worked with engineers that had the oil lamp and they'd be telling you about it. And they wanted to go to electric lights. You'd think the company was gonna go broke. And that was their biggest savings. They had a big argument, even go to Congress to get a back curtain. And when the stokers come, they were really gonna go broke. It always turned to the company advantage, but they had to fight it.

It seems like they felt, We can't lose power over that man. We're gonna make him do what *we* think is right.

We have a meeting once a month with the Brotherhood. Most of them that's working now is just griping about the help you got now. If these younger ones had to do what we had to do, they wouldn't be around. The engineer was respected then, and now there's no respect for him. He's just a dummy, the same as the rest of us.

The old days, when you had an engineer, he was the boss. He was respected as a man and his judgment was respected from the top of the ladder to the bottom. That's gone now. They can get an eighteen-year-old kid out of high school and make him a train master, and you try to tell him right from wrong, he's liable to have you up for insubordination. In the old days, you had judgment on your trains and what you could do. When you figured you had too much, you'd tell the train dispatcher. Your word was law. Respect's lost.

I'll show you one of their half-a-century cards. (He digs out a gold paper pass: "Mr. William J. Norworth, locomotive engineer, Chicago Northwestern Railroad, in recognition of fifty years of service.") That's it.

You can ride on the trains free with this?

On the Northwestern only. But there's no trains.

Was there a ceremony?

No sir. He just called me up and told me on the way to work to stop at his office, that he had something for me. When I got there, he handed me my fifty-year card. That's it.

Did he shake your hand?

No. It wasn't that him and I are just like brothers or that. There was no ceremony. He just called me in to hand it to me. That's it.

POSTSCRIPT: *"If they had good trains again, people would ride. But they discourage you. The last time the wife went to New Jersey, that was awful."*

MRS. NORWORTH: *I left Newark at five o'clock in the evening and I got into Chicago at eight o'clock the next morning—and like to froze to death in that car. We were putting sweaters on or whatever we had on our feet. We are all cold and to ride all night like that. And what did they want for a berth? Forty-four dollars. So the next time, he said, "Fly."*

JOE ZMUDA

He lives by himself in a tidily kept basement apartment on Chicago's West Side. There is a large-screen TV set with a vase of daisies on top of it. A small radio is on the table. An electric fan keeps things fairly cool on this hot July day. "Three weeks from now I'll be seventy-five years old." Ten years ago he voluntarily retired.

"I was a shipping clerk for twenty-five long years. The firm went kerflooey. Then I put in fifteen years at a felt works. I was operating a cutting machine. Before that, I was a roving Romeo. I worked as a kid before they asked for your birth certificate. Box factories."

Some people told me, "Joe, you got your health and you shouldna done it." But it was too late. I don't know why I retired. It's just a habit, I guess. (Sighs.) Yeah, I have no regrets.

The first two years, I was downhearted. I had no place to go, nothin' to do. Then I gave myself a good goin' over. You can't sit at home like that and waste your time. So I kept travelin'. I went to see one of my old friends. Two days later, I'd go see another one. Three days later, they'd both come over and see me. That's the way life went.

The day goes pretty fast for me now. I don't regret it at all that I've got all this time on hand. I'm enjoying it to the best of my ability. I don't daydream at all. I just think of something and I forget it. That daydreaming don't do you any good. What the heck, there's no reason to have a grouch on or be mad at the world. Smile and the world smiles with you, that's an old slogan.

I live on a pension and social security. I don't get much pension because I only put in fifteen years at that place. I get thirty-six dollars a month from there and I get $217 from Social Security. If I manage my money, I'm fifteen, twenty dollars to the good every end of the month. I do most of my cooking.

(He reaches for a looseleaf book on the nearby shelf. He reads from it.) Here's cash on hand and here's my list of expenses. They're painting our church, so I contributed seven dollars. That was July first. The next day the grocery was $6.12. Gas and electric for the month was $16.48. Miscellaneous was $2.22. I don't remember what that was for. Rent is (mumbles) so-and-so. Dr.—that's not doctor, that's drink—$6.80. That's an awful, awful big bill for drink. Last Sunday, lodge meeting, $5.73. I have to keep track. If you don't, who in the hell will? If you come to the twenty-fifth of the month and you ain't got any money . . .

I stay up till one o'clock every night. I sleep late. I get up between nine and ten thirty in the morning. The first thing you do is take ahold of the coffee pot handle and you find out it's empty, so you gotta make coffee. Then I take that goddarn pipe and I fill it up with tobacco, and the day is started. I just had three soft boiled eggs about a half-hour ago. I just about wiped my chin when you come in.

I linger around till about one and one thirty. Right now I can't go out much because I just got this cataract operation about three weeks ago. I still can't look at the sun. They're fittin' me for new glasses. I can see that picture. I can see that flower. The vision is comin' back to me real nice. I have no difficulty watchin' television.

In the evening I like to turn on the news for a half-hour or so. That Watergate's gettin' on everybody's nerves lately. I don't even understand what it's about, to tell you the truth. They say politics is politics. I'm tired of it. Tonight I suppose I'll listen to the White Sox game and lay around. At ten o'clock the Cubs will go on television. They play San Francisco. On Sunday I'll go to Church.

I like baseball. I can listen to baseball on the radio and television and I don't get tired of it. In the wintertime I love bowling on television. Oh, I love that bowling. I remember one year we went out to Mundelein, Illinois. That's the only place in my life I saw bowling on the outside. Believe it or not, I bowled on those wooden alleys.

During the summer I used to go fishin' an awful lot. I

had a brother-in-law, he was a great fisherman. For ten long years we spent two or three weeks in Hayward, Wisconsin. We had the nicest times ever. And then come back home and wait for next year. On the first day of December, 1961, he was drivin' to work and had a heart attack. He smashed into a car, he hit a post, and he ran right into a tavern, and that was that.

Just about ten years ago I went to a golden jubilee wedding. My mother's only living sister's daughter. What an affair that turned out to be, somewhere's in Elmhurst. Believe it or not, there was a dozen scrap books on two tables. It brought back memories of my grandfather, my grandmother, my mother, sisters, and all. And now all of that's gone. I call some of my relatives now and then. I got quite a number of them. I usually take a little ride to the cemetery to visit my wife's grave. And I go to the other cemetery a week or so later to see my folks' grave, and that's that.

Sunday evenings my landlord—I've known him since childhood—he likes to shoot pool. I do too. We don't shoot pool for nothin'—a buck a game. Sunday I beat him three in a row and he was cryin' about it all the way: "You dirty dog." (Laughs.)

I go to the tavern Saturday or Sunday. I meet my old gang there. There's another fella, may his soul rest in peace, he died about six months ago. He liked pool very much. I'd beat this guy and he'd start hollerin', "That nasty old man beat me again." (Laughs.)

There are times when we make a foursome. Each guy takes a coin, tosses it up, and you pick your partner that way. You lose, you buy the drinks. If you win, you get the drinks for nothin'. There's conversation in-between. I liked pool when I was a kid and I still like it today. I won't say I'm a sharpie. I won't challenge Minnesota Fats, but I'll play the average guy in the tavern.

Like Sunday, we had a lodge meeting. There was seven of us. Each guy puts two dollars in the pot and we drink the rest of the afternoon with that. I like about three or four shots a week, and three, four games of pool and that's my evening.

The tavern I go to is just three blocks away. I walk there, but I'm driven home by my landlord. So we don't have to worry about gettin' held up. The idea is you gotta be careful so you don't keep all your money in your wallet. Sometimes you gotta put a ten spot behind the collar. I got held up in this neighborhood on the twenty-second of March about four years ago. I'm glad they didn't beat me. They took the money but they gave me my wallet back. I was so scared I didn't even know they put it back in my shirt.

I have two friends that are living on the South Side, just about a block away from the National Biscuit Company. I get a big thrill of it when I go by there. Boy, you should see the nice aroma from that place.

I go by my cousin, he stood up at my wedding. I spend two, three hours with him and he says, "I'm gonna call Whitey." He's another retired man. He's got that goddamn habit. He's at the park every day in the week watchin' them pinochle players and card sharks. My cousin calls him up, he comes over, and we start shooting the boloney all over again.

Like I say, when we were young fellas, there used to be one of them amusement parks. I'll never forget that place as long as I live. I had an occasion to take my girl friend out there. That was about 1920. They had that ride they called the Big Dipper. That thing went up and then down and up again. She had a great big white hat and a great big wide brim and she had what they call a stole, some fur piece. When that goddarn thing went down, she like fainted. I had to hold her. I had to hold her hat. I had to hold her fur piece. I had to hold myself. When we got off, the words she used are not allowed to be printed. Outside of that, she was a sweet kid. About fifty-three years ago. This is what we talk about.

Another man that stood up at my wedding, he's also retired. But he has asthma or something. Believe it or not, he pulled out a grocery bag about that big and he said, "Joe, here's what I got to compete with." He just dumped the contents out and he had about twelve different bottles of medicine. He says, "Joe, you don't know how lucky you are."

Sometimes when I get kind of wild, I take a train and go out to Glen Ellyn by my daughter. I surprise her because I hate to impose on people. I got two granddaughters. When I go out there, how they beg me, "Grandpa, stay for dinner." I say, "Not this time. I'm goin' home by train the same way I came out." Occasionally I stay there. There's two Slovenian families across the street. They're

brother-in-laws. They love to come to the tavern with
their wives and have a drink or two. One of them got a
real beautiful voice and he loves to sing. So we start
singing in the tavern and their wives join in. Believe it or
not, we dig up songs that are fifty years old. (He sings.)

I'm so happy, oh, so happy, don't you envy me?
I leave today at three for my home in Tennessee.
Dad and mother, sis and brothers are waiting for me
    there
And at the table, next to Mabel, there's a vacant chair.
Oh my, you ought to see the world she showed me.
Right on my mother's knee, she showed the world to
    me.
(He pauses, hesitates: "I'm a little mixed.")
All I can think of tonight is the field of snowy white
The banjoes hummin', the darkies drummin',
All the world seems right.
The rose 'round the door make me love mother more.
I'll see my sweetheart glow and friends I used to know
When I—

(He pauses, stops.) Somehow or other, I'm losin' out on
that song. But that's all right.

I go to fires every once in a while. That fire we had on
Milwaukee Avenue about three months ago, that was supposed to start in the morning. I was there at four o'clock
that afternoon. I was surprised that goddarned all the windows was broke and yet the smoke was comin' out there
heavy as hell, but you don't see the flame. They had about
thirty units there. You get the news on the radio. I was
gonna go to that Midway Airport accident. My two
friends, they said, "Joe, you can't see nothin' there no
more. That's all cleaned up, leveled off and everything."
They work fast on that.

I tell you what I did see. In 1915 I was workin' as an
errand boy. I saw that Eastland disaster about two minutes after it happened. I was right on the bridge when it
toppled over. You should hear the screams. I was chased
off. That was that Western Electric picnic outing. Seven
hundred or something was drowned.

I usually go to the Exchange Building downtown just to
get myself a nasty headache. I have a brother there. He
makes up packages of dollar bills in a canvas bag and puts

a wire around. One-dollar bills come four hundred in a package. Sometimes he's got stacks about two foot long and two foot wide and three foot high. You can imagine he's got a couple of million there. That's the headache.

This coming December, it'll be three years I made the trip to California. I got a sister out there. I stayed out there over the Christmas holidays and we went to Disneyland. Believe it or not, honest to God, I didn't think such beautiful things existed in this world of ours. It was somethin'.

I'm hopin' to be around here for at least five more years. I don't care. Twenty more years? Oh God, no. When people get old, they get a little bit childish.

I have a very, very good, darn good memory. I'll tell you another one. On the eighteenth of June, 1918, I went to a dance. Another guy and me. There was two girls dancin'. They were sisters. He grabbed one, so I grabbed the other. You know what they played. (Sings) Smile a while, you bid me sad adieu. I kissed that girl on the cheek. She told the world and me, "If I don't marry you, Joe, I'll never marry another person in this world." She was seventy years old last week. I called her up, wished her a happy birthday, and that's all. I could've married her, but—

I know a lot of songs. Sometimes when I'm washin' dishes, that's when the old time songs come to you. (He sings.)

> Everybody loves a baby
> That's why I'm in love with you
> Pretty baby, pretty baby
> Won't you let me rock you in the cradle of love
> And we'll cuddle all the time.
> Everybody loves a baby
> That's why I'm in love with you, pretty baby of mine.

That's all. That's over. There's more I know. I pride myself with that. Many of my friends will tell you, "If there's anything you want to know, ask Joe."

a wire around. One-dollar bills come four hundred in a package. Sometimes he's got stacks about two feet long and two feet wide and three feet high. You can imagine he's got a couple of million there. That's the headache.

This coming December, it'll be three years, I made the trip to California. I got a sister out there. I stayed out there over the Christmas holidays and we went to Disney-land. Relieved or not honest to God, I didn't think such beautiful things existed in this world of ours. It was something . . .

I'm hoping to be settled before I get much older, I don't care. Twenty-three more years. Oh God, no. When people get old they get a little bit childish.

I have a very, very good cherished memory. I'll tell you another one. On the eightieth of June, 1918, I went to a dance. Another guy and me. There was two girls there. They were sisters. He grabbed one, so I grabbed the other. You know what they played? (Sings) Sang a while. You and me and adieu. I kissed her just on the cheek. She told the world and me, "I'll love, marry you, too. I'll never marry another person in this world." She was sixty-eight years old last week. I called her up, wished her a happy birthday, and that's all I could've thought out, huh.

I know a lot of songs. Sometimes when I'm washing dishes, that's when the old time tunes come to you. (He sings.)

Everybody loves a baby,
That's why I'm in love with you, A-
Pretty baby, pretty baby.
Won't you let me rock you in the cradle of love
And we'll cuddle all the time.
Everybody loves a baby
That's why I'm in love with you, pretty baby of mine.

That's all. That's over. There's more. I know. I made my-self with that. Many of my friends will tell you. "If there's anything you want to know, ask Joe."

BOOK EIGHT

THE AGE OF CHARLIE BLOSSOM

CHARLIE BLOSSOM

He is twenty-four years old, of an upper-middle-class family. His father and grandfather are both doctors. His parents are divorced; each has since remarried. He attended a college on the west coast for one year, dropped out, and has been on his own ever since. "My main concern was political activity. I was then supported by my parents. It was a struggle for a lot of people I knew, whether to continue taking money from their parents."

His long hair is be-ribboned into a ponytail; his glasses are wire-rimmed; his mustache is scraggly and his beard is wispy. He is seated on the floor, having assumed the lotus position. The account of his life, adventures—and reflections—is somewhat discursive.

My first job was in a dog kennel, cleaning up the shit. It was just for a couple of days. My real first job was in a factory. I was hired to sweep the shit off the floor. They saw I was a good worker and made me a machine operator. I was eighteen and a conscientious objector. I told 'em at the factory I didn't want to do any war work, any kind of contract with any military institution. I tried to adhere to my politics and my morality. Since that time and through different jobs I've been led into compromises that have corrupted me.

They said, "You don't have to do any war stuff." They were just not telling me what it was, figuring I'd be cool. I was going along with it because I wanted to keep my job. I didn't want a confrontation. I was punching out some

571

kind of styrofoam. It was for some burglar alarm or something weird. You twist it around and ream it out. I was getting really angry about it. It's just not worthy work for a person to be doing. I had a real battle with myself. If I had any real guts, I'd say, "Fuck it," and walk out. I would be free. All this emotional tension was making me a prisoner. If I would just get up, I would put this down and say, "This is bogus, it's bullshit, it's not worthy. I'm a *human being*. A man, a woman shouldn't have to spend time doing this"—and just walk out. I'd be liberated. But I didn't.

One afternoon I was sorting out the dies and hangin' 'em on a pipe rack. In order to make room to hang more up, I had to push 'em like you push clothes in a closet. It made a horrible kind of screeching sound—metal on metal. I was thinking to myself—somewhat dramatically—This is like the scream of the Vietnamese people that are being napalmed. So I walked over to the foreman and I said, "Look, no longer is it enough not to do war work. The whole plant has just not to do any kind of work associating with killing people of any kind. Or I'm not gonna work at all." It was sort of like a little strike. I said, "I'm going home." He said, "Yeah, come back in a day or so." So I came back in a day or so and some high-up guy said, "Maybe you better look for another job." I said, "Okay." That was my first real job.

I worked in VISTA for a couple of years. I got assigned as a youth worker, with no real supervision, no activities. I just collected my paycheck, cashed it, and lived. I suppose I did as good as anyone else with a structured job. Freeing myself of a lot of thought habits, guilt, and repressiveness. Getting better acquainted with my own feelings, my own sensations, my own body, my own life. After they fired me, I worked with guerilla theater. I worked for a leftist printer. It didn't work out. I didn't have a car, didn't have money. Couldn't get a job. Not that I was really trying. Finally I was recommended for a job as copy boy on a Chicago paper.

I had very long hair at that time. It was halfway down my back. In order to get the job, I tied it up in such a way that it was all down inside my shirt. From the front it looked like a hillbilly greaser kind of haircut. The kind like Johnny Cash has. I borrowed some ritzy looking clothes, advertising agency clothes.

I went down to the paper and I talked to this guy and told him how much I wanted to be a journalist. It sounded like some Dick and Jane textbook. A lot of people like to pretend that's the way the world is. He liked me. He thought I was bright and hired me. I had a tie on.

Within a couple of weeks after working there, I reverted to my natural clothes. I was bringing organic walnuts and organic raisins and giving it away. Coming to work was for me a kind of missionary kind of thing. Originally I was gonna get some money and leave, but I had to get involved. So I tried to relate.

After a couple of weeks, the editor called me into his office. He said, "Read this little speech I wrote and tell me what you think of it." It was just a bunch of platitudes. Objectivity was the one thing he mentioned. I started telling him stuff: I think a newspaper should be this, that, and the other thing. We talked about an hour. I thought we were in fine agreement, that he was eating it up. I was paraphrasing exactly what he said. In the business world, you gotta play the game. I was leading around to asking for a scholarship.

We were exchanging rhetoric about how wonderful a newspaper is as a free institution and all this bullshit. *All of a sudden* he said, "I was walking through the office last week and I said, 'Who is that dirty, scummy, disgusting filthy creature over there?' And I was told that's one of our new copy boys. I was told he was bright and energetic."

He was talking about *me!* That struck me as a weird way of relating to somebody. He started by saying that clothing is unimportant, "so that's why I'm asking you to change your clothes." It was just so bizarre. I told him, "Look, now that I've got a job, I'll buy fancy clothes, I'll rent an apartment, I'll take a shower." He seemed pleased, but he wanted me to cut my hair. I balked at that. He rose from his desk and stood up. The interview was over. He said blah, blah, blah, blah and hustled me out of the office. I was very shaken by it and went out and cried. Or maybe I didn't cry at that time. But once he was pissed off at an assistant editor and took it out on me and yelled, "You got to look like a young businessman tomorrow or you're out!" That's one time I'm pretty sure I did cry, 'cause I just don't know how to relate to it.

I was enjoying my job, because I was answering the

phone most of the time. People would call up and complain or have a problem. I'd say, "This is a capitalist newspaper and as long as it's a capitalist newspaper it's not
gonna serve you, because its purpose is not to serve you.
Its purpose is to make money for its owner. If you want
some help ..." And I'd refer them to the Panthers or the
*Seed.** People were very grateful. They'd say, "Thank you
very much." After they talked to me forty-five minutes or
so, they'd say, "I'm glad I talked to you. I didn't know the
Panthers were like that."

Were there any complaints?

About what?

About your—uh—commentary and suggestions?

No complaints, no hassles. I was very polite. At that
stage of the game, I was in a very mellow mood. I was
giving organic raisins and walnuts and sunflower seeds to
everybody—to reporters and rewrite men. I was bright
and cheerful and everything. The city editor was very
short and rude to people that called up and hung up and
stuff like that. I'd say, "That's a *person* on the phone." I
used to walk around the office and say, "How can grown
people spend their time doing this?" I got into long raps. I
actually got one, who'd been a reporter for twenty years,
to seriously question himself: Am I doing anything worthwhile? I liked doing this, to persuade people to think. It
was my contribution to the world. That's why I told people who called for help that they should write letters or
call up the editor or come down and take over the paper.
A lot of people responded very well to those suggestions.

And no complaints about your persuasions . . . ?

(A throwaway.) Sometimes. What finally happened
was—I was involved in a severe personal relationship and
I really got obnoxious. I was very alienated and very hostile. I stopped bringing in organic food. I started taking a
couple of hours off on my dinner break—which is very
cool. I'd grab two, three beers and smoke a joint or two

* A popular Chicago underground newspaper at the time.

on my break. The grass and the beers put me in a very mellow state. The straw broke when somebody called up and the reporter hung up on him. The guy called back and I answered the phone. I got real mad at the guy, too, and called him a bigot, racist, and hung up on him, too. The guy complained. And I was the one who got in trouble. It was a big thing, with the editor coming down on me for my attitude on the phones. I guess he found out about those other calls. I couldn't understand his anger. I was just trying to convey my feelings to the people.

My fantasies all spring at the paper was getting a machine gun and coming in and shooting them. Getting psychedelic hallucinogens and putting them in their drinks. Getting a gun and walk into the editor's office and shooting him. Maybe pointing the gun at him first and say, "Okay, how do you face your death?" I saw a Japanese movie once where two guys met their deaths in two different ways. That's the kind of fantasies I had, cutting 'em up with knives.

Other people's fantasies, from what I could observe, were sexual. They were not connected with the political realities. They would look at the young women—attractive by white, bourgeois standards, the ones with long blonde hair and miniskirts—and draw erotic stimulation.

There was one hired as a copy girl, through some uncle who had pull, and within a month she was an editorial assistant. There were two copy boys that had worked there for a couple of years, that were married and had kids, and weren't getting fucking paid as editorial assistants.

A copy boy is a kind of nigger. You stand around in a room full of people that are very ego-involved in a fantasy—they think they're putting out a newspaper. These are the reporters and editors. Somebody yells, "Copy!" Sometimes they yell, "Boy!" You run over—or you walk over—and they give you a piece of paper. You take that piece of paper someplace, and you either leave it there and go back to waiting around or you get another piece of paper and bring it back to the person that originally called you.

The other thing you do is go down, when the editions come off the press, and you get three hundred copies of the paper on a big cart and you wheel it around and put one on everybody's desk. And stuff like that. "We've got a pack of photographs to pick up at Associated Press, go

over and get it." "Somebody's in town making a speech, go
and get it." Or, "Take this over to city hall and give it to
the reporter that's over there ..."

Copy boys are also expected to do editorial assistant's
work. That's answering the phone and saying, "City
Desk." If it's a reporter, you connect him with the editor
or whatever. If an individual is calling about a story that
says, "Continued on page seven," but it's not on page
seven, I look through the paper until I find where the
story is and tell him. Or I go get clips out of the library.
You take one piece of paper and exchange it for another.
It's basically bullshit.

When I first worked there, I ran. They'd say, "Copy!"
and I'd run. Nobody noticed. It didn't make any difference. Then I started walking. Why the fuck should I run
for them? This spring, I started to shuffle. That's when the
people started to complain about me. I started in February,
1970, and I was fired May 20, 1971. I was out with hepa-
titis for six months.

Want to know why I was ultimately fired? I had a pair
of shoes, the soles were loose. I didn't want to spend
money on shoes. I was taking home seventy bucks a week
and saving fifty. I wasn't hanging around the paper because that was my destiny. I was just some little pinball
that had dropped in a slot. I was there because a bunch of
accidents put me there. I also had a will and energy and I
was moving. I was in motion, creative.

I wanted to have a computer at the paper. I wanted an
arrangement where you could get up in the morning and
call up and say, "Okay, this is Charlie. I can work on
Tuesday, Thursday, Friday, and Saturday in the evenings.
And on Wednesday morning. I absolutely cannot work
Wednesday evening." Everyone would be calling up and
the computer would put it all together. They would call
back and say, "Okay, these are your hours this week."
'Cause it doesn't make any difference who shows up, the
way they run the paper. These are the kinds of ideas I
had. I wanted decision making in the hands of the people
who did the work. I wanted to fuck capitalism.

I saw those things in terms of classes. The seventh floor
was the executive. The fourth floor was the middle
class—editorial, reporters, and all that. The ruling class
had their offices there too, not up with the executives. I
used to see Marshall Field in the hall. I was thinking, If

they kill Bobby Seale, maybe I should get a gun and come in here and shoot Field. Maybe that's a reason for me to keep this job. I'm not accomplishing anything else here. I don't want money. Money isn't worth it.

What would you accomplish by killing Marshall Field?

Oh well, you can't look at it as accomplishing anything. Like one of the editors told me, "If you behave yourself, you won't get fired." I wanted to take a baseball bat and smash his head in, except I wanted to do it with my hands. He made me so angry. Here is this motherfucker, who is comfortable, he's not struggling—in truth, there's not a hell of a lot for him to struggle about, 'cause he's a fuckin' marshmallow in a bag of marshmallows. He's a nice guy. I mean, I like him. But he's a fuckin' marshmallow.

Your shoes, the soles were loose ...

Yeah. What I did was put glue on 'em. And then somebody suggested I put tape on 'em. So I did. People kept suggesting that I buy shoes. I kept saying, "No. I don't want to buy shoes. These shoes are fine." There was no reason for me to stay in their culture.

Still I was making friends with different people. I was trying to get the foreign editor to do an article about opium that the CIA is responsible for bringing into this country as heroin. I read it in *Ramparts*. They just laughed at it. A week later, another paper ran a column by Flora Lewis about the *Ramparts* article. I was incensed by these pigs. This guy thinks he's my friend. I mean, I like him a lot. He's really a nice person. I don't know if I would get any pleasure from shooting him up with a .50-caliber machine gun and seeing his body splatter to pieces. I'd be emotionally disturbed by an act of destruction as total as that. But I would get some satisfaction out of it, because of the rage I feel towards these guys. The way they wrote about the demonstrations and the Panther grand jury. I'm so enraged by these swine ... They pretend they're liberals. They pretend to be concerned. They never fight over an issue. This editor told me, "I fight every day for space." God!!

I had my most hostile fantasies on the job. I just

reached a point where I just didn't want to hand out the fucking newspaper. I wanted to burn it. It's like you get a job in a prison. It's the only job in town. Your job is to go around the cells and hand out a washcloth. I don't want to be just handing out washcloths. You begin to realize this guy that's locked up is just another human being. Maybe I could help him out. I'll bring him cigarettes. I think that was the real reason I passed out organic walnuts and raisins. And my thoughts.

The job was also a corrupting thing. I realized I could get a lot of free books, a lot of books came in to review. And records, I could cop records. You sort of be nice to this guy because he'll give you the records. I was getting corrupted.

How pitiful these people are! They kept telling me I should try to keep the job. It was security. I could look at these guys that worked twenty, thirty fucking years, and they were telling me if I cut my hair and wore different clothes, I would be like them. They don't want to have to say, "Jesus! I blew it! I'm sixty years old and I've wasted it all." I'm not stupid. I can work. I'm lazy, most of us are. But we're lazy because we've got nothing worthwhile to do. I lost a year of my life working there. Was it worth it?

I'm saying godly things, that's what it's all about. How can we get that boot to step three inches over to the left or the right, so it won't trample that flower. Look at these rich motherfuckers who don't know shit. We don't have to have a society in which you work because you're tricked, cajoled, manipulated, or pressured into it.

How many jobs in this country consist of locking things or counting things, like money—the banks, the cashiers. Or being a watchman of some kind. Why in the hell do these jobs exist? These jobs are not necessary to life. This guy I was talking to yesterday said, "Money makes the world go around. Brothers kill each other over money." And that's true. I pointed to the sun. "What makes that go around? You're not gonna tell me money makes that go around." So there's something else besides money. You can't eat money, you can't fuck money, you can't do nothin' with money except exchange things. We can live without money. We can live with people and grow food and build a table and massage a neck that has a sprain . . .

Your shoes, you had them taped . . .

Oh yeah. You wanna know why I was ultimately fired? I'm very interested in Oriental stuff. Sometimes I fantasize about being a samurai, especially after I see a Japanese movie. So I used to sit Japanese-style on my knees on the floor. (At this point, he shifts from the lotus position to that of a samurai.) I'd pick a quiet corner of the room.

(Softly, hardly audible) The city room . . . ?

In front of the desk of the religion editor. I thought it was appropriate. Sitting and breathing. People tried to ignore it. Some people thought I was meditating. I said, "Sure I'm meditating." I don't know what meditation is exactly, so I would be reluctant to call it that. I used to do this, before, on the floor of the mail room. One day a guy objected because he thought if a guy came in wheeling a thing, he wouldn't be able to see me. I showed him I could move extremely quickly. That put his fears to rest.

One day the head librarian, he's such as ass-hole—I really hate to call people ass-holes because they're all nice, I'm more obnoxious than a lot of people I call ass-holes. But he's the kind of guy only interested in himself, which to me is a very outdated point of view. I mean, if you study Zen or ancient philosophy, they all say the same thing, and that is that no man is an island. Okay, so he came in and said, "Don't sit like that." I said, "Why not? I'm not bothering anybody." He said, "I don't want you to."

I said, "Man, let me explain . . ." He said, "Do you want me to talk to the editor?" I said, "No, no, no, don't talk to him, he'll fire me." So he said, "I don't want you sitting there, it looks just terrible." I said, "Okay, I won't sit in the corner, I'll sit in the middle of the room." He said, "No, no, no, don't do that either." So I left. I went down and sat in front of the desk of the religion editor.

About a week or so later—one of my stops with the paper is the public relations office. There was a vase with some flowers in it. So I sat down in the chair and looked at the flowers in it—maybe five minutes, six at most—and I got up and left. A couple of days later, the editor called me into his office and says, "I got three complaints I want to discuss with you. One was from the librarian. He told

me about your sitting on your knees and I told him if you
ever do that again to throw you out. The second is about
you and the flowers. They complained you disrupted the
office." I said, "I was sitting there with my back straight
and breathing (breathes slowly, deliberately, deeply) in-
instead of (gasps frantically)—right?" *That* disrupted them?

In a way I did disrupt. It's the kind of thing Gandhi or
Thoreau or Christ would say. If you really want to strike
a blow at the corruption of society, come into eternity. I
have to concede that a human being who sits down and
meditates—tries to get in touch with God or whatever—is
the most threatening fucking thing of all. On a physical
plane, I wasn't interfering with them at all. But the fact
that I sat with my back straight and most people at their
jobs don't sit with their backs straight, that's weird. They
looked at me and they felt guilty. I wasn't trying to irritate them. I wasn't trying to throw any magic their way. I
was just looking at the flowers.

Most of all, I wanted to be touched by these flowers. I
stroked a couple of petals really gently. I was trying to
reach out and say, "Hey plant, I know you're here in this
office and it's probably a drag and you're lonely. But I
love you." I took a couple of petals that had fallen off the
table and put them in my pocket.

The third complaint . . . ?

. . . was about my shoes. He said, "It's entirely unacceptable to have tape on your shoes."

*Were you fired because of the shoes, looking at the flowers,
or assuming the samurai position?*

No. On Monday morning I called up the paper and said
I'd be fifteen minutes late and I was fifteen minutes late.
Tuesday morning I called and said I'd be fifteen minutes
late and I was fifteen minutes late. He said that was entirely unacceptable. So he gave me a written memo.

So that was it?

No. Originally they pissed about my clothing. I said,
"When I wore my good clothes they got ruined here, tearing against the typewriters. You ought to provide some

kind of smocks." Surprisingly, he accepted the idea and gave us smocks. Hell, it was hot and it was summertime. So I started wearing just the smock and no shirt. And he said that was entirely unacceptable. "Suppose somebody comes in and sees you. This is a business office."

Nobody complained about my work except the head copy boy, and I made a deal with him. I said, "Let me do all the paper rounds and I won't be in the city room." I hated the way they treat you in the city room.

I got great satisfaction from the paper rounds, far more than going to a library or hanging around the city room. I'd go down and fill up the cart and that fucking thing's heavy. I'd have to push it and it would take strength and I'd sweat. It's like 250 or 300 papers to go around on each edition. I liked it 'cause I sweated and I got into conversations with people. I'd get done and I would say, "I did something."

I'd do the rounds and go sit outside in the flower garden. After a week or so, the head copy boy said, "Look, the other copy boys see you sittin' around while they're working and it makes them uptight." I said, "Okay, I'll come back, do more work, but I won't do *all* the paper rounds." They were uptight not because they saw me sitting around—because dealing with these reporters, these pigs, who called them "Boy!" all the time, *they* wanted a chance to get out.

(Mumbles) Then it wasn't the shoes or the samurai position or the flowers or being late . . . ?

No. I was going through all this upset. I said to the head copy boy, "I'm going through all this weirdness and I haven't gone to lunch. I might as well leave early." People do that kind of shit all the time. Come five o'clock, I started getting my stuff together and changing. I would come to work in blue jeans and change into a pair of pants and a shirt. At the end of the day I could change back into blue jeans. At five thirty, I would just (snaps fingers) walk out the door.

At five thirty somebody walked in and said to me, "Here are some clips. Can you go and get 'em?" I said, "No, I'm leaving." Another copy boy says no, too. The next morning the editor came to me and said, "You left early . . . blah, blah, blah, blah . . . And you refused to get the clips." I said, "Let me explain." And he said, "That's entirely unacceptable. This is the straw that broke the camel's back." To me it was more like the one that broke the pig's back.

I had been thinking for months, What will I do when I get fired? Will I smoke a joint in the city room? Will I meditate in the library? I wanted to do something to show, Hey, I'm better than you motherfuckers. I'm getting fired because I'm different. I don't want to be a cipher. I was thinking, How could I show that? By kidnapping Marshall Field? By shooting him? I had to think fast, so I looked at the editor and said, "I hope you can live with the conditions you're creating." And I just turned around and walked out and started to cry.

He hurried after me and said, "Wait a minute. I'm not creating these conditions, you are." I said, "No, no, no, I'm not the one that has the power. You're the one that has the power." I walked out of there. Then I hung around the office most of the day selling copies of *Rising Up Angry*.* (Laughs.)

I've gotten myself on unemployment. They were nice to me the first few times, then a woman told me to get a number. I wanted to tell her, Fuck you. I can wait outside your apartment and knock you over the head and steal your money. Fuck your money. It's not your money in the first place. It's mine. I worked for it. And if you don't give it to me, I don't give a fuck, 'cause I'll live anyway. When I was younger and applied for a job and the guy wouldn't give me a reason for not hiring me, I would say, "It's okay." I wouldn't yell at him, "You're a racist pig." I'd think, Fine. Mao Tse-tung will hire me to kill you. Or I could be a bank robber. But that bitterness, I don't like being bitter. I'm a pacifist.

I have picked a career for myself. I want to practice the kind of traditional medicine that is more spiritually oriented than modern Western medicine. I want to learn herbs and massage and things like that, and meditation. I don't want to be dependent on other people. This notion of self-reliance is peculiar to day. The frontiersman lived by his own effort. Today nobody does that. I want to be a frontiersman of the spirit—where work is not a drag.

* The most militant of all the Chicago underground papers at the time.

STEVEN SIMONYI-GINDELE

We're in the offices of the Capitalist Reporter, *a sixty-four-page monthly tabloid. It's in one of the older office buildings along a mid-Manhattan street. Though the quarters are cramped, an air of busyness pervades. At work, among half-filled paper coffee cups and ash trays, higgledy-piggledy, are several young people, long-haired, casually dressed.*

He, the publisher, is twenty-six. Born in Hungary, he emigrated to Canada after the revolution. He is as informal as the others. On his lapel is a large "Jesus Loves You" button; on his feet, sneakers. His dog scrounges about on a blanket in this inner office.

"We report on people making it. How to start out on a small investment, how to invest outside the stock market and get a rich return. Like buying cheap land, antiques, farms ... We do well-researched stories of people actually succeeding, with little or no capital, going into business for themselves and making a go of it.

"We've done what we preach. We started out with thirty thousand dollars—ten thousand dollars in capital and twenty thousand dollars in loans. After our preview issue we had only eight thousand dollars in the bank. We're now in our second year—we had a hundred thousand trial subscribers and have a fifty thousand dollar newsstand distribution—and circulation is growing. Right now, we're undercapitalized, so we're penny pinching. Each person has to do the work of two or three.

"Pat* and I became partners in business eight years ago. It was several years of struggling, saving our money, putting it into ventures, and losing it and investing it again. Finally we found we have the ability of conveying a sales message in print."

I went to work when I was nine years old. I used to get up at three-thirty in the morning and deliver four hundred newspapers. I was bored by school and left in the last year.

---

* Patrick Garrard, editor of the *Capitalist Reporter.*

I was never afraid of working. I always enjoyed the challenge and I always enjoyed the reward. I did all kinds of things.

I was a bus boy when I was thirteen. It took me six weeks of steadily looking for a job. It was high unemployment at that time in Canada. I realized then the only security a person has is what he himself can do. There's little security in a job, working for somebody else. I like to control my fate as much as possible.

I don't believe the answer lies in making money. It didn't for me. By the time I was twenty-one I was driving a Cadillac and I could afford a fifteen-hundred-dollar-a-month seashore apartment in Florida, go to shows, and spend two hundred dollars a night and take my mother out, my grandfather, and live like a king. But I was more frustrated than when I was making thirty-four cents an hour delivering for a drugstore in Toronto.

I couldn't understand why I wasn't happy. Happiness is not related to money. Being successful at what you're doing is the measure of a man. The measure of a man is standing on his own two feet. To succeed by himself without leaning on other people to support him.

My quest I have already found. I found that in the Bible. Until I was twenty-four, I never read the Bible. But I heard that God had a plan for every human being and I could have a direct contact with God through Jesus Christ. I asked Christ to come into my life. At that point, I realized what life is all about. My life became really worth living.

Before I found Christ, I learned how to ski, how to sail, how to fly, how to speak French. All these things I dropped after I had a mastery of it, because they didn't satisfy me. You can master making money like you can master algebra. After you get the basic essence, any person can do it.

Before I accepted Christ, I didn't feel I had a good deal until I really crushed a guy and squeezed the last penny out of it. So when I accepted Jesus, I realized I was a slave to this money. I called up Patrick, who was my partner at the time in another venture, and I told him I wanted to get out. We were in publishing. We were selling books through the mail. Self-improvement, educational, sex manuals. Quite acceptable, normal for the trade. We had a very successful campaign selling the book. We sold about 150,000 copies. It was a very profitable item. But I would not do it today.

I feel I could start any business. It boils down to a formula. You find there's a need for something. Then you supply that need. There is a spread between what it costs you and what you sell it for. That's what's called a profit. I don't know a fairer way of rewarding a man than by profit. What a man sows, so shall he reap.

Each man has a calling. The gifts God has given me is to be a businessman. To be able to organize, to be able to sell, to be able to understand figures and what not. I want to use these gifts for the glory of God. I don't want to do anything in my business life that would shame my Saviour. So I always look to guidance from the Bible on how the business should be run. My principles of doing business have changed altogether from two years ago.

Previously my guideline was: what you could get away with, that was right. The only mistake you could make is to get caught. You had this gut fear inside: What did I tell this guy last time he was here? That no longer worries me. I always tell the same story to everybody. Everything I do in business must be aboveboard—must be something I can face God with once I appear before Him after I die.

An issue of the magazine features in graphic detail the successful exploits of a strikebreaker in Canada. "Maybe strikebreaking is the wrong word to use. What that person does is supplies, in a competitive system of labor and management. Strikes is one of the legitimate weapons labor can use. Management also has a right to keep functioning. Because of physical threats made upon management, most companies are not willing to continue to function. Law enforcement has not been able to guarantee the personal safety of people for their right to run their business if their employees don't wish to work. What this company does is take photographic evidence of physical violence on people who continue to work for the strike-bound company, and takes them to court to restrain them . . . That's the essence of what I gathered in the story."

Patrick Garrard reflected another point of view: "Steve doesn't like unions. I merely have a mild distaste for them because they're bureaucratic. Steve regards the article as getting back at unions—let's sock 'em. To me, it was a good story, that's all. I was a bit worried about it because

it was the only one in all our issues that could be con-
strued as a right-wing kind of story. I don't want our mag-
azine to get that reputation."

We're different from other business publications. *For-*
tune and *Forbes* and *Business Week* talk about corporations and corporation executives. We talk about individuals and small companies. We have a lot of subscriptions
from prisoners, who transfer nine dollars from their com-
missary account for the *Capitalist Reporter.* It's a substantial amount of money when you make twenty-seven cents
a day. Many prisoners are natural entrepreneurs that have
gone outside the accepted norms that society has set, and
they've ended up rightfully where they are.

We have kids coming in here, long-haired hippies, who
are very excited and want to buy back issues of the magazine or run an advertisement in it. I think a lot of hippies
today have decided it is more fun to be successful than to
be a failure. (Laughs.) I think it's become a fashionable
thing now to be successful.

There are two kinds of people—some are gifted leaders,
some are followers. The young leaders in the past few
years have been negative, nihilistic, destructive—have run
their course. Young people are now looking for other
ways. Why am I alive? One answer is: A person must support himself. He can't expect people to bring him everything on a silver platter. The unhappiest people are the
young ones who have everything at home.

What a lot of young people rebel against is having to go
into corporations where they have to spend thirty years of
their lives and come out as a wornout human being on a
pension. They say, "Why on earth should I do that? There
must be something more to life." It's more challenging to
strike out on your own.

The Bible says if a man doesn't work, he shouldn't eat.
I'm in full agreement. Unless he's crippled or mentally disabled, a man should work. When I was twelve in Canada,
I found a bus boy's job. I searched door to door looking
for work. If I would have dictated what I wanted, I would
never have found work. I was willing to take anything . . .

The Depression in the thirties was a unique period. People were willing to work and there wasn't work around. I
think the mentality of the thirties and the mentality today
is different. Then people really wanted to work. Now the

thing is to want something *meaningful.* I despise that word. They must be willing to take whatever they find and they must grow from that. *Fulfilling,* that's another one they stumble on. I didn't start out as president of a company with a hundred thousand subscribers. It was necessary for me to scrub toilets. I scrubbed them. Not that I liked doing it. But I didn't feel debased by it. It was better than doing nothing. *Any* work is better than no work. Work makes a person noble.

This is a lie about meaningful work. It comes from teachers, Ph.D.'s who've never really worked. They feel they have a special knowledge to impose upon a lower being, who goes to work when he's thirteen or fifteen and settles down and goes forward . . .

If I've done my best, I find my work meaningful. If I haven't done as well as I could, I don't find it meaningful. I don't think my work is any more important than a man sweeping the streets. It's important to me only because it provides my livelihood. Whether it's important to society only time will tell.

The only truth as far as I'm concerned is the word of God in the Bible. That is the only reliable proven fact that has been uncontested. You can read it in all the papers, Jesus Christ is becoming an issue today. Jesus Freaks is the wrong term. They're very normal young people. They don't take drugs any more. They don't promiscuously screw around with everything that walks any more. They live very healthy lives. Maybe compared to others, they're freaks.

I run three miles every morning. I come into the office around eight o'clock. I spend a half-hour reading five psalms and a proverb—and praying. Then I make a schedule of what's to be done during the day. I try to assign as many tasks as possible to my staff, so I can reduce my work. I need two or three additonal people. A couple who are not pulling their weight I'm in the process of replacing. This is very painful. You have to interview a great many people before you can find that person who has the talent plus the right attitude. This is not a normal time for us, so my work runs until nine o'clock at night. Generally my workday would be over at one o'clock in the afternoon.

No, I don't take my work home with me. You can become a slave to work. To be a successful executive, you must always be in control of your work, not let work control you. You make sure details have been assigned to others. After you check these things out, you look for new profit avenues. You search elsewhere. Who knows? I may be interested in starting another business. Now I'm interested in studying the Bible. I want to spend more time doing that. I like to read. I'm sadly lacking in my knowledge.

If God calls me, I may one day become a missionary. I don't see beyond that. I certainly could be just as happy living on fifty dollars a week as I could on five hundred dollars a week. I can adjust my living standards. I somehow feel there is some kind of destiny ahead of me—that God wants me to use the gifts He's given me in different ways than just making me rich. I think there'll be something along that line in the future.

TOM McCOY

He is twenty-three years old. He is a proofreader in the printing plant of a national weekly magazine. His father is a retired policeman; his mother, a retired social worker. "My father never saw himself as a cop. He became one during the Depression when there weren't any other jobs. He was worried about survival."

He majored in sociology at Northwestern University "'cause it was just about the easiest thing. I wasn't really fascinated. The only reason I was in school: I was either too young to object or, when I was a sophomore in college, I figured I might as well stay out of the draft." It took him five and a half years to graduate. "I was dropping in and dropping out."

One of the things I like about my job is that the time will vary each week. I'll work a Wednesday night one week, a Thursday afternoon, and a Saturday night. Next week it'll be Tuesday during the day, Friday at night . . . I never know when I'll be working, and it almost doesn't seem like working. The hours are weird, so I don't get caught in a rush hour. You don't get in a rut. I dig it.

It bothers me when the boss is there. He's usually in during the day. In the evening there's no supervision and I won't be worrying how I look. It's really pleasant. When the boss is around, if he sees you reading a newspaper or something, it grates him and he'll find something for you to do. That's the part of the job I dislike the most, having to look busy.

One of the older guys was telling me how amazing he found it that I would sit there totally oblivious to the boss and read a paper. That's something he would never do. It ran against his ethic. I think there's too much of an attitude that work has to be shitty.

I noticed somebody talking on the phone the other day, one of the older guys. He said he was at the office. It dawned on me when a guy says, "I'm at the office," it means, "I'm a white-collar worker." It means, "I don't dirty my hands." He wasn't at work, he was "at the office." It really blew my mind. I don't think I've used that phrase in my life. I say, "I'm at work."

I'm not afraid of the boss. I think he's sort of afraid of me, really. He's afraid of the younger people who work there because they're not committed to the job. The older person, who's got his whole life wrapped in the organization, has a sword hanging over his head. The boss can keep him from getting a promotion, getting a raise. If he screws up, he can be fired. His career is hanging in balance. If I make a little mistake, I'll say, "That's too bad, I'm sorry it happened." This guy'll freak out because his career is dangling there. Consequently, the boss doesn't have that power over us, really. The tables are sort of reversed. We have power over him, because he doesn't know how to persuade us. We do the job and we do it fine. But he doesn't know why. He knows why the older guys work—because they want to get ahead. He doesn't know why we work.

I can't figure him out. It's a weird mixture of condescension, trying to be a nice guy—"Wouldn't you do this?"—and trying to be stern, a fatherly sort of image. He doesn't know whether to be nice or be stern. Part of it comes out of his own fear. He doesn't realize younger people resent this. I object to seeing this guy as my father. I would rather see him as some sort of equal or as a boss. Older people, he tells them what to do and they do it, because that's the way it is. But he never feels sure the younger people are going to do it. They want to know why.

Nobody refused to do anything, but we want to know why.

If there's a lull in the work, the kids'll go in the main office, which is plush, where the big boss works—and they'd sleep on the couches. The big boss complained to my boss that people were sleeping on the couches on Saturdays. He asked if I would pass the word along not to sleep on the couches any longer. I said, "Why? It doesn't make any sense. If there's nothing to do and it's the middle of the night and the people want to grab a nap and the couch is there . . ." He said, "Well, that's what the boss said." I just told him, "No, I wouldn't feel right telling them. You'll have to tell them yourself." It's really stupid. If the couch is there and somebody's tired, he should lay down on the floor to keep this guy's couch neat for the next Monday?

RALPH WERNER

"I'll be twenty tomorrow." His parents are divorced and have since remarried. He lives with his stepfather and mother in the area of the steel mills, where most families own their own homes; the archetype, a frame bungalow. "We're one of the last neighborhoods in the city that is just about all white. There is a fear of black people. Why, I don't really know. They bus a lot of kids in from the West Side, but there hasn't been any trouble at school. I do have certain questions about them, but I try to view things from a Christian standpoint . . ."

He graduated from high school as "an average student. My initiative didn't carry me any further than average. History I found to be dry. Math courses I was never good at. I enjoyed sciences, where I could do things instead of just be lectured to. We called it labs. Football was my bag in high school. My senior year I made all-city halfback."

He is small, wiry, agile, intense. He wears an American flag pin on the lapel of his suit coat.

In my neighborhood the kids grow up, they get married right after high school, and they work in the mills. Their whole life would revolve around one community and their certain set of friends. They would never get out and see what the world's like. It seemed terrible to me.

I was planning to go to Western Illinois on a football scholarship. I didn't get it. My attitude was kind of down. I couldn't really see myself working in the mills. I did, when I was a junior, full-time after school for about two months. I would work from two in the afternoon to eleven at night. Fortunately I never had much homework. I hated it. It's dirty. It's the same old routine day in and day out, and it's your whole life.

I was a laborer. That's where everybody starts in the mill unless you have a college education. I worked on the scarfing dock. We would burn the shavings off the steel. I would shovel 'em up and put 'em in a big tub, which would be carried off and remelted and made into steel again.

It wasn't that the work was so hard. You had a lot of time to rest. It was just demoralizing. I consider my morals high. Their whole life revolved around the mills, the race track, the tavern. They talked about sex in a very gross way. The language was unheard of in a public place. (Laughs.) It just wasn't my kind of living.

After five o'clock all the important people had gone home. The office people left, and things would kind of darken after that. By six o'clock the mills were pretty well run by the foremen. Those two months heightened my awareness of what the neighborhood was like.

I can remember as a child I was scared of the mills. I used to see pictures on a steel mill calendar of a big strong guy shoveling coal. Big pits where there was fire. I wanted to get in. I found out it's not a nice place. There are foremen and something new called sub-foremen. The mills used to be rough, but now they're getting wild. It's racial tensions. It's not where I want to spend my life.

As I knew a few white-collar workers, I associated with them on breaks. I was afraid to get too close to those that worked labor. Not because I was afraid of them themselves. They were all nice to me. It was just that I didn't care for their conversation. So I stayed with the white-collar workers. There were different cliques all over the mill, like I found in high school. There's cliques just about everywhere you go.

I think a lot of people who are in a higher position, the upper-class people with a lot of money, who don't have calloused hands, don't have quite the appreciation of a dollar as someone who has worked in a mill, who knows what it's like to earn your money by physically working. And if you're sick, you know it's gonna hurt you. And if something happens to you where you no longer have your capabilities, they're gonna get rid of you. They have a deeper concern for life. They have a deeper feeling for the political system than someone who's upper class. Because they've worked, they keep our nation moving, they turn the steel out. They put their hearts and their fists behind it. They don't sit there and let the brain do their work. I think they have a little stronger character.

Yesterday was my last day of working as a salesman in a store in the big shopping center. I worked there six months. An expensive store, high class. You don't come in there looking for a pair of socks. People are expected to spend a lot. It goes from upper class to middle, several doctors, execs, important people who have a lot of money.

We had cards that were color-coded depending on how good the credit rating is of the person. Naturally the best being gold. They were a higher quality of people. I myself would only shop there because I needed dress clothes to work. Otherwise I wouldn't shop there.

There was a gray card or silver, which was a good credit rating, but these people weren't as financially well off as the gold. Then there was a blue card, which they'd pass on to the employees or those with new accounts, where we would call downtown every time they would buy something. Most people would dress alike, so it was hard to tell what somebody did by the color of their card.

With the blue card, they wouldn't release any merchandise until we would call downtown. Several times we couldn't get through on our phones. There was a constant waiting. So we would tell 'em, "We can't release the merchandise to you. We'll have to send it out." I saw several occasions where people with blue cards as well as silver cards would tear them up and throw them. I didn't feel it was right to classify people like that. If you give 'em a credit card, whether they can work in a mill or can be a doctor, I feel everybody should be on an equal scale.

When I got out of high school, I thought I'd go into retailing. That's what my father did, my real dad. He was a salesman. This is what he's been all his life. But I didn't care for it. It's too seasonal. A lot of standing around.

My stepfather works in the mill. He used to be a pipe inspector. He's gone to be a clerk now, a better job. He's a lot more satisfied with life than my natural father. He gets along fine with the guys in the mill. He's happy when he comes home. He knows exactly what he's got to do in life. He talks very little about it. He doesn't express feelings, but he seems content. He's never said anything against it. It's a good paying job. He's looking for retirement in a number of years. Ten years, something like that. He's just going to last out his time until he can, which I think is great.

He also has a part-time job, which helps him waste his time anyway—collecting on a paper route for a news agency. The pay isn't that good, but it's something he likes to do. It gives him money which he uses on a fishing trip every year. Oh, he's good at home. He likes to clean up the garage, cut the grass, take care of the house, keep it clean. I believe he's forty-five, give or take a year or two. This is how old my real dad is, too.

My real dad, up in Minnesota, he's constantly traveling. He does sales. Constantly having to talk his way to his next dollar. I have a little brother and sister which are ten and eleven, which he wishes he could spend more time with. He longs to just get a cabin up at the lake and just relax in life. But he knows that won't come for a long time. He seems very tired for his age, very wornout.

This past summer, I spent quite a bit of time with him, and he's had many inspiring words for me. He's told me several things that have echoed in my mind as I found depressing things in life. He told me: "Sometimes you have to make a decision in life, right or wrong." Those few words have kept my head above water several times. Nobody's gonna take your hand and walk you through life. My dad has a lot of intelligence about things like that. He knows what life's about. He knows what you have to do in life to get ahead. This is why he's so successful as a salesman. Even though he's tired.

He doesn't—(a pause)—he no longer can really appreciate his job. Again, he's been at it for an awful long time. He's been with several firms, he's restless. He wants to be an individual. But he's growing older. He's growing older than he should. Time's catching up with him. He's caught up in his environment as well as somebody who got caught up in the mill.

My stepfather doesn't express himself. The other day he put an American flag sticker on his car—which some people might think a big deal. When he put that flag on his window, it kind of classed him. There he is, a typical middle-class American. I joked around with him about it, telling him he's become a capitalist and things like this. But he doesn't take an open stand. He's a quiet person who enjoys the natural beauty of life. This can be reflected on these fishing trips he goes on up to Canada, Wisconsin, Minnesota. He enjoys the outdoors.

I thought, I gotta make a goal for myself in life. I have to try to reach something. In my junior year I got interested in photography as a hobby, which I eventually put quite a bit of money into. This is what I want, something I can enjoy doing, something I can express myself. And it won't be a drag of a nine-to-five job five days a week for the rest of my life.

He is about to enroll for a forty-week course at a photography school. "They can't guarantee a job, but she said they place every one of their students within two days after they leave."

It's something where I'll be able to take my camera ... I hope I get in advertising. I can develop the pictures myself. I can see the result of my work. I'll know if I'm good, if I'm doing bad. I enjoy taking pictures of scenes, of people, of creating moods. I want to create a better mood than the next guy, so they'll use my pictures. If I'm put in as a photographer for a certain company and there's no competition—no matter how the picture comes out, they'll have to use 'em if I am the only one—this is what I don't want. Because you're caught up in a rut. I have nothing to strive for, no one to beat. And if I can't beat no one, I don't want to play. (Laughs.)

Competition has always been an aspect in my life. I hate to lose and I love to win. Competition has been involved in me since grammar school. It gives a person a goal. It makes you push yourself to be better. Some people are satisfied with placing second or third in life. I don't. I want to be the best at it and I don't want to be overtaken.

I was short in football and many people thought I wouldn't make it. But I didn't let that take advantage against me. I worked hard. I put a lot of time into it. All year round we were constantly playing football. When I got on the varsity team, I weighed about 130. I felt it an advantage to be small. I turned what a lot of people thought was a handicap into an advantage. I worked on speed, on brain over brawn. I'm not gonna knock that big guy over, so I'm gonna work on how I'm gonna get around him. It was almost like a business. You had to know what you have to do, what your opponent can do, and try to beat him at his weakness. Knowing your enemy is half the battle.

You noticed the American flag on my lapel, which I wore every day for a year now. I got four stickers all over my car. I think America is the greatest country in the history of the world. One of the reasons? Free enterprise. You can go to your heart's content in life. You can set your goals anywhere you want to set 'em in America. This is all part of the American spirit, to compete, to be better, to be number one. To go as far as you can. If the next man can't go that far, don't stop and wait for him. Life will pass you up.

There are times when I shoot my mouth off and times when I shouldn't. I don't want to create hard feelings about me, especially at the store. I was careful what I'd say and who I'd say it to. The length of my hair, I kept it clean, I kept it combed, it didn't fall in my eyes. But it was covering my ears a bit. I was classified right away as a radical. Management didn't come right out and attack me, but I couldn't help feel something behind closed doors was going on about it.

And I was wearing a conservative suit, and I had the flag on my lapel. But I was still heckled about my hair. I didn't wear my hair to be a leftist, I'm a right-winger. But I wanted to see what it was like. I enjoyed it for a while, but last Friday I got a haircut. Now it's straight where I had it most of my life. I like it better. At the store I felt a warmer feeling.

Oh, yes, I can see myself in the future with a family, with a home, being called a typical middle-class American. I don't see myself going up to the upper class. I would like to stay just middle class. I feel you can get a better taste of life.

My—quote—dream girl—unquote—has long brunette hair, doesn't have to wear a lot of make-up or put a lot of spray on her hair, because she's going to be naturally pretty. She'll be natural in the way she's dressed. I want her to have a lot of personality, because when she's fifty and I'm fifty and we're going up the ladder (laughs), there's going to have to be a lot more than just looks. It's going to be someone I can communicate with, who needs my guidance and my leadership. And she's someone I can depend on. And she'll be a good mother. At first she'll probably be working. She can stay home for our first child and from that time on. I feel that her place is to take care of the house, to have my dinner ready when I come home. I hope to have three children, two boys and a girl. And I hope my daughter will grow up like her. My daughter will be protected by the two boys. She'll have security in them if I shouldn't be around. Plus I think it's great to have two boys in sports.

Competition I hope is one of the things I can communicate to 'em. It creates a feeling of pride in yourself. When I've been beaten in a sport, I respect the guy. It's important that when you're beaten you should be gracious about it. But I really don't think about losing. Winning's the only thing.

I would like a colonial house of some sort, possibly one that leans toward a Mediterranean style. I like a lot of bold things in my house. I'd like a nice recreation room in the basement, possibly a pool table. I hope my wife can play pool.

Eventually, I'd probably go into my own business. Once I get into something I'll strive to be the leader in it. I want to be in command. Like the football team. I strived to be a captain. My junior year I was. I enjoyed being looked up to, to be expected to come up with the answers. I don't want to be on the bottom. I want to go for the top. I want to win.

BUD FREEMAN

He is sixty-five years old, though his appearance and manner are of William Blake's "golden youth." He has been a tenor saxophone player for forty-seven years. Highly respected among his colleagues, he is a member of "The

World's Greatest Jazz Band." It is a cooperative venture, jointly owned by the musicians, established jazz men.

"I'm with the young people because they refuse to be brainwashed by the things you and I were brainwashed by. My father, although he worked hard all his life, was very easy with us. Dad was being brainwashed by the people in the neighborhood. They'd come in every day and say, "Why don't your boys go to work?" So he made the mistake of awakening my brother at seven thirty. I pretended to be asleep. Dad said, "You're going to get up, go out in the world and get jobs and amount to something." My brother said, "How dare you wake us up before the weekend?" (Laughs.) I don't recall ever having seen my father since. (Laughs.)

I get up about noon. I would only consider myself outside the norm because of the way other people live. They're constantly reminding me I'm abnormal. I could never bear to live the dull lives that most people live, locked up in offices. I live in absolute freedom. I do what I do because I want to do it. What's wrong with making a living doing something interesting?

I wouldn't work for anybody. I'm working for me. Oddly enough, jazz is a music that came out of the black man's oppression, yet it allows for great freedom of expression, perhaps more than any other art form. The jazz man is expressing freedom in every note he plays. We can only please the audience doing what *we* do. We have to please ourselves first.

I know a good musician who worked for Lawrence Welk. The man must be terribly in need of money. It's regimented music. It doesn't swing, it doesn't create, it doesn't tell the story of life. It's just the kind of music that people who don't care for music would buy.

I've had people say to me: "You don't do this for a living, for heaven's sake?" I was so shocked. I said, "What other way am I going to make a living? You want to send me a check?" (Laughs.) People can't understand that there are artists in the world as well as drones.

I only know that as a child I was of a rebellious nature. I saw life as it was planned for most of us. I didn't want any part of that dull life. I worked for Lord and Taylor once, nine to five. It was terribly dull. I lasted six weeks. I couldn't see myself being a nine-to-five man, saving my money, getting married, and having a big family—good God, what a way to live!

I knew when I was eight years old that I wasn't going to amount to anything in the business world. (Laughs.) I wanted my life to have something to do with adventure, something unknown, something involved with a free life, something to do with wonder and astonishment. I loved to play—the fact that I could express myself in improvisation, the *unplanned*.

I love to play now more than ever, because I know a little more about music. I'm interested in developing themes and playing something creative. Life now is not so difficult. We work six months a year. We live around the world. And we don't have to work in night clubs night after night after night.

Playing in night clubs, I used to think, When are we going to get out of here? Most audiences were drunk and you tended to become lazy. And if you were a drinker yourself, there went your music. This is why so many great talents have died or gotten out of it. They hated the music business. I was lucky—now I'm sixty-five—in having played forty-seven years.

If jazz musicians had been given the chance we in this band have today—to think about your work and not have to play all hours of the night, five or six sets—God! Or radio station work or commercial jingle work—the guys must loathe it. I don't think the jazz man has been given a fair chance to do what he really wants to do, to work under conditions where he's not treated like a slave, not subject to the music business, which we've loathed all our lives.

I've come to love my work. It's my way of life. Jazz is a luxurious kind of music. You don't play it all day long. You don't play it all night long. The best way to play it is in concerts. You're on for an hour or two and you give it everything you have, your best. And the audience is sober. And I'm not in a hurry to have the night finish. Playing night clubs, it was endless.

If you're a creative player, something must happen, and it will. Some sort of magic takes place, yet it isn't magic. Hundreds of times I've gone to work thinking, Oh my God, I hate to think of playing tonight. It's going to be awful. But something on a given night takes place and I'm excited before it's over. Does that make sense? If you have that kind of night, you're not aware of the time, because of this thing that hits you.

There's been a lot of untruths told about improvisation. Men just don't get up on the stage and improvise on things they're not familiar with. True improvisation comes out of hard work. When you're practicing at home, you work on a theme and you work out all the possibilities of that theme. Since it's in your head, it comes out when you play. You don't get out on the stage and just improvise, not knowing what the hell you're doing. It doesn't work out that way. Always just before I play a concert, I get the damn horn out and practice. Not scales, but look for creative things to play. I'll practice tonight when I get home, before I go to work. I can't wait to get at it.

I practice because I want to play better. I've never been terribly interested in technique, but I'm interested in facility. To feel comfortable, so when the idea shoots out of my head I can finger it, manipulate it. Something interesting happens. You'll hear a phrase and all of a sudden you're thrown into a whole new inspiration. It doesn't happen every night. But even if I have a terrible night and say, "Oh, I'm so tired, I'll go to sleep and I'll think of other things," the music'll come back. I wasn't too happy about going to work last night because I was tired. It was a drag. But today I feel good. Gonna go home and blow the horn now for a while.

Practicing is no chore to me. I love it. I really do love to play the horn alone. They call me the narcissistic tenor (laughs), because I practice before the mirror. Actually I've learned a great deal looking in the mirror and playing. The dream of all jazz artists is to have enough time to think about their work and play and to develop.

Was there a time when you were altogether bored with your work?

Absolutely. I quit playing for a year. I met a very rich woman. We went to South America to live. We had a house by the sea. I never realized how one could be so rich, so unhappy, and so bored. It frightened me. But I did need a year off. When I came back, I felt fresh.

The other time was when I had a band of my own. I had a name, so I no longer worked for big bands. I was expected to lead one of my own. But I can't handle other people. If I have a group and the pianist, let's say, doesn't like my playing, I can't play. I don't see how these band leaders do it. I can't stand any kind of responsibility other than the music itself. I have to work as a soloist. I can be the custodian only of my own being and thinking.

I had this band and the guys were late all the time. I didn't want to have to hassle with them. I didn't want to mistreat them, so I said, "Fellas, should we quit?" I wouldn't let them go and stay on myself. We were good friends. I'd say I'd quit if they didn't come on time. They started to come on time. But I wasn't a leader. I used to stand by in the band! A bit to the side. (Laughs.) Now we have a cooperative band. So I have a feeling I'm working for myself.

I don't know if I'll make it, but I hope I'll be playing much better five years from now. I oughta, because I know a little bit more of what I'm doing. It takes a lifetime to learn how to play an instrument. We have a lot of sensational young players come up—oh, you hear them for six months, and then they drop out. The kid of the moment, that's right. Real talent takes a long time to mature, to learn how to bring what character you have into sound, into your playing.* Not the instrument, but the style of music you're trying to create should be an extension of you. And this takes a whole life.

I want to play for the rest of my life. I don't see any sense in stopping. Were I to live another thirty years—that would make me ninety-five—why not try to play? I can just hear the critics: "Did you hear that wonderful note old man Freeman played last night?" (Laughs.) As Ben Webster† says, "I'm going to play this goddamned saxophone until they put it on top of me." It's become dearer to me after having done it for forty-seven years. It's a thing I need to do.

---

* Mme. Lotte Lehmann often spoke of art and age. She recalled a wistful conversation with Maestro Bruno Walter. In his eighties, he reflected on the richness and wisdom of the aged artist and of the long way the young virtuoso had to go—"but he's less tired." It is said that Arturo Toscanini, in his last years, often was thus reflective.

† The eminent tenor sax man whose highly creative years were with Duke Ellington.

KEN BROWN

He is twenty-six. He is the president of four corporations: American Motorcycle Mechanics School, Evel Knievel's Electrocycle Service Centers, Triple-A Motorcycle Leasing, and AMS Productions.

The first: The largest motorcycle mechanics' school in the country. "I started out before they had any. It's a 350-hour course, twelve weeks, six hours a day. It's three hours on the night shift, twenty-four weeks. Now we're having home study courses. We're doing new courses on the Wankel rotary engine. They're gonna go big in the next five years. Most of your cars are gonna have 'em. They don't pollute."

The second: A franchise—"service centers and accessory sales. The machine I designed for Sun Electric tests motorcycles and electronically spots the problem. I'm partners with Evel Knievel.* We're going nationwide. We expect to have them in every city. I've got fifteen salesmen around the country selling franchises. You walk in, get your motorcycle tuned up, and buy accessories. We sell 'em the initial package, we set 'em up, we have our own design for the buildings and everything. It's going to be like McDonald's or Kentucky Fried Chicken."

The third: Another franchise—"You can lease a motorcycle just like you can an automobile for a season, a month, a day. We're going nationwide here also."

The fourth: It's for shows where Knievel performs. "We have three salesmen selling program ads and booth space. This year we're doing ten shows. At show time you need about fifty people.

"In the next few years there's gonna be a lot of big things going on. It's just going to skyrocket. In the last year I had plenty of ups and downs. When you're down you've gotta keep climbin' six times as hard."

---

* The celebrated motorcycle stunt man. "He broke his back yesterday. Down in Atlanta—jumping. I was just on the phone with him, since he's part of our group insurance policy."

I'm enjoying what I'm doing. I'll make a good chunk of money in one thing, stick it back in the other thing, and just watch it grow. I'd get more out of it than hoarding it away somewhere. I'd say I'm better off than most twenty-six-year-old guys. (Laughs.)

Any one of these companies would probably be twice as big if I put all my time into it. But it wouldn't be a challenge any more. There are some new ideas I'm working on that are really something. I don't even know whether I should say anything . . .

I started working pretty young. When I was six I had my first paper route. At nine I worked in a bicycle repair shop. At the same time I was delivering chop suey for a Chinese restaurant. I worked as a stock boy in a grocery store for a year. This had no interest to me whatsoever. This was all after school and weekends. I always liked the feeling of being independent. I never asked my parents for financial help. Anything I wanted to buy, I always had the money. I didn't have them watching over me. They wouldn't have cared had they known.

I was lucky in school. Subjects everybody had trouble with—mathematics, algebra—they just came natural to me. I never did any studying. I was more interested in my work than in school. I liked drafting and machine shop. History and English bored me.

"I won a scholarship to Francis Parker.* My mother wanted me to go there. They said, 'Nobody will ever know you're on scholarship.' I don't think anybody there didn't know I was there that way. I never got invited to any of the parties. They just put up with you because you were there. Got in a lot of fights. Ended up paying for a window. After two years I quit and went to Lane Tech† where I really wanted to go."

I had my first full-time job as a tractor mechanic for International Harvester. They had an opening for an industrial designer. I studied that at IIT. I was to start at eighty-five hundred dollars a year, plus they were gonna pay for my education. I was supposed to start Monday at eight. They called me about six thirty in the morning and

* An upper-middle-class private elementary and high school.

† A public high school attended predominantly by lower-middle-class boys. (It is now coeducational.)

said they've got a guy with a college degree and ten years' experience. I said, "You need tractor mechanics, I'll take that job." I bullshitted my way into it. They gave me a test which was ridiculous. Instead of making eighty-five hundred as an industrial designer, I was making ten five to start as a tractor mechanic. (Laughs.)

I worked there for about a year. I was getting maybe a couple of hours' sleep. I was putting in about a twenty-hour day. I was just rundown completely. I was in the hospital for three months. Had a relapse, was back in for another month. This is when I did a lot of thinking. I decided to go into business for myself. I rented a place for forty-five dollars a month and I opened up a repair shop for motorcycles, lawn mowers, and bicycles. That was nine years ago. I was about seventeen.

This drive I had—maybe it went back to Francis Parker. Seeing those kids drive up in chauffeur-driven cars—what I thought were the finer things. I wanted to make something of myself. I felt if I worked hard while I was young, I could take it easier later on. If I'd come from a wealthy family, I probably never would have had this drive. The other kids were laying around at the beach and screwing around. Here I was already in business. I felt I really accomplished something.

My interest in motorcycles was for the money originally. I saw this was going to be a big field. Later, business becomes a game. Money is the kind of way you keep score. How else you gonna see yourself go up? If you're successful in business, it means you're making money. It gets to the point where you've done all the things you want to do. There's nothing else you want to buy any more. You get your thrill out of seeing the business grow. Just building it bigger and bigger . . .

When I started making money I just went crazy. I bought a limousine and had a chauffeur. I bought two Cadillacs and a Corvette. Bought a condominium in Skokie. I just bought a home out in Evanston. I'm building a ranch out in Arizona. Once you get something, it's not as important as it was. You need something else to keep going. I could never retire. It gets inside you. If you don't progress every day, you feel you've wasted it. That's a day you'll never get back.

You get enemies in the business, especially if you're successful. Ones that have grown up and started with you.

You want to be liked and you want to help people. I've found out you can't. It's not appreciated. They never thank you. If you're successful in business, you're around phonies all the time. There's always some guy slappin' you on the back, tryin' to get you to buy something from him or lend him money.

You remember old friends and good times. This relationship is gone. The fun you used to have. They're envious of what you have. They wonder why they didn't do it. When I opened the repair shop in Old Town I was paying my partner $250 a week. I gave him a car and helped him with his tuition in college. Someone offered him double what I paid. I said, "If you go, there's no comin' back." So he left. We grew up together, went to grammar school. I lived with him. There's no loyalty when it comes to money.

I'm younger than most of the guys who work for me, but I feel older. It's like a big family. I have the feeling they're not here for the money. They want to help me out. They respect me. They feel that what I'm doing is, in the end, gonna work out for them. I don't like an employee that comes in and it's a cut and dried deal: "I want so much a week," and walks out at five o'clock.

I usually get out of here at one o'clock in the morning. I go home and eat dinner at two. I do my best thinking at night. I can't fall asleep until seven in the morning. I turn the TV on. I don't even pay attention to it. They got the all-night movies. You actually feel like an idiot. I just sit there in the living room, making notes, trying to put down things for the next day to remember. I plan ahead for a month. Maybe I'll lay down in bed about four in the morning. If something comes in my head, I'll get up and start writing it. If I get three, four hours' sleep, I'm okay.

That's when I come up with my ideas. That's when I put this Electrocycle idea together. I sold Sun Electric on the idea of building them for me. Then I sold Evil Knievel on the idea of putting his name on it. He's on nationwide TV.

Knievel is a good example of doing something for fame and money. He takes all the beatings and breaks himself like he does because he feels it's that important to be famous and make money. When you really enjoy something, it doesn't seem like work. Everybody in the world could do something if they wanted to. I guess there's some people that don't want to do anything. If they could, they wouldn't be fighting with each other.

The world is full of people who don't have the guts or the balls to go out on their own. People want to be in business for themselves, but they don't want to take the chance. That's what separates me from the majority of people. If I've got an idea, I'll go ahead and put everything on the line.

A lot of young people are getting into business now. The shops and bars and places where young people go. Who knows better than a young person what's gonna attract young people? Companies are beginning to realize this.

The hardest problem I had was getting mechanics. If I hired an older guy, a good mechanic, I couldn't tell him what to do. He might have been doing it for twenty years, and he didn't want to hear from a kid like me. But if I took a young kid who knew nothing but had ambition, I could make a better man for me out of him. This is what the bigger companies are finding out.

What motivates a lot of young people who work here is they see somebody like me who made it. They think, Christ! What the hell's wrong with me? When the article came out about me in the paper,* Jesus! I had so many calls from young people, "This is great! I'm gonna get my ass going." I had a call from a sixteen-year-old kid. He felt he really wanted to do things. I was amazed at the number of young people who read it.

A guy I went to grammar school with—hadn't seen him since sixth grade—was out in the hall here. His brother has cancer. He was telling me how happy they both were to read something like this. It gave 'em a boost. They had known somebody that had made a success.

This hippie deal and flower child, I don't believe in giving anybody anything. I think everybody should work. The world problem that bothers me more than anything is the attitude of younger people. The opportunities they have, and no desire. I hate to see anybody that feels the world owes them a living. All this welfare. The largest percentage of them don't want to do anything.

I'm down at the office Saturdays too. Sundays, about

* The financial section of the *Chicago Daily News* had a full-page feature story on him.

half the time. The other half of the time maybe my wife and I will go horseback riding or visit a friend's house. Even when you're visiting with them, you can't get away from your work. They ask about it. It's a kind of a good feeling. There's not too many Sundays like that. I've been traveling more than ever with these franchises.

When I first started to get successful, people in the business tried to hurt me. One of my biggest kicks is getting beyond them. There's nothing they can do. I'm in a position where there's no competition. If somebody tries to do something to me, bum rap me, why hell, I can just open my franchise right next door to 'em.

When I was younger—I was applying for a Yamaha franchise or a Honda—these dealer reps would come in and ask for Ken Brown. I'd say "I'm Ken Brown." They'd say, "I want to talk to your father." I fought to get in Old Town. The chamber of commerce didn't want me there. They still had this black leather jacket image. They felt all these Hell's Angels would be coming down and wrecking. We opened up and had three hundred thousand people there on a weekend. You didn't even have to advertise. I had the place full. They saw money being made there. A young punk comes in and rents an alley for $125 a month and I made about $125,000 over the summer out of that alley—leasing bikes. That really killed 'em.

When you're young and in business, it's not an asset. The first time I walked into a bank they didn't want to deal with me. I used to be nervous. I'd look at the guy across the desk with a tie and suit and everything. You could see what he was thinking. You oughta see that guy now when I come in. (Laughs.) When I go into banks now, I feel I'm better than them. And they know it.

You've been noticing my Mickey Mouse watch? (Laughs.) I like something like this because nobody would expect me to be wearing this. No matter what I've done, it's always been they never expected it. When I rented the Amphitheatre for the first show, they turned me down. I rented the Colosseum and had a success. The next year they were happy to deal with me.

It bothers them that somebody new should come in and be so successful. It wasn't easy. When other people were going out and just having fun and riding motorcycles and getting drunk and partying, I was working. I gave up a lot.

I gave up my whole youth, really. That's something you never get back.

People say to me, "Gee! You work so damn hard, how can you ever enjoy it?" I'm enjoying it every day. I don't have to get away for a weekend to enjoy it. Eventually I'll move to Arizona and make that my headquarters. I'm young enough. I'll only be thirty-one in five years. I can still do these things—horseback riding, looking after animals. I like animals. But I'll never retire. I'll take it a little bit easier. I'll have to. I had an ulcer since I was eighteen.

(Indicates bottle of tablets on the table. It reads: "Mylanta. A palliative combination of aluminum, magnesium, hydroxide to relive gastric hyperacidity and heartburn.") I chew up a lot of Mylantas. It's for your stomach, to coat it. Like Maalox. I probably go through twenty tablets a day.

I guess people get different thrills out of business in different ways. There's a lot of satisfaction in showing up people who thought you'd never amount to anything. If I died tomorrow, I'd really feel I enjoyed myself. How would I like to be remembered? I don't know if I really care about being remembered. I just want to be known while I'm here. That's enough. I didn't like history, anyway.

KAY STEPKIN

We're in The Bread Shop. "We've taught all sorts of people how to make bread. The Clay People are across the street. They teach people ceramics. The Weaving Workshop is a block down. They give lessons in weaving and teach people how to make their own looms. Nearby is The Printing Workshop. They teach ... It's an incredible neighborhood. Within four blocks, there's every possible type person, every nationality."

There are posters in the window and stickers on the door: "Peace and Good Will Toward People"; "Children of the New Testament"; "Needed: Breadmakers, Hard Work, Low Pay"; "We have bread crumbs and scraps for your birds."

There are barrels of whole wheat flour. There are huge

cartons and tins of nuts, vanilla, honey, peanut butter. Varieties of herb tea are visible. On the counter are loaves—whole wheat, cinnamon raisin, oatmeal, rye, soy sunflower, corn meal. "People come up with suggestions we love to hear. People will say, 'Why don't you make this?' 'Why don't you make that?' We try it out. We average 200 to 250 loaves a day. We use any ingredient that's in its natural state. We don't use white flour."

Among her customers, as well as health food stores, are conventional groceries, including a huge supermarket. "The stores pick it up. We don't have a car. It's about half-wholesale and half-retail. The retail part is the most enjoyable, because we meet people and talk to 'em and they ask questions." *A matronly woman who has just bought a loaf pauses.* "I tried this soy sunflower bread about three weeks ago and it's really great. Gave it to two people as Christmas gifts."

There is an easy wandering in and out of customers and passersby, among whom are small boys, inhaling deeply, longingly, in comic style. It is late afternoon and a few of her colleagues are relaxing. She is twenty-nine years old.

I'm the director. It has no owner. Originally I owned it. We're a nonprofit corporation 'cause we give our leftover bread away, give it to anyone who would be hungry. Poor people buy, too, 'cause we accept food stamps. We sell bread at half-price to people over sixty-five. We never turn anybody away. A man came in a few minutes ago and we gave him a loaf of bread. We give bread lessons and talks. Sometimes school children come in here. We show 'em around and explain what we're doing.

Everything we do is completely open. We do the baking right out here. People in the neighborhood, waiting for the bus in the morning, come in and watch us make bread. We don't like to waste anything. That's real important. We use such good ingredients, we hate to see it go into a garbage can. And it may be burned and go into the air some way.

We have men and women, we all do the same kind of work. Everyone does everything. It's not as chaotic as it sounds. Right now there's eight of us. Different people take responsibility for different jobs. We just started selling tea last week. Tom's interested in herbs. He bought the tea.

We hire only neighborhood people. We will hire anyone who can do the work. There's been all ages. Once we had a twelve-year-old boy working here. A woman of forty used to work here. There isn't any machinery here. We do everything by hand. We get to know who each other is, rapping with each other. It's more valuable to hear your neighbor, what he has to say, than the noise of the machine. A lot of people are out of work. Machines are taking over. So we're having people work instead of machines.

The bread's exactly like you would make it at home. You can make it sloppy or very good. If you're into bread making, you know just when to start and when to stop kneading and how much flour to add. The machine just can't do as fine a job. I started doing things for myself when I realized our food supply is getting more and more poisoned. I didn't have anybody to show me. I just made the dumbest mistakes.

"It was about nine years ago. I would read books on it. But there was no one to talk to. I was doing different jobs. I was teaching. I was a waitress. I never did anything satisfying. About two years ago, I started realizing how bad things really are out here—on the planet. (Laughs.)

"I see us living in a completely schizophrenic society. We live in one place, work in another place, and play in a third. You have to talk differently depending on who you're talking to. You work in one place, get to know the people, you go home at night and you're lonely because you don't know anyone in your neighborhood. I see this as a means of bringing all that together. I like the idea of people living together and working together."

We start about five thirty in the morning and close about seven at night. We're open six days a week. Sundays we sell what's left over from Saturday and give bread lessons. We charge a dollar a lesson to anyone who wants to come. It about covers the cost of the ingredients. Each person makes three loaves of bread. We tell why this shop uses certain ingredients and not others. Just about everything is organic. We have a sign up saying what isn't.

We try people out. We take them as a substitute first. You can't tell by words how someone's gonna do. We ask people to come as a sub when someone is absent. Out of those we choose who we'll take. We watch 'em real close. We teach 'em: "This is the way your hands should move." "This is how you tell when your bread's done, if it feels this way." "Why don't you feel my bread?"

We try to discourage people from the start, 'cause it's hard having a high turnover. If someone applies for a job, I tell 'em all the bad points. Some of 'em think it's something new or groovy. I let 'em know quickly it's not that way at all. It's *work*. Each person's here for a different reason. Tom's interested in ecological things, Jo enjoys being here and she likes working a half-day . . .

I get here at six thirty. I stand at the table and make bread. I'll do that for maybe two hours. There might be a new person and I'll show him. . . At eight thirty or so I'll make breakfast and read the paper for half an hour. Maybe take a few phone calls. Then go back and weigh out loaves and shape 'em.

We each make seven dollars a day. At first we didn't make any salaries at all. After two weeks, we each took out five dollars. It sounds unscientific, but most of us could get by. Everyone was living with someone. We all get help from one another. We also buy the ingredients at the store. We get our food real cheap. We can each take a loaf a day out of the store. The store pays all our taxes.

Our prices are real reasonable. I went into a grocery store and saw what they were selling bread for. Machine-made whole wheat was selling at forty-five cents. So we made it at fifty cents a loaf. It would cost fifty cents to make that bread at home using the same ingredients. We priced it that way on purpose.

We have about eleven different kinds of bread. All the other loaves are sixty cents a pound. If we were doing real good, we'd lower the prices. It's been working out. Wholesale is a dime less. We put a reseale price on the bread 'cause some people were selling our bread for ridiculous prices likes eighty and ninety cents a loaf. Now they're only allowed to sell it for a nickle more than we sell it here. We check the stores. I always like to see the bread and how they display it.

We started out real strict. We'd sell only what we *make*. Otherwise, we were middlemen, profiting off somebody else's labor. But now we're selling ingredients too, because there's no other store around that has them available. We sell honey, oil, flour, nuts. We buy honey in sixty-pound tins, and we're able to sell real dark good honey for about twenty cents less than the big supermarkets.

Our customers have to bring their own bottles and bags. We don't have any bags around at all. We figure any penny we save here is passed on to the customers one way or the other. I don't see how we'll ever make a profit because of the nature of what we're doing. There's a limit to how many loaves of bread one person could make. As there's a demand for more bread, there have to be more people here. We never have any money left over. We had thirty-five hundred dollars in loans. We put twenty-five dollars a week away toward the loan. We've paid back a thousand dollars already.

But we're growing in other ways. We're looking for ways to get our product to people cheaper without resorting to machinery. One way is to get the ingredients cheaper—without sacrificing quality. Right now, there's only one distributor of organically grown grain in bulk in the entire Midwest. He gets all his grain from Texas. There's an exorbitant shipping charge passed on to us. Furthermore, we don't know that these grains are *really* organically grown. So we've purchased a mill. It's going to make big changes here.

We'll grind our own grain. We'll be able to buy organically grown grain right here in the Midwest. Buying right from the farm, it's going to be maybe a third or fourth of the price. We'll be able to go to the farm and see for ourselves. If there's not one weed growing between these rows of wheat, you know they use chemicals. Even our customers will go to these farms and see for themselves.

We use about a thousand pounds of wheat a week. We can say to the farmers, "Stop using this chemical and we'll buy your whole field." His neighboring farmers will see that he can sell this for a profit and maybe they'll catch on too. People can do anything. (Laughs.) It's such a good feeling. Somebody'll come in and say, "Your bread is delicious." It's like your making dinner in your own house and giving it to someone. People come in like guests. They have an idea and we might take their advice. One man, who had been to a baking school, worked here three months. He enjoyed it a lot. At first he was horrified by what we were doing. We don't measure flour and he couldn't believe it. Our bread rises at different rates every day, depending on the temperature. We don't have automatic rising things. He taught us a lot. He taught us how to shape loaves better, in a more efficient manner.

We taught him a lot too. He found out you don't have to measure the whole wheat flour. You can tell by the feel of it when the bread is done and you have enough flour. It also gives you more satisfaction than just doing it machinelike. You're putting more of yourself into it somehow.

We try to have a compromise between doing things efficiently and doing things in a human way. Our bread has to taste the same way every day, but you don't have to be machines. On a good day it's beautiful to be here. We have a good time and work hard and we're laughing. It's a good day if we don't make too many mistakes and have a good time. I think a person can work as hard as he's capable, not only for others but for his own satisfaction.

In the beginning our turnover was huge. It's slowing down now. I noticed as I was doing this tax thing at the end of the year, we've had only eleven people here the last three months, which is beautiful. That means only three people have left. In our first three months we had eighteen people. (Laughs.) The work was unbearably hard at the beginning. As we've learned more, our work has gotten easier. So there's a big feeling of accomplishment.

I get the same money as the others. I don't think that's the important issue. The decisions have been mainly mine, but this is getting to be less and less. Originally all the ideas were mine. But I'd taken them from other people. Now we have meetings, whenever anyone thinks we need one. Several times people have disagreed with me, and we did it the way the majority felt.

I believe people will survive if we depend on ourselves and each other. If we're working with our hands instead of with machines, we're dealing with concrete things, personal, rather than abstract things, impersonal. Unless we do something like this, I don't see this world lasting. So I really have no future to save money for. (Laughs.) I don't know what this bread shop is gonna mean in a year or two or so. I'd say times are worse for this planet than they've ever been, so each tries to be the best he can, she can. I am doing exactly what I want to do.

Work is an essential part of being alive. Your work is your identity. It tells you who you are. It's gotten so abstract. People don't work for the sake of working. They're working for a car, a new house, or a vacation. It's not the work itself that's important to them. There's such a joy in doing work well.

When people ask what you do, what do you say?

I make bread. (Laughs.)

POSTSCRIPT: *A drunk, who had obviously had a hard day's night, enters. There is a soft discussion. She hands him a loaf. He leaves.* "He asked me for a quarter. I gave him one this morning. Now he said he's still hungry. So I offered him bread. He said, 'If you don't give the quarter, I'm not gonna take the bread.' So I said, 'Okay, don't.' He took the bread."

CATHLEEN MORAN

She is nineteen years old.

What is your work?

Makin' beds and bed pans and rotten stuff like that.

What are you called?

Nurse's aide, dumb aide.

Presently she is working at a middle-class hospital. It's her third. Her previous jobs were lower-middle-class and upper-middle-class institutions. She has been at it since she was fifteen.

I really don't know if I mind the work as much as you always have to work with people, and that drives me nuts. I don't mind emptying the bed pan, what's in it, blood, none of that bothers me at all. Dealing with people is what I don't like. It just makes everything else blah.

How often do you work?

As least as possible. Two days on a weekend, just to get me through school, like money for books and stuff. We start to work at seven, but I get up as late as possible, get everything on and run out the door. I ride my bike to work. I usually have someone punch me in, 'cause I'm never on time. You're gonna think I'm nuts, but I do my work well. If I come a quarter after seven, they're surprised. They don't mind, because I get my work done before the allotted time. I won't have anybody saying I did something lousy. I don't know why.

We get on the floor and you have to take thermometers and temperatures or you have to weigh people or pass water, and you go in the rooms, and they yell when you get 'em up so early in the morning. Then they don't want to get out of bed when you weigh 'em. They complain, "How come the water wasn't passed earlier?" "We couldn't sleep all night with the noise." Or else you'll walk in the room and you'll say, "Hello," and they'll say, "Good morning, how are you?" So I'll say "Fine," and some of 'em will say, "Well, gee, you're the one that's s'posed to be asking me that." They don't even give you a chance."

I really wonder why I do have such a rotten attitude towards people. I could care less about 'em. I'll do my work, like, you know, good, I'll give 'em the best care, but I couldn't care less about 'em. As far as meeting their emotional needs, forget it. That's why (a little laugh) I don't think I should go into nursing.

I work on a floor that's geriatric. Old people and psychiatric, so there's never anyone in their right minds. They're out of it or they're confused. After you pass out trays, and there's rarely a tray that has everything on it, they start hollering, "I didn't get two sugars," and then you spend half the time running to all the rooms gettin' all their stuff. Then you have to feed all of them, and half the patients are out of it and they spit stuff at you and they throw their food. They throw their dishes on the wall and floor. And I hate feeding patients that are always coughing. They cough right at ya. (Laughs.) That I don't mind, cleaning stuff up. It's just that you're s'posed to calm 'em down and talk to 'em, forget it. I won't be bothered.

I used to work in a hospital, it was more of a cancer ward. Young women, men. I got along great with the men, they could care less. But I always hated working with the women. They drive you nuts. I really can't sympathize with 'em unless sometimes, rarely, I think, What if I was in their place? Like the younger girls, they want you to feel sorry for them. I just can't feel that. Some of 'em are okay, but they're always crying. That doesn't depress me. I have no feelings at all. A lot of nurses come in and they sit with the patients and they talk with 'em. Forget it.

A patient will be in pain and they'll be crying. They put the nurse's light on and want to talk and stuff. I really don't care. It's rotten, you know? Lots of times I try to think as to why I have this attitude. I really think it was from my background in boarding school.

"Living in a dorm with kids all the time, you didn't have to be accepted, but you always had to be on top—or else you'd be pushed around and all that. At Maryville I never really was close with anybody. Couldn't afford to be or else you got hurt. So I just turned everybody off. I just kept to myself. I was there from when I was just three until I was sixteen.

"There were kids whose parents had money, but they didn't want 'em for some reason. When we first went out to high school, everybody started calling us orphans. I couldn't understand that, because they had money, they had clothes, they had parents to come to see 'em. But there were a few who didn't have parents.

"My mother, she makes about six thousand dollars a year. She really couldn't afford to take care of me at home. When I was born my dad took off. He was an alcoholic. My mother was also an alcoholic. I was raised in Maryville from loneliness and stuff. My mother always came to see me, no matter what the weather was.

"In the eighth grade you had to get stupid to survive, no kiddin'. I wouldn't let anybody push me around. I have people tell me I have a chip on my shoulder or I'm sensitive if someone barks at me. I could see how girls were pushed around, socked and stuff. But I was good in sports, I came to be the best swimmer, basketball, and I was looked up to. So I could afford to be on my own and left alone. They were allowing us to go out and get jobs. When you get out, you're not worth nothing."

She worked for several months at a hospital "which was really a dump. It was mostly black and low-income whites, though there were a number of patients from middle-income high rises nearby. I really couldn't understand it, af-

ter Holy Family. I thought that was a typical hospital—it was spotless. When I saw this one, it was filthy, with bugs on the food cart, I thought, 'Oh God.' I only stayed there for two months.

"I used to have to be forced to get out of bed in the morning and go there. I'd rarely work a weekend when I was supposed to. (Laughs.) Which isn't me. That's why I said I gotta get outa here, because it was getting to me, and that's goofy. They never had any sheets. They never had anything the patient needs. Like they were paying so much money for a room. I'm not lying, don't think I'm nuts. There wasn't a morning when we had linen before ten, eleven o'clock. The patients, they're awakened at seven. We never had adequate help and the other aides, they didn't really fulfill the patient's needs. I was about the only white aide in the hospital and they were wondering what I was doing there."

I have a hard time dealing with black patients, because they're really sensitive. You're gonna think I'm rotten, but when I go into a room I don't have a great attitude. I'm not blah, but if I don't feel like talking, I don't talk. I'll give 'em a bath, but I'm not making up a bunch of conversation just to make them feel good.

It happened just last week. I was in a room with a black patient and she had her hair set in rollers, and she looked like about twenty something. I couldn't see her hair, whether it was graying. She happened to be forty-one. I asked her what she was in for and she said arthritis. I said, "God, you look like about twenty-something." She felt great. She said, "Gee, thanks." I said, "I really can't tell a black's age, they always seem so much younger." If you call 'em colored they have a fit. If you call 'em black, they'll have a fit. So you don't call 'em. So she got so upset. "Why are blacks so different? You mean you can't tell a white person's age?" They just don't show it, not as much, in my opinion. Oh, she started yellin'. I was patient with her.

I think blacks demand more attention—like little piddley stuff she could reach for, she wanted me to get her. I mean, they're going to take advantage of being waited on like whites. Because she's black, she'll get white service, too.

I'm not prejudiced really, but they all put their money

under their pillows, while the whites put it in a drawer. I was making her bed, so I turned her on the side and I put her purse on the window. I walked out of her room and I heard her saying, "That white bitch stole my purse!" She was really yelling. I looked on the window and it was right in front of her. And then she said, "Well, stay here, you probably stole something out of it anyway." I was going to walk out of the room and she said, "Hey, white girl, can you come back and fix the blankets up a little neater?" They were really perfect. By that time, you felt like kickin' her right in the mouth. Rarely do I put up with it. I just say, "Do you want your bed made? Get somebody else."

Like I was going to give a black person a bath and I was too lazy to walk and get some soap way down in the utility room, so I got the soap that was in the bathroom. So she said to me, "What do you think I am, a dog? That I'm going to use that soap that white hands have washed their hands on." So I told her it was a fairly new bar and I said, "What does color got to do with a bar of soap?" She went on and on, so I told her I wasn't going to give her a bath, because sometimes you can't do anything right for 'em.

White patients are just as bad. But the blacks always bring up their color. The whites are just a pain in the neck too. Black are more offensive, but whites nag you more about the stuff they don't get.

When I first started at Holy Family, I really couldn't stand it, 'cause I really didn't want the job. I was just doing it to get out of Maryville for a couple of hours. When I got on the floor, I didn't know beans. I was dumb. You may think I'm nuts, but I really feel myself capable in whatever I do. So I learned what was up fast, and went out of my way to do extra stuff, to take care of blood pressures and bandages and stuff, so I'd be left alone so I could do my work. I wouldn't have anybody on my back checking me. If they wanted something done, they could get it done, you know? I was real good friends with the nurses and aides, I liked it.

You always get a nurse, you wonder what she's doing there. They're blah, bad news, crabby, they try to push you around—which is how I'm afraid I'm going to turn out. Most nurses, they sit at the desk. They chart and take care of the medications. As far as patient contact, they don't get any at all. It's the aides, you know? The nurses don't do anything except give a shot. The head nurse is at the desk constantly, with the doctor's orders, so the aides get all the contact. That's why I figure if I'm going into nursing, I won't have any contact with the patients anyway.

I'd go nuts. I'm just doing it because it's a good job and if times ever become like the Depression, they always need nurses. I'd still like to get a master's, go into law school or something. Everybody thinks I'm nuts: "What are you going to nursing school for if you hate it?" Because I can do my work well and I can put up with it, even if it drives me nuts.

You either get patients who don't want a bath at all and then report you for not giving them a bath, or patients who fake near bath time that they have chest pains so you'll give them a bath, and the next minute you see them walking around the hall and they're visiting.

With orthopedics, with the geriatric, it's really discouraging. The nursing homes have given them terrible care and they have sores you wouldn't believe—bones, tendons, everything showing. I change the dressings and soak them and try to position them where they're not on a sore. But anywhere you put them they're on a sore. You feel like they're aching.

Lots of times they get bladder infections. You'll just make a bed and they'll urinate right on the clean side. You'll have to, okay, man, start again. You turn them over on the clean side and then they'll have a BM. Sometimes this goes on four or five times. You have to make a patient's bed at least three or four times a day to do good work. It takes about four hours to get all the patients really clean. By the time you're done, you feel so good. But a nurse comes up and says, "So-and-so needs their bed changed, they crapped all over." It really gets discouraging. Each time you go in that room you want to kill them.

I get done at three-thirty. But lots of times it's three-thirty and someone falls out of bed or pulls out their IVs or you know ... Well, I'll stay. But a lot of kids cut out at even a quarter to three. I usually punch them out, 'cause they're good about it in the morning.

She straightens out a cushion behind me. "Uh ... do you want to lean back, so you can get more comfortable?" "You're talking like a nurse's aide interested *in the patient." "I forgot what we were talking about."*

If you ever hear someone crying out in pain ... ?

I could care less. If the nurse gets there right away or next year, I don't care. That's a rotten attitude, it really is. God, I'd go nuts if I was in the hospital and someone treated me that way. What gets me so mad is: if I'm ever in the hospital, I'd be a typical patient. I'll probably be worse than all of them. And yet I can't stand them.

But I don't know, you get to like some of them. There was this old man, he died recently. He came in terrible from nursing homes and we got him really good care. He was bad news. Like he'd never eat because he thought he'd have to pay for it and he didn't have the money. He was just stubborn. He'd do everything to get you. But you knew he was confused and senile. He went back to the nursing home and I saw him and he was all shriveled up, and you wouldn't believe the sores on his body. I was so mad. I was going to write a note to the nursing home and really do something about it.

I think what am I going to do when I get about seventy and depend on somebody. And what am I going to do if I'm laying in bed—a lot of times they aren't conscious— you wonder, God, what am I going to do? I say, hey, when I reach seventy, here I go—I'm committing suicide. But I'm too chicken to commit suicide, no matter what treatment I get.

I'm not the same as if they were conscious and I really couldn't get away with it. I don't treat a patient as well as if they were with it. We had an elderly patient, she was eighty—she claimed she had a Ph.D.—and she was deaf. Aw, she was terrible, taking everything and throwing it at the wall, hitting me in the head with her spoon, as I was feeding her. I wasn't as nice as I should have been. I was kinda having fun, which was pretty terrible. I knew I had to feed her and she'd spit it out. So I had fun. She was getting so mad I was getting a kick out of putting the food in her mouth. I remember thinking that night, God, that was pretty rotten. I never hit a patient, even though I got slugged a couple of times. But I could have been more gentle with her. Oh, I was terrible. The nurses see me as something different, as somebody really good with patients, when in fact I'm not. I put up a front. But they wouldn't believe. Patients are always reporting me for my attitude, but the nurses don't see that side of me.

I do good work. A couple of times when I've been reported, it's not for the care I've given, it's what I say to them. And that's not really nice. You're supposed to be sympathetic. My attitude, it's rotten. I stop and wonder why I don't really care about people. I want to be accepted and them to think I'm okay, you know? It's funny. Yet I don't give anyone else the time of the day.

"I think it's something about Maryville. There was this rigid discipline. We had this one nun, but oh, I couldn't stand her. If you cried, you were really bad news. She literally made everybody cry. She was always yelling and never paid attention to who she was hitting. I remember walking out the door with this girl and hearing her tell this nun to go to hell. The nun called me back and said, "What'd she say?" Oh, I'm not gonna tell her. So she made me work for her from eight thirty in the morning until ten o'clock at night. I had to wash all the stairs, scrub 'em. I was done about four o'clock, I did it pretty fast. I had a system of sweeping. I thought I showed her, hmm, only four o'clock and I'm through. She made me do it all over again.

"She had to teach, take care of our dorm, keep the library, and be dean of our high school. You're going to think this is strange, she was so tough, so brutal, I sort of admired her because she was good at her many jobs."

Has she been your model . . . ?

"I know! Don't mention! (Laughs.) She had me when I was three. I could never get rid of her. Every time I moved up, she was there. Where we ate and where our dorms was was quite a distance. When we were not even five years old, we had to go from where we slept to where we ate in single file and freezing weather and not say a word. Not touch the snow. You couldn't drop your mitten. I remember a night where I was feeling around in the snow, so she punished everybody for it. She kept you in

*line. If somebody got out of line, she punished everybody.
She had this big paddle and she had a strap in the other
hand and, boy, that was bad news. She's spank kids and
hit 'em and they'd go to bed and everybody was crying.
(Giggles.)*

*"Someone dared me get out of line and go sneak to my
bed. I was the one why everybody was getting punished. I
faked I was asleep, so she said, 'Cathleen Moran, get over
here!' And boy, do I remember! She beat me and I had to
kneel and say the rosary a couple of hours. So everybody
had this fear of her, always punching. She used to say she
had these five brothers and every time you got out of line,
you got punched. Her fist—her knuckles, they're each her
brother. Oh, she was a terror.*

*"As I got into high school I didn't see her as much. I'd
be studying late and she'd come up. She'd be depressed. I
never noticed that side of her. She started telling me
things—how she'd hit someone and didn't want to. She
was really a sensitive person. She really cared. And
that's—I remember understanding her more, but not liking
her any more. I thought she was weak and I couldn't understand it."*

Before, even though you feared her and she beat you . . . ?

*"She was great. She was good in everything she does. It
gave me the creeps to listen to her now. It's like weak patients complaining and stuff like that. That's how she was.
I can't put up with that and she wouldn't put up with that
with me. I know I'm just as weak as everybody else and I
don't like that. Some of the nurses are nice and care about
patients, and I don't really want to be bothered."*

I don't know any nurse's aide who likes it. You say,
"Boy, isn't that rewarding that you're doing something for
humanity?" I say, "Don't give me that, it's a bunch of boloney." I feel nothin'. I like it because I can watch the ball
games in the afternoon.

That's why if I'm a nurse, I'd go into administrative
work and I'd work in surgery. The only thing you have to
deal with in surgery is who you work with. You don't
have to deal with the patient—like sympathize with them
and say, "Gee, we couldn't get all the cancer out," and

stuff like that. I like working in ICU* because they're all half-dead, and you can give a patient good care and not have to deal with them. I'd enjoy that. It's terrible.

You're always saying it's terrible.

You feel kinda rotten when you see somebody else dealing with them ...

Your conscience bothers you?

Um ... rarely. After I leave the hospital I forget all about it. What gets me the most is that if I was in the hospital, I'd be a pain in the neck. I know I'm very weak and that's why I don't get involved with patients, because I'm just like them. A lot of nurses say, "God, it's great that you're not able to get involved and do your work well. It's good that you're not sympathetic, that you could care less."

There are a lot of good nurses who do feel something towards the patient. When someone dies they feel kinda: "Oh, so-and-so died." So I say, "I'll take them to the morgue." I'll get 'em wrapped up, because it doesn't bother me. Usually when they die they crack all over and you have to get them cleaned up and tie their hands up and their feet and put a white sheet over their head, put them on a cart and take them to the morgue.

That really gets me, though—the morgue. It's down in the basement, isolated from everything. It's a long hall. They got little dark lights and it's a funny sound from the boiler room—mmmmmm (humming). That sometimes gets me. It doesn't make me afraid of death, though I am. It doesn't give me the creeps. You open the freezer and see all the dead bodies and everything seems meaningless. Couple years and I'll be there and someone's gonna take me down ...

Couple years ... ?

Well, you never know. God, when it's my turn ... Usually orderlies do it, because it's tough getting them into this little box. When I go down, rarely do I think I'm put-

* Intensive Care Unit.

ting a human being, someone with a life, into this freezer. They have jars of eyes and stuff and I find it interesting, and everybody's screaming and running out. For kicks, someone locked the door on me. But that doesn't bother me, because I don't get involved. There's no fear if you're never involved in something. I go in and look at the autopsies and stuff. Everybody's saying, "Oh, God, I think if I was laying on that table, what if I——." Then, boy, I got problems, because I start to think and it bugs me. I'm a very sensitive person, and if I start to think of myself as a patient, forget it. I don't want no part of it.

Do you ever get the feeling you're like a machine?

I never thought of myself in terms of a machine—though that's what I am. I don't have no feelings. I do, but somehow I don't have them any more. I can't explain. It's kinda goofy. My brother just went into the service. I got along well with him. He was really good to me. He filled out forms for me. My mother said, "Aren't you gonna miss him?" Well, I'll miss him 'cause I'll have to fill out all the forms myself. And because he was a good companion. But I never let myself think about a real feeling for him.

If I daydream about him or anything, I find it a sign of weakness. Sometimes I think of the good times I had at Maryville. Sometimes I can't even remember making a bed. I'll know I've done something, but I can't really think of when I done it.

When I'm through at three-thirty, I'm usually watching the ball game. And then I'll ride my bike for hours, along the lake, or anyplace that you haven't got a million people in the way. I'll read for a couple of hours, then I'll ride back. I do a lot of reading. I like philosophy. It's sort of like a struggle, what I'm going through. I love Jean-Paul Sartre. I read all his books. I try to find out about myself and relate it to the world around me. I know I can't, because I don't relate. I always get a negative attitude about myself. But I do feel quite capable of anything I do. I was going to go into physical education. But she said, "That's for dummies."

Who said?

The nun. But that's dealing with people, too. You know

what? I had no patience for someone who didn't get it like this (snaps fingers), because I got it. That's why I knew I couldn't be a teacher. No matter what I'd do, I'd have the same attitude. And I'm trying to get rid of the attitude.

I had to coach a team a couple of months ago. To me, when you're going to do something, it's not for fun. Nothing's ever for fun. They wanted to have a good time and play. I said, "Have a good time and play when you're practicing on your own, but when you're in a tournament, it's not for fun. You're working." You have to strive and be the best. Number one. But I don't care if you lost, if you played a good game. If they have a rotten attitude and won, I tell 'em they've lost.

Nurses tell me to go into sports because it's something I enjoy. But it's the same thing no matter what I do. I'd be detached. I've won trophies. I would walk up there and get the trophy and it was no big thing. Everybody's saying, "Boy, you act like you're mad about getting it." I can't stand when someone shows emotion, if someone's excited. If I'm excited about something, I'll keep it to myself, I repress it.

One night, Christmas Eve, I was working and a patient had a colostomy and couldn't accept surgery. He's fighting off the drugs. He's such a strong guy. We heard a loud crash and this guy had taken out his IVs, thrown it against the wall, taken the TV, thrown that against the wall, threw his tables outside the window. It was all a mess. And he had been tied down, leather restraints. Everybody was panicking. They called the police, and all the patients were crying. I thought I could deal with him and I wasn't afraid of what he was up to. But I couldn't deal with the patients crying. The nurse told me to quiet them down. I said, "I can't be bothered." Everybody was nervous and I just wasn't.

He wasn't weak, he was fighting. He doesn't know that he's got strength then. I didn't care that he was having problems. It didn't bother me. It was a difficult task to get him settled and to straighten him out. And that I enjoyed. Because he wasn't laying in bed, he was fighting.

I love to work with 99s, emergencies, when patients are kicking the bucket and they're trying to save 'em. You don't have to deal with the patient, you deal with the work. You're trying to save his life. Though I don't think of it as a life, I think of it as a job.

Do you care whether he lives or dies?

No, I really don't. It's not that I won't give him my care. My attitude doesn't affect my work. If someone's almost dead, I'll spend hours putting the tube through their nose, suctioning out the stuff, so they'll live. But I don't care. But yet I know that's not right. I'm just trying to figure it out . . .

CRADLE TO THE GRAVE

RUTH LINDSTROM

She is nearing eighty. She came to America from Sweden in 1913 and immediately was engaged in housework at ten dollars a month. In 1918 she became a practical nurse. "I took training for baby care. How to give shots, take temperatures . . . I used to pick them up at the hospital and stay with them a week, two weeks, whatever they'd want. Two months, that's average. I've stayed with one child for four years. Wages at times were seven dollars a week."

As she recollects, past and present intertwine.

A baby nurse is one that changes diapers and loves 'em dearly. Get up at all hours of the night to give 'em the bottle and change their pants. If the baby coughs or cries, you have to find out the need. I had my own room usually, but I slept in the same room with the baby. I would take full charge. It was twenty-four hours. I used to have one day a week off and I'd go home and see my own two little ones. It's been so long I've almost forgotten what it was.

I learned how to cope with things. I have never had to look for a job, because one customer recommends me to the other one. I have taken care of a lot of children in my day. I have pictures of four hundred children.

In the morning, six o'clock, they get their first bottle. You put them back in bed again. About eight, you pick 'im up, change his diaper, and give him his bath. Then he has another bottle. You put 'im back in bed again. He sleeps until ten, eleven, twelve. You do the same thing again. That's just a routine. Sometimes it's eleven o'clock at night before you settle down. In the afternoon, you sometimes take 'em out in the buggy if the weather's permissible, so they can get some fresh air.

I usually do the family washing, the children's washing and their bottles, and get all the formulas ready. The mother might be resting or she might have other children she looks after or she might go out shopping. Sometimes I take a nap when the kids take a nap.

I worked for very wealthy families and for very poor families. I sometimes worked for nothing because they were so poor ... I felt sorry for them. I slept on an army cot and fell out every time I turned around. (Laughs.) I once worked six weeks without pay. These people lost everything in the Depression, and they needed me. I didn't get cash, but I got some lovely paintings. I worked for them sixteen years.

When the mother comes home from the hospital she's tired and nervous, high strung. She needs someone to rely on. Today a baby nurse gets twenty-five, thirty dollars a day. If they couldn't afford it, I'd go for less. I worked for very, very high-grade rich people, too. Sometimes they're more tight than middle-class. (Laughs.)

Most of the time I go to the hospital and pick 'em up—just born, about a week or ten days old. It's always nice to see them grow up and get nice and round and fat and chubby and smiling at you. I've seen 'em learn how to walk and talk and help themself, and they run away from you when you try to catch 'em. (Laughs.)

In one place, the baby was nine months old. They went on a trip for two weeks. When she came back, the baby wouldn't go near her. He cried and he clung to me and he puts his arms around my neck when she talked to him. I said to her, "Don't feel bad about it." She said, "I'm happy because I know he had good loving." He's nineteen now.

Another boy, when he came home, all the blood was drained out of him, he had leukemia and was very sick. I stayed up nineteen hours. I walked the room with him. He cried and I cried and she cried, too. But he grew up to be a very nice boy. They moved to California. One year I was there and he was seven. When he saw me, he put his arms around me. It's so rewarding to find that. He's forty-seven now. One family, I took care of her children and her grandchildren. The children of the very ones I baby nursed.

Sometimes it's really hard to leave 'em, I tell you. I took care of two little girls, their mother passed away. Their father was all alone. The little girl was one year old and the older one was four. I stayed with them for two years. That was my hardest job to leave. That little girl, she stood there by the door and she pulled my skirt and she said, "Mommy, don't leave me." Oh, how that affects you! I have letters from 'em yet. Oh yes, you get very attached. They cry and they reach out their hands to you. You want to stay. That's the worst, to leave them. That's really hard.

You've got to be careful how to treat them when they're little. It's a wonderful profession. It's a responsible profession. I never worked in a place where they looked down on me, even people that was of means and had help. Sometimes they'd call me into the living room, "Sit down, let's talk." When I first came to this country, being a maid was a low caliber person. I never felt that way. I felt if you could be useful and do an honest job, that was not a disgrace.

"I was a ladies' maid before. For Mrs. Rockefeller McCormick. When they have company, you take their wraps and you see that they have powder in the powder room. If they have a run in their stockings, you see that it gets mended. Then you take them into the room where the hostess is to introduce her.

"You clean silver. You change beds, even if nobody's sleeping in the room. I arranged all the flowers. We had fresh flowers every day on the table. You do a lot of things. We had Mrs. Rockefeller out there once. She had lunch. Of course, we were all on our toes. There were thirteen servants there. That's something of the past. Nobody appreciated my work there."

Babies are rewarding. No matter what, they cry all night, I like 'em. I go baby-sitting for those that need me, two-, three-, five-year-olds. I even baby-sat last week.

I'm never gonna retire. What for? As long as I can be useful and needed someplace, I'll work. Even if I can't scrub floors, I'll do some other things. When that day comes when I can't work, I'll be a lost soul.

ROSE HOFFMAN

I'm a teacher. It's a profession I loved and still love. It's been my ambition since I was eight years old. I have been teaching since 1937. Dedication was the thing in my day. I adored teaching. I used to think that teachers had golden toilets. (Laughs.) They didn't do anything we common people did.

She teaches third grade at a school in a changing neighborhood. It is her second school in thirty-three years. She has been at this one for twenty years. "I have a self-contained group. You keep them all day."

Oh, I have seen a great change since January 6, 1937. (Laughs.) It was the Depression, and there was something so wonderful about these dedicated people. The teachers, the children, we were all in the same position. We worked our way out of it, worked hard. I was called a Jewish Polack. (Laughs.) My husband tells me I wash floors on my knees like a Polack. (Laughs.) I was assigned to a fourth grade class. The students were Polish primarily. We had two colored families, but they were sweet. We had a smattering of ethnic groups in those times—people who worked themselves out of the Depression by hard work.

I was the teacher and they were my students. They weren't my equal. I loved them. There isn't one child that had me that can't say they didn't respect me. But I wasn't on an intimate basis. I don't want to know what's happened in the family, if there's a divorce, a broken home. I don't look at the record and find out how many divorces in the family. I'm not a doctor. I don't believe you should study the family's background. I'm not interested in the gory details. I don't care if their father had twenty wives, if their mother is sleeping around. It's none of my business.

A little girl in my class tells me, "My mom's getting married. She's marrying a hippie. I don't like him." I don't want to hear it. It is not my nature to pry. Even a child deserves a certain type of privacy in their personal life. I don't see where that has anything to do with what a child studies. I came from a broken home. My mother died, I was eight years old. Isn't that a broken home? I did all right.

I have eight-year-olds. Thirty-one in the class and there's about twenty-three Spanish. I have maybe two Appalachians. The twenty-three Puerto Ricans are getting some type of help. The two little Appalachians, they never have the special attention these other children get. Their names aren't Spanish. My heart breaks for them.

They have these Spanish workers that are supposed to help the Puerto Rican children in their TESL program.* I'm shocked that English is the second language. When my parents came over I didn't learn Jewish as a first language at the taxpayers' expense. The Polish didn't learn Polish as a first language. But now they've got these Spanish-speaking children learning that at our expense. To me, this is a sin. As long as they're in this country, English should be the first language. This is my pet peeve. One of these teachers had this thick Spanish accent. So they picked up this accent too. He pronounces dog "dock." That's horrid.

The language! I could never use some of the words I hear. Up to five years ago I could never spell a four-letter word. Now I can say them without any embarrassment. The kids come right out and say it: "Teacher, he said a bad word." I said, "What's the word?" He said "Jagoff." I said, that's not a bad word. And they all started to laugh. I said, "Jagoff means get out of here." They laughed. I came home and asked my husband, "What's jagoff?" So he explained the gory details to me. I didn't know it before. These children know everything. It's shocking to me because I think that anyone that uses that language doesn't know any better. They don't have command of any language. (Sighs.) But maybe I'm wrong, because brilliant people use it nowadays, too. I must be square.

There's a saying: Spanish people don't look you straight in the eye because of their religious background. It isn't respectful. I don't believe that. These children, they look you straight in the eye when they use those words. I have never learned how to use these four-letter words until I came into contact with them. I never could even swear. Now I'm brazen. I had a fight with my husband one day. You know what I said to him? "Fuck you." (Laughs.)

* Teaching English as a Second Language.

And I never talked that way. (Laughs.) I hear it all the time from the students. They use it the way we use "eat" and "talk." They don't say "pennies," they say, "f-pennies." Every word. It's a very descriptive adjective.

They knew the words in the old days, I'm sure. But they knew there was a time and place for it. I have never had this happen to me, but I was told by some teachers that the children swear at them. A child has never done that to me.

I loved the Polish people. They were hard-working. If they didn't have money, they helped out by doing housework, baby-sitting for ten cents an hour. No work was beneath them. But here, these people—the parents—came to school in the morning. This is a social outpost for them. They watch their kids eat free breakfasts and lunches. There isn't any shame, there isn't any pride. These Polish people I knew, there was pride. You didn't dare do anything like that. You wouldn't think of it.

I see these parents here all the time. A father brings his kids to school and he hangs around in the hall. I think it's dangerous to have all these adults in the school. You get all these characters. I'm afraid to stay in my room unless I lock the door.

We see them at recess. They're there at lunch time. These people, they have a resentment that everything is coming to them. Whereas the Polish people worked their way out of the Depression. They loved property. They loved houses. My father loved his little house and if anyone would step on the grass, he would kill them. (Laughs.) He'd say, "Get out of here! This is mine!" (Softly.) There was a great pride. These people, they have no pride in anything, they destroy. Really, I don't understand them.

They take the shades. They take the poles. Steal everything. Every window is broken in our school. Years ago, no one would ever break windows. These kids, if they're angry with you, they'll do terrible things. (Sighs.) Yes, the neighborhood is changing and the type of child has been changing, too. They're even spoiling a nice little Jewish boy who's there.

There were middle- and upper-class people in this neighborhood when I first came. They were very nice people and their children were wonderful. There was an honor system. You'd say, "I'm going to the office for a moment. You may whisper." And they would obey. I was really thrilled. I don't dare do that now. I don't even go to the toilet. (Laughs.) I'm a strong teacher, but I'm afraid to leave them.

In the old days, kids would sit in their seats. If I had to leave the room for a few minutes, I'd say, "Will you please be good?" And they were. These kids today will swear, "We'll be good, we'll be good." I don't know what it is, their training or their ethnic background—or maybe it goes back to history. The poor Spanish were so taken they had to lie and steal to survive. I tell them, "You don't have to lie and cheat here. Everyone is equal." But their background . . .

The first contingent of Puerto Ricans that came in were delightful. They were really lovely kids. I adore some of them. I don't care what ethnic group you belong to, if you're a low-down person, I don't like you.

Today they have these multiple chairs instead of the pedestals, seats that were attached. The kids slide all over the room. Anything to make life more difficult. (Laughs.) If I didn't laugh at these things, I couldn't last. Whereas it was a pleasure to teach a motivated child, how do you motivate *these* children? By food? By bringing cookies to school? Believe me, these children aren't lacking in anying. If I ask for change for a dollar, I can get it. They have more money . . . We have seventeen that get free lunches, and they all have this money for goodies.

I've always been a strong disciplinarian, but I don't give these kids assignments over their head. They know exactly what they do. Habit. This is very boring, very monotonous, but habit is a great thing for these children. I don't tell them the reason for things. I give them the rote method, how to do it. After that, reasoning comes. Each one has to go to the board and show me that they really know. Because I don't trust the papers. They cheat and copy. I don't know how they do it. I walk up and down and watch them. I tell you, it's a way of life. (Laughs.)

At nine o'clock, as soon as the children come in, we have a salute to the flag. I'm watching them. We sing "My Country 'Tis of Thee." And then we sing a parody I found of "My Country 'Tis of Thee."

To serve my country is to banish selfishness
And bring world peace

I love every girl and boy
New friendships I'll enjoy
The Golden Rule employ
Till wars shall cease.

And then we sing "The Star-Spangled Banner." I watch them. It's a dignified exercise. These children love the idea of habit. Something schmaltzy, something wonderful.

I start with arithmetic. I have tables-fun on the board—multiplication. Everything has to be fun, fun, fun, play, play, play. You don't say tables, you say tables-fun. Everything to motivate. See how fast they can do it. It's a catchy thing. When they're doing it, I mark the papers. I'm very fast. God has been good to me. While I'm doing that, I take attendance. That is a must. All this happens before nine fifteen, nine twenty.

The next thing I do is get milk money. That's four cents. I have change. I'm very fast. Buy the milk for recess and we have cookies that I bring. To motivate them, to bribe them. (Laughs.) I also buy Kleenex for them, because they'll wipe their nose ... (Laughs.) By nine forty, which is the next period, I try to finish the marking. Two of the children go to a TESL program. (Sighs.)

Then I have a penmanship lesson on the board. There it is in my beautiful handwriting. I had a Palmer Method diploma. On Mondays I write beautifully, "If we go to an assembly, we do not whistle or talk, because good manners are important. If our manners are good, you'll be very happy and make everyone happy, too." On Friday we give them a test. They adore it. Habit, they love habit.

They drink their milk. I have to take them to toilet recess. I have to watch them. No one goes unless they're supervised. We watch them outside. If there's too much monkey business, I have to go in and stop them. When they raise their hands in class, I let them go, even if they're lying. I tell them, "If you're lying and get in trouble, you won't be able to go again." So I hope they tell me the truth every once in a while.

About eleven o'clock, I give them an English workbook. I pass the free lunch tickets out about a quarter to twelve. Sometime during the day I give them stretching exercises. Sideways, then up and down, and we put our hands on our hips and heads up and so on. I'm good at it. I'm better than the kids.

I have reading groups. One is advanced, one is the middle, and one is the lowest. At a quarter to two we have our spelling—two words a day. Six words a week, really. If I did any more, it's lost. I tried other ways, they did everything wrong. I didn't scold them. I researched my soul. What am I doing wrong? I found out two words a day is just right. Spelling is a big deal. We break the words. We give them sentences. I try to make it last till two o'clock. Fifteen, twenty minutes, that's their attention span. Some days it's great. Some days I can't get them to do anything.

I take them to the toilet again because they're getting restless. Again you watch them. From a quarter after to about two thirty we read together. I give them music, too. That's up to me, up to my throat. They love music. I have it two, three times a week. At two thirty, if they're good, I give them art. I make beautiful Valentines. We show them how to decorate it. And that's the day. If they're not good—if they scream and yell and run around—I don't give them art. I give them work. If they're not nice to me, I'm not going to be nice to them. I'm not going to reward them.

Three fifteen, they go home. You walk them all the way down to the door. You watch them all the way. (Laughs.) I go home. I'm never tired. I go shopping. I give every store on my way home a break. At twelve o'clock I go shopping, too. I have to get away from the other teachers. They're always talking shop.

I don't take any work home with me. With these children, you show them their mistakes immediately. Otherwise they forget. When I'm home, I forget about school, absolutely, absolutely, absolutely. I have never thought of being a principal. I have fulfilled my goal.

As for retirement, yes and no. I'm not sixty-five yet. (Laughs.) I'm not tired. It's no effort for me. My day goes fast, especially when I go out the night before and have a wonderful time. I'm the original La Dolce Vita. If I have a good time, I can do anything. I can even come home at two, three in the morning and get up and go to work. I must have something on the outside to stimulate me.

There are some children I love. Some have looks and brains and personality. I try not to play favorites. I give each one a chance to be monitor. I tell them I'm their school mother. When I scold them, it doesn't mean I hate them. I love them, that's why I scold them. I say to them, "Doesn't your mother scold you?"

These children baffle me. With the type of students we had before, college was a necessary thing, a must. They automatically went because their parents went. The worship of learning was a great thing. But these children, I don't know . . . I tell them, "Mrs. Hoffman is here, everybody works." Mr. Hoffman teases me: "Ah, ah, here comes Mrs. Hoffman, everybody works." Working is a blessing. The greatest punishment I can give these children is not to do anything. If they're bad, you just sit there and we fold our hands. I watch them. They don't want a teacher, they want a watcher. I say, "Mrs. Hoffman is too dumb to do teaching and watching. If you want me to be a teacher, I'll be glad to be a teacher. If you want me to be a watcher, I'll have to watch you."

The younger teachers have a more—what is their word?—relaxed attitude. It's noisy and it's freedom, where they walk around and do everything. I never learned to teach under conditions like that. The first rule of education for me was discipline. Discipline is the keynote to learning. Discipline has been the great factor in my life. I discipline myself to do everything—getting up in the morning, walking, dancing, exercise. If you won't have discipline, you won't have a nation. We can't have permissiveness. When someone comes in and says, "Oh, your room is so quiet," I know I've been successful.

There is one little girl who stands out in my mind in all the years I've been teaching. She has become tall and lovely. Pam. She was not too bright, but she was sweet. She was never any trouble. She was special. I see her every once in a while. She's a checker at Treasure Island.* She gives no trouble today, either. She has the same smile for everyone.

PAT ZIMMERMAN

He is "headmaster" and administrator of the Southern

* A "super" supermarket in the community.

School in Uptown.* It's an alternative school. It began in 1969. "I knew the kids were getting in trouble around here. I simply felt I could teach them and make their troubles less. Someone offered me a storefront church which was used only on Sundays. Someone gave us desks and a couple of tables. I scrounged up some textbooks, and we began—even though there was no income for a while. There was none of the planning and campaigning that many free schools have for months . . . It began with about eight kids.

"It's changed in its four years. We're much more diverse now. No more than fifty percent are poor Southern whites. The others are Chicago kids—blacks, Puerto Ricans, and a couple of Indians. Mike Mayer teaches a class of boys between the ages of eight and sixteen. Jean Fisher and Mary Ryan have a class of girls between the ages of seven and fifteen. I have a class of boys between the ages of twelve and seventeen. There are three classrooms, a large recreation room, and a TV area. We're up for accreditation in May."

He is thirty-one from South Carolina, of a working-class family. He "drifted until '67. Suddenly I had the urge. At one time, I'd have said I had the calling. I started teaching . . ."

I'm a strict kind of teacher. When I say something to one student in a very quiet voice all the way across the room, I want it quiet enough to reach him. I don't have to tell them to shut up very much. It's self-enforced.† I make a lot of demands on my students and I get honestly angry if they don't live up to their possibilities. The importance is not whether a teacher is strict. Is it for the kid's benefit or

---

* A Chicago area in which many of the Southern white *émigrés* live; furnished flats in most instances.

† When I was there last year for a commencement talk, the parents, many of them wives of *émigré* black lung miners, were attentive. The students were excited and voluble, what with soda pop and cake. A casual look from Pat, momentary silence—in fact, profound attention—and the ceremonies began. Later, I found out that the whispers and giggles concerned me. They were anticipating my surprise and speechlessness at the presentation of their gift—a railroad man's gold watch, inscribed.

is it to make his teaching role easier and not get involved? My idea of being a teacher is influenced by my idea of being a particular person. I'm dealing with a particular kid.

I don't have any idea what any of them will end up being. So I'm an unsettled teacher in a classroom. A certain tenseness, nervousness about me because I don't like facing a lot of kids who have the cards stacked against them. They catch on and have some hope and that helps a little.

It isn't the kind of free school you read about. We're involved in picking up basic skills that others have neglected to teach the kids. Some of them have feelings of rage, undefined, and they're acting it out in school—dangerously. We try to calm them down.

In a neighborhood like ours it's very dangerous. It's low income and there are many ethnic groups. This community has experienced its war on poverty and hasn't changed. The kids now don't believe in politics. They don't believe things will get better for them. There's a feeling of hopelessness and despair.

They're from ages six to seventeen. The age difference doesn't really . . . Certainly a fifteen-year-old kid is not going to see an eight-year-old as his equal. But kids do throw off the age barrier and relate to each other as human beings. Because they see us doing the same with them.

The person who's sixteen realizes he has a lot of catching up to do, work. He knows I'm not gonna embarrass him. Other kids are having the same problems. I discourage competition in the classroom. The only one I accept is the student's competition with himself. He has to compete against where he is, against where he wants to be, and against where he has been. I think every kid understands that. They don't have to prove anything to me. Each kid has to prove to himself that he's worthwhile. There's no cheating here. There's no reason for it.

We're not trying to jive 'em into learning. We lay out powerful materials in front of them, and tell 'em they're perfectly capable of doing it—and not to make any excuses about it. We use newspapers, too, and catchy urban stuff—but more as diversions. If you con someone into learning, you really believe they're not capable of it. So we're straightforward. Our learning materials are very hard. That's tough.

I have some that may end up in college, but I don't push them. I sent a boy to Latin School.* He got a scholarship. He was so unhappy there he did everything he could until I took him back. I thought he would have everything to make him happy. Bright, colorful people who smelled of the security of success, friendly teachers, a magnificent building, all the books he could read. But he was missing something—friendship.

I don't think they want to be doctors or lawyers. It's not because they don't know. It's that they have no expectations. Some have vague feelings of wanting to be teachers. They aren't interested in professional roles. See? They just want the security of working—a steady job. Something their parents haven't had in Chicago. These kids are living out their parents' hopes. It's popular today to look at success of minority groups in terms of upward mobility. I don't know that upward mobile groups are so happy.

The majority of our parents are on welfare. When they screw up, they get ashamed and hide from us. The family's falling apart and we've known them for a long time. They can't face the fact. They know it doesn't have to be as bad as it gets sometimes. They know what they're capable of.

We only get to know the families if they want to know us. If a kid doesn't want us involved, we trust that that's the best thing for him, that somehow he needs us all to himself, not to share with his family. If there's a real problem between the kid and his family, the greatest respect we can show him is not to get involved. To give the kid a chance to pull himself out by himself. We trust the kid enough to be an autonomous individual. Hopefully, if he feels better about himself, the family will pick up on that. Very often the kids become effective—quote—therapists—unquote—in the family situation. One kid has carried the major load in helping his father get through some difficulties.

I try to be fairly aware of their feelings. Sometimes I feel guilty that I identify too much. I always let them know when they touch on my feleings, and what those feelings are like. I think children are unaware of what

* A posh private school—upper-middle-class.

adults' feelings are like. Some of these kids that I've taught for a while—I've had some for four years—who are sixteen and seventeen, are getting a taste of those feelings. On the other hand, adolescents have new feelings, different from the ones I had when I was their age. So they're willing to share my feelings as an adult, because they know that I know they have new kinds of feelings. Maybe that's the pain—trying to share it with them. They're reaching across and trying to touch something they've never experienced before—adulthood. In a specific situation of urban life—poverty.

In my school the teachers have the decision about who they want to take or not. No administrator does that. He decides what he wants to teach and how he teaches it. My only requirement, as an administrator, is that he teaches well.

Our classes are segregated by sex. It's easier for them to study. They don't have to play out the traditional sexual roles demanded of them in the neighborhood. They're not secure in being men, so they play at being rough around their women. They have to be. The girls overact and become overseductive and overteasing. We give them a chance to have one place in their lives where they can put aside these roles. Our students have a chance to become more natural in their sex roles as they get away from the defenses that their parents have felt.

We spend so many hours here. Our lives, fortunately or unfortunately. It's very hard for us to get away from it. My work is everything to me. I find myself trying to get an hour or two of personal life now and then—in vain. I'd rather die for my work life than for my personal life. I guess you can't really separate them. The school's not an institution. We have a building, that's where the school exists. But it also exists when we leave.

We often work after six. The people we work for—the National Institute of Mental Health—once wanted us to do an honest time sheet. After they saw our honest time sheet they said, "Just please put in eight hours a day on the time sheet." (Laughs.) Weekends? What weekends? (Laughs.) I work Saturday morning, writing letters, administrative details. I usually work Sunday afternoons and Sunday evenings.

My first year I taught at an all-black school on the South Side. I worked with a very strong woman teacher who was well liked by the students. I picked up a lot of her strength. My second year I was on my own and very unhappy. The students were holding back and I was holding back. I couldn't get involved in their lives and they couldn't in mine. We were playing roles. It was like a polite dance. I liked them, they liked me. We both knew there was a great deal missing.

I have to have complete freedom in what I'm going to teach, and what words I use in the classroom. If I want to cuss at them for something, I cuss at 'em. A certain kind of cussing is an emotional release. If I want to discuss intimate matters with them, I want to be free to do so without justifying it to an administrator. I want to go to the parent's house and scream and yell at 'em if I feel that's gonna shape the kid up.

If I see the day's gonna be a rotten day because everybody's in a lousy mood, I want the freedom to pick up and go someplace and not pretend it's going to be an okay day. I don't tell them, "Let's be happy today, have fun." Sometimes I say the opposite. (Laughs.) I say, "I'm very unhappy today and we're not gonna have fun, we're gonna work." They pull me out of it. And when they're in a lousy mood, they don't hide it. They certainly let me know it.

We hosted a free school from Minneapolis. I thought the students were unhappy because they didn't have a whole lot of direction. There was a great deal of liberty that I don't think the kids wanted. The teachers seemed more interested in theory than in the actual work of teaching. It was incredibly well funded with a staff of twenty-five to 180 kids. There wasn't much I could say to them. In these situations adults are robbing adolescents of their childhood. Children deserve a chance to be irresponsible, to learn from mistakes. You lose your childhood soon enough in a low-income neighborhood.

I don't think these kids are capable of being adults—or want to. In some free schools adults are ready to give away their adulthood and take away from the students their childhood. It's fraudulent and becomes chaos. They're forcing a young person to be older than he really is. The freedom of our school is bounded by two obligations: learning and no violence against another person, physical or emotional. That includes me too.

Our school has sixty-eight students and we're still too

big. I wanted to set the limit at fifty. But I'm too tender-hearted. (Laughs.) If someone knocks on our door long enough, they can get it open. I make a distinction between people who deserve to be cared about and some who have completely given up. They don't deserve the attention because they take too much away from the others, who somehow want to pull some worth out of their lives.

The self-destructive ones deserve someone to completely mother and father them. If someone is willing to commit his or her life to that one person, okay. But not in a classroom with other people who want to care as a group. You see a kid who's been fine for six months just suddenly collapse, and there's no way ... What happens is the other kids spend an awful lot of time ignoring the fact that it's happening. They expend a lot of energy protecting themselves emotionally—from it catching on to them. A teacher goes through an awful lot of anguish watching someone they care about give up.

I was very upset yesterday. A kid collapsed in October and was sent away for criminal activites. He reappeared on a furlough, begging to come back when he gets out. Though I care about him very much—I don't know. It's like a ping-pong game. I haven't decided.

Grades? I give grades, but they aren't entered on anything. I simply keep them in mind as a trend ... Kids like grades, 'cause they like to know where they are right now. Records? No. They have enough records. They have police records, social history records, welfare records. (Laughs.) I should have to keep records?

I think the parents are glad we're around. We take a great deal of pressure off them. We give them a chance to get on with other things in their lives. We've had a lot of families move back South. A great deal of our neighborhood has gone under the bulldozer of urban renewal. Families who haven't done so well after eight, nine years have now decided they'll give the South another try. Kids are getting in neighborhood trouble. City life may be just a bit too hard.

We're really content when our students get a full-time, good paying job. We're always around for him to learn if he wants to. He's still interested in learning about himself. He realizes his life doesn't end when he gets a job. Or when he gets married, his life doesn't end. He doesn't end up in heaven or hell because he got married.

From what I've read about concentration camps, there's a similarity in feeling to ghetto areas. The walls aren't built, they're there. How your life can become concentrated. Rather than escape from it, I've tried to do what some survivors did—find meaning in it to share with other people. Not in any martyr kind of a way, because I can always leave. But it's something beautiful to me. Being able to be hurt by things and then understanding how it happened and explaining to others who have been hurt by the same things.

I run into people who say how much they admire what I do. It's embarrassing. I don't make any judgments about my work, whether it's great or worthless. It's just what I do best. It's the only job I want to do. I work hard because I have to. I get tired. At four I feel as though I'm ready to die. (Laughs.) I don't feel bad about it. This is my life. I just *am*.

KITTY SCANLAN

She is assistant professor of the medical-surgery unit at a Midwestern university's medical center. "That's just a title. I'm an occupational therapist. It's an emerging profession—like medicine was, maybe a hundred years ago.

"We get a heart attack patient. We try to help him find a life style that is satisfying. We had one wealthy man who could see nothing but work. If it meant dying in three days, he'd rather die working than live another fifteen years in a way he wasn't accustomed to. Some of our patients are death-oriented."

A hospital is a dehumanizing institution. People get in and they become arms or legs or kidneys or bladders or something besides Joe Smith the human being. If a hospital was a good place for people to work, it would meet the patient's needs. There would be no need for me.

The nurses, the doctors, the medical students, are set up on a rigid status kind of system. If you buy into this kind of system, you buy the idea that "I'm not quite as good as the guy above me." The resident doesn't strike back at the attending man when he has a bad day. He strikes out at the nurse. The nurse strikes out at the hospital aide or the cleaning lady.

Many patients tell me the best person for them has been the cleaning lady. Yet the doctors and nurses, everybody is saying that the cleaning lady just does a rotten job—"That dirt's been on the floor three days!" The cleaning lady deals with the patient on a human level. She's scrubbing the floor in the room and the patient says, "My son didn't come to visit me today." The cleaning lady smiles and says, "I know how you feel. I know how I'd feel if my son didn't come to visit me if I was sick." The cleaning lady doesn't see the patient as a renal failure or an ileostomy. She just sees a poor lady who's sick.

Until recently, I wasn't sure how meaningful my work was. I had doubts. A surgeon does a really beautiful job. That's meaningful to him *immediately*. But it's not the kind of sustaining thing that makes a job meaningful. It must concern the relationship you have with the people you work with. We get hung up in the competition: "Who's responsible for saving this life?" "Who's responsible for the change in this dying patient?" Rather than saying, "Isn't it beautiful that we all together helped make this person's life better?"

I worked in the leading rehab hospital in the country. The schedule was very rigid. Everybody punches time clocks when they come to work and when they leave. You get so many minutes for coffee break. The patient's day was regimented as my day was regimented. You have a quadriplegic who at eight o'clock goes to occupational therapy—nine o'clock goes to physical therapy—ten o'clock sees the social worker—twelve o'clock goes back to occupational therapy. We see him as a quadriplegic rather than as a person. We're, both of us, things.

That's what happens in hospitals—not because people are unfeeling or don't care, but because they feel put-down. You have to protect yourself in some way. Many things in the institution frustrate me. The doctor who refuses to deal with the patient who knows he's dying. He says, "He doesn't want to know anything." Or the alcoholic with cirrhosis. What's the use of putting him in this hospital bed, prolonging his life, to send him back to the lonely, isolated world where he'll sit in his room and drink and nobody to cook for him? You know there's no place to send him. Or the old lady who's had a stroke, who lives alone. She's been very dear to all the staff and you know you can't keep her in that hundred-dollar-a-day bed, and she's shipped to some rotten nursing home that welfare put her into. She can't live alone. And the bastards you have to deal with—sarcastic doctors. They're not really bastards—it's the way the institution makes them. You think, "What's the use?"

For several months I worked with hemiplegics, elderly people who've had a stroke. Half their body is paralyzed. First thing in the morning I'd get to the old men's ward and I'd teach them dressing. They didn't think they could do anything, but they could dress themselves. If people can take care of themselves, they have more self-esteem.

They were in long wards and they had curtains around the bed. I'd start out with just the shirt, work on getting the affected arm into the sleeve. Some people, it would take ten days to learn. Some could do it in one day—getting their shirt on, their pants on, how to wash themselves with one hand . . . The patients taught me a lot. They have better ways they've learned on their own. They'd say, "Wouldn't it be better if I did it this way?" I learned a lot about self-care from them. I try to tell my students to listen to the patients.

Being sick can be like going through early developmental stages all over again. It can have profound growth potential for people. It's like being a child again, to be sick. The doctor is like the parent. I've seen it happen with kidney transplant patients. People who've been seriously ill may come out much stronger, happier . . . Some kind of learning. Something can happen in the sick role. It's one of the areas where we say it's okay to be dependent, as an adult, in our society. It's not intellectual learning.

I think the luxury of individual patients is coming to an end—and I'm glad. Group treatment is far more effective. Patients I've worked with helped each other much more than I helped them. If I get five old men together—hemiplegics—and do some crazy thing like tie a red ribbon on their affected arm, it gets to be a game or a joke. They look at what the other guy is doing—he didn't know he had that side of his body—and say, "Hey, what you're doing is wrong." I could say it over and over and over and it wouldn't mean anything. They learn about survival from each other. They learn it by discussing what their lives were like, what they're like now. I can't tell them. I don't know what it's like. I've never been paralyzed from the neck down.

The kind of thing we do can be done by anybody in a general hospital. It's easy for a nurse to learn how a hemiplegic dresses. If they were able to take time with the patient, they could do what I do. The best I am is a good cleaning lady in medicine-surgery.

I had so many doubts about my work. I'd think, Oh God, the doctor doesn't see what I'm doing as important. I finally learned it didn't matter what he thought. If I believed in what I was doing, I didn't give a damn what the doctor thought of it. I began to see his own protective cover.

There's a doctor who thought we were play-ladies. Occupational therapy uses crafts, fun things. I thought of it as a loss of status. I saw it as not nearly as important as taking temperatures and all these vital, life-saving things. Now I find it exciting, more important than the other matters. I see it as the kind of thing missing in a lot of people's lives. It wasn't the people higher up who didn't recognize the importance of our work. It was *I* who didn't recognize it.

She quit her job for a time and worked as a waitress at a popular neighborhood restaurant. After her return to the medical center she kept at it, as a part-time waitress. "It put my life back in perspective for me. I pretend being assistant professor's a big deal. I fell into this status trap because people do act impressed. I'm no different when I'm waitressing than I am as an assistant professor. They made me quit as a waitress. There's a policy at the university that if you carry two jobs, you have to fill out all these forms. I thought, Oh hell, it isn't worth it."

When I had resigned from the university, I told them I was as great a pain in the ass to them as they were to me. I didn't like this rigidity—you have to be here at eight. It doesn't matter if you stay till ten at night, if you're one minute late, people will think OTs are not dedicated. I told them to go to hell. They liked my fight, so they said, "What will it take for you to stay?" I said, "A leave of absence." I think I've been good at this job and good for the students. But if I'm not good for me, I'm not good for anybody else.

They needed me, so they got off my back. When I first took this job, they said I couldn't wear earrings. Only sluts wear pierced earrings. I told them to go to hell. And I said I wouldn't wear the white uniform. Everyone is supposed to wear it. They said, "Okay, wear a lab coat." I said, "I won't wear one." Now the whole staff isn't wearing uniforms. This is very destructive in a status-conscious institution that controls people with these kind of things.

Through working on this job I'm coming to learn that I do have some influence, at least over my own happiness. I could have been here, wearing uniforms, fighting, being angry—feeling ridiculous, but helpless. Now I say, "The hell with the uniform." And I do wear pierced earrings and they can't pull them off. I was lucky or smart when I challenged them. They gave in, and now I'm learning something of my own power.

I do get some mileage out of my title, I hate to admit it. When, I'm uncomfortable with somebody new and they ask me what my job is, I make a joke of telling them. But the fact is, I do tell them. It's status, of course. When I'm free of the fear of losing it, I'll be a much healthier person.

BETSY DELACY

I'm called a patients' representative. My job is to admit them into the hospital. I'm the first one they see when they walk in the door and the last one to see when they leave. When they get their bills in the mail, they think of me. I think my name is listed along with the fire and police department on their telephone. (Laughs.) Who to call in emergencies.

She works in a 540-bed hospital, and thirty-five patients are in her charge. She wears a navy-blue dress with a yellow collar and yellow sleeves. "They get to know me not only as a person but as a uniform. I've become sick of navy-blue. I don't have any identification marks as a person. I'm recognized as a department when I wear this uniform. I go home with it. I crawl out of bed and get into it. I don't look in my closet and decide what I'm going to wear that day."

I handle patients A, B, J, and K. We call insurance companies and find out what their benefits are. Then we code the count for the computer. We type up all the necessary forms. This is called pre-admit. We let you know what your benefits are so you won't have to worry about your hospital bill. Our rooms are seventy-five dollars a day. If the insurance pays only twenty-five dollars, that man's going to owe fifty dollars out of his own pocket every day he's here. I get the money ahead of time. You don't have insurance, there must be a five-hundred-dollar deposit. You have to come walking in here with five hundred dollars if you're going to be put to bed.

When you ask for money first thing he comes in, it tends to upset the patient sometimes, unless you put it in a way that they're most grateful. I find the best way to do that, without myself being yelled at and called names, is to charm the patient and they calm down. "Are you aware what your benefits are? Do you have the means to pay the other fifty dollars a day?" They think you're informing them rather than demanding money. But you are demanding money.

When I visit you, I've warned you and I've joked about it. I've taken the edge off the whole thing. So it's not a big shock. I'd rather go up to you and say, "Sir, you owe two hundred dollars," than not bother you and one day you walk out, and you owe fifteen hundred dollars and have to drop your teeth and have another heart attack. Health care is expensive, you know.

I don't feel I represent the patient. I represent the hospital. I represent the cashiers. I'm the buffer between the patient and the collection department. This job could be done with a little more finesse. There are times when we dun the patient while he's in bed: "Tomorrow, can you have three hundred dollars paid on this bill?"

I have no problems. A few patients think this is a little crude. Also doctors are very good about warning patients to bring some deposit in the hospital if your insurance is not adequate. If he can't bring in five hundred dollars, you ask him how much he can raise. We work out weekly, monthly payments. Most patients are very understanding and cooperative.

We've had a few we've asked to leave. The doctor is the only one can discharge the patient. If he suggested you be in ten days, maybe you could go home in five. This is brought to the doctor's attention because it affects the bill. Then the doctor decides he can go home. You're doing the patient a favor. You might be saving him five hundred dollars. The guy's not kicked out of bed: "Sorry, sir, no more money, no more bed." It is done with finesse.

We visit our patients as often as we can, so they get to know us as their representative. "Are you comfortable?" "Are you satisfied with your food?" Then, when he gets to know me—"I know your account is going to be a problem ..." I'm not looking for money, but if the patient doesn't ask such questions, I mention it. I sort of joke with 'em and then lay it out and sock it to 'em.

"They want the bill explained. It's computerized, and it had taken me about three weeks to understand when I started out on this job. The patient's just looking at all these figures and doesn't know what's coming off.

"Computers make it worse than before. You used to have three cashiers. You now have seven. There's the coding, there's the sorting, there's the tearing apart of pieces of paper. At one time all you had to do was write a little figure in the corner and that was it. Something very simple you used to do in five minutes takes you five days. Hospital costs have gone up since computers. The cost of an error is so fantastic. Where if you've paid ten dollars and I've written down a receipt for a hundred, it's a simple little mistake. All I had to do was scratch out the hundred and write ten. Now if that kind of error's made, it ties everything up for five days."

I really do like to visit patients and chatter. Most of 'em, they're laying in bed watching the same old soap operas they've been watching all day. I walk in the room. I can walk down the hall with my chin draggin', I'm tired and hot. The minute I hit that room, shoulders back and a big smile on my face. I go bursting in there like gangbusters. They sit up in bed, straighten their gowns, pull up the sheets, and turn off the TV. They're really glad I've come. One guy turns up the set when I come in. He doesn't need me and he's tellin' me that.

I won't mention the bill to a dying patient, if I can talk

with the family. A relative will be grateful to me because I didn't pester the patient. There's no problem here. That's the worst thing about my job, though. I really hate to say, "Oh, did I mention the four hundred dollars to you?" Sometimes I'll sit there and chat for fifteen minutes and sort of squeeze that into the conversation. All of a sudden the visit is canceled and the business has begun. I try to avoid it, but sometimes I have no choice.

People see hospitals as money first and health second. On our admitting forms we ask all these questions—next of kin, who's gonna pay the bill?—and fill out all these blank squares. The *last* question is: "What is wrong with you, sir?" I'd rather see patient care first and your financial problems second.

Not all my visits are for collection. A guy just had his leg amputated, doesn't have anybody. I go visit, then shoot the breeze with him. Is he going to be able to take care of himself once he gets home? If he's going to live in a third-floor flat and he doesn't have anybody home, this bothers me. He's my patient because he's my letter in the alphabet. When the account's taken care of, I become his friend.

Isolated patients are on my mind. I had one little girl who had rheumatic fever. She was very ill. Spanish. They had very limited insurance and her bills were just soaring. I talked to the oldest son who was seventeen. I took their application to public aid. It was denied because both parents were working. I got her transferred to La Rabida.* They still owe us fifteen hundred dollars. They've made arrangements to pay forty dollars a month. Sad. But this is an eight-hour-day thing. I can walk away from the job and not worry about it.

I used to work at Wieboldt's.* In head cash. Counting all the money taken in the day before, getting it ready for the bank. I never saw the customer, I only saw his money. I've worked in drugstores managing a cash register. Everything I've done is money, some way or another. It's hard for me to deal with the emotional factors.

When people ask me, I don't like to say I'm in collections. If I'm gonna work in collections, I'd rather say I

---

* A hospital for children with heart conditions.

* A department store whose customers are primarily lower-middle-class and working-class people.

work at Wieboldt's. It seems strange that you should have a collection department in a hospital. Patient representative has a better sound. Nobody knows what it's all about. It's like any organized business. They give people such titles that nobody knows what it's all about.

I'd like to see one insurance for all people, one plan—socialized. Free medical care would be wonderful, but I don't know how it would be supported. We'd only end up paying for it through taxes. That would tend to irritate people. Intelligent people realize health care is expensive. They realize hospitals don't make profits. Hospitals misuse money badly. But that's poor management.

That's what I was in at the other hospital. We were on a cash basis. If you didn't have insurance, you paid cash. It hurt those other girls to sit there and ask for money. It didn't bother me. I wasn't out there doing it. I'd say, "If he doesn't have the money, he can come back tomorrow. He's not gonna die." It was easy to have an attitude like that. But I'm the other end of the stick now.

I don't get into many arguments with patients. They're more or less at my mercy. They can't say too much. Once you're in the hospital and you owe me money, if I talk to you in a sympathetic way, you're not gonna get too sarcastic about it. If you owe me money, I can't ignore that fact. You may be sick and dying and I like you a lot and you make me cry and all that, I still got to go in and talk to you about your bill. That's what's hard.

POSTSCRIPT: *She has since been transferred to the accounting department. She is in charge. She has—and this occupies most of her leisure time—joined Jehovah's Witnesses.*

CARMELITA LESTER

She arrived from the West Indies in 1962. She has been a practical nurse for the past five years. "You study everything about humanity, the human body, all the way through. How to give the patient cares, how to make comfortable ... Most of the time I work seven days."

We're in a private room at a nursing home for the elderly. "Most of them are upper, above middle class. I only work for private patients. Some may have a stroke, some are maybe confused. Some patients have nothing wrong with them, but relatives just bring them and leave them here."

*As she knits, she glances tenderly at the old, old woman lying in the bed. "My baby here has cerebral thrombosis. She is ninety-three years old."**

I get in this morning about eight-thirty. I shake her, make sure that she was okay. I took her tray, wipe her face, and give her cereal and a cup of orange juice and an egg. She's unable to chew hard foods. You have to give her liquids through a syringe. She's supposed to get two thousand cc per day. If not, it would get dry and she would get a small rash and things like those.

The first thing in the morning, after breakfast, I sponge her and I give her a back rub. And I keep her clean. She's supposed to be turned every two hours. If we don't turn her every two hours, she will have sores. Even though she's asleep, she's got to be turned.

I give her lunch. The trays come up at twelve thirty. I feed her just the same as what I feed her in the morning. In the evening I go to the kitchen and pick up her tray at four o'clock and I do the same thing again. About five thirty I leave here and go home. She stays here from five thirty until eleven at night as floor care, until the night nurse come.

You have to be very, very used to her to detect it that she's having an attack. I go notify that she's having a convulsion, so the nurse come and give her two grains of sodium amytal in her hips. When she gets the needle it will bring down her blood pressure. Because she has these convulsions, her breathing stops, trying to choke. If there's nobody around, she would stifle.

Some days she's awake. Some days she just sleeps. When she's awake she's very alert. Some people believe she isn't, but she knows what's going on. You will hear her voice say something very simple. Other than that, she doesn't say a word. Not since she had that last heavy

* Four years before, I visited "her baby" when she was eighty-nine years old. It was a gracefully appointed apartment; she was most hospitable. Bright-eyed, alert, witty, she recounted her experiences during the Great Depression.

stroke last year. Before that, she would converse. Now she doesn't converse any more. Oh, she knows what's going on. She's aware. She knows people by the voices. If a man comes in this room, once she hears that voice, I just cannot undress her. (Laughs.)

She knows when I'm not here. If I'm away too long, she gets worried, sick. But she got used to it that I have to go out sometimes. She knows I'll be back, so she's more relaxed now. Oh, sometimes I sit here and get drowsy. I think of the past and the future. Sometime I think when I was a little girl in Cuba and the things I used to do.

If I'm not doing nothing after I get through with her, it's a drag day. I laugh and I keep myself busy doing something. I may make pillows. I sell 'em. Sometimes I'll be writing up my bills. That's my only time I have, here. If I don't feel like doing that, well, I'll make sure she's okay, I'll go down into the street and take a walk.

The work don't leave my mind. I have been so long with her that it became part of me. In my mind it's always working: "How's she getting along?" I worry what happened to her between those hours before the night nurse report. If I go off on a trip, I'll be talking about her. I'll say, "I wonder what happened to my baby." My girl friend will say, "Which baby are you talking about?" I'll say, "My patient." (Laughs.) I went to Las Vegas. I spent a week there. Every night I called. Because if she has these convulsions . . .

My baby, is not everyone can take of her through this illness. Anybody will be sittin' here and she will begin to talk and you don't know it. So you have to be a person that can detect this thing coming along. I called every night to find out how she was doin'. My bill was seventy-eight dollars. (Laughs.) If she's sick, I have to fly back. She stays on my mind, but I don't know why. (Laughs.)

She works through a nurses' registry. "You go where they send you. Maybe you get a little baby." She had worked at a general hospital before. "I used to float around, I worked with geriatric, I worked with pediatric, I worked with teen-agers, I worked with them all. Medical-surgical. I've been with her two years. As long as she's still going." (Laughs.)

In America, people doesn't keep their old people at

home. At a certain age they put them away in America. In my country, the old people stay in the home until they die. But here, not like that. It's surprising to me. They put them away. The first thing they think of is a nursing home. Some of these people don't need a nursing home. If they have their own bedroom at home, look at television or listen to the radio or they have themselves busy knitting ... We all, us foreigners, think about it.

Right now there's a lady here, nothing wrong with her, but they put her away. They don't come to see her. The only time they see her is when she say, "I can't breathe." She wants some attention. And that way she's just aging. When I come here, she was a beautiful woman. She was looking very nice. Now she is going down. If they would come and take her out sometimes ...

We had one lady here about two years ago, she has two sons. She fell and had a broken hip. They called the eldest son. He said, "Why call on me? Call the little one. She gave all the money to that little one." That was bad. I was right there.

All these people here are not helpless. But just the family get rid of them. There is a lady here, her children took her for a ride one day and push her out of the car. Let her walk and wander. She couldn't find her way home. They come and brought her here. And they try to take away all that she has. They're tryin' to make her sign papers and things like those. There's nothing wrong with her. She can dress herself, comb her hair, take a walk ... They sign her in here, made the lawyers sign her in. They're just in for the money. She will tell you, "There's nothin' wrong with me."

Things that go on here. I've seen many of these patients, they need help, but they don't have enough help. Sometimes they eat and sometimes they don't. Sometimes there's eight hours' wait. Those that can have private nurse, fine. Those that can't suffer. And this is a high-class place. Where *poor* old people ... (She shakes her head.)

"The reason I got so interested in this kind of work, I got sick. One evening my strength just went. My legs and everything couldn't hold. For one year I couldn't walk. I had twelve doctors. They couldn't find out what was wrong. I have doctors from all over the United States come to see. Even a professor from Germany. A doctor from South

Carolina came, he put it in a book. My main doctor said, 'You have to live with your condition 'cause there's nothing we can do.' I said to him, 'Before I live this way, I'd rather die.' 'Cause I couldn't feed myself, I couldn't do nothin'. This life is not for me.

"They took me home. I started prayin' and prayin' to God and things like those and this. Oral Roberts, I wrote to him several letters. Wrote from my heart. Still I was crippled. Couldn't put a glass of water to my mouth. The strength had been taken away. I prayed hard.

"One night I was in bed and deeply down in my sleep, I heard electricity. Like when you take an electric wire and touch it. It shot through both my legs. Ooohhh, it shocked so hard that I woke up. When I woke up, I felt it three times. The next morning I could raise this leg up. I was surprised.

"The next night I felt the same thing. The third night I felt the same thing. So I got up and went to the bathroom. I went back to the doctor and he said, 'That's surprising.' Ooohhh, I can't believe it. There is a miracle. This is very shocking."

What do you think cured you?

"God."

Did Oral Roberts help?

"Yes."

How?

"By prayin' sincere from his heart.

"I was a nurse before, but I wasn't devoted. I saw how they treated people when I was there. Oh, it was pitiful. I couldn't stand it. And from that, I have tender feelings. That changed me. That's when I decided to devote myself."

I feel sorry for everybody who cannot help themselves. For that reason I never rest. As soon as I'm off one case I am on another. I have to sometimes say, "Don't call me for a week." I am so tired. Sometimes I have to leave the house and hide away. They keep me busy, busy, busy all the time. People that I take care of years ago are callin' back and askin' for me.

Plenty of nurses don't care. If they get the money, forget it. They talk like that all the time. They say to me, "You still here?" I say, "Yes." "Oh, you still worry about that old woman." I say, "That's why she pays me, to worry about her." Most of the nurses have feelings.

If I had power in this country, first thing I'd do in nursing homes, I would hire someone that pretended to be sick. 'Cause that's the only way you know what's goin' on. I would have government nursing homes. Free care for everybody. Those hospitals that charge too much money and you don't have insurance and they don't accept you, I would change that—overnight.

Things so bad for old people today—if I could afford to buy a few buildings, I would have that to fall on. You got to be independent. So you don't have to run there and there and there in your old age. They don't have enough income. I don't want to be like that.

An elderly person is a return back to babyhood. It give you a feeling how when you were a teen-ager, you're adult, you think you're strong and gay, and you return back to babyhood. The person doesn't know what's happening. But you take care of the person, you can see the difference. It makes you sad, because if you live long enough, you figure you will be the same.

POSTSCRIPT: *A few months after this conversation, her "baby" died.*

HERBERT BACH

We are called memorial counselors. We use telephone solicitation. We use direct mail. We put ads in papers. In any kind of field you look in the haystack for needles.

We call ourselves the Interment Industry. The funeral industry is a little bit different. You conduct a funeral, it takes one or two or three days, and that's the end of that. But we're responsible for fifty, a hundred, two hundred years. People will come in and say, "Where is my great-grandfather?" If you don't have a record of that, we're in trouble.

We're in a creative field. We get into engineering, into landscaping, into purchasing for flowers. We get into contracting and road building. We cover areas from working with a bereaved family to dropping a sewer thirty feet into the ground so it will properly drain. Oh yes, there have been significant changes in cemetery management.

In the old days the cemetery was strictly a burial ground. When somebody died, they would dispose of the remains. They left it to each family to put in some sort of tombstone. Today the cemetery is a community institution. It should be a thing of beauty, a thing of dignity.

It the old days the cemetery served a simple purpose. Today we think of it in terms of ecology. Green acres in the center of residential and commercial areas, newly built. We have 160 acres here. Around us are industrial parks. Still, we have this green . . . The cemetery field has become professionalized.

In the old days each little church, each little synagogue, would buy a piece of land, and the sexton would keep the records of who and what was buried where. There was no landscape design, there were no roads, there was no draining. Our landscaper does the annual World Flower Show. One of our architects had done the Seagram Building. We use forward-thinking people who make the cemetery serve the whole community.

In the olden days, the maintenance of the cemetery was left to the individual family. One family would pay and the others didn't. You would have weeds in one area and someplace else cared for. Today, in a modern cemetery, you have trust funds. Whenever a family purchases, a part of that money is put into a trust. This trust is inviolate. In this state it's held by a third party, a bank. You know that cemetery is gonna be cared for.

We have eliminated tombstones and monuments. We use level bronze memorials. You get away from this thing of a marble orchard—and the depression of cold, cold stone. What you see are shrubs and flowers and trees. The beauty represents something for the entire community.

We are only fifteen years old and our trust has close to a million dollars to help pay for the maintenance. When the park is complete, the trust will run between twelve and fourteen million dollars. Only the interest can be used. So we put in works of art.

I am not a grief psychologist. (Laughs.) I think death is a personal thing. We feel we have to do something to help people overcome their grief. At every interment service we erect a chapel tent. We have an outdoor chapel. We call it the Chapel in the Woods. We hold annual memorial services. So the family knows—even if they don't come to the service—their loved ones are being remembered. We have a lowering device—the casket is put on that—covered with green. So people don't see the bare hole in the ground, which is very traumatic.*

Funerals are more restrained today. In the past people got very, very emotional. Today there is a dignity to the service. They don't have to get emotional. They don't have to do the kind of thing they did in the past to show everybody how much they loved the one that went away. The one big thing at the time of death is the guilt complex. We always felt we haven't done enough for the person who passed away. So we try to overcome this at the time of death.

One of the big things people say at the time of death is: "Oh, I loved him so much. I want him to get the very best." I want to get the finest of this and the finest of that. They are subjected to emotional overspending. At the funeral chapel they'll buy the casket they can't afford. At the cemetery they'll buy the interment space they can't afford. We try to avoid that. We say it should be planned, like you plan life insurance. You wouldn't drive a car without au-

---

* Joe Matthews, a clergyman, recalls his aged father's funeral: "I sat alone with my father the day before his burial. The cosmetics shocked me. It wasn't my father as I had known him. I wanted to see his wrinkles again. I helped put those wrinkles there. My brothers and sisters helped put those wrinkles there. My mother helped put those wrinkles there. Those wrinkles were part of me. They weren't there that day. It was as if they had taken away *my* life. It was as if I were ashamed of my father as he was. No. The mortician was friendly, though bewildered. He brought me the soap, sponge, and basin of warm water I asked for. I took the make-up off of papa. I never got him to look ninety-two again. But he didn't look fifty any more when I was finished."

tomobile insurance. You wouldn't move into a house without fire insurance. Why not memorial insurance?

They can budget it over a period of time. If people don't budget, they have to pay cash, right? If you don't pay for a refrigerator, they can repossess it. If somebody passes away and you make an interment, you can't very well repossess the body. (Laughs.) So they have to pay cash here in advance. It's a matter of budgeting.

ELMER RUIZ

Not anybody can be a gravedigger. You can dig a hole any way they come. A gravedigger, you have to make a neat job. I had a fella once, he wanted to see a grave. He was a fella that digged sewers. He was impressed when he seen me diggin' this grave—how square and how perfect it was. A human body is goin' into this grave. That's why you need skill when you're gonna dig a grave.

He has dug graves for eight years, as the assistant to the foreman. "I been living on the grounds for almost twelve years." During the first four years "I used to cut grass and other things. I never had a dream to have this kind of job. I used to drive a trailer from Texas to Chicago." He is married and has five children, ranging in age from two to sixteen. It is a bitter cold Sunday morning.

The gravedigger today, they have to be somebody to operate a machine. You just use a shovel to push the dirt loose. Otherwise you don't use 'em. We're tryin' a new machine, a ground hog. This machine is supposed to go through heavy frost. It do very good job so far. When the weather is mild, like fifteen degrees above zero, you can do it very easy.

But when the weather is below zero, believe me, you just really workin' hard. I have to use a mask. Your skin hurts so much when it's cold—like you put a hot flame near your face. I'm talkin' about two, three hours standin' outside. You have to wear a mask, otherwise you can't stand it at all.

Last year we had a frost up to thirty-five inches deep,

from the ground down. That was difficult to have a funeral. The frost and cement, it's almost the same thing. I believe cement would break easier than frost. Cement is real solid, but when you hit 'em they just crack. The frost, you just hit 'em and they won't give up that easy. Last year we had to use an air hammer when we had thirty-five inches frost.

The most graves I dig is about six, seven a day. This is in the summer. In the winter it's a little difficult. In the winter you have four funerals, that's a pretty busy day.

I been workin' kinda hard with this snow. We use charcoal heaters, it's the same charcoal you use to make barbeque ribs or hot dogs. I go and mark where the grave is gonna be tomorrow and put a layer of charcoal the same size of a box. And this fifteen inches of frost will be completely melt by tomorrow morning. I start early, about seven o'clock in the morning, and I have the park cleaned before the funeral. We have two funerals for tomorrow, eleven and one o'clock. That's my life.

In the old days it was supposed to be four men. Two on each end with a rope, keep lowerin' little by little. I imagine that was kinda hard, because I imagine some fellas must weigh two hundred pounds, and I can feel that weight. We had a burial about five years ago, a fella that weighed four hundred pounds. He didn't fit on the lowerin' device. We had a big machine tractor that we coulda used, but that woulda looked kinda bad, because lowerin' a casket with a tractor is like lowerin' anything. You have to respect ... We did it by hand. There were about a half a dozen men.

The grave will be covered in less than two minutes, complete. We just open the hoppers with the right amount of earth. We just press it and the we lay out a layer of black earth. Then we put the sod that belongs there. After a couple of weeks you wouldn't know it's a grave there. It's complete flat. Very rarely you see a grave that is sunk.

To dig a grave would take from an hour and a half to an hour and forty-five minutes. Only two fellas do it. The operator of the ground hog or back hoe and the other fella, with the trailer, where we put the earth.

When the boss is gone I have to take care of everything myself. That includes givin' orders to the fellas and layin' graves and so on. They make it hard for me when the fellas won't show. Like this new fella we have. He's just great but he's not very dependable. He miss a lot. This fella, he's about twenty-four years old. I'm the only one that really knows how to operate that machine.

I usually tell 'em I'm a caretaker. I don't think the name sound as bad. I have to look at the park, so after the day's over that everything's closed, that nobody do damage to the park. Some occasions some people just come and steal and loot and do bad things in the park, destroy some things. I believe it would be some young fellas. A man with responsibility, he wouldn't do things like that. Finally we had to put up some gates and close 'em at sundown. Before, we didn't, no. We have a fence of roses. Always in cars you can come after sundown.

When you tell people you work in a cemetery, do they change the subject?

Some, they want to know. Especially Spanish people who come from Mexico. They ask me if it is true that when we bury somebody we dig 'em out in four, five years and replace 'em with another one. I tell 'em no. When these people is buried, he's buried here for life.

It's like a trade. It's the same as a mechanic or a doctor. You have to present your job correct, it's like an operation. If you don't know where to make the cut, you're not gonna have a success. The same thing here. You have to have a little skill. I'm not talkin' about college or anything like that. Myself, I didn't have no grade school, but you have to know what you're doin'. You have some fellas been up for many years and still don't know whether they're comin' or goin'. I feel proud when everything became smooth and when Mr. Bach congratulate us. Four years ago, when the foreman had a heart attack, I took over. That was a real tough year for myself. I had to dig the graves and I had to show the fellas what to do.

A gravedigger is a very important person. You must have hear about the strike we had in New York about two years ago. There were twenty thousand bodies layin' and nobody could bury 'em. The cost of funerals they raised and they didn't want to raise the price of the workers. The way they're livin', everything wanna go up, and I don't know what's gonna happen.

Can you imagine if I wouldn't show up tomorrow morning and this other fella—he usually comes late—and sometimes he don't show. We have a funeral for eleven o'clock. Imagine what happens? The funeral arrive and where you gonna bury it?

We put water, the aspirins, in case somebody pass out. They have those capsules that you break and put up by their nose—smelling salts. And we put heaters for inside the tents so the place be a little warm.

There are some funerals, they really affect you. Some young kid. We buried lots of young. You have emotions, you turn in, believe me, you turn. I had a burial about two years ago of teen-agers, a young boy and a young girl. This was a real sad funeral because there was nobody but young teen-agers. I'm so used to going to funerals every day—of course, it bothers me—but I don't feel as bad as when I bury a young child. You really turn.

I usually will wear myself some black sunglasses. I never go to a funeral without sunglasses. It's a good idea because your eyes is the first thing that shows when you have a big emotion. Always these black sunglasses.

This grief that I see every day, I'm really used to somebody's crying every day. But there is some that are real bad, when you just have to take it. Some people just don't want to give up. You have to understand that when somebody pass away, there's nothing you can do and you have to take it. If you don't want to take it, you're just gonna make your life worse, become sick. People seems to take it more easier these days. They miss the person, but not as much.

There's some funerals that people, they show they're not sad. This is different kinds of people. I believe they are happy to see this person—not in a way of singing—because this person is out of his sufferin' in this world. This person is gone and at rest for the rest of his life. I have this question lots of times: "How can I take it?" They ask if I'm calm when I bury people. If you stop and think, a funeral is one of the natural things in the world.

I enjoy it very much, especially in summer. I don't think any job inside a factory or an office is so nice. You have the air all day and it's just beautiful. The smell of the grass when it's cut, it's just fantastic. Winter goes so fast sometimes you just don't feel it.

When I finish my work here, I just don't remember my work. I like music so much that I have lots more time listenin' to music or playin'. That's where I spend my time. I

don't drink, I don't smoke. I play Spanish bass and guitar.
I play accordian. I would like to be a musician. I was
born and raised in Texas and I never had a good school.
I learned music myself from here and there. After I close
the gate I play. I don't think it would be nice to play music when the funeral's goin' by. But after everything . . .

I believe we are not a rich people, but I think we're
livin' fair. We're not sufferin'. Like I know lotsa people
are havin' a rough time to live on this world because of
crises of the world. My wife, sometimes she's tired of
stayin' in here. I try to take her out as much as possible.
Not to parties or clubs, but to go to stores and sometimes
to go to drive-ins and so on.

She's used to funerals, too. I go to eat at noon and she
asks me, "How many funerals you got today? How many
you buried today?" "Oh, we buried two." "How many
more you got?" "Another." Some other people, you go to
your office, they say, "How many letters you write today?"
Mine says, "How many funerals you had today?"
(Laughs.)

My children are used to everything. They start playin'
ball right against the house. They're not authorized to go
across the road because it's the burial in there. Whenever
a funeral gonna be across from the house, the kids are not
permitted to play. One thing a kid love, like every kid, is
dogs. In a way, a dog in here would be the best thing to
take care of the place, especially a German Shepherd. But
they don't want dogs in here. It's not nice to see a dog
around a funeral. Or cats or things like that. So they don't
have no pet, no.

I believe I'm gonna have to stay here probably until I
die. It's not gonna be too bad for me because I been livin'
twelve years already in the cemetery. I'm still gonna be
livin' in the cemetery. (Laughs.) So that's gonna be all
right with me whenever I go. I think I may be buried
here, it look like.

BOOK NINE

THE QUIZ KID AND THE CARPENTER

BRUCE FLETCHER

Nobody likes to grow old, but I'm afraid I grew old at a very early age. The years went by quickly when I was very young, and all too quickly in the years when I should have been having fun. I became a concerned old man at a very early age. I began to grow gray when I was twenty-one . . .

He was one of the original Quiz Kids—first program, June, 1940. He was the youngest. "I was seven, going on eight." He participated in the network program for three years, 1940 to 1943. He is thirty-nine years old.

"My specialty was Greek mythology and natural history. These two subjects were what they asked me about on the show. At home I'd sit on the floor and go through the book and recite off the names of the birds. My Aunt Louise thought this was very great and very wonderful. So she called in the neighbors to have me perform. One of the neighbors called the newspapers and they came and photographed me and reported on me. I was considered a child prodigy.

"After three years as one of the Quiz Kids, I was eleven and pretty obnoxious, I'm afraid. When you're seven years old, these things are tolerable. When you're eleven and becoming an adolescent, these things become intolerable. It was considered wise that I retire earlier than age fifteen, which was considered the graduation age for the Quiz Kids. I wondered what happened. From then on, I was just plain Bruce Fletcher."

My big ambition was to go to New York and Columbia University. When a Midwestern hick arrives in New York, you start at the bottom—and I did. I worked in a factory and was amused by the way it was run. Eight o'clock the bell rang, all the machines started, and you started working like little machines yourself.

I found a job at a very exclusive men's club for the social register only. What amused me was something that existed far beyond its time: servants were treated as servants. I cleared twenty-nine dollars a week plus two meals. They were slip-cowish, and this hateful chef sought to give it to the employees. Things became so desperate that one of the servants went up to a club member with some sausage that you wouldn't feed a puppy that was starving, and he said, "Here, *you* eat this." Six months was a bellyful, I assure you.

I liked the factory much better, aside from the money. I was glad to be a cog in the wheel. At least it wasn't humiliating. I felt that I could just go through the day's work, make enough money, oh, that I could go to the Met three times a week or Carnegie Hall, and I could more or less live my life properly when my time was my own.

I was a young Columbia man while I worked in a cafeteria from 6:30 A.M. to 3:00 P.M. I was much respected by the management, even though I drove the people that I worked with insane, because I had standards they couldn't cope with. I cannot stand laziness and neglect when I'm breaking my neck and somebody else is holding up the wall. I would scream bloody murder and carry on like a demon and a tyrant.

Through Columbia,* I got a job as a proofreader at one of the biggest law firms in New York. Whatever the case, the law firm brought me back to the fact that I was not just somebody's scullery maid. The people either liked me very much or hated me with a purple passion. But I was respected. I've been respected on every job I ever had.

It wore out my eyes, just like you had them grated on a grindstone. You have to read small print all day long and keep your eyes glued to it. Also, we had handwritten documents that the lawyers would send in. Some of their handwriting was like Egyptian hieroglyphics. We ran into

* "When I went to Columbia I was at the head of my class in music history, European history, and French."

ridiculous situations. If something went wrong, we would be blamed and heads would roll like cabbage stalks.

I left under circumstances of considerable honor. I was given a farewell luncheon by half the staff of the law firm, meaning the lawyers themselves. I was asked to make a speech and I was much applauded.

The most I made was seventy-five dollars a week. I consider making good money in this life where you can walk into a supermarket and you can fill up the grocery cart with everything you choose without having to add the prices of every item. This should have gone out in the thirties, when there was never enough money to go around. Ha ha. I did in New York what I do now. I add up the prices when I put things in the grocery cart to make sure that the purse matches the fancy.

During the years 1960 to 1968 he was on the west coast and in Texas. He worked as an announcer for three different radio stations, favoring classical music. With his collection of ten thousand phonograph records, he made tapes for broadcasts. One job "consumed me day and night for a year and a half. Those were the happiest times of my life."

"Since coming back to Chicago in 1968 I have considered myself in retirement. At thirty-six I was no longer young. People hire people at age twenty. They don't hire people age thirty-six. Oh, I've felt old since my twenties."

I now work in a greenhouse, where we grow nothing but roses. You walk in there and the peace and quiet engulfs you. Privacy is such that you don't even see the people you work with for hours on end. It is not always pretty. Roses have to have manure put around their roots. So I get my rubber gloves and there I go. Some of the work is rather heavy.

The money isn't good. The heat in the summer almost kills me. Because there you are under a glass roof where everything is magnified. There's almost no ventilation, and I am literally drenching with perspiration by the time the day is over and done with. But at least I don't have somebody sneak up behind you and scream in your ear abuse. I had enough of that.

The reason I like this job is because my mind is at ease all day long, without any tensions or pressures. Physically it keeps me on my toes. I'm a little bit harder and tougher than I was. I'm on my feet all day. I have an employer who's the best one I ever had in my life. There has never been the slightest disagreement, which is a miracle. Everyone says, "Bruce is hard to get along with." Bruce is not difficult to get along with if I had intelligent people to work with, where people are not after me or picking on me for that and that and another thing.

I tend to concentrate so much on what I'm doing. That's why I scare very easily. If anyone comes up behind me and speaks to me very suddenly when I'm at work, I'm concentrating so thoroughly I nearly jump through the roof.

I start at seven fifteen in the morning, and the first thing I do is cut roses. They have to be cut early in the morning. The important thing is to cut them so that they're rather tightly closed. Bees and butterflies don't last very long because there's no nectar and pollen. We cut the roses when they're so tightly closed that they can't get at them. If they're kept in refrigeration and in water with the stems trimmed properly, they'll be fresh a week later.

Of course, there's always the telephone. That is a big problem. The greenhouses extend what seem to be miles from the telephone, but you can always hear it, even at a distance. It means a great big long run to get it, and pray that they won't hang up before you can answer it. That usually means orders to be taken. Sometimes the day gets too much and I feel I want to die on the spot.

When the day is over I go to the library. If it's a night of operas or concerts, I time myself accordingly. I always do as I did in New York. Unless I had to go stand in the standing room line at the Met, which meant getting there right after work, I'd go home, take a nap, so that I won't fall asleep at the performance. And then come back and get as much sleep as I possibly can. The day isn't complete unless I fall asleep with the reading light on and a book in my hand.

I don't know what's going to happen to me. It would be much more convenient if I had cancer and passed away and say, "Oh, how tragic," and I could have the peace of the grave. I don't know. I'd love to be back in radio, in the classical music business. I blossomed forth like the roses in the greenhouse ... I was in my own kind of work.

Peace and quiet and privacy have meant a great deal to me in the years since I made my escape. I didn't feel free as one of the Quiz Kids. Reporters and photographers poking you and knocking you around and asking ridiculous questions. As a child you can't cope with these things. I was exploited. I can't forgive those who exploited me.

I would have preferred to grow up in my own particular fashion. Had I grown up as others did, I would have come out a much better person. In school, if I would fail to answer a question, the teacher would lean forward and say in front of the class, "All right! Just because you were one of the Quiz Kids doesn't mean that you're a smart pupil in my class." I wish it had never happened.

(Softly) But we were unique at the time. The Depression was over. America was the haven and all good things were here. And I was the youngest of the Quiz Kids. Of course, I'm a has-been. The Quiz Kids itself has been a has-been. But it brought forth something that was not a has-been. It achieved history, and that is where I'm proud to have been a part of it. (Laughs.) Ah, the time of retirement has come and I'm in it! I'm in it!

NICK LINDSAY

Though he lives in Goshen, Indiana, he considers his birthplace "home"—Eddystone Island, off the coast of South Carolina. At forty-four, he is the father of ten children; the eldest, a girl twenty-six, and the youngest, a boy one and a half years old.

He is a carpenter as well as a poet, who reads and chants his works on college campuses and at coffeehouses. "This is one of the few times in my life I had made a living at anything but carpentry. Lindsays have been carpenters from right on back to 1755. Every once in a while, one of 'em'll shoot off and be a doctor or a preacher or something.* Generally they've been carpenter-preachers, carpenter-farmers, carpenter-storekeepers, carpenters right

---

* His father, Vachel Lindsay, was a doctor as well as a celebrated poet.

*on. A man, if he describes himself, will use a verb. What
you do, that's what you are. I would say I'm a carpenter.*

"I started workin' steady at it when I was thirteen. I
picked up a hammer and went to drive in nails. One man
I learned a lot from was a janitor, who didn't risk the ebb
and flow of the carpentry trade. You can learn a lot from
books about things like this—how nails work, different
kinds of wood."

He dropped out of high school. "It's a good way to go.
Take what you can stand and don't take any more than
that. It's what God put the tongue in your mouth for. If it
don't taste right, you spit it out."

Let me tell you where the grief bites you so much. Who
are you working for? If you're going to eat, you are working for the man who pays you some kind of wage. That
won't be a poor man. The man who's got a big family and
who's needing a house, you're not building a house for
him. The only man you're working for is the man who
could get along without it. You're putting a roof on the
man who's got enough to pay your wage.

You see over yonder, shack need a roof. Over here
you're building a sixty-thousand-dollar house for a man
who maybe doesn't have any children. He's not hurting
and it doesn't mean much. It's a prestige house. He's
gonna up-man, he's gonna be one-up on his neighbor, having something fancier. It's kind of into that machine. It's a
real pleasure to work on it, don't get me wrong. Using
your hand is just a delight in the paneling, in the good
woods. It smells good and they shape well with the plane.
Those woods are filled with the whole creative mystery of
things. Each wood has its own spirit. Driving nails, yeah,
your spirit will break against that.

What's gonna happen to what you made? You work like
you were kneeling down. You go into Riverside Church in
New York and there's no space between the pews to
kneel. (Laughs.) If you try to kneel down in that church,
you break your nose on the pew in front. A bunch of
churches are like that. Who kneels down in that church?
I'll tell you who kneels. The man kneels who's settin' the
toilets in the restrooms. He's got to kneel, that's part of
his work. The man who nails the pews on the floor, he
had to kneel down. The man who put the receptacles in the
walls that turn that I-don't-know-how-many horsepower

organ they got in that Riverside Church—that thing'll blow you halfway to heaven right away, pow!—the man who was putting the wire in that thing, he kneeled down. Any work, you kneel down—it's a kind of worship. It's part of the holiness of things, work, yes. Just like drawing breath is. It's necessary. If you don't breathe, you're dead. It's kind of a sacrament, too.

One nice thing about the crafts. You work two hours at a time. There's a ritual to it. It's break time. Then two hours more and it's dinner time. All those are very good times. Ten minutes is a pretty short time, but it's good not to push too hard. All of a sudden it comes up break time, just like a friend knocking at the door that's unexpected. It's a time of swapping tales. What you're really doing is setting the stage for your work.

A craftsman's life is nothin' but compromise. Look at your tile here. That's craftsman's work, not art work. Craftsmanship demands that you work repeating a pattern to very close tolerances. You're laying this tile here within a sixteenth. It ought to be within a sixty-fourth of a true ninety degree angle. Theoretically it should be perfect. It shouldn't be any sixty-fourth, it should be 00 tolerance. Just altogether straight on, see? Do we ever do it? No. Look at that parquet stuff you got around here. It's pretty, but those corners. The man has compromised. He said that'll have to do.

They just kind of hustle you a bit. The compromise with the material that's going on all the time. That makes for a lot of headache and grief. Like lately, we finished a house. Well, it's not yet done. Cedar siding, that's material that's got knots in it. That's part of the charm. But it's a real headache if the knots fall out. You hit one of those boards with your hammer sometime and it turns into a piece of Swiss cheese. So you're gonna drill those knots, a million knots, back in. (Laughs.) It's sweet smelling wood. You've got a six-foot piece of a ten-foot board. Throwing away four feet of that fancy wood? Whatcha gonna do with that four feet? A splice, scuff it, try to make an invisible joint, and use it? Yes or no? You compromise with the material. Save it? Burn it? It's in your mind all the time. Oh sure, the wood is sacred. It took a long time to grow that. It's like a blood sacrifice. It's consummation. That wood is not going to go anywhere else after that.

When I started in, it was like European carpentering.

But now, all that's pretty well on the run. You make your joints simply, you get prehung doors, you have machine-fitted cabinet work, and you build your house to fit these factory-produced units. The change has been toward quickness. An ordinary American can buy himself some kind of a house because we can build it cheap. So again, your heart is torn. It's good and not so good.

Sometimes it has to do with how much wage he's getting. The more wage he's getting, the more skill he can exercise. You're gonna hire me? I'm gonna hang your door. Suppose you pay me five dollars an hour. I'm gonna have to hang that door fast. 'Cause if I don't hang that door fast, you're gonna run out of money before I get it hung. No man can hurry and hang it right.

I don't think there's less pride in craftsmanship. I don't know about pride. Do you take pride in embracing a woman? You don't take pride in that. You take delight in it. There may be less delight. If you can build a house cheap and really get it to a man that needs it, that's kind of a social satisfaction for you. At the same time, you wish you could have done a fancier job, a more unique kind of job.

But every once in a while there's stuff that comes in on you. All of a sudden something falls into place. Suppose you're driving an eight-penny galvanized finishing nail into this siding. Your whole universe is rolled onto the head of that nail. Each lick is sufficient to justify your life. You say, "Okay, I'm not trying to get this nail out of the way so I can get onto something important. There's nothing more important. It's right there." And it goes—pow! It's not getting that nail in that's in your mind. It's hitting it—hitting it square, hitting it straight. Getting it now. That one lick.

If you see a carpenter that's alive to his work, you'll notice that about the way he hits a nail. He's not going (imitates machine gun rat-tat-tat-tat)—trying to get the nail down and out of the way so he can hurry up and get another one. Although he may be working fast, each lick is like a separate person that he's hitting with his hammer. It's like as though there's a separate friend of his that one moment. And when he gets out of it, here comes another one. Unique, all by itself. Pow! But you gotta stop before you get that nail in, you know? That's fine work. Hold the hammer back, and just that last lick, don't hit it with your hammer, hit it with a punch so you won't leave a hammer mark. Rhythm.

I worked at an H-bomb plant in South Carolina. My work was building forms. I don't think the end product bothered me so much, 'cause Judgment Day is not a thing . . . (Trails off.) It doesn't hang heavy on my heart. It might be that I should be persuaded it was inappropriate . . .

They got that big old reactor works with the heavy water and all that. This heavy equipment runs there day and night, just one right after another, going forty miles an hour, digging that big old hole halfway to hell. They build themselves a highway down there, just to dig that hole.

Now you're gonna have to build you a building, concrete and steel. You ship in a ready-mixed plant just for that building. A pump on the hill. It starts pumping concrete into the hole. It's near about time for the carpenters. We're building forms for the first floor of that thing. I was the twenty-four-hundredth-and-some-odd carpenter hired at the beginning. That's how big it was. There was three thousand laborers. Each time we built one of these reactors there would be a whole town to support it. We built a dozen or so towns in this one county.

We all understood we were making H-bombs and tried to get it done before the Russians built theirs, see? That's what everybody thought. It was one of those great secret jobs where you had guards at the gates, barbed wire around the place, spies, and all that kind of foolishness.

Some people call it the hard lard belt, some call it the Bible belt. Mostly just farmers who stepped from behind the plow, who had tenants or were tenants themselves. It was a living wage in that part of the country for the first time since the boll weevil had been through. And boy, you can't downrate that. It seems like the vast comedy of things when a Yankee came and got us to build their H-bomb, part of the fine comedy that she should come and give us the first living wage since the War of Northern Aggression—for this.

In Bloomington, Indiana, I saw a lot of women make their living making bombs. They had a grand picnic when they built the millionth bomb. Bombs they're dropping on people. And the students came to demonstrate against the bombs. Maybe these women see no sense in what they're doing, but they see their wages in what they're doing . . .

Some people will say, "I'm a poet. I'm better than you. I'm different. I'm a separate kind of species." It doesn't seem to me poetry is that way. It seems to me like mockin'birds sing and there's hardly ever a mockingbird that doesn't sing. It's the same way with poetry. It just comes natural to 'em, part of what we're made for. It's the natural utterance of living language. I say my calling is to be a carpenter and a poet. No contradiction.

(Chants) Work's quite a territory. Real work and fake work. There's fake work, which is the prostitution. There is the magic of payday, though. You'll say, "Well, if you get paid for your work, is that prostitution?" No indeed. But how are you gonna prove it's not? A real struggle there. Real work, fake work, and prostitution. The magic of payday. The groceries now heaped on the table and the new-crop wine and store-bought shirts. That's what it says, yes.

IN SEARCH
OF A CALLING

NORA WATSON

Jobs are not big enough for people. It's not just the assembly line worker whose job is too small for his spirit, you
know? A job like mine, if you really put your spirit into it,
you would sabotage immediately. You don't dare. So you
absent your spirit from it. My mind has been so divorced
from my job, except as a source of income, it's really absurd.

As I work in the business world, I am more and more
shocked. You throw yourself into things because you feel
that important questions—self-discipline, goals, a meaning
of your life—are carried out in your *work*. You invest a
job with a lot of values that the society doesn't allow you
to put into a job. You find yourself like a pacemaker
that's gone crazy or something. You want it to be a million things that it's not and you want to give it a million
parts of yourself that nobody else wants there. So you end
up wrecking the curve or else settling down and conforming. I'm really in a funny place right now. I'm so calm
about what I'm doing and what's coming . . .

*She is twenty-eight. She is a staff writer for an institution
publishing health care literature. Previously she had
worked as an editor for a corporation publishing national
magazines.*

*She came from a small mountain town in western Penn-
sylvania. "My father was a preacher. I didn't like what he
was doing, but it was his vocation. That was the good part
of it. It wasn't just: go to work in the morning and punch*

675

a time clock. It was a profession of himself. I expected work to be like that. All my life, I planned to be a teacher. It wasn't until late in college, my senior year, that I realized what the public school system was like. A little town in the mountains is one thing . . .

"My father, to my mind, is a weird person, but whatever he is, he is. Being a preacher was so important to him he would call it the Call of the Lord. He was willing to make his family live in very poor conditions. He was willing to strain his relationship to my mother, not to mention his children. He put us through an awful lot of things, including just bare survival, in order to stay being a preacher. His evenings, his weekends, and his days, he was out calling on people. Going out with healing oil and anointing the sick, listening to their troubles. The fact that he didn't do the same for his family is another thing. But he saw himself as the core resource in the community—at a great price to himself. He really believed that was what he was supposed to be doing. It was his life.

Most of the night he wouldn't go to bed. He'd pull out sermons by Wesley or Spurgeon or somebody, and he'd sit down until he fell asleep, maybe at three o'clock in the morning. Reading sermons. He just never stopped. (Laughs.)

I paper the walls of my office with posters and bring in flowers, bring in an FM radio, bring down my favorite ceramic lamp. I'm the only person in the whole damn building with a desk facing the window instead of the door. I just turn myself around from all that I can. I ration my time so that I'll spend two hours working for the Institution and the rest of the time I'll browse. (Laughs.)

I function better if they leave me alone more. My boss will come in and say, "I know you're overloaded, but would you mind getting this done, it's urgent. I need it in three weeks." I can do it in two hours. So I put it on the back burner and produce it on time. When I first went there, I came in early and stayed late. I read everything I could on the subject at hand. I would work a project to the wall and get it really done right, and then ask for more. I found out I was wrecking the curve, I was out of line.

The people, just as capable as I and just as ready to produce, had realized it was pointless, and had cut back.

Everyone, consciously or unconsciously, was rationing his time. Playing cards at lunch time for three hours, going sun bathing, or less obvious ways of blowing it. I realized: Okay, the road to ruin is doing a good job. The amazing, absurd thing was that once I decided to stop doing a good job, people recognized a kind of authority in me. Now I'm just moving ahead like blazes.

I have my own office. I have a secretary. If I want a book case, I get a book case. If I want a file, I get a file. If I want to stay home, I stay home. If I want to go shopping, I go shopping. This is the first comfortable job I've ever had in my life and it is absolutely despicable.

I've been a waitress and done secretarial work. I knew, in those cases, I wasn't going to work at near capacity. It's one thing to work to your limits as a waitress because you end up with a bad back. It's another thing to work to your limits doing writing and editing because you end up with a sharper mind. It's a joy. Here, of all places, where I had expected to put the energy and enthusiasm and the gifts that I may have to work—it isn't happening. They expect less than you can offer. Token labor. What writing you do is writing to order. When I go for a job interview—I must leave this place!—I say, "Sure, I can bring you samples, but the ones I'm proud of are the ones the Institution never published."

It's so demeaning to be there and not be challenged. It's humiliation, because I feel I'm being forced into doing something I would never do of my own free will—which is simply waste itself. It's really not a Puritan hang-up. It's not that I want to be persecuted. It's simply that I know I'm vegetating and being paid to do exactly that. It's possible for me to sit here and read my books. But then you walk out with no sense of satisfaction, with no sense of legitimacy! I'm being had. Somebody has bought the right to you for eight hours a day. The manner in which they use you is completely at their discretion. You know what I mean?

I feel like I'm being pimped for and it's not my style. The level of bitterness in this department is stunning. They take days off quite a bit. They don't show up. They don't even call in. They've adjusted a lot better than I have. They see the Institution as a free ride as long as it lasts. I don't want to be party to it, so I've gone my own way. It's like being on welfare. Not that that's a shameful thing. It's the surprise of this enforced idleness. It makes you feel not at home with yourself. I'm furious. It's a feeling that I will not be humiliated. I will not be dis-used.

For all that was bad about my father's vocation, he showed me it was possible to fuse your life to your work. His home was also his work. A parish is no different from an office, because it's the whole countryside. There's nothing I would enjoy more than a job that was so meaningful to me that I brought it home.

The people I work with are not buffoons. I think they're part of a culture, like me, who've been sold on a dum-dum idea of human nature. It's frightening. I've made the best compromise available. If I were free, economically free, I would go back to school. It galls me that in our culture we have to pay for the privilege of learning.

A guy was in the office next to mine. He's sixty-two and he's done. He came to the Institution in the forties. He saw the scene and said, "Yes, I'll play drone to you. I'll do all the piddley things you want. I won't upset the apple cart by suggesting anything else." With a change of regimes in our department, somebody came across him and said, "Gee, he hasn't contributed anything here. His mind is set in old attitudes. So we'll throw him out." They fired him unceremoniously, with no pension, no severance pay, no nothing. Just out on your ear, sixty-two. He gets back zero from having invested so many years playing the game.

The drone has his nose to the content of the job. The politicker has his nose to the style. And the politicker is what I think our society values. The politicker, when it's apparent he's a winner, is helped. Everyone who has a stake in being on the side of the winner gives him a boost. The minute I finally realized the way to exist at the Institution—for the short time I'll be here—was not to break my back but to use it for my own ends, I was a winner.

Granted, there were choices this guy could have made initially. He might have decided on a more independent way of life. But there were all sorts of forces keeping him from that decision. The Depression, for one thing. You took the job, whatever the terms were. It was a straight negotiation. The drone would get his dole. The Institution broke the contract. He was fired for being dull, which is what he was hired to be.

I resist strongly the mystique of youth that says these kids are gonna come up with the answers. One good thing a lot of the kids are doing, though, is not getting themselves tied up to artificial responsibilities. That includes marriage, which some may or may not call an artificial responsibility. I have chosen to stay unmarried, to not get encumbered with husband and children. But the guy with three kids and a mortgage doesn't have many choices. He wouldn't be able to work two days a week instead of five.

I'm coming to a less moralistic attitude toward work. I know very few people who feel secure with their right just to be—or comfortable. Just you being you and me being me with my mini-talents may be enough. Maybe just making a career of being and finding out what that's about is enough. I don't think I have a calling—at this moment—except to be me. But nobody pays you for being you, so I'm at the Institution—for the moment . . .

When you ask most people who they are, they define themselves by their jobs. "I'm a doctor." "I'm a radio announcer." "I'm a carpenter." If somebody asks me, I say, "I'm Nora Watson." At certain points in time I do things for a living. Right now I'm working for the Institution. But not for long. I'd be lying to you if I told you I wasn't scared.

I have a few options. Given the market, I'm going to take the best job I can find. I really tried to play the game by the rules, and I think it's a hundred percent unadulterated bullshit. So I'm not likely to go back downtown and say, "Here I am. I'm very good, hire me."

You recognize yourself as a marginal person. As a person who can give only minimal assent to anything that is going on in this society: "I'm glad the electricity works." That's about it. What you have to find is your own niche that will allow you to keep feeding and clothing and sheltering yourself without getting downtown. (Laughs.) Because that's death. That's really where death is.

WALTER LUNDQUIST

He's fifty; a commercial artist, designer. "I deplore the whole idea of commercialism. I find it degrading."

I was a kid in 1942 when I got out of art school. I wanted to make a lot of money and become famous. In five years I'll own the world. I'll be in New York driving a Cadillac and owning my own plane. I want gold cuff links and babes and the big house in the country. The whole bit. The American Dream. (Laughs.) That beautiful, ugly, vicious dream that we all, in some way, have. I wanted to be a key man in the industry. Over the years I realized there isn't any key man—that every man, every human is a commodity to be exploited. And destroyed and cast aside. For thirty years I've been a commercial hack.

The problem isn't the work itself. Does it have a real meaning or is it a piece of commercial pap? The question gets down to who the hell pays for it. Okay. You want a living, you want to eat. Say you're a bookkeeper. Are you counting something of human value or are you counting for the Syndicate or the Pentagon? Are you a bookkeeper counting dead bodies or children at school? What kind of an individual are you? Do you feel you're something because you create a cute commercial spot that sells a product that has no human value? Is it all purely style? Is there no content?

I had my own organization, fifteen people. "Let's go out and do a job for the client. Yes, sir. Let's lick his boots." Who's the man with the checkbook? What does he want from you? Now you take nice things and make them into some dumb package. Some plastic thing which is not biodegradeable, which will not decompose, which fills the society where you want to scream, "We're drowning in plastics!"

You think of the advertiser and his influence on our sexual climate. Vaginal sprays are now on the market. Why is a woman spraying her vagina? Because she's tastier? Who's going down there sniffing? You see two young girls on TV talking about a date. One tells the other she's using a vaginal spray. Why doesn't her girl friend do it? God! What a cunt-lapping society we've become!

I wanted to be at the drawing board, creative, doing something I believed in. But I became a pimp. I didn't start drinking until I was thirty. I surprised myself. I found I could outdrink any of my clients. They got drunk and I didn't. What an absurd way to live! To make money because you could booze it up and cater to someone else's frailty. His need for a boot licker's comradeship, listening to his cheap jokes at some expensive bar. I got the work all right, but it made me sick. I couldn't stand it.

We had a client who was providing additives to meats and food preparations. My job was to make it into a trade publication ad. I'm sitting at these meetings with the president of the company and the sales manager. We're out to provide a service to the meat packers so they can cheat government analysts who are going to inspect the sausages. They don't see it as cheating. I say, "Why are we doing this ad for mustard?" They say, "Mustard acts as a binder." It holds together the globules of fat the client is putting in. So we make a living selling mustard because the guy wants to put fat instead of meat protein in there. So the public's been cheated and these sons of bitches are out there playing golf . . .

We were doing a beautiful job for a big brewer. They'd just bought a new brewery and found out the beer was too nutritious. It had a lot of food value. They did market research and found out that psychologically inadequate young men consumed beer as a way of competing with one another—the kids in college. "Can you drink fourteen bottles of beer while I drink fourteen bottles of beer?" How many can you drink before you puke? The beer that sells the best is the weakest and the thinnest and doesn't fight you. The first thing they did was to take the richness out of it. They got it down to alcohol and water.

My role was to create a fun-filled image, an exciting boy-girl gaiety in the competitive market of light beer. "Light beer"—that's the ad phrase for watered and thin beer. So the schmucky kid thinks he's a stud fighting for the babe by consuming all that alcohol.

You begin to say, "What the fuck am I doing? I'm sitting here destroying my country." The feeling gets stronger and stronger and suddenly your father dies.

The turning point in my life was the death of my father. It was a funny thing. Here you're watching a beautiful guy with white hair lying in his bed, dying of a heart attack. You hear him ramble and wander and talk about his life: "I was never anything. I didn't do a job even in raising my children. I didn't mean anything . . ." You watch death. Then you say, "Wait a minute. What's going on with him is going to hit me. What am I doing between now and my death? If you take actuarial tables of insurance companies, I'm running on borrowed time." You begin to assess yourself and that's a shock. I didn't come up smelling like a rose. "Am I going to go on forever being a goddamn pimp? What's the alternative? Is there another way of earning a living?"

I had a client who was my best friend. I'd known him twenty years. We'd been sitting together talking casually. I was telling him my feelings. He was shocked. "For Chrissake," he says, "you're my enemy. From now on I'm never going to deal with you again." I haven't seen this poor guy in four years.

At this moment I have a job on the drawing board that's pretty good. This one client has some degree of conscience. It's an ecology poster for children, given away as a premium. It's a beautiful thing to hang on the wall, acquainting a child with the cycle of life. I'm working on two film strips for education. One's on Luther Burbank and the other's on Franz Boas. But—little dough.

Now fifty percent of my time is taken up with antiwar work. Of course, nobody pays for this kind of message. The big problem I'm facing is how to support my family. I'm straddling two worlds and I'm trying to move over into the sane one. But I can't make a living out of it.

I have a very small office. As soon as I come in, the phone starts ringing. All free jobs. Usually my paying jobs get done later. (Laughs.) They're the ones I take home with me. My family watches TV and I sit down beside them and work through the evening to turn out the paying job, so I can get my bread and spend the rest of the day doing what I think is important. I put in a sixteen-hour day. It's a crazy cycle. It's been a trying experience for my wife. She thinks I'm psychologically sick. She goes one way and I go the other. My kids pay a terrible penalty for me . . .

I'm struggling to survive. I'm running out of funds. I may have to pimp again for survival's sake. But I'll not give up the sane work. I'm scurrying about. If it doesn't work, I may do somewhat what young people do and drop out. I'll stop existing in this society. I'll work on a road crew. I'll cut lumber or whatever the hell it'll be. But I'll never again play the full-time lying dishonest role I've done most of my life.

Once you wake up the human animal you can't put it back to sleep again. I guess I'm pretty schizophrenic. Obviously all the schizophrenics are not locked up in asylums. (Laughs.)

REBECCA SWEENEY

"I never felt that I'd been searching for a calling. Circumstances made me look around and keep right on looking. Over the last years I've been fired sixteen times. (Laughs.) I'd have to dig up all my records to tell you all the jobs I was fired from." She is thirty-five.

I grew up in a devout Irish Catholic family. By the time I was eighteen I decided to be a nun. I wanted to be a doctor too. So I found a religious order, the Medical Mission Sisters. I was never assigned to a hospital. I did farm work and office work and I cooked. I took care of the property too. I enjoyed it. But after six years I was asked to leave. I didn't know why. I think it was a personality difference between myself and the Superior. I was hurt because I had been rejected. All I did was cry about it. As soon as I walked out my spirits picked up. I was looking for something new and adventurous.

I was twenty-four and too old to study medicine. So I just went ahead for my degree in sociology. I attended the university at night and got a job as a bank teller. I realized there were no black people employed at the bank. So I went in and talked to the personnel man and the president. Before I knew it, people were no longer talking to me. I used to come in all smiles and people'd say, "Hi." Now I was getting the cold shoulder.

One young woman—I had talked religion with her, she was a Lutheran—said she agreed with me but didn't want to lose her job. She warned me to be careful. I said no, the president had a nice Irish Catholic name and everything. (Laughs.) I called the Labor Board. They said they could only protect me if I was organizing a union. So I immediately began talking union. The president called me in. "First you talk about this integration stuff and now you're talking union. If you're not careful, we'll let you go."

One day a Negro girl applied for a job. As soon as I

saw her leave the bank I followed her. I told them I was going on my pass. Caught her on the street. She thought I was nuts. I told her if she wasn't hired, to go to the FEPC and keep in touch with me. A few days later she called me. And a few days after that I was fired.

I got a job in a girls' detention home. The girls were coming to me with their problems instead of going to the nuns, 'cause I was younger and wasn't in a habit and joked around with them a little. I was asked to leave.

Then I got a job in a hospital as an aide and surgical technician, scrubbing operations. There was a group organizing the hospital help. I wasn't able to do much because I was going to school and active in the peace movement and knocking myself out. But I was talking it up. I put the laundry people in touch with the union. The personnel director called me in. My work reports were excellent but he did fire me.

I was pumping gas in a Standard station because I was tired of working indoors. I knew something about cars. I was fired from that job because I wouldn't sleep with the boss. That job lasted only a couple of months.

When I finished my education I knew I wanted to get into union work. So I started doing work in different factories, making contacts—nonunion shops. I worked in one plant as a machine operator, makin' nuts and bolts and drill press work. I've always liked mechanical work, work with my hands. Work you can put your energy into.

I just went around and got different jobs in other plants and got regularly fired. In the meantime, to pick up money, I was driving a cab. I've always liked to drive a car. I didn't really like that so much. It was hard on my eyes and my neck. I had fun. Since I was white, they'd say, "I suppose there's some places in this city you don't like to drive." I'd say, "Yeah, there's one place." They'd say, "What?" They'd be expecting me to say the South Side. I'd say, "The Loop. I tell you driving there is terrible." (Laughs.) They'd stop all conversation. That job I quit, believe it or not.

I took some census work in '70. It's such a bureaucracy. They keep bringing up different supervisors and firing people and transferring them and everything. Rather than come out and say it's a temporary job—two, three months—they pick on you and lay you off. When you're fired it goes on your record. People were mad about it. I got fired for using vulgar language. (Laughs.) I called a supervisor a goddamn motherfucker. That was it.

I was doing automatic lathes in another plant. The Steel Workers Union was there. I went to meetings right away and would give my opinion. The plant had about five thousand people. Maybe thirty would come to meetings. I was raising issues all the time, mostly health and safety in the plants. The local president was a company man but about half a dozen people told him, "We'd like you to assign Becky to the Health and Safety Committee. She's really good." I'd go to the local fire department and find out about regulations. Some doors were blocked off because they stacked materials there. I'd raise the issue.

I really liked doing that work. I studied chess while I was working. People would laugh at me 'cause I would buy a paperback chess book, tear a page out, and stick it up on the machine. When I'd have a three-minute pause, while the pieces were running through, I'd be reading that thing over. They'd say, "You read all your books that way? A page at a time?" They got a kick out of it.

I got along fine with 'em. We had good friendships. One woman, May, was a lathe operator. Only the men had the bigger lathes and they got more dough. She knew the company wouldn't give it to her, so she never applied. I got mad at her. I really gave it to her. I went and applied for the job myself. I got another young girl to do it too. Just to make an issue. Then May went in and applied. The personnel guy called the three of us in. He started telling us how hard it was. So I reached in my back pocket and pulled out a brochure from the Equal Employment Opportunities Commission, with Title Seven of the 1964 Civil Rights Act. I laid that on the table. He didn't stop to catch his breath. He said, "Of course, May, if you want this job you're welcome to it. You're the most qualified." She got the job.

Eventually they did fire me. For falsifying my application. I had left off that I worked in the bank. I knew they wouldn't give me good references and I'd never get the job. And I didn't put down that I had a college degree. That was suspicious—somebody that is too smart to be doing this dumb work.

I filed a grievance and the union had to take it to arbitration. Oh, I'm telling you. Something else they brought up—I was involved with CORE and the civil rights thing around the bank. They had really dug. Anything written about me, they dug up. HUAC* had investigated me 'cause I was involved in the Students' Mobilization Committee.

So the arbitrator ruled in favor of the company. The workers felt bad about it. They said they'd like to help me, but they were afraid to make statements on my behalf. They were really scared.

My health was running down quite a bit. I had arthritis. I was thrown from a horse. I had broken bones. I was wearing a neck brace. I had pimples all over my face. The specialist said, "Don't strain yourself." But I started taking karate. I had been raped and I was interested in self-defense. I went to a naprapath. He agreed with my doing karate. He changed my eating habits and my health improved completely.

I got on the staff of UE.† My union work transferred me to Ohio. I joined a karate club down in the hills. I dropped out because I was hit a couple of times and it hurt. So I decided to do some yoga. I found that more to my liking. While I was doing organizing I would do yoga every day. I made it a way of life. I teach it.

I was very busy in union work in Ohio. I was organizing a plant of thirteen hundred, mostly women. It was an electrical plant and they had lightweight stuff. I would get so wound up in the work and be running around so much that the only way I could unwind was yoga.

I was fired from UE. It was not political. It had more to do with the fact that I'm an outspoken woman, that I have been involved with Women's Liberation, and that I'm unmarried. There has also been a development in the openness of lesbians. Some men lumped all these together. So . . .

My way of dealing with this question is the same way I deal with communism. Any time anyone was challenging me, "Are you a communist?" I'd say, "What is the issue?" It's the same way in dealing with Women's Liberation. Only instead of calling it communism, they call it lesbianism. I think that's why I was fired. The innuendoes.

* House Un-American Activities Committee.
† United Electrical Workers of America.

Many people have suffered because of this. Not because of the loss of me. Lord knows I can be replaced very easily. But this plant in Ohio is going to cost the union. It was a very difficult campaign. People tried five times before to organize it. The company would hire high-school girls and they could care less about the union. They always voted it down. I was in touch weekly with about sixty desperate people who wanted the union. They were behind me. But one of the factory workers in the plant was dead set against me. He didn't want any "broad" telling him what to do. The other people didn't care about him, but he reached the union's higher-ups.

Some of the best people at the plant were furious when I was fired. "If they do this to Becky, what are they gonna do to us?" Even one of the better union officials refused to stand up for me. He said, "It's one thing to fight for the working class, but it's another thing to take a fight on for lesbianism."

I'm collecting unemployment while I'm teaching yoga once a week at a Catholic girls' high school. So now I've enrolled in a college to study naprapathy, which is a form of drugless healing. I'd like to show people how to cure themselves while letting nature cure. I'm also studying colon therapy. Our system isn't clean.

The first few times I was fired, I cried because my feelings were hurt. When I was fired from UE, the first thing I did was to call the doctor and ask him if I could get into college right away. He said yes. So everything's fine. When I was in high school I thought a vocation was a particular calling. Here's a voice: "Come, follow me." My idea of a calling now is not: "Come." It's what I'm doing right now, not what I'm going to be. Life is a calling.

I pretty well flow with the tide. You know what I'd like to do someday? I would like to be a heavy equipment operator. These big earth movers . . . If I don't get it done in this life, maybe I'll get it done in my next life.

SECOND CHANCE

FRED RINGLEY

We have a small farm in Arkansas. It's a mile and a half off the highway on a dirt road on top of a hill. It's thirteen and a half acres. We call it Lucky Thirteen. We are in the process of building a cattle herd, because you can't make a living as a farmer unless you have thousands of acres.

We have five children, six to eleven. Three girls and two boys. The eleven-year-old boy takes care of the cattle. The ten-year-old girl takes care of the chickens. The nine-year-old boy takes care of the two hogs. And the youngest girls take care of the dog.

We purchased a dairy bar—a combination ice cream parlor and hamburger joint. My wife and I alternate from ten in the morning until ten at night. This is a carry-out joint. It's a mama-and-papa operation. A Benedictine abbey sits on top of the hill. It's a boarding school for boys. They don't like the food in their dining room and they furnish our daytime business.

He is forty years old. Until a year ago he had lived all his life in the environs of Chicago. He was born in one of its North Shore suburbs; he was raised, reached adulthood, and became a paterfamilias as a "typical suburbanite." His was a bedroom community, middle-class, "of struggle for the goods of the world." He had worked in advertising as a copywriter and salesman.

We were caught up in the American Dream. You've

gotta have a house. You've gotta have a country club. You've gotta have two cars. Here you are at ten grand and getting nowhere. So I doubled my salary. I also doubled my grief. I now made twenty thousand dollars, had an expense account, a Country Squire—air-conditioned station wagon given by the company—a wonderful boss. We began to accumulate. We got a house in the suburbs and we got a country club membership and we got two cars and we got higher taxes. We got nervous and we started drinking more and smoking more. Finally, one day we sat down. We have everything and we are poor.

The superhighways were coming through. Ramada Inn moved in and Holiday Inn moved in. We used to sit around until three in the morning, my wife and I, and say, "There's gotta be a better way." We own a travel trailer. We said, "Suppose we hook the trailer up to the car and just went around these United States and tried to figure out where would be a good place to live—where we could make a living and still have the natural background we want. How could we do it? We're only average people. We don't put any money away. Our equity is in our home."

We sold the house, paid off everybody we owe, put our furniture in storage, and started driving. We had everything in the big city and quit while we were still ahead. We had seen what we wanted to see in the East. It's time to go West.

We had two criteria: water and climate. We ruled out the North and the deep South. That left us a straight line from Indianapolis to New Mexico. We decided central Arkansas was the best for environment. They've backed up the river and made these fantastic lakes. We bought this farm.

Our neighbors came over. They're sixty-eight. They're broiler farmers.* She plays piano in the church, by song-

* "Arkansas is the leading producer of poultry in the United States. The broiler farmer invests somewhere between twenty and thirty thousand dollars in two chicken houses. They hold up to seven thousand baby chicks. The packing company puts the chicks in and supplies the feed and medicine. At the end of eight weeks they're four and a half pounds. The companies pick 'em up and pay you for 'em. Ralph Nader's been after them. It's almost white slavery. The farmer invests and the com-

books written in do-re-mi notes. I brought a record out—
hits of the last sixty years. It was from Caruso to Mario
Lanza or something. She didn't recognize one piece of music on that record except Eddy Arnold. They didn't get a
radio down there until about 1950, because they weren't
wired for electricity.† So we've got one foot in the thirties
and one in the seventies.

We have a milk cow, a Jersey. I had never put my hand
on a cow. The people we bought the home from taught us
how to milk her. We discovered a cow can be contrary
and hold her milk up if she wants to tighten certain muscles and doesn't like your cold grip. People would come
over and watch us and laugh.

All through this eight-thousand-mile trip, Daddy is
thinking, Maybe I haven't done the right thing. Everywhere I went, they said, "You'll never make money."
Friends said, "Oh, Fred's lost his beans." We were digging
into our backlog money for food. Time was passing. It
was winter.

I realize there are only two ways to do things: work for
somebody else or be an owner. There are two classes of
people, the haves and the have-nots. The haves own. I
went to the local bank and discovered that this dairy bar
was for sale. I said, "I can cook a hamburger." But I'd
never worked in a restaurant, even as a bus boy or a soda
jerk. We borrowed a hundred percent of the money from

---

pany can say, 'This is a lousy lot, we're not gonna pay you
the full price.' But you're still putting in twelve hours a day."

† Clyde Ellis, a former congressman from Arkansas, recalls,
"I wanted to be at my parents' house when electricity came.
It was in 1940. We'd all go around flipping the switch, to make
sure it hadn't come on yet. We didn't want to miss it. When
they finally came on, the lights just barely glowed. I remember
my mother smiling. When they came on full, tears started to
run down her cheeks. After a while she said: 'Oh, if only we
had it when you children were growing up.' We had lots of
illness. Anyone who's never been in a family without electricity—with illness—can't imagine the difference. . . . They had
all kinds of parties—mountain people getting light for the
first time. There are still areas without electricity . . ." (quoted
in *Hard Times* [New York: Pantheon Books, 1970]).

the bank, fourteen thousand dollars. We revamped the entire place because it hadn't been kept up.

We don't have car hops. You come to the window. We serve you a to-go meal through the window. Inside we have five tables, and in the alcove a little game room with three pinball machines. We serve hamburger, fried chicken, pizzaburger—we introduced it in the area—chili dogs, Tastee Freeze, candy. Bubble gum's a good seller. We sell a plastic bag of shaved ice for a quarter to tourists, fishermen. Coke, Dr. Pepper, Sprite. Fish sandwiches.

We've had the bar only six months. We're trying to get it to a point where we spend less and less time there. The owner has to be there, 'cause they come in to see you as much as they come in to eat. They come in and say, "How's the cow?" They've never forgotten. They say, "How's the farm and how are the ticks?" And so on. And, "The place looks nice." They get all dressed up for this. The wife puts on her best dress and comes to the dairy bar for dinner. It's a big deal.

If all goes well and we've doubled the business, we'll close when school closes. Maybe we'll close for Easter week. And then close another week when the boys in the abbey have off. So we'll end with a month's vacation. We're only a day's drive from New Orleans. We'll go there this winter.

My wife opens the place at ten. Help comes from eleven to one—high-school girls. At three she comes home and gets me. We traded our Country Squire for a used pickup truck. At about three thirty the boys come from the abbey and play pinball machines and have hamburgers. I stay until ten at night.

I'm a short order cook and bottle washer and everything else—until ten. Shut the lights off, clean the grill. Sometimes I'll stop off at the tavern across the street and shoot the breeze until he closes at eleven. I'll come home and my wife is watching the news or Johnny Carson. That's when we talk. She tells me how the animals are doing and the kids are doing. We go to bed about midnight and it starts all over the next day. Except Monday.

Monday we're closed. Now we begin to reap the benefits of what we went there for. On Monday we put the kids on the bus to school. We get in the truck, we throw the boat in the back. Six minutes from our front door, we put it in one of the world's largest man-made lakes and go

fishing and picknicking and mess around until four o'clock
when the kids come home. We sit out there, where I don't
suppose three boats go by us all day long. Sit and watch
the copperheads on the shore and the birds overhead. Discussing Nixon and Daley and fishing and the dairy bar and
whatever. What's astonishing is we can climb a mountain
right across from our home. There's a waterfall at the top.
And no jets going over. No people. Just a pickup truck
down the road now and then.

A man stood on Eden's Highway* and took a survey of
guys driving to work. Their jaw muscles were working. I
was one of those guys. I was this guy with his eyes bulging
and swearing and saying, "You rotten guy, get out of my
way." For what? So I could get to work to get kicked
around by a purchasing agent because his job is five minutes late? That forty-five minutes' drive to work. I would
usually have about five cigarettes. Constant close calls,
jam-ups, running late, tapping the foot on the floor,
thumping that wheel, and everything that everybody does.

I would get to the office. You might find the paper
hadn't been delivered, the press had broken down, the boss
might be in a foul mood. Or you might have a guy on the
phone screaming that he had to see you in half an hour or
else the whole world would end. They always had to have
an estimate first. So you'd do your paper work as fast as
you could. Then you'd start your round of daily calls.
Then came the hassle for parking space. Are you lucky
enough to get one of those hour jobs on the street or do
you go in the lot? If you go in the lot, what're they gonna
do to your car before they give it back to you? How many
dents? So you go through that hassle.

Then it would be lunch time. You'd take a guy to lunch,
have two or three drinks. Rich food ... You come out of
the darkened restaurant back into the summer afternoon.
At four you'd take whatever jobs you had assembled or
proofs you had to look over. Maybe work until five thirty
or six. Then you're fighting the traffic back to the suburb.

I'd be home at a quarter to seven. We would just sit
down and eat. We would finish at eight, with dinner and
conversation, looking at the kids' report cards and whatever. Then we'd watch TV if something decent was on. If it
was daylight saving time, we'd play ball with the kids until

* An expressway leading into and out of Chicago.

nine or ten. Then we'd go to bed. Or else we'd start hacking away at our personal problems. Mostly it was fighting the bills. On weekends we'd go to the country club for dinner. I belonged for three years and never played the course. I never had time.

Just the intolerable strain of living here is fantastic, especially when you've been away for a year.* I haven't been as nervous in one day driving mountains with radiators blowing out as I was the half-hour it took my father to drive me down here this morning—in his Oldsmobile.

If you decide to cut and run, you've got to do it in one clean break. You'll never do it if you piddle away and if you wait until you're sixty. A fellow I know, he was sixty-three, bought a piece of land in Taos, on a mountain top, forty acres. He and his wife were gonna go in three years and move there. He told me this on a Tuesday. On Saturday his wife was dead in the garden. The day he buried her he said to me, "Boy, you're so smart to get out while you're young." Our decision to make this journey evolved over a period of years. Not so strangely, it came about with our achievement of what is called the American Dream.

People say, "You're wasting your college education." My ex-employer said to my father, "You didn't raise your son to be a hash slinger." I've lost status in the eyes of my big city friends. But where I am now I have more status than I would in the city. I'm a big fish in a little pond. I'm a minor celebrity. I can be a hash slinger there and be just as fine as the vice president of the Continental Bank. If I were a hash slinger in the suburbs, they'd ask me to move out of the neighborhood. I said to myself as a kid, What's Mr. So-and-so do? Oh, he only runs a cleaners. He's not a big wheel at all. My personal status with somebody else may have gone down. My personal status with myself has gone up a hundred percent.

I think an education is to make you well-rounded. The first room we built in this house was the library. But I believe we've gotten too far away from physical work. I found this out working around my house in the suburb. I could have one terrible day and come home and hang a wall of wallpaper and get so involved, do the edges, make

* The conversation took place in Chicago during his visit, the purpose of which was the delivery of some cattle.

sure there are no air bubbles under it—that I could forget all my frustrations. I don't think jogging is enough. I believe most suburban guys are happier and easier to get along with when they're out cutting the grass than when they're in that Cadillac. I work on the house in Arkansas. It's just an old oak frame. There's no finish. I'm remodeling all the way through. You're rehanging doors and moving thresholds. Just by trial and error. When I walked out of my old life I weighed 185 pounds. As you see me today I weigh 160. I feel healthier than I've ever felt in my life.

I don't say I'm gonna end up the rest of my life as a hash slinger, either. I may buy more land and get more involved in cattle. I would like to go a hundred percent in farming, but it would require ten times the land I've got, and it takes time ... In the cattle business there's enough demand for meat, so you can make a comfortable living between the cattle and the broilers. I might expand the dairy bar into a regular restaurant, make it a little fancy. I've got a lot of different ways to go.

But one thing we've still got—the one thing my wife would not let me get rid of—is we still got the trailer. We can go again if we have to. If we found something better, maybe a higher mountain top to live on, we'd go live there.

PHILIP DA VINCI

He is a lawyer, twenty-nine years old. Until three years ago he had been working for the house counsel of a large insurance company. Though "doing very well," he and a colleague suddenly quit and took off—wandering out West.

I was defending the company against people who had been hit by cars. I honestly took that job because it was the first rung on the ladder. The next thing would have been to jump sides in the game, become a PI—a personal injury lawyer for the plaintiffs. Passing out cards to policemen and start getting referrals and making a lot of money and on and on and on and on. Had I remained with the company for twenty-five years, I would have walked out with $350,000 in profit sharing. (Laughs.)

The first three months were novel. Getting up there and playing the advocate. The novelty wore off when I found out what I was really doing. Spending eight, ten hours a day defending an insurance company was a waste of time. If I had this education, I might as well do something useful.

I drove a cab. Somebody told me about Legal Aid. I went there with the intention of staying only six weeks, make a grubstake, and go to New York. I started working in Uptown.* When it came time to go to New York I said, "No, I'm gonna stay." I finally got into something where I actually felt useful. It's been two years now. I'm still a lawyer, but it's different.

My clients are Appalachians, blacks, senior citizens, people in landlord-tenant cases. We're in Juvenile Court. We represent people abused by police. We represent inmates of the state penitentiary. My clients are people who've been dumped into Uptown as a result of overcrowding in state hospitals.† They're like camps, some of them—six to a room. They're dying. After you pressure the hell out of them and threaten an exposé, the Building Department files a suit and they move the people to a better place. All the day labor agencies are down the street, the slave marts.

For the last nine months I've been fighting with the Illinois Department of Financial Institutions. They are twenty-six companies that call themselves debt planners. There's one that advertises on a Spanish-speaking TV program. It preys on the people. They get 'em in there and they have 'em sign these contracts in English which they can't read. Making debts that don't exist, charging exhorbitant fees. Finally they said they'll investigate—a slap on

* A slum area of Chicago, inhabited primarily by poor white immigrants from the deep South and Appalachia.

† In the area are halfway houses for people who have been released from mental institutions. They are hotels that in earlier times, when the neighborhood was less transient in nature, were patronized by middle-class guests. Some are operated responsibly and with a modicum of tender loving care. There are others . . .

the wrist. So we filed our own law suit attacking the companies directly. It's intentional malfeasance on the part of the bureaucracy not to enforce the laws, not to impinge on the mercantilism of the slumlords, shylocks, et cetera. We're constantly attacking the bureaucracy.

He works out of a storefront office. "We have a group of law students from the school where I teach—two classes a week. Plus two Mexican women and one black woman, who help us run the office." It is funded by the Office of Economic Opportunity. "Had I stayed downtown practicing law, I'd be making slightly more money, more than slightly . . ." (Laughs.)

Every day is different. There's no boredom 'cause there's so much going on. A typical day? We walk out of our office and all of a sudden two guys in topcoats walk up behind us and start taking our picture. As we walk in the restaurant, they're looking at us. As we walk out, our pictures are taken again. Red Squad, Chicago Police Department.* Because we represented the Young Patriots.† That was at the time when they established the free medical clinic. The city was trying to close it down. They were keeping a file on the activist lawyers in the city.

I walk back to the office and interview people. Calling finance companies, trying to find defenses on contracts where people have signed, not knowing what the hell they signed because they can't read English. Their car gets repossessed, their wages are garnisheed ... You can work four days straight, sixteen hours a day, and never feel tired. Until your eyes start falling out, and then you know you have to go to bed.

There's a new thing going on—the legal commune. Four or five people out of law school get together. They'll just work out of their apartment. We'd make exhorbitant fees if we were in private practice. But we charge one-tenth of what a lawyer would normally charge. You know,

---

* It has been officially known as the Industrial Squad. It came into being in the thirties, during the battles to organize the CIO.

† An organization of young Southern whites: the "hillbilly" equivalents of the Black Panthers and the Young Lords.

lawyers who behave are well paid in our society. (Laughs.)

At the insurance company it was all competition. You've got to push the other guy down and crawl on top of him and move up that way. If you don't push him down, you know he's gonna get over you and pass you up. He's gonna get that job and you're not gonna make as much money and you're not gonna get that title. Oh, the day dragged on! I was always sneaking out, going to a show downtown to pass a few hours. It was so boring. You have a stack of a hundred files on your desk. All you do is make check marks. Go into the court and make the same motion. The same thing, over and over, day after day. And why? To save the company money.

Here you're aware of the suffering of your client. You know the type of landlord he has. You know what his apartment looks like. You know the pressure he's under. It makes you all the more committed. We don't help them only with their legal problems. If they're suffering from a psychological problem we try to hook them up with a psychiatrist. Or try to get them in school. They're so pushed down, so depressed.

You get to know them intimately. We're very close. I've been in their houses. They come to my house. I know them all by their first names. We go out drinking. They're my friends. The people I worked with at the company, I never saw them after five o'clock. I would never think of sharing my thoughts with those people. The people I work with here are my life.

My work and my life, they've become one. No longer am I schizophrenic. At the other place you had to go to work with a suit and tie on. When it hit five you would run out, hop on a bus, and go home. I would immediately strip myself of my suit and put on levis, sandals, and a T-shirt. Of course, I still wear a suit and tie in court. I don't want to hurt my clients. But the falseness has passed. People have to accept me for what I am.

(Suddenly he is fatigued.) I don't consider myself a real lawyer. I'm not a lawyer in the sense that the better job I do, the more money I get from my client. I'm just trying to help . . . (Sighs wearily.) You can change a few things. But not much progress is being made. There are about two thousand of us in the country. The legislatures are not controlled by us. For every law we have declared unconstitutional, they rewrite five more. For every step we make, we're pushed back four. Some days I'm optimistic. Other days . . . (Trails off.)

Because of the commitment in this type of work, the amount of hours per day, per week, per month you put in, there's a burn-out process. Usually guys last here two years and they just burn out. It's just physically too much—and emotionally, God! That's what happened to Bud. (Laughs and indicates his colleague seated nearby.)

Bud, too, had previously worked for an establishment law firm. He became a "poor people's lawyer," and now, after two years at it, is taking time out. He chuckles ruefully: "They complained about small things on LaSalle Street. 'I didn't get my five hundred bucks from this guy.' Doesn't mean anything. Up here it's a wearing process. I go down to the office and I've got 110 cases and their lives are involved. You feel overcommited and overextended . . ."

In the past ten years I find myself unable to sit through it for another ten hours. You just become emotionally sick because of your powerlessness. You'd like to pick up a gun and get that cop who beat up that thirteen-year-old kid. You prepare that one brief and file that one complaint and go before the jury and get twenty-five bucks for a kid that's had his skull split open by five police officers. You know it's bullshit. Maybe the best way is to give the kid a gun and say, "Okay, square it." But those are the depressing moments.

It's a matter of maintaining a grasp on hope—that more people will become aware. Maybe things will get better in my lifetime. Maybe twenty, thirty, forty years from now. You're overwhelmed by so much, you just gotta turn off and say, "Man, I can't go back for two days." This happens a lot.

You live for two years in the ghetto and you get so absorbed, you don't see what's going on outside. I need more escape from this job than from my old one. At the insurance company you're not being battered from all sides. You have a few hassles but they're meaningless. Here, things are so heavy . . .

I have no regrets. On my bad days I feel I have wasted three years working here in the ghetto. But not over-all. It has helped me see a lot of things and made me aware of what's going on in our society—what the system does to people. I would have died on the other job. I would have become an alcoholic or a drug addict or something. It would have driven me to that, I'm sure.

SARAH HOUGHTON

It's a farmhouse in New Jersey. A Sunday brunch with her husband, Dave, who works in Manhattan. He spends long weekends here. She is a librarian at a private school.

She attended library school for four years, 1960 to 1964. Most people who went there had other jobs. She was forty-six. "We were referred to as second chancers, because we were all hoping for more rewarding work. All were looking to this as a release, as a 'now I'll live' kind of thing.

"I'd been out of college for twenty-five years. When I got out, it was during the Depression. If you had a liberal arts education, you couldn't get very much. Everybody went to Macy's." She did secretarial work, taught temporarily at a girls' college. "When I was very little I had a picture in my mind of how life was going to be." She worked as a newspaper reporter, edited trade union journals, and in 1949 "drifted" into the new field of television.

I was the first television producer the agency had hired. They had done a Wildroot commercial and the client didn't like the negligee the girl wore. Somebody said, "The only way to do it right is to hire a woman." So I was hired.

I didn't think I ever worked on anything I thought was terrible, really. Though I didn't think there was that much difference between Wildroot and someone else's shampoo. I know Coty has one kind of smell and another has another kind—a new lipstick, there's not that much difference.

I took pride in what I did. I made myself do it right. But it became increasingly ridiculous to spend all that time and energy making sure a print got to the station on Thursday the twenty-second at six o'clock. I dropped the film off myself on the way home because you couldn't be sure a messenger would get it there on time. What difference did it make if the film was there on Monday or Thursday? I felt, to live miserably under such pressure, to knock yourself out—it should be for something more important. Life was too short for this.

It was obvious, too, that the men were getting much more than I was. They were getting raises more regularly. They were getting twice as much as I was getting for the same work. That kind of stuff—which any woman gets used to, after a while.

Every time they'd lose a big account the pink slips would come out. Is it going to be me? Or somebody else? This is nervous-making. There'd be times when you were terribly busy and times when you'd sit around with nothing to do. You'd try to look busy. You'd sit there and knit or read or do double-crostics. You had to be by the telephone in case somebody'd call. I never took my work home with me. I took the tension home. You couldn't help doing that. If you're going to be tense, it should be for something worthwhile.

I could probably have stayed at the agency for ages. Perhaps being squeezed into one thing or another. The time would come when they'd say, "You will clean the film or get out." It happened to some people. They certainly weren't going to keep a sixty-five-year-old film producer. (Laughs.) So I had to think of something else.

I had known so many women—the only thing they could do after they left their jobs was to be a receptionist. I had seen too many ladies that had to earn their living doing these miserable things—receptionist, companion. Or going back to being a secretary. I didn't want this. Suddenly I had the inspiration. Why didn't I go to library school?

In the winter of 1960, I started thinking about library work. I don't know whether it was my sense of insecurity at the office or whether I just felt I had to get out. I heard there was no age limit, that you could be a librarian until you practically keeled over. I accepted the notion that I would probably work until I dropped. Anyway, I think people and books are a nice combination. It was comfortable to feel that you could probably do this for as long as you wanted to. So I went to Columbia Library from seven till eleven at night for four years.

An offer came from a private school in the small town near the farmhouse she and Dave bought. "My salary would be cut at least half. We talked and talked and talked. He said, 'I didn't sit around in our apartment four nights a week for four years for nothing. Take the job. It's what you want to do, for Christ's sake. Jesus, take it.' Dave convinced me.

"When I was very little, I had a picture in my mind of how life was going to be. You go straight ahead until you curve slightly to the right, until you get to be about twenty-one. Of course, after college you got married, and there was nothing after that. Everything was fine. This is what happened to all the people I knew. Maybe a couple of them worked a little bit. You had children and then everything was dandy.

"At Smith there were two thousand girls. This was during the Depression. There were no jobs. There was no vocational training. You could have taken education and taught, although it wasn't very fashionable. You knew you were going to do something very nice. I was brought up to know there was nothing I couldn't do. If I wanted to be President, I could be President. Nobody could beat me in anything. But I wasn't particularly good in anything. I wasn't a musician or a writer. No, I don't remember having a talent for anything. There was no set pattern to my life. I sort of went along accidentally from thing to thing. Until Dave forced me into this decision . . ."

I had never been behind a library desk in my life. At library school there is no practice teaching. It was another world. There was no pressure, nothing. There were books. The worst thing you could think of is whether the kids are gonna remember to unlock the library on Sundays so it'll be open. Nobody behaved as if I'd never been in a library before. The kids were great. There hasn't been a tense day since. A charmed life. Don't miss the city, don't miss the job, don't miss the expense account (laughs), don't miss any part of it.

There was another reason I didn't want to get stuck as a little lady receptionist, smiling and directing someone. I'd go out of my mind. On this job, you can *use* your mind. Things that are challenging. Find out what some of the new math phrases mean. Selecting books is a complicated matter. If you have thousands and thousands of dollars in your budget, it doesn't make that much difference if you make a few mistakes. But we're limited here. I must be very frugal.

It's one big room. We're bursting now. Last week we had fifty-eight kids there and there are only seats for fifty-seven. It's a tribute that they like to come there. It's an agonizing night, though, when you have to go around shushing. It's just too much. I'm old-fashioned. I think it has to be a quiet place.

We don't lock our doors here at the house. It never occurs to me. In the city, you would go to the subway and follow everybody and try to get a paper. Here I drive down to school and just make a turn at the corner and see the whole Appalachian spread out for miles and miles. And I'm ready to go to work.

I feel free as a bird. I'm in a unique position because I'm the boss. I buy what I like. I initiate things. I can experiment with all kinds of things I think the kids might be interested in. Nobody interferes. For me, it's no chore to go to work. I'm fortunate. Most people never get to do this at any time in their lives.

My father was a mechanical engineer, hated every day of it. He couldn't wait forty-six years, or whatever it was, until he retired. When we were little, we knew he loathed his job. One of the things he hated most was having to take customers out for dinners. He almost didn't make it because he had a very bad heart attack a couple of months before retirement age. Fortunately, he lived for almost twenty years afterwards. He retired at sixty-five and started to live. He took guitar lessons, piano lessons, art lessons. He was in little theater productions. Work for him was something he hated. He went through the motions and did it very well. But he dreaded every minute of it.

I assumed he became an engineer because his father was one. He attended the same university. His brother was an engineer too. It was just assumed. But it wasn't for him. I have a sister who can't wait until next December, 'cause she's going to retire at a bank. She's just hanging on. How terrible.

I don't think I could ever really retire. There's not enough time.

MARIO ANICHINI

In the yard outside the shop are statues in marble and stone of saints, angels, and fountains. The spirit of Look Homeward, Angel *and W. O. Gant hovers tempestuously. Yet, M. Anichini, artisan, has never been more relaxed. His son and colleague, Bob, interjects a contemporary note: "We also work in foam, fiberglass, polyurethanes . . ."*

In Italy I was working in marble a little bit. I was a young kid. In Lucca, a young kid do this, do that. Little by little I learned. When I was about twenty I came to this country here. I couldn't do anything like that, because of here we had a Depression. From '27 year to '55 I was a butcher. For twenty-eight years . . .

I started to get a little ulcer in my stomach. I had sciatica. So I hadda quit. So I stay for one year. I don't do nothing. But after, I feel I could do something. The plaster business, the tomb business. As soon as I started it, I started to feel better.

BOB: *He was about fifty-five years old when he started this business again. My mother thought he was losing his mind. But he insisted. Everybody from the area where he came from in Tuscany has a relative or somebody in the art business. You have Florence . . .*

There's change a lot. We use rubber to make a mold now. We used to use some kind of glue. It was only good for about ten pieces. Now with a rubber mold we can make three hundred, four hundred pieces. In Italy you gotta go to school one year to make a mold. Before, I used to make one piece, stone or marble. Maybe you a millionaire and you want to make it your bust. Okay, how much you pay? Now nobody want to spend that much money. Over here I don't see so much good stone to work with.

BOB: *We used to sell statuary and fountains: a nymph*

*holding a jug, pouring water. All of a sudden, with the
ecology bit, people want to hear water running. In the city
they want to be close to the country. So there's a combination of art and nature. When we started, I was quite
against it. Who's going to buy a fountain? We put 'em indoors now as humidifiers. People are putting statues in
their yards. There is such a demand for it we built a factory.*

I remember when I quit the butcher business, I was
sick. When I started this business, I became better and
better and I feel good and enjoy myself.

BOB: *For grave sites people in the old days wanted a certain statue, St. Anthony or St. Anne or something like
that. We don't have much call for saints these days, especially now with the Church . . .*

People will laugh. Every time they see me, they see me
better and better. I used to work in the basement. They
say, "You eat too much dust down there, and you getting
better and better. Before you work in the butcher shop,
very nice, very airy, everything, you used to be sick. How
come?"

BOB: *My dad had another man that didn't feel too well at
what he was doing. He worked with my father in this—
what he did as a kid, too—and he got healthy and fat and
stuff like that. (Laughs.) My dad was an old man fifteen,
twenty years ago. Today he's a young man.*

FATHERS AND SONS

GLENN STRIBLING

A casual encounter on a plane; a casual remark: he and his wife are returning from a summer cruise. It was their first vacation in twenty-five years. He is forty-eight.

He and his son are partners in the business: Glenn & Dave's Complete Auto Repair. They run a Texaco service station in a fairly affluent community some thirty miles outside Cleveland. "There's eight of us on the payroll, counting my son and I. Of course, the wife, she's the bookkeeper." There are three tow trucks.

"Glenn & Dave's is equipped to do all nature of repair work: everything from transmission, air conditioning, valves, all . . . everything. I refer to it as a garage because we do everything garages do.

"We have been here four years." He himself has been at it "steady" for twenty-nine years. "When I was a kid in high school I worked at the Studebaker garage part-time for seven dollars a week. And I paid seven dollars a week board and room." (Laughs.) It more or less runs in our family. My great-grandfather used to make spokes for automobiles back in Pennsylvania when they used wooden wheels. I have a brother, he's a mechanic. I have another brother in California, he's in the same business as I'm in. My dad, he was a steam engine repairman.

"Another reason I went into this business: it's Depression-proof. A good repairman will always have a job. Even though they're making cars so they don't last so long and people trade 'em in more often, there's still gonna be people that have to know what they're doing."

I work eight days a week. (Laughs.) My average weeks usually run to eighty, ninety hours. We get every other Sunday off, my son and I. Alternate, you know. Oh, I love it. There's never a day long enough. We never get through. And that's a good way to have it, 'cause people rely on you and you rely on them, and it's one big business. Sometimes they're all three trucks goin'. All we sell is service, and if you can't give service, you might as well give up.

All our business has come to us from mouth to mouth. We've never run a big ad in the paper. That itself is a good sign that people are satisfied. Of course, there's some people that nobody could satisfy. I've learned: Why let one person spoil your whole day?

A new customer comes to town, he would say, "So-and-so, I met him on the train and he recommended you folks very highly." Oh, we've had a lot of compliments where people, they say they've never had anything like that done to a car. They are real happy that we did point out things and do things. Preventive maintenance I call it.

A man come in, we'd Xed his tires, sold him a set of shocks, repacked his wheel bearings, aligned his front, serviced his car—by service I mean lubricate, change oil, filter ... But he had only one tail light working and didn't know it. So we fixed that and he'll be grateful for it. If it's something big, a matter of a set of tires or if he needs a valve job, we call the customer and discuss it with him.

Sometimes, but not very often, I've learned to relax. When I walk out of here I try to leave everything, 'cause we have a loud bell at home. If I'm out in the yard working, people call. They want to know about a car, maybe make a date for next week, or maybe there's a car here that we've had and there's a question on it. The night man will call me up at home. We have twenty-four-hour service, too, towing. My son and I, we take turns. So this phone is hooked up outside so you can hear it. And all the neighbors can hear it too. (Laughs.)

Turn down calls? No, never. Well, if it's some trucking outfit and they don't have an account with us—they're the worst risk there is. If they don't have a credit card or if the person they're delivering won't vouch for them, there's gotta be some sort of agreement on payment before we go out. Of course, if it's a stranger, if it's broke down, naturally we have the car.

Sometimes if we're busy, bad weather and this and that, why we won't get any lunch, unless the wife runs uptown and grabs a sandwich. I usually go home, it varies anywhere between six thirty, seven, eight. Whatever the public demands. In the wintertime, my God, we don't get out of here till nine. I have worked thirty-seven hours non-stop.

I don't do it for the money. People are in trouble and they call you and you feel obligated enough to go out there and straighten them out as much as you can. My wife tells me I take my business more serious than a doctor. Every now and then a competitor will come down and ask me to diagnose something. And I go ahead and do it. I'll tell anybody anything I know if it'll help him. That's a good way to be. You might want a favor from them sometime. Live and let live.

You get irritated a lot of times, but you keep it within yourself. You can't be too eccentric. You gotta be the same. Customers like people the same all the time. Another thing I noticed: the fact that I got gray hair, that helps in business. Even though my son's in with me and we have capable men working for us, they always want to talk to Glenn. They respect me and what I tell 'em.

If I'm tensed up and there'll be somebody pull in on the driveway, ring all the bells, park right in front of the door, then go in and use the washroom—those kind of people are the most inconsiderate kind of people there is. If you're out there in the back, say you're repacking wheel bearings. Your hands are full of grease. In order to go out in that drive, you have to clean your hands. And all the customer wanted to know was where the courtroom is. When I travel, if I want information, I'll park out on the apron. Sometimes we have as high as fifty, sixty people a day in here for information. They pull up, ring all the bells ... You can imagine how much time it takes if you go out fifty, sixty times and you don't pump gas. I call 'em IWW: Information, wind, and water. It's worse the last four years we've been here. People don't care. They don't think of us. All they think of is themself.

Oh, I lose my temper sometimes. You wouldn't be a red-blooded American if you wouldn't, would you? At the same time you're dealing with the public. You have to control yourself. Like I say, people like an even-tempered person. When I do lose my temper, the wife, she can't get over it. She says, "Glenn, I don't know how you can blow your stack at one person and then five minutes later you're tellin' him a joke." I don't hold grudges. Why hold a grudge? Let people know what you think, express your opinion, and then forget it. Of course, you don't forget, you just don't keep harpin' on it.

In the summertime, when I get home I don't even go in the house. I grab a garden tool and go out and work till dark. I have a small garden—lettuce, onions, small vegetables. By the time you're on your feet all day you're ready to relax, watch television, sometimes have a fire in the fireplace. At social gatherings, if somebody's in the same business, we compare notes. If we run into something that's a time saver, we usually exchange. But not too much. Because who likes to talk shop?

There's a few good mechanics left. Most of 'em in this day and age, all they are is parts replacers. This is a new trend. You need an air conditioner, you don't repair 'em any more. You can get exchange units, factory guaranteed and much cheaper, much faster. People don't want to lay up their car long enough to get it fixed. If they can't look out and see their car in the driveway, they feel like they've lost something. They get nervous. It's very seldom people will overhaul a car. They'll trade it in instead.

This is something hard to find any more, a really good, conscientious worker. When the whistle blows, they're all washed up, ready to go before they're punched out. You don't get a guy who'll stay two or three hours later, just to get a job done.

Take my son, Dave. Say a person's car broke down. It's on a Sunday or a Saturday night. Maybe it would take an hour to fix. Why, I'll go ahead and fix it. Dave's the type that'll say, "Leave it sit till Monday." I put myself in the other guy's boots and I'll go ahead and fix his car, because time don't mean that much to me. Consequently we got a lot of good customers. Last winter we had a snowstorm. People wanted some snow tires. I put 'em on. He's a steady customer now. He just sold his house for $265,000.

When we took this last cruise, my customers told me Dave did a terrific job. "Before, we didn't think much of him. But he did a really good job this last time." I guess compared to the average young person Dave is above average as far as being conscientious. Although he does sleep in the morning. Today's Wednesday? Nine o'clock this morning. It was ten o'clock yesterday morning. He's supposed to be here at seven. Rather than argue and fight about it, I just forget it.

Another thing I trained myself: I know the address and phone number of all the places we do business with and a lot of our customers. I never even look in the phone book. (Dave had just made a phone call after leafing through the directory.) If he asked me, I coulda told him.

DAVE STRIBLING

He is twenty-three, married, and has two baby children. He has been working with his father "more or less since I was twelve years old. It's one of those deals where the son does carry on the family tradition.

"I actually worked full-time when I was in junior high school. School was a bore. But when you stop and look back at it you wish to hell you'd done a lot more. I wanted to go get that fast buck. Some people are fortunate to make it overnight. My dad and I had a few quarrels and I quit him. I used to work down at Chrysler while I was in high school. I worked at least eight hours a day. That was great. You don't work Saturdays and you don't work Sundays. Then I came back and worked for my dad."

How would I describe myself? Mixed up really. (Laughs.) I like my work. (Sighs.) But I wish I hadn't started that early. I wish I would have tried another trade, actually. At my age I could quit this. I could always come back. But I'm pretty deep now. If I were to walk out, it would be pretty bad. (Laughs.) I don't think I'll change my occupation, really.

I think I'da tried to be an architect or, hell, maybe even a real top-notch good salesman. Or maybe even a farmer. It's hard to say. The grass is always greener on the other side of the fence. You turn around and there's an attorney. It makes you feel different. You work during the day and you're dirty from this and that. The majority of the people overlook the fact as long as you're established and this and that. They don't really care what your occupation is as long as you're a pretty good citizen.

Where it really gets you down is, you're at some place and you'll meet a person and strike up a conversation with 'em. Naturally, sometime during that conversation he's going to ask about your occupation, what you do for a living. So this guy, he manages this, he manages that, see? When I tell him—and I've seen it happen lots of times—there's a kind of question mark in his head. Just what is this guy? You work. You just sweat. It's not mental. 'Cause a lot of these jobs that you do, you do so many of the same thing, it just becomes automatic. You know what you're doing blindfolded.

It's made me a pretty good livin' so far. But I don't have a lot of time that a lot of these guys do that are in my age and in the same status that I am. I put in every week at least sixty, sixty-five hours. And then at night, you never know. If somebody breaks down, you can't tell 'em no. You gotta go. My friends work forty hours a week and they're done. Five days a week. I work seven, actually. Every other Sunday. I have to come and open up.

I don't really like to talk about my work with my friends. They don't really seem to, either. A lot of times somebody will ask me something about their car. How much will this cost? How much will that cost? I don't really even want to quote my price to them. A couple of 'em work for the state, in an office. A couple of 'em are body men. One's a carpenter, one's a real estate salesman. A few of 'em, they just work.

I come home, I gotta go in the back door, 'cause I've got on greasy boots. (Laughs.) If it does happen to be about six thirty, then I won't get cleaned up before I eat. I'll sit down and eat with the wife and kids. If they've already eaten, I'll take a shower and I'll get cleaned up and I'll come down and eat. If it's a nice night, I might go out and putz around the yard. If it's not nice outside, I'll just sit and watch the TV. I don't really read that much. I probably read as much as the average American. But nothing any more. Sometimes you really put out a lot of work that day—in general, I'm tired. I'm asleep by ten o'clock at night. I come to work, it varies, I might come in between eight and nine, maybe even ten o'clock in the morning. I like my sleep. (Laughs.)

He's the one that opens it up. He believes the early bird gets the worm. But that's not always true either. I might come in late, but actually I do more work than he does here in a day. Most of it probably is as careful as his. I can't understand a lot of the stuff he does. But he can't understand a lot of the stuff I do either. (Laughs.) He's getting better. He's kinda come around. But he still does think old-fashioned.

Like tools. You can buy equipment, it might cost a lot more money but it'll do the job faster and easier. He'll go grab hand tools, that you gotta use your own muscle. He doesn't go in for power tools.

Like judging people. Anybody with long hair is no good to him—even me. If he caught me asleep, he'd probably give me a Yul Brynner. Hair doesn't have anything to do with it. I've met a lot of people with hair really long, just like a female. They're still the same. They still got their ideas and they're not hippies or anything. They go to work every day just like everybody else does. It gets him. Especially if someone will come in and ask him to do something, he'll let them know he doesn't like them. I don't give people that much static.

When somebody comes in and they're in a rage and it's all directed at you, I either go get the hell out of there or my rage is brought up towards them. I've definitely lost customers by tellin' 'em. I don't know how to just slough it off. In the majority of cases you're sorry for it.

I've seen my father flare up a lot of times. Somebody gives him a bad time during the day, he'll take it home. Whereas instead of tellin' 'em right there on the spot, he'll just keep it within himself. Then half-hour later he might be mumblin' somethin'. When I used to live at home, you could tell by thirty seconds after he got in the door that he either didn't feel good or somebody gave him a bad time. He just keeps it going through his mind. He won't forget it. Whereas when I go home to the wife and the two kids, I just like to forget it. I don't want to talk about it at all.

I yell a lot, cuss a lot. I might throw things around down here, take a hammer and hit the bench as hard as it'll go, I'm getting better though, really. I used to throw a lot of stuff. I'd just grab and throw a wrench or something. But I haven't done that in a long time now. When you get older and you start thinking about it, you really have changed a lot in the last few years. (Laughs.) It'll stay inside me. You learn to absorb more of it. More so than when you were a kid. You realize you're not doing any good. Lotta times you might damage something. It's just gonna come out of your pocket.

When I was younger, if there was something I didn't agree upon, I was ready to go right then against it. But now I don't. I kinda step back a half a step and think it out. I've gotten into pretty good arguments with my buddies. It never really comes down to fists, but if you're with somebody long enough, it's bound to happen, you're gonna fight. You had a hard day and somebody gave you a hard time and, say you went out to eat and the waitress, she screwed something up? Yeah, it'll flare up. But not as much as it used to be.

As far as customers goes, there's not too many of 'em I like. A lot of customers, you can joke with, you can kid with. There are a lot of 'em, they don't want to hear any of it. They don't want to discuss anything else but the business while they're here. Older people, yeah, they're pretty hard. Because they've gone through a change from a Model T to what you got nowadays. Nowadays a lot of 'em will put up the hood and they just shake their heads. They just can't figure it out.

Some of 'em, when they get old they get real grumpy. Anything you say, you're just a kid and you don't know what you're doin'. (Laughs.) They don't want to listen to you, they want to talk to somebody else. There's a lot of 'em that'll just talk to him. But there's a lot of 'em that want to talk to me and don't want to talk to him. My-age people. It's a mixed-up generation. (Laughs.)

I have pride in what I do. This day and age, you don't always repair something. You renew. Whereas in his era you could buy a kit to rebuild pretty near anything. Take a water pump. You can buy 'em. You can put on a new one. I wouldn't even bother to repair a water pump. You can buy rebuilts, factory rebuilts. Back in his time you rebuilt water pumps.

His ideas are old, really. You gotta do this a certain way and this a certain way. There's short cuts found that you could just eliminate half the stuff you do. But he won't. A lot of the new stuff that comes out, he won't believe anybody. He won't even believe me. He might call three or four people before he'll believe it. Why he won't believe me I don't know. I guess he must figure I bull him a lot. (Laughs.)

When he was working for a living as a mechanic, his

ability was pretty good. Actually, he doesn't do that much work. I mean, he more or less is a front. (Laughs.) Many people come in here that think he does work on their car. But he doesn't. He's mostly the one that meets people. He brings the work in. In his own mind he believes he's putting out the work. But we're the ones that put out the work.

He's kind of funny to figure out. (Laughs.) He has no hobbies, really. When he's out he'll still talk his trade. He just can't forget it, leave it go.

I'd like to go bigger in this business, but father says no for right now. He's too skeptical. We're limited here. He doesn't want to go in debt. But you gotta spend money to make money. He's had to work harder than I have. There's nobody that ever really gave him anything. He's had to work for everything he's got. He's given me a lot. Sometimes he gives too much. His grand-kids, they've got clothes at home still in boxes, brand-new as they got 'em. He just goes overboard. If I need money, he'll loan it to me. He's lent me money that I haven't even paid back, really. (Laughs.)

(Sighs.) I used to play music. I used to play in a rock group. Bass. I didn't know very much on the bass. Everybody that was in the band really didn't know all that much. We more or less progressed together. We played together for a year and a half, then everything just broke up. Oh yeah, we enjoyed it. It was altogether different. I like to play music now but don't have the time ... I like to play, but you can't do both. This is my living. You have to look at it that way.

STEVE DUBI

We're in Pullman, an industrial neighborhood on the far South Side of Chicago. It is a one-family dwelling, much like all the others on the block. He has lived in this area all his life. "I was born in the shadow of them steel mills." He has worked as an inspector at the South Works of U.S. Steel for forty years.

"I was hired in '29 as a water boy. I was sixteen. I had to be seventeen, but in those days they overlooked a little

*thing here, a little thing there. I worked for a year. Then
came the Crash. I was rehired in June '33 and I've been in-
specting ever since. I'm ready for retirement. But the
home we live in isn't paid for yet. The car I'm driving isn't
paid for yet. Nothing to show for forty years of work."*

*His wife is a licensed practical nurse who "works with
geriatrics." They have two sons. Robert, a Vietnam war
veteran, is married. He's in the field of sales. Their other
son, Father Leonard Dubi, is one of the city's most
renowned activist priests. As a passionate spokesman for
the blue-collar community in which his parish is located,
he has on numerous occasions challenged some of the
city's most powerful men and institutions.*

*During the visit, as his weariness is evident, his wife
joins the conversation.*

When we were kids we thought the steel mill was it. We'd
see the men comin' out, all dirty, black. The only thing
white was the goggles over their eyes. We thought they
were it, strong men. We just couldn't wait to get in there.
When we finally did get in, we were sorry. (Chuckles.) It
wasn't what it was cut out to be.

You're on your feet all day, on concrete. They lay the
steel out on the skids. It's like a long horse, and they lay
the steel across. You get your flashlight and you walk over
it and you chalk it and mark the defect. You look for the
defect in the steel. You watch the tolerances for lengths
and thickness and what not. You have a chipper or a grinder to smooth it out. If it comes within the tolerance the
customer allows, it's all right. If it goes too deep, you
scrap the bar or recut it. When we broke in, the older
men showed us what defects to look for. A crack in the
bar is called a seam. Some would be wide open where you
couldn't miss 'em. Some were real tight and you would
have to look close. It's hard on the eyes. Oh, your eyes do
get tired. I put some drops in my eyes.

I'm getting up in the age now where I can't take it any
more. In my younger days I used to work eight hours, go
out and play a doubleheader of softball, go out and drink
a shot, and sleep it off (laughs), and go back to work in
the morning. And not feel too much pain. (Sighs.) But
now I can't take it any more. I'd like to retire. I think I've
worked hard enough and long enough, but I still can't see
my way out. I don't know if I'll make it. I got sore legs

and a sore back, sore arms, arthritis, bursitis, and every other thing is catching up on me. (Laughs.)

Everyone looks forward to retirement, but there's a lot of 'em not makin' it. That's all they talk about is retirement. Where are you gonna go? What are you gonna do? And the poor soul never makes it. A lot of 'em, they're countin' the months instead of the years—and pass away. A lot of my friends are passed away already.

I can take it any time I want, but I won't be fifty-nine until December. I don't get on social security until I'm sixty-two. Why, that'll be another three years. I don't want to go just yet, but maybe I won't be able to take it any more. It's gettin' tougher. I'm not like a machine. Well, a machine wears out too sometimes.

And they're forcin' more work on ya. It's knockin' off men, makin' cut-backs here and there to save money. They've knocked off an awful lot of jobs. With the foreign imports of steel they're losin' money. That's what they say. I suppose in order to make a profit they have to cut somewhere. But I told 'em "After forty years of work, why do you take a man away from me? You're gonna force me into retirement." All of us were real angry. But there's nothin' we can do about it. What can I do? Quit?

I try not to take this home with me. I don't tell her nothin' about it. It'll cause her to worry. There's nothin' I can do about it. About four o'clock I'll sit down here and watch TV, maybe get my dinner on a TV table and watch the finish of the ball game or the finish of a good movie. I'll sit back here and work the crossword puzzle and read the sports news and fall asleep. (Laughs.)

I had to ask this coming Sunday off because I'm going to a golf outing. Otherwise I'd have had to work from three to eleven. They're working us twelve days in a row. When I'm workin' on the day shift I'll work Monday through Saturday, seven to three. The following week I'll be lined up on the three to eleven shift. It's a forty-hour week, but it's always twelve days in a row.

If they're in a slack time, they go down to one shift. You can't make any long-range plan. When we bought this house fourteen years ago, the real estate man wanted to sell me a lot more expensive house. I said no. With the job I have I don't know if I'll be workin' three, four months from now. We might go out on strike. We may go down to four days a week. Been like this all these years.

I got nothin' to show for it. I live in a home the bank has a mortgage on. (Laughs.) I own a car the finance people have the title to. (Laughs.) I don't know where they got the idea that we make so much. The lowest class payin' job there, he's makin' two dollars an hour if he's makin' that much. It starts with jobs class-1 and then they go up to class-35. But no one knows who that one is. Probably the superintendent. So they put all these class jobs together, divide it by the number of people workin' there, and you come up with a fabulous amount. But it's the big bosses who are makin' all the big money and the little guys are makin' the little money. You hear these politicians give themselves a thousand-dollar raise, and they scream when the steelworker asks for fifty cents an hour raise.

You pack your lunch, or you buy it at the vending machine. We used to have a canteen in there, but they cut that out. The vending machine is lousy. It hurts a man when he'll put his quarter or thirty-five cents in there for a can of vegetable soup and it takes the coin but don't kick anything out. There's no one there to open the machine and give him his quarter back or a can of food. (Laughs.) A lotta machines are broken that way. Every day it occurs.

You're not regarded. You're just a number out there. Just like a prisoner. When you report off you tell 'em your badge number. A lotta people don't know your name. They know you by your badge number. My number is 44-065. When your work sheet is sent in your name isn't put down, just your number. At the main office they don't know who 44-065 is. They don't know if he's black, white, or Indian. They just know he's 44-065.

Of course, there are accidents. They're movin' a lot of steel—a lot of crane movement and transfer buggy movement and switchin' and trucks. And there's machinery that straightens the bars and turning lathes. Always movement. You eat the dust and dirt and take all the different things that go with it. How you gonna grind a defect out of a bar without creating dust? How you can scarf the billet without makin' smoke? When a man takes off sick, he's got a chest cold, how do you know what he's got? A lot of people died, they just had a heart attack. Who knows what they die of?

We have to slog our way through dirt and smog and

rain and slush to get to our place of work. From the mill gate to where I work is about a fifteen-, twenty-minute walk. In-between that you have puddles. We don't have a nice walkway with an overhead ramp. We don't have a shuttle bus. If it's raining, you walk through the rain. If it's snowin' or blowin', you're buckin' that snow and the wind. In the wintertime that wind is comin' off that lake, it's whippin' right into your face.

That place is not inside a building. It's just under a roof. There's no protection against the winds. They won't even plug up the holes to keep the draft off you. Even the snow comes through and falls on you while you're workin'. The roof is so leaky they should furnish you with umbrellas.

His wife murmurs: "He's sick all the time."

The union squawks about it, but if the steel mill don't fix it, what are you gonna do? The washrooms are in terrible shape. But when they get around to fixin' 'em, there's five hundred men usin' one bowl to sit on. The union's helped a great deal, but the steel mill is slow in comin' across with things like they should.

If I retire right now, I would make $350 a month. There's a woman across the street got a half a dozen kids and no husband, and she's probably gettin' five hundred dollars a month from ADC. She gets more money than I would right now after workin' for forty years. If I retire now, my insurance is dropped. I belong to this Blue Cross-Blue Shield insurance now. If I go on a pension, I would get dropped automatically. The day you retire, that's the day it's out.

I told my sons, "If you ever wind up in that steel mill like me, I'm gonna hit you right over your head. Don't be foolish. Go get yourself a schooling. Stay out of the steel mill or you'll wind up the same way I did." Forty years of hard work and what have I got to show for it? Nothing. I can't even speak proper. When you're a steelworker (laughs), you don't get to speak the same language that you would do if you meet people in a bank or a business office.

"When I was going to school I really loved mechanical drawing. I really excelled in it in high school. I was gettin'

*good marks. But my dad died. Well, most of the children
had saloon keepers and grocery store keepers, they had
dads workin', and they were able to buy things. I felt embarrassed because I couldn't buy the proper paper. I
would use the other side of someone else's discarded paper. I did love mechanical drawing and I was good at it.
Well, I had to get a job . . ."*

I was hopin' Leonard would be a doctor. When he entered the seminary, I thought: Gee, what caused him to
go in there? When he was an Andy Frain usher he was assigned to Holy Name and he got acquainted with a lot of
priests there. A lot of the ushers were at the seminary.
They probably influenced him. He's happy, so I'm happy
for him. At first I wasn't sure he was gonna stay, 'cause he
loved life too much. He loved everything, people and animals. (Muses) Maybe that's why he became a priest . . .
(Trails off.)

In the past, it was strictly parish. They come out once a
year to bless the house and shake the hand. But now, with
the younger set, things have changed. All the priests are
goin' without their collars and doin' a lot of things that the
old-time priest would never think of doin'. I don't think
they were allowed to.

*Henrietta Dubi reflects: "I'll never forget those women,
my neighbors, they were sittin' out on the porch and they
couldn't understand why I'm grievin' that Leonard went
into the seminary. They said, 'Oh, it's such an honor.' I
said, 'Yes, but it's gonna be a hard life.' No freedom, no
privileges. We could only see him once a month. I figured
he was in prison. One day I said to him, 'Leonard, are you
happy?' He said, I can't begin to tell you how happy I am.
Please don't ask again. I chose this life and this is the life
I'm going to lead.' When he was havin' his senior prom, I
should have known then. Everything he was buying was
black. It never dawned on me. The first time I seen Skid
Row in my life was when my son took me down there. He
said, 'I want to save people like this.' In a kidding way I
said, 'These people are beyond saving.' He said, 'As long
as there's breath in 'em, they can be saved.' I was sad
and depressed when he first went in. I couldn't understand
why. Now I'm very proud of him. I wish there were more*

like him to speak out, but some are afraid. We pray for him all the time."

Sometimes I worry about him. He takes on the real big shots. He might buck the wrong person. They've been shooting Presidents and senators. He could be shot at too—if he says the wrong thing or gets the wrong man angry. When you're foolin' around with a politician, why you got troubles. But he's for the people, he wants 'em to have a square deal. And I'm glad. If the people don't like what he's sayin', why that's too bad.

You know the big joke? When Len was an Andy Frain usher, he used to seat Mayor Daley in his box at Comiskey Park. Ten years later he's fightin' him on the Crosstown Expressway business and the county assessor's office. (Laughs.) When we first started visiting Leonard at the seminary we weren't even allowed to bring him a newspaper. He wasn't allowed to have a radio. It was so strict at that time. What amazes me now, I turn on the TV and I see him arguin' with the mayor, (Laughs.) Or the county assessor and them politicians. It's so different, it's fantastic.

When he started on this pollution against the steel mills, I told Leonard everybody knows the steel mill is polluting. How can you make steel without polluting? I'm not gonna bite the hand that feeds me. They been doing it for a hundred years. It could be cut down a great deal, I suppose, if they wanted—which they are trying to do. They're putting in a lot of new buildings. I don't know what they are, but they claim it's for ecology. Who knows?

This pollution business. He helped them people on the West Side where he lived. When we used to go to visit him it seemed you are going into a valley. It seemed you hit a fog bank. We learned later it was smog from the Edison plants. And he cleared it up. So we're for him one hundred percent. But this fightin' with the mayor and the aldermen, that scares me. (Laughs.)

Mrs. Dubi interjects: "When I see him on television, I run. There might be a nut in the audience who'll shoot."

She's scared. We're real proud of him. All my friends cut clippings out of the newspaper and bring 'em to me and they'll say, "Hey, I heard Leonard on the radio on my way to work." They'll tell me they're all for him. My sister was tellin' us the other day that her doctor was speakin' of a young priest who was doin' so much for the people in the neighborhood. She said, "That's my nephew." He said, "Gee, he's wonderful."

You know what I told him to start on next? He's fightin' for lower taxes, which is all right. And better livin' conditions, which is all right. And this road that he's against, it's all right. Like he said, they're gonna demolish a lotta homes, a lotta people are gonna be put out. So the next thing I want him to do is lower this age of retirement, social security to about sixty, so I can get out of the mill sooner. If they lowered the age to about sixty, maybe they'd get a year or two benefit out of the pension before they die.

Hard workin' never killed a man, they say. I say workin' in the steel mill is not like workin' in an air-conditioned office, where politicians and bankers sit on their fannies. Where you have to eat all that dust and smoke, you can't work hard and live a long life. You shouldn't be made to work till sixty-two or sixty-five to reap any benefit. We're paying social security, and most of us will never realize a penny from it. That's why they should give it to him at a younger age to let him enjoy a few years of the life he ruined workin' in the factory. I told him. "Leonard, you get to work on that next." (Laughs.)

Yeah, we're proud of Len. At least he's doin' somethin'. What have I done in my forty years of work? I led a useless life. Here I am almost sixty years old and I don't have anything to show for it. At least he's doing something for his people. I worked all my life and helped no one. What I'm happy about is that them two boys took my advice and stayed out of the steel mill. (Laughs.) We're a couple of dummies. We worked all our lives and we have nothing.

MRS. DUBI: *You know what we have? We got two million dollars in our children. Even in this angered world, both these kids turned out good, right? So we're still winners. (To him) Even though we don't have the cash, Father, we don't have nothin' to retire with we still got two million dollars.*

You gotta show it to me.

MRS. DUBI: *You see him on TV, don't you?*

No thanks to me. I had nothin' to do with makin' him what he is. I told you I am nothing. After forty years of workin' at the steel mill, I am just a number. I think I've been a pretty good worker. That job was just right for me. I had a minimum amount of education and a job using a micrometer and just a steel tape and your eyes—that's a job that was just made for me. But they don't appreciate it. They don't care. Bob worked in the mill a few months during a school vacation. He said, "I don't know how you done it all these years. I could never do it." I said, "I been tellin' you all your life never get into that mill." (Laughs.)

FATHER LEONARD DUBI

He is associate pastor of St. Daniel the Prophet. He has just turned thirty. "This is a big year for the parish. It's twenty-five years old. Tonight I have a meeting with the book ad committee. I have a person coming in for coun-selling this evening. My day will end around ten-thirty. It's a fourteen-hour day, sometimes longer. I wear two hats. I'm a full-time priest and I'm co-chairman of a commu-nity organization, CAP." *

"My day begins about six o'clock in the morning. We have three masses: six forty-five, seven-thirty and eight. I rotate with my boss, the pastor, Father Brennan, and Fa-ther Tanzi. We come back to the rectory. We put on a cup of coffee, we'll sit around, read the papers, chat. The kids start arriving for school. The doorbell will ring several times before that. A little kid wants to ask a ques-tion or see one of the priests to bless religious articles.

"The phone starts ringing and rings all day. Simple re-quests. Somebody's in the hospital: 'We'd appreciate your

* Citizen's Action Program. It was originally called Com-mittee Against Pollution. It is a grass-roots organization that began in Father Dubi's community and has expanded in membership as well as in aims. It has challenged, on specific occasions, the political as well as the industrial power brokers of the city.

going to see him.' Kids call up for premarriage instruc-
tions. There are calls about funeral arrangements—mass,
burial, wakes. The morning is spent answering the mail
and checking with the CAP office. I try to do some read-
ing in the afternoon or run out to the hospital for a visi-
tation or I'm called to a meeting. After school I'll meet
with the altar boys to plan for the masses, for special lit-
urgies, for the annual picnic. I don't know where the time
goes. The weekends are the busiest time for a priest—
weddings, confession schedules, mass schedules. Sunday's
a great time to meet our people."

I never thought I'd be a priest. I didn't even know what a
seminary was until I was seventeen. I started working for
Andy Frain as I entered my senior year in high school.
Frain hired a lot of seminarians. In the process of knowing these fellows, I started going back to church. One of
my friends kept nagging at me: "Why don't you consider
being a priest?"

My mother went to work when I was about four years
old just to be able to make the weekly and monthly bills.
My father completely discouraged me from ever thinking
of a life as a steelworker. Where others would admire
their fathers for their work in the mills, my father challenged me to lift my horizons beyond that.

The steel mill's been a hard thing for my father. He's
always suffered from back trouble. There were times when
just the burden of walking and bending over those steel
ingots just knocked his back out and he'd be in pain for
days and weeks at a time. He felt life was like that because
people like him went to work too early, had no education.
They didn't really discuss, they didn't read. When they'd
get off work it was a release to go to the tavern and have
a couple of drinks. He didn't want that for his children. He
agonized. He was so unhappy with himself. Sometimes it
caused serious strains in the house. I think he has tremendous ability. But because he was caught up in the system
so young, the system that kept him so humiliated, he was
just frustrated in his life. He didn't want it to happen to
his sons.

I know my father had much more potential, but he was
locked into a system day after day, and he didn't want me
to get locked in. He encouraged me to go college—"to
make something of yourself" were the words he used. My

mother was lobbying very strongly that I go into the medical field.

When I entered the seminary, I can remember my mother would cry and cry and cry. My father was so frustrated, he thought I was going to be a priest to save his soul, that I did it to make up for all his sins, that I was doing penance for him. I said, "Hell no, Dad, I'm going because I'm choosing to go, not because of your life. I want to do it." Even today if I decided I could not be happy and personally fulfilled, I'd step out as a priest. The work of a priest is to bring life to people. If I don't have that life inside me, I can't give that life away.

My parents were raised in Catholic families, but they were not that deeply religious. They were married in court and did not have it validated by the Roman Church until I entered the seminary. My father was turned off by what he considered the religious hypocrisy of many of the Catholics he was raised with. My mother grew up in a Polish home, and many people of ethnic backgrounds looked upon the clergy as people who were just interested in money.

The priest would come on Easter to bless the baskets and pick up a five-dollar bill. My grandmother—she didn't have much money—used to embarrass me every time I'd go over as a priest. She would hand me money. That would hurt me. I'd say, "I don't want it." She was a poor old lady. That's part of her tradition. When the priest comes you give him money. I started going over there less and less . . .

When I got out to St. Daniel's three years ago, I had an agenda for myself. I was trained in a very liberal seminary. I saw social action issues—war and peace and poverty. I spent my deacon years—before I was ordained—at Catholic Charities. It was one of the most frustrating experiences of my life. I was fisherman pulling people out of troubled waters. Trying to bring them back to life with artificial respiration and Band-Aids. Then I'd put them back on the other side of the river into the same society that pushed them in. I knew I'd have to do more than just be a social worker and patch up people.

When I got there I decided I would listen rather than just act. I kept hearing people talk about their problems and it blew my mind. I had stereotyped white middle America. I came from a steelworker's family. We lived in

a cold water flat until I was fourteen. We had plenty of
problems. But I hadn't been listening to these people. I put
them all in the same bag: they were all prejudiced, they
all hated black people, they were all for the war in Vietnam, they could hardly care less about poor people. As I
listened, I saw they were as powerless as anybody.

We had a congregation of about twenty-four hundred
families, two thousand attend regularly. We get about four
thousand people at St. Daniel's every single weekend. It's
a working-class, a lower-middle-class community. Most of
the people are laborers. We have a high proportion of city
workers, people who have migrated to the outer edge because of changing racial patterns. We're in the Twenty-
third Ward. About twenty-four hundred policemen and
their families live here. We have very few professional
people.

The one high school here, John F. Kennedy, was built
for fourteen hundred. Now thirty-six hundred kids go to
this school. It's integrated because there's a public housing
project nearby. Two white kids or two black kids can jostle and if they have a fight, it's just a fight. If a black kid
and a white kid happen to jostle in the hall and a fight
breaks out, it's a racial incident.

It's just one example of poor city planning of a community where taxes have doubled over the past ten years.
People who were paying $350 are now paying $700.
They're just about wild about that. They feel they're not
getting the services they're paying for. They have been neglected by the city.

They couldn't do anything about their kid's poor education, the pollution caused by Commonwealth Edison and
the Sanitary treatment plant that poured nine and a half
tons of greasy aerosols on them every day. They couldn't
do anything about the Crosstown Expressway when it was
announced from on high. They wrote letters, they called
the alderman, but nothing happened year after year. I was
listening.

In January 1970 I got a call from a young Jesuit semi-
narian. He was working with a new organization known as
CAP. I had lunch with him, and the next day I was off and
running. It was like a roller coaster ride. It took off like
wildfire. At St. Daniel's the women especially got active.
I'm an advocate of the Women's Lib movement. I try to
have as many women as possible participate in the church

services. Many of the extraordinary ministers at St. Daniel's are women. The women understand exactly the need for power. They became commited organizers for CAP.

There's a great difference between textbook civics and the actual civics of the streets. When people, fifty or a hundred, go to see the alderman or the mayor, they can't believe what they hear. They're resented by the men they put in power. For the first time in their lives they learn that politics is power. People with the big money—the big institutions, corporations—have worked out deals in back rooms with politicians. They're not going to break these deals until they're forced to by the people.

We had five hundred down at Mayor Daley's office during our battle with Commonwealth Edison. They were peaceful. Some of them for the first time in their lives had ever been to city hall. They were just digging it. They're really looking around and enjoying it. Out come two aldermen, Tom Keane and Paul Wigoda* and they yell at the people, "You should be home with your kids. Why do you have your kids down here?" Who are you, sir?" said one lady. She couldn't believe an alderman would talk to her that way. The next thing, she's being shoved by a policeman. A middleclass woman who loves the system, who's a friend of the police because they're for law and order. All of a sudden she's pushed. She came up to me with tears in her eyes: "I didn't do anything. I would have moved if he'd asked me, but he just shoved me. I could understand what those kids went through in Lincoln Park in 1968." She hated these kids before.

Funny thing, a lot of the police are for CAP. Some of them are from our community. Their wives have actually participated. The people who delight me are the policemen and their wives. We have many of them involved. They can't take out-front roles, but they're silent supporters. They know the system needs an overhaul, that change must come.

Ours is a white community, except for the housing project. A strict racial balance was kept in the area adjacent to the project, fifty percent white, fifty percent black. During the civil rights decade, black organizations pressured for the removal of the quota system. Consequently, white

* Two of Mayor Daley's most perfervid spokesmen in the city council.

people moved out and black people came in. Homes were
built in this area, where you put five hundred dollars down
and the rest of your life to pay. The community there is
now ninety percent black. Youth gangs keep the black
people of this area in fear.

This affects my parish nearby. "Where are we gonna
go? We don't want to live in a black neighborhood." The
blacks say, "We don't want to live in a white neighborhood." Both want to live where they can have good
schools, good services, good transportation, and feel safe.
I blame the CHA,† which couldn't care less about these
blacks and whites.

Yet in the process of organizing we have seen black
people and white people share the same problems. The
small home owners. The community has been built up
around Midway Airport. When the airlines, in their over-
scheduling, clogged up O'Hare, Mayor Daley wanted a lot
of them transferred to Midway, with their 747 jets. That's
why we're fighting the Crosstown Expressway. It would
gut the city and demolish many of the homes. Black and
white together have united to stop the Expressway.*

Another fight. The Sanitary District had been processing
waste into sludge, dehydrating the sludge, and the gases
had been polluting the community. We had attended Sanitary District meeting after meeting, with one hundred, two
hundred, three hundred people. It kept escalating. Finally
all the trustees but two came to the rally in the school
basement at St. Daniel's. The room holds eight hundred.
Over fifteen hundred were there. They were standing in
the aisles, on the window sills, up on the doorway, out in
the parking lot. We had testimony from the people who
were being terribly affected by this pollution.

† Chicago Housing Authority.

* This battle was apparently won. The newly elected
governor, Dan Walker, had committed himself to opposing its
construction. Mayor Daley still insists he'll go ahead . . .
At the moment, the issue is joined.

As for the most recent development: "Mayor Daley has won
the right to bypass Governor Walker and build the Crosstown
Expressway with city funds under terms of a compromise
federal highway bill approved by a House-Senate conference
committee" (*Chicago Sun-Times*, July 22, 1973). Moral: The
fight to save a neighborhood is forever.

I gave a speech and demanded that the trustees sign a contract with the people, setting a date to end that pollution at their next regular meeting. The five trustees present made little speeches and signed their names. The people were just absolutely elated. The roof almost went off. For the first time in their lives they saw the culprits responsible for the smoke that was polluting their neighborhood. The people felt they had won. The trustees—I'll give them credit—have lived up to the agreement. It's a much cleaner neighborhood now. If it wasn't for the pressure of the people, this air would still be polluted.

In 1971 we started to fight U.S. Steel because of pollution. That's the company my dad works for. This company broke the agreement about cleaning up. How could we fight it? We didn't have a consumer angle. Ordinary people don't buy steel ingots. We started investigating U.S. Steel's tax history. We discovered it was under-assessed by P. J. Cullerton† to the tune of sixteen million dollars a year. Here were people being polluted to death by a company they were actually subsidizing, because the money lost by the county had to be made up by the small people. As we investigated further, we found out other companies and banks and race tracks were also under-assessed. We went to the county building, en masse, and demanded redress.

The people have now learned the importance of coming out in large numbers. We're peaceful. We trust ourselves not to be violent. Our strongest weapon is the volume of our voices. Confronting a person up to now considered unapproachable and making him show his face—and state his position in our presence. The people have become politically independent. They recently threw out an alderman . . .

Tremendous changes have occurred in their lives. They are able to understand that their problems in society are not just caused by what they used to consider goofy little minority groups. They're becoming extremely politicized. They're able to see people—even black people—as allies, rather than enemies you have to run away from if they move next door to you. What these people are seeing now is a common enemy. It can be called city hall. It can be

† County assessor.

called the private corporation. It can be called big money.
God, have I seen attitudes change!

The most exciting moment in my life? Picture this. It's
the annual meeting of the shareholders of Commonwealth
Edison, one of the largest public utilities in the entire
country. The chairman of the board and all the directors
are up on the stage. We had about two thousand people in
the lobby.* It was like a festival—people dancing. About
twenty of us entered the hall. The chairman heads for the
podium and is about to gavel the meeting to order. We
walk down the aisle. Here is the symbol of the establishment of the United States—the annual meeting of a large
corporation. I look up at the chairman and I tell him,
"We're here to find out what you're going to do about pollution. You have a half-hour to give us your answer." People were on their feet: What is this priest doing here, dis-
rupting this meeting? We did it.

It was a liberating experience for me. I never believed I
would be able to do that kind of thing. I had always been
taught to be polite. To say, Yes sir, No sir. To stay in my
place. I should be seen and not heard. But I felt, Hell, if
you're not heard, you're never gonna be seen.

We had the rally outside. A half-hour later we came
into the hall again. They let us in, one at a time. Only
about ten of us were allowed. They tried to seat us in different parts of the hall. I made a break for this aisle and
the others broke away and followed. I faced the chairman
again and asked for his answer. There was no answer. He
threatened to adjourn the meeting. I said, "Okay, here's
our answer. You won't listen to the people, but we're not
gonna take it. We're gonna go to city hall and force this
issue through law." By this time one of our women who
had been wrapped in an arm lock by a security guard—
she didn't know whether to be a lady or kick him or bite
him—broke away. She told the chairman a thing or two.
We all walked out together.

At the city council we forced them to pass one of the
strongest air pollution ordinances in the country. We tangled with the all-powerful Commonwealth Edison and
forced them to purchase six million tons of low sulphur
coal. They've retired much of their antiquated equipment.

* I was present at the lobby rally. I had been invited to act
as the MC. It was my most exhilarating experience, too.

It's not over yet. There's a lot of struggle ahead. But we've had a touch of victory and it's sweet.

To be free is to have some kind of say-so about your life. I have no vote on the board of directors of Commonwealth Edison. I count for absolutely nothing. But that company is polluting my environment, is shaping my life, is limiting it and the chances of the kids at St. Daniel's parish. It's killing me as a person, as life in the steel mill is killing my father. I have to fight back. That brash act— that rude act—of interrupting the chairman of the board did it. I felt free. I don't have to be afraid of him. He goes to the toilet the same way I do. What makes him better than me? His hundred thousand dollars a year? Hell no. Well, that act made me free. You can't emerge as a person if you're a yes-man. No more yes, Mr. Mayor. No more yes, Mr. Governor. No more yes, Mr. Chairman.

JACK CURRIER

It was a chance encounter on the Illinois Central. He is a teacher of English at a branch of the City College. At night he conducts adult education classes at an urban university; among his students are ADC mothers. He is thirty-seven.

My father is the comptroller, treasurer, and a member of the board of directors of a large corporation. His title, salary, his house in the suburbs, everything about his life— the successful American life—is right out of the picture book. But I wouldn't trade places with him for a million dollars.

My father's spent his life adding up numbers for somebody else. Any connection between his real life and his work seems to be missing. I feel, with all my doubts about the institution I work for, with the sense of hypocrisy, there's a connection.

In order to do a better job, I have to become a better man. In the business world, in order to do a better job, you have to become ruthless. In order to make more money, you have to care for people less. In order to succeed, you have to be willing to stab your competitor in the back.

A couple of years ago I was in my father's office. I think we were getting ready to go out for lunch. He got a phone call. His boss was chewing him out for something—in a tone and language that was humiliating. Here's my father who had worked for this company for thirty years.

My father's a dignified man and he works hard. God knows he's given that company all the years of his life. He doesn't have anything else. There are no hobbies. He wasn't close to any of his children. Nothing outside of work. That was it. He would get up in the morning and leave the house and come home twelve, fourteen hours later, six days a week. That was it. Yet here he is at sixty and here's a guy chewing him out like he's a little kid. I felt embarrassed being there. I felt sorry that he knew I was watching that happen. I could see he was angry and embarrassed. I could see him concealing those feelings. Sort of shufflin' and scratchin' his head, in the face of higher authority. We went to lunch. We didn't talk about it at all.

I would hate to spend my life doing work like that. If work means something to you, it doesn't matter what the boss . . . I can imagine being fired from my job. I can imagine an administrator at the college disapproving my teaching methods. But there's no way he could deprive me of the satisfaction that comes from doing my job well.

If my father were ever let go, I don't know what he would do. I suppose he could find somebody else to add up numbers for, although at his age that would be hard. There ought to be a reason behind what men do. We're not just machines, but some of us live like machines. We get plugged into a job and come down at nine o'clock in the morning and someone turns us on. At five o'clock someone turns us off and we go home. What happens during that time doesn't have any connection with our real lives.

I have a lot of respect for my father. He worked hard. During the Depression he went to night school in Washington, D.C., and got a law degree. He was a soda jerk in the drugstore of the Mayflower Hotel and he worked his way up to be the chief accountant. He gave his whole life to that corporation. I don't know any man more honest, more conscientious than my father. But what is it worth? What has it gotten him?

His family and his children got away from him. When I got old enough to go to college, I went off and that was it for me. My sisters graduated from high school and, soon as possible, moved out. It was a place where we all slept, but it wasn't home.

I felt, as long as I stick to talking about his job, we could have a pleasant, superficial conversation. As I became interested in music and politics, I found no comfortable way to pursue those things with him. His job was the only topic . . . He makes some contribution to the Republican party, he always votes, and he reads the newspaper every day on the train, but the job is really it. After all those years, that's his life. To ask whether he loves the company or not—it's irrelevant.

I had a series of jobs in the early fifties, after flunking out of college. I worked for a bank, sold insurance . . . I ended up with a job as a traveling salesman for a business machine company. I was twenty-three years old and making ten thousand dollars a year. I probably could have made it seventeen thousand the next year. I could see it was going right up.

I began to run into conflicts with my own feelings. I couldn't accept the way my boss did business or the way in which everybody in the field did business. If I had remained, I'd be sitting on top of a business of over a million dollars. One of the outfits that had become disenchanted with my boss offered to take me on as their manager and buy them out. It looked like a beautiful proposition. But I just . . . it wasn't my life. I didn't know what I wanted to do, but I knew I wasn't doing it.

I think about guys that were in college with me in the early fifties. They sell real estate, insurance, they're engineers, they're bankers, they're in business. They probably make a lot more money than I do. It's like they're twenty years older than me. They seem a lot closer to my father than they do to me. They're in a groove, they're beyond change. They're caught into something which is so overpowering—it's as though their life was over. It's all settled. I think my job is keeping me young, keeping me alive.

*He went back to school, the experimental St. John's Col-
lege in Maryland. He taught elementary school for a year
in a depressed rural area. "I just felt I had to get into
teaching and really try my hand at it."*

Laing* says in a sick society almost anything that is
done is harmful. I have that feeling about my classes. You
walk into a classroom and you've got an enormous
amount of power. I'm six seven and here were these
fourth graders. You can imagine how much power I had
there. They all listened when I spoke. I was the big father
figure. They all loved me and I took care of them and it
was a great thing for my ego. But I felt it wasn't really
using enough of me dealing with fourth graders. There
was something missing for me.

I ended up teaching adults. Again, that's very satisfying
for the ego. You get into a classroom and you have all the
power of the institution. You tell people what to do and
they do it, what to read and they read it. You tell people
what to think, how to interpret things ... You can make
them feel guilty because they haven't read certain things,
because they're not familiar with them. Teachers are
playing that kind of game all the time. And I was right in
there, with both feet.

I was scared of my students when I began. I did everything I could to keep from being caught in an error, in a
lapse of knowledge. I used all the authority I had to keep
them at a distance, to keep them in their place. If any of
the students didn't hate my guts, it wasn't because I gave
them no reason. There was no communication going on in
that classroom at all.

The traditional education sees the school as a place
where the student gets poured into him the accumulated
knowledge of the past. I've gone very much from one end
of the pole to the other in the last seven years. I'm very
interested in listening to my students. But I still feel hypo-
critical about my work. I suspect people in the business
world have to stay away from thoughts like that. Yet
there are things I feel pretty good about. I know there are

* R. D. Laing, *The Politics of Experience* (New York: Pantheon Books, 1967).

students I've helped. I'm not sure I ever helped anyone when I was selling business machines or insurance.

. I've become suspicious of the teacher who automatically thinks he's superior to somebody who's out there working as a salesman. I don't think there is anything automatic about it. I am working for an institution that turns out students so they will be salesmen.

When I began teaching at college, I pretended to be this authoritarian figure who knew everything. Gradually, over the years, it's become possible for me to walk in the class and to admit to my own confusion. As I present the person I really am to my students, they present the people they really are to me.

When I was a salesman, there was never a day in which I felt I could be absolutely honest. It was essential that the role be played. I was on somebody else's trip. I would fit into that slot and behave in a certain way. In order to do that, it meant wearing a mask every minute on the job.

One summer I took a job out in Missouri, selling insurance. After I learned the pitch and got out in the territory I realized it was a crooked operation, a con game. Oh God, they were a terrible outfit. (Laughs.) I needed the money and I was a salesman. I found out I couldn't do it. I'd be driving down the country road and I'd come to the farm where I was supposed to make my pitch. It was difficult just to turn the car into the driveway. I'd drive around the place three or four times before I could pump myself up enough to go in and talk to the guy. I sold one policy in seven weeks and then quit.

I feel that my unwillingness to settle into a groove—my fear of being caught in a rut—is related to my father and his job and his success. While my contemporaries have been out pursuing exactly what it is my father has, I got a good look at it early enough. So I knew it wasn't the way I'd spend my life.

The corporation really wants that person's whole life. They like to have a guy who will join a country club for the corporation, marry an appropriate wife for the corporation, do community work for the corporation. These are the people that really make it. That's my father's life.

It's hard to think of a friend that my father has. I don't know of one. There are people he works with. These are people in the family. That's it. Because of his particular job he's less in contact with people than a lot of business-men. He's an accountant, a bookkeeper.

I can't talk to him about my social life. I'm sure he'd disapprove of a lot of people I'm close to, a lot of things I do. I really feel my life is wide open. I've got problems, there are things that get me down, but on the whole, I feel younger than I did ten years ago. I have a lot of friends, students, who have affected my life.

When I think of my father, the strongest memories are the very, very early ones. He hadn't been completely sucked into that business. He still had a life separate from the job. I must have been less than four. There was a parking lot across the street. I can remember sitting with my father at the window and he would name all the different kinds of cars for me. I remember his taking me out on a Sunday morning in the park. I'd be riding the tri-cycle and he'd be walking ... I can't remember a time we spent together after that.

By the time I was ten I was aware of the distance be-tween us. I was aware he didn't understand me. I was aware he didn't know what I was thinking. what I was feeling. That gap continues ... (Pause.) When I got old enough to go out on my own there was nothing to hold me back. His job is the key to his life and, I think, the key to mine.

HAROLD PATRICK

He is small, compactly built; his battered face has seen all sorts of weather. His shoulders are stooped—reluctantly, it would seem. He is sixty-two. Two of his sons are city firemen and one is a policeman.

I started workin' when I was eleven years old. With a ped-dler on Saturdays, at five o'clock in the morning until it was done. For twenty-five cents. The peddler used to yell out the wares and the woman would holler out the win-dow, "Bring me up the potatoes." I'd run upstairs and give it to the woman. Fifty years later I'm runnin' a freight elevator. I been runnin' it for the past thirteen years. A man does a certain job and it becomes so repetitious there's no imagination left . . .

There's all kinds of problems in retiring. The inflation makes it difficult for a man to retire because the money he gets is wiped out and the number of years he has to be in a union in order to acquire a pension is such that he never reaches it. Most of my friends died on the verge of getting pensions. I have pictures of when I was a truckdriver. There's eight guys in the picture. Me and one other fellow are left. All the rest are dead. So retirement for the average man is pretty rough. He feels he's finished and even then he can't be finished because he hasn't got the means to live on, or has to depend on his family. And he doesn't want that.

He recounts past jobs, more than a half-century's worth, with the detail and in the manner of a Leporello cataloguing the amorous adventures of Don Giovanni: "I was an errand boy, I drove horses, I drove automobiles, small ones, and I drove trailers and trucks about twenty-five years. I worked as a seaman, I was on ships and fired below as a fireman. I worked as a longshoreman, loaded coffee on ships, workin' for the Panama Pacific and Morgan Line and the various Cunard lines. I drove a winch on a ship. For a while I was a sailor on deck. I worked as a rigger. I worked as a bricklayer's helper. I worked cutting trees down, cleaning roads to put up telephone poles. I guess I done most every kind of work."

There's not the same fraternalism today. There was a pride. A fireman on a ship, he took a certain pride. Then, he was a truckdriver amongst truckdrivers.* He was proud of being a truckdriver, he wasn't ashamed. Today it's impersonal.

Oh, there was a certain amount of adventure to it. In 1933 I drove a trailer from New York to Pittsburgh. They didn't have the roads they have today and the lights. You went over the Alleghany Mountains, you didn't go through short cuts. You arrived at places where drivers always

* His son Tom recalls his father's craftsmanship: "If there was the tiniest space, he could swing back the biggest truck in there, one, two, three, wit' maybe one inch to spare. This little guy up there in 'at truck . . ."

met. These roadhouses had logs and the driver would jot
down who he was and where he came from. They would
meet in Pittsburgh at four, five in the morning in a bar,
and they had a party. Everybody got charged up and went
to bed and then went back to work again. Everybody
seemed to know each other.

*He re-creates the conditions at sea before the birth of the
National Maritime Union: eight men in a room, no doctor aboard, tensions, fights ... As for the longshoreman's
lot, it was purgatory ashore: the shouldering of two-hun-
dred-pound bags from one end of the dock to the other,
hour after hour ... "The only break was if you went to
take a crap or five minutes to steal off a smoke." At six
dollars a day, "It was during the Depression and you were
glad to get it. When the ship was loaded, you wasn't
workin' no more—till you caught the next ship. You drove
a taxi all day and came home with a quarter. It don't
leave you untouched. That's a physical grind. If you don't
think sittin' in a chair and bitin' your nails to the elbows
wasn't physical . . ." (Laughs.)*

Operatin' a freight elevator doesn't take too much
imagination. Plenty opportunity to think. You think
maybe I shoulda did this or I shoulda did that. But ah,
what the hell, you don't worry too much. After all, I recognize my limitations. Ninety percent of the freight eleva-
tors is automatic today. That's the thing that's going down
with the gandy dancer. He's gone too.

You have all kinds of problems, especially with the dis-
gruntled. If the elevator isn't there fast enough ... there's
speed-up in everything. A truckdriver comes, he's got a
load, he wants to get rid of it, right? He's in a hurry. You
have to have a certain amount of patience to understand
his problem. It's not easy to be an elevator operator, because you get all kinds of abuse unless you understand
why the other guy's upset. He understands that you know
it, then you become friends.

The boss gives the guy a bad time. He says, "Where the
hell are ya hangin' out?" Jesus Christ, the guy's sittin'
there, he's givin' me a call, "Why the hell don't you hurry
up?" He says to his boss, "I had to wait for the elevator."
Then the elevator man becomes the guy who you can
blame all your problems on. That's the way it is.

Each boss on each floor—say I have twelve floors—seems to feel he's the guy that pays the elevator's wages. If there's no heat in the buildin', he gets the elevator man, "Where the hell's the heat?" Or the water or the lights go out or the hallway gets dirty. He says, "Where the hell is the elevator? The hallway's got no lights, my workers are gonna fall down." He's worried about his workers only so far as it affects his production, where his profits are involved. The elevator man, you're young, you can be more demanding. But as you get older, it's not so easy to be as demanding. Once you get white it's not so easy to walk around and say you want a job. Soon as the snow gets on top of your head you ain't wanted no more.

The elevator man is usually older, he's on his way down. But he can out-survive the truckdriver. Because the truckdriver at forty, his kidneys are beginning to kick up or he's got his whole prostate gland giving him a bad time. Forty, forty-five, many of them I know, they begin to get ulcers because the pressures—the traffic cop, the lights, the speed-up . . .

Of course, there's humiliations with the elevator man. There's no measure of intelligence. It's a simple job and you gotta survive. Now there's limitations . . . Don't think the elevator man just takes shit. He's as abusive as the next guy. He got the chip there too. He knows the guy's comin' in and the guy's gonna holler at him and he's gonna holler back at the guy, right? What the hell, nobody's mad, really. They call each other names, but that doesn't mean nothin'. If you didn't have that, you'd really blow, you're finished.

Every worker looks down at the other. Let's say he's a guy who's on top of the skyscraper and he's tossin' these things and he's walkin' out on the beam: I'm number one. Here, boy. I'm makin' the biggest buildin'. He's proud, right? The truckdriver that drives the big trailer in and out and backs it into . . . he's got a certain pride. And he looks down. Now the guy who sweeps the floor in one of the shops, the elevator man can look over him, he's a little bit lower. (Laughs.) Each one has their guy . . . But what pride is there in lookin' down?

The guy that opens the door, could he have pride? Even the elevator man has pride. But the guy that opens the door for the rich man and holds the umbrella on his head, it's a little more harder for him to take pride in it.

You have to understand the worker in this society. This is a society of profit, right? But in the socialist society the elevator man could be an honored person, too, just the same as the highest person. Because they don't get there unless the elevator man lets them up . . .

I believe socialism is gonna be the future. I believed that fifty years ago and I believe that today. I never lost my doubts which way the human race is gonna go. The capitalists are puttin' together cars, it's socialized, the production. But the means of returns are not socialized. It goes into a few, but it's produced by the many. You see the results in the workers around you. Some of 'em are broken at thirty, at forty, some of 'em at fifty.

If you could live your life over . . . ?

It's been so busy I've never really thought, Oh, I'd love to be this. But I never dreamt of being boss. I tried to influence the drivers to get better conditions for themselves. I participated as one of the leaders of the two biggest teamster strikes in the history of New York—1938 and 1947. In '38 we tied up the entire city of New York. We won conditions for the drivers, but I never enjoyed those conditions. Immediately following I was never able to get a job any more.* That's the way it went, but I don't regret it. I'm proud of the fact that the drivers got those things. I don't begrudge 'em. I wish they'd got 'em sooner, that's all.

Only a few of 'em enjoy it. That's the sad part of it. It's the same in medicine, same in everything. The wealthy, the ruling crowds, they enjoy all the things that workers produce. They're greedy, they're just like animals. I've seen dogs that they have just filled themselves and they couldn't eat another bite, but they would not tolerate another animal comin' near the food. The human animals, too, some of 'em are the same. No matter how much they have, they wouldn't part with any of it and they wouldn't let nobody else get it if they could help it.

I'm proud of my sons. They have principles and they

* His son Tom recalls: "My father was blacklisted in 1949 and used to have a bodyguard and all this . . ." Bob, his other son, remembers: "At the time of the strike my father went on the radio with Mayor LaGuardia."

have courage. We mustn't put a stigma around a uniform. A postman delivers mail, and he can be a very kindly man and you have lots of respect for him. So why shouldn't we respect a policeman or a fireman? But he must be the kind of man that justifies the respect of the people, that's all.

POSTSCRIPT: *"I have a piece of land in New Jersey and now my boys are building their places on it for their children. I run up there on Friday and get the place tidied up. I like farmin'. I like to grow it and I like to eat it better. (Laughs.) When you get your corn, you never taste corn like that in the store. And you have your big red tomatoes come in and cabbage, and make sauerkraut. In the fall you can tomatoes and you can string beans and you make grape jelly and blackberry jelly. Now I put a pond in and I had fish put in, and now wild birds come, and ducks and geese and swans and pheasant and all that. Deer come down and they drink out of the pond . . .*

"Oh yeah, I work like hell on that. I work harder than I work on my elevator. Of course, you take pride. I go around to the fairs and I make comparisons of my vegetables with the others. I feel mine are just as good. Oh, I love it. I would have liked that—if I had been a boy. But I was city-bred. The children and the grandchildren are going up there and we have a hell of a good time." (Laughs.)

BOB PATRICK

Harold's son. He is thirty-three, married, and has a child. He has been a member of the city police force for six years. For the past three years he has been an emergency service patrolman.

"Emergency service is like a rescue squad. You respond to any call, any incident: a man under a train, trapped in an auto, bridge jumpers, psychos, guys that murdered people and barricaded themselves in. We go in and get these people out. It is sometimes a little too exciting. I felt like I wasn't gonna come home on two incidents."

He finished among the highest in his class at the police academy, though he was "eleven years out of high school."

Most of his colleagues were twenty-one, twenty-two. "I al-
ways wanted to be with the city. I felt that was the best
job in the world. If I wasn't a cop, see, I don't think I
could be anything else. Oh, maybe a truckdriver."

I got assigned to foot patrolman in Bedford-Stuyvesant. I
never knew where Bedford-Stuyvesant was. I heard it was
a low, poverty-stricken area, and it was a name that people feared. It's black. Something like Harlem, even worse.
Harlem was where colored people actually grew up. But
Bedford-Stuyvesant is where colored people migrated from
Harlem or from North Carolina. They were a tougher
class of people.

Myself and two friends from the neighborhood went
there. We packed a lunch because we never really ven-
tured outside the neighborhood. We met that morning
about six o'clock. We had to be in roll call by eight. We
got there a quarter after six. We couldn't believe it was so
close. We laughed like hell because this is our neighborhood, more or less. We were like on the outskirts of our
precinct. It was only ten minutes from my house.

When we got our orders, everybody said, "Oh wow, forget it." One guy thought he was going there, we had to
chase him up three stories to tell him we're only kidding.
He was ready to turn in his badge. Great fear, that was a
danger area.

I was scared. Most people at Bedford-Stuyvesant were
unemployed, mostly welfare, and they more or less didn't
care too much for the police. The tour I feared most was
four to twelve on a Friday or Saturday night. I'm not a
drinker, I never drank, but I'd stop off at a bar over here
and have a few beers just to get keyed up enough to put
up with the problems we knew we were gonna come up
against.

I would argue face to face with these people that I
knew had their problems, too. But it's hard to use selective
enforcement with 'em. Then get off at midnight and still
feel nervous about it. And go for another few drinks and
go home and I'd fall right to sleep. Two or three beers
and I would calm down and feel like a husband again with
the family at home.

I rode with a colored guy quite a few times. They
would put you in a radio car and you'd be working with

an old-timer. One of the calls we went on was a baby in convulsions, stopped breathing. The elevator was out of order and we ran up eight flights of stairs. This was a colored baby. It was blue. I had taken the baby from the aunt and my partner and I rushed down the stairs with the mother. In the radio car I gave the baby mouth to mouth resuscitation. The baby had regurgitated and started breathing again. The doctor at the hospital said whatever it was, we had gotten it up.

The sergeant wanted to write it up because of the problem we were having in the area. For a white cop doin' what I did. But I didn't want it. I said I would do it for anybody, regardless of black or white. They wrote it up and gave me a citation. The guys from the precinct was kidding me that I was now integrated. The mother had said she was willing to even change the baby's name to Robert after what I did.

The guy I worked with had more time on the job than I did. When we went on a family dispute, he would do all the talking. I got the impression that they were more aggressive than we were, the people we were tryin' to settle the dispute with. A husband and wife fight or a boyfriend and a husband. Most of the time you have to separate 'em. "You take the wife into the room and I'll take the husband into the other room." I looked up to my partner on the way he settled disputes. It was very quick and he knew what he was doing.

I've been shot. The only thing I haven't been in Bedford-Stuyvesant is stabbed. I've been spit at. I've been hit with bottles, rocks, bricks, Molotov cocktails, cherry bombs in my eye ... I've gotten in disputes where I've had 10-13s called on me. That would be to assist the patrolman on the corner. Called by black people to help me against other black people.

After three years at Bedford-Stuyvesant he was assigned to the emergency service patrol. "Our truck is a $55,000 truck and it's maybe $150,000 in equipment. We have shotguns, we have sniper rifles, we have tear gas, bulletproof vests, we have nets for jumpers, we have Morrissey belts for the patrolman to hold himself in when he gets up on a bridge, we have Kelly tools to pry out trapped people, we give oxygen ..."

Fifty to seventy-five percent of our calls are for oxygen. I had people that were pronounced DOA by a doctor—dead on arrival. We have resuscitated them. I had brought him back. The man had lived for eight hours after I had brought him back. The doctor was flabbergasted. He had written letters on it and thought we were the greatest rescue team in New York City. We give oxygen until the arrival of the ambulance. Most of the time we beat the ambulance.

We set up a net for jumpers. We caught a person jumping from twenty-three stories in Manhattan. It musta looked like a postage stamp to him. We caught a girl from a high school four stories high. If it saves one life, it's worth it, this net.

A young man was out on a ledge on a six-story building. He was a mental patient. We try to get a close friend to talk to him, a girl friend, a priest, a guy from the old baseball team . . . Then you start talkin' to him. You talk to him as long as you can. A lot of times they kid and laugh with you—until you get too close. Then they'll tell you, "Stop right where you are or I'll jump." You try to be his friend. Sometimes you take off the police shirt to make him believe you're just a citizen. A lot of people don't like the uniform.

You straddle the wall. You use a Morrissey belt, tie it around with a line your partner holds. Sometimes you jump from a ledge and come right up in front of the jumper to trap him. But a lot of times they'll jump if they spot you. You try to be as cautious as possible. It's a life . . .

Sometimes you have eleven jobs in one night. I had to shoot a vicious dog in the street. The kids would curse me for doin' it. The dog was foaming at the mouth and snapping at everybody. We come behind him and put three bullets in his head. You want to get the kids outa there. He sees the cop shooting a dog, he's not gonna like the cop.

We get some terrible collisions. The cars are absolutely like accordions. The first week we had a head-on collision on a parkway. I was just passing by when it happened and we jumped out. There were parents in there and a girl and a boy about six years old. I carried the girl out. She had no face. Then we carried out the parents. The father had lived until we jacked him out and he had collasped. The whole family was DOA. It happens twenty-four hours a day. If emergency's gonna be like this, I'd rather go back to Bedford-Stuyvesant.

The next day I read in the papers they were both boys, but had mod haircuts. You look across the breakfast table and see your son. My wife plenty times asked me, "How can you do that? How can you go under a train with a person that's severed the legs off, come home and eat breakfast, and feel ... ?" That's what I'm waiting for: when I can go home and not feel anything for my family. See, I have to feel.

A patrolman will call you for a guy that's DOA for a month. He hanged himself. I'm cuttin' him down. You're dancing to get out of the way of the maggots. I caught myself dancing in the middle of the livingroom, trying to get a ring off a DOA for a month, while the maggots are jumping all over my pants. I just put the damn pants on, brand-new, dry cleaned. I go back to the precinct and still itch and jump in the shower.

And to go under a train and the guy sealed his body to the wheel because of the heat from the third rail. And you know you're gonna drop him into the bag. A sixteen-year-old kid gets his hand caught in a meat grinder. His hand was comin' out in front. And he asks us not to tell his mother. A surgeon pukes on the job and tells you to do it.

One time we had a guy trapped between the platform and the train. His body was below, his head was above. He was talking to the doctor. He had a couple of kids home. In order to get him out we had to use a Z-bar, to jack the train away from the platform. The doctor said, "The minute you jack this train away from the platform, he's gonna go." He was talkin' and smokin' with us for about fifteen minutes. The minute we jacked, he was gone. (Snaps fingers.) I couldn't believe I could snuff out life, just like that. We just jacked this thing away and his life. And to give him a cigarette before it happened was even worse.

While you're en route to the job, to build yourself up, you say, This is part of the job that has to be done. Somebody's gotta do it. After this, there couldn't be nothing worse. No other job's gonna be as bad as this one. And another job comes up worse. Eventually you get used to what you're doin'.

Homicides are bad. I seen the medical examiner put his

finger into seventeen knife wounds. I was holding the porto-light so he could see where his finger was going. Knuckle deep. And telling me, "It's hit the bone, the bullet here, the knife wound through the neck." I figure I've seen too much. Jeez, this is not for me. You wouldn't believe it. Maybe I don't believe it. Maybe it didn't hit me yet.

I'm afraid that after seein' so much of this I can come home and hear my kid in pain and not feel for him. So far it hasn't happened. I hope to God it never happens. I hope to God I always feel. When my grandmother passed away a couple of months ago, I didn't feel anything. I wonder, gee, is it happening to me?

One time a guy had shot up a cop in the hospital and threw the cop down the stairs and his wheel chair on top of him. He escaped with a bullet in him. He held up a tenement in Brownsville. They called us down at three o'clock in the morning, with bullet-proof vests and shotguns. I said to myself, This is something out of the movies. The captain had a blackboard. There's eight of us and he gave each of us a job: "Two cover the back yard, you three cover the front, you three will have to secure the roof."

This guy wasn't gonna be taken alive. Frank and me will be the assault team to secure the roof. We're loaded with shotguns and we're gonna sneak in there. We met at four o'clock in the morning. We're goin' up the back stairs. On the first stairway there was a German shepherd dog outside the doorway. The dog cowered in the corner, thank God. We went up three stories. We secured the roof.

We could hear them assaulting in each apartment, trying to flush this guy out. He fled to the fire escape. As he was comin' up, we told him to freeze, Tony, it was all over. He started to go back down. We radioed team one in the back yard. We heard shots. The rooftops had actually lit up. The assault man had fired twenty-seven bullets into this guy and he recovered. He's still standing trial from what I heard. This was one of the jobs I felt, when I was goin' up the stairs, should I give my wife a call? I felt like I had to call her.

If a perpetrator's in a building, you either talk to him or contain him or flush him out with tear gas rather than runnin' in and shoot. They feel a life is more important than anything else. Most cops feel this, yes.

I went on the prison riots we had in the Tombs. I was the first one on the scene, where we had to burn the gates out of the prison, where the prisoners had boarded up the gates with chairs and furniture. We had to use acetylene torches. My wife knew I was in on it. I was on the front page. They had me with a shotgun and the bullet-proof vest and all the ammunition, waiting to go into the prison.

I wonder to myself, Is death a challenge? Is it something I want to pursue or get away from? I'm there and I don't have to be. I want to be. You have chances of being killed yourself. I've come so close . . .

I went on a job two weeks ago. A nineteen-year-old, he just got back from Vietnam on a medical discharge. He had ransacked his parents' house. He broke all the windows, kicked in the color television set, and hid upstairs with a homemade spear and two butcher knives in one hand. He had cut up his father's face.

We were called down to go in and get this kid. He tore the bannister up and used every pole for a weapon. We had put gas masks on. All the cops was there, with sticks and everything. They couldn't get near him. He kept throwing down these iron ash trays. I went up two steps and he was cocking this spear. We cleared out all the policemen. They just wanted emergency, us.

If you wait long enough, he'll come out. We had everybody talk to him, his mother . . . He didn't come out. The sergeant gave orders to fire tear gas. I could hear it go in the windows. I went up a little further and I seen this nozzle come out of his face. I said, "Sarge, he's got a gas mask on." We fired something like sixteen cannisters in the apartment. When he went back to close one of the doors, I lunged upstairs. I'm very agile. I hit him in the face and his mask went flying. I grabbed his spear and gave him a bear hug. He just didn't put up any resistance. It was all over.

The patrol force rushed in. They were so anxious to get this guy, they were tearing at me. I was tellin' him, "Hey, fella, you got my leg. We got him, it's all over." They pulled my gas mask off. Now the big party starts. This was the guy who was agitating them for hours. "You bum, we got you." They dragged him down the stairs and put him in a body bag. It's like a straitjacket.

When we had him face down a patrolman grabbed him by the hair and slammed his face into the ground. I grabbed his wrist, "Hey, that's not necessary. The guy's handcuffed, he's secure." I brushed the kid's hair out of his eyes. He had mod long hair. My kid has mod hair. The guy says, "What's the matter with you?" I said, "Knock it off, you're not gonna slam the kid."

The neighbors congratulated me because the kid didn't get a scratch on him. I read in the paper, patrolman so-and-so moved in to make the arrest after a preliminary rush by the emergency service. Patrolman so-and-so is the same one who slammed the kid's face in the ground.

I'm gonna get him tonight. I'm gonna ask if he's writing up for a commendation. I'm gonna tell him to withdraw it. Because I'm gonna be a witness against him. The lieutenant recommended giving me a day off. I told my sergeant the night before last the lieutenant can have his day off and shove it up his ass.

A lot of the barricade snipers are Vietnam veterans. Oh, the war plays a role. A lot of 'em go in the army because it's a better deal. They can eat, they can get an income, they get room and board. They take a lot of shit from the upper class and they don't have to take it in the service.

It sounds like a fairy tale to the guys at the bar, in one ear and out the other. After a rough tour, a guy's dead, shot, people stabbed, you go into a bar where the guys work on Wall Street, margin clerks, "How ya doin? What's new?" You say, "You wouldn't understand." They couldn't comprehend what I did just last night. With my wife, sometimes I come home after twelve and she knows somethin's up. She waits up. "What happened?" Sometimes I'm shaking, trembling. I tell her, "We had a guy . . ." (Sighs.) I feel better and I go to bed. I can sleep.

The one that kept me awake was three years ago. The barricaded kid. The first night I went right to sleep. The second night you start thinking, you start picturing the kid and taking him down. With the kid and the tear gas, the sergeant says, "Okay fire." And you hear the tear gas . . . Like you're playing, fooling around with death. You don't want to die, but you're comin' close to it, to really skin it. It's a joke, it's not happening.

I notice since I been in emergency she says, "Be careful." I hate that, because I feel jinxed. Every time she says be careful, a big job comes up. I feel, shit, why did she say that? I hope she doesn't say it. She'll say, "I'll see you in the morning. Be careful." Ooohhh!

Bad accidents, where I've held the guys' skulls . . . I'm

getting used to it, because there are younger guys comin'
into emergency and I feel I have to be the one to take
charge. 'Cause I seen a retired guy come back and go on
a bad job, like the kid that drowned and we pulled him
out with hooks. I'm lookin' to him for help and I see him
foldin'. I don't want that to happen to me. When you're
workin' with a guy that has eighteen years and he gets
sick, who else you gonna look up to?

Floaters, a guy that drowns and eventually comes up.
Two weeks ago, we pulled this kid out. You look at him
with the hook in the eye ... You're holdin' in because
your partner's holdin' in. I pulled a kid out of the pond,
drowned. A woman asked me, "What color was he?" I
said, "Miss, he's ten years old. What difference does it
make what color he was?" "Well, you pulled him out, you
should know." I just walked away from her.

Emergency got a waiting list of three thousand. I have
one of the highest ratings. I do have status, especially with
the young guys. When a guy says, "Bob, if they change the
chart, could I ride with you?" that makes me feel great.

I feel like I'm helpin' people. When you come into a
crowd, and a guy's been hit by a car, they call you. Ambulance is standing there dumbfounded, and the people
are, too. When you give orders to tell this one to get a
blanket, this one to get a telephone book, so I can splint a
leg and wrap it with my own belt off my gun, that looks
good in front of the public. They say, "Gee, who are these
guys?"

Last week we responded to a baby in convulsions. We
got there in two minutes. The guy barely hung up the
phone. I put my finger down the baby's throat and pulled
the tongue back. Put the baby upside down, held him in
the radio car. I could feel the heat from the baby's mouth
on my knuckles. At the hospital the father wanted to
know who was the guy in the car. I gave the baby to the
nurse. She said, "He's all right." I said, "Good." The father was in tears and I wanted to get the hell out of there.

This morning I read the paper about that cop that was
shot up. His six-year-old son wrote a letter: "Hope you
get better, Dad." My wife was fixin' breakfast. I said,
"Did you read the paper, hon?" She says, "Not yet." "Did
you read the letter this cop's son sent to his father when
he was in the hospital?" She says, "No." "Well, he's dead
now." So I read the part of it and I started to choke. I

says, "What the hell . . ." I dropped the paper just to get my attention away. I divided my attention to my son that was in the swing. What the hell. All the shit I seen and did and I gotta read a letter . . . But it made me feel like I'm still maybe a while away from feeling like I have no feeling left. I knew I still had feelings left. I still have quite a few jobs to go . . .

TOM PATRICK

Bob's brother.

He has been a city fireman for two years. During the preceding four years he had been a member of the city's police force. He is thirty-two, married. "It's terrific for a guy that just got out of high school with a general diploma. I don't even know English. My wife is Spanish, she knows syllables, verbs, where to put the period . . . I wish I was a lawyer. Shit, I wish I was a doctor. But I just didn't have it. You gotta have the smarts.

"There was seven of us. Three brothers, myself and my sister, mother and father. It was a railroad flat. Me and my brother used to sleep in bunk beds until we were twenty-seven years old. And they're supposed to be for kids, right?"

He owns his own house and can't get over the wonder of it, mortgage or not. A back yard, "it's like a piece of country back there. It smells like Jersey. We have barbecues, drink beer, the neighbors are good.

"Twenty years ago it was all Irish, Italian, Polish. I went in the army in '62 and everybody was moving out to Long Island. There's a lot of Puerto Ricans now. They say the spics are movin' in, the black are movin' in. They're good people. They don't bother me and I don't bother them. I think I'm worse than them. Sometimes I come home four in the morning, piss in the street. I think they might sign a petition to get me out.

"The guys in this thing were prejudiced. I'm probably prejudiced too. It's a very conservative neighborhood. A lot of the cops are here. Up to the fifties, these guys were my heroes, these guys in the bar. You hear this guy was in the Second World War . . . I was a kid and a lot of these

*guys are dead now. Forty-eight, fifty years old, they died
young, from drinking and shit. You just grow up into this
prejudice—guy's a spic, a nigger. When I was in the army
I didn't think I was prejudiced, until the colored guy told
me to clean the floor five, six times, and I was calling him
nigger. You express yourself, get the frustration out.*

*"One o'clock in the morning, in August, we had a block
party. They were dancing on the fire escapes. People were
drinking. We had three, four hundred people there. We
had a barricade up on the corner and the cops never came
around. The fuckin' cops never came around. We don't
need 'em. I think when you see a cop everybody gets
tense. Instead of concentrating on the music and drinkin'
beer, you keep lookin' over your shoulder: Where's the
cop? You know."*

I got out of the army in '64. I took the test for transit police, housing police, and city police. It's the same test. It
was in March '66 when I got called. I got called for the
housing police. For the first six months you just bounce
around different housing projects.

I was engaged to this other girl and her father was mad
that I didn't take the city police, because I could make
more money on the side. He said I was a dope. He said,
"What are you gonna get in the housing projects? The
people there don't pay you off." Because they were poor
people. I said, "The money they give me as a cop is good
enough." Most of the people around here don't go on to
be doctors or lawyers. The thing to get is a city job, because it's security.

I worked in Harlem and East Harlem for three years.
There was ten, eleven cops and they were all black guys. I
was the only white cop. When they saw me come into the
office they started laughin'. "What the fuck are they sendin' you here for? You're fuckin' dead." They told me to
get a helmet and hide on the roof.

This one project, there were five percenters. That's a
hate gang. They believed that seventy percent of the black
population are Uncle Toms, twenty-five percent are alcoholics, and five percent are the elite. These fuckin' guys'll
kill ya in a minute.

This project was twenty-five buildings, thirteen stories
each. Covered maybe twenty acres. It was like a city. I
remember the first night I got there, July fourth. It was

105 degrees out. I had come in for the midnight to eight tour. I had an uncle that was a regular city cop. He called me up the night before and he said they expected a riot in this project. He said the cops had helicopters going around above the people and a lot of cops in plain clothes and cars. He was worried about me: "Be careful."

This one black guy said, "You stay with me." That night we went on the roof and we're lookin' down and people are walkin' around and drinkin' on the benches. This colored guy was drinkin' and I went down there seven in the morning. I told him to move. "Somebody's gonna rob you." He said, "Man, I ain't got a penny on me. The most they could do is give me somethin'." And he went back to sleep.

The thing is you gotta like people. If you like people, you have a good time with 'em. But if you have the attitude that people are the cause of what's wrong with this country, they're gonna fuckin' get you upset and you're gonna start to hate 'em, and when you hate, you get a shitty feeling in your stomach that can destroy you, right?

When I went to the housing project, I said, There's a lot of people around here and you meet 'em and the older people want you to come in and have a beer with 'em. I used to go to some great parties. I'd go up there nine o'clock at night and I'm in uniform with my gun on and you'd be in the kitchen, drinking Scotch, rye, beer, talking to these beautiful Spanish girls. These are people, right? Poor people. My family's poor. They talk about the same thing and the kids come over to me and they'd pet you or they'd touch the gun.

I made an arrest. Some kid came over and told me a guy across the street had robbed his camera. So I ran over and grabbed the guy. It was petty larceny. The colored cop said I broke my cherry. So he took me to the basement that night and they had a party. A portable bar, record player, girls come down, they were dancin'.

I couldn't wait to go to work, because I felt at ease with these people. Sometimes I'd look in the mirror and I'd see this hat and I couldn't believe it was me in this uniform. Somebody'd say, "Officer, officer." I'd have to think, Oh yeah, that's me. I wouldn't really know I was a cop. To me, it was standin' on the corner in my own neighborhood. Poor. I'd see drunks that are like my father. A black drunk with a long beard and his eyes ... He'd bring back memories of my father. I'd be able to talk to the kids. They'd be on the roof, fuckin', and I'd say, "I'll give you ten minutes." It took me two minutes to come. "Ten minutes is enough for you right?"

One project I worked out of I made nineteen arrests in one year, which was tops. I didn't go out lookin' to make 'em, I ran into shit. If you run into a person that's robbin' another person, man, that's wrong! My mind was easy. I just figured if a guy was drunk or a guy's makin' out with a girl, it shouldn't be a crime. I was with this one cop, he used to sneak up on cars and look in and see people gettin' laid or blow jobs. I used to be embarrassed. I don't like that shit.

I made all these arrests and they transferred me out. I didn't want to leave, 'cause I knew the people and I thought I could be an asset. It was Peurto Rican, black, I had like a rapport. Jesus Christ, I loved it. They're sending me to Harlem because I'm so good. Bullshit! That jerked me off. I wanted East Harlem because you had every thing there. You had Italians, still. I used to go up the block and drink beer. I used to listen to Spanish music. And the girls are beautiful. Jesus! Unbelievable! Spanish girls. My wife's from Colombia. She's beautiful. I love it when her hair's down. I think that's where I got the idea of marrying a Spanish girl. In East Harlem.

I wasn't against Harlem, but there was no people. It was a new project. I was just there to watch the Frigidaires. I was a watchman. Sewers open, the ground wasn't fixed, no grass, holes. We used to stand in lobbies of an empty building. I want to be where people are. So I got pissed off and put a transfer in. After six months people started moving in—and I liked it. But they transferred me to Canarsie. Middle-income white. And all these bullshit complaints. "Somebody's on my grass." "I hear a noise in the elevator." Up in Harlem they'll complain maybe they saw a dead guy in the elevator.

I never felt my life threatened. I never felt like I had to look over my shoulder. I was the only white cop in that project. The kids'd be playin', come over and talk to me. Beautiful. But sometimes they just hate you. I'm in uniform and they just go around and say, "You motherfucker," and stuff like that. I can't say, "Wait, just get to know me, I'm not that bad." You haven't got time. If you start explainin', it's a sign of weakness. Most people, if you try to be nice, they're nice. But you get some of these guys that got hurt, they really got fucked, they got arrested for not doing anything.

I was with a cop who arrested a guy for starin' at him! Starin' at him! The cop I was with, Vince, he had a baby face and the guy on the bus stop kept lookin' at him because this cop never shaved. He said, "Motherfucker, what're you lookin' at?" The guy said, "I'm just lookin'." I said, "The guy probably thinks you're not a cop 'cause you got a pretty face." Vince puts the night stick under the guy's chin. Naturally when a guy puts a night stick under your chin, you push it away. As soon as you do that, you got an assault. He arrested the guy. The guy was waitin' for a bus!

With this same Vince, another kid came around, a Puerto Rican seventeen years old. They all knew me. He says, "Hi, baby," and he slapped my hand like that. "How you doin', man?" Vince said, "What're ya lettin' the kid talk to you like that for?" I said, "This is the way they talk, this is their language. They ain't meanin' to be offensive." He says, "Hey fucko, come over here." He grabbed him by the shirt. He said, "You fucker, talk mister, sir, to this cop." He flung the kid down the ramp. We had a little police room. His girl started crying. I went down after this Vince, I said, "What're you doin'? You lock that fuckin' kid up, I'm against you. That fuckin' kid's a good friend of mine, you're fuckin' wrong." He said, "I'm not gonna lock him up, I'm just gonna scare him. You gotta teach people. You gotta keep 'em down."

Just about that time twenty kids start poundin' on the door. The kid's brother was there and his friends. We're gonna get a riot. And the kid didn't do anything. He was just walkin' with his girl.

I was in the riots in '67 in Harlem. I saw a gang of kids throwin' rocks and they hit this policeman. The cops inside the car couldn't see where the rocks was comin' from. When they all piled out, the kids was gone. They thought the rocks was comin' from the roof. So these guys come out shootin' to the blues. One big white guy got out, he says, "Come out, you motherfuckin' black bastard." I was with five black cops and one said to me, "Get that fucker away from me or I'll kill him."

City cops, they got clubs, they think they're the elite. Housing is H.A.—they call us ha-ha cops. Transit cops are called cave cops because they're in the subway. These are little ribs they give. Who's better, who's New York's Finest? . . . I was in the park three years ago with a transit cop. We're with these two nice lookin' girls—I was still single. It's about one o'clock in the morning. We had a couple of six-packs and a pizza pie. We're tryin' to make out, right? Cops pull up, city cops, and they shine the light on us. So my friend shows the cop his badge. The cop says, "That's more reason you shouldnt' be here. You're fuckin' on the job, just get the fuck outa the park." 'Cause he was a transit cop they gave him a hard time. My friend was goin' after this cop and this cop was goin' after him. I grabbed him and the driver in the police car grabbed his buddy and they were yelling, "Keep outa the park." And the other guy's yellin', "Don't come down in the subways." I coulda turned around and said, "Don't ever come in the housing projects." It was stupid shit, right? A guy'll pull out a gun and get killed.

You can't laugh at a gun. I had a gun put to my head in a bar, over the Pueblo incident. A cop. I got a load on and argue with these guys about shit in Vietnam. I said, "Saigon's got a million-dollar police station and my brother's got a station a hundred years old. Where's the money come from? The cops and firemen are paying taxes and they're not fixin' up their stations." This guy, Jim, who's a city cop for twenty-four years, is everything you want a cop to be. When I was eighteen he was thirty-eight, he was a supercop. But the hate just fucked him up, and the war.

I was in the bar and Jim had his load on, too. He's got personal problems, he's married twice, divorced. He said, "We should invade Korea, bomb it." I said, "You're ready to drop a bomb on a country with civilians." He said, "Ah, you fuckin' commie." So I turn my back. I feel this thing on my tenple, he had a gun to my head. Two guys next to me dived for the ground. With my left hand I came towards his fuckin' left wrist. The gun went to the ground and I grabbed him in a headlock. Three other cops in civilian clothes broke it up. You gotta watch that gun.

I coulda been like Jim or Vince. I started seein' the problems of people. Ten people in an apartment and there's no place to go except sit out on the street drinkin' beer. I guess I got this feeling from my father.

My father's a great man. I see what he went through

and the shit and hard times. I don't see how he lived
through it. I used to lay awake when I was drinkin' and
listen to him talk all right. And I used to cry. He talked
about the shittin' war, all the money goin' for war. And
the workers' sons are the ones that fight these wars, right?
And people that got nothin' to eat ... I tell ya, if I didn't
have an income comin' in ... These kids hangin' around
here, Irish kids, Italian kids, twenty-five years old, alcoholics, winos. One guy died of exposure. He went out with
my kid sister and he's dead now.

I was in a four-man detail in Harlem for about six
months, just before my transfer to Canarsie. It's four
thirty-story buildings, and the people'd be movin' in there.
Every day I have a list of names of people that are movin'
in. One black family came with eight kids. They had seven
rooms on the twentieth floor. The mother, this big, fat
woman, asked could I show her the apartment. The kids
just wanted to see it. Beautiful painting, real clean. The
kids started crying, little kids. I could cry when I think of
it. They ran into the bedrooms and they laid on the floor.
They said, "This is mine! this is mine!" The kids said,
"Look at the bedroom, it's clean." These little black kids
with sneakers and holes in their pants, crying. It was
empty, but they wouldn't leave that room. The woman
asked me could they stay over night. Their furniture was
gettin' delivered the next day. You get people a job or decent housing, you won't have no trouble.

*"What led me to be a cop? I'm not that smart to be a
lawyer. I failed in Spanish. I'm lucky I can talk English. A
good day in school for me was when the teacher didn't
call on me. I used to sit in the back of the room and slide
down into the seat so she didn't call on me.*

*"When I got pimples on my face, that made it worse. I
was shy with girls. One thing I told my father, 'I'm gonna
kill myself, I got pimples.' He said—I'll never forget it—
'The world's bigger than the pimples on your face.' At
that time I didn't think it was. I used to pile Noxzema on
my face and I was with a girl makin' out and she'd say, 'I
smell Noxzema.' It used to be in my hair, up my nose ...*

*"I liked mathematics. I could add like a bastard. I start-
ed gettin' to algebra, but then I got lost. I didn't want to
raise my hand because I had this skin problem. It's crazy,*

right? I sunk down and the teacher never called on me for two years."

The more arrests you make, they got the assumption you're a better cop, which is not right. They put pressure on me to make arrests. You gotta get out and you gotta shanghai people because you got the sergeant on your back. It comes down to either you or the next guy. You got a family and you got everybody fuckin' everybody ... It's crazy, know what I mean?"

The project I worked in in East Harlem, you grab a kid doin' wrong: "Come here, you fuck." That's it. He don't argue. But the middle-income, the kid'll lie to you. He won't tell you his right name. His name is a fireman or a cop. He tells his son, "Don't fuckin' give any information." They know the law better.

Like the last project I was on, white middle-income. They were all kids with long hair, right? This cop, he'd be seein' me talkin' to the kids, playing guitars. I'd be talkin' about records. He'd call me, "Hey, what're ya talkin' to those fags?" I'd say, "They're all right." One of the kids with long hair, his father's a cop. He said, "Aw fuck that, they're all commies."

A couple of times the kids burned me. I saw five kids smokin' pot. They're passin' around the pipe. I grabbed them and threw the shit on the ground. I didn't want to arrest them. I let 'em all go. The next day one of the kids told this cop, "That Tommy's a good cop, he let us go." It got back to the sergeant and he says, "You're gonna be hung." So a few times I got charges brought up on me.

I didn't want to be a cop. Money comes into it. I was twenty-six and I worked in the post office and I wasn't making' money, $2.18 an hour. I was young and I wanted to go out with the girls, and I wanted to go down to the Jersey shore, I wanted to buy a car, I just got out of the army. That's why I took it.

When I became a cop I thought I was going against my father. Cops are tools of the shittin' Rockefeller. Cops can't understand when they built a new office building in Harlem the people in that community want a hospital or a school. Rockefeller built that office building, right? Built by white construction workers. And these people demonstrate. Suppose they built in this neighborhood a state office building and black people built it and black people work in it. The cops go in there and break up the demonstrations and who gets it? The cops. Rockefeller's a million miles away. Cops are working guys, they don't understand.

You got cops that are fuckin' great cops, they're great people. Your supercops. The man in the front line, the patrolman, they do all the work. The sergeants aren't in with the people. They'd be doin' paper work. That's what got me mad.

I know a lot of cops that even liked people more than me. And some were fucks. You got black cops in the projects who were harder on their own people than a white guy. They think the poor people are holdin' them back. But a lot of them are supercops. Maybe if it was the other way around, if the whites were down and the blacks were top dog, you'd get better white cops.

Know why I switched to fireman? I liked people, but sometimes I'd feel hate comin' into me. I hated it, to get me like that. I caught these three guys drinkin' wine, three young Spanish guys. I said, "Fellas, if you're gonna drink, do it in some apartment." 'Cause they were spillin' the wine and they'd piss right in front of the house, in the lobby. I came back in a half-hour and they had another bottle out. They were pissin' around. I'm sayin' to myself, I'm tryin' to be nice. I walked over. There was two guys facin' me and one guy had his back to me. So he says, "What the fuck's the mick breakin' our balls for?" He's callin' me a mick. He's changing roles, you know? He's acting like they say a cop does. So I said, "You fuckin' spic." So I took the night stick and I swung it hard to hit him in the head. He ducked and it hit the pillar. He turned white and they all took off. It scared me that I could get this hatred so fast. I was fuckin' shakin'.

A few times I pulled my gun on guys. One time I went to the roof of this project and there's this big black guy about six seven on top of the stairs. He had his back to me, I said. "Hey fella, turn around." He said, "Yeah, wait a minute, man." His elbows were movin' around his belt. I was half-way up. I said "Turn around, put your hands up against the wall." He said, "Yeah, yeah, wait a minute." It dawned on me he had a gun caught in his belt and he was tryin' to take it out. I said, "Holy shit." So I took my gun out and said, "You fucker, I'm gonna shoot." He threw his hands against the wall. He had his dick out and he was tryin' to zip up his fly, and there was a girl standin' in the corner, which I couldn't see. So here was a guy gettin' a hand job and maybe a lot of guys might have killed him. I said, "Holy shit, I coulda killed ya." He started shaking and my gun in my hand was shaking like a bastard. I said—I musta been cryin'—I said, "Just get the hell outa here, don't . . ."

I took the fire department test in '68 and got called in '70. I always wanted to be a fireman. My other brother was a fireman eleven years. He had a fire and the floor gave way, he was tellin' me the story. He thought it was just a one-floor drop. But the guys grabbed him by the arms. They said, "If you go, we all go." He couldn't believe this kind of comradeship. They pulled him out. He went down to get his helmet and it was two floors down. He really woulda got busted up.

I like everybody workin' together. You chip in for a meal together. One guy goes to the store, one guy cooks, one guy washes the dishes. A common goal. We got a lieutenant there, he says the fire department is the closest thing to socialism there is.

The officer is the first one into the fire. When you get to captain or lieutenant, you get more work not less. That's why I look up to these guys. We go to a fire, the lieutenant is the first one in. If he leaves, he takes you out. One lieutenant I know got heart trouble. When he takes a beatin' at a fire he should go down to the hospital and get oxygen or go on sick. He don't want to go on sick. I used to go into a fire, it was dark and I'd feel a leg and I'd look up and see the lieutenants standing there in the fire and smoke takin' beatings.

When I was in the army I didn't respect the officers, because the men did all the work. That goes for the police department, too. Cops get killed. You never see a lieutenant get shot. Ten battalion chiefs got killed in fires in the last ten years in the city. The last three guys in the fire department were lieutenants that got killed. 'Cause they're the first ones in there. I respect that. I want to respect an officer. I want to see somebody higher up that I can follow.

You go to some firehouses, these fuckin' guys are supermen. I'm not a superman, I want to live. These guys are not gonna live. Every day orders come down, guys are dyin', retirement. I don't think these guys get their pensions too long. I never heard a fireman livin' to sixty-five.

When you get smoke in your lungs, these guys are spittin' out this shit for two days. A fireman's life is nine years shorter than the average workingman because of the beating they take on their lungs and their heart. More hazardous than a coal miner. The guy don't think nothing's wrong with him. You don't think until you get an x-ray and your name's on it. We got this lieutenant and when he takes a beating he can't go to a hospital because they'll find something wrong with him. He was trapped in a room and he jumped out of the second-story window. He broke both his ankles, ran back into the building, and he collapsed.

There's more firemen get killed than cops, five to one. Yet there's only one-third of the amount of men on the job. We get the same pay as policemen. These politicians start to put a split between the departments. I'd like to take some of these politicians right into the fuckin' fire and put their head in the smoke and hold it there. They wouldn't believe it. They don't give a shit for the people. Just because they wave the flag they think they're the greatest.

The first fire I went to was a ship fire. I jumped off the engine, my legs got weak. I nearly fell to the ground, shakin', right? It was the first and only time I got nerves. But we have to go in there. It's thrilling and its scary. Like three o'clock in the morning. I was in the ladder company, it's one of the busiest in the city, like six thousand runs a year.* The sky is lit up with an orange. You get back to the firehouse, you're up there, talkin', talkin' about it.

I was in a fire one night, we had all-hands. An all-hands is you got a workin' fire and you're the first in there, and the first guy in there is gonna take the worst beatin'. You got the nozzle, the hose, you're takin' a beating. If another

---

* "You go on false alarms, especially two or three in the afternoon, kids comin' home from school. And four in the morning when the bars are closed. Drunks. Sometimes I get mad. It's ten, eleven at night and you see ten, twenty teenagers on the corner and there's a false alarm on that corner, you know one of 'em pulled it. The kids say, 'What's the matter, man? What're ya doin' here?' and they laugh. You wanna say, 'You stupid fuck, you might have a fire in your house and it could be your mother.' "

company comes up behind you, you don't give up that nozzle. It's pride. To put out the fire. We go over this with oxygen and tell the guy, "Get out, get oxygen." They won't leave. I think guys want to be heroes. You can't be a hero on Wall Street.

There's guys with black shit comin' out of their ears. You got smoke in your hair. You take a shower, you put water on your hair, and you can still smell the smoke. It never leaves you. You're coughin' up this black shit. But you go back and you have coffee, maybe a couple of beers, you're psyched up.

You get a fire at two, three in the morning. The lights go on, you get up. I yelled, "Jesus, whatsa matter?" It dawned on me: Where else could we be goin'? All the lights goin' on and it's dark. It's fuckin' exciting. Guys are tellin', "Come on, we go. First Due." That means you gotta be the first engine company there. You really gotta move. It's a pride. You gotta show you're the best. But what they're fightin' over is good. What they're fightin' over is savin' lives.

You go in there and it's dark. All of a sudden smoke's pourin' outa the goddamn building. It's really fast. Everybody's got their assignments. A guy hooks up a hydrant. A guy on the nozzle, I'm on the nozzle. A guy's up to back me up. A guy's puttin' a Scott Air Pack on. It's a breathing apparatus. It lasts twenty minutes.

Two weeks ago we pulled up to this housing project. On the eighth floor the flames were leaping out the window. We jumped out, your fuckin' heart jumps. We ran into the elevator. Four of us, we rolled up the hose, each guy had fifty feet. We got off on the seventh floor, the floor below the fire. We got on the staircase and hook into the standpipe. The guys were screamin' for water and smoke was backin' up. You're supposed to have a wheel to turn on the water and the wheel was missin'! Someone stole it in the project. You get these junkies, they steal brass, anything. They steal the shittin' life. A guy with a truck company came with a claw tool and the water came shootin' out.

They started yellin' for a Scott. It weighs about thirty pounds, got the face mask and cylinder. I couldn't get the damn thing tight. There's three straps, I tied one. They need me upstairs. They push you into the room. (Laughs.) This is it. One guy's layin' on the floor and I'm crawlin',

feeling along the hose. The second company comes in with
Scotts on. One guys got his face piece knocked to the side,
so he's gotta get out because the smoke is gettin' him. The
other guy yells, "Give me the nozzle." It started whippin'
around, fifty, sixty pounds of pressure. Knocked my helmet off. I grabbed the nozzle. I looked up and saw this orange glow. I start hittin' it. The damn thing wouldn't go
out. It was a fuckin' light bulb. (Laughs.) A bulb in the
bathroom.

I felt this tremendous heat to my left. I turn around
and this whole fuckin' room was orange, yellow. You can't
see clear through the plastic face piece. You can just see
orange and feel the heat. So I open up with this shittin'
nozzle to bank back the smoke. The guys come in and
ventilated, knocked out the windows. A seven-room apartment, with six beds and a crib. That's how many kids
were living there. Nobody was hurt, they all got out.

There was a lot of smoke. When you have two minutes
left on the Scott, a bell starts ringin'. It means get out,
you got no oxygen. The thing I don't like about it, with
the piece on your face, you feel confined. But as I went to
more fires, I loved the thing because I know that thing's
life. Ninety percent of the people die from smoke inhala-
tion, not from burns.

You got oxygen, it's beautiful, but you can't see. It's a
shitty feeling when you can't see. Sometimes a Scott's bad
because it gives you a false sense of security. You go into a
room where you're not supposed to be. You'd be walkin'
into a pizzeria oven and you wouldn't know it. You can't
see, you feel your way with the hose. You straddle the
hose as you get out. You gotta talk to yourself. Your
mind's actually talkin'. I'm sayin' things like: It's beautiful,
I can breathe, the fire's over.

In 1958 there was a fire across the street from where I
live. It was about one o'clock in the morning. There's
flames on the second floor. I ran up the stairs and grabbed
this little girl. She was burnt on the arm. I ran down the
street and yelled to the firemen, "I got a girl here got
burnt." They went right past me. I hated the bastards.
Now I understand. You gotta put the fire out. There's
more life up there you gotta save. This girl's outside . . .
It's real . . .

When you're with the police, it wasn't real. I heard guys
makin' arrests, they found a gun in the apartment. In the

paper they say the guy fought with the guy over the gun. When you know the truth, the story's bullshit. But in the fire department there's no bullshit. You gotta get into that fire—to be able to save somebody's life.

About two years ago a young girl ran to the firehouse. She's yellin' that her father had a heart attack. The guy was layin' in the kitchen, right? He pissed in his pants. That's a sign of death. The fella was layin' there with his eyes open. Angie pushes the guy three times in the chest, 'cause you gotta shock his heart. The son was standin' in the room, just starin' down. I got down on his mouth. You keep goin' and goin' and the guy threw up. You clean out his mouth. I was on a few minutes and then Ed Corrigan jumped on the guy's mouth. The captain bent down and said, "The guy's dead. Keep goin' for the family." We took over for ten minutes, but it was a dead man. The son looked down at me and I looked up. He said, "Man, you tried everything. You tried." You know what I mean? I was proud of myself. I would get on a stranger, on his mouth. It's a great feeling.

We had this fire down the block. A Puerto Rican social club. The captain, the lieutenant, and the other firemen took the ladder up and saved two people. But downstairs there was a guy tryin' to get out the door. They had bolts on the door. He was burnt dead. Know what the lieutenant said? "We lost a guy, we lost a guy." I said "You saved two people. How would you know at six in the morning a guy's in the social club sleeping on a pool table?" He said, "Yeah, but we lost a guy." And the lieutenant's a conservative guy.

You get guys that talk about niggers, spics, and they're the first guys into the fire to save 'em. Of course we got guys with long hair and beards. One guy's an artist. His brother got killed in Vietnam, that's why he's against the war. And these guys are all super firemen. It's you that takes the beating and you won't give up. Everybody dies . . .

My wife sees television, guys get killed. She tells me, "Be careful." Sometimes she'll call up the firehouse. I tell her we had a bad job, sometimes I don't . . . They got a saying in the firehouse: "Tonight could be the night." But nobody thinks of dying. You can't take it seriously, because you'd get sick. We had some fires, I said, "We're not gettin' out of this." Like I say, everybody dies.

A lotta guys wanna be firemen. It's like kids. Guys forty years old are kids. They try to be a hard guy. There's no big thing when you leave boyhood for manhood. It seems like I talked the same at fifteen as I talk now. Everybody's still a kid. They just lose their hair or they don't fuck that much.

When I was a kid I was scared of heights. In the fire department you gotta go up a five-story building with a rope around you. You gotta jump off a building. You know the rope can hold sixteen hundred pounds. As long as you got confidence in your body and you know the guy's holding you, you got nothing to be scared of. I think you perform with people lookin' at you. You're in the lime-light. You're out there with the people and kids. Kids wave at you. When I was a kid we waved at firemen. It's like a place in the sun.

Last month there was a second alarm. I was off duty. I ran over there. I'm a bystander. I see these firemen on the roof, with the smoke pouring out around them, and the flames, and they go in. It fascinated me. Jesus Christ, that's what *I* do! I was fascinated by the people's faces. You could see the pride that they were seein'. The fuckin' world's so fucked up, the country's fucked up. But the fire-men, you actually see them produce. You see them put out a fire. You see them come out with babies in their hands. You see them give mouth-to-mouth when a guy's dying. You can't get around that shit. That's real. To me, that's what I want to be.

I worked in a bank. You know, it's just paper. It's not real. Nine to five and it's shit. You're lookin' at numbers. But I can look back and say, "I helped put out a fire. I helped save somebody." It shows something I did on this earth.

Born in 1912, Studs Terkel grew up in Chicago. He graduated from the University of Chicago in 1932 and from the University of Chicago Law School in 1934. He has acted in radio soap operas; been a disk jockey, a radio commentator, and a TV emcee; and traveled all over the world doing on-the-spot interviews. Currently, he has a daily radio program on WFMT in Chicago that is syndicated throughout the country. He is also a winner of the Pulitzer Prize for his best-selling book, *"THE GOOD WAR."*

Born in 1912, Studs Terkel grew up in Chicago. He graduated from the University of Chicago in 1932 and from the University of Chicago Law School in 1934. He has noted for radio soap operas, became disk jockey, radio commentator, and a TV emcee, and traveled all over the world doing on-the-spot interviews. Currently he has a daily radio program on WFMT in Chicago that is syndicated throughout the country. He is also a winner of the Pulitzer Prize for his best-selling book.